Penn's Treaty with the Ind

ANNALS

OF

PHILADELPHIA AND PENNSYLVANIA,

IN THE OLDEN TIME;

BEING A COLLECTION OF

MEMOIRS, ANECDOTE, AND INCIDENTS

OF THE

CITY AND ITS INHABITANTS,

AND OF THE

EARLIEST SETTLEMENTS OF THE INLAND PART OF PENNSYLVANIA,

FROM

THE DAYS OF THE FOUNDERS.

INTENDED TO PRESERVE THE RECOLLECTIONS OF OLDEN TIME, AND TO EXHIBIT SOCIETY IN ITS CHANGES OF MANNERS AND CUSTOMS, AND THE CITY AND COUNTRY IN THEIR LOCAL CHANGES AND IMPROVEMENTS.

EMBELLISHED WITH ENGRAVINGS, BY T. H. MUMFORD.

BY JOHN F. WATSON,

MEMBER OF THE HISTORICAL SOCIETIES OF PENNSYLVANIA, NEW YORK, AND MASSACHUSETTS

IN TWO VOLUMES.

VOL. II.

"Oh! dear is a tale of the olden time!"
Sequari vestigia rerum.

"Where peep'd the hut, the palace towers;
Where skimm'd the bark, the war-ship lowers;
Joy gaily carols where was silence rude,
And cultured thousands throng the solitude."

PHILADELPHIA:
J. B. LIPPINCOTT & CO.
1870.

CONTENTS OF VOL. II.

LIST OF EMBELLISHMENTS

IN VOLUME II.

☞*And Directions to the Binder.*

ANNALS

OF

PHILADELPHIA AND PENNSYLVANIA.

OLDEN TIME AFFECTIONS AND RESEARCHES.

Our love of antiquities,—the contemplation of *by-gone days*,—is an impress of the Deity. It is our hold on immortality. The same affection which makes us reach forward and peep into futurity, prompts us to travel back to the hidden events which transpired before we existed. We thus feel our span of existence enlarged even while we have the pleasure to identify ourselves with the scenes or the emotions of our forefathers. For the same cause relics are so earnestly sought and sedulously preserved,—"they are full of local impressions," and transfer the mind back to "scenes before."

As *Americans*, we see in a short life more numerous incidents to excite our observation and to move our wonder, than any other people. The very newness of our history and country ministers to our moral entertainment, and increases our interest in contemplating the passing events. A single life in this rapidly growing country, witnesses such changes in the progress of society, and in the embellishments of the arts, as would require a term of centuries to witness in full grown Europe. If we have no ruins of Pompeii and Herculaneum to employ our researches, no incomprehensible Stonehenge, nor circle of Dendara to move our wonder, we have abundant themes of unparalleled surprise in following down the march of civilization and improvements,—from the first landing of our pilgrim forefathers to the present *eventful* day!

The wealth and ambition of a potent prince may have accomplished a magnificent city in shorter time upon the banks of the Neva; but in this country we have many equal wonders by the energies and resources of a people, until lately "no people." The wisdom of our free institutions has made our land the desired asylum of the oppressed. Here human life is not wantonly wasted in ambitious broils for sovereignty; we therefore behold our population quadrupled in a term of forty years; and our hardy pioneers subduing the soil, or advancing their settlements from the Atlantic to the Pacific wave. Canals, rivaling in magnitude the boasted aqueducts of imperial Rome, are in successful operation. By these and rail roads, inaccessible districts are brought nigh; mountains charged with metallic treasures are entered, and their deposits of iron, coal, and lead, &c., lavished over the land. Cities, towns, and villages, arise in the west, as if by enchantment. Many of their present inhabitants redeemed their soil from a waste howling wilderness. In less than twenty years our exports have grown from twenty to eighty millions. Our navy, from "cock-boats and rags of striped bunting," has got up to power and renown. Our private law, commercial code, and bold diplomacy, have grown into a matured and learned system. Our inventions and improvements in the arts, which began but yesterday, make us, even now, "a wonder unto many;" and our vapour vessels, while they crowd our waters and overcome the rapids of the Mississippi and Missouri, are accomodating and enriching the old world by their adoption and imitation. Here we have no lordly potentates in church, "lording it over the conscience of the people;" no standing armies to endanger their liberties: no despots to riot in the oppression of the subject. Nay, so exalted are *our* privileges as a *self-governed* people, that the fact of our example and happiness is bidding fair to regenerate other nations, or to moderate the rigour of despotic government throughout the world!

If topics like these,—which enter into the common history of our growing cities, may be the just pride and glory of an American, must not the annals, which detail such facts, (and to such these pages are specially devoted,) be calculated to afford him deep interest; and should it not be his profit, as well as amusement, to trace the successive steps by which we have progressed, from comparative nothingness, to be "a praise in the earth!"

There are minds, feeling and cultivated, which can derive rich moral pleasure from themes like these, for

"Is there a man, with soul so dead,
Who never to himself hath said—
This is my own, my native land!"

Such views and such feelings impressed and imbued the mind of the author, else he had never attempted these pages. His stimulus was purely *con amore;* recompense he did not contemplate, and time he could ill spare from other engagements; wherefore, indulgence for casual imperfections is but justly due from the considerate reader. He wrote at first for his sole gratification, never intending his collections for the public eye, nor does he encounter that ordeal but by the encouragement of those friends who are willing to accept the performance by their sense of his *limited means* to perfect it. If it should stimulate others to add to these materials, it will be a grateful service. And if *the example*, thus set to the sister cities of New York, Boston, &c., should engage minds of kindred feelings and adequate industry to make similar collections of their domestic history, the usefulness of the present publication will be still more felt and acknowledged; and the eventual aim of the author still more accomplished.

We should not forget these things: our land and our fathers have been the subject of many heaven-descended mercies. They who love to contemplate the cause of the numerous effects, so indicative of our blessings as a nation, will regard it not less a duty of piety than of patriotism *to thus preserve their memorial.*

"Go call thy sons,—*instruct* them wnat *a debt*
They owe their ancestors, and make them vow
To pay it,—by transmitting down entire
Those *sacred rights* to which themselves *were born!*"

In writing these memorials of the times by-gone, I have often felt the suggestion pressed upon my mind, whether I was indeed pursuing inquiries and preserving facts which will have the sympathies and countenance of others, or am I so peculiar, as to be only amusing myself. I have thought the contemplation of *time past* has something inherently attractive; not indeed in the notice of our personal waste of years, when sufficiently old to see our sun declining, but in the recollections of the exhilarating sunshine beams of our youth. Not that, when the past was the present, we were all satisfied with our situations and ourselves, but that vexations have been forgotten in the lapse of years, and we remember pleasures alone; as, in looking back on the landscape we have passed over, the rude hills become softened by distance, and the cliffs, that were so difficult to surmount, seem dissolving in the purple sky. For this reason, the recollections of *childhood* are so captivating to every unperverted mind, though to him whose soul is stained with crimes, they are fraught with pain and remorse.

The causes which operated to induce *me* to form the present *museum* of incidents of "*men and manners*" are curious even to myself. The resolution to execute them, was only a concern of a few years; but the love to such objects in general was as early as my childhood, and has indeed "grown with my growth and strengthened with my strength." I may now say, I feel gratified that my mind has been thus led to chronicle incidents. Many of them ought to be preserved as the eventful facts of a land peculiarly favoured of Heaven, and as destined, perchance, to future renown. *We should not forget these things;* and the record of them, in such manner as I have adopted, should be deemed a generous service to all those who, with grateful hearts, love to consider the *causes* of their blessings. Piety and patriotism equally cherish such sentiments.

I have had frequent occasions to lament that this kind of inquiries was not instituted sooner, even by myself; they might have been advantageously begun much earlier, by still older persons. In now recollecting the aged of my early days, of whom I might have inquired, how many are remembered from whom nothing was attempted! To illustrate these ideas, what a treasure might Dr. Franklin have imparted of all he had seen or knew, from the years 1723, to 1790, when he died! He was remarkably qualified to have given us the materials for such a history as I have attempted in these pages He must have been familiar with the *traditions* of the primitive settlers; must have *seen* many who *saw* Penn, &c. But his mind appears never to have been drawn to the consideration of their value to us, their posterity. The truth is, very few minds are so abstracted from the daily concerns of life, as to perceive that the things which at any given moment every man knows, may, thereafter, become highly interesting. Another reason may be, that Franklin never saw, at any period, any such astonishing improvements, as, since his death, every where arrest attention. Colonial things were too uniform and tame to arouse the mind. All things, in his day, were regularly progressive, gliding to their end with the smoothness of a stream. But if a person of my inquiring mind had had opportunities of drawing from such an observing mind as Franklin's, what a fund of entertainment and information could have been derived for posterity!

For reasons like the above, I, who am but little past middle aged, am better qualified to ask various questions which would never occur to the mind of much older men. To me, the field was all new and unexplored, and therefore, with the eagerness of a child which asks questions about every thing, I felt constantly awake to inquiries on topics which would not affect the minds of old persons; things in which they had long ceased to be curious. Owing to this faculty of the mind, the most interesting travels, like Silliman's, are those which record every *new* thing which most surprises or pleases it. Then such a writer must speak *feelingly enough* for those who, like himself, have never seen what he so discovers to them. And even to those who have, he refreshes their memories in a way most grateful.

About twenty-seven or twenty-eight years ago, I desired to see some such work as the present effected. Not thinking to attempt it myself, I suggested some such scheme to a friend. It met the approbation of the late Mr. Delaplaine, who set upon it with great ardour. My ideas were expressed in the form of a prospectus, which procured a subscription list, it was said, of four thousand subscribers, before the book was even written. With such a patronage, there was a defect of labour or enterprise in producing the *materials*, and Dr. Mease was resorted to as composuist, to bring out something to answer the claims of the subscribers. It received the name of "*The Picture of Philadelphia*,"—but how far like my present result, the reader must judge. The doctor has managed his materials unexceptionably; but the defect was, that he had not the proper staple to weave into his fabric. Had he succeeded better in what were *my* aims, I should never have made this attempt; but, untouched as my scheme had been, I have made at last, though thus late, my own efforts, although subject to the disadvantage of residing six miles from the city, about which my inquiries and observations are employed, and being withal fettered with daily *official* duties, and cares of paramount consideration. From reasons like these, those who know me best will be readiest to excuse imperfections, whether of style or selection,—and critics, if they deign to notice such labours, did they know the irregular hours and intervals in which fragments of time were seized for the purpose might rather wonder it has been so well, than that it should have been so ill executed. To judge beyond this may savour of ill-nature,

> "Which taught them still to say,
> Whate'er was done, *might* have been better done!"

To such I need only say,—"What is writ, is writ,—would it were worthier."

Many of my selections of *local* facts were derived from a very great mass of court papers, and had to be hunted out among files of petitions, recognisances, special presentments for assaults, batteries, felonies, tippling and disorderly houses, &c., being the *usual* accompaniments of "*quarter sessions*," as is well known to those in any degree acquainted with the criminal docket. Most probably, such a search they have not had before, since packed away as the lumber of office, and such another, I presume, they will *never have again!* Some local notices may appear too trivial for notice; but who knows what future discoveries may be made, in digging into some of the former "*fillings up?*" as, for instance, the late discovery of *sub-terrane* logs in Chestnut street, by Hudson's alley, (the remains of the old bridge, &c.,) which no living persons could explain from memory! If a *jewel*, or some pieces of *coin*, (as may occur!) should hereafter be dug out of some of the "breaches" of Front street, (afterwards filled up,) some of the foregoing facts may tend to elucidate the *cause* of their deposit there. As *Boswell* said, in an apology for his minute mention of the "*oak cudgel*,"—it was because it might afterwards become the hero of a *good* tale, in the hands of so interesting a character as Johnson! Johnson's Rambler, too, justly remarks, "nor can it be always safely determined, which should be rejected or retained; for they may sometimes unexpectedly contribute to the illustration of history, and to the knowledge of the natural commodities of the country, or of the genius and customs of its inhabitants."

Poulson's paper of March 6th, 1821, contains an article by me, entitled "Old Times" of 1769, &c. It requests others to communicate similar facts. I thus tried to set others at this kind of service, and to *exempt* myself;—but none heeded my counsel,—and afterwards I made my own attempt. Fame or reward never entered into my motives. Like quaint John Bunyan,

> "'Twas mine own self to gratify!"

The service was sufficiently pleasing in itself, to be a positive recreation and amusement, furnishing its own reward by the way:

"For having my method by the end,
Still, as I pulled, it came;
Till at length it came to be,
For size, the bigness which you see!"

If I were to give the history of my troubles or profits in the publishing of my three books, it might startle some and discourage others. The Annals went off heavily, and allowed a profit equal to the pay of a copyist, if I had used such a help; and the two books of Historical Tales produced *nothing* for authorship. It had been a pity, indeed, if *their readers* had not been obliged or benefited, since their author was not.

I have deemed it my duty, in many cases, to support my facts with the *names* of the credible relators. Not that they alone mentioned them to me, for it was my practice to confirm surprising facts by concurrent testimony, so far as the things told were susceptible of being known to others. Several authorities too, deemed awkward or indelicate to introduce into the printed text, may be found in their connexion, in the original MS. Annals, in the City Library, and in the Historical Society.

There is another remark concerning *names* which might be appropriately mentioned here, as showing that I was aware that *names* and *personalities* are sometimes too sensitive to bear the touch. Yet I found it needful to retain them in general, and especially in my MS., as *my* necessary proofs and vouchers, in case of dispute or reference. Some that I designed only in initials, the inadvertency of the printer sometimes retained. In other cases, the names were sanctioned by the informants or persons themselves—and finally, as an imposing reason, some names occasionally became a necessary appendage to the story.

Searching for some of these facts was like seeking for the "living among the dead." Only a few of the very aged, as by accident, had preserved their memory. And very often, persons equally old, or even older, dwelling on the spot of interest or inquiry, knew nothing, or nearly nothing, about it. The comparative intelligence of different men of equal ages was often very dissimilar. To exemplify this, I have only to say, that not one aged man in fifty, now in Philadelphia, could tell me where was "Guest's Blue Anchor tavern, in Budd's long row"—nor the "Barbadoes lot,"—nor the "Swamp,"—nor the adjoining "Society hill,"—nor "Bathsheba's bath and bower,"—the "Schuylkill baptisterion,"—the "*old* Hospital,"—Hudson's orchard,"—"Penny-pot landing,"—"Penn's cottage,"—the "Swedes' house,"—and *many other things* spoken of in these pages. *I* came at them by reading ancient papers, and then, by recalling forgotten things to their memories, their minds were enabled to seize on long forgotten facts. Sometimes, when I have asked ancient persons to tell me what they knew of antiquity, such would seem to have nothing to relate: all seemed a blank to them. But when I have transported myself back to the cotemporaneous occurrences of their youth, and warmed their imaginations with recitals, with which they were once familiar, I have been rewarded, by receiving many of the lively images of things which my conversation had generated. Without vanity, I may say that I have often made my company agreeable to the aged, and have seen them quickened to many emotions younger than their common feelings or their years. On other occasions I have visited such as were past sensibility,—the body enfeebled and the memory decayed; I laboured in vain to revive the expiring spark of life. They were looking for their "appointed change," and this not unwisely engrossed all their thoughts. Finally, earlier questions might have been more successful, and any thing later than my attempt would have been absolutely fatal! What I rescued was "trembling on the lips of narrative old age," or "tumbling piece-meal into the tomb." My regret is, that some of those of whom, or from whom, I write, will scarcely stay to have the chance of reading some of these pages. I might perhaps pertinently hint at my being fully aware of occasional repetition of facts in substance, though not in language,—this necessarily occurred occasionally from the design of making given chapters more complete on given subjects.

In connexion with the foregoing, it may not be inappropriate to add, that many of the *little histories of places and things* set down in this book have been often since used in substance, by publishers and orators, as a part or parcel of their own explorations and insight into the past,—not even hinting at the source whence derived. It gives me no offence, since I wished them to be known,—but it is but justice to myself to here suggest, in self-protection, that I came not at them, from *their* discoveries and researches, but as the results of my own industry.

With some I shall doubtless need an apology for the little estimation in which they may regard some of my collections; I am con tent to say, I have only written for kindred minds. Such affections as mine have had precedents enough in feeling minds; for instance, "the oak," immortalized by Cowper's muse, became so precious that the owner, the Marquis of Northampton, to keep it from its frequent pious thefts, was obliged to enclose it by a strong fence, and to affix to it a notice of prohibition. The chair in which the poet Thomson composed, is exhibited at his commemorative festivals. How many pious thefts have been made upon Shakspeare's mulberry tree; and cups made from that, and from the "royal oak," have sold at great prices. Learned doctors still deem it an honour to shroud themselves in Rabelais' old cloak at Montpelier. The taking of the sword of Frederick the Great, by Buonaparte, from Berlin to Paris, while it shows his estimate of relics, is treated by Scott and the world as a heinous offence to all other men. Of all such things, says Edgeworth, and truly too, "we contemplate such with deep curiosity, because they are full of local impressions, and by the aid of these we create the ideal presence." They connect the heart and the imagination with the past.

We may take as another evidence of the appreciation of relics, the fact of the late proceedings of congress, upon receiving from the heirs of Washington, the gift of his sword and the cane of Doctor Franklin—called "two most interesting and valuable relics connected with the past history of our country,"—and saying of them, that "associations are linked in adamant with their names, and with those sacred symbols of our golden age." The sword was a plain hanger, with a green hilt and silver guard, made at Fishkill, in 1757,—the same which he had worn first as colonel in the Virginia service in Forbes' campaign, and afterwards through the whole period of the Revolutionary war.

Among the encouragements to such reminiscences, I may mention such evidence as results from public celebrations of fetes intended to revive and cherish such recollections. They prove to me that my anticipations from such records as the present have not been vain.

Already have the semi-historical sketches of Irving's muse, in this way, given rise to a drama, in which is portrayed the costumes and manners of the primitive Knickerbockers. The prologue to his "Rip Van Winkle" has some sentiments to my taste and to my future expectations of what may be hereafter set forth in poetry, painting, or romance, to arrest the attention of modern Philadelphians, to what were the primitive manners of their forefathers. The poet thus speaks, to wit:

"In scenes of yore endear'd by classic tales
The comic muse with smiles of rapture hails;
'Tis when we view those days of *Auld Lang Syne,*
Their charms with Home—that magic name—combine.
Shades of the Dutch! how seldom rhyme hath shown
Your ruddy beauty, and your charms full blown!
How long neglected have your merits lain!
But Irving's genius bids them rise again."

Since the publication of my former edition, my friend, William Dunlap, Esq., of New York, while stirring up his recollections of the past, at my suggestion and for my use, found that he could compile enough to make a work for himself *in my way*, viz., his History of New York for schools and youth; and afterwards, as his mind expanded with his theme, he felt impelled to bring out his large work, the General History of New York State. Thus every way, the fund of historical truth is increased. J. R. Broadhead, Esq., also is procuring state papers, &c., in Holland, for a future publication.

The Annals of Portsmouth, Lewis' History of Lynn, Gibbs' Collections of Salem, and Davis' Notices of Plymouth, are such works as we wish to see multiplied in our country. So also is Johnson's Early Notices of Salem, N. J.

Such works furnish occasions for imaginative works and tales, such as we have already seen deduced from my Annals, in the story of "Meredith, or the Meschianza,"—and in "a Tale of Blackbeard the Pirate."

Our country has been described abroad, and perhaps conceived of at home, says Flint, as sterile of moral interest. "We have, it is said, no monuments, no ruins, none of the colossal remains of temples, and baronial castles, and monkish towers, nothing to connect the heart and the imagination with the past, none of the dim recollections of the gone-by, to associate the past with the future." But although we have not the solemn and sombre remains of the past, as the remains of the handy work of man, we have every thing in the contemplation of the future. For when our thoughts have traversed rivers a thousand leagues in length, when we have seen the ascending steamboat breasting the mantling surge, or seen her along our opening canals, gleaming through the verdure of the trees, we have imagined the happy multitudes that from those shores shall contemplate their scenery in ages to come, in times when *we* shall have "strutted through life's poor play," and "been no more!"

As our desires conspire with our feelings in wishing to promote and excite a love of the study of the past, we purpose herein to add a few of such articles as have most ably sustained the arguments which we wish to enforce—viz.:

Walter Scott had early habits of antiquarian study. He dwelt with fondness on the rude figures of the olden time.

Blackwood's Magazine says that anecdotes of men and things will have a charm as long as man has curiosity.

"Hudibras (says Dr. Johnson) is one of those compositions of which a nation may justly boast, [mark the reason,] as the images which it exhibits are *domestic*, the sentiments *unborrowed* and *unexpected*, and the strain of diction *original* and *peculiar*."

Hutton, speaking of Birmingham, says, "while the historian only collects matter of the day, the antiquarian brings his treasures from remote time—*calls things back into existence which were past*—collects the dust of perished matter, remoulds the figure and stamps the past with a kind of immortality,—*by his recreative power*."

Blackwood's Magazine says, "things that may appear *trifling now*, when *present* and *familiar*, may become very different, when they are read after the accession of a totally different set of manners. They are the materials from which alone a graphic and interesting history of the period can be formed. With what delight do we read the glowing pictures in Ivanhoe, and the Crusaders, in Quentin Durward, and Kenilworth, of the manners, customs and habits of *those* periods!"

"Instructed by the antiquarian times,
He must, he is, he cannot but be wise."

The author of Scott's Memoirs (*George Allen*) presents many facts to prove how very much the readers and admirers of Scott are indebted, for their interest in his writings, to his affection for talking with, and gathering up, *the recollections* of "the ancient crones and gaffers." When a young man, Scott was wont to make frequent journeys into the country, *among strangers*, going from house to house, with his boy George,—and particularly seeking out the residences of *the old people*, with whom he delighted to enter into conversation, and exciting them to dilate upon the reminiscences of their youth. Finally, says his biographer, "all who know his works must feel how much of their amusement they owe to his gypsy strolls." All this he did too from his innate love of antiquity; and not merely from the design of drawing pictures of common life for books, —for it was earlier than the time of his career of authorship. These facts are worth consideration.

Hannáh More, in writing to Mrs. Gwatkins, on the occasion of her first visit to London, says "I have rambled through the immediate shades of Twickenham; I have trodden the haunts of the swan of the Thames."—"I could not be honest for the life of me; from the grotto I stole two bits of stones; from the garden a sprig of laurel: and from one of the bed chambers a pen; because the house had been *Pope's*." On another occasion, speaking of her visit to Kent, where had once dwelt Sir Philip Sidney, and Sacharissa, she says, "I pleased myself with the thought, that the immense oaks and enormous beeches, which had once shaded them, now shade me." [This last is the very thought I have expressed in passing the woods to Harrisburg, and thinking they were *the same* trees which had shaded the aborigines, now so wasted and expelled.]

The Edinburgh Review, in discussing the leading objects of history, says, "the perfect historian is he in whose work the character and spirit of an age is exhibited in miniature; by judicious selections, rejections and arrangement, he gives to truth *those attractions*, which have been usurped by fiction. He considers no anecdote, no *peculiarity of manner*, no familiarity of saying, as too insignificant for his notice, which is not too insignificant to illustrate the operations of laws, religion, and of education, and *to mark the progress of the human mind.* Men must be made intimately known to us, by *appropriate images* presented in every line. Sir Walter Scott has succeeded to illustrate history, by using up those fragments of truth which historians have scornfully thrown behind them, *in a manner* which may well excite their envy. A truly great historian would reclaim those materials which the novelist has appropriated; society should be shown from the highest to the lowest. Instruction derived from history thus written would be of a vivid and practical character. It would be received by the imagination as well as by the reason. An intimate knowledge of the DOMESTIC history of nations *is therefore absolutely necessary.*" [I have aimed at this last.]

Hone's "Every Day Book," which I have only lately seen, is an expensive and embellished work, published in 1827, in London, got up on purpose to illustrate, *after my manner*, the perishing memorials of by-gone men and things in London. The chief difference between us seems to be, that he is often supported by the written contributions of others, from all parts of England, and of course producing the pleasing varieties of many minds, whereas I never could enlist the help of any competent mind to furnish me with any personal reminiscences. Hone manifests much tact and good feeling and good taste for his subject—giving us many interesting actions of men and things—several of them disused and obsolete—which in that cause enhances their value and character to us as moderns. His "Every Day Book" abounds with sentences commendatory of olden time affections, and shows that, in the estimation of men of sense, they are decidedly worthy of all praise. It may also be remarked, that in many cases, much smaller matters than I have preserved, and which some might deem trifles, are deemed of sufficient value to be embellished with drawings, or gravely supported with proofs. The whole is calculated to prove that the *memorial of times by-gone* is certainly valued, because of the insight it affords into the character and action of a departed age; and for that very reason is most valued by those who are most intellectual. Those whose imaginations are most occupied about their readings of any given people or place, are those who most like to have the pictures and images, which their fancies may instinctively draw, *satisfied and settled by facts;* and hence the love for those portraits and delineations of olden time, which bring up the "very age and picture of the past."

Chambers' "Traditions of Edinburgh," which I only saw in 1834 —after the publication of my Annals, has much the spirit and purpose of my own book; it is even more minute in sundry articles than I ventured to be: such as characteristics of crazy or silly persons and beggars, under the chapter "objects;" also "the hangman;" some memorable "old maids," &c. His leading topics are "characters" of sundry peculiar or remarkable men and women; sundry "closes and places;" taverns, clubs, and convivial places and parties; sundry remarkable "old houses" and their inmates; and many miscellaneous facts of men and manners, in the former age. The whole in two volumes, 12mo.: 2d edition, Edinburgh, 1825. The author speaks of his performance, as a subject which had engrossed his leisure *for many years*, and that the praise which it has received is to be ascribed to the accidental *excellence of his subject*, rather than to any personal merit of his own. He gives several pages on ladies' dresses, such as "calashes, bongraces, (a bonnet of silk and cane,) negligees, stomachers, stays, hoops, lappets, pinners, plaids, fans, busks, rumple, knots, &c., then worn and now forgotten." Gentlemen's dresses he appears to have *overlooked*, save that he incidentally says that they wore a small black muff, hung by a cord from the shoulder, and seen dangling at the side, when not in use, like a child's drum!

A life or a book of observation may always be useful; and this idea is supported by Mr. Walpole, from the opinion of a poet, saying, that "if any man were to form a book, of *what he had seen or heard himself*, it must, *in whatever hands*, prove a most useful and interesting one." I am fully of the same opinion, from numerous facts known to me in my researches among the aged for reminiscences and traditions; and with such sentiments, I would make the above sentence my motto, to such future observations or passing events as I may record.

Our eloquent countryman, *Everett*, has touchingly commended to our notice a just regard for our *national recollections*,—saying of them, "it is thus a free people is to be formed, animated and perpetuated. With such fine examples and studies at home, we need not to be eternally ringing the changes upon Marathon and Thermopylæ. From the lessons of our forefathers, let us glean our instructions. Let us consult with profit their prudent councils in perplexed times; their exploits and sacrifices, either as settlers, or as citizen soldiers, contending for themselves and posterity. The traditionary lore still dwelling in the memories of the few revered survivors among us is worth our preservation. Let us seize it all as the rich inheritance of our children; as a legacy from our progenitors, virtually saying,—"My sons, forget not your fathers."

Some have taken it for granted that I must have a decided preference for every thing olden, as if age alone made things valuable; but they mistake my bias and feelings; mine is a poetical attachment. I go into it as into the region of imagination. The Edinburgh Review, in noticing the works of Sir Walter Scott, has ascribed principles of action to him, the force of which, in its degree, I also felt and can appreciate, viz.: "his attachment to the manners of antiquity is to be considered merely as a poetical attachment. He is won by their picturesqueness, and by their peculiar applicability to purposes of romance." *I* write of olden time, because *I* think the facts, if so preserved, will eventually furnish the material of future legendary story and romance. I also, as I think, am thus preserving useful facts for national recollections and reflection.

The public in general have very little conception of the really pleasing character of olden time inquiries. They view the volume as so much accumulated facts, attained, as they suppose, by laborious delving, and exploration, and inquiry. They wholly overlook the real *poetry* of the subject; the stimulus and gratification which a mind duly constituted for the pursuit acquires, by opening to itself the contemplation and the secrets of a buried age. Such an inquirer examines a world of beings known only to himself; and while he walks and talks with them, he learns facts and incidents *known only to themselves*. By comparing in his mind the things which may have been so unlike the present, he learns how to estimate the measure of changes which may probably occur in the future, and thus opens to himself additional subjects of gratification and consideration. Thus his mind is busied in the contemplation of things—calm and soothing in their nature, which others do not consider and cannot enjoy. The present race are mostly engrossed in themselves, and their various bounds of action and concern. Their ideal images are limited; but the lover of olden time, revels in the regions of past events, and peoples his intellectual reveries with persons and society all his own; not of fairy creatures like Shakspeare's, but of sober reality, and of such *choice selection* as may best minister to his entertainment and edification. He sees the forefathers of our land, fresh and ardent as they were, when first set upon the enterprise of cultivating a new Eden for us; he enters into their spirit, and feels their sympathies at home and abroad; he hears their deliberations in the domestic circle, and in the public councils; he is present at every new inland settlement; sees how new plantations are effected, and how towns are created; sees original lands, now dense with population, just as they were in their state of wild nature, then savage with beasts of prey and tawny aborigines. He sees aged oaks and hemlocks, and visits uncultivated spots, like the many still undisturbed scenes on the banks of the Wissahiccon, and cheers his imagination with the fact that *he* sees *the same* unaltered objects, which they had once seen and considered:

> "It soothes to have seen what they have seen,
> And cheers to have been where they have been."

The poet who expressed that sentiment, had a soul which anticipated and felt all which is meant to be here embodied by these *few* remarks. To an imaginative mind rightly cultivated, the very few hints here suggested will present an unlimited field of amplification. To such, every thing of the past is filled with imagery: and the possessor of the faculty is always enabled to evoke from the store-house of his memory the ideal presence, and is at all times ready "to walk and talk with men of other days." Surely there is positive gratification in faculties like these. "A fool and an antiquary (says Hutton) is a contradiction—they are, to a man, people of letters and penetration."

Superficial observers and thinkers may think lightly of the contemplation of facts and things that are past, or grown gray and neglected with years, only because they do not think with the same class of thoughts and associations, or the same character of emotions, which actuate the minds of the real lovers of the times and things *by-gone*. The affection for such pursuits and studies is wholly intellectual. There are occasions when the soul feels irrepressible reverence, and a hushed silence, in the contemplation of a known relic, or the remains of what was once memorable and peculiar. The soul has a ready facility in investing the perishing, or rescued remains, with an impersonation and ideal presence which enables it, as it were, to speak out to our arrested and excited senses, and recites to us, mentally, *the long tale* of its notices and observations on men and things, which, through days of by-gone time, it may have witnessed or considered. From such a cause of operation, who can behold an ancient mummy, for instance, and not instinctively revert in reflection to Campbell's touching apostrophe to such an impressive relic! saying within ourselves:—

"Statue of flesh—immortal of the dead!
Imperishable type of evanescence!
Come, prithee *tell us something of thyself;*
Reveal the secrets of thy prison house:—
Since in the world of spirits thou hast slumber'd,
What hast thou seen—what strange adventures numbered?"

I cannot but observe it as a fact in *our history*, which may perhaps be applied in general to most other early history, that the chances for a true account of *the origin of things*, are but few and difficult—because I cannot but perceive that such is the little of investigation employed thereon by competent minds, and so little are the topics within the cognizance of the mass of the people, that there remains scarcely any to detect a fraud or misconception; but almost all tacitly concede to the first writer or compiler, the complaisance to *believe all that he asserts* of times by-gone. I have, in after time, detected some such lapses, especially in *typographical* errors of dates, &c., in my own pages; but which none of the vigilant reviewers—*so fond of faults*, had the sagacity or skill to expose! Sometimes very old people assert things as facts, which they verily believe and have often told, only because their extreme age has destroyed the power of accurate discrimination,—*they confound things*—and yet they seem so sure and so plausible, that we are constrained to believe them, until subsequent official or written data of the true time and circumstances, disclose the truth. A remarkable instance of what I mean, is verified in the incident related by old Butler, aged 104, respecting General Braddock's marching *from Philadelphia*, when he landed at Virginia and travelled westward, via the Potomac! If these never come to light to contradict the former assertion, *the oft repeated tale* goes down to posterity unmolested *for ever*. In this manner the oldest persons in Philadelphia had all a false cause assigned for the name of "Arch street," and it was only the records of the courts which set me right. The historian of North Carolina gave a wrong case as the cause of the origin of "Yankee Doodle;" and if I had not discovered another cause, it would have stood as confirmed history for ever. Mr. Heckewelder has given us much detailed history of our Pennsylvanian Indians, and of the Delawares, and has said these last were an original people, and more powerful than all the other Indians; but a late writer, in Mr. Vetake's New Review, endeavours to prove that it was an illusion of the good missionary. He had said too, that the name of "Manhattan" was given to New York by the Indians, as meaning "*the place* where they all got drunk." This is in opposition to the facts told one hundred and fifty years before, by De Laet, a cotemporary, who twice asserts that the

Manhattes was *the name* of a tribe there. We do not pretend to decide in this last matter, but we can discern hereby, how it is, that given facts take a "local habitation and a name." Truth, therefore, requires much wariness, in seeking.

My notices of olden time were wholly of my own conception and suggestion. I had never read any similar works,—and even to this day, (1842,) although I have *named* them in my "Annals." I have not read Lewis' Lynn, Gibbs' Salem, Notices of Plymouth, &c., none of which have been made a part of the Philadelphia Library.

We had thought to have here concluded this chapter, already longer than we had purposed, when we began it—but we think that a few beautiful remarks which we shall here give from Alison's Notices of the Beautiful and Sublime, will be willingly read by every intellectual reader. He says: "The delight which most men of education receive from the consideration of antiquity, and the beauty that they discover in every object which is connected with ancient times, is in a great measure to be ascribed to their perceptions of beauty. Surrounded by relics of former ages, we seem to be removed to ages that are past, and indulge in the imagination of a living world. 'Tis then that all that is venerable or laudable in the history of those times, present themselves to the memory; then the imagination and fancy are stimulated. The subjects of consideration seem to approach him still nearer to the ages of his regard: the dress, the furniture, the arms of the times, are so many assistances to his imagination in guiding or directing its exercises; and offering him a thousand sources of imagery, provide him with an almost inexhaustible field in which his memory and his fancy may expatiate."

"There is no man who has not some interesting associations with particular scenes. The view of the house where he was born, of the school where he was educated, and where the gay years of infancy were passed, is indifferent to no man. The scenes which have been distinguished by the residence of any person, whose memory we admire, produce a similar effect. The admiration which the recollections afford, seems to give a kind of sanctity to the place where they dwelt."

"It is not the first prospect of Rome, as Rome only, which creates our emotions of delight. It is not the Tyber, diminished to a paltry stream. It is *ancient* Rome, with all its associations, which fills the imagination. It is the country of Cæsar, and Cicero, and Virgil, which is before him. All that he has read and studied opens at once before his mind, and presents him with a mass of high and solemn imagery which can never be exhausted."

I cannot but be aware, that my mind has been instinctive in its perception of matters and things in their state of *transitu*, that are habitually overlooked by many others. In the consciousness of my own peculiarity therein, I cannot but feel the force of remarks made by Colonel Trumbull, in his autobiography,—tending equally to show that in his department of national painting, which is, in fact, his desire for preserving his *pictorial images of the past*, we have been actuated measurably alike. "His aim (he says) has been to transmit to those who come after us, the personal resemblance of those who have been the great actors in those scenes that are past,—to portray which he had some superiority, because he had been an actor and a willing observer of things, for which no one then lives with him, possessing *the same advantage;*—and withal, no one can come after him to divide the honour of their truth and authenticity. He may therefore cherish an honest pride (he says) in the accomplishment of a work—*such as never has been done before*, and in which *it is not easy that he should find a rival.*"

PENNSYLVANIA INLAND.

The whole of Pennsylvania—such as it was for the first half century of the settlement,—was comprised within the three counties of *Philadelphia*, *Bucks*, and *Chester;* of these, therefore, we are chiefly to speak in the following pages. All beyond these—westward and northward, until of latter years, consisted of unsettled lands or Indian hunting grounds;—so very modern is every thing of improvement and civilization in Pennsylvania, which we now behold. Such a country, so rapid in its progress—so lately rising from comparative nothingness, to be "a praise in the earth," may well demand our admiration and regard.

Cotemporary with the first settlement of Philadelphia, the colonists proceeded into the country, and laid the foundation of sundry towns and neighbourhoods; as this was done while the country was in a wilderness state, and in the midst of the Indian nations, it may justly interest our readers to learn the earliest known facts concerning several of such settlements. To this end, we shall relate sundry incidents concerning Pennsbury, Bucks county, Chester, and Chester county, Byberry, Germantown, Frankford, Lancaster, &c. We begin with Germantown, the largest and oldest town begun in Philadelphia county, to wit:

Germantown.

The Germantown settlement was first taken up by Francis Daniel Pastorius, the 12th of the 8th month, 1683, by a purchase from William Penn, and was surveyed and laid out by the surveyor general, 2d of 3d month, 1684; under a grant to him for himself and others for 6000 acres. It proved, however, to contain but 5700 acres.

It was a *part* of *Springetbury Manor*, and was distributed among the proprietaries as follows, viz.:

200	acres to Dr. Francis D. Pastorius himself, on *Chestnut Hill*,
150	do. to Jurian Hartsfielder (the same who in 1676 owned *all* Campington,)
5350	do. To Pastorius, as *agent* to German and Dutch owners, called the Francfort company.
5700	do.

Pastorius and Hartsfielder were to pay yearly 1*s*. per 100 acres, quitrent: and all the others at the rate of 1*s*. per 1000 acres, ("they having bought off the quitrents,") for ever to William Penn and *heirs*.

The patent for all the preceding land from Penn is executed by William Markham, secretary for Pennsylvania, at Philadelphia, the 3d April, 1689, and it therein specifies "the purchasers," as follows, viz.:

Jacobus Vandewalle	535	acres
Johan Jacob Sheetz	428	do.
Daniel Spehagel	356⅔	do.
John W. Uberfeld	107	do.
George Strauss	178⅓	do.
Jan Laurens	535	do.
Abraham Hasevoet	535	do.
	*2675	do.

Jacob Tellner	989	acres
Jan Strepers	275	do.
Dirk Sipman	588	do.
Gobart Renckes	161	do.
Lenert Arets	501	do.
Jacob Isaacs	161	do.
	2675	do.

The distribution of the lands was made as follows:

Germantown (proper) contained	2750	acres
Cresheim	884	do.
Somerhausen	900	do.
Crefelt	1166	do.
	5700	do.

* All the above 2675 acres were sold in 1708, for £3000, to one Sprogel, by Daniel Faulkner, as agent to the Frankford Company, but as it was contrary to the wish of his principals, it was always deemed a fraud, and did not convey a transfer.

Germantown was incorporated as a borough town by a patent from William Penn, executed in England in 1689. Francis Daniel Pastorius, *civilian*, was made first bailiff; and Jacob Tellner, Dirk Isaacs op den Graff and Herman op den Graff, three burghers, to act ex-officio as town magistrates, and eight yeomen; the whole to form a general court to sit once a month. They made laws and laid taxes.

The town lost its charter for want of a due election, officers not being found willing to serve; somewhere about 1706. In a letter from Pastorius to William Penn, dated in 1701-2, he states his concern that he should not be able to get men to serve in the general court for "*conscience sake;*" and he trusts, for a remedy, to an expected arrival of emigrants. This difficulty probably arose from the oaths used in court proceedings.

All the settlers in Cresheim built on the Cresheim road, before settling a house on the Germantown road through Cresheim. There is an old map, made in 1700, in which all their residences and barns at that time are marked.

The Germantown *town* lots (55) were located in 1687, and were drawn for by lot in 1689, being 27½ lots on each side of the road. Their side lots up town began from Abington lane, (at Samuel Johnson's) and went up to the foot of the hill by Leibert's board yard. The original price of the township of Germantown was 1*s.* per acre.

The *original* of the following curious paper is in the hands of John Johnson, Esq.

" We whose names are to these presents subscribed, do hereby certify unto all whom it may concern, that soon after our arrival in this province of Pennsylvania, in October, 1683, to our certain knowledge Herman op den Graff, Dirk op den Graff, and Abraham op den Graff, as well as we ourselves, *in the cave* of Francis Daniel Pastorius, *at Philadelphia*, did *cast lots* for the respective lots which they and we *then began* to settle in Germantown; and the said Graffs (three brothers) have sold their several lots, each by himself, no less than if a division in writing had been made by them. Witness our hands this 29th Nov., A. D. 1709.

Lenart Arets	Thomas Hunder	Abraham Tunes
Jan Lensen	William Streygert	Jan Lucken
	Reiner Tysen.	

The Frankford Land Company gave titles to much of the lands on each side of Germantown Main-street. The company at first consisted of *ten* gentlemen living in Francfort, on the Maine, in Germany; their articles were executed in that city on the 24th November, 1686. They bought 25000 acres of land from William Penn. The Germantown patent for 5350, and the *Manatauney* patent for 22,377 acres. F. D. Pastorius was appointed the attorney for the company, and after his resignation Dan. Faulkner was, in 1708, made attorney.

Most of the old houses in Germantown are plastered on the inside with clay and straw mixed, and over it is laid a finishing coat of thin lime plaster; some old houses seem to be made with log frames and the insterstices filled with wattles, river rushes, and clay intermixed. In a house of ninety years of age, taken down, the grass in the clay appeared as green as when cut. Probably twenty houses now remain of the primitive population. They are of but one story, so low that a man six feet high can readily touch the eves of the roof. Their gable ends are to the street. The ground story is of stone or of logs—or sometimes the front room is of stone, and the back room is of logs, and thus they have generally one room behind the other. The roof is high and mostly *hipped*, forms a low bed chamber; the *ends* of the houses *above* the first story are of boards or sometimes of shingles, with a small chamber window at each end. Many roofs were then tiled.

In modern times those houses made of logs have been lathed and plastered over, so as to look like stone houses; the doors all divide in the middle, so as to have an upper and a lower door: and in some houses the upper door folds. The windows are two doors, opening inwards, and were at first set in leaden frames with outside frames of wood.

The Germans who originally arrived, came for conscience sake to this land, and were a very religious community. They were usually called *Palatines*, because they came from a Palatinate, called Cresheim and Crefelt. Many of the German Friends had been convinced by William Penn in Germany. Soon after their settlement, in 1683, some of them who were yet in Philadelphia, suffered considerably by a fire, and were then publicly assisted by the Friends.

The original *passports* of the first inhabitants coming from Germany to Germantown were written with golden ink on parchment, and were very elegant.

Wishert Levering, a first settler, lived to the age of 109, and died at Roxborough in 1744.

Jacob Snyder lived to be 97.

Francis Daniel Pastorius was a *chief* among the first settlers; he was a scholar, and wrote Latin in a good hand, and left a curious manuscript work called "*the Bee*," containing a beautiful collection of writing, and various curious selections. He once owned all Chestnut hill on both sides of the road. He was a member of assembly in 1687; and attorney for the Frankford Land Company. He died about the year 1720. I have been indebted to the kindness of James Haywood, of Cambridge, Massachusetts, for an explanation of the old German pamphlet, 12mo., in the Cambridge Library, done by F. D. Pastorius, as a "Description of Pennsylvania." Its consists of sundry subjects, printed in Holland, viz.:

A voyage from London to Pennsylvania, in 1683.

Pastorius' Account of the condition of Pennsylvania, in 1683.

The Charter by Charles II. to William Penn, of March 1681—Penn's Constitution,—a Geographic Description of the Country, its Trade, and a History with some account of the Aborigines,—and

Extracts of several letters of Pastorius to his friends in Germany,—An extract of William Penn's account of Pennsylvania, in a letter to his friends in London, &c.

The whole seems to be an extract (im anszug) *with notes*, done from some larger work.

Arents Klincken came from Holland with William Penn in his first voyage in 1682. He had seen and known Penn in Holland. He built the first *two* story house ever raised in Germantown; and Penn was present and partook of the raising dinner; the same old stone house on Justus Johnson's premises. He died at the age of 80. He left a son whose name was

Anthony Klincken, a great hunter, who spent a long life in such exercises. He used to have the garret of the house filled in the winter with wild game, and had it marked with the date when he killed it, so as to eat it in due succession as an epicure. The same house next to Justus Johnson's premises. He even purchased a German *Yager*, celebrated for shooting, to aid him in his field sports; he had iron prickers to the hands and feet to aid in climbing lofty trees for crows' scalps, which bore a premium. He used to wade the Wissahiccon in the depth of winter; finally contracted rheumatism and gout, which so ossified the flesh of his knuckles, that he could scrape chalk from them when old! He never went to Philadelphia without taking his gun with him in the spring and fall, and never came home without several geese or ducks, which he had killed in a spatterdock pond, then at the corner of Fourth and High streets! He called it the best game pond any where to be found. This was probably about the years 1700 to 1710. He used also to speak with wonder of seeing hundreds of rats in the flats among the spatterdocks at Pool's bridge, and that he was in the habit of killing them for amusement as fast as he could load. He was born about the year 1677, and died about 1759, aged about 82 years.

As early as 1700 there were four *hermits* living near Germantown—John Seelig, Kelpius, Bony, and Conrad Mathias. They lived near Wissahiccon and the Ridge. Benjamin Lay lived in a cave near the York Road, at Branchtown.

John Kelpius, *the hermit*, was a German of Sieburgen in Transylvania, of an eminent family, (tradition says he was noble,) and a student of Dr. John Fabritius, at Helmstadt. He was also a correspondent of Mæcken, chaplain to the Prince of Denmark in London. He came to this country in 1694 with John Seelig, Barnard *Kuster*, (Coster,) Daniel Falkener, and about forty-two others, being generally men of education and learning, to devote themselves, for piety's sake, to a solitary or single life; and receiving the appellation of the "Society of the Woman in the wilderness." They first arrived among the Germans at Germantown, where they shone awhile "as a peculiar light," but they settled chiefly "*on the Ridge*," then a wilderness. In 1708, Kelpius, who was regarded as their leader, died "in the midst of his days," (said to be 35,)—after his death the members began to fall in with the world around them, and some of them to break their avowed religious intentions by marrying. Thus the society lost its distinctive character and died away; but previous to their dispersion they were joined about the year 1704 by some others, among whom was Conrad Mathias, (the last of the Ridge hermits,) a Switzer, and by Christopher Witt, (sometimes called Dr. Witt of Germantown,) a professor of medicine, and a "*magus*" or *diviner*.

After the death of Kelpius, the faith was continued in the person of *John Seelig* who had been his companion, and was also a *scholar*. Seelig lived many years after him as a *hermit*, and was remarkable for resisting the offers of the world, and for wearing a coarse garment like that of Kelpius. This Seelig records the death of his friend Kelpius in 1708, in a MS. Hymn Book of Kelpius', (set to music,) which I have seen—saying he died *in his garden*, and attended by all his children, (spiritual ones, and children whom he taught gratis,) weeping as for the loss of a father. That Kelpius was a man of learning is tested by some of his writings; a very small-written book of one hundred pages, once in my possession. It contains his writings in Latin, Hebrew, Greek, German and English: and this last (which is very remarkable, he being a foreigner,) is very *free* and *pure*. The journal of his voyage to this country, in sixteen pages, is all in Latin; some of his letters (of which there are several in German, and two in English) are in Latin: they are all on religious topics, and saving his peculiar religious opinions, reason very acutely and *soberly*. From venturing with the thousands of his day to give *spiritual* interpretations to Scripture, where it was not so intended, he fell upon a scheme of religion which drove him and other students from the Universities of Germany, and under the name of *Pietists*, &c., to seek for some immediate and strange revelations. He and his friends therefore expected the *millennium* year was close at hand—so near that he told the first Alex. Mack (the first of the Germantown Tunkers) that he should not die till he saw it! He believed also that "the woman in the wilderness," mentioned in the Revelations, was prefigurative of the great deliverance that was then soon to be displayed for the church of Christ. As she was "to come up from the wilderness leaning on her beloved," so the beloved in the wilderness, laid aside all other engagements, (i. e. being hermits, and trimming their lamps and adorning themselves with holiness, that they may be prepared to meet the same with joy.) "Therefore they did well to observe the signs of the times, and every new phenomenon (whether moral or preternatural) of meteors, stars, or colours of the skies, if peradventure the *harbinger may appear*." He argued too, that there was a *three-fold* wilderness, like state of progression in spiritual holiness: to wit, "the barren, the fruitful and the wilderness state of the *elect of God*." In the last state, after which he was seeking, as a highest degree of holiness, he believed it very essential to attain it by dwelling in solitude or in the *wilderness*: therefore he argues Moses' holiness by being prepared forty years in the wilderness—Christ's being tempted forty days in the wilderness as an epitome of the other—John the Baptist coming from the wilderness, &c. He thought it thus proved that holy men might be thus qualified to come forth among men again, to convert whole cities, and to work signs and wonders. He was much visited by religious persons. Kelpius professed love and charity with all—but desired to live *without* a name or sect. The name they obtained was given by others. There are two of Kelpius' MS. Hymn Books still extant in Germantown: one of his own composing, in German, is called *elegant*; they are curious, too, because they are all *translated* into English poetry (line for line) by Dr. C. Witt, the diviner or magus. The titles of some of them may exhibit the mind of the author:

"Of the wilderness—or Virgin-Cross love."

"The contentment of the God-loving soul."

"Of the power of the new virgin-body wherein the Lord revealeth his mysteries."

"A loving moan of the disconsolate soul."

"Colloquium of the soul with itself."

"Upon *Rest* after he had been wearied with *Labour* in the wilderness."

Although he looked for a *qualification* to go forth and convert towns and cities in the name of the Lord, it is manifest, that neither he nor his companions were enthusiastic enough to go into the world without such endowment. They often held religious meetings in their hermitage, with people who solicited to come to them for the purpose. Kelpius' hut or house stood on the hill where the widow Phœbe Riter now lives. Her log house has now stood more than forty years on the same cellar foundation which was his; it is on a steep descending grassy hill, well exposed to the sun for warmth in the winter, and has a spring of the hermit's making, half down the hill, shaded by a very stout cedar tree. After Kelpius' hut went down, the foxes used to burrow in his cellar; he called the place the "Burrow of Rocks, or Rocksburrow"—now Roxborough.

Doctor Christopher Witt was born in England (in Wiltshire) in 1675: came to this country in 1704, and died in 1765, aged 90. He was a skilful physician and a learned man; was reputed a magus or diviner, or in grosser terms a *conjuror;* and was a student and a believer in all the learned absurdities and marvellous pretensions of the *Rosicrucian* philosophy. The Germans of that day, and indeed many of the English, practised the casting of *nativities* —and as this required mathematical and astronomical learning, it often followed that such a competent scholar was called "a fortune teller." Doctor Witt "cast nativities," and was called a conjuror: while Christopher Lehman, who was a scholar and a friend of Witt, and could cast nativities, and did them for all of his own nine children, but *never for hire*, was called a notary public, a surveyor, and a gentleman.

SHOEMAKER'S FIRST FARM, GERMANTOWN.—Page 23.

MARKET SQUARE AND CHURCH, GERMANTOWN.—Page 24.

Benjamin Lay, the hermit, called the "Pythagorean, cynical, Christian philosopher," dwelt in a cave on the York road, near Dr. De Benneville's. He left it in the year 1741, and went to reside with John Phipps, near Friends' meeting house at Abington. He was suddenly taken ill when from home, and desired he might be taken to the dwelling of his friend Joshua Morris, about a mile from Phipps', where he died on the 3d of February, 1759, aged 82 years. He was the first public declaimer against the iniquities of holding slaves. He was in communion with the Germantown *Friends*. It is to the honour of the German *Friends* of Germantown, that as early as 1688 they addressed the Philadelphia Yearly Meeting at Burlington, "protesting against the buying, selling, and holding men in slavery, and declaring it, in their opinion, an act irreconcileable with the precepts of the Christian religion."

Friends.—Their first meetings were held at Dennis Conrad's house, (then spelt Tennis Kundert,) as early as 1683. Part of the wall of that ancient house may now be seen on the north-west end of the two houses rebuilt and occupied by Lesher, as an inn. On the site where Dr. George Bensell's house now stands, there was an ancient house, pulled down by Dr. Bensell, in which William Penn preached: it was low and built of frame work and filled in with bricks. He also preached at Schumacher's ancient house, built in 1686, and till lately standing in Mehl's meadow—of which see a picture.

In 1705, the Friends built a meeting house of stone, in their present graveyard on the street. It has been taken down. From the original subscription and account book, it appears that they bought fifty acres for £60, raised by subscription of individuals and other meetings, in sums of from 20s. to £10, 4s. In Philadelphia, one hundred and thirty persons of that meeting gave £12, 7s. 8d. Eighteen Friends in Frankford contributed £22, 8s. In Abington, thirty-seven persons gave £21, 6s. chiefly in wheat at 4s. Byberry meeting gave forty bushels of wheat, £8, 3s. The prices of labour were then 3s. 6d., apples 1s. 6d. per bushel, boards 10s. per hundred, lime 14d., oats 2s. 6d., malt 4s. 6d., bricks 22s. per thousand, linseed oil 8s., nails 1s. 2d., shingles 10s. per thousand, timber 6s. per ton, sawing 10s. per hundred.

Tunkers.—In 1709, the *Tunkards* from Germany and Holland emigrated to Pennsylvania, and settled *first* at Germantown. Their first collected meetings were held in the *log house* in front of their present stone church in Beggarstown. Alex. Mack was then their principal leader. He was a very rich miller in Cresheim, gave all his property in common, and came with 8 or 10 to Germantown in 1708. He died old: and his son Alexander lived to be near 91 years of age. That *log house* was built in 1731, by John Pettikoffer, for his dwelling, who procured his funds, by asking gifts therefor from the inhabitants. Because it was the first house in the place and procured by begging, it was called "Beggarstown." The stone church on the same premises was built in 1770. Alex. Mack, junior, succeeded his father as minister, and Peter Baker had been their minister as early as 1723. The original Tunkers from Ephrata, used to dress alike, and without hats covered their heads with the hoods of their coats, which were a kind of gray surtout, like the Dominican friars. Old persons now living remember when forty or fifty of them would come thus attired on a religious visit from Ephrata, near Lancaster, to Germantown, walking *silently* in Indian file, and with long beards; also girt about the waist, and barefooted, or with sandals.

The *Mennonists'* first meeting house was built here in 1708, and was a log house, in the same lot where their present stone house (built in 1770) now stands. The log house was also a school house, kept by Christopher Duck, in 1740.

The *German Reformed* erected their first meeting house, opposite to the market house, about the year 1733. The front half part was first built; the back part was added in 1762. This old church, (of which a picture is given,) in the market square, originated as a Dutch Reformed, and was built and used as one directly under the Reformed church in Holland. From thence it had its first pastor. It had an ancient shingle roofed steeple after the Dutch manner, and was surmounted by a well finished iron *cock*, being the Dutch sign of a church. From its low elongated form, of stone, with its adjunct additions and affixes, and *bare* beams to the gallery—with high and narrow pulpit and sounding board—it was in itself a venerable specimen of the *olden time*, and for that cause was to be prized for its *associations.* It seemed in itself calculated to bring up the recollections of the forefathers who once worshipped there. It seemed the very place to inspire the descendants with hallowed reminiscences of those who had gone before them. Among its recollections was that of its being the place, in 1793, where General Washington and his family regularly went, as often as they had English preaching, which was sometimes done by Doctor Smith, from the Falls of Schuylkill. But time, and the passion for newness, resolved them "to pull down and build greater." They therefore lately made a new brick church in its place. The steeple was taken down with much skill, entire, and taken away to be preserved as a graceful summer house, by one who had the fancy for thus preserving it as a relic of the past; and the rod and vane were taken and set up again upon Mr. Stokes' hall. The steeple at the summit had many rifle bullets in it, shot there by the Paxtang boys, when they shot at the vane as a mark. The old organ, too, with its trumpet angels in their golden array, just as the whole came from Holland, was discarded and cast aside.

The whole subject forcibly brings to mind the poetic description made by Mrs. Seba Smith, saying,

They all are passing from the land,
Those churches old and gray,
In which our fathers used to stand,
In years gone by, to pray—

They never knelt,* those stern old men
  Who worshipp'd at our altars then.

No, all that e'en the semblance bore
  Of popedom on its face,
Our fathers as the men of yore
  Spurn'd from the holy place—
They bow'd the heart alone in prayer
  And worshipp'd God thus sternly there.

Through coarse gray plaster might be seen
  Oak timbers large and strong,
And those who reared them must have been
  Stout men when they were young—
For oft I've heard my grandsire speak,
How men were growing thin and weak.

His heart was twined, I do believe,
  Round every timber there—
For memory loved a web to weave
  Of all the young and fair,
Who gather'd there with him to pray
For many a long, long Sabbath day.

He saw again his youthful bride—
  His white hair'd boys once more
All walk'd demurely by his side,
  As in those days of yore.
Alas! those boys are old and gray,
And *she* hath pass'd in death away.

That *sounding board!* to me it seem'd
  A cherub poised on high—
A mystery I almost deem'd
  Quite hid from vulgar eye.
And that old pastor, wrapt in prayer,
Look'd doubly awful 'neath it there.

I see it all once more; once more
  That lengthen'd prayer I hear—
I hear the child's foot kick the door,—
  I see the mother's fear—
And that long knotty sermon too,
My grandsire heard it all quite through.

But as it deeper grew and deep—
  He always used to rise—
He would not like the women, sleep—
  But stood with fixed eyes,
And look'd intent upon the floor,
To hear each dark point o'er and o'er.

Aye pull them down, as well ye may,
  Those altars stern and old—

* It was one of the points of early opposition to *the Church*, that *dissenters* should not *kneel*, as they said the others did, *too much* by rule.

They speak of those long pass'd away,
Whose ashes now are cold.
Few, few are now the strong arm'd men
Who worshipp'd at our altars then.

And they reproach you with their might,
The pious, proud and free—
The wise in council, strong in fight,
Who never bow'd the knee.
And those gray churches only stand
As emblems of that hardy band.

Then pull them down and rear on high
New-fangled, painted things,
For these but mock the modern eye,
The past around them brings.
Then pull them down, and upward rear
A pile which suits who worship here.

The Lutheran Church.—It is not accurately known when this was built, but it had an addition of its front part made to it in 1746. It is certain, too, that there was a church in Germantown *before* the first one in Philadelphia, which was erected in 1743. The first ordained minister, Dr. H. M. Muhlenburg, came to Philadelphia in 1742, and of course before that time their services in Germantown were conducted by their schoolmaster, as is their practice in similar cases. In 1754 a lottery of five thousand tickets, at $2 each, was drawn in Philadelphia, to net £562 to purchase a messuage and lot of ground in Germantown for the minister of the Lutheran church and school house, &c., for the benefit of the poor of the society, the minister to instruct the poor children. In 1761 the Lutheran church at Barren-hill was also built by a lottery.

Nothing but German was preached in the Lutheran and German churches till of late years, and the present *Presbyterian* church was formed by the seceders from those churches, because the other members would not agree to have English preaching for *half* the time. They built their stone church in 1812, under the patronage of the Rev. Dr. Blair.

The *Methodists* began to preach in Germantown about the year 1798, and in 1800 they built their stone meeting house, in the lane opposite to Mr. Samuel Harvey's house. In 1823, their former church being too small, they built a new and larger meeting house.

The *Protestant Episcopal Church* of St. Luke was built in the year 1819: the first Rector was the Rev. Charles Dupuy: previously the society assembled for worship at the house of James Stokes, at the corner of the church lane.

The lower burying ground of half an acre was the gift of John Streeper, of Germany, per Leonard Aret; and the upper one was given by Paul Wolff. The potter's field in Bowman's lane was bought in 1755 for £5 10s. containing one hundred and forty perches.

The first grist mill set up in Philadelphia county was that now called Roberts' mill, in Church lane, just one mile north-east from the market square. Roberts' mill was erected as early as 1683, by Richard Townsend, a public Friend, who brought the chief materials from England. Some years afterwards, in his printed address to Friends, he speaks of this mill and his early difficulties, and the kind providence extended to him there, which are very interesting. He states that his was the only mill for grain in all the parts; and was of great use to the inhabitants. That they brought their grist on men's backs, save one man, who had a tame *bull* which performed the labour. That by reason of his seclusion in the midst of the woods, he had but little chance of any supply of flesh meat, and was sometimes in great straits therefor. On one occasion, while he was mowing in his meadow a young deer came near to him, and seemed to wonder at his labour; it would follow him up while he worked, but when he stopped or approached it, it skipped away; but an accident made him stumble, and so scared the deer, that he rushed suddenly aside against a sapling, and being stunned, he fell and was taken alive and killed, to the great relief of the family. See Appendix, p. 511.

The first paper mill in Pennsylvania was built by Garret Rittenhouse. It stood about a hundred yards higher up the stream than where old Martin Rittenhouse now lives, at C. Markle's. It was carried off by a freshet. William Penn wrote a letter soliciting the good people to give some aid in rebuilding it with their money. The grist mill, now Nicholas Rittenhouse's, on Wissahiccon, below Markle's, was built without the use of carts, or roads or barrows.

The Academy.—There were numerous scholars here in the German school, sixty-five years ago; now there are none taught. The public school now called the Academy was first commenced in building in 1760, by a subscription chiefly raised in Philadelphia; but it not being likely to be finished thereby, in 1761 they made a lottery to draw in Philadelphia, of 6667 tickets, at $3, to raise $3000 at 15 per cent. to finish it. In 1821 the legislature granted $1000 to help it out of debt. Their first teacher was Dove, distinguished in Philadelphia as a scholar: and he had considerable fame as a satirical poet in political controversies. He used to send a committee of boys with a lantern and candle *in day time*, ringing a bell, to find absent scholars, and bring them with shame to school. His name was David I. Dove. He differed with the trustees, and built the house next to the Academy as an opposition seminary, and found himself unsuccessful and mortified. Pelatiah Webster succeeded him; all that time there was also a German master and scholars, and all the education there was at 10s. per quarter, and now English is $5, and the languages $10.

The *market house and prison* was built in 1741. The ground was granted for that purpose by James de la Plaine in 1701; the said De la Plaine lived in and owned James Stokes' house. There was once a *pound* in the market square at the south-east end, and near it stood a small log prison, in which one Adam Hogermoed was imprisoned for a small offence of intemperance. His friends pried it up at one corner and let him out at night. Some time after he made the prison his free house, for when the charter was lost, it was sold to him and he moved it to where it now forms part of Joseph Green's group of houses.

In 1761 Jacob Coleman began, from the King of Prussia Inn, the first *stage* with an *awning*, to run to Philadelphia, three times a week, to the George Inn, south-west corner of Second and Arch streets. He afterwards ran a stage to Reading.

I have not seen any ancient inhabitant who had a correct knowledge respecting the terms on which they once held *court*. They had a tradition that they held courts here *before* it was done in Philadelphia! But I have seen the record of the original patent, from which I abstract as follows, viz.—A patent of William Penn, dated *London*, August 12, 1689, and on the back thereof, this endorsement, viz.: "12 8mo. 1689, let this pass the great seal. To Thomas Lloyd, keeper thereof, in Pennsylvania. (Signed) William Penn." On the *inside* was affixed, "passed under the great seal of the province of Pennsylvania, on the 3d day of the 3d mo. 1691." This therefore marks the period, I presume, at which they began to live subject to the laws of a *borough town*. The patent grants "that Francis Daniel Pastorius, *civilian*, and J. Tellner, merchant, Dirk Isaacs op den Graeff and eight other freemen of Germantown, (named,) shall be a body corporate by the name of the bailiff, burgesses and commonalty of Germantown, in the *county of* Philadelphia. To have *perpetual* succession, and at *all times* thereafter shall be able and capable in law with a joint stock to trade, and with the same to take, purchase, &c., messuages, lands, &c., of a yearly value of £1500 per annum. To have and to use a common *seal*. That there shall be elected *one bailiff* (Pastorius) and four burgesses and six persons committee-men, all from the aforesaid *eleven* nominated corporation, which shall constitute 'and be *called* the General Court of the Corporation of Germantown.' The then appointed corporation to continue in office till the 1st December next ensuing, and *from thence* UNTIL there be a new choice of other persons to succeed them, 'according *as therein directed*.'

The bailiff and the two eldest burgesses for the time being shall be *justices of the peace*. The bailiff and the oldest burgesses, and the *recorder* for the time being, shall hold and keep one *court of record*, to be held every *six weeks* for hearing all civil causes according to the laws of the province. And also to hold and to keep a *market* every *sixth* day, in such places as *the provincial charter doth direct*."

[Recorded at Philadelphia, 13th 3d month, 1691.]

The government of Germantown *began* the 6th of 8mo. 1691, and terminated 25th of 12th mo. 1706-7, being fifteen years.

The borough and court records of Germantown were ordered to the Recorder's office in Philadelphia, by an act of the General Assembly in 1769. From those records I have extracted the following

GREEN'S HOUSE, GERMANTOWN.—Page 28.

primitive and "simple annals" of that *beginning era* of settlement and civilization, to wit:

The Records of the Courts of Record held in the Corporation of Germantown, from the 6th day of 8th month, anno 1691, [the year of their getting their charter from William Penn,] and thenceforward from time to time;—*thus transcribed* by order of a general court held at the said Germantown, the 26th day of 10th month, in the year 1696.

Anno 1691. The 6th day of the 8th month *the first court of record* was held at Germantown, in the public meeting house, [of Friends,] before Francis Daniel Pastorius, bailiff, Jacob Tellner, Dirk Isaacs op den Graef, and Herman Isaacs op den Graef, the three eldest burgesses. Isaac Jacobs van Bebber, recorder; Paul Wolf, clerk; Andrew Souplis, sheriff; Jan Lucken, constable. Proclamation being made by Andrew Souplis, the charter was read, and the officers attested. Caspar Carsten and his wife, who were both bound over to this court for menacing the constable, when about to serve a warrant upon them, were called, and, submitting to the bench, were fined two pounds, ten shillings. The court adjourned until the 17th of November next.

1692, the 29th day of 9th month. John Silans (upon Jacob Schumacher's complaint) promised before this court to finish the said Jacob Schumacher's barn within four weeks next coming. [Observe there are no fines or penalties in the case—only a *promise* of better action!] Walter Simons and James de la Plaine, for themselves and in behalf of their neighbourhood, protested against the road from the Mill street towards Thomas Rutter's, as not being laid out by the governor's order.

1692–3, the 21st day of 12th month. By reason of the absence of some, for religious meeting over Schuylkill, this court was adjourned till the 4th of 2d month, 1693. [How considerate and accommodating!]

1693, the 8th day of 6th month. Francis Daniel Pastorius, as attorney of the Frankford Company, delivered unto Wigart Levering a deed of enfeoffment containing fifty acres in Germantown. James de la Plaine, coroner, brought into this court the names of the jury which he summoned the 24th day of 4th month, 1701, viz.—Thomas Williams, foreman, Peter Hearlis, Herman op den Graef, Reiner Peters, Peter Shoemaker, Reiner Tissen, Peter Brown, John Unslett, Thomas Potts, Reiner Hermans, Dirk Johnson, Herman Turner. Their verdict was as followeth: We, the jury, find that through carelessness the cart and the lime killed the man; the wheel wounded his back and head, and it killed him.

1701, the 20th day of 11th month. Reiner Peters, for calling the sheriff, on open street, a rascal and liar, was fined 20 shillings.

1703, the 28th day of 12th month. When the cause of Matthew Smith against Daniel Faulkner being moved, the plaintiff, by reason of conscience, viz., that this day was the day wherein Herod slew the innocents, as also that his witnesses were and would for the aforesaid reason not be here, desired a continuance to the next court of record to be held for this corporation; which was allowed of, provided the said Daniel Faulkner do then appear and stand to trial.

1703–4, the 8th day of 12th month. George Müller, for his drunkenness, was condemned to five days' imprisonment. Item, to pay the constable 2 shillings for serving the warrant in the case of his laying a wager to smoke above one hundred pipes in one day.

[At this place there seems to be a stoppage of court proceedings, until the next opening in 1706–7, which was then made *final.* A letter of Pastorius to Wm. Penn, when in Philadelphia in 1701–2, which I have seen, says, he believes there will be a difficulty to get men to serve in the general court, "*for conscience sake*"—meaning the oaths.]

On the 17th of 12th mo., 1701, the general court of Germantown present to Wm. Penn, their "honourable and dear governor," newly arrived, "the petition of the Germantown corporation"—to the effect, "that seventeen years preceding they had laid out the township in lots and more compact settlements than elsewhere had been done, so that some dwelling so near each other, had not enough of timber to make their separate fences, whereby they were compelled to fence in four quarters—[meaning, it is believed, on the four angles of the oblong square, on the outside only]—consequently requiring much care, lest by carelessness of one or other, the rest [within the enclosure] should suffer harm or injury."

They also represent, "that by reason of the charter of 1689, granted unto Germantown—construing the same most beneficially to the grantees, they have hitherto refused to pay those taxes, levies and impositions, which the county courts do lay upon those under *their* jurisdiction—for being by the said charter exempted from the county court of Philadelphia, and having our own court of record, as well as our general court, we cannot but believe that we are freed from all charges towards the said county—seeing that it would be rather a burthen than a privilege to pay *both* the county taxes and the taxes of our own corporation. [Just the very thing which *citizens* of Philadelphia now do.] As to the provincial taxes we make no exceptions, and are willing to bear our share, as good and loyal subjects should."

"We implore thy benevolence, that thou wilt so defend and support our township, by way of explanation to thy aforesaid charter, that our corporation *may be exempted* from all and every *county* tax; and whereas, we before represented a difficulty of finding persons to serve in the corporation, for conscience sake, we hope it may be remedied, *as it is already in part*, by arrivals of new comers among us."

1706–7, the 11th day of 12th month, (January,) before Thomas Rutter, bailiff, &c. The court was opened; the queen's attorney

George Lowther laid the following points before this court: 1st, that the general court of this corporation did lay taxes, &c.; 2d, that the justices wanted their qualifications; 3d, that this court did clear by proclamation, &c., and 4th, bind over to the peace, and not to the Philadelphia county; 5th, that Johannes Kuster married a couple without the limits of the corporation; and [he, the said queen's attorney,] desired the court's answer to the government: whereupon this court adjourned till two o'clock in the afternoon, and having given their answers to the said attorney-general, further adjourned to the 25th day of this instant.

N. B. The said attorney-general *promising then* to procure the government power to qualify them himself—the which, nevertheless, *he did not, though often required and well paid; and therefore, from thence, no more courts were kept at Germantown!* And the above charged points being partly false, and the others sufficiently answered, convinced the said attorney-general, as by his own hand-writing, hereunto affixed, may appear.

Old Mr. J. W., about the year 1720, purchased five hundred acres of land at 2*s.* per acre, adjacent to where his descendant now lives; when he afterwards sold much of it at £3 per acre, he thought he was doing wonders; some of it has since been worth $200 to $300 per acre.

The price of labour in and about Germantown, sixty years ago, was 3*s.* a day in summer, and 2*s.* 6*d.* in winter. The price of hickory wood was 10 to 11*s.* per cord, and oak was 8 to 9*s.* Hickory now sells at $8, and oak at $6, and has been $2 higher.

In 1738 a county tax was assessed of 1½*d.* per pound on the city and county, (including Germantown,) for "*wolves* and *crows* destroyed, and for assemblymen's wages," at 5*s.* per day.

The blackbirds formerly were much more numerous than now; a gentleman mentioned to me that when he was a young man, he once killed at one shot (with mustard seed shot) one hundred and nineteen birds, which he got; some few of the wounded he did not get; they had alighted in an oat-field after the harvest, and he was concealed in a near hedge, and shot them as they rose on the wing. There was a law in 1700 made to give 3*d.* per dozen for the heads of blackbirds, to destroy them.

A person, now 80 years of age, relates to me that he well remembers seeing colonies of Indians, of twenty to thirty persons, often coming through the town and sitting down in Logan's woods, others on the present open field, south-east of Grigg's place. They would then make their huts and stay a whole year at a time, and make and sell baskets, ladles, and tolerably good fiddles. He has seen them shoot birds and young squirrels there, with their bows and arrows. Their huts were made of four upright saplings, with crotch limbs at top. The sides and tops were of cedar bushes and branches. In these they lived in the severest winters; their fire was on the ground and in the middle of the area. At that time wild pigeons were very numerous, in flocks of a mile long; and it was very common to shoot twenty or thirty of them at a shot. They then caught rabbits and squirrels in snares.

The superstition then was very great about ghosts and witches. "Old Shrunk," as he was called, (George S., who lived to be 80,) was a great conjuror, and numerous persons from Philadelphia and elsewhere, and some even from Jersey, came to him often, to find out stolen goods and to get their fortunes told. They believed *he* could *make* any thieves who came to steal from his orchard "*stand*," if he saw them, even while they desired to run away. They used to consult him where to go and dig for money; and several persons, whose names I suppress, used to go and dig for hidden treasures of nights. On such occasions, if any one "*spoke*," while digging, or ran, from "*terror*," without "the *magic ring*," previously made with incantation around the place, the whole influence of the "*spell*" was lost. Dr. Witt, too, a sensible man, who owned and dwelt in the large house, since the Rev. Dr. Blair's, as well as old Mr. Frailey, who also acted as a physician, and was really pretty skilful, were both U——e doctors, (according to the superstition then so prevalent in Europe,) and were renowned also as conjurors. Then the cows and horses, and even children, got strange diseases; and if it baffled ordinary medicines, or Indian cures and herbs, it was not unusual to consult those persons for relief; and their prescriptions which healed them, as resulting from witchcraft, always gave relief! Dr. Frailey dwelt in a one-story house, very ancient, now standing in the school house lane. On each side of his house were lines of German poetry, painted in oil colours, (some of the marks are even visible now); those on one side have been recited to me, viz.:

	Translated thus.
Lass Neider neiden,	Let the envious envy me,
Lass Hasser hassen;	Let the hater hate me;
Was Gott mir giebt	What God has given me
Muss mann mir lassen.	Must man leave to me.

An idea was very prevalent, especially near the Delaware and Schuylkill waters, that the pirates of Black Beard's day had deposited treasure in the earth. The fancy was, that sometimes they killed a prisoner and interred him with it, to make his ghost keep his vigils there and guard it. Hence it was not rare to hear of persons having seen a *sphoke* or ghost, or of having dreamed of it a plurality of times, which became a strong incentive to dig there. To procure the aid of a professor in the black art, was called *Hexing;* and Shrunk, in particular, had great fame therein. He affected to use a diviner's rod, (*a witch-hazel*) with a peculiar angle in it, which was supposed to be self-turned in the hands, when approached to any minerals; some use the same kind of rod now to *feel* for hidden waters, so as to dig for wells. The late Col. T. F. used to amuse himself much with the credulity of the people. He pretended he could *hex* with a hazel rod; and often he has had superstitious persons to come and offer him shares in spoils, which they had seen a *sphoke* upon! He even wrote and printed a curious old play,* to ridicule the thing. Describing the terrors of a midnight fright in digging, he makes one of the party to tell his wife,

> "My dearest wife, in all my life
> Ich neber was so fritened;
> De spirit come, and Ich did run,
> 'Twas juste like tunder, mid lightning."

Mr. K., when aged 78, and his wife nearly the same age, mentioned to me, that in their youthful days they used to feel themselves as if at double or treble the distance they now do from Philadelphia, owing to the badness and loneliness of the roads; they then regarded a ride to the city as a serious affair. The road before it was turnpiked was extremely clayey and mirey, and in some places, especially at Penn's creek, there was a fearful quicksand. Several teams were often joined at places along the bad road to help out of mires, and horses were much injured, and sometimes killed, thereby. Rail stakes used to be set up in bad places to warn off.

In those times the sleighing used to continue for two or three months in the winter, and the pleasure parties from the city used to put up and have dances at old Macknett's tavern, where his son since lived. It was then very common for sailors to come out in summer to have frolics, or mirth and refreshments at the inns. The young men also made great amusement of shooting at a target. They used no wagons in going to market, but the woman went, and rode a horse with two panniers slung on each side of her. The women too carried baskets on their heads, and the men wheeled wheel-barrows—being six miles to market! Then the people, especially man and wife, rode to church, funerals and visits, both on *one* horse; the woman sat on a pillion behind the man. Chairs or chaises were then unknown to them; none in that day ever dreamed to live to see such improvements and luxury as they now witness.

The first carriage of the coach kind they ever saw or heard of belonged to Judge Allen,† who had his country seat at the present Mount Airy College; it was of the phaeton or Landau kind, having a seat in front for children, and was drawn by four black horses: he was of course a very opulent man, a grandee in his generation—such phaetons cost £400. The country seats then were few. Penington had his country house where Chew's now stands, and the present kitchen wings of Chew's house sufficed for the simplicity of gentlemen of those days. Another country house was Samuel Shoemaker's, a mayor of Philadelphia, and is the same now a part

---

* A copy of it is in the Athenæum Library.

† There were three or four earlier carriages in Philadelphia, viz.: Norris, Logan, and Shippen's.

of the house of Mr. Duval's place, and enlarged by Col. T. Forrest. In their early days, all the better kinds of houses had *balconies* in the front, in which, at the close of the day, it was common to see the women at most of the houses sitting and sewing or knitting; at that time the women went to their churches generally in short gowns and petticoats, and with check or white flaxen aprons. The young men had their heads shaved, and wore white caps; in summer they went without coats, wearing striped trowsers, and barefooted; the old Friends wore wigs.

In their day every house was warmed in winter by "jamb stoves," and Mr. Sower, of Germantown, (the printer,) cast the first stoves perhaps thus used in the United States. They were cast in Lancaster; none of them are now up and in use, but many of the *plates* are often seen lying about the old houses as door steps, &c. A jamb stove was set in the chimney jamb, (or side,) in the kitchen fire-place; it was made something like the box form of the present ten-plate stoves, but without a pipe or oven, and it passed through the wall of the chimney back into the adjoining sitting rooms, so as to present its back end (opposite the *fire door*) in that room. The plate used to be made sometimes red hot; but still it was but a poor means of giving out heat, and could not have answered but for their then hardy constitutions, and the general smallness of their rooms in that day.

Mr. K. remembers very well, that when he was a lad, there was yet a little company of Delaware Indians, (say 25 or 30 persons,) then hutted and dwelling on the low grounds of Philip Kelley's manufactory ground. There was then a wood there through all the low ground, which now forms his meadow ground and mill race course. Some of the old Indians died and were buried in Concord burying ground, adjoining Mr. Duval's place. After they were dead the younger Indians all moved off in a body, when Keyser was about 14 or 15 years of age. Indian Ben among them was celebrated as a great fiddler, and every body was familiar with Indian Isaac.

In going to the city there was a thick woods on the south-west side of the turnpike below Naglee's hill—where Skerrett's house now stands, called Logan's swamp and woods. The road then went on the low ground to the south-westward of said hill and house. At Penn's creek, (or Three-mile run, now Albanus Logan's place,) and at the opposite side on Norris' place, began a deep and lofty wood, which extended on both sides of the road nearly into the suburbs, and from thence the woods continued many miles up the Delaware. There was then no inlet into the city but by the *Front street* road. The Second and Third streets were not then formed.

On the 20th of October, 1746, a great public fair was held at Germantown.

In 1762, the Paxton boys, from near Lancaster, halted at the market square, preparatory to their intended invasion of Philadelphia, to kill the friendly Indians sheltered there; they yielded to negotiation and went home. There were several hundred of them.

Rittenhouse, the celebrated philosopher, as well as Godfrey, the inventor of Hadley's quadrant, were of the neighbourhood of Germantown. Captain Miller, who was basely killed at Fort Washington, after its surrender, was of Germantown.

The old road of Germantown continued in a line with the first bank of Germantown, (to the south-west of the present,) ran near the poor house, by S. Harvey's, up through R. Haines' low lands, and came out by the Concord school house, by the Washington, or Abington lane. Some of the logs now lie sound under ground, back of Justice Johnson's, on which the road ran by the *swamp*.

The quantity of Indian arrow heads, spears, and hatchets, all of flint and stone, and attached to wooden or withe handles, still ploughed up in the fields, is great. I have seen some of a heap of two hundred together, in a circle of the size of a bushel; some of them, strange to tell, are those taken from chalk beds, and not at all like the flint of our country.

The creek on which Wm. L. Fisher's mill stands is the head of Frankford creek, and was called by the Indians *Wingohocking*. The creek at Albanus Logan's, called Penn's creek, was called *Tumanaxamaming*, and goes out at the upper end of Kensington.

Anthony Johnson, who died in 1823, aged 78, saw, when a lad, a large bear come across the road in daytime from Chew's ground, then a wood; he has seen abundance of wild turkeys, and has often heard the wolves howl at night near his father's house; the one rebuilt at the corner of S. Harvey's lane. The woods then came up near the house. He has seen several deer in the woods, but they were fast going off when he was young. Near the same house, when the old road passed in the swamp behind it, his father told him he once saw six wolves in daytime.

After James Logan's house was built, in 1728, at Stenton, a bear of large size came and leaped over the garden fence.

Jacob Keyser, now 88, tells me that he and others pursued and killed a small bear, about sixty-five years ago, on one of the back lots; it was, however, then matter of surprise and sport.

Mr. K. remembers that a Mr. Axe, in his time, killed a bear on Samuel Johnson's place, not far from the *Wissahiccon*. Foxes and rackoons were then quite plenty.

Only about fifty years ago a flock of six wild turkeys came to Enoch Rittenhouse's mill, and remained about there till his family shot the whole of them; and in the winter of 1832 they shot a lynx there.

In 1721 a bear was killed *in* Germantown, and *so published*, and two more nearer to Philadelphia.

In the house of Reuben Haines, built by Dirk Johnson, a chief and his twenty Indians have been sheltered and entertained.

Anthony Johnson, when a boy, has seen near two hundred Indians at a time on the present John Johnson's place, in a woods on the hollow adjoining to the wheelwright's shop. They would remain there a week at a time, to make and sell baskets, ladles, fiddles, &c He used to remain hours with them and see their feats of agility. They would go over fences without touching them, in nearly a horizontal attitude, and yet alight on their nimble feet. They would also do much at shooting of marks. One Edward Keimer imitated them so closely as to execute all their exploits. Beaver and beaver dams A. Johnson has often seen.

The earliest settlers used to make good linens and vend them in Philadelphia. They were also distinguished, even till modern times, for their fabric of Germantown stockings. This fact induced the Bank of Germantown to adopt a seal, with such a loom upon it. The linen sellers and weavers used to stand with the goods for sale on the edge of the pavement in Market street, on the north side, near to Second street corner. The cheapness of imported stockings is now ruining their business.

Professor Kalm, who visited Germantown in 1748, says: "The inhabitants were so numerous, that the street was always full."

Old Mr. W., in 1718 or '20, shot a stout deer between Germantown and Philadelphia, and the rifle he used is now in possession of his grandson.

John Seelig predicted men's lives when requested, by the rules of nativities; and he had a mysterious *cane*, or rod, which he commanded to be cast into the Schuylkill in his last sickness, and which, as the tradition goes, exploded therein! Kelpius too kept his diary by noting the signs of the Zodiac.

Doctor Witt left all his property to strangers by the name of *Warmer*, saying, they had been kind to him on his arrival, in bestowing him a *hat* in place of his, lost on shipboard.

The tombstone of C. F. Post, the missionary and interpreter, so often named in Proud's history, is in the lower burying ground. He died in 1785, aged 75 years.

The Germantown newspaper, by C. Sower, was printed but once a *quarter*, and began in the year 1739; and what was curious, he cast his own types and made his own ink! It eventually was printed *monthly*, but from and after the year 1744, it was printed every *week*, under the title of the "Germantown Gazette," by C. Sower, Jr., and was not discontinued till some time in the war. A copy of these papers would be a kind gift to the Germantown Library. Sower published *first* in the United States a quarto Bible, in German.

Germantown was a place of great interest during the war of the revolution, and at the celebrated battle there. It occurred on the morning of the 4th of October, 1777. The main body of the British army, under Gens. Howe, Grey, Grant and Agnew, were attacked by the Americans in the following order: Washington, with the division of Sullivan and Wayne, flanked by Gen. Thomas Conway's brigade, entered the town by Chestnut hill road. Gen. Armstrong, with the Pennsylvania militia, attacked the left and rear, near Schuylkill. The division of Generals Greene and Stephens, flanked by Gen. M'Dougall's brigade, were to enter by taking a circuit at the market house, and attack the right wing, and the militia of Maryland and Jersey, under Generals Smallwood and Freeman, were to march by the old York road and fall upon the rear of the right. General Sterling, with Generals Nash and Maxwell's brigade, formed a corps of reserve. Admirably as this attack was *planned*, it failed, from those fortuitous events in warfare, over which Gen. Washington had no possible control. Lieut. Col. Musgrave, of the British army, as the Americans advanced, threw himself, with six companies of the 40th regiment, into Chew's large stone house, which stood full in front of the main body of the Americans. Musgrave, before the battle, encamped back of Chew's house in excellent huts, and Col. Webster's regiment (33d) lay back of John Johnson's in huts also; they were as regular and neat as a town. Gen. Read, it has been said, was for pushing on immediately, and was opposed by Gen. Knox as against military rule, to leave an enemy *in a fort* in the rear. Any how, in attempting to induce the surrender of Lieut. Col. Musgrave, the precious moments were lost, and gave Generals Grey, Grant, and Agnew, (who dwelt in Germantown,) time to come up with a reinforcement. Much blame, too, was attached to Gen. S.'s division, who was said to have been intoxicated, and to have so far misconceived and broken his orders as to have been afterwards tried and broken. The morning was exceedingly foggy, which would have greatly favoured the Americans, had not those, as well as part of Greene's column, remained thus inactive. Col. Mathews, of Greene's column, attacked with great spirit and routed the parties opposed to him, and took one hundred and ten prisoners; but, through the fog, he lost sight of his brigade, and was himself taken prisoner with his whole regiment, (on P. Kelley's hill) and his prisoners released. Greene and Stephens' division, formed the last column of the retreating Americans. Count Pulaski's cavalry covered their rear. Washington retreated to Skippack creek—his loss amounted to one hundred and fifty-two killed, and five hundred and twenty-one wounded, upwards of four hundred were made prisoners, amongst whom were fifty-four officers.

The *cannon* which assailed Chew's house were planted in front of the present John Johnson's house; Chew's house was so battered that it took four or five carpenters a whole winter to repair and replace the fractures. The front door which was replaced was filled with shot holes—it is still preserved there.

A cousin of mine, who was intimate with Gen. Washington's aid-de-camp, told me that he told him he had never heard the general utter an oath, but on that day, when he seemed deeply mortified and indignant, he expressed an *execration* at General S—— as a drunken rascal.

The daughter of Benjamin Marshal, Esq., at whose house General

Washington stopped after the battle, told me he reached there in the evening, and would only take a dish of tea, and pulling out the *half* of a biscuit, assured the family the other half was all the food he had taken since the preceding day.

The general opinion then was, that but for the delay at Chew's house, our army must have been victorious, and we should have been sufficiently avenged for our losses the preceding month at the battle of Brandywine, and would have probably caused the British to evacuate Philadelphia. But Gen. Wilkinson, in his late memoirs, who has described minutely the battle therein, and was but a few years ago here on the spot, examining the whole ground, has published his entire conviction that it was a *kind providence*, which overruled the disaster for our good: for had we been successful and pushed on for the city, Gen. Howe was coming on with a force sufficient to have captured or destroyed the whole American army. He states, that Washington relied on information from a deserter, that Howe intended a movement of his troops towards Fort Mifflin, which, unknown to Gen. Washington, he had countermanded, and so enabled him to come out in full force. See Appendix, p. 554.

There were as many as twenty thousand British, &c., in and about the town under Gen. Howe. He was a fine large man, and looked considerably like Gen. Washington: he lived some time at Logan's, and also in the present Samuel Morris' house; he walked abroad in plain clothes in a very unassuming manner. Gen. Grant occupied the house now Michael Staiger's, near the lane. The artillery lay on the high ground in rear of the poor house; two regiments of Highlanders half a mile in the rear of Reuben Haines' house: and the Hessians lay on the Ridge *Hill* above Peter Robeson's, near the road; all the infantry were on the commons about where J. Price's seat now is.

In the time of the battle Gen. Howe came as far as the market square, and stayed there giving his commands. Gen. Agnew rode on at the head of his men, and when he came as far as the wall of the Mennonist grave yard, he was shot by Hans P. Boyer, who lay in ambush, and took deliberate aim at his star on the breast: he fell from his fine horse, and was carried to Mr. Wister's house, where he died in his front parlour. He was a very civil and gentlemanly man. The man who killed him was not an enlisted soldier, and died not long since in the poor house.

At that same place is a rising hill, at which the severest of the firing and battle was waged, except what occurred so disastrously for us at Chew's house. The British advanced no farther than the said hill on the road, until after the retreat.

Several have told me, who saw the dead and dying after the action, lying on the ground, that some in their last moments were quite insane: but all who could speak were in great *thirst* from anguish, &c. In Samuel Keyser's garden many bodies were lying: and in the rear of Justice Johnson's, Gen. Morgan of the rifle corps came up with a small body after the action was supposed to be closed, and very daringly and unexpectedly killed nineteen Hessians and an officer, all of whom were buried there, save the officer, who was next day removed to the city. Boys were suffered to get very near the combatants on the flanks. Benjamin Lehman was one, who has told me, there was no order nor ranks after the first fire, and soon every face was as black as negroes' about the mouth and cheeks, from biting off the cartridges; British officers, especially aids-de-camp, rode at full rate up and down through the men, with entire unconcern as to running over them. The ranks, however, gave way.

When the British burned seventeen houses at one time, between Philadelphia and Germantown, in retaliation for some aggressions made, they said, by Col. Ayres, from some of those houses, they ordered Stenton house to be included: two men came to execute it, they told the housekeeper there, to take out her private things—while they went to the barn for straw to fire it. A British officer rode up, inquiring for deserters; with much presence of mind she said they had just gone to the barn to hide themselves in the straw—off he went, crying, "Come out you rascals, and run before me back to camp!" In vain they protested, and alleged their commissions; and thus Logan's venerable house was spared. This house was built in 1727–8, by James Logan, secretary for Penn, and in which he resided; it was a palace-like structure in that day, and was surprisingly well built. Gen. Howe stayed part of his time there.

A fence of cedar boards is now standing in Peter Keyser's yard, which was very much perforated with musket bullets in the time of the battle.

On the 19th of October, the British army removed from Germantown to Philadelphia, as a more convenient place for the reduction of Fort Island.

After the battle, the British surgeons made use of Reuben Haines' hall as a room for amputating and other hospital operations requiring prompt care; the Americans who were wounded were carried to the hill where Thomas Armatt's house is, and were there temporarily attended by surgeons, previously to being sent to the hospital in the city.

Capt. Turner of North Carolina, and Major Irvine, and six men, were all buried in one grave, at the N. E. corner of the burying ground by the school house. We have set them a stone there.

On the north-east side of Three-mile run (Fox Chase Inn now) was a wood in the time of the war. In it were thirty Oneida Indians, and one hundred of Morgan's riflemen, who raised a warwhoop and frightened Lord Carthcart when in a conference with M'Lane.

A British picket lay in the present yard of Philip Weaver, and several were shot and buried there. The most advanced picket stood at Mount Airy, and was wounded there.

Gen. Agnew and Col. Bird, of the British army, are both buried in the lower burying ground, side by side, next to Mrs. Lamb's grave.

stone, (south-west side of it,) at ten feet from Rapp's wall, in a line with the south-west end of his stable. Gen. Agnew showed great kindness to old Mrs. Sommers. Col. Bird died in Bringhurst's big house, and said to the woman there, "woman, pray for me, I leave a widow and four children." The late Mr Burrill, whose father was grave-digger, told me he saw them buried *there*. They now have a stone.

When the British were in Germantown, they took up all the fences and made the rails into huts, by cutting down all the buckwheat, putting it on the rails, and ground over that. No fences remained. Gen. Howe lived a part of his time at the house now S. B. Morris', so said B. Lehman. B. Lehman was an apprentice to Mr. Knorr, a carpenter, and went to the city with half a calf on his shoulder, for which he got quickly 2s. 6d., metal money, per pound, he also sold his old hen for 1 dollar! He saw there men come stealthily from Skippack, with butter carried on their backs in boxes, which they sold at 5s. There were woods all along the township line to near the city, and they could steal their way through them. Lehman was out two months in the militia draft, but never in battle, he got 200 dollars paper money; for 100 dollars he bought a sleigh ride, and for the other 100 dollars a pair of shoes! Samuel Widdes, in Germantown, used to go to the city with a wheelbarrow to take therein apples and pears, which he sold high. Lehman, and all the other boys, *went to meeting* in tow trowsers and shirts, without jackets or shoes. What homely days! At that time, and during all the war, all business was at a stand. Not a house was roofed or mended in Germantown in five or six years. Most persons who had any substance lived in part on what they could procure on loan. The people, pretty generally, were mentally averse to the war—equal, certainly, to two-thirds of the population of the place who felt as if they had any thing to lose by the contest. So several have told me.

Mrs. Bruner, who died in Germantown, in 1835, at the age of 80, the wife of a blacksmith, in respectable circumstances, had been the mother of twelve children, and kept her house with such a family more than sixty years of her life without ever having had any hired help. She had done all her own work and done it well; and very often, in her younger days, she had sat down every night, after her house work was done, to make leather gloves for pay as a seamstress. She was but a specimen of many of her day, who looked to such industry as a means to acquire a small estate at the end of a long life. Industry became so habitual to both husband and wife, that they knew not, in time, *how to rest* when idle. The family was pious, benevolent and kind. When shall we see such people among the moderns?

The trustees of the Academy of Germantown, in the year 1793, had applications from the *State*, and *United States*, to rent their academy for their use. It was thereupon resolved by the trustees, on the 26th October, 1793, that they would take measures to accommodate the *Congress of the United States*, at their next session, with the use of the same, for the sum of 300 dollars. Only think of such a school-house, of eighty by fifty feet, being seriously purposed for the use of the American congress. The congress was *then* so small; it is now so great.

The circumstance which led to the intended application of the house, grew out of an inquiry made by Gen. Washington, who then resided in Germantown, in the house afterwards for many years the summer residence of the Perot family—now of Samuel B. Morris. In 1793, when Gen. Washington dwelt in Germantown, the town was held as the government place of the state of Pennsylvania and of the United States; and this was because of the necessary retreat of the officers and offices, from the city of Philadelphia, where the yellow fever was raging with destructive effect. At that time the office of state, &c., of Pennsylvania, was held in the stone house next above B. Lehman's. There you could every day see Governor Mifflin and his secretary of state, A. J. Dallas. The house now the Bank of Germantown was occupied by Thomas Jefferson, as secretary of state of the United States, and by Mr. Randolph, as attorney general. The Bank of the United States was located in the three-storied stone house of Billings, and when its treasure was brought, it was guarded by a troop of horse. Oellers, once celebrated for his great hotel for the congressmen, in Chestnut street, had his hotel here, in the house since Clement Bringhurst's; and, at that house, filled with lodgers, the celebrated Bates, of comic memory, used to hold musical soirees at 50 cents a head, to help to moderate the gloom of the sad times. At that time, the whole town was crowded with strangers and boarders; and especially by numerous French emigrants, escaped from the massacre of St. Domingo.

It was then expected that the next, or future years, might be again visited by yellow fever; and, therefore, numerous engagements of houses, and purchases of grounds at increased prices were made, to insure a future refuge. In this way, the Banks of North America and of Pennsylvania found a place in the Academy in the next fever, which occurred in 1798.

It ought to be mentioned as a peculiar circumstance connected with Perot's house, before mentioned, that it had been the residence severally of Gen. Howe, the British commander in the war of the revolution, and *at the same time*, the home of the then youth, Prince William, the late king of England, William IV.; afterwards, in 1793, the residence of Gen. Washington, while President of the United States. Look at its size as then regarded good enough and large enough for a president, in contrast with the present presidential palace at Washington city! It is thus that we are rapidly growing as a nation from small things to great things!

The French West India residents that were in Germantown, were of various complexions, were dressed in clothing of St. Domingo fashion, presenting a peculiarity of costume; and showing much gayety of manners. They filled the streets with French conversation by day—for they were all idlers; and with much of music at night. They were withal great shooters, and killed and eat all manner of birds without discrimination—they saying that crows, swallows, &c., were as good as others, as all depended upon the style of the cooking.

I have seen or known of several officers of the Revolution, who had been in the battle of Germantown, who came again, in advanced age, to revisit the active scenes of their military prowess; so came Capt. Blakemore and Capt. Slaughter, both of the Virginia regiment; so Col. Pickering, of New England; so some of the relatives of Gen. Agnew, who was killed, &c. What scenes for *them* to remember afresh.

Intimately connected with the fame and reputation of Germantown is the now frequently visited stream, the Wissahiccon, made attractive by its still native wildness, and rugged, rocky, woody character; there is also there, under the name of the "*Monastery of the Wissahiccon*," a three-storied ancient stone building of an oblong square, situated on high ground, near to a woody, romantic dell, through which the Wissahiccon finds its meandering way. About this house, so secluded and little known to the mass of the people, there have been sundry vague and mysterious reports and traditions of its having been once occupied as a monastery. A name, and purpose of use, sufficiently startling, even now, to the sensibility of sundry protestants.

The place was last owned and occupied by Joshua Garsed—a large manufacturer of flax-thread, twine, &c.—who has shut up many of the windows, which were formerly equal to four to every chamber, making two on every front or angle of the square. Those who saw the structure sixty years ago, say that it then had a balcony all around the house at the floor of the second story. The tale told in the early days of the present aged neighbours was, that it once contained monks of "the Seventh-day Baptist order," and that they used wooden blocks for pillows [like those at Ephrata,] scallopped out so as to fit the head. Some have also said that they remembered to have seen, near to the house, small pits and hillocks which indicated a former burial place, since turned into cultivation.

With such traditionary data for a starting point, it has become matter of interest to many, who are curious in the history of the past, to learn what further facts we can produce, concerning the premises. If the house should have been built as early as 1708--when Kelpius, the hermit, died "at the Ridge," it may have been constructed by the forty students from Germany—the Pietists who came out in 1694, with Kelpius, to live a single life in the wilderness; but if it was built, as is most probable, and as has been said, by Joseph Gorgas, a Tunker-Baptist, who intended it as a branch of the brotherhood established at Ephrata near Lancaster, and to whom he afterwards moved and joined himself,—then he must have built it before the year 1745, when Conrad Matthias, "the last of the Ridge her-

SCENE ON THE WISSAHICCON.—Page 42.

mits" died. It is known, by "the Chroniea Ephrata,"—a folio, that there was a brotherly affinity between "the Ridge hermits" (of Roxborough) and those of Ephrata. After Joseph Gorgas had gone to Ephrata, the premises, with a farm of seventy acres and a grist mill, fell to his son John Gorgas; from him it was sold about the time of the Revolution, to Edward Miller;—thence to Peter Care, fifty years ago, who held it till about the year 1800. Then it was bought by John Livezey, miller; next by Longstreth, who made it a paper mill; and lately and lastly, by Joshua Garsed & Co. Since their possession of the premises, they have considerably increased the numbers and size of the buildings along the creek; and the Monastery House they have converted into an agreeable dwelling, changing and modernizing the internal forms of the rooms—taking out all the corner chimneys, &c.

The scenery from this house, and from the dell below, is very romantic, rugged, and in nature's wildest mood,—presenting, particularly, very high and mossy rocks, studded with stunted trees—the whole standing out very perpendicularly into the line of the Wissahiccon, and turning it off very abruptly in another direction.

It was in the year 1732, that the religionists of Ephrata first agreed to quit their former solitary life, and to dwell together in monastic society as monks. This they did first, in May 1733. Their book of chronicles says, that "the society was enlarged by members from the banks of the Wissahiccon." Of course, intimating and confirming the idea already advanced, that there was a brotherhood of their order, dwelling at or near the place now called the Monastery.

Christopher Ludwick, once an inhabitant of Philadelphia and Germantown,—interred at the Lutheran ground in said town, in 1801, at the age of 81 years, was quite *a character* in his day; and deserves some special notice. A short memoir of his life has been drawn up and published by Doctor Rush; he deeming him to be a person fully worthy the effort of his pen to report him, as an exemplary and valuable citizen. He was by birth a German, born in 1720; by trade a baker. In early life he enlisted in the Austrian army and served in the war against the Turks. At Prague he endured the hardships of the seventeen weeks' siege. After its conquest by the French in 1741, he enlisted and served in the army of Prussia. At the peace, he entered an Indiaman, and went out to India under Boscawen; afterwards he was in many voyages, from 1745 to 1752, from London to Holland, Ireland and the West Indies, as a sailor. In 1753, he sailed to Philadelphia with an adventure of £25 worth of clothing, on which he made a profit of $300, and again returned to London. He had taken the idea of becoming *a gingerbread* baker in Philadelphia; and in 1754 he came out with *the necessary prints*—a seemingly new idea among the simple cake eaters then! He began his career *in Lætitia court*, and began to make money fast by his new employment. He proved himself an industrious, honest and good neighbour, which led to a deserved *influence* among the people, and to the *soubriquet* of the "governor of Lætitia court."

At the commencing period of the Revolution in 1774, he had become rich, and gave his influence and his money freely, to help on the resistance of the colonies. He was elected readily on all the committees and conventions of the time, for that object. On one occasion, when it was proposed by General Mifflin to procure fire arms by private subscriptions, and whilst several demurred to it as unfeasible, he put down the opposition, by saying aloud, let the poor gingerbread baker be set down for £200! In the summer of 1776, he acted as a volunteer in the flying camp, *without pay.* He possessed great influence there among his fellow soldiers; he stimulated them to endurance; and on one occasion prevented their revolt when complaining of inadequte rations, by falling on his knees before them, and imploring them to *patience* and better *hopes.* When eight Hessians were captured and brought to camp, he interceded to have them handed over to him to manage; which was to take them to Philadelphia, to there show them the fine German churches, and the comfort and good living of Germans in humble pursuits of life, and then to release them to go back to their regiment, and to tell the Germans that we had a paradise for his countrymen, if they would but desert their service. Desertion did follow whenever occasion offered; and the most of these lived prosperous citizens among us. So much for the war *for them!* With the same good design for his countrymen he solicited and obtained the grant to visit the Hessian camp on Staten Island, as a disguised *deserter.* There he succeeded fully to impress them with the happiness of Germans settled in Pennsylvania, and to return safely, with a full assurance of the usefulness of his mission.

In the year 1777, he was cordially appointed by Congress as baker general of the American army, and to choose freely his own assistants and necessaries. In their instructions to him, they expected to require from him one pound of bread for every pound of flour, but Christopher readily replied, "Not so: I must not be so enriched by the war. I shall return 135 lbs. of bread for every 100 lbs. of flour:" an increase of weight by baking, seemingly not then understood by the rulers! and not much by *families* now.

As a proof that he was respected and valued in his sphere, he was often invited to dine with Washington, in large companies, besides having many opportunities of long conferences alone with him, as commander of the army, in relation to the bread supplies. The general appreciated his worth, and usually addressed him in company as "his honest friend." In his intercourse with the officers, he was blunt, but never offensive. By common consent he was privileged to say and do what he pleased. His German accent, his originality of thought and expression; and his wit and humour, made him a welcome guest at every table in the camp. He took with him to camp a handsome china bowl brought by him from China; around its silver rim was engraved his name, &c., and from it he was accustomed to offer his punch or other beverage with his own leading toast, to wit: "Health and long life to Christopher Ludwick and wife." That bowl still exists as *a bequeathed* legacy, to be perpetuated. At the return of peace, he settled on his farm near Germantown. In his absence it had been plundered of every thing by the British. A certificate of his good conduct, in the proper handwriting of General Washington, given in 1785, was much valued, was put under frame, and kept hung up in his parlour, as his diploma. In that, he much gloried; and considered it a full recompense for losses which he had sustained by a depreciated currency, paid to him by sundry persons, for his bonds for good money lent them. He owned at one time eight houses in Philadelphia, and had out £3000 of money lent on bonds and interest. He left a great deal of his money to public charities, especially a fund for educating poor children. He delighted to find out objects of charity, and to relieve their wants. In the time of the yellow fever of 1793, he went into Fraley's bakery in Philadelphia, and worked at bread baking gratuitously, to relieve the wants of the poor. He had a great respect for religion and its duties, which he said he inherited from his father, who had given him, in early life, a silver medal, on which was inscribed, among other devices, "the blood of Christ cleanseth from all sin." This he always carried with him as a kind of talisman; and with a view to enforce its remembrance and its precepts, when he left it to his family, he had it affixed to the lid of a silver tankard, and on the front he had inscribed a device of a Bible, a plough, and a sword, with the motto, "May the religious industry and courage of a German parent, be the inheritance of his issue!" Such a man leaves the savour of a good name, and a good example, to posterity. His remains now rest beneath an expensive monument, where the reader may read of his worth, and go, if he can, *and do likewise!*

His last house of residence in Philadelphia was No. 174 North Fifth street. He had had two wives; but left no children to survive him. Their relations became his heirs.

Colonel Gray's Powderhorn.—In July 1841, there was found in digging about two feet below the surface, in the lot of the New Lutheran church in Germantown, a very curiously wrought powder-horn of the Revolution, used and lost in the battle of Germantown, by Elijah Lincoln, a volunteer of Windham, Connecticut. This, when found, showed the way to its ownership, and the facts connected therewith,—by being published as a curious relic, in the Germantown Telegraph. It was a large white bullock-horn, and had engraved thereon, besides the name of the owner—E. Gray—several pictures and devices: such as a sketch of Boston and its environs, Bunker's hill, Dorchester, and encampments of the military, the British fleet and positions. The facts in the case were these:—

Ebenezer Gray, and William Hovey—the inscribed maker of the horn, with Elijah Lincoln, were young volunteers of Windham, going to begin the war at Bunker hill. While encamped near there under Washington, the horn was engraved by Gray. At this time, we are to presume that regular cartouch boxes were not supplied. Upon the regular organization of the army, Gray, who was an educatad man, received a commission, which he honoured by his after services and bravery, and rose to the rank of colonel. When promoted, he gave his horn to Lincoln, under his promise to use it faithfully for his country. That he did in many battles; till at last it was lost in the affair at Germantown, by being pulled from his side by the grasp of a dying comrade, shot by his side, in the very act of drawing a load from it, for his musket! The company, with Lincoln, rushed forward without the horn, and soon after he found another well filled for his purpose. When the present horn was found and published, it came out, from the publisher of the Democrat, of Columbia county, Pennsylvania, that *he* had been formally engaged in making out a pension claim for Lincoln, and had all these facts, before told, in his possession! Colonel Gray is deceased, but his widow and son and daughter are alive at Windham, and have been informed of their opportunity to repossess this long lost relic of a patriot's service and glory.* It is something to be valued and perpetuated in a family! This circumstance reminds me of the following facts, of Captain George Blackmore, of the Virginian line.† He made my acquaintance in Germantown in 1832, desiring to go over the battle ground, where he had fought, side by side with his brother, in Chew's field. The brother was killed, and left near a spring house, found to be at Duval's fish pond in the rear of his house. He wanted to find that place again, and to shed a tear; and he had a difficulty to find the positions and places in his memory, since so changed by elegant improvements. It was a feeling concern to travel once more with his eyes and explanations "o'er the tented field to book the dead." Every thing interested him, and especially a choice of bullets, which I gave him, gleaned from Chew's house. He chose a battered leaden bullet which had been picked out from Chew's door. That, he said, he should incase in silver and hang to his watch chain, and bequeath to his heirs. I was glad thus to minister to his mournful pleasures. I might add, that I introduced him to Mr. Jacob Keyser, who had buried that brother, with four others, in the place at the spring house, since made the fish-pond,—in one hole, all in their clothes. Alas, poor *undistinguished*, yet meritorius sufferers for their country!

It was once a remarkable characteristic of Germantown, in its early history, say about the year 1700,—when it was described by Oldmixon, that the whole street of one mile in length was fronted with blooming *peach trees.* To think of a state of society where their

---

† He was of Berrysville, Frederick county, Virginia.

* His grandson has since got the horn.

shade trees along a public highway, should consist of the most delicious fruit!

An original paper, by F. D. Pastorius, found at Stenton, of March 1708–9, presented to the council, sets forth his difficulty of getting redress against one John Henry Sprogel, through the plotting and contrivance of Daniel Falkner, pretended attorney for the Frankford Company, for lands in Germantown—and to effect his fraudulent purposes, he had feed or retained *the four known lawyers of the province*, so as to deprive the said Pastorius, (himself a civilian,) and John Jawart, of all advice in law; and being in himself unable to *fetch lawyers from New York*, he therefore prays the interference of the governor and council, so as to restrain further proceedings, until further action from the principals in Germany.

I have seen an old family Bible, 8vo., of the *Shoemaker* family, which came out with the first settlers in 1682, printed at Zurich in 1538, by Christoffel Froschouer, in Switzer-German, done so early as to be *without verses.* In many pages, verses are marked with a pen, and many passages are underscored to add to their force. It was marked as being bought for 50*s.* at second hand, in 1678. In it was a record of family marriages, births, and deaths. Isaac Schumacher, the head of the family, was born in Cresheim in Germany, married in Pennsylvania Sarah Hendricks, who was born in the same town, the 2d of 10 mo., 1678. She died a widow the 15th June, 1742, her husband having died the 12th February, 1732. Benjamin, a son of the above, was born in Germantown, the 3d August, 1704, married in Philadelphia, the 18th June, 1724, to Sarah Coates, daughter of Thomas and Bulah Coates. Benjamin died at Philadelphia in 1767; the wife died the 8th June 1738, leaving four children. I have indulged in this lengthened detail, because this venerable old relic has got out of the family, by some means, and fallen into the hands of strangers; and thus shows, how strangely families will sometimes allow their records to sink into oblivion! It is since given by me to Samuel M. Shoemaker, in Baltimore.

There is, I presume, a great mass of citizens, who having never been in battle, feel a desire to have a close insight into the incidents which must there occur;—this, as a means to remove some of the vagueness of their imaginings and conjectures. Such feelings I have had myself; and which have been in part relieved, by such enquiries as I have occasionally made among the few remaining individuals who had witnessed the doings in the battle, and at the British encampment, &c., in Germantown, to wit:

The most of the conflict was on the north-eastern side of Germantown. That part of our troops which encountered the Hessians and British, near the junction of the Wissahiccon with the Schuylkill, had defiled for that purpose, after they arrived at Chestnut hill, going thence, as led by two guides, of whom Geo. Danenhower, lately alive, was one.

When the battle began, the fathers of families were quickly busied in disposing of their children and women in cellars. In the present C. M. Stoke's house, then belonging to Squire Feree, there were collected two dozen of weeping and terrified women. George Knorr and other boys ran towards Philadelphia, as far as Nicetown, where they met the Hessians coming out, and then stopped. One cannon ball struck a tree at Haines' brewery, as they passed, and then went before them down the street.

Boys were very curious and venturous; and several of them plucked up courage and got to the tops of houses, and even into the streets. to see what could be seen. Such as some of them saw, I shall relate:—Such as the battallion of *tall* Virginians, under Col. Matthews, brought in prisoners from Kelley's place, and lodged in the church at the market house. The faces of the prisoners and their guards were well blackened about their mouths with gunpowder, in biting off their cartridges. These Virginians had just before captured a party of British in the fog, and set up a hurrah, which brought a greater force upon them, and caused their own capture.

The roar and rattling of discharges of musketry and cannon, was incessant: and the whistling of balls, were occasionally heard. Combatants could be seen, from the house top, occasionally in conflict, then obscured by smoke, and then again exposed to view.

The battle, though begun at day light, was continued till after 10 o'clock. The retreat, when it began, a little before 11, must have been skilful as to general arrangement and orders, for it went off *with entire silence.* It seemed like a conflict and a great outbreak, suddenly hushed.

The battle was but little witnessed *in the town*, after the first onset, and but few of the military were seen along the main street. It was chiefly on the north-eastern side, on the tillage ground; and the fences were mostly down. A great deal of fighting must have occurred in Joseph Magarge's field, near Branchtown, (probably with Stephens' division,) ascertained from the great number of leaden bullets found in his ten acre field, for years afterwards. Stephens himself had been set aside some time before, by his own officers, as too much inebriated to command. This was told me by one of his captains.

The present Dr. George de Benneville, of Branchtown, now aged 83 years, was a lad of sixteen, at the time of the battle of Germantown, and saw much of the fight, and of the preceding and succeeding operations of the two armies. They had the Highlanders and British cavalry quartered in his neighbourhood. They were always cheerful, and always seemed to go gaily and confidently into expected fights. On such occasions, the kilted Scots went off in full trot, keeping up with the trot of the cavalry. The soldiers made free to take and kill the cows of his family, and their neighbours; but the officers were gentlemanly in their deportment, and seemed to try to put them in a way to get some recompense. Several of the British officers were quartered in Thomas Nedrow's house the same now Butler's house, opposite to the residence of the present Pierce Butler. When the battle came on, the British made a barricade across the York road, at the place of those two houses. Our militia, in the time of the battle, made no stand of resistance in the neighbourhood of Branchtown, but seemed quickly to make their retreat; and for this non-defence, as many of them were known in the neighbourhood, they did not fail, afterwards, to receive the jibes and jeers of the people. They accused them of throwing away their cartridges, as a feint of having exhausted them in fight! Dr. de Benneville saw the British army come down the York road, on their return and defeat, after they had had their affair at Edge hill, where Gen. Morgan, with his riflemen, had so ably discomfited them. The British still looked well, and as if able to make a bold stand, if pressed to it. The doctor has described to me, with lively vivacity, his vivid recollections of those days; and says they were daily of the most stirring interest to him, and others of his neighbourhood. They kept them daily excited, and interested in every thing doing around them; and almost every day brought something new to pass, which in some way or other, might engage the feelings, or the wonder, of himself, and his youthful companions. Such recollections, to their possessors, at least, are even now *felt* to be worth a whole age of lesser years!

A British officer, wounded, was seen near the market house, in Germantown, led by two soldiers;—he unexpectedly met there a surgeon, and said to him, all pale and faint, "I believe it is all over with me, doctor—I have got a mortal wound?" The doctor opened his breast, while still standing in the street, and turning aside his linen, soon said,—"Don't fear, I shall save you—go on." On he went, quite a renovated man.

Mr. John Ashmead, still alive, and then an intelligent lad of twelve years of age,—as soon as the battle ceased, started from the market house, with a young companion, to "range o'er the tented field to note the dead." He saw several lots of dead, in parcels of sixes and sevens; none of the wounded remaining. They visited Chew's house—there they saw before the house about thirty dead, whom citizens were already beginning to bury, north-west of the house. They went into the house and all over it—saw blood in every room—noticed where a six pounder, which had come in at the front window, had gone through four partitions, and then out at the back of the house. Observed that some of the British therein, had used the back windows on the roof to get out, and under the shelter of that roof, to fire upon assailants approaching the front. They saw a dead American soldier, lying by his still smoking fire brand, who had evidently gotten there under the shelter of a board fence, joining the house to the kitchen out-house, and had been shot, (vainly seeking "the bubble reputation,") as he was about setting fire to the same, by a soldier from the cellar window. Another, a fine young warrior, volunteering to effect the same purpose, with a bundle of straw at a window, at the north-west corner, was also shot down on the spot. The same persons saw some six or seven bodies of soldiers, partially interred, back of the Methodist meeting-lane; ground was heaped upon them just where and as they fell. Their feet were partly uncovered, *and told their tale.*

In R. Smith's woods, in Branchtown, were lately taken up the remains of three American soldiers, buried there, and reinterred by him with a head stone; part of their clothes and caps still remained, also their buttons and flints. They were there as an advanced picket guard, and were surprised.

Persons who saw our retreating men at Chestnut hill, say they passed there with some show of order and control. It is, however, surprising how very few seem to have seen the whole scene, with sufficient intelligence to afford a picture to any inquirer now. One wants to know how they looked and did, how fared the wounded, and how they got on, &c., &c. Some of those in the retreat passed by the way of Oxford, thus showing a wide dispersion. Sundry of our wounded were deemed far enough removed when taken into the Episcopalian church, as their hospital, at Flour town.

The British, shortly after the battle, concentred in Philadelphia and vicinity. Directly after they left Germantown, a troop of American horsemen came through the town upon their rear, so closely, that a British surgeon, who had just left dressing the wounds of three American officers, prisoners in the Widow Hess' house, was overtaken on foot in the street. When they were about to arrest him, W. Fryhoffer, who saw it, and knew the facts in the case, proclaimed his useful services, and he was told to walk to the city at his ease. In the mean time, the three officers were taken as prizes, and thus unexpectedly liberated. The same troop, advancing a little further, encountered a Quaker looking man in a chaise, who, in trepidation, made a short turn at Bowman's lane and upset, and thus exposed a large basket full of plate. He and his treasure were captured and ordered off to head-quarters.

One of the boys of that day has told me how he used to go to mill, to bring flour to an individual in Germantown, who used to deliver it out *to women* coming from Philadelphia,* at high prices, and carrying it in small parcels concealed about their persons. These were probably petty dealers for the wants of the town, and thus made their gain. The same returned with salt, &c.

British officers were generally quartered in houses in the town, and demeaned themselves very civilly to the families therein. The officers, very many of them, were young; only the superior grades were aged. The soldiers were well disciplined, and did not commit any severe aggressions. The 33d one night stole a neighbour's cow, killed her, and covered her with straw, behind the late Wm. Keyser's

---

* It was carried to Philadelphia, and brought $8 per cwt. I knew a man to carry ½ cwt., and boys that carried ¼ cwt., but they had to take a by-road for fear of losing it.

bark house; a sham search was made next morning, but it was soon hushed, and the cow cut up. They were said to be the clearings of the jails. The 33d were noted thieves, but they had to do it quietly.

Two of the inhabitants of the town, Andrew Heath and young Sowers, became guides to the British, and wore their green uniform when so acting, intending, probably, to pass unnoticed; but they did not, and had to leave the place till the peace. At the same time, the brother of Sowers was an active whig. The honest father was abused as a tory, although he had actually given many blankets to the town militia.

Sundry of the whig persons, engaged with the army, used to make, occasionally, hazardous excursions to visit their families stealthily, by night, &c. On one occasion, Mr. Denny, who was a militia lieutenant, came to his father's, near the market house, and when going away on horseback, at midnight, he chanced, as he was intending to turn into the church lane, to encounter the advance of a secret silent detachment going against La Fayette, at Barren hill. As he whipped up to turn the corner, they let fly a platoon, a ball from which, passed through his thigh, scarcely making him sensible of a wound, for he actually got over to the Branchtown tavern before he stopped. Such an alarm, at midnight, soon startled the whole town, and rapidly brought up the whole force of the expedition, at the same time breaking the intended secrecy.

On another intended secret invasion of the British at midnight, a Mr. Lush, who was an acting wagoner for the gunpowder for the American army, was apprised to be on his guard. He geared up his team, and had it ready at the door for a start if needful; finding no approach, he concluded to ride down the city road to reconnoitre, and there he soon fell into their hands a prisoner. But his wagoner, more alert than his master, saw the approach in time to mount his team, and at full whip, dashed up the street, waking up all the inhabitants, to look abroad for something strange, and to see the exposure of the British array.

Mr. John Ashmead, when a lad of twelve, had the exciting spectacle of seeing the whole British army come down the main street of Germantown, at their first entry. He was allowed, unmolested, to set in the street porch. Their whole array seemed in complete order—the display of officers, the regular march of red coated men, and refugee greens, the highlanders, grenadiers, their burnished arms, &c. There was, however, *no* display of colours, and *no* music—every thing moved like machinery in silence. In all their progress there was no violence and no offence. Sundry men occasionally came up and said, "Can you give us a little milk or any cider." On being referred to the father, who purposely kept in door, as he was a known whig, it was deemed expedient to give out readily. In time, the cider barrel began to fall low, when it so occurred that a young officer came to ask a like indulgence;—when it was said to him he was welcome, but others had been before him, and left it muddy; he expressed his surprise at their exaction, and said it should be corrected. Quickly there appeared a sentinel before the house, who kept his place till superseded by another and another, for six or eight changes, until the whole army had passed. It showed discipline, and a decorous demeanour in an enemy, which it is but honest justice to record. This discipline could be confirmed in another thing:—An insolent refugee soldier used to come to the cow yard of a family, who had officers quartered in their house, and to take his quantum of milk as his right. At last it became a grievance, which was hinted to one of the officers; he replied, ask his name, or notice the number of his button, and I shall soon have him punished. The culprit was cautioned by the aggrieved, and begged pardon, and never came again.

In going over these incidents of the battle, and while yielding to emotions of compassion for the dead and the wounded, it cannot but occur to the mind, that even the fortunate and the victorious then, are *now* nearly all whelm'd in one common lot;—scarcely any now survive!

Jacob Keyser, now an aged citizen of about 89 years of age, was then a lad; he, with his father's family, lived where is now the house of the Rev. Mr. Rodney. Its high position above the street enabled them, by placing an apple under the cellar door, to peep abroad and see the battle in the opposite field, distinctly. He could see there, those who fell under successive peals of musketry.

After the battle he went abroad; he saw at the gate, adjoining his present house, many bullet marks; also an Adjutant Lucas dead, and his fine clothes divested. He was buried in the ground near by.

Before the door of Jacob Peters' house, lay a fine large American officer dead, on the pavement. In a little while, when he again passed there, he was nearly stripped, and while he beheld him, a man forced off his shirt as his own lawful prey! His body was interred in the north-east corner of the burying ground opposite.

His brother, Abraham Keyser, saw several officer looking persons, much divested of their clothing, laying dead along the inside of Chew's front wall-fence. It was understood that these inhumanities were inflicted by the followers of the camp—sometimes by soldiers' wives.

These two brothers saw seventeen bodies put into one pit, near Chew's house, under a cherry tree. There was a row of cherry trees from the gate up to the north side of the house, and behind these trees men approached towards the house, as their shelter; some were dead, or wounded, at the foot of those trees. A fine large soldier, from Reading, lay dead at the gate; also, a lad, a son of Col. Chamberlane, of New Jersey.

Soon after the battle, British officers came to the houses, and asked for young men to come out and bury. While they were so burying, a British soldier came and said, "Don't bury them with their faces up, and thus cast dirt in their faces, for they also 'are mothers' sons.'" An officer came to a speechless, dying man, and said kindly, "Pray now for your soul." One of the bodies, very slightly buried, south of the house, was scented and dug after by the dogs, and afterwards corn was noticed to grow there with wonderful luxuriance.

Very few girls were known to have formed any attachments for the enemy—a Miss Servor, and another, were the only two known to have gone away.

In going into Chew's house, they noticed that the rooms were all much blackened by the smoke of their firings—not much blood observed. Saw only one man who had been wounded in the house, and he was dying.

One Isaac Wood, at the present John Andrews' place, on Lime Kiln road, was killed at his cellar door, while peeping out at the battle, which was near him, along side of Dr. Betton's woods.

An elderly lady and her nephew came to Germantown, about seven years ago, making inquiries for the remains of Gen. Nash, which, it is believed, none could then inform them about. He was shot through the thigh, and the same shot killed his horse, and his aid, Major Witherspoon.

Very few accidents occurred to cattle during the fight. A cow, which belonged to John Smith's father, and which was in the field between the combatants, was bought after the fight for ten joes (80 dollars); at that time her beef would bring 50 cents a pound. They had hard fare then, and all lived on the coarsest and cheapest kind of food. A cow, killed by a bullet in Peters' stable, was cut up, and eaten willingly.

The house now Duval's, (then Christopher Huber's, and once Samuel Shoemaker's, a mayor of Philadelphia,) had the floor at one time covered with army tailors, making up clothing. The shoemakers and smiths would go to shops in squads, and use the tools for their work, in which the owners would join them, for the sake of keeping an eye on the preservation of their tools and materials.

At and about the spring house of the same Duval's place, (at the rear of his garden lot,) the premises being then in the tenure of Ch. Huber, the Virginia troops became engaged. On that occasion a soldier was shot and killed along side of *Wm. Dolby*, who, from that circumstance, became averse to war; soon after left his station in the ranks, found a retreat at Thomas Livezey's, (a miller and Friend,) then a very secluded place amid the wilds of the Wissahiccon. There he became fully convinced of Friends' principles, joined the society, and was afterwards a very acceptable and approved public Friend. He afterwards settled in Delaware state—often visited the yearly meetings in Philadelphia,—and at the end of forty years after the above mentioned battle, revisited the spot of his outward and inward conflict, and told the facts to Abraham Keyser, my informant, now 80 years of age.

I once had a similar fact of convincement from my old friend

John Baylie, who was engaged as a non-commissioned officer, a volunteer, under Wayne, at Trois rivers; and while *fearlessly* entering into battle, all at once, one of the men in the ranks near him, (a militia man,) beginning audibly to pray for the salvation of those who might fall, he had such a conviction of *his* unpreparedness for death and eternity, that he felt himself to tremble from head to foot under the divine power—he also ejaculated prayers—resolved instantly *to kill no man*—fired above his mark—became tranquil and self-possessed—went fearlessly into all danger,—and as soon as he got home, joined the Friends in Bucks county, and relinquished his pay.

There was much woods on the north-east side of Beggarstown, up to Leibert's board yard; and along these woods were many dead and wounded. Houses along the town were much fewer in number than now, and generally lower and smaller—not such as we now see them in the same places.

John Smith saw an American trooper driving dashingly along the poor house lane, towards Germantown, then turned off the road and hid himself and horse in a cider mill, on present John Wistar's place. Soon there came a troop in pursuit, and missed him

When Smith first left his father's house, at the beginning of the battle, to seek a refuge, he saw walking on the street two wounded British soldiers, bloody, and going to the rear. He ran to Nicetown before stopping, and there met the British coming out from the city, in a kind of half running march.

In Jacob S. Wunder's lot, he saw two of our men wounded, who had lain there all night, and he took them cider to drink. They were shot in the limbs, so that they could not walk, or help themselves.

The British army were covered with dust, when they first passed through Germantown; they were at other times kept very clean. Their horses were heavy, clumsy and large. Horsemen of both armies would occasionally pass rattling through the streets of Germantown by night, and in the morning it was clearly designated of which side the horsemen were, by the English horse being so very much larger in the hoof. The Hessian cavalry were gay ponies, much decorated with leather trappings.

Women coming from Philadelphia, when met by our scouts, were very rudely searched for forbidden things about their persons, and often shamefully plundered of real necessaries.

There were several rich young gentlemen, volunteers, attached to the British light infantry army, without commissions, seeking opportunities of promotion. There were three or four brothers of the name of Bradstreet among them. They used carbines.

A. K. thinks that there was not much fighting along the street; he had often seen Col. Musgrave, who defended Chew's house. On one occasion the Colonel asked him if he had heard that Burgoyne was taken, and whether he was a citizen of Germantown; and on his answering "Yes," the Colonel repeated sternly, "Yes, yes!"

meaning to reproach him for not adding *sir*, to a gentleman! He had been shot in the mouth, and had his face disfigured thereby, with a hole in his cheek. None of the officers were observed to have had any ladies with them, and had no intercourse as visiters in the families of the place. Indeed, the society then was very plain and unfashionable, and generally talked more German than English. The soldiers alone were most at home among the people, and they freely admitted the boys and old men of the place to visit their camp before the battle; but afterwards, they changed greatly, and kept often changing their grounds, and finally drew themselves wholly into and about the city.

A large body of Hessians were hutted in Ashmead's field, out the School lane, near the woods; their huts were constructed of the rails from fences, set up at an angle of 45°, resting on a crossbeam centre; over these were laid straw, and above the straw grass sod—they were close and warm. Those for the officers had wicker doors, with a glass light, and interwoven with plaited straw; they had also chimneys made of grass sod. They no doubt had prepared so to pass the winter, but the battle broke up their plans. One of the Hessians afterwards became Washington's coachman.

Lieut. Craig, of the cavalry, was often adventurous; on one occasion, being alone and pursued up Germantown by the British horse, he purposely led them across a marsh at Cresheim, where one of their horses so mired, that he could not get out; this stopped the pursuit, and they had to kill the horse on the spot.

Col. Pickering, in speaking of his recollections of the battle of Germantown, says, Washington's army started the evening preceding the battle, and marched all night. In the march, Gen. Washington followed Sullivan's column, and when the battle began, said to Col. Pickering, "Go ahead, and say that I am afraid he is throwing away his ammunition, and to try to reserve himself for a more general action." The colonel then passed Chew's house without seeing any demonstrations of fight there; and he thinks the unseen troops therein were then barricading the premises. He overtook Gen. Sullivan three or four hundred yards beyond that house, and when returning, saw for the first time, that they were firing from that house across his road. He soon rejoined Gen. Washington, with his officers, at Billmeyer's house A flag was sent forthwith to the house to summon their surrender, which Lieut. Smith, of Virginia, volunteered to carry, and got shot as he was advancing, and afterwards died from the wound. Sullivan's division, therefore, was *never delayed* by the force in the house. Gen. Greene's column on the left did not get into action till three quarters of an hour later than those on the right, because of the greater circuit which they had to make; whereas, those on the main street, went more directly to the point of attack. In Col. Pickering's opinion, Judge Johnson's "Life of Greene" has given erroneous statements respecting Gen. Washington's hesitancy to pass Chew's house; and he distinctly says, that only Gen. Knox could have been present, to obtrude any advice in that matter; all the rest of the general officers were in their places, with their commands. The first of the retreating began for *want of more ammunition*, they having exhausted it, as the commander-in-chief had before apprehended.

The boys of Germantown made play-work of the war, making themselves three forts (upper, middle, and lower,) along the town. They had regular embankments, and fought with stones, under a show of wooden guns. On one occasion, an American officer, in passing, called out, "Who commands there?" and they called out his own name, "Proctor!"

An aged gentleman, who has been a contributor of many of the facts of Germantown, and to whom I have submitted the perusal of the preceding pages, has commended them for their accuracy, and has furnished some additional illustrations, which I have added, viz.:

Christopher Ludwick, the baker-general, usually bore, and received, the appellation of *general*. He once owned the plantation, now belonging to John Haines. He lived many years in a very independent manner, in the house next Mrs. Sarah Johnson. He was of a very social cast, talking freely along the street with all he met, and in so loud and strong a voice, as every where to announce his vicinity;—so much so, that it was usual in families, in doors, to say, "There goes the general!" The frankness which characterized him, encouraged the woman, who became his second wife, to say to him, in meeting him in the street, that as she felt concerned for his loneliness as a widower, she would offer herself to him for a companion, in case he thought it might conduce to their mutual happiness. He took it, as he said, into a short consideration, and they became man and wife; she being a good wife, and both of them a happy couple, in the opinion of all! He had but one eye.

My informant has seen many of the brotherhood of Ephrata, passing through Germantown, following in Indian file, all dressed alike, *and all their clothes, from head to foot, was without colour!*

Flourtown, in old Shronk's day, was, as remembered, the peculiar head-quarters of witchcraft, and witch-credulity. There, almost every body credited the evil influence; and from that cause old Shronk was under frequent requisition to go there, from his house at Schuylkill falls. When seen riding from home along the town, it was common for old and young to run to the windows to take a look at the rare man, and to say, surely he is again called off to Flourtown. When arrived there, he would fling his arms about and proclaim that, here and there, in given directions, are many, many witches! The whole place was in serious trouble and confusion for several years; one and another accusing and charging the other with being witches; and all referring to Shronk, to know the verity of their several apprehensions.

An eye witness has thus described the British array, viz.:—The trim and graceful grenadier, the careless and half savage highlander, with his flowing tartaned robes, and *naked knees*; then the immovably stiff German—here a regiment of Hessians,—and there slaves of Anspach and Waldeck, the first sombre as night, the second gaudy as noon. Here dashed a party of dragoons, and there scampered a party of *yagers*. The British officers gay in spirit and action, and the German officers stiff in motion and embroidery; the whole forming a moving kaleidoscope of colours and scenery.

Mr. Jacob Miller, when aged about 82, told me of his observations in Germantown, when a youth of sixteen. He lived, while the British were in Germantown, in the house now of George W. Toland; then the house of George Miller, a captain in the American army.* The first night of the arrival of the British army, upwards of a dozen of the British officers made their quarters in that house. While they were all present in one large room, they sent for him, and questioned him about his knowledge of many of the localities. In such inquiries, they always called every thing American "rebel;" and upon his saying he did not know what they meant to ask by the word rebel, some were rough, and charged him with wilful ignorance, and some others justified him, and said he was not obliged to acknowledge the term, even if he understood it. His mother was soon employed to be their baker, and daily after she received their flour, and made it into bread, pound for pound, leaving her a good supply of gain, for the use of her family.

He did not dare to go much abroad among the encampments, unless with some of the retainers of the army, for fear they might arrest him; therefore did not see much of their doings. The boys and girls of the place, he believes, kept very close house; he heard of no violence or insult to any of the inhabitants. Ming, Lightfoot, and Heath made themselves most useful to the British, and were afterwards regarded, and treated by ourselves, as tories; they were once afterwards paraded through the town to disgrace them, and were threatened with tar and feathers. The most outrageous conduct was committed on the person and property of Christopher Sower, a worthy, innocent, good man, on account of his son Christopher, who had taken the enemies' side.

When the battle began, he and several others went across the street to Lorain's old house, and secured themselves in the cellar, from the door of which they peeped out and saw the cannon balls making their streaks through the air, towards Toland's woods; they also heard the whistling of many musket bullets.

The British cavalry were hutted on the lots of Mehl's and Royal' present open fields.

Just as the battle began, and when he was going to the cellar before mentioned, he saw Gen. Howe ride up with several officers, from his quarters at Logan's house, (the owner, Wm. Logan, being

* He afterwards became a colonel, and distinguished himself with the Germantown militia at Princeton.

then deceased,) and stopping near Lorain's house, he heard General Howe say, quite loud, "My God, what shall we do? we are certainly surrounded!' They then rode onward up the town.

After a while they left the cellar and ventured abroad; finding the firing had ceased, and seeing wounded men, on foot, coming there as to the rear, he ventured to go towards Chew's house, by the back lots, the fences being all cut down. He saw many dead, and a soldier stripping an officer who had a fine watch. When he got near there, he found himself unexpectedly near some renewed firing—one of the balls went through the porch where he was standing—he retreated rapidly homeward. When again at home, he found a gathering at his neighbour Mechlin's house, (the present Wagner's,) and went in, where he found, in the large stable in the yard, a British hospital, where surgeons were beginning to arrange long tables, made of the doors, on which to lay men, (friends and foes,) for amputation. They soon pressed him to assist them, but he not liking the employ, soon managed to get off and hide himself. He saw as many as two dozen there, wounded; they cut off arms and legs, and cast them, when done, into the stone quarry near, where they were afterwards covered with a little earth. He knew that, afterwards, dogs got at some of them; he took from a dog a leg, which he buried at Mehl's gateway.

He knows that there was a great deal of fighting on his present lot in Danenhower's lane; and also on Armstrong's hill, by the mill. There, he and other boys have collected several hatfuls of leaden bullets; even to this day, he finds bullets and flints in his lot, whenever he ploughs the place. He supposes he gathered as many as a bushel of them, not long after the battle, getting usually a hatful at any one time of searching; and these he used to hide in post holes for the time.

He used to steal to Philadelphia occasionally, to get things wanted for the family. His way was to watch occasions when parties of the British came out, then to follow closely in their rear; and afterwards to get home by by-paths and back roads, and always keeping a good look out to shun Capt. Allen M'Lane, who was always on the scout, and was often seen by him and others close upon the British outposts. He has seen him pursued several times, from near his house. Dover and Howard were officers also in the same service.

He saw Gen Agnew and Col. Bird buried, in the lower burying ground, with very little parade. There was also a British officer buried there, from Ottinger's house, where he died of sickness. He saw several dead soldiers buried in Mechlin's tanyard after the battle; they were probably from the hospital there, and at Armat's house.

One of the officers, who was unwell, the night of their first arrival, wanted him to go up the town to purchase something for his relief, and he being afraid to go alone, expressed his reluctance, when the officer said, "I'll give you a scrip which will pass you." So he went, and at every little distance he found a sentinel along the street, by whom he was challenged, and showed his passport, and proceeded till he got what he wanted.

On Taggart's ground were a great many of the British encamped in huts, made up from the fences, and overlaid with sods. On the same ground, he afterwards saw Count Pulaski's cavalry, of four hundred men, in their whitish uniform, where they made a grand display of military evolutions, in exercising in a mock battle. They were formed mostly from the prisoners of Burgoyne's army, Germans, and others. Their exercises made a deep impression on his youthful fears; for when he beheld their frequent onsets with drawn swords, he felt quite persuaded they must turn it all to earnest. One of them got killed in the onset.

At one time, it was said that the British were intending to take into their service all the half grown boys they could find in the place; to avoid which, he and others got off to a public house near Flourtown. He supposes that it was a false report.

He was present, with the brother and sister of Major Witherspoon, (aid to Gen. Nash,) when he was disinterred, in Philip Weaver's front lot. They had brought a coffin, and outer case, intending to take him home to Princeton, but his body was too decayed and offensive to bear such a removal. He was in the same pit with six other bodies; but he was known from the rest, by the loss of part of his skull, and by being the only one wrapped in a blanket. The sister cut off a lock of his hair. What an affecting scene for relatives!

The English cavalry pursued the Americans eight miles, on the Skippack road, fifteen and a half miles from Philadelphia, into Whitpaine township, as far as the Blue Bell. We have heard from an old friend, a witness now at that place, that our militia was already there when the British cavalry arrived, and wheeled about to make good their retreat and return. He describes the confusion that existed among the Americans as past the power of description; sadness and consternation was expressed in every countenance. While the dead and dying, (which had preceded this halt at the Blue Bell,) were before seen moving onward for refuge, there could be seen many anxious women and children rushing to the scene to learn the fate of their friends, and to meet, if they could, the fathers, brothers, or other relatives, who had been before sent forward for the engagement. Again and again, the American officers were seen riding or running to the front of the militia with their drawn swords, threatening, or persuading them to face about and meet the foe. But all efforts seemed to fail; and officers and men were still seen every where borne along on the retreat. They broke down fences and rushed away in confusion, as if determined no longer to hazard the chances of war in another onset. Some few, however, still held on to the moving mass of dead and wounded—for some had died, while still in the course of their removal.

General Nash, of North Carolina, Col. Boyd, Major White, of Philadelphia, aid to Sullivan, and another officer, who were among the wounded, were carried onward, so far, as that when they died they were all buried side by side, at the Mennonist burying ground and church in Towamensing township, a place beautifully shaded with forest trees. Their graves there I have visited, twenty-six miles from Philadelphia.* I have learned from the sons of one De Haven, that their father had assisted in carrying Gen. Nash, who was brought into his house, and then taken two miles further to his brother's house, where he died,—having in his profuse bleeding for his country's good, bled through two feather beds before he died. A Mr. Godshalk, who is alive at Kulpsville, saw his interment; Major White was deemed the finest looking officer in the service—his beauty and dress had conferred on him the soubriquet of "beau White." He was an Irishman by birth, married to a London lady, and the father of the present Judge John M. White, of Woodbury, New Jersey. He had gone on after the battle, wounded, but riding on his own horse. He had reached the house of Abram Wentz, on Skippack road, where he had before quartered. As the alarm of the pursuing army came onward, he undertook to ride six miles further, when he took a fever from his exertions, of which he died. A lady who saw him at Wentz's house, and who is still alive, has told me he came there with Gen. Furman, and that the major was gay and cheerful, and declined any bed or assistance. In the same company there was a very young officer from Virginia, (supposed to be Lieut. Smith,) wounded in the shoulder, who also went onward. An old German, a soldier, has informed that four of our officers were buried side by side at Whitemarsh, [most probably non-commissioned ones.] In that neighbourhood there are still some remains of the former entrenchments.

A large portion of the American army lay encamped on the Skippack road, twenty and a half miles from Philadelphia, and while there, Gen. Washington, and several of the officers, were quartered in the house of Mr. Morris---since known as the large country house and residence of the late Dr. James, of Philadelphia. Gen. Washington had also his quarters at Jacob Wampole's farm house (the father of the late Isaac Wampole, the eminent city scrivener,) located near a woods, and three quarters of a mile from the aforesaid Mennonist burying ground. That family had known that the general was in the practice of retiring to pray.

It occurs to me here to say a little of the state and class of people settled in this section of country. Such as are known to me of Towamensing and Franconia. They were generally German Mennonists and Tunkards. The latter have a meeting-house and a well dressed congregation, by the Indian creek; all the farms are well cultivated, and evince prosperity,—far different from what their forefathers could have enjoyed in their own country. Such a country as this is now, so little distant from Philadelphia, was only first settled in 1719—at the cost of but £10 for fifty acres. When first settled, several small remains of Indians still lingered about; and the

* We have since given them a monument there.

name of Indian creek, given by the settlers when the first surveys were made in 1718 to J. Steel, shows their then understood vicinage and home. There I have been shown their grave ground, &c. When Henry Funk settled there in 1719, in Franconia, he was six miles northward of any neighbour, and although his place is now a mill, he then had no mill nearer than the present Mather's mill at Flourtown, (so called most probably as the earliest known place of supply,) to which place the family used to send a single bag of grain on horseback.

The late Gen. Cobb, who was long a member of Gen. Washington's military family during the war, has informed us of some of the habits of the chieftain. Every thing was to be precise and punctual there—at the breakfast hour, the general was sure to be punctual, and then he expected to find his aids, Cobb, Hamilton, Humphreys, awaiting him. He came then dressed for the day, bringing with him the letters and despatches of the preceding day, with short memoranda of the answers to be made; also the substance of orders to be issued. After breakfast, these papers were distributed among the aids, to be put in form. Soon after, he mounted his horse to visit the troops, and expected to find on his return, before noon, all the papers prepared for his inspection and signature. There was no familiarity in his presence; it was all sobriety and business. Throughout the war it was understood in his military family that *he gave a part of every day to private prayer and devotion.* Gen. Cobb, though so long closely connected with so grave a leader, was himself a man strongly disposed to enjoy a laugh; and yet he says, that in his long intercourse with him, he had only met with one officer—Col. Scammel, who had the power of affecting the risibilities of the general. Scammel was full of ludicrous anecdotes, and when dining at the general's table, was allowed to *take the command*, and to excite, beyond any other man, the general himself.

It may afford interest to some, to learn some of the local facts incident to the management and retreat of La Fayette, at Barren Hill, where he was intended to be surprised and broken up by Gen. Gray, such as I learned them to be, from Samuel Maulmsby, a respectable Friend, dwelling then and since at Plymouth meeting-house.

He was at the time an active and observing boy. The whole British force arrived early in the morning at the meeting-house, in the *rear* of La Fayette, and halted in the public road, remaining there about an hour and a half, seemingly perplexed and disappointed; and, as it is believed, debating between the choice of going either to Spring mill, or Madson's ford. The men seemed unwearied, but chagrined and angry.

He had then an uncle—a Capt. Davis, of the Pennsylvania militia, who being then with the American army, and familiar with all the localities of the country, was much consulted and often used as a guide, &c. From him Mr Maulmsby learned many facts concern-

6

ing the retreat of La Fayette across the Schuylkill at Madson's ford Such as that the British made their approach with all possible quiet ness and secrecy, in the night (as before mentioned, through Germantown, &c.) They turned at Mather's mill to go on to Plymouth. At that mill lived a Capt. Stoy, who having occasion to get out of bed, chanced to see the army passing his door. He immediately ran across the fields and nigh cuts, to give La Fayette the alarm; but his breath failing him, he called up one Rudolph Bartle, who ran on to Barren hill and gave the intelligence. La Fayette immediately sent off his artillery to the other side of Schuylkill, at Madson's ford, and going himself to the same place by the way of Spring mill. There were Oneida Indians attached to his command, who took their own course, and had to swim the river. In doing this, they left behind them a young prince of twelve years of age, whom they there lamented in strong cries and yells of distress, as being captured or drowned. He soon after appeared, when they all kneeled in solemn praise and thanksgiving, to the Great Spirit, for his safety. The force of La Fayette moved on to Valley Forge to join Washington's army, then there.

Mr. Maulmsby saw among the British several refugees, who seemed to be very active advisers. Some of them had been his neighbours. They were dressed in greenish uniforms.

He told me a fact, which should be remembered, as it helps to illustrate many cases, I presume, of alleged cruelty and plunder. A party, from the force in the road, came into his mother's house under pretext of getting water. They seemed to be highlanders; these immediately ran over the house and up stairs, forcing open chests and drawers with their bayonets, and taking off what they liked. Had the matter rested there, the whole might have been deemed a common violence; but an accident showed another system. An officer came in to ask if they could spare a pair of swingle-trees, which when young Maulmsby had found, the price was asked, and none being required the officer gave him a guinea. At this time, a soldier was observed running to the house for his musket which he had forgotten, and out of this fact grew an explanation of the previous plunder. The officer forthwith entreated the widow to come out to the men to designate the depredators, assuring her the property should be restored, and the men punished before her face; he saying, they had already been threatened with death, if they attempted to plunder. Just then firing was heard at a distance, when they all hastily marched off.

General Washington was often to be seen riding abroad, with a black servant, having a guard and some officers in company. How different things *then*, from what he must have afterwards witnessed them when a summer resident in Germantown, and going occasionally over the same happy and prosperous neighbourhoods, witnessing their changes and improvements.

In preserving the remembrance of the past, I may mention that the house in which I dwell was the residence of *Thomas Jefferson*, in 1793, when he was secretary of state. The same house was before occupied by John De Braine, a French-German, distinguished as an astronomer; who published, while here, several small publications, and diagrams, too occult to be understood!

Persons now visiting Germantown, and witnessing its universal *English* population, could hardly imagine that a place so near Philadelphia could have retained its *German character*, down to the year 1793. Before that time, all the public preaching was in German; and nearly all the plays of the boys, and their conversation, was in that tongue. The yellow fever of 1793 brought out here all the officers of the general and state governments, and of the banks, and filled all the houses with new inmates. In the next and subsequent years, sundry families from the city became summer residents. Then English succeeded rapidly; and soon after, increased desires for English preaching, in part, began to be manifested among the young, and to be resisted by the aged. Then, Runkle, Wack, and others, who could preach in both languages, were inducted. Now, Mr. Richards is the only one who preaches in German, and that only once a month; the chief of his sermons are in English. The Methodists were the first who introduced English preaching—they beginning in the school house, at first.

While the British were here, the chaplains of the Hessians preached in the German churches, and two remained in this country after the war. One of them, the Rev. Mr. Schaeffer, took the Lutheran church, in Germantown.

The yellow fever could make no headway in Germantown, although so near Philadelphia; only six or eight persons died of it here, and they had derived it from Philadelphia. The place is always pre-eminently healthy.

General Washington, when residing here, in 1793, was a frequent walker abroad, up the main street, and daily rode out on horseback, or in his phaeton. So that every body here was familiar with the personal appearance of that eminent man. When he and his family attended the English preaching, in the Dutch church, at the market house, they always occupied the seat fronting the pulpit. It was also his own practice to attend the German preaching, thus showing he had some knowledge of that language. His house was closed on the Sabbath, until the bell tolled, when it was opened, just as he was seen coming to the church. I chance also to know, that he had some knowledge of the French, because, when my friend, Jacob Roset first arrived in this country, about the year 1792, he, with four or five of his countrymen, met the general in the street, in Philadelphia; and stopping to let him pass, he held out his hand to Mr. Roset, and said to him and his friends, *Bien venu en Amerique*. A salutation which delighted them.

When he left Germantown, to go onward to Carlisle, to join the western expedition, and was intended to have been escorted by a troop of horse, from Philadelphia, he wishing to shun the parade, went off in his *single seated* phaeton, drawn by four fine gray horses, out the School lane, and up the rugged back road of the township line, so as to escape their notice and attention.

Many remember his very civil and courteous demeanour to all classes in the town, as he occasionally had intercourse with them. He has been seen several times at Henry Fraley's carpenter shop, and at Bringhurst's blacksmith shop, talking freely and cordially with both. They had both been in some of his campaigns. His lady endeared herself to many, by her uniform gentleness and kindness. Neither of them showed pride or austerity. I could illustrate the assertion, by several remembered incidents in proof.

Those who now visit Germantown, and notice the general neatness and whiteness of the front faces of the houses, and see the elegance of some of the country seats, can have little idea how differently it looked in 1814, when the writer first became a resident in the place. Then, most of the houses were of dark, moss-grown stone, and of sombre and prison-like aspect, with little old fashioned windows, and monstrous corner chimneys, formed of stone. Now the chimneys are rebuilt of brick, and taken from the corners; and nearly all of the front walls are plastered over in imitation of marble; besides this, the whole town is laid with good foot-pavement, and thus relieving the street-walkers from the great annoyance of muddy feet These changes were effected by the frequent expostulations and suggestions of writers in the Germantown Gazette, among whom the present writer was to be numbered. Numerous shade-trees were also introduced along the streets, so as to add to the charm of the promenade, the whole length of this remarkably long town;—sometimes called *Long-ville*, in reference to this, its peculiar characteristic. Many of the old houses, now of two stories, have been raised from one and a half stories. Before the Revolution, the most of the houses were but one and a half stories, with high double-hipped roofs.

Gilbert Stuart, the great painter, dwelt in Germantown, in 1794–5. His dwelling was the same now David Styers'; and his paintings were executed in the barn in the rear, with one light. There he executed that memorable head—*his second Washington;* the first being destroyed by himself, voluntarily, as insufficient to meet his views of that extraordinary man. The head, only, was finished—the drapery having never been executed. The same head is now owned by the Boston Athenæum, procured after the death of Stuart, from his widow, at a cost of 1000 dollars. From that head he executed all his other portraits, including his full length portrait, done at Germantown, for Lord Lansdown, and afterwards badly, as an engraving, by Heath, in London. Stuart had a great aversion to the drudgery of making drapery to his pictures, and used to employ another hand to execute them. At his house Gen. Washington and his lady were frequent visiters, seen here, as such, by many. Mrs. Washington had a great desire to have possession of that finished head of the general; but as it was his *chef-d'œuvre*, and he had no hopes to be able to execute another as well, it was conceded to him as an indulgence, to retain it for himself during his life. While here, he executed a full length portrait of Cornplanter, the celebrated Indian chief. Mr. Stuart was noted for his eccentricity, and his love of good eating and drinking. To the latter, he was much addicted after his dinner, showing therefrom a much inflamed face, and much of recklessness in his actions when excited by his drink. In this he dealt in wholesale way;--buying his wine, brandy, and gin, by the cask. On one occasion he was seen kicking a large piece of beef across the street from his own house over to Diehl's, his butcher, and tumbling it into his premises; as if to say, such beef was not only unfit for his table, but too bad to be handled. On another occasion, he took a fancy to paint for Riters' tavern a finely executed sign of the King of Prussia on horseback, (the painter to be unknown!) it stood for years worthy of admiration, and at last got painted over *with letters* "The King of Prussia Inn," none knowing that it was, in fact, a curiosity and a relic. At my request this sign is now preserved, and will be given to any company of artists who may wish to preserve it, by taking off its last covering of paint. The history of his life, as told in Dunlap's Arts of Design, shows many singular characteristics of this remarkably gifted man; he was great in his person, and extraordinary in all he did; highly honourable in his sentiments, and independent in his actions.

Another *character* of Germantown, but of quite another cast, was *Redheifer*, the pretender to perpetual motion. For a while he enlivened the town with his numerous visiters, to see his machinery in perpetual motion, at the extraordinary price of one dollar each visiter. It was at last found to be moved by a crank, which was wound perpetually, by a concealed little old man in an upper loft! The machinery was elegant and expensive; and might have produced something, had it been preserved for exhibition, as a curious and amusing toy. But he and his apparatus disappeared together. He was himself said to be an immoral man, and a gambler.

Among the *characteristics* of the place was its unrivalled manufacture of superior stockings—all done by hand weaving, as originally brought into use by the first settlers; these have been in modern times driven out of use. The place was also, since the revolution, pre-eminent for its superior build of coaches and vehicles; but, in late years, the workmen of Newark have drawn off the business by their reduced prices.

The first introduction of carriage building was somewhat curious. Mr. William Ashmead, a smith, observing the heavy build of the coaches of his day, and that they were mostly imported, if intended to be of a superior kind, bethought him to form an open-front light carriage, on his own plan. When it was done, it was admired by many, and was often called for by the wealthy who wished to travel to distances;—among these was Mr. Bingham. They engaged it at one dollar a day; and it was in constant demand. At last, a gentleman from Maryland, who had seen it, came to the place to buy it. It was not for sale; but he offered £120 for it, and took it. Then another and another was built, and orders were renewed upon Mr. Ashmead. Soon, increased demands occurred; and his son John being made a carriage maker, received numerous orders for many kinds of light carriages, and especially for phaetons. About the same time, (the time of the revolution and afterwards,) Mr. Bringhurst, who was at the time a chaise maker, went largely into the making of carriages. Coaches and chariots were made for £200 and phaetons for £100.

The same William Ashmead, as a smith, had made himself a plough with a *wrought iron* mould-board, which was found to be a great improvement; and was so much admired by La Fayette, who saw its utility, that he purchased four of them, for his La Grange farm in France. No patent was taken; and in time some other person, following the hint, made the same thing of *cast* iron,—such as is now in general use.

Germantown was the first place in our country to declare against the practice of *slavery.* The declaration proceeded from the Friends' meeting, of whom the chief members at the time were Germans.

The old inhabitants have been old observers of "*Lammas' floods,*" to prevail from the 1st to the 10th or 12th of August, and well it is marked, while this work is going through the press, in August 1843, flooding Philadelphia; drenching the military encampments *daily;* carrying away fifty bridges in Delaware county, &c.! St. Lammas is of record in the German almanacs—and mind! make no appointments *for pleasure* in Lammas' times!

It may justly surprise the present generation to have a little insight into the state of farming before the revolution, and before the introduction of *clover and plaster of Paris.* These were the things which enriched the cultivators and beautified our fields. It was first started about the year 1780, at Chestnut hill, by Abraham Rex, and at Germantown, by Leonard Stoneburner. It became a wonder to see men making grass, and hauling it in from *upland* fields. Every body was delighted to see the effect of this new era in farming. The aged now can well remember the stirring interest which was every where excited by this important improvement. Before this time, a farmer at Germantown would consider one hundred acres of land as inadequate to provide his frugal living *then*, unless he had also a good portion of *natural* meadow to supply his stock. It soon came to be experienced that fifty acres of land, well tilled, produced enough to fill a barn of double the size before used! The horses and cattle soon found a joyous change to their benefit, and well they *showed* the difference of their feeding. We tell these things for the sake of the *gratitude* and *acknowledgment* which such benefits, conferred on us, deserve.

Another great era of public benefit, now but little considered, was the formation of the Germantown turnpike—a measure got up chiefly through the exertions of Casper Haines. The common road through Germantown, before this time, at the breaking up of the winter, as well as at some other times, was impassable for *wneel* carriages. To that cause it was that the most of the marketing, going through the place to Philadelphia, was all carried on horseback with side panniers and hampers, and the most of the horses were ridden by *women*. Think what a relief they have had since those days! It is a well known fact that horses and carriages have been *swamped* and *lost!* In going through the town, (now all well paved,) their horses would enter the mud to their knees at every step, and not being able to progress faster than two or three miles an hour, and then often endangered. Now what a change do we witness!—No men or women now on horseback with marketing, but going with easy spring dearborns at five and six miles an hour, as easy and safe as if in state carriages. Even wagon loads of hay can be seen sometimes passing in a trot! The young farmers now know almost nothing about former difficulties and poor returns; and they are not sufficiently aware that the fine barns and fine houses, as they have since seen them, have all been the result of clover cultivation and improved husbandry. We aim, therefore, to keep these facts "before the people," that they may thus know "the rock from which they were hewn."

I ought to take this suitable occasion to explain why it formerly was, that *great country stores* could be so well sustained at Germantown and Frankford, and out on Lancaster road. It arose from the extreme badness of all great roads leading into the city, in particular seasons. To avoid such, farmers bringing produce could sell out their whole loads to Rex, and others, on Chestnut hill, or at Stoneburner's, Fry's, and Miller's, in Germantown. In return they could get salt, fish, plaster of Paris, clover and grass seed; all kinds of groceries and dry goods. Such stores were granaries for all kinds of grain, and received and cured hogs and beef. They all made money. You might see a dozen country wagons at a time about their premises. All this continued until turnpikes insured safe passages into the city; and then the stores began fast to decline, and finally to give up, or to contract themselves into small affairs.

The present aged Jacob Keyser was told by A. Cook, a primitive inhabitant, that he could well remember Germantown street as being an *Indian foot-path*, going through laurel bushes.

John Miller, Esq., a respectable gentleman and a magistrate, dwelling in Germantown, in the house now belonging to the Chanceller family, kept a diary of passing events, during the time the British occupied that place and the city of Philadelphia. He was a strong whig, and eventually lost a great deal by the continental money. From his MS. book of twenty pages, quarto, I select the following notices, to wit:

Sept. 18th, 1777, he speaks of much alarm among the people from the expected approach of the British, and the apprehended capture of Philadelphia. He and his wife go to the city to consult with their children there, to settle to what places they should remove for refuge. They determine to wait a little.

September 19th. On a second visit to the city, found his son-in-law, Mease, and family, had, in the interval of a day, fled from their house at four o'clock in the morning, and had gone towards Trenton. He finds there, that great numbers had fled the last night and this morning. The roads were full of persons going away.

September 20th. He states that the roads are still full of poor people flying off from their good homes, to fall perhaps into greater danger. To-day, his wife went to the city to endeavour to save some of the furniture, left behind by her daughter.

September 22d. The news and reports, of to-day and yesterday, are all uncertain. They heard a cannonading up the Schuylkill; cause unknown.

September 23d. The alarm this morning is great. The militia are returning in great haste; tell us the British passed the Swedeford last night, and are since in full march for Germantown. From this news many fled this night. Among them was Doctor Bensall and family, which went to Horsham. He left a well furnished house and a large shop of medicines, which the enemy, as he was a known whig, destroyed, or carried off.

September 25th. The British army entered Germantown at eleven o'clock, and encamped around them, and occasions much fear, especially from the foreign mercenaries. They burnt and destroyed all his fences, grain, potatoes, turnips, &c., and endeavoured to inveigle away some of his negroes. To his person they were complaisant, and readily gave him a safeguard to keep his effects in door, from harm. A heavy rain fell at night.

September 26th. The morning was cool from the rain. General Lord Cornwallis marches into Philadelphia in great state,—the incidents of which were inscribed in pompous language, and at much length, on the Coffee House books.

September 28th. He hears that his daughter's family, which had gone to Summer Seat for refuge, had to change their place, and were going to Lancaster for greater security. Her husband, Mr. Mease, was with the camp. This day, for the first time, General Howe made *his* entrance into Philadelphia, and made his call upon Lord Cornwallis, then at Richard Penn's mansion, in High street, near Sixth street. [The same afterwards Washington's residence.]

September 29th. The army seem all quiet—have a fine season—are hourly destroying the property of all within their reach.

September 30th. This day, and at other times, he speaks of visiting Galloway in the city for a pass, to visit his daughter, but is always refused or put off.

October 2d. He hears the attack begun on the Fort at Mud

Island. He mentions hearing, from day to day, for near *two months* after this, the heavy cannonading continued on that fortress—(so gallantly and long defended). It sensibly shook the ground, he says, at Germantown!

October 4th. He returned to Germantown this morning from the city, and finds that a hot engagement had occurred between the two armies at Germantown. His poor wife was *alone*, up two pair of stairs, when a cannon ball passed through a window very near her.

October 6th. Great numbers came out from the city to satisfy their curiosity respecting the battle of yesterday. After the battle, the Hessian camp is placed just by him, and makes him much dislike their presence.

October 7th. Several were executed for desertion and others were flogged for offences. An aid of General Knyphausen, (one Copenhouse,) robbed him of a Map of Pennsylvania, and otherwise behaved unlike a gentleman. In the evening, a great number of the Highlanders were encamped up town,—and the following morning were again moved off.

October 10th. He notices the army to be in great motion this morning; and it is the opinion of some, that Washington is approaching:—others say, (so uncertain is the news!) that he has crossed the Delaware.

October 11th. He notices the first white frost. Before day light the soldiers went off to try to surprise the Americans, and by eight o'clock, A. M., returned without falling in with any of them.

October 17th. Orders came for all horses in Germantown and the environs to be sent to Philadelphia by eight o'clock, with their harnesses. About five hundred were so sent and appraised, but only tories received their pay! His horse was exempted by the kindness of Sir William Erskine. At this time, his house being marked for the quarters of General Sterne, it is occupied below stairs by his aids; and next day, there came a great suite of his officers, and fixed their sentinels around the house—filling the stables with their horses;—but in an hour, much to his joy and comfort, came an order for their return, and to say, he would not come.

October 18th. Three regiments marched as high as Barren hill in quest of rebels, as they said. In the evening he heard thirteen cannons and volleys of small arms,—which proved afterwards to be a *feu-de-joie* from the Americans, for the capture of Burgoyne's army.

October 19th. The army is in motion at day light, to march from here and not to return. By ten o'clock, they were all gone for the city. In about an hour, the American light horse appeared, and soon had some skirmishing down the road. They took three or four prisoners and some wagons.

October 20th. A part of General Wayne's division marched down through Germantown, and returned in the evening. He speaks of several American officers as being entertained at his house as friends·

such as General Reed, Colonel Bradford, &c., and then, as returning to their camp in the afternoon.

October 23d. A part of General Washington's army began to march by ten o'clock at night through Germantown, and continued till day-break. They formed on the heights near the city and drove in the pickets. The enemy not venturing out, the troops withdrew, as they did not wish to attack *the city*. They hear the cannonading at the fort, and two violent shocks of explosion, shaking the earth,—which afterwards proved to be the Augusta man-of-war blown up, &c.

November 10th. Several parties from our camp pass through town to forage. Several deserters from day to day from the city confirm the scarcity of bread, &c., there. The cannonade at the fort is still very heavy, and still shaking the very earth.

November 11th. A hard frost, and next day seems to begin the first of the winter—snow having fallen all the preceding night.

November 15. The weather clear and cold. They can *see* from a house in Germantown, by the aid of a spy glass, two men-of-war, closely bombarding the poor little fort, which has held out nobly since the 2d October, and only yielded at the end of seven weeks.

November 17th. Several women of the British camp were caught last night plundering the gardens, and were carried to head-quarters, to look and feel very awkwardly.

November 20th. Several *women* came from the city to look up a little provision for their families. Desolation and famine seem to threaten us.

November 22d. In the afternoon the British burnt the house of John Dickinson, Esq., (the same now known as J. P. Norris' house,) also the tavern of the whig lady, Mrs. Nice, at the Rising Sun, and several others in that neighbourhood, on the Germantown road. They also burnt the house of Jonathan Mifflin; Peale Hall, Francis' place, &c. This to their great shame!

November 25th and 26th. There was much alarm in Germantown, from reports that it was the purpose of the enemy to burn this place. It was even said, that the party for this purpose was resting at the Rising Sun. In consequence of this fear, he conveyed away a trunk of valuables as far as Chestnut hill.

November 27th. There appeared a great and surprising northern light—as red as blood.

December 4th. The enemy were much in motion—had pressed yesterday numerous horses, wagons, &c.

December 5th. The whole of the enemy's force, last night and this morning, passed through Germantown on their way to surprise General Washington at Whitemarsh. They did much damage as they went—wantonly burning and destroying houses and property in the night time. At ten o'clock, A. M., was heard a heavy firing begun on Chestnut hill, and lasting for two or three hours. They returned on the 8th instant.

December 6th. The enemy and our light horse place us in much danger, as they patrol our streets alternately.

December 10th. He finds many of the inhabitants of the town deploring their losses. Several had sent their goods for safety to Chestnut hill—where the enemy took some and burnt the rest. He, however, found that his trunk, which had been left at Mr. Bush's house, had escaped the pillage, although the house itself had lost much, while occupied as the temporary quarters of General Howe and his attendants. [This house was, since, Lentz's house, at the fork of the road.] When they returned, the night of the 7th, down the Old York road, they spared neither friends nor foes, but burnt and robbed all along the road. They carried with them about forty loads of wounded. Mrs. Bush was so frightened by the violence of some towards her son, Dr. Bush, then a wounded officer in bed, in threatening to stab him, &c., that she miscarried with *her twentieth* child, and was interred at Philadelphia, on the 21st December.

December 20th. The navigation at Philadelphia was stopped for ten or twelve days by the ice.

In January, 1778, the weather being severely cold, the British army goes into winter quarters—often sending out foraging parties to rob the country around, and on market days to protect the country people bringing them produce.

The 19th of May, a large detachment of British marched up the Old York road; and next day a second party came through Germantown, and had a skirmish. They returned about five o'clock, P. M. in some haste, with several wagons of dead and wounded. The Indians killed seven British horsemen on the banks of the Schuylkill.

May 28th. A large detachment of the enemy came up and returned, without permission to do any harm.

June 3d. The British army came up and went through the town by break of day, and returned by nine o'clock, A. M. They rob gardens and steal fowls, as they pass along.

June 6th. They came up again in force and returned by nine o'clock, A. M.—having with them a few wounded in a skirmish.

June 10th. The enemy came up again by different routes, and joined forces at Allen's lane, (now Mount Airy,) and returned before nine o'clock in the morning—effecting nothing but the plundering of gardens, &c.

The English commissioners came up strongly guarded as far as Chew's house, and returned just after the above force.

June 13th. The army marched up for *the last time*, and got as far as Mount Airy. They returned in two hours.

June 16th and 17th. They are embarking and making all preparations for a departure from Philadelphia; and on the 18th, the *Americans* again took possession of the city. *Laus Deo!*

☞ The foregoing, it will be observed, speaks more of the predatory aggressions of the enemy, than was generally complained of, by others. We give the facts as they have been told us.

Such are the leading facts of the ancient town of Germantown—first, of its antiquities, as old as Philadelphia itself; and next of its stirring incidents as a captured country, and a battle field. We conclude with a single additional recital and confirmation, to wit:

Mrs. Hall, of Philadelphia, gave a short notice of the retreat of her family to Jersey—which, like many others, was by market wagons, carts, and other rough vehicles. She went away with others in a wood flat, fully crowded, sitting in smoky cabins, or wrapped in blankets and laying on the decks. Many were thankful to get into barns and out-houses in the country on their first arrival. Those who met abroad felt an instinctive brotherhood, and all did what they could to help and accommodate each other. Some went down to Delaware and along the Chesapeake, and were again driven from their asylums in the following summer, by new alarms. When they afterwards met at their desolate homes, marvellous and amusing were the adventures recounted at the firesides. "Sir, (said a gentleman, whose name was eminent among the patriots,) *these stories will be told by our children when we are dead and gone!*" And so they shall,—*Ecce res facta!*

Frankford.

There has been an opinion prevalent about Frankford village, that it derives its name from *Frank*, a black fellow, and *his ford*, where he kept a ferry for passengers on foot; but, besides its looking too artificial to be true, there are obvious reasons against that cause of its name. It is called Frankford creek in Holmes' map, in 1682. I see it, as early as 1701, referred to in a public petition concerning a road under the name of Frankford: besides, it lies on the creek, the Indian Wingohocking, which comes from the "*Frankford* Company's land" in Germantown. It was their proper water passage to the river.

Jonathan Dickinson, in 1715, writing respecting Fairman's land at "Frankford creek," says, "*a ford* there will be very needful, and very expensive, as the winds drive the waters from the Delaware *over* much marshy land."* For two hundred and twenty acres he offers £400. It falls short in the survey thirty-seven acres, thus showing how vaguely it was first done. He says it cannot be surveyed on the marsh [now all converted into productive meadows, &c.] till the winter is so as to go over it on the ice. He states that one hundred loads of timber were cut off it, because untenanted in the last winter, *by moonlight night.* Thus there were great depredators *then!* They probably cut it for staves and ship timber.

In the year 1814, Christopher Kuhn, at Frankford, in digging a cellar foundation for a small store house, on Kinsey and Hilles' present tanyard, came to a pot of old coin, hid perhaps by pirates.

* Thomas Fairman had been a surveyor, who dwelt at the *Treaty tree.*

This tanyard, on the Frankford creek, was close to the bank where it is high; and at three feet depth, he came to an earthern vessel highly glazed, which held about half a pint, and contained one hundred pieces of various sizes and shapes of *silver* coin. None of it was left to be shown to me; the whole having been sold soon after to the silver-smiths as old silver! On questioning him as to their character, he stated that there were many *cut pieces* of the size which would re main in cutting quarters and halves of dollars into sections of four pieces each. He observed dates to some as much as three hundred years old. One piece was as large as a crown, and was *square*. Two pieces had a tree on one side, and were marked *Massachusetts*, such a coin I have myself, of the year 1652. On the whole the vessel contained quite a treasure for a collector, and yet none were saved.

The aged Giles Gillingham, who died at Frankford in 1825, at the age of 93 years, said that when he was a boy, it was quite common with him to play with Indian boys in the neighbourhood. Frankford then had but very few houses, and was often called Oxford, after the name of its township. About the time of Braddock's defeat, there came an Indian from a distance, blowing a horn as he entered the Indians' place; they soon went off with him, and were no more seen near the place.

The Frankford mill, now possessed by Mr. Duffield, was originally used as a mill by the *Swedes* before Penn landed. The earliest house in the place, now T. W. Duffield's, near the same mill, was deeded to Yeamans Gillingham, by Penn's commissioners, in 1696. The "Swedes' mill" was probably a *saw* mill, as *wind* mills were first used for grist.

It appears, by the minutes of council, that the inhabitants of Frankford petition, in 1726, that the road may be *altered* so as to have but one bridge in use, instead of the two then existing.

Some very *old tombstones* are still in existence near Crescentville, in Bristol township, on the country seat of James N. Dickson, which have been intended to designate the remains of a mother and her two sons, of the name of Price, of Welsh origin, who died there in 1702. They were members of the community of Seventh-day Baptists,—the same which afterwards took the name of Keithian Baptists, from their union in sentiment with George Keith, who had been a Friend. They owed their origin to Abel Noble, who arrived in 1684, and formed a society of Baptists in Upper Providence, Chester county, where he baptized Thomas Martin, a public Friend, and others. This last, as a public minister, baptized Rees Price, in 1697.

In the year 1702, Rees and John Price, and others, built a meeting house in Oxford township, on a lot given to them by Thomas Graves; but neglecting to get their deed in due time, it came to pass that the Episcopalians got both the lot and house,—the same premises on which now stands the Oxford Episcopal church.

The tomb stones referred to are thus inscribed, to wit:

No. 1.

FOR THE
MEMORY FOE
ELIZABETH PRICE
WHO DIED
AVGVST THE 2st
1697.

No. 2.

FOR
THE MEMORY
OF JOHN
PRICE WHO
DIED JVNE THE
11th DAY 1702
AGED 20
YEARS

No. 3.

FOR
THE MEMORY
OF REES
PRICE WHO
DIED JVLY
THE 17 DAY
1702
AGED 23
YEARS.

Back of No. 2.

This YOVNG man was
So much with sence indved
That of his own and
Brothers Death contlvde
Saying Dear Brother
This know well Do i
'Twill not be long
Before we both must die.

Back of No. 3.

These *are first*
Thats in this Dust i say
Gods sabbath kept
To wit ye seventh Day.
in faith they DY'D
Here side by side remain
Till Christ shall come
To raise them up again.

It may not be inappropriate to mention another old tombstone, of the same vicinity. It is one to the memory of *Ralph Sandiford*, and is now in the possession of Jesse Griffith, at the place where R. Sandiford was buried—at Sandy hill—on the Bustletown road. The stone, to some, will be regarded as a curiosity, because he was a Friend, and was withal the early protestant against negro slavery—to wit:

IN MEMORY OF
RALPH SANDIFORD
SON OF JOHN SANDIFORD
OF LIVERPOOL. HE BORE
A TESTIMONY AGAINST THE
NEGRO TRADE, AND DYED
YE 28th OF YE 3d MONTH
1732, AGED 40 YEARS.

Byberry.

This township was settled as early as Philadelphia itself. The first Englishmen who explored it were four brothers of the name of *Walton*, who had landed at New Castle, and set out on foot to make their discoveries and choice of location. When they came to Byberry, they were much pleased with a spot of open grass land, and determined to make it their permanent home. They soon got a few acres into wheat, although they had to go back as far as Chester to procure their seed.

These were soon after joined by other settlers, among whom were Comly, Carter, Rush, and others,—the latter named was the ancestor of the distinguished Dr. Rush. The greater part of the first settlers were Friends, which for numerous years afterwards gave to the country the ascendency of Friends' principles and manners. It was therefore, for many years, the preferred spot of visitation for the remaining Indians, numbers of whom used to gather annually from Edge Pillock and other places in New Jersey, forming little colonies, which would set down at favourite places in the woods, and subsist a while on the land turtle they could catch, and the game they could kill. In these woods they gathered their supply of materials for making baskets, spoons, and ladles, bows and arrows, &c., and saying, as their apology, that their forefathers had reserved such rights in their disposal of the territory. The people were too kind to them to dispute their privilege, and they continued to visit, unmolested, until the period of the revolution.

The frank and generous hospitality of the Indians to the original settlers deserved a kind and generous return. The descendants of the original settler, (Carver,) have told me of a striking case of kindness. When his family was greatly pinched for bread-stuff, and knew of none nearer than Chester or New Castle, they sent out their children to some neighbouring Indians, intending to leave them there, until they could have food for them at home; but the Indians took off the boys' trowsers, tied the legs full of corn, and sent them back thus seasonably loaded.

Byberry is remarkable for having been once destined as the location of Philadelphia city! At the lower or southern side of the mouth of the Poquessink creek is a pretty elevation of table land, conforming to the line of the river Delaware, covered with a range of pine trees and others, intermixed, and showing now a primitive state and character, such as we understand Philadelphia itself originally had. Our youth who pass it in the steamboats should observe it. This site had once been surveyed and plotted as Philadelphia; and circumstances, for numerous years afterwards, caused it to be called popularly, "Old Philadelphia." It is now a part of the country seat of Mr. Morgan;—and his present mansion, altered and repaired, was once celebrated as "the bake house," at which, on a large scale, biscuit were baked for sea service, and for the continental army.

So many of the descendants of the primitive inhabitants still occupy in prosperity the places of their forefathers, and give perpetuity to the names of so many original settlers, that it is gratifying now, to ride through their township, and to witness the comforts enjoyed by them.

This love of visiting and contemplating places filled with local impressions, generated by the events and doings of our forefathers, is one of the strongest and purest feelings of our nature, and one which we wish to foster, with warm hearted interest, in these pages. It flings over the imagination a delightful spell, where fancy draws those pictures of the past, more homebred, social and endearing, when viewed glimmering through the mist of years. With thoughts like these, we are prompted to add, in conclusion, some extracts from a letter written with pathos and feeling by the celebrated Dr. Rush, to the Hon. John Adams—his warm and social friend, on the occasion of his visit to Byberry, in 1812, to see the old *homestead*, and to revive the images of his childhood and departed kindred;—even its length, in this place, will be excused by those who know how to appreciate such pure emotions, so prompted by country and home. Such feelings are full of poetry and sensibility, and may some day present to some future Byberry poet, the theme of a touching poem!

When silent time, with lightly foot,
  Had trod o'er fifty years,
He sought again his native spot
  With grateful thoughts and tears;—
When he drew nigh his ancient home
  His heart beat all the way,—
Each place he pass'd seem'd still to speak
  Of some dear former day.

"I was called," says he, "lately to visit a patient in that neighbourhood, and having with me my youngest son, I thought I would avail myself of the occasion to visit *the farm* on which I was born, and where my ancestors for several generations had lived and died. In approaching it, I was agitated in a manner I did not expect. The access was altered, but every thing around was nearly the same as in the days of my boyhood, *at which time I left it.* The family there, though strangers to me, received me kindly, and discovered a disposition to satisfy my curiosity and gratify my feelings. I soon asked permission to conduct my son up stairs to see the room in which I drew my first breath and made my first *unwelcome* noise in the world, and where first began the affection and cares of my beloved and excellent mother. I next asked for a large cedar tree which once stood before the door,—planted by my father's hand. It had been converted into the pillars of the piazza before the house. Filled with emotion, I embraced the one nearest me. I next inquired for the orchard planted by the same hand, and was conducted to an eminence behind the house, where I saw a number of apple trees which still bore fruit, to each of which I felt something like the affection of a brother. The building, which is of stone, bears marks of age and decay. On one of the stones near the front door, I discovered the letters J. R. Before the house flows a small but deep creek, abounding in pan fish. The farm consists of ninety acres, in a highly cultivated state. The owner did not want to sell; but I begged, if he ever should incline to dispose of it, to make me or one of my surviving sons the first offer. While I sat in its common room, I looked at its walls, and thought how often they had been made vocal by my ancestors—to conversations about wolves, bears and snakes, in the first settlement; afterwards about cows and calves, and colts and lambs, &c., and at all times, with prayers and praises, and chapters read audibly from the Bible; for all who inhabited it, of my family, were pious people—chiefly of the sect of Quakers and Baptists. On my way home, I stopped to view a family graveyard, in which were buried three and a part of four successive generations, all of whom were the descendants of Captain John Rush, who, with six sons and three daughters, followed William Penn to Pennsylvania, in 1683. He had been a captain of a troop of horse under Oliver Cromwell; and when I first settled in Philadelphia, I was sometimes visited by one of his grandsons, a man of eighty-five years of age, who had, when a boy, often seen and conversed with the former, and especially concerning his services under the Protector. I retain, as his relics, his sword, watch and Bible leaf, on which is inscribed, in his own hand, his marriage, and children's births and names. My grandfather, James Rush, after whom my son, the physician, is named, has his gravestone and inscription in the aforesaid grave ground—as "departed this life, March 16, 1727, aged 48 years, &c." He was a farmer and gunsmith, of much ingenuity in his business. While standing and considering this repository of the dead, there holding my kindred dust, my thoughts ran wild, and my ancestors seemed to stand before me in their homespun dresses, and to say, what means *this gentleman*, by thus intruding upon our repose; and I seemed to say—dear and venerable friends, be not disturbed. I am one who inherits your blood and name, and come here to do homage to your Christian and moral virtues; and truly, I have acquired nothing from the world, (though raised in fame), which I so highly prize as the religious principles which I inherited from you; —and I possess nothing that I value so much as the innocence and purity of your character. After my return from such a visit, I recounted in the evening to my family, the incidents of the day, to which they listened with great pleasure; and heartily they partook of some cherries from the limb of my father's tree, which my little son brought home with him as a treat to them."

Such a letter, from such an eminent man, consecrates to kindly remembrance such hallowed localities;—It gives to me, if I needed it, a sufficient apology for thus enlarging this chapter on recollections and incidents of Byberry. They will come home to the bosom of many.

There is not a spot in this wide-peopled earth,
So dear to the heart as the land of our birth;
'Tis the home of our childhood, the soul-touching spot,
Which mem'ry retains when all else is forgot!

A letter written under such circumstances does more to illustrate the character and the *heart* of the writer, than a volume of common biography. The visit of such a man to the graves of his ancestors, creates a stirring at the heart of the sensitive reader. There is piety in it—an enthusiasm and holiness of feeling devoted to the dead, which give character and immortality to him who cherished them. His feelings were far better and more pure than to be borne aloft *by his renown*, amidst the hosannas of the people. In such a place for thought—for mental abstraction, how withdrawn from the tempests which sweep over the world's affairs! What a rest to the heart!—The fancy only is busy, when it there cons over the former employments, business, joys, sorrows, hopes and fears of those now beneath his tread. The world's glory—its highest ambition, quickly fades and dies before the tranquil pleasures of such an hour as this. Such *a home* is consecrated by such a letter, and should be perpetuated and visited as the *solum natale* of a man both good and great. One cannot forbear the wish that the sons of such a father should long possess the home, and there preserve the simple and touching narrative of such a parent! I would inscribe such a letter upon *its walls* for ever—*Esto tu perpetua.*

Gwynedd—in Montgomery county.

The late venerable Jesse Foulke stated, in substance, the following facts concerning what he knew of the settlement of Gwynedd, to wit:—

In the year 1698, the township was purchased of William Penn, by William, John, and Thomas Evans, and distributed among original settlers, to wit: William, John, Thomas, Robert, Owen and Cadwallader Evans, Hugh Griffiths, Edward Foulke, Robert Jones, John Hughs, and John Humphreys. Only the two eldest were then Friends—all were Welshmen; and all, except the two Friends, were churchmen. These held their meetings at Robert Evans'; and there Cadwallader Evans was in the practice to read from the Bible to the people.

But as Cadwalladar Evans himself related, he was going as usual to his brother Robert's, when passing near to the road to Friends' meeting, held at John Hughs' and John Humphreys', it seemed as if he was impressed "to go down and see how the Quakers do." This he mentioned to his friends at the close of his *own* meeting, and they all agreed to go to the Friends the next time; and where they were all so well satisfied, that they never again met in their own worship.

In 1700, they built a log meeting house, near where the present one stands. This gave place to a larger one of stone, in 1712; and in 1823, that was removed for a still larger one.

The Friends' meeting house, at Gwynedd, was made a hospital for the wounded of the army after the battle of Germantown.

I have given the foregoing recital of the manner of Evans' convincement, in the words of Mr. Foulke; but his kinswoman, Susan Nancarro, who died lately at the age of 80 years, told it to me a little variant. She said that the brothers read the *public* services of their church, and convened in a summer house. As one of the brothers was once going to that place, he passed where William Penn was speaking, and willing to hearken to *him*, he became so earnestly convinced that way, that he succeeded to bring over all his brethren.

Mrs. Nancarro had often seen and conversed with her grandfather, Hugh Evans, who lived to be ninety years of age. When he was a boy of twelve years of age, he remembered that William Penn, with his daughter Letitia and a servant, (in the year 1699 or 1700,) came out on horseback to visit his father, Thomas Evans. Their house then was *superior* in that it was of *barked* logs, a refinement surpassing the common rank. The same place is now E. Jones', near the Gwynedd meeting house. At that house William Penn ascended steps *on the outside* to go to his chamber; and the lad of twelve, being anxious to see all he could of so distinguished a man, went up afterwards to peep through the apertures at him; and there he well remembered to have seen him on his knees praying, and giving thanks to God for such peaceful and excellent shelter in the wilderness! What a subject for a painter! I heard Mrs. D. L. say that she had also heard the same facts from old Hugh Evans.

There was at this time a great preparation among the Indians near there for some public festival. Letitia Penn, then a lively young girl, greatly desired to be present, but her father would not give his consent, though she entreated much. The same informant says she ran out chagrined, and seeming to wish for something to dissipate her regret, snatching up a flail near some grain, at which she began to labour playfully, when she inadvertently brought the unwieldly instrument severely about her head and shoulders; and was thus quickly constrained to retreat into the house, with quite a new concern upon her mind! This fact made a lasting impression upon the memory of the lad aforesaid, who then was a witness.

Norristown.

This place, now so beautiful and numerous in houses, is a town wholly built up since the war of independence. At that time, it was the farm of John Bull; and his original farm house is now standing in the town, as the inn of Richard Richardson.

As early as the year 1704, the whole *manor*, as it was then called, which included the present township of Norrington, was sold out by William Penn, Jr., for £850. From Isaac Norris, one of the purchasers, the place has since taken its name.

The original settlers about the neighbourhood of Norristown, Swedes' ford, &c., were Swedes, who much inclined to settle along the banks of the Schuylkill, and, like the Indians, to make free use of their canoes for travelling conveyances. The Swedes' church, not far off, was much visited by worshippers going there in their boats; and in still later times, when horses became a means of conveyance, it was common for a man and woman to ride together on one horse, the women wearing for economy "safe-guard petticoats," which they took off after arrival, and hung along the fence until again required.

There are still remains below Norristown, nearly fronting the ford, of a long line of redoubts, made by the Americans, under the direction of Gen. Du Porteuil, to defend the passage of the ford against the British approaching from the battle of Brandywine, and which had the effect to compel them to pass six miles higher up the river, at "Fatland ford." Some of the cannon, in an angle of the redoubt, have since washed into the river bank, and may at some future day surprise a discoverer!

It was on the river bank, at Norristown, that the *first spade* was set to excavate *the first public canal* attempted in the United States' This should be remembered! It was indeed abortive for want of adequate funds, as well as economy; but it tested the early spirit of enterprise of *our* leading citizens,—acting a few years in advance of the age in which they dwelt. This fact, in connexion with the MS. account of Mr. John Thompson, of Delaware county, of his early adventure in a boat, the White Fish, by a navigation from Niagara to Philadelphia, by the water courses in New York state; showing *beforehand*, the practicability of the Grand canal of New York, are so many evidences of *our* early efforts in the "canal system!" The boat, after so singular a voyage, was laid up in the State-house yard, in the year 1795, and visited as a curiosity. A sight of that boat, and a knowledge of the facts connected with it, is supposed to have prompted President Washington, at that early period, to write of his conviction of the practicability of *a union* of the waters of the lakes with the ocean. A subject, happily for all, now no longer a problem.

Chester County.

At the time the European emigrants first settled in this county it was principally overshadowed by forests—only a small patch here and there around the Indian huts having been cleared by the natives, for the purpose of growing their corn. *But the woods at that time wore a very different appearance from what they do now.* Owing to the Indian custom of firing them once or twice in a year, the small timber and bushes were killed in their growth, and of course the forests were *but thinly set.* I am informed that one of the first settlers said that, at the time of his first acquaintance with the county, he could have driven *a horse and cart from one end of its extremi-*

ties to the other, in almost every direction, without meeting with any material obstruction.

For a number of years the process of agriculture by the new settlers was extremely rude and imperfect. No regular rotation of crops was observed. A field was frequently appropriated to one kind of produce for several successive years. No man's care in relation to his ground extended beyond the sowing and gathering of his crops, and by *total neglect of manuring and fertilizing* their lands, the strength of the soil was yearly and daily exhausting itself. This was so much the case within the memory of one ancient now living, that when he departed from the common course, and began to endeavour to recruit his soil, his plan became the subject of general ridicule among his neighbours; and the saying was applied to him on all hands, " a penny wise, a pound foolish." His success, however, began to have its influence in his neighbourhood; but still they did not then know the beneficial effects of *lime*—little use was made of it before the revolution, and so little was it valued in itself, as to be often sold for five or six cents a bushel. Wheat, rye, oats and barley, were the principal productions. Indian corn was so little regarded, that many depended upon getting the little they used from the lower counties, in preference to raising it themselves. Clover was almost wholly unknown, and timothy quite so. Meadows which were irrigated furnished the grass for hay and pasturage. How very differently managed is every thing now! Now all the farmers are becoming wealthy and happy. Thus proving that *conduct is luck.*

This county originally contained within its limits the present county of Delaware, and they together formed one of the first settled counties in the state. The first settlers were generally of the society of Friends, and now their descendants mostly occupy the south eastern and middle townships. The Welsh settled along the " Great Valley," a fine region of land, of from one to three miles wide, traversing the whole county from east to west; the Irish Presbyterians settled in the south-west; and the English intermixed generally throughout the whole county. Many of the townships are of Welsh origin, as is indicated by their names,—such as Tredyffin, Uwchland, the Calns, Nantmels, &c. Other names indicate lands formerly belonging to the London company, such as London Grove, New London, London Britain, Birmingham, &c.

The appearance of the fruitful and picturesque country of the "Great Valley," is well worth a visit from the youth of our city. It comprises nearly fifty thousand acres of the choicest lands, and is bordered on either side by long continuous ranges of high ridges, called North and South hills. From their summits, there are sometimes very extensive and beautiful views—such as might lead out the young mind to conceive of those much greater elevations, "the Blue mountains," and the great Allegheny " backbone of the state."

The Brandywine, running through this county, is a fine stream, affording much profitable " water power," and some very picturesque scenery. Brantewein (brandy) is a word of Teutonic origin, which might have been used equally by the Swedes and Dutch to express its brandy-coloured stream. Certain it is, that at all early periods, after the river lost its Indian names of *Minquas*, and *Suspecough*, it was written *Brandywine*.

Since the county sustained the separation of Delaware county, the county town has been located at West Chester, a very growing place and possessing a genteel and intelligent population. At this place, are the original records of Chester county, and of course affording to the curious inquirer the means of exploring the antiquarian lore of the primitive days.

As our business is to show to the present rising generation the great difference between the present and the remote past, when all was coarse and rustic, we shall subjoin some scraps of information illustrative of such change, to wit:

Mr. William Worrell, who died but a few years since,—an inhabitant of Marple township, at the advanced age of nearly one hundred years---says, that in the country there were no carts, much less carriages; but that they hauled their grain on sleds to the stacks, where a temporary thrashing-floor was made. He remembered to have assisted his father to carry *on horseback* one hundred bushels of wheat to mill in Haverford, which was sold there for but 2*s.* a bushel. The natural meadows and woods were the only pasture for their cattle; and the butchers of Philadelphia would go out and buy one, two, or three head of cattle, from such as could spare them, as all their little surplus.

He recollected when there were great quantities of wild turkeys; and a flight of pigeons which lasted two days! Only think of such a spectacle! They flew in such immense flocks, that they obscured the rays of the sun! One night they settled in such numbers at Martin's bottom, that persons who visited them could not hear one another speak, by reason of their strong whirring noise. Their weight on the branches of the trees was so great as to break off numerous large limbs!

He never saw coffee or tea until he was twenty years of age: then his father brought some tea from Philadelphia, and his aunt did not know how to use it, till she got information first from a more refined neighbour. On another occasion a neighbour boiled the leaves and buttered them!

In going to be married, the bride rode to meeting behind her father, or next friend, seated on a pillion;—but after the marriage, the pillion was placed with her behind the saddle of her husband. The dead were carried in coffins on the shoulders of four men, who swung the coffin on poles, so that they might proceed along narrow paths with most ease.

Another ancient inhabitant, William Mode, who died on the west branch of the Brandywine, in 1829, at the age of eighty-seven years, said he well remembered the Indians—men, women and children,—

coming to his father's house to sell baskets, &c., and that they used to cut and carry off bushes from their meadow, probably for mats to sleep on. The deer, in his boyhood, were so plenty, that their tracks in the wheat field, in time of snow, were as if marked by a flock of sheep: at one time his father brought home two of them on his sled. Wild turkeys in the winter were often seen in flocks, feeding in the corn and buckwheat fields. Foxes often carried off their poultry; once their man knocked one down near the barn. Squirrels, rabbits, rackoons, pheasants and partridges abounded.

Samuel Jeffrey, too, a man of eighty-seven years, who died at West Chester in 1828, said he could well remember when deer were plenty in the woods of Chester county, and when a hunter could occasionally kill a bear. He also had seen several families of Indians still inhabiting their native fields. N. Marcer died in 1831, aged one hundred and one years.

This county still contains some of the oldest inns known in the annals of our country. Thus, Powell's Journal, of 1754, speaks of his stopping on the way to Lancaster, at "the Buck," by Ann Miller—at "the Vernon," by Ashton, (now "the Warren")—"the White Horse," by Hambright—"the Ship," by Thomas Park—"the Red Lion," by Joseph Steer—and "the Wagon," by James Way, &c.

Chester county is also distinguished as being the theatre of some important events in the revolution,—such as "the battle of Brandywine," the "massacre of Paoli," and the winter quarters of our army at "the Valley Forge." The battle ground of the Brandywine, near where La Fayette was wounded, may be still visited at the Birmingham meeting-house of Friends. There, if you see the grave-digger turning up the grave ground, you may possibly see the bones of some British soldier at only two feet under the ground, with fragments of his red coat, his stock-buckle, buttons, &c.! You may even be shown some old gold coin, found concealed once in the great cue of a buried Hessian! If you ramble down to "Chadsford," not far distant, you may still see remains of the little redoubt which disputed the ford; and there, as a relic of silenced war and bloodshed, pick up an occasional bullet or grapeshot. The county was at one time much disturbed, and made withal remarkable, by a predatory hero in the time of the revolution. He was usually called "Captain Fitz," but his real name was James Fitzpatrick. He roamed the country in stealth, as a "British refugee," making his attacks upon the chattels of the "stanch whigs," and seemingly delighting in his perils and escapes. His whole character made him a real Rob Roy of his time. At last he was seized and executed.

The state of the American army at the Valley Forge, in the drear winter of 1777–8, was an extremely perilous and suffering one. They were kept in necessary fear from so superior a force as Howe's well appointed army; whereas, ours was suffering the need of almost every thing. An officer, an eye-witness, has told me, that a sufficiency of food or clothing could not be had; that so many men were without whole shoes, that several actually marked the snowy ground with their bloody footsteps; some, while on duty as sentinels, have doffed their hats to stand in, to save their feet from freezing; of salt beef or pork, they could not get a supply, and fresh beef was wholly impracticable to get at all; of vegetables they got none. *One* wooden or pewter dish answered for a whole mess; and *one* horn tumbler, in which whisky rarely entered, served for several. Much of their diet was salted herrings, too much decayed to bear separation; but were dug out of the cask *en masse.* Sugar and coffee were luxuries not seen; and paper money, with which they were paid for such severities, was almost nothing!

If *such* were the calamities of war, and such *the price* they paid for our *self-government*, oh! how greatly should we, their descendants, prize the precious boon! Maddened be the head, and palsied be the hand, that should attempt to despoil us of a treasure so dearly purchased!

A public journal of Philadelphia, of August, 1778, thus describes the circumstances of the conduct and capture of the aforesaid Captain Fitz, saying, "The celebrated bandit of Chester county was taken and brought to Philadelphia in August. He had been made prisoner by Robert McPhee (McAfee) and a girl. Fitz entered the house of McPhee's family while they were at tea, armed with a rifle, a sword, and a case of pistols, saluting them as friends; upon their saying they did not recognize him, he swore he would soon be better known, as 'Captain Fitz, come *to levy his dues* on the cursed rebels.' He soon demanded his watch and buckles, and soon after ordered them all up stairs before him, whilst he should search for his money. When he had got up stairs, he, thinking he was safe, began to arrange his shoe buckle on the edge of the bed, when McPhee (McAfee) signing to the girl, Rachel Walker, a young woman, they sprang upon him, and so held him that he could not escape." The reward was 1000 dollars, which was divided between them, and Captain Fitz was hung. While in Philadelphia he broke his hand cuffs twice in one night. At Chester, afterwards, he filed off his irons and got out of his dungeon, and would have escaped but for the extraordinary vigilance of his jailer. His real name was James Fitzpatrick, he was hanged at Chester: was a blacksmith.

The New London Academy, of New London, though not much spoken of now, furnished, in colonial days, some of the leading scholars, such as Dr. Francis Allison, Charles Thomson, Gov. Thomas M'Kean, Dr. John Ewing, Dr. Hugh Williamson, M. C.; Dr. David Ramsey, historian; the Rev. James Latta, &c.

The "battle ground of Brandywine," so eventful in our revolutionary period, will ever tend to consecrate it as a place of remembrance, and by some as a place of visitation. To those who may choose with us "to wander o'er the bloody field to book the dead," we shall here furnish such *notitia*, and notes by the way, as will serve as a companion to others:—

"Our direction was to the forks of the Brandywine, on Jeffrey's ford, the point at which Lord Cornwallis crossed the river on the 11th of September, 1777—the day of the battle, known by the name of the river on the banks of which it was fought.

"It was near the close of July of that year, that the British army, under Sir William Howe, and their Hessian auxiliaries, under Gen. Knyphausen, embarked from New York on the meditated invasion of Pennsylvania. The squadron had a long and unpleasant passage. Finding the Delaware too well prepared for defence, to allow of a very favourable ascent of that river, the British commander bore away for the Chesapeake—thence ascended Elk river into Maryland, as far as that stream was navigable, at which point the army disembarked, and on the 23d of September took up its march for Philadelphia. In the mean time General Washington returned from Jersey, for the defence of that important city, and public opinion seemed to require the hazard of a pitched battle. The American commander, therefore, marched upon the Brandywine to intercept the advancing foe, and crossed the river with a part of his forces. The British forces advanced until they were within two miles of the Americans; but, after reconnoitring the enemy on the night of the 8th of September, General Washington, apprehending the object of the enemy to be to turn his right, and, by seizing the heights on the north side of the river, to cut off his communication with Philadelphia, changed his position by recrossing the river, and taking position on the heights near Chadd's ford, several miles below the forks.

"From the dispositions of the enemy, it was supposed that he would attempt to cross with his whole force, at this place; but while the Americans were making preparations to receive them at this point, Lord Cornwallis, at the head of the enemy's column, took a long circuitous march to the left, until he gained the forks, and crossed at Trimble's and Jeffrey's ford, without difficulty or opposition. Continuing east from the ferry, about three quarters of a mile, he took a road turning short down the river to the right, in order to fall upon the right of the American forces. The movement was a partial surprise upon the American commander, who, however, as soon as he was apprised of it, took all possible measures to provide against the effect, by detaching General Sullivan, with all the force he could spare, to oppose Cornwallis. General Sullivan took an advantageous position, on commanding grounds, near the small Quaker meeting house of Birmingham, his left extending towards the Brandywine, his artillery advantageously disposed, and both flanks covered with woods. Wayne's division, with Maxwell's light infantry, remained at Chadd's ford to keep Knyphausen in check, while the division of General Greene, accompanied by the commander-in-chief, formed a reserve at a central position between the right and left wings.

"In the interesting excursion we are now describing, we took the track of the division of Cornwallis, where it turned south after crossing the forks of the river. It was at two o'clock in the afternoon;

and such was the deliberation of the British troops, that they stopped for dinner upon the brow of a hill, about midway between the corner and the position occupied by the Americans. An old resident, yet living near the spot, and who was forced into the service of Cornwallis, affirms, that it was a merry though a brief dinner frolic amongst the officers. The American forces being no where even in sight, though scarcely two miles distant—another hill intervening to cut off the prospect—the young officers felt but little apprehension—probably supposing that the "rebel Yankees" would hardly make a stand even when they did come in sight. Among the gayest of the gay, as a volunteer in the suite of one of the British generals, as tradition informs us, was a sprightly and chivalrous descendant of the Percies—not the Lord Percy who brought the ill-fated British detachment back from Lexington, at the commencement of the revolution, (who was the last duke of Northumberland, and died in 1817,) but a younger one still. He was a noble and generous youth, and had volunteered on the present occasion, as an amateur, to see how fields were won. He wore a splendid uniform, and rode, like a Percy, a noble steed richly caparisoned. The column resumed its march at half-past three, and by four o'clock ascended the intervening hill before mentioned, which brought them in full prospect of the American troops, in battle array, and coolly awaiting the onset. Instant dispositions were made for battle. As the young Percy came over the brow of the hill, he was observed suddenly to curb in his impatient steed, and the gay smile upon his lively features, changing at first to gravity, soon became sad and pensive, as he glanced his bright eye over the extensive rolling landscape, now rife with animation. It was a glorious spectacle. The wide prospect of gentle hill and dale, with forest and farm-house, the bright waters of the Brandywine, just appearing in one little winding section in a low and beautiful valley on the right, formed of itself a picturesque view for the lover of the simple garniture of nature. But enlivened, as it now was, by the presence of two hostile armies, both eager for the onslaught—on *that* side the American line resting upon their burnished arms in order of battle; and on *this* the brisk note of preparation, the displaying of columns, and other manœuvres necessary to the sudden change of position and circumstances—

> "'The neighing steed, and the shrill trump,
> The spirit-stirring drum, the ear-piercing fife,
> The royal banner, and all quality,
> Pride, pomp, and circumstance of glorious war,'

all combined to make up a scene which it would hardly be supposed would have damped the ardour, or clouded with gloom the fine features of a young officer, whose proud lip would at any other moment have curled with scorn, and his eye kindled with indignation at the remotest intimation of a want of firmness in the hour of trial. Yet, with a subdued and half-saddened eye, the young Percy, who but a moment before was panting to play the hero in the contest, paused for a moment longer. Then calling his servant to his side and taking his diamond-studded repeater from his pocket—'Here,' said he, 'take this and deliver it to my sister in Northumberland: I have seen this field and this landscape before, in a dream in England: Here I shall fall; and'—drawing a heavy purse of gold from his pocket—'take this for yourself.' Saying this, he dashed forward with his fellows. The lines were formed, and at four o'clock the battle commenced. The onset was impetuous, and the Americans received their haughty invaders with coolness and courage. But their right wing being overpowered by numbers, was at length compelled to give way. The remaining divisions being now exposed to a galling fire on the flank, continued to break, until a route ensued, although several strong posts were successively defended with intrepidity for a time.

"The most obstinate fighting, during the engagement, took place near the centre, which rested upon the little stone meeting house of the Quakers, and in the grave yard, walled on all sides by a thick stone mason-work, which, with the church, are yet standing as firmly as at the period of which we are writing. This enclosure was long and resolutely defended by the Americans, and it was near this place, about the middle of the action, that the noble young Percy fell, as he believed he had been doomed to do. The enclosure was at length scaled, and carried by the bayonet. The wounded were taken into the meeting-house, built by peace-makers, for the worship of the God of peace, though now the centre of the bloody strife; and the dead were inhumed in one corner of the burying ground, in which they had many of them been slain. Just before our visit, a grave had been dug, and the remains of a British soldier disinterred. A part of his shoes remained; a few pieces of red cloth, which fell to pieces, however, on being exposed to the air, were discovered; a button, likewise, marked '44th Reg't.,' and a flattened bullet—probably the winged messenger of death to the wearer,—were also found, both of which were given to us by the good man near by the meeting house.

"There is a scrap of unwritten history attached to this little obscure meeting-house,—true, though living only in tradition,—which is full of interest. A few years before the revolutionary war, the little parish of Birmingham was favoured on one occasion by the presence of one of the most gifted and eloquent preachers of their peaceable sect. The spirit moved him to preach, and as he proceeded, he seemed to rise to an unwonted measure in his thoughts; an unusual ardour possessed him, and his words fell with a holy unction upon his listeners. He proceeded, in language still more glowing and lofty, until his kindling eye seemed to catch glimpses of things unseen, and to penetrate the curtain of things yet to come. At length a vision broke upon him, and he burst forth, in language similar to that of Milton—

"'Oh what are these?
Death's ministers, not men; who thus deal death
Inhumanly to men; and multiply
Ten thousand fold the sin of him who slew
His brother!'

He then, in words of one 'rapt—inspired,' predicted the coming conflict with its attending scourges, and declared that there, even in that quiet community—whose precepts and conduct breathed nothing but peace on earth and good will to men—the angel of destruction should spread his wings—even there, the blood would flow to their horses' bridles—even there, within the walls of that little sanctuary, would be piled up heaps of the dying and the dead! The fulfilment was as exact as the prediction was surprising.

"The little meeting-house, and the grave-yard, were alike opened to our examination, and were both viewed with that interest which the associations connected with them would naturally inspire. The space here consecrated for the repose of the dead is of ample size for a country town, but it has been thus occupied for more than a century and a half. There is no clustering of houses adjoining this hallowed spot. There are spreading elms around, and one within the enclosure—and a cedar of more than a century's growth, which is as funereal in its appearance as the yew tree; and as 'the air its solemn stillness holds,' one standing here could hardly refrain from quoting the inimitable and deathless Elegy of Gray—particularly as nearly the whole area is now closely filled with the little grassy mounds which cover the dead:—

"'Beneath those rugged elms, that yew tree's shade,
Where heaves the turf in many a mouldering heap,
Each in his narrow cell for ever laid,
The rude forefather's of the hamlet sleep:'
* * * * * * *

And onward; [the sentimental reader, however, must quote for himself.] But of all the dead who repose here, not a single stone, nor the slightest discriminating memorial, indicates the spot where slumber the ashes of any particular individual. This neglect of such memorials, or marks of respect for the dead, we are aware is in strict and uniform accordance with the usages of that peculiar people; although it little accords with the views and feelings of others. True, as the same beautiful poet above quoted, intimates, neither 'storied urn,' nor 'animated bust,' can call back the 'fleeting breath;' nor can the flattery of inscriptions, deserved or undeserved, 'soothe the dull cold ear of death.' And it is likewise a sad—a melancholy reflection, how very short a period do nearly all the memorials reared to the memory of the dead, by the hand of surviving friendship and affection, endure! A few—a very few brief years, and the headstone has sunk—the slab is broken—the short column or pyramid overturned. Yet while they *do* remain, they are often mementoes of many interesting incidents, or endearing recollections. An incident of this description now rises upon the memory, and as its relation will wound none among the living, we will repeat it. There is an humble freestone standing in Trinity church-yard, New York, so near the street, that the bright and laughing eyes of beauty and pleasure can look upon it any day as their possessors are tripping along Broadway. It stands beneath the tree at the corner, by Doctor Bliss' book store, and the inscription yet retains the name of Mrs. ——— Johnson. The deceased was young and beautiful, full of intelligence and vivacity, when she was married, a few months before the breaking out of the pestilence which desolated New York in 1798. One Sunday afternoon, soon after the fever had commenced, and before there was much alarm, walking down the Broadway, upon the arm of her husband, by whom she was adored, and whom she adored in turn, in company with a friend who was also newly married, the epidemic was among the natural topics of conversation. Mrs. Johnson, whose natural buoyancy of spirits, perhaps, imparted, even at that moment, an appearance of light-heartedness she did not feel, was remarkably lively and cheerful. In passing the spot we have indicated, where the tree was then casting its refreshing shade upon the green sward beneath, she suddenly stopped, and looking up into her husband's face, with a sweet though slightly pensive smile, remarked with the utmost *naïvete* :—' There, Johnson : if I die of the yellow fever, bury me here.' On the very next Friday, she *was* buried there!

" But we have strayed a wide distance from Brandywine, without finishing the battle. Return we then to that part of our narrative. No sooner had Cornwallis defeated the Americans at Birmingham, than Knyphausen, after successfully keeping the attention of Wayne's division all day with an apprehension of an attack, which he did not intend, made the passage of the river, and carried the entrenchments, and took the battery and cannon intended to cover and defend the ford. After a severe conflict, the Americans posted in this quarter were compelled to give way, and thus the defeat became complete. The retreat continued that night and the day following to Philadelphia."

In examining the records of Chester county—beginning with its origin in 1681, we have found sundry items and facts, which may tend to give us an insight into the *men and things and doings* of the olden time, to wit:

The *first* court is recorded as being opened the 13th September, 1681, at Upland (Chester)—the justices present, William Clayton, William Warner, Robert Wade, Otto Ernest Cock, William Byles, Robert Lucas, Lassey Cock, Swan Swanson, Andreas Bankson, Thomas Fairman. Sheriff, John Test. Clerk, Thomas Revell.

The *first* action is a case of assault and battery—being Peter Erickson *vs.* Harmen Johnson and wife. The jury of twelve find for the plaintiff an award of 6*d.* damages, at his costs of suit.

Whereupon, the same Harmen Johnson and wife reverse the

action, and become plaintiffs against the same Peter Erickson, for assault and battery, and recover 40*s.* damages and cost. There must have been some adroitness in the use of law, to have so managed a defence as to turn about and mulct the accuser!

In the same court it was granted, by proclamation, that if any person present had aught against one of the justices, they might declare it. Whereupon, Daniel Brenson and Charles Brigham, upon oath, and Walter Pumphray upon attestation, declare that they had heard certain Indians speak against him, and also against Captain Edward Cantwell, a former sheriff. Then the said Lassey Cock upon oath declared his innocency, and that he had not spoken such words, whereupon the case was quieted or quashed.

At the court held November 30th, 1681, William Markam, Esq., governor and president, present with ten justices.

John Anderson is accused by Richard Noble, Peter Rambo and L. Lawrenson, of stealing and concealing sundry articles of pork; and on examination is acquitted.

The overseers for the highways were nominated and elected at the court, March 14th, 1681, to serve for one year, for repairing the roads, &c., to wit: Woolley Rawson, from Marcus creek to Naman's creek; Robert Wade, from thence to Upland creek; William Oxley, from thence to Amos' land; Mauns Stawkett, from thence to Karkus' mill; Peter Yokeham, from thence to Schuylkill falls; Andreas Rambo, from thence to Tacony creek; Erick Mullickay, from thence to Poetquessin creek; Claus Johnson, from thence to Samuel Cliff's; John Akraman, from thence to Gilbert Wheeler's. The foregoing arrangement for earliest roads evidences *the line* of the first routes of intercourse, beginning from *Marcus Hook*, keeping nigh to the Delaware till they reach the Schuylkill, (then spelt Schorekill) and thence to go up along its line to the falls, (thus going behind Philadelphia) and thence across the country (above the city) to the Tacony creek; thence up the country to Wheeler's place; that is as far as Pennsbury manor, then the end of all travelling!

At the court held at Chester, on the 27th of 4 mo., 1684, William Penn, Esq., proprietary and governor, was present.

At the court held the 6th of the 8 mo., 1685, it was ordered that, for defraying the public charges, there be a levy upon land of 2*s.* 6*d.* per hundred acres, and a poll tax of 2*s.* 6*d.* The same may be paid in wheat at 4*s.* 6*d.*, rye at 3*s.* 6*d.*, and corn at 2*s.* 8*d.*

David Lewis, a servant to Robert Dyer, is seized upon suspicion of treason; as having been concerned, by his own say-so, with the duke of Monmouth in the west country. He gave the security of his master to answer at the next court.

James Sanderlaine, *bestows* in the 10th mo., 1686, a convenient piece of land in the town of Chester, for the erection of a court house and prison.

At the court of the 7th of 4 mo., 1687, the grand jury present

Thomas Colborne, of Chester, for selling rum to the Indians, contrary to the laws of the province.

John Blumstone made a record of a deed of one acre of land in the township of Darby, to build a meeting house thereon for the use of said township, *for the exercise of the true worship of God.*

Richard Crosby is arraigned for drunkenness and abusive language; he submitted himself to the court and was fined 5*s.*

Elias Keach is arraigned and reprimanded, for speaking *false news*, contrary to law; "remitted, provided he do so no more." ["Elias Keach" was the first Baptist minister at Pennepeck, in 1687; he married Mary, the daughter of Nicholas Moore, of Moreland.]

William Coblett, of Concord, is presented for travelling on the highway with his wain drawn by oxen and horses *on the first day of the week;* showing that they then reverenced the *Sabbath.*

At the court held at Chester, 1689, John Maddock, of Ridley, is arraigned for speaking scandalous words against William Penn, the proprietary, and against his present governor, John Blackwell,—whereupon he is fined £5 and costs.

On the 27th of 6 mo., 1689, a case of Crim. Con. occurs. The parties confess their guilt before the grand inquest, whereupon a *jury of women* is called to make further inquisition. They report that "they cannot find that she is (as charged,) neither be they sure she is not."

Isaac Brickshaw, having offended John Simcocks, is dimissed on making humble confession.

At the court of 8 mo., 1691, the grand jury present Henry Barnes, for swearing several oaths.

Also, Edward Eglinton, for breaking the stocks in the town of Chester, and letting the prisoner free.

Also, Richard Thompson, for ranging the woods and taking up horses, saying he was *ranger*, "but we find him not fit for that honest trust."

At the court held March 7th, 1692, John Maddock, is *again* arraigned for abusing John Simcocks and John Bristow, two of the justices, calling them rogues; he boldly averred the same before the court, saying they were the greatest rogues that ever came to America. He was *again* fined £5 and costs.

At the court of 1st mo., 1693, John Clews and Eleanor Arme, now his wife, being presented by the grand jury for immoral intercourse, pleaded guilty, and were adjudged to pay 50*s.* fine, and that the said Eleanor shall stand at the whipping post a quarter of an hour, with a paper on her breast, written thereon,—"I here stand for an example to deter all others," &c. One feels some revoltings at such manner of publicity, and cannot but reflect how few juries of twelve men, all opportunities considered, might be able—all of them, to stand such searching self-rebukes as our Lord once inflicted upon those who brought him a similar sinner to condemn. "He tho is without sin, *let him* cast the first stone: and they went out one by one," till no accusers were found!

At the court held at Chester the 2d October, 1695, the grand jury state that the country is in debt, and that the prison is not yet finished, and that, besides, *there are several wolves' heads to pay for;* wherefore, they recommend a levy, to wit: on all real and personal estate of 1*d.* per pound, and 3*s.* per head poll-tax. The *valuation* then given is important now, as showing values then, to wit: All cleared land under tillage to be valued 20*s.* per acre; rough land by the river £10 per hundred acres; lands in the woods at £5 per hundred acres; horses and mares at £3; cows and oxen 50*s.*; sheep 6*s.*; negroes, from sixteen to sixty years, at £25; females at £20. Then come *five mills* at the earliest places, to wit: Chester mill £100; Joseph Coebarn's £50; Darby mill £100; Hartford mill £20; Concord mill £10.

At the court of 10th December, 1695, Patrick Kelly and Judith Buller are presented for marrying against the law of 2d December. It is ordered that they appear at the next court, and that in the mean time, they marry *again*, as the law directs.

The grand jury present Robert Reman of Chichester, for practising *geomancy* according to Hidon, and *divining by a stick.* He submits himself to the bench, and the court fines him £5 and costs, and never again to practise the arts.

They also present the following books: Hidon's Temple of Wisdom, which teaches Geomancy, and Scot's Discovery of Witchcraft, and Cornelius Agrippa's, teaching *Necromancy.* The books are ordered to the next court.

At the court at Chester, of 24th of 12 mo., 1701–2, the court then allows the charge of £26, incurred in running and settling the *circular* boundary line next to New Castle.

Chester.

In April, 1827, we made a visit to Chester, with a view to see and examine the venerable *remains* of that once distinguished town. We had for a companion a gentleman whose soul is alive to such inquiries. In our ride we often noticed the unusual indications of a very forward spring—such as has not before occurred since the year 1791: the wild flowers of the fields and woods were in bloom on the 23d April, which formerly appeared only in May. We were necessarily frequently pleased to notice the air of comfort and improvement indicated by various farms on the road side, contrasted with the few, still remaining, small *log houses:*—houses which Kalm, in his Travels, on the same road eighty years before, said were the general structures of that day. The numerous wild grape vines which he then noticed were gone, as well as the extended woods. Red clover—then unknown as to any practical benefit, now assisted with plaster of Paris, every where enriched the farmer and gratified our senses. The wild bees, which then sheltered their cells in the depths of the forest, now having lost that refuge by the clearing of the country, have become domesticated in the bee-boxes, seen by the wayside in the most of the gardens—then the road was but little travelled,—by *pleasure carriages*, scarcely ever, when but very few existed. The few travellers who could be be met were on foot, or if on horse back,—often having a female up behind—or if a female going to market, having two great panniers poised on either side of the animal. Wilson has thus described them when going home.

"There market maids, in lively rows,
With wallets white were riding home;
And thundering gigs, with *powder'd* beaux,
Through Gray's green festive shades to roam."

The women and girls on these occasions were clad in homely, useful "homespun," and the beast was a real *pacer*. A chaise you could but seldom meet: but we were frequently met by gigs, sulkies and coaches, sometimes effulgent in glittering plate! So, times are altered!

Having reached Chester, we could not make our entry without thinking of those primitive founders, all of whom had gone down to the dust. Our busy imaginations could not forbear to frame conjectures, and to weave, in fancy's loom, the images of things as we presumed they generally were in their early state. For the inhabitants whom we now saw in the streets, in modern habiliments, and some of modish mien, we substituted, instinctively, the homespun yeomanry of other appearance, manners and feelings. We peopled the streets and houses with Swedes and Quakers, with such men, and their wives and children, as Sanderlaine, David Lloyd, Robert Wade, Caleb Pusey, the Parkers, Richard Townsend and others; and instead of ancient and decayed houses, as several of them had now become, we contemplated all, as if then lately built or building. Instead of a dreary old court house, old prison, old church, &c., we saw them, in fancy, in the finish and brightness of a new thing, as buildings, of which the labour and expense of erecting was past, and the community was reposing in complacency, resting from their works.

But to come more immediately to facts, as we *now* found them:—Our first wish was to see the house of Parker, the colonial register, &c., and the father of that excellent and eminent lady, Mrs. Deborah Logan. There her good father and her mother lived and died. It was a two-storied brick house, of respectable dimensions, built in 1700, had much of old-fashioned wooden wainscotting. In the chambers up stairs the pannels were curiously painted in a congeries of colours, not unlike yellow mahogany. The house had originally small glass panes, set in leaden frames, of which a few specimens still remained in the casements on the stairway, large closets were on each side of the chimneys, large enough for small beds, which were lighted by small windows in the outer walls; on the side of the house stood a one-story office, which had long contained the records of Chester county, from the earliest dates, and which being since removed to West Chester, might prove curious, if now examined with antiquarian tact and skill.

James Sanderlaine, often written Sanderlin, was a wealthy *Swedish* proprietor of all Chester, and extending back into the country a considerable distance on the Chester side of the creek; from him descended all the land titles. Robert Wade, of the Essex house, was an equally extended proprietor of all the lands on the other side of the creek. Sanderlaine appears to have been an eminent *Episcopalian*, and probably the chief founder of the old Episcopal church there, of St. Paul, as I find his memory peculiarly distinguished by a large and conspicuous mural monument in that church, covering a space of six and a half by three and a half feet. It is formed of fine *sand-stone*, and is chiseled in *relief* and ornament, in a very elaborate and skilful manner. It is in itself a curiosity, as expressive of a death of a citizen which occurred as long back as 1692. Not one of the name of Sanderlaine remains! His daughter was married to Jasper Yates.

Jasper Yates, at an early period, built a great building, still standing, called the *Granary*, and sometimes the Bake-house, it having been formerly used for both purposes. In the cellar part was the bake-house, and above it were the grain rooms, intended in their day to receive and use up the grain from the fruitful fields of Lancaster county—a commerce disused for several years. The bakery, while it lasted, made biscuit by wholesale for shipping.

Near to that building was shown me the first used court house of brick, now a dwelling house and cooper's shop, and owned by John Hart. Near to it is *a part* of the stone wall of the first prison, now converted into a dwelling house.

The second, or present, court house and prison were built in 1724.

We next visited the house of David Lloyd, a name of perpetual occurrence in our early annals, as a leading member of assembly *opposed* to proprietary interests; as a disturbing *Friend*, an educated lawyer—a man who had once been a captain in Cromwell's army, and who sought his peace by coming to this country. His house is the same building facing the river, now known as the altered house of Commodore Porter. It was built in 1721. Pestilent and refractory as D. Lloyd appeared in public life, he was excellent and amiable in his social relations. The body of himself and wife are marked by head stones in the Friends' ground.

In 1798, Chester was visited with yellow fever in its most appalling form, derived from the families who fled from Philadelphia to Chester for refuge. It spread in Chester with frightful rapidity, and depopulated whole families and streets.

Chester has been often called "Upland," in the early history Few, or none, have a right conception of the cause. The name, I am satisfied, was applied to the whole land held by the Swedes *at and above Chester.* They called the *country* of Philadelphia county, *Upland County*—wherefore the *court town* took the name of *the country.* The name was *first* given to contradistinguish the *Up*-Delaware country, from the *Low*-Delaware country, or *lower* counties, where the Swedes first settled.

Bucks County.

This county had its first settlers located nearest to the neighbourhood of Bristol and Pennsbury. They were nearly all of them of the society of Friends; among these, James Harrison and Phineas Pemberton were most influential and conspicuous. Strong expectations were entertained by these first settlers, that the city of Philadelphia might have been located at either of those chief places; but it was deemed that the river channel was too shallow for ship navigation.

All the first settlers who arrived were obliged to bring certificates of acceptable character, and to be enrolled in a record book, which I have seen, kept by P. Pemberton, as clerk of the court, giving therein the names of the parents, number of children, names and number of servants, and the vessels by which, and at what time, arrived. This, it must be granted, forms a curious record of consultation now, and may show some families their "ancestorial bearings" then.

The Indians were round about in small settlements in almost every direction. Some, long after, dwelt on the "Indian field," near Penn's estate at Pennsbury, and some at Ingham's spring; others were on the Pownall tract, the Streiper tract, and Fell tract. The last of the Indian race went off from Buckingham in a body, in the year 1775. The general state of woody wastes was much the same as has been already described in the county of Chester. The Indian practice of burning the underbrush in the woods, made the woods in general easy of traversing and exploring.

The people of Bucks county have been, from the earliest settlement, trained and disciplined to a kindly spirit of good neighbourhood and frank hospitality. It arose at first from their universal brotherhood and mutual dependence; and it was long kept alive by the unreserved welcome, for ever cherished, under their eyes, by the Indians settled about them. A true Indian never deems any thing too good for his friend or visiter.

The greater part of the centre grounds of Bucks county were located as early as 1700. Such was Buckingham and Solesbury. Among the first of those settlers there, were Thomas and John Byle, William Cooper, George Pownall, Roger Hartley, and other Friends, from the neighborhood of the "Falls Meeting." Thomas Watson arrived and settled among them in 1704. For the first few years, considerable of their supplies of grain for any new comers had to be drawn from the Falls, or Middletown; and until 1707, they had to take all their grain on horseback, for grinding, to Gwin's mill, on the Pennepeck, near to the Billet. In the mean time, many persons had to be content to pound their grain at home in wooden mortars. Several of the houses of the original settlers are still standing. Such a house, built for Thomas Canby, now belongs to Joshua Anderson. The great portion of the houses were constructed of logs, and called log-houses, a rude but very comfortable kind of building.

Improved land was generally sold by the acre, at the nominal price or value of twenty bushels of wheat; so that when wheat was at 2s. 6d. a bushel, the land was actually sold at 50s.

The women were always industrious, clothing their families in general by their own hands—spinning and weaving for all their inmates, all the necessary linen and woollen clothing. For common diet, milk and bread, and pie, formed the breakfast meal; and good pork or bacon, and a wheat-flour pudding or dumplings, with butter and molasses, were given for dinner. Mush, or hominy, with milk and butter, and honey, formed the supper. Chocolate was only occasionally procured, and used with maple sugar; and deer-meat and turkeys, when the season answered.

Only a few of the wealthiest farmers had any wagons before the year 1745; about the year 1750 was the time of their more common use. Carts were the most in use in going to market. John Wells, Esq., was the only person who then had a riding-chair. Taverns were scarcely known any where; the one at Coryell's ferry was the first.

After the year 1750, a new era seemed to commence, by the influx of more wealth among the people. Bohea tea and coffee were introduced, and sundry articles of foreign fabric for the farmers' wives, brought among them by the pedlers,—such as silk and linen neck-handkerchiefs, some silk or figured gowns. The men, too, began to wear vests and breeches of Bengal, Nankin, fustian, or black everlasting, and cotton velvet. Coats also were made of the latter, But no man or woman, in any condition of life, ever held themselves above the wear, for common purposes, of home-made "linsey-woolsey," of linen or woollen fabric.

Bucks county has the honour of having had located, at the forks of the Neshamony, the once celebrated "Log College," so called, of the Rev. William Tennant, commenced there in 1721; and from it issued some of our best men of earliest renown. It was then "the day of small things."

Bucks county, in the period of the revolution, was made conspicuous, by a daring "refugee family," called the *Doans*. Their numerous perilous adventures, in scouring the country for "whig families," and to make their plunder on such, brought them into great renown as bold desperadoes. There were five brothers of them, severally fine looking men, and expert horsemen. Great rewards were offered for them; and finally, two were shot in combat, and two were apprehended and executed. They were far above ordinary robbers, being very generous and humane to all moderate people. The whigs had injured them, and they sought revenge at the hazard of their lives.

Dr. John Watson, of Bucks county, contributed to the Historical Society of Pennsylvania a very interesting account of the primitive state of society in Buckingham and Solsbury. From his account I add a few particulars. See Appendix, p. 119.

When wheat and rye grew thick and tall on new land, and all was to be cut with sickles, many men, and *some women*, became dexterous in the use of them, and victory was contested from many a violent effort. About the year 1744, twenty acres of wheat were cut and shocked in half a day in Solsbury. Rum was drunk in proportion to the hurry of business on all such occasions. In fact, rum being a *British* liquor, had to be used, if at all, as the common beverage. A bottle of rum was handed about at vendues, each taking his draw from the neck of it, by a swallow or more. At wedding regales, and even at funerals, mixed and stewed rum, called spirits, was an expected and common entertainment. Rum was even put on their toasted bread occasionally. It led to its evils, and serious and considerate persons got an act of assembly prohibiting the use of spirits at vendues. Now temperance societies impose its disuse in every thing; and we know of good apple orchards there, now, of which they will no longer make even cider. Apple pies, both green and dried, have ever been in plentiful use all the year round in this county.

The first settlers, and many of their successors, were accustomed to wear a strong and coarse dress—such as enduring buckskin. It was used for breeches, and sometimes for jackets; oznaburgs, made of hemp tow at 1*s.* 4*d.* a yard, was used for boys' shirts; sometimes flax, and flax and tow were also used. Coarse tow for trowsers, wool hat, strong heavy shoes, brass buckles, two linsey jackets, and a *leathern apron*, made out the winter apparel. Such apparel for the labouring class was common down to 1750.

A higher class, however, had means to procure such suits as would have purchased two hundred acres of land! The coat of broad-cloth had three or four plaits on the skirts; they were wadded to keep them smooth, as thick as a coverlet. The cuffs very large, went nearly up to the elbows. The hat was a good broad-brimmed *beaver*, with double loops, drawn nearly close behind, and half raised on each side. The ladies, in full mode, wore stiff whalebone stays, worth eight or ten dollars. The silk gown much plaited in the back. The sleeves were short and nearly twice as large as the arm; the rest of the arm covered with a fine linen sleeve, nicely plaited, locket buttons and long-armed gloves. The head was covered with a Bath bonnet and its cape. On marriage occasions the bride dressed in a long black hood without a bonnet. Two yards of rich *paduasoy* made such a hood, and used to be *loaned* for nuptial occasions. In time, came up the straw plait, called the bee-hive bonnet, and with it the blue or green apron.

Before the use of upland grass and clover, they could only form or procure their grass in plains or swamps—often at several miles from home, in which case it was stacked on the spot, and hauled home as needed, on sleds during the winter.

In those days it was common to go ten or twelve miles to mill on horseback; the same distance to get any smith work and repairs. Horses were seldom shod, and blocks to pound hominy were used, in imitation of the Indians.

The Indians were still much among them, very often bringing presents of game, beans, &c., and refusing any pay. The Indian children were very sociable and fond of play.

The prices, from 1724 to 1735, as seen marked in books of the time, set wheat at from 3 to 4*s.*; rye, 2 to 3*s.*; middlings, fine, 7 to 8*s.*; coarse, 4*s.* 6*d.*; bran, 1*s.*; salt, 4*s.*; beef, 2*d.*; bacon, 4*d.*; pork, 2*d.* Swine were easily raised and fattened. Venison roasted and in stew-pies, were luxuries of frequent use in their homely log cabins.

Indian corn was not attempted to be raised in large quantities before the year 1750. Wheat was the great article for making money, it was cultivated with open fallows, and was generally ploughed three times a year.

In the neighbourhood of Doylestown is considerable of Indian remains, such as their graveyard, &c.; and on the Neshamony near there, is said to be the grave of the celebrated chieftain *Tamanee*, after whom we have now the popular name of "Saint Tamany."

It is said also, that the *first court* held in Pennsylvania was held in this county; and *the oldest record* to be found in our state, is to found in the county office at Doylestown. It is a record, or register of *ear marks*, for sheep and cattle, and showing, by a drawing of the head of the animal, the different *crops* upon the ears, as well as an accompanying description in words, and in the name of the individual who assumed it as his designating property. This record, it is said, was made a little before Penn's landing, and was continued in practice for a number of years subsequently. The date is now effaced, but was certainly as early as 1681.

The next record, in point of time, is a record of the *Orphans' Court*, No. 1; its first entry bears date the 4th day of 1st mo., 1693, and was held at the private dwelling of *Gilbert Wheeler*. "Present, the governor, Wm. Penn, with justices James Harrison, Jonathan Otter, Wm. Yardley, Wm. Beaks, and Thomas Fitzwater. Phineas Pemberton, clerk." The next court was held at *Pennsbury;* the next again at Gilbert Wheeler's, on the 7th of 8 mo., 1684.

At a court of *Quarter Sessions*, held the 10th of 10th mo., 1684, the eldest of Clark's orphans was bound to Richard Noble, until she attained the age of twenty-one, and was then to receive as her freedom, *one cow and calf, and one sow.* The above record book is complete to October 1692; and after that time the court was suspended or omitted for several years, having at times the record, "No court then held." On the 10th of 8 mo., 1697, a court is again held, when the record *closes* with "No court then, nor since, *for orphans.*" The first record book *for deeds* commences in 1684.

It is to be supposed, that if all the records were well examined by an industrious hand, and by a mind of proper *tact* for olden time inquiries, that something strange, amusing, or useful, might be found to gratify the present generation. But who shall do it?

The "Crooked Billet," now known as Hatborough, was originally settled by John Dawson, a hatter, of London. The first name was derived from the first house there built, it being used as a public inn, with the sign of a crooked billet of wood hung out as its token, and the place, when made a town, was changed to the name of Hatborough, in reference to the employment of the first resident. His descendants have informed me, that when he first came there he built a cabin, and afterwards a stone house, with his own hands; and was assisted with stone and mortar, by his daughter Ann, who married Bartholomew Longstreth, who came from Yorkshire in 1699. The same John Dawson moved to Philadelphia in 1742, and dwelt in the house south-west corner of Second and Church alley, made notable there as "*the first built brick house.*" His relative, Wm. Clinkenbeard, a farmer in Plymouth, lived to be one hundred and eight years of age.

Bartholomew Longstreth first opened the York road from the Billet to Neshamony. When he built his house, one hundred and twenty-eight years ago, now occupied by Daniel Longstreth, he sawed all his joist with a whip saw, from hewn squared logs. That family still retain the bell-metal mould in which he used, like other farmers, to make his own pewter spoons Think of that specimen of household economy then! They have also preserved the same iron with which old John Dawson used to smooth beaver hats.

Old Jacob Heston, who died about ten years ago, had resided at, and died on the spot, and perhaps at the same house, that was first built in Wrightstown by his ancestors, who emigrated from New England at the time of the Quaker persecution. A remarkable providence attended them, deserving of some record here. The family was obliged to escape in the night, and eventually to cross the Delaware, not knowing whither they were going. They sat down in the woods, and to their surprise and satisfaction, found an old neighbour who had also fled on the same night, without the knowledge in either of them of their several intentions! Here, amongst wild beasts and Indians, they found that security and repose that was denied them elsewhere.

The road from Philadelphia to Buckingham, prior to the opening of the York road, was across the Neshamony at Galloway's *ford*, one mile above Hulmeville, through Langhorne park, thence by Attleborough, &c.

Near that ford, once stood Growden's old fire proof, in which were kept the *records of Bucks county;* and when Joseph Galloway went off with the British in '78, the office was broken open, and the records strewed about, to the use of any who might choose to possess them. Thomas Paxson, who saw them so strewed about on *the ground* the next morning, got hold of a MS. journal of a voyage down the Ohio, that was curious and interesting, and being lent about, has disappeared.

The first built mill on the Pennepeck was Gwin's mill, the same place where James Varee now has his rolling mill. An old log house of a Swede still remains, near the Neshamony, which has such superior construction as to be remarkable. All the logs are so grooved thus, ⌒ one above the other, as to turn all winds and rains, without the use of intermediate mortar, except in very thin quantity.

John Watson, now of Buckingham, who is in himself a walking library in matters of local antiquity, especially in Buckingham valley, where the family first settled in 1691,—besides the MS. book of occurrences, (made by his father, Dr. John Watson,) which he has bestowed on the Historical Society of Pennsylvania, has been a strenuous advocate of the "poor Indians," who, as he and others of Bucks county allege, were *cheated* out of their lands by the agents of the Penn family, at the time of the notable "great walk." He has written and given to the Philosophical Society, for their library, his circumstantial *narrative* of that "great walk." It was once a very exciting subject of animadversion and general discussion in Bucks. The agents publicly advertised a fee of £5 for the greatest walker for one day, and procured Marshall, who *ran* over four times as much ground as the Indians expected. He argues, and supposes, that all the country north-west of Wrightstown meeting-house, was taken from the Delawares without compensation. [Nicholas Scull, the surveyor general, made oath, in 1757, that he was present when James Yeates, and Edward Marshall, together with some Indians, walked one and a half days back in the woods from Wrightstown; that they walked but eighteen hours, and made out fifty-five miles; did not run, or go out of a walk; that B. Eastburn, surveyor general, and T. Smith, sheriff, were also along, and were satisfied of the same; and that no objections were expressed by the Indians at the time.] The Indians always cherished a spirit of revenge against Marshall; and a party of warriors once came from their settlement, at Wyoming, to seek his life. He was from home, but his wife was made prisoner, and his children escaped, by an Indian thoughtlessly throwing his match coat over a bee hive, which caused the party to be so attacked and stung, that they went off without the children. The mother, being pregnant, could not keep up with the party, and her bones and remains were found, six months afterwards, on the Broad mountain.

In the revolutionary war, the Indian warriors again returned from west of the Ohio, into Tinicum, or Noxamixon townships, still aiming at Marshall, and he again escaped by being from home; they then went back through Jersey. This they told themselves after the peace. The most of these facts, above told, are not in his "Narrative of the Walk," as above mentioned; but, coming from his own mouth, are to be respected and believed, as the relations of an honest and intelligent gentleman: for such he is.

The "Log College," of Tennant, still remains near the Neshamony; and lately it was so, that a gentleman called and offered five dollars for a piece of its log, and scared the occupants, as if the enthusiast was demented!

It would seem, from family names existing in Bucks, that many of the *Dutch* must have been primitive settlers there, most probably under grants from Governor Andros, of New York. There is a place, beyond Abington, called *Holland*, which even now is much settled with Dutch names, such as Wynkoop, Vanmeter, Vansant, Corell, &c. The Presbyterian church too, at Abington, founded in 1717, was originally got up by the people near there of the Reformed Dutch faith, the descendants of Dutch forefathers. These facts were confirmed to me by the present pastor, the Rev. Mr. Steele. New Britain was settled by the Welsh.

Pennsbury.

This was the name of Penn's country place and mansion—sometimes called his "palace,"—in Bucks county, situated on the margin of the Delaware river, below Bordentown. There William Penn and his family lived, during part of his stay among us in the years 1700 and 1701. There, he often entertained Indians, and held treaty covenants, religious meetings, &c. The place was constructed in 1682-3, at great expense for that day, having cost £7000, and having considerable of the most finished or ornamental materials brought out from England. The mansion was sixty feet in front, by forty feet in depth; the garden, an ornamental and sloping one, lay along the river side in front of it, and numerous offices were in a front line with the dwelling. All that now remains is the house now occupied by Robert Crozier—the same building of wood which was originally formed for Penn's family "brew-house."

After Penn had gone back to England, his place was retained some time in hopes of his return. His furniture was long preserved there, and finally got sold and spread about in Bucks county. His clock, and his writing desk and secretary, I have seen. For many years the people of Burlington used to make visits to the place, because of its associations with so distinguished a man—"a hallowed haunt, though but in ruins seen." Beneath a great grove of walnut trees they used to regale, and take their refreshments. A leaden reservoir on the top of the house, kept there for retaining water as a security against fire, got to leaking, and caused the building to fall into premature decay, so that at the era of the revolution, it was torn down, with an intention to rebuild another; but the war prevented

9*

that design. While it rested in a state of decay, it had a furnished chamber, hung with fine tapestry, and in which the family descendants were intended to be lodged in case of visits. This, from its being so seldom opened, and when seen, presenting so many tokens of musty and cob-web interior, got the reputation of "the spirit-room," and was deemed to be a haunted chamber! All who used to visit the premises in years long since, were accustomed to take away some relics of the place. Some such I have preserved,—such as the carved side of the door, and a piece of the bed cover, curiously worked by Letitia Penn. In the Pennsylvania Hospital is Penn's chair, taken from this mansion.

The country immediately around, through Penn's manor, presents a generally level and rich soil; but its aspect from the river side is quite low and tame. Formerly a creek (now dry) ran round behind the mansion, at some distance, forming the farm into an island, and being crossed at places by bridges. At those places Penn once had his pleasure barge, and some small vessels.

It has been matter of surprise to some, why Penn so soon provided for *a country residence*, even when *society* for mutual benefit was so necessary in the early rise of Philadelphia. A cause may perhaps be found in his predilections for a *country life*, as expressed in his admirable letter of *family counsel*, to wit: "Let my children (he said,) be husbandmen and housewives. This leads to consider the works of God and nature, and diverts the mind from being taken up with the vain arts and inventions of a luxurious world. Of cities and towns of concourse *beware*. The world is apt to stick close to those who have lived and got wealth there. *A country life and estate I like best for my children.*"

A letter of William Penn says, the place cost him £7000, and he intended to settle permanently there, saying, "I should have returned to it in '86 or '89 at furthest."

In 1705, he says, "whether I surrender to the crown, or not, shall make no difference as to my coming and inhabiting there." He says he bought there of an old Indian king. Of course it was a royalty once! It was called Sepessin.

The original tract of Pennsbury contained, in 1684, about 3431 acres, from which were abstracted, at various times afterwards, about 1888 acres granted to others, and 400 acres besides to Arthur Cook, a public Friend of Philadelphia.

John Richardson, a public Friend, speaks in his journal of living with William Penn, at Pennsbury, in 1701—saw there a public meeting and a marriage; also, an Indian assemblage to renew and revive former covenants with Penn before his departure for England—they held a cantico or worship, sitting around a fire, and singing a very melodious hymn, after which they joined in a dance, &c.

Having had, in my possession, the book of MS. letters from William Penn to James Harrison, his chief steward—*i. e.*, his general agent of the years 1681 to 1687,—[vide the letters in form in my MS. Annals, pages 164 to 171, in the Historical Society of Pennsylvania.] I have here selected such extracts, as will serve to show the character of the houses, &c., once made or intended as the residence of the proprietary and his future generations, to wit:

In August, 1684, he says, he sends Ralph, his gardener, some walnut trees to set, and some seeds of his own raising, which are rare good. He urges Ralph to stick to his garden, and to get the yards fenced in, and doors to them. By an Irish ship, he says, he sends butter, cheese, shoes, &c.—Some beer at £10 a tun, and some wine.

On the 18th of 11th month, 1684–5, he says, "I have sent herewith four servants—three carpenters, and a gardener; he had three more, but they failed him. I would (says he) have a kitchen, two larders, a wash-house, a room to iron in, a brew-house, and a Milan oven for baking, a stable for twelve horses; all my rooms I would have nine feet high, and my stables eleven feet, and overhead half a story. What you *can*, do with *bricks*. What you can't, do it with good timbers, and case them with clap-boards, about five feet, which will serve other things, and we can brick it afterwards."—[Probably this was never done so afterwards, and furnished a cause of premature decay.]

"Pray, let the court-yard be levelled, and the fields and places about house be cleanly and orderly kept: so let me see thy conduct and contrivance about grounds and farm accommodations. I hope *the barge* is kept safely. Let Ralph take the lower grounds of the garden, and the other, his helper, the upper grounds and courts—have too a convenient well, or pump, for the several offices.

"I desire that a pair of handsome plain steps be made at the landing right against the house, also the bridge more passable going to John Rowland's, unless one over the creek near the New England people may be better done.

"I would have a walk to the falls [meaning in the direction to them,] and to the point where S. H.'s son built, cleared so as two may walk a foot. It would be pleasant if the old *Indian paths* were cleared up.

"Pray, secure the refusal of the New England people's farms—I ave some in my eye that will buy them.

"Let there be a two-leaved door back, and have a new one in one for the front, as the present is most ugly and low. I would have a rail and banisters before both fronts. The pales will serve *round*, though they are sad ones."

The 19th of third month, 1685, he writes and says, "I like all thou hast sent me. I hope they go on with the *houses* and *gardens*, and let them *finish* that which is built as fast as they can. The partition between the left parlour and the great room the servants used to eat in, should be wainscotted up. The doors had best be large between the other parlour and the withdrawing room.

"If the cattle of Col. Lloyd are not brought home from Maryland, dissolve the bargain, because I will supply beef from Ireland. The last I sent went by way of Barbadoes.

"Let Ralph this fall get about twenty young poplars, of about eighteen inches round, beheaded to twenty feet, to plant in the walk below the steps to the water.

I mentioned the kinds of out-houses *wanted*, but I know how to shift. I am a man of providence tost to and fro."

"The 11th of 5th month, 1685, he writes and says, "Tell Ralph I must depend on his perfecting his gardens—hay dust [is not this seed?] from Long Island, such as *I* sowed in *my* court yard, is the best for our fields. I will send divers seeds for gardens and fields. About the house may be laid out into fields and grass, which is sweet and pleasant. I trust to provide myself at my coming with carpenters, husbandmen, bricklayers and makers. I hope care is had of my three mares and their colts. I intend to bring more when I come, and a fine horse. A good dairy my wife will love."

The 4th of 8th mo., 1685, he says, "I hear poor Ralph is dead. Let Nicholas then follow it (the garden) diligently, and I will reward him. Do not much *hiring* of carpenters and joiners. That I sent will do. Assure my servants, if they prove faithful and diligent, I will be kind to them in land and other things at my return. By this ship, I purpose to send some haws, hazelnuts, walnuts, garden seeds, &c."

In another letter he says, "I have now sent a gardener (in place of Ralph, deceased,) with requisites. Let him have help of two or three men when needful. He is to have his passage paid and £30, and sixty acres of land, at three years, and a month in each year to himself; he to train me a man and a boy. There comes also a Dutchman, a joiner and a carpenter, that is to work one hundred and fifty days, and pay me £5 or £7 country money, for £7 sterling lent him. Let him wainscot and make tables and stands: but chiefly help on the out-houses, because we shall *bring much furniture*."

"I would have Nicholas (the gardener) have as many roots and flowers next spring, by transplanting them *out of the woods*, as he can."

7th of 9th month, 1685, he writes and says, "I am glad the Indian fields bore so well. Lay as much down as you can with hay dust, and clear away the wood up the river to open a prospect upwards as well as downwards. Get some wooden chairs of walnut, with long backs, and two or three eating tables for twelve, eight, and five persons, with falling leaves to them."

17th of 9th month, 1685, he says, "P. Ford has sent James Reed more trees, seeds, and sciences, (scions) which James, my gardener *here*, bought. Tell James I would have him lay in a good stock before he parts with any thing I send him. I would send free stones for the steps, if he had the dimensions. What you build is best done with bricks. The man I sent can make them. A better kitchen would do well, with milk-house, stable, &c., but all by degrees. There is gravel *for walks*, that is *red* at Philadelphia, near the swamp. In what you build, let there be low lodgings over head of eight feet. Let all be *uniform*, and not *ascu* from the house. Get and plant as much quick, as you can, about fields, and lay them out large, at least twelve acres in each."

In 1686, he writes: "I send a wheelwright, who can also work as a carpenter. I should be glad to see a draft of Pennsbury, [and so might we!] which an artist would quickly make, with the landscape of the house, out-houses, their proportions and distance from each other. Tell me how the peach and apple orchards bear. Of what are the out-houses built, and how do they stand to the house. Pray don't let the fronts of the house be common. I leave thee whether to go on with my son's land above Welcome creek or no."

Such is the early history of the munificent expenditures and intentions of Penn.

A letter of Wm. Penn to James Logan, of the 23d of 5th mo., 1700, *then at Pennsbury*, says, "That, because of an injury done his leg, he is unable to meet the council, &c., and therefore desires that four of the counsel, the collector and minister, and witnesses, to come up to him *by his barge*, which he will send to Burlington." He adds, too, "Let the Indians come hither, and send in the boat more rum, and the match coats, and let the council adjourn *to this place*. Here will be victuals." At this time he speaks also of his coach or "calash" and horses, then in Philadelphia, and of his man John (a black man) to drive it.

The above letter seems to indicate an assemblage or gathering for a treaty. It would seem there must have been a plurality of such Indian assemblages; for, in 1701, John Richardson, in his journal, tells of his being there when many Indians and chiefs were then *to revive* their covenants with Wm. Penn, before his return home. There they received presents, and held their cantico or worship, by dancing around a fire prepared on the ground.

In 1703–4, when young William Penn came to this country, there assembled as many as one hundred Indians, and nine kings, at Pennsbury, to greet his arrival there.

It may further serve to give us a more direct insight into household economy and domestic concerns of such a man as Penn, and as marking the state and style of the grandees of olden time, to give here a list of the furniture and plate, which once was deposited at Pennsbury, to wit:

J. F. Fisher got from Stoke Pogis, of John Penn, two papers containing an account of what goods and plate Penn had at Pennsbury, and left there on the 3d of 10 mo., 1701, to wit:

In *the best chamber*, sundry tables, stands, cane chairs, a bed and bedding, and a suit of satin curtains, &c.

In the next chamber, a bed and bedding, six cane chairs, a suit of camblet curtains, &c.

In the next chamber, one wrought bed and bedding, six wooden chairs, &c.

In the nursery, one pallet bedstead, two chairs of master John's, and sundries, &c.

In the next chamber, one bed and bedding, one suit of striped linen curtains, four rush-bottomed chairs, &c.

In the garrets, four bedsteads, two beds, three side saddles—one of them my mother's, two pillions.

In the lower rooms. Best parlour, two tables, one couch, two great cane chairs and four small ditto, seven cushions—four of them satin, three others green plush, and sundries more.

The other parlour, two tables, six chairs, one great leather chair, one clock, a pair of brasses, and other mentioned things.

In the little hall, six leather chairs, five maps.

In the great hall, one long table and two forms, six chairs, pewter dishes, five mazarins, two cisterns, and sundries others.

Linen and plate, damask, Irish diaper, fine Dutch diaper, hugabag, five sideboard cloths, one large tankard, one basin, six salts, one skillet, five plates, seven spoons, two forks, two porringers, &c., small articles. A chest of drawers containing an invoice of linen, all marked W. P. H.

In the closet and best chamber, bed and bedding, two silk blankets and white curtains, also two damask curtains for windows, six cane chairs, one hanging press.

In the kitchen, a grate iron, one pair of racks, three spits, one pair of great dogs, &c.

I see also another paper entitled, "Plate carried to Pennsylvania," from which I extract some of the items: one large tankard, one caudle cup, three tumblers, six spoons, two forks, three chafing dishes, with things to burn spirits, one large plate with the *Springet arms*, that Springet's grandmother gave him, one little strong-water bottle, G. M. S., one save-all, G. S., six spoons with a cross, six egg spoons, W. P. G., six porringers, G. W. P., eighteen spoons, G. W. P., six forks with W. P.'s arms, one skillet, J. P. M., one sucking bottle, M. P.—W. P., one sugar dish, J. J. M., one large chafing dish with gridiron, a top, which Letitia's grandmother Penington gave her, also one skimmer, from the same to her, one large plate with the Springet arms, that Springet's grandmother Penington gave him. (Several other items are named.)

In conclusion, we add hereto three original letters of Penn, to John and Mary Sacher, while overseeing his concerns at Pennsbury. They are so primitive, frank and friendly, as to set the spirit of the man before us, while we read them.

Lond. 12, 8 *mo.*, 1705.

Honest John and Mary.—My reall love is to you, and desire you and your little ones preservation heartily, and I know so does my dear wife and loving mistress. We are all, through the Lord's mercy, well, save little Hannah at Bristoll, whose arme has a weakness. She is a sweete childe, as Thomas and little Margaret.

I doubt not your care and good husbandry, and good housewifery, to make that place profitable to me, after the hundreds, yea thousands, yt have been sunk there from the beginning. Though if that could be lett, to one yt would not misuse it, and you upon a plantation for my deare Johnne, I should like it better, and pray tell James (Logan) so; for I think I have spent too much there already. Johnne grows a fine childe, tall, brisky as a bird, his mother's limbs, but my countenance, and witty, as others say, and as healthy as any of them. Let me hear from you how Sam and Sue attend, and if the black boy and little Sue begin to be diligent. The Lord be with you, and all his humble and faithful ones, on both sides the water. Farewell: your reall friend,

Wm. Penn.

Lond. 18, 3 *mo.*, 1708.

John Sacher—Loving friend.—I had thy letter with satisfaction, and glad to hear of thy and family's welfare. I am glad to hear of the good condition of poor Pennsbury, beloved of us all, and there, in the will of God, we wish ourselves. If thou leavest it, give J. Logan an acct. of ye fruit of thy labour, as acres cleared, and fence, and of both plow and sow land. Likewise, deliver all ye plate, linnen and household stuff into his possession and care. [This may account for my Penn-chair received from Mrs. Logan.] I bless God, we are all alive and well, save our dear sweete Hannah, whom the Lord took four months ago, at 4½ years, the wittiest and womanliest creature that her age (of 4½) could show, but His holy will be done.

Thy loving friend,

Wm. Penn.

To Honest Mary.—I had thine by our frd. Mary Dannester, with the pair of gloves to Johnne, which both pleased and fitted him well. I was well pleased to heare of yr well doing while at that place of my pleasure, poor Pennsbury, which I like for a place better than I have ever yet lived at, and I hope *since 'tis lett*, (which to be sure James (Logan) does to our advantage,) it will be kept as it deserves, and be fitt to receive me, if the Lord please to make way for our coming thither again. My dear father has been dangerous ill, which hurry'd me to Bristoll lately. There I saw thy brother, who has three children, and thrives in person and trade.

With true love to thee and thy husband, and honest friend Jane, remain thy friend, W. P.

Græme Park. Mrs. Hart, an aged lady, remembered the park when, in the affluence and circumstance of the Græme family, it was stocked with deer, and when all the woods, of five hundred acres, was cleared of underwood, and through the whole were several open avenues, (since grown up.) One place only was left uncleared, called *the thicket.* The place was surrounded by privet hedge. Miss Stedman, who dwelt with, and survived Mrs. Furguson, the talented daughter of Doctor Græme, retained all the poetic and other papers of Mrs. Furguson, and at the death of Miss Stedman, the papers fell into the hands of Mr. Smith, of Lehman and Smith, druggists in Philadelphia. Mrs. Furguson was a remarkably ready talker, even when a very aged woman, and always talked well. She was habitually called "Lady Furguson" by the neighbours of Græme Park. This same place was sold to French, in 1836, as a *poor farm*, at a very small price. *Sic transit gloria mundi!* Mrs. Furguson, it will be remembered, was the lady who was employed, as it was said, to offer the British bribe to Governor Read.

Historical Notices of Lancaster, and Lancaster County.

Lancaster was laid out as a town in 1728.

In 1729 Lancaster county was erected out of part of Chester county. The German settlers, in consequence of the new county being formed, applied to the proper authorities for leave to enjoy the rights and privileges of British subjects, which was granted. The law containing their names and their petition is signed by Emanuel Zimmerman, (now Carpenter,) in behalf of others. A large number of Irish emigrants settled at Pequea, also sundry Welsh.

A court house and prison is begun at Postlewaite's, and £300 were lent by the governor upon bills of credit to defray the same. £300 additional were afterwards lent to the same object.

1730, Stephen Atkinson built a fulling mill at great expense upon the Conestoga, but the inhabitants on the upper part of the creek assembled and pulled down the dam, as it prevented them from rafting and fishing. Mr. Atkinson then altered his dam with 20 feet passage for boats and fish.

In 1731 a great excitement was caused throughout the settlements, by the shameful murder of three Indians, by the settlers on Swatara creek. This creek was called after a town in Ireland, by Mr. Patterson, one of the original settlers.

In 1732 a violent contest for a member of assembly took place between Andrew Galbraith and John Wright. On that occasion Mrs. Galbraith rode throughout the town at the head of a numerous band of horsemen, friends of her husband. In consequence of her activity, her husband was elected.

In 1734 an Episcopal church was built in Conestoga, fifteen miles from Lancaster. The same year a Lutheran church was built in Lancaster.

The seat of Justice is removed from Postlewaite's to Lancaster, which last place, Hamilton laid out at the request of the proprietaries.

In 1739, at the request of the Scots Presbyterian ministers and people, they were excused from "kissing the book," when giving their evidence on oath; the practice being contrary to the doctrine and worship of the church of Scotland.

In 1742, a number of Germans stated that they had emigrated from Europe by an invitation from the proprietaries, and being attached to the *Omish* doctrines, and that being conscientious as to oaths, they cannot procure naturalization by the present laws. Whereupon a law was made in conformity with their request. [These Omish people wear long beards like the Dunkards, but have no places of worship, save their own private houses, and always retiring to a private and retired place, when inclined to pray. They have been excused from juries, in criminal cases, from their known inclination to acquit in cases of taking life.]

In 1743, at an election to supply the vacancy of Thomas Linley, the Irish compelled the sheriff to receive such tickets as they approved, and to make a return accordingly. The assembly cancelled or so altered the return as to give the seat to Samuel Blunston.

Note.—The proprietaries, in consequence of the frequent disturbances between the governor and Irish settlers, after the organization of York and Cumberland counties, gave orders to their agents to sell no lands in either York or Lancaster counties to the Irish; and also to make advantageous offers of removal to the Irish settlers on Paxton and Swatara, and Donegal townships, to remove to Cumberland county, which offers being liberal, were accepted by many. "Du verfluchter Irischer" used to be a frequent ejaculation of reproach in former days.

. In 1774, Murhancellin, an Indian chief, murdered John Armstrong and his two men on Juniata, and was apprehended by Captain Jack's party, but released after a confinement of several months in Lancaster prison.

This year a treaty was made with the Indians, in Lancaster, by Conrad Weiser, interpreter and agent, &c.

John Musser complained to the governor that the Indians barked his walnut trees, which stood in the town, designing the bark as covers to their cabins; he asked £6 for damages, and was granted £3.

In 1745, the Episcopal church was partly completed.

In the year 1745, the German pastor of the Lutheran church (built in 1734) united a portion of his congregation with the Moravians. A great ferment was excited among the Lutherans. The Lutherans alleged that they were compelled to hear a doctrine which they did not approve, or else to resign their church.

The "dark swamp," once in the centre of Lancaster, was attempted to be cleared of wood, and a drain made to carry off the water.

In 1749, James Webb complained to the general assembly of

the undue election and return of a member from Lancaster county, and stating it was done by violence, and by many persons voting five to ten times severally, making 2300 votes out of 1000! The election was confirmed, but the managing officers were brought to the house and reprimanded.

In 1751, at a large meeting held at Lancaster, it was resolved that a house of employment should be erected specially for the use of settlers, who had severely suffered from the hardships of new settlers and from the hostilities of Indians. A farm was procured and also implements for manufacturing, &c. They made *stockings* there, which soon gave celebrity to Lancaster in that article.

In 1758, the freemen of the county, by reason of the badness of the roads to Philadelphia, in spring and fall, pray to be excused from attendance there in the supreme court, and request a county court in lieu thereof.

In 1759, in consequence of the distracted state of the country by Indian cruelties and French hostilities, a barrack was erected in Lancaster, to contain 500 men, for the security of the country.

A petition of 1763, by settlers along the Conestoga, complains of its dams, as destroying the former fishery of shad, *salmon* and rock fish, which were before in abundance, and the tributary streams had plenty of *trout*,—all now gone.

In 1764 occurred the terrible massacre of the Indians in the prison of Lancaster, where they were placed for security. A company of fifty men from Paxton, with blackened faces, armed and mounted, entered the town in full gallop, went to the prison and effected their cruel purposes. They had before destroyed the town of Conestoga manor, murdered six of the Indians, and burnt the place!

The Ephrata institution near Lancaster has hitherto been little understood; prejudice has served to distort facts in the case, so that, from Carey's Museum,—in an article written by a British officer, down through Hannah Adams' "View," &c., Buck's Theological Dictionary, and even the Historical Society of Pennsylvania, there has been a succession of misconceptions and mistatements concerning the community. They had nevertheless traits of character, which might redound more to the credit of the state and themselves than has been hitherto appreciated. For many years the institution was the seat of learning and the fine arts; and many families of Philadelphia and Baltimore resorted thither to have their children educated; and well the children loved the brotherhood. It contained some of the most learned men of the colony. Peter Miller, the prior, was employed by the government, and translated the Declaration of Independence into *seven* different languages, to be sent to the courts of Europe. They had one of the first printing presses in the state; and for a period of twenty years, did *more* book-printing than was done elsewhere in the whole province; and more *original* works were *written* and *printed* at Ephrata, during the time it flourished, than in any province of the union! *The first Sabbath school too, on record*, was established there: for as early as 1740, full forty years earlier than Robert Raikes' much applauded system was known in England, this one at Ephrata was begun by *Ludwig Strecker* and others, which continued under good auspices, down to the year 1777.

Music was much cultivated; BEISSEL was a first rate musician and composer. In composing sacred music he took his style from the music of nature; and the whole, comprising several large volumes, are founded on the tones of the Æolian harp—the singing is the Æolian harp harmonized. It is very peculiar in its style and concords, and in its execution. The tones issuing from the choir imitate very soft instrumental music; conveying a softness and devotion almost superhuman to the auditor. Their music is set in two, four, five, and seven parts. All the parts, save the bass, are led and sung exclusively by females, the men being confined to the bass, which is set in two parts, the high and low bass—the latter resembling the deep tones of the organ, and the first, in combination with one of the female parts, is an excellent imitation of the concert horn. The whole is sung on the *falsetto* voice, the singers scarcely opening their mouths, or moving their lips, which throws the voice up to the ceiling, which is not high, and the tones, which seem to be more than human, at least so far from common church singing, appear to be entering from above, and hovering over the heads of the assembly. Their singing so charmed the commissioners who were sent to visit the society by the English government, after the French war, that they requested a copy to be sent to the Royal family in England; which was cheerfully complied with, and which I understand is still preserved in the National Library. About twelve months afterwards a box was received of three or four feet long, and two or two and an half wide, containing a present in return. What the present was is not now certainly known—none having seen it but FRIEDSAM and JABEZ, who was then prior, and into whose care it was consigned. It was buried secretly by him, with the advice of BEISSEL. It is supposed, by a hint given by JABEZ, that it was images of the king and queen, in full costume, or images of the Saviour on the cross, and the Virgin Mary; supposing, as many in this country have erroneously thought, that the people of Ephrata possess many of the Catholic principles and feelings. The king, at whose instance they were sent, was a German, and we may presume that he considered that they retained the same views as the monastic institutions of Europe. They have nearly a thousand pieces of music, a piece being composed for every hymn. This music is lost entirely now, at Ephrata—not the music books, but the style of singing: they never attempt it any more. It is, however, still preserved and finely executed, though in a faint degree, at *Snowhill*, near the Antietam creek, in Franklin county, of this state; where there is a branch of the society, and which is now the principal settlement of the Seventh Day Baptists. They greatly outnumber the people of Ephrata, and are in a very flourishing condition. There they keep up the institution as originally established at Ephrata, and are growing rapidly. Their singing, which is weak in comparison with the old Ephrata choir, and may be likened to the performance of an overture by a musical box, with its execution by a full orchestra in the opera house, is so peculiar and affecting, that when once heard, it can never be forgotten.

The *Pequea valley*, besides having been the loved home of the Delawares, is still the chosen and fruitful region of their successors, the prosperous farmers of Lancaster county. At the first settlement of the county, it was selected as the preferred residence of sundry *French families* of the persecuted Huguenots. They bore the names of Dubois, Boileau, Larroux, Lefevre; and some of their descendants remain there to the present day. A large quarto Bible, which Isaac Lefevre brought with him from France at that time, is now in the possession of John C. Lefevre, Esq., and held as a prized relic. The aforesaid names were also united with those of Charles De La Noe, a minister, and Andrew Dore, and some other Frenchmen, who had come out under the influence of William Penn, to form *vineyards*, and to cultivate *grapes*, "up the Schuylkill." They, however, not succeeding to their expectation, felt prepared to avail themselves of a change to the Pequea valley, which was produced by the arrival, in 1712-13 of *Madame Mary Feree*, a widow lady, having with her three sons and three daughters, and coming to this land to seek a peaceful asylum from the persecutions of religious intolerance abroad. She had just lost her husband, a gentleman of eminence in France, by such persecution; and reaching England for refuge, she found friendship in William Penn and Queen Anne, by whom she was aided in her embarkation for America. She became possessed of four thousand acres of the best land in Pequea, recommended by Penn's agent, in this country, to her special notice: two thousand acres of which came by grant, and the other two thousand acres by purchase. To this place *all those French people* went for settlement, and were there heartily welcomed by the Indian king, Tanawa. When he died, soon after, all the Huguenots attended his burial; and his grave was marked with a pile of stones, which long remained to mark the place,—on what is now called La Fayette hill, near Paradise. The church of All Saints now stands on what was the Indian burial ground.

The name of Madame Feree is still remembered and venerated in the neighbourhood of Paradise, where she settled, and gave, by grant of deed to trustees, the ground for general burial, as now used by the people there.

Isaac Lefevre, before named, had lost both his parents by the massacre in France, and he arrived at Philadelphia, a youth of seventeen, in 1686; afterwards he became the husband of Catharine, the daughter of Madame Feree, and their son, by this marriage, was *the first born* white child in Pequea. Philip Feree married Leah a

HARRIS' FRONTIER HOUSE, HARRISBURG.—Page 113.

BLOCK-HOUSE AND LOG-HOUSE SETTLERS.—Page 147.

daughter of Abraham Dubois. One of the Ferees became a Friend. I have been indebted for sundry of these facts, to R. Conyngham, Esq., who has made himself acquainted with them by his residence in the town of Paradise.

Harrisburg, &c.

This place, now the seat of government, was originally located and settled by John Harris, and the place was founded, in 1762, by his son, John Harris, Jun'r. The son of the latter, Robert Harris, now alive at the age of seventy years, has informed me of many facts connected with his family and the original settlement. I herein relate them, much in the manner I received them from himself, *viva voce*, in the year 1835, when visiting the place. Considering how recently it was but an Indian wild, and now so populous and richly settled as the growing *seat of government*, it cannot but prove interesting to the reader, as being in itself a proof of the varied enlargement and advancement of our prosperous country, to wit:

John Harris the first, and his wife Esther, the first settlers here, sat down as Indian traders on the frontier while the Indians were still settled in their town close by, at the mouth of the Paxton creek. Many of their graves were in Harris' orchard. They were both born in Yorkshire, England, and came out to Philadelphia as first emigrants with William Penn. He died in advanced age, in 1749. His wife survived him ten years, having married again to William Chesney, a resident on the other side of the river.

Robert has heard his grandfather and grandmother Reed, in Hanover, fourteen miles off, (where they had a stockade defence,) tell of the Indian alarms, and of the people running in for protection; they had seen some tomahawked.

The first lots *in town* were valued by commissioners at from 10 to £60.

From the market house back to the hills, and up to, and over the state house hill, was in woods when he was a boy.

He, Robert Harris, was born in the present stone house, in 1768. The other old house stood six or seven years afterwards, as a kind of store-house. Two hundred people at a time came there to stop to find boats, &c., to go on with. He has seen three different houses, there, one hundred and fifty feet long, filled with skins.

The fields cultivated were cleared before he was born, and were back of this house, and from the river to beyond the market house.

He thinks that John Harris saw William Penn here, or at Conois creek; he always heard that he (William Penn) visited him *on the Susquehanna*; and that he did much business for Penn's interest, and even talked of buying lands of him, over on the other side, down to the Yellow Breeches creek.

The wild turkeys and the deer were plenty in the revolution. They used to have as many of the former as they chose to shoot

He and his father have killed as many as twenty bears seen crossing the river.

The Paxton boys assembled here; they came from Cumberland and Hanover, and even as far as Franklin. John Harris, the second, tried to prevent them. Col. Smith was their principal man, and Col. Wilson Smith, of Waterford, in Erie county, of the legislature, is his son.

Esther Harris, up near Juniata, must have been John Harris' wife; she was resolute, masculine, capable of writing, and was the best trader of the two. Would box Indian chiefs' ears if they got drunk and unruly.

She carried her son John, born in 1726, to Christ church, in Philadelphia, to be baptized; he died in 1791, aged sixty-five. He was *the first born white child* hereabout, and the father of the present Robert Harris.

He had not his title confirmed by Shippen until 1733, but bought long before; it was about £5 per hundred acres, at first at 50*s*.

There was an Indian town opposite to Harris' ferry, just where are heaps of muscle shells—they ate them much; another town was at the mouth of Canodoquinet creek, two miles above; and there was one below, about two miles, at the mouth of Yellow Breeches, or Haldeman's bridge, which was once James Chartier's landing, Indian agent.

He has heard that they could assemble here seven hundred people by firing a gun—all came over then to this side.

They had a battle at Mokonoy, six miles this side of Shamokin, John Harris, the second, was along; one hundred went up from here to inquire, they surprised the party on the return, and killed sixteen to twenty men. John Harris, the second, in crossing the river had the man behind him, a *doctor*, shot off.

At the old church at Paxton, under Parson Elder, three miles from Harrisburg, on the road to Reading, they used to take guns and stack them while in the church. A party of Indians came and hid themselves for a week, to attack them; they lost two as prisoners, who told the fact. They shot at some on their return; killed and wounded some. They broke Major Burnett's arm, he died five years ago only.

Robert Harris has seen five hundred pack-horses at a time in Carlisle, going thence to Shippenburg, &c.

The road from John Harris', on the Susquehanna, in or near Paxton, towards Philadelphia, by way of Lancaster and Chester counties, was procured, in 1736, by petitions of sundry inhabitants in said counties.

John Harris, the first, is buried at the mulberry tree before his house, and close to the block-house on the river bank. He had seven children. This Robert Harris saw the remains of the block-house and stockade—were old when he was young.

The large stone house where he dwells was built in 1766, by his father, John Harris, the second.

His grandfather, John Harris, had a stockade round his old house (in front of the present one.) There an Indian came in with his gun, and fired upon the British officer therein; his gun flashed. His grandmother, then there, blew out the candle for concealment. This was in the log-house before the present residence.*

John Harris, the first, and his wife, who came from Yorkshire, were at first livers at Philadelphia. He often assisted at clearing lands in and about Philadelphia. He moved to Chester county; then to a place above Lancaster, at the mouth of Canoy creek—the same place where Haldeman's mills now are, three miles above Columbia. Then moved up to his place about a quarter of a mile below here; then moved here for the sake of being nearer the ferry. It was a ford in summer time, and chosen because of the better landing on the other side.

There were troops at the block-house, and furnished guards to travellers. Several travellers were occasionally wounded; some killed. Robert has seen one man that was scalped above Sunbury, and one here afterwards.

The Indians came to John Harris' trading store to get rum and ammunition; a party got angry and tied him to the tree to burn him, for refusing more rum. Another party came and released him. He valued the tree, and requested to be buried there; also two of his children are there. His faithful old black man *was not* buried there, (as some talk,) but where the *new* Methodist church is built, near by. He got money of Mrs. Logan's mother, at Chester, and called to pay interest once a year.

John Harris procured his patent of Shippen, in 1733. But the land was purchased much earlier.

John Harris owned all the town ground, eight to nine hundred acres; it was laid out in 1785, and sold off in fee simple. Lots in town sold first at 10 to £15, but now some would bring 2500 dollars to 5000 dollars! Robert Harris sold his family mansion and ground, in 1835, to Elder, for 5000 dollars, built in 1766.

The first old log-house was gone before Robert Harris was born. He saw the orchard there, all killed since, one old cherry tree only is standing.

There are several present log-houses still in the town, but now weather-boarded. Houses here are generally brick of two stories; several of white frame. The bridge across to M'Clay's island, in two divisions, done 1816—began three years before. This is the only stone house, save that of M'Clay at the other end, in the town. It is very large, and fronts the river at the lower end.

His grandmother rode once on urgency to Philadelphia, the same horse, in one day! At one time, when at Big Island, on trade, and hearing of her husband's illness, she came down in a day and a night in a bark canoe!

* We give many of the following notitia, from memoranda we had made when at Harrisburg.—J. F. W.

His grandfather farmed fields; he was the first who used a plough along the Susquehanna. He was a brewer in England.

The Indians went away to Shamokin and Seeling's Grove, and Muncey, and there lived, while John Harris, the first, lived down here. He traded for furs. Robert Harris often saw *many families* in bark canoes come down here to trade, and go down to Lancaster. Harrisburg built up very fast, even in the first year; five to six hundred people in three years. Government came here in 1809–10.

Esther Harris laid the foundation of the brick house, now Carson's, five miles up the Susquehanna. When the Indians made an invasion they shunned to attack it, because the scaffold holes in the walls scared them off, as supposing they were loop holes for guns!

One of the Harrises was a *wild devil*, of great agility and strength, who liked to encounter five or six Indians at once at grip and wrestle. He could beat them too, at their play at foot-ball.

Once Esther Harris showed her courage and management, when on an occasion of sending her maid up stairs she put her lighted candle into a powder cask as a stand, upon a sudden call down stairs, thinking it was flaxseed! Mrs. Harris ran up and took it out carefully with her own hands.

June 19th, 1733, Shekallamy, a chief, by Conrad Weiser, as interpreter, said, that he had *before*, together with Sassoonar, sent a letter to *John Harris*, to desire him to desist from making a plantation at the mouth of *Choniata*, (Juniata,) where Harris had only built that house for carrying on his trade, that his plantation, on which he has houses, barns, &c., at Paxton, is his *place of dwelling*, and that he has *no warrant* for any settlement at Choniata, and might have only intended to clear some land to raise corn for his horses, but that they should give the necessary orders in it. Shekallamy, acting for the Six Nations, then said, he had no ill will to John Harris, but that he is afraid that the warriors of the Six Nations, in passing there, will *see it* and take it ill.

Mrs. Esther Harris, was an excellent swimmer, and could use fire arms like a hunter. Even her grandaughter, Mrs. Mary Hana, the widow of Gen. Hana, who is now alive, aged about sixty-eight, could swim half across the river, and has learned several girls of her day to swim, as seen by Mr. Fahnestock.

The Indians were all great friends to John Harris, and afterwards became as friendly to his wife.

A letter from the justices of the peace in Berks county, of the 23d July, 1755, sent express to Governor Morris, signed by Conrad Weiser and five others, says, as all our Protestant inhabitants are very uneasy at the behaviour of the Roman Catholics, *who are very numerous in this county*, some of whom show *great joy* at the bad news lately come from the army, we have thought it our duty to inform your honour, and to ask that they may be disarmed. We have reason to believe that those who live in Cussahoppen, believed to be now present Summany town, where they have a very magnificent chapel, and have had large processions, *have bad designs*, and besides it is reported and believed generally, that in that neighbourhood there are thirty Indians lurking for prey and well armed. [This is another reason, *perhaps*, why the people of Paxton, &c., all Scotch-Irish Presbyterians, believed that their own Indians were misled and made hostile, as expecting great support from distant Indians in the French and papal pay and interest.]

A letter from the Rev. John Elder, of Paxton, to the secretary, R. Peters.

Paxton, 9th November, 1755.

I have just now received an express, informing me that out of a small party on guard last night in Tullyhoe's gap of the mountain, five were killed and two wounded. Such shocking accounts we frequently receive, and though we are careful to transmit them to Philadelphia, and remonstrate and petition from time to time, yet to no purpose, so that we seem to be given up into the hands of a merciless enemy.

There are within this few weeks upwards of forty of his majesty's subjects massacred on the frontiers of this and Cumberland counties, besides a great many carried into captivity, and yet nothing but unseasonable debates between the two parties of our legislature, instead of uniting on some probable scheme for the protection of the province. What may be the end of these things, God only knows; but I really fear that unless vigorous methods are speedily used, we in *these back settlements* will unavoidably fall a sacrifice, and this part of the province be lost.

If I have expressed my sentiments with too much warmth, you will be kind enough to pardon me, as it proceeds from a hearty regard to the public good.

Sir, your obedient servant,

JOHN ELDER.

[The subscriber was the first minister of the Paxton church.]

[*Note.*—He had also a colonel's commission—was born in Ireland, and was sixty years minister of the Presbyterian church.

"The flying rumours gather'd as they roll'd,
Scarce any tale was sooner heard than told;
And all who told it, adding something new,
And all who heard it, made enlargement too!"

Letter from Edward Biddle, at Reading, to his father, James Biddle, in Philadelphia.

I am in so much horror and confusion, I scarce know what I am writing, [at Sunday, one o'clock.] The drum is beating to arms, and the bells ringing, and all the people under arms. This moment express has arrived from Michael Reiss, at Tulpehoccan, eighteen miles off, who left about thirty of their people engaged with an equal number of Indians at said Reiss'. This night we expect an attack. Truly alarming is our situation. The people exclaim against the Quakers, and are scarce restrained from burning *the houses* of those few who are in this town. Oh my country! My bleeding country!—My love to sister and Jemmy.

Your affectionate son,

E. Biddle.

Peter Spycker, writing from Tulpehoccan, says that the people, hearing a firing, and running there, found the Indians (four) sitting on children scalping them: three of them are dead and two alive without scalps. Thence went to the watch-house of Derrick Sixth, and found six dead bodies, four being scalped. They have burned four plantations.

In council, 25th August, 1757.—A petition was received from the inhabitants of the township of *Paxton*, setting forth that the evacuating of *fort Hunter* is of great disadvantage to them, that fort Halifax is not necessary to secure the communication with fort Augusta, and is not so proper a station for the batteaux parties as fort Hunter, praying that the governor would please to fix a sufficient number of men at *Hunter's*, under the command of an active officer, with strict orders to range the frontiers daily. It is said at same time that fort Halifax was built by Colonel Clapham, without the orders of Governor Morris, and is in a bad situation, where none could be protected by it in batteau parties, it having no command of the channel. Although the fort or block-house at Hunter's (mills) was not tenable, being hastily erected and not finished, yet it was the best situation upon the river for every service, as well as for the protection of the frontiers.

In September, 1755, Conrad Weiser, in his letter to the governor, states that on the 7th inst., he went by orders to meet the Indians at John Harris' ferry. He found several had gone up the river to settle about Shamokin. He found there, however, "the Belt" and Seneca George, and five or six other elderly men, and fifty or sixty others. The Belt said the Six Nations were now resolved to revenge the death of Braddock, and drive away the French, "which the great general could not do because of *pride and obstinacy*, and for which the most High had thus punished him."

Harris' ferry, the 8th January, 1756. The governor, R. H. Morris, held a treaty here, having Conrad Weiser as interpreter, and James Hamilton, Richard Peters and Joseph Fox, commissioners, present; the Belt of Wampum and the Broken Thigh, with their families, the former a Seneca, the other a Mohock, which was adjourned to Carlisle, because of only *one house* at Harris' to accommodate them. At Carlisle, they were also joined by John Hamilton and William Logan, and by Mr. George Croghan, from his residence at Aucquick, [also Awkwick.]

Mr. Hamilton informed the council, that in November, 1755, he was at John Harris', and finding the people collected there in the utmost confusion, and in continual fear of being fallen upon by a large body of French and Indians, who were said to have passed the Allegheny hills in their march towards this province, he was induced to offer a great reward to Aroas, (Silver Heels,) to go up the east side of Susquehanna as far as Shamokin, to ascertain the facts in the case, and he being since returned and now present, was asked to relate the facts of his journey. He had gone as far as Nescopecka, where he found one hundred and forty warriors in their dance, and who expressed much anger against the English, and an intention to fall upon them to the eastward.

Abraham Horn, of Northampton, and Peter Frailey, of Orwickburgh, (now dead,) were the leading and influential persons, who most caused *the removal* of the seat of government from Philadelphia to Lancaster, by a resolution of March, 1799. They were supported by the members from Bucks county, and all along the Delaware, (so says secretary Trimball.)

The subject had been before agitated several times, and it would have been carried on one occasion, but for the casting vote of John Channon, of Huntingdon, in the senate.

The sale of the state lands was procured by the influence of banqueting parties, and good suppers, by "the committees of vigilance," so called, and *since* called *borers*, so first named after 1812, at Harrisburg. This measure gave great offence to many back members.

The most offensive case, and most prominent as a final and leading measure of removal, was the case of *the removal of* the court of justice in Wayne county to Bethany. This was procured by old Samuel Preston, (died in 1836,) a surveyor and postmaster, who acted in Wayne county as agent for Henry Drinker's lands. The last was a Philadelphian.

When they went to Lancaster, it was called a temporary object, for ten years only. They continued there until 1812.

The Paxton boys, being memorable in their day, and being often spoken of in these pages, we here add some special facts concerning them, to wit: Thomas Elder, a gentleman of the bar at Harrisburg, now about seventy-five years of age, tells me that his father, the Rev. Mr. Elder, rode after the Paxton boys, and got at their head to turn them back, and they declared they would shoot him down They were generally from Hanover, fourteen miles off. They took sacrament at the Paxton church, before going.

Elder's father was a Scotch-Irish Presbyterian minister, the first for Paxton church. He came from Ireland to it, about the year 1732; lived to be eighty—died in 1792, and had been the minister there sixty years. The Indians came twice to destroy his congregation, in time of worship; one time they laid about, seeking their chance, for a week; but having come on Monday, and laying about so long, they had to go away; in doing so they killed and wounded some whom they met. Major Burnett was wounded in his arm. Two prisoners who escaped told these things. At another time, they saw all the congregation bring their arms and stack them at the door. One of their prisoners escaped and gave the alarm, and they were repulsed with some blood on both sides. Mr. Elder remembers several Indian families still near here in his early days.

Mr. Fahnestock, aged sixty-six, remembers to have seen several of the leaders of the Paxton boys; he named Stewart, Colhoun, Smith, and Dickey. This last was the grandfather of the present Robert Dickey, who is doorkeeper to the senate. They lived to be aged men, in and about Harrisburg.

The Love rock, near M'Clay's house, was a place of Indian resort and council—part of it has been blown off.

A letter from Harris, to Conrad Weiser, dated June 30, 1755, at Paxton, to wit:

"I am sorry that I have occasion to inform you of such melancholy news. On Monday, the 22d inst., was killed and scalped three persons by Indians, near our fort, at Wills' creek. [Wills' creek was near Chambersburg.] And within three days after, upwards of twenty of our inhabitants have been killed or taken near Fort Cumberland. William Chesney is come home, who saw a little boy in our fort who was scalped last week, and likely to live. In short there seems to be nothing but desolation on the Potowmac. There was not scarce an hour since the army marched, but news of alarm comes down the road, that it will probably be stopped by the enemy; one soldier was found upon it killed. Our *own Indians* are *strongly suspected* for several reasons; first their deserting our army, all except about six men, and also, by English goods or arms found on one Indian killed last week by one Williams, which articles were delivered but lately out of our fort to Indians then there. I think it advisable that you should use endeavours to find out, if our own Indians are concerned, so that we might with the least delay, *lay some schemes for revenge*, before they can find time to use us as they have done our fellow subjects and acquaintances. We need men to be directly raised for our defence, and to guard provisions, &c., to our camp and army." [The foregoing letter shows perhaps the grounds of the massacre of the Conestoga Indians by the Paxton boys. They believed too, that the two or three persons killed at Quitepahilla, not far from Harris' ferry, eighteen miles towards Reading, were destroyed by their own Indians, just before they went off. John Harris above was *son* of the first John Harris, an original settler.]

A letter from John Harris, at Paxton, October 29, 1755, to Edward Shippen, Esq., Lancaster, says:

"We expect the enemy upon us every day, and the inhabitants are abandoning their plantations, being greatly discouraged at the approach of such a number of cruel savages, and no present sign of assistance. I had a certain account of fifteen hundred French and Indians being on their march against us and Virginia, and now close upon our borders; their scouts scalping our families on our frontiers daily. Andrew Montour and others at Shamokin, desired me tc take care, that there was a party of forty Indians out many days, *and intended to burn my house and destroy myself and family.* I have this day *cut loop holes* in my house, and am determined to hold out to the last extremity if I can get some men to stand by me. But few can be had at present, as every one is in fear of their own families being cut off every hour. Great part of the Susquehanna Indians are no doubt actually in the French interest, and I am informed that a French officer is expected at Shamokin this week with a party of Delawares and Shawnese, no doubt *to take possession of our river.* We should raise men immediately to build a fort up the river to take possession, and to induce some Indians to join us. We ought also to insist on the Indians to declare for or against us, and as soon as we are prepared for them, we should *bid up the scalps*, and keep our *woods* full of our people upon the scout, else they will ruin our province, *for they are a dreadful enemy!* I have sent out two Indian spies to Shamokin; they are Mohawks. [John Harris went up with a party of forty men to make discoveries, and to fight as far as Shamokin, they there saw strange Indians painted and dancing, and received advice from Andrew Montour to hasten back, and by the longest route on the eastern side, but they chose the western, and were attacked, and lost half a dozen of their men, &c.]

Paxton was the earliest name; it at first embraced several townships now nearest to it. The present Thomas Elder, Esq., remembers when there was but *one* German family in all the country. The first settlers were all Scotch-Irish. Their minister, Mr. Elder, was also a *colonel* at the same time—thus showing what a fighting race they must have all been against the heathen.

I visited Paxton church, built of lime-stone, quite old. The graveyard near, is surrounded by a good stone wall, and has many head-stones. The tombstones of marble, were of James and John Harris, William M'Clay, William Wallace, Hugh Wilson, Gen. Simpson, Thomas Forster, Krauch, Kelso. The Rev. John Elder had a double width of marble. There are headstones of Duncans, Stephens, Acols, Fulton—this last, perhaps, of steam memory! Older stones were of red slate stone, and the inscriptions illegible and rude. I thought many of these may have been of persons killed in Indian wars.

In this church there have been several cases of public confession, before the congregation, of *fornication*, saying, after the covenanters' way, "for my own game, have done this shame, pray restore me to my lands again," &c. The present Thomas Elder has seen these things of both sexes! Mr. Walters also saw it done up the Juniata, Mifflin county. The church is near to the woods, behind and aside of it; and its front opens to a beautiful cultivated country, lying below it. It is three miles from Harrisburg, near the turnpike to Lebanon.

The tombstone of Gen. Simpson says that his family settled in Paxton in 1720. It must have been earlier than any lands were sold on patent.

In continuation with Harrisburg, we may pertinently mention that even *Carlisle*, a few miles off, though settled so late as 1750, was so far a frontier then, as often to be subjected to Indian alarms in its vicinage, and to have had many characteristics of a *frontier town.* It was a place originally noted for its "beaver dams," probably formed out of the Le Tort creek; a name it received from James Le Tort, once a noted French trader and interpreter, as early as 1712. This was once *his* frontier and home. When this town was begun, it was then the Shawnese home, they dwelling until then round and about the "beaver pond." They moved off, leaving only one of their families behind, in the wigwam of "Doctor John." Doctor John and his family were all killed in 1768, by some of his neighbours, and it excited much indignation among the better portion of the white settlers.

Many aged persons, still alive in Carlisle, remembered very well when all the carriage of goods and stores westward from Carlisle was done wholly on pack horses, coming and going in whole companies. Only as long as twelve years ago, there were not more than three wagons in all Shearman valley—all was drawn on sleds, in summer as well as winter.

A Mrs. Murphy, who died in that valley in 1830, aged nearly one hundred years—having lived a long life there among the Indians. She remembered seeing the first *wagon* arrive at Carlisle, and the indignation it excited among the packers, as likely to ruin their trade!—even the widening of the roads, when first ordered, offended them! The pack-horses used to carry bars of iron on their backs, crooked over and around their bodies—barrels were hung on them, one on each side. She remembered that the *first Indian tract* to go westward, was to cross at Simpson's, four miles below John Harris' (Harrisburg); then across Canodoquinet, at Middlesex; thence up the mountain across Croghan's gap, (now Sterrett's); thence down the mountain and across Shearman's creek at Gibson's; then by Dick's gap; then by Shearman's valley by Concord, to the Burnt Cabins; then to the waters of the Allegheny, and down the river.

Shearman's valley was named after an Indian trader, who lost his life in fording it, with his horse and furs. In this valley I saw a real "leather stocking," in the person of a Mr. Stewart:—twenty-five years ago he had killed as many as sixty-three deer in a season; he goes out in snow time in preference, and lays out all night. It was in this valley that I heard of Wm. Penn's iron spur, left on his visit to Susquehanna, near Columbia, and now in the possession of Lewis Pennock, in London grove, Chester county.

Wyoming and its Massacre.

Among the claims set up by the state of Connecticut was the following,—that by their charter they owned all lands lying between those parallels of latitute forming the northern and southern boundary of their state, and extending west to the Pacific ocean. This claim, it will readily be perceived, would cover a large portion of the southern part of New York, and of the northern parts of Pennsylvania and Ohio. In prosecution of this claim, a colony from Windham, in Connecticut, obtained a state grant for a large tract of land, lying along the Susquehanna, in the state of Pennsylvania, whither they removed. The valley they occupied was called Wyoming, said to mean "field of blood;" so called on account of a bloody battle fought in the neighbourhood of the settlement by the Indians, at a period anterior to the removal of the whites.

The following account of the battle and massacre is taken from an interesting history of Wyoming, written by Isaac Chapman, Esq., late of Wilkesbarre. Judge Chapman lived upon the spot, and could hardly have failed to collect accurate materials, and to give a correct narrative of the events which transpired there during the revolutionary war. The inhabitants had collected in Forty fort—the principal fort in the valley. The number of men in the fort was three hundred and sixty-eight.

On the morning of the 3d of July, 1778, the officers of the garrison at Forty fort held a council to determine on the propriety of marching from the fort, and attacking the enemy wherever found. The debates in this council of war are said to have been conducted with much warmth and animation. The ultimate determination was one on which depended the lives of the garrison and safety of the settlement. On one side it was contended that their enemies were daily increasing in numbers; that they would plunder the settlement of all kinds of property, and would accumulate the means of carrying on the war, while they themselves would become weaker; that the harvest would soon be ripe, and would be gathered or destroyed by their enemies, and all their means of sustenance during the succeeding winter would fail; that probably all their messengers were killed, and as there had been more than sufficient time, and no assistance arrived, they would probably receive none, and consequently now was the proper time to make the attack. On the other side it was argued, that probably some or all the messengers may have arrived at head quarters, but that the absence of the commander-in-chief may have produced delay; that one or two weeks more may bring the desired assistance, and that to attack the enemy, superior as they were in number, out of the limits of their own fort, would produce almost certain destruction to the settlement and themselves. and captivity, and slavery, perhaps torture, to their wives and children. While these debates were progressing, five men belonging to Wyoming, but who at that time held commissions in the continental army, arrived at the fort; they had received information that a force from Niagara had marched to destroy the settlements on the Susquehanna, and being unable to bring with them any reinforcement, they resigned their appointments, and hastened immediately to the protection of their families; they had heard nothing of the messengers, neither could they give any certain information as to the probability of relief.

The prospect of receiving assistance became now extremely uncertain. The advocates for the attack prevailed in the council, and at dawn of day, on the morning of the 3d of July, the garrison left the fort, and began their march up the river, under the command of Colonel Zebulon Butler. Having proceeded about two miles, the troops halted for the purpose of detaching a reconnoitring party, to ascertain the situation of the enemy.

The scout found the enemy in possession of fort Wintermoot, and occupying huts immediately around it, carousing in supposed security; but on their return to the advancing column, they met two strolling Indians, by whom they were fired upon, and upon whom they immediately returned the fire without effect. The settlers hastened their march for the attack, but the Indians had given the alarm, and the advancing troops found the enemy already formed in order of battle, a small distance from their fort, with their right flank covered by a swamp, and their left resting upon the bank of a river. The settlers immediately displayed their column and formed in corresponding order; but as the enemy was much superior in numbers, their line was much more extensive. Pine woods and bushes covered the battle ground, in consequence of which, the movements of the troops could not be so quickly discovered, nor so well ascertained. Colonel Zebulon Butler had command of the right, and was opposed by Colonel John Butler, at the head of the British troops, on the left; Colonel Nathan Denison commanded the left, opposed by Brant at the head of his Indians on the enemy's right. The battle commenced at about forty rods distant, and continued about fifteen minutes, through the woods and brush, without much execution. At this time Brant with his Indians having penetrated the swamp, turned the left flank of the settlers' line, and with a terrible warwhoop and savage yell, made a desperate charge upon the troops composing that wing, which fell very fast, and were immediately cut to pieces with the tomahawk. Colonel Denison having ascertained that the savages were gaining the rear of the left, gave orders for that wing *to fall back.* At the same time Colonel John Butler, finding that the line of the settlers did not extend as far toward the river as his own, doubled that end of his line which was protected by a thick growth of brushwood, and having brought a party of his British regulars to act in column upon that wing, threw Colonel Zebulon Butler's troops into some confusion. The orders of Colonel Denison for his troops to *fall back*, having been understood by many to mean a *retreat*, the troops began to retire in much disorder. The savages considered this a flight, and commencing a most hideous yell, rushed forward with their rifles and tomahawks, and cut the retiring line to pieces. In this situation it was found impossible to rally and form the troops, and the rout became general throughout the line. The settlers fled in every direction, and were instantly followed by the savages, who killed or took prisoners whoever came within their reach. Some succeeded in reaching the river, and escaped by swimming across, others fled to the mountains, and the savages, too much occupied with plunder, gave up the pursuit. When the first intelligence was received in the village of Wilkesbarre that the battle was lost, the women fled with their children to the mountains, on their way to the settlements on the Delaware, where many of them at length arrived, after suffering extreme hardships. Many of the men who escaped the battle, together with their women and children, who were unable to travel on foot, took refuge in Wyoming fort, and on the following day, (July the 4th,) Butler and Brant, at the head of their combined forces, appeared before the fort, and demanded its surrender. The garrison being without any efficient means of defence, surrendered the fort on articles of capitulation, by which the settiers, upon giving up their fortifications, prisoners, and military stores, were to remain in the country unmolested, provided they did not again take up arms.

In this battle about three hundred of the settlers were killed or missing, and from a great part of whom no intelligence was ever afterward received.

The conditions of the capitulation were entirely disregarded by the British and savage forces, and after the fort was delivered up, all kinds of barbarities were committed by them. The village of Wilkesbarre, consisting of twenty-three houses, was burnt; men and their wives were separated from each other, and carried into captivity; their property was plundered, and the settlement laid waste. The remainder of the inhabitants were driven from the valley, and compelled to proceed on foot sixty miles through the great swamp, almost without food or clothing. A number perished in the journey, principally women and children; some died of their wounds; others wandered from the path in search of food, and were lost, and those who survived called the wilderness through which they passed *the shades of death*, an appellation which it has since retained.

Catrine Montour, who might well be termed a fury, acted a conspicuous part in this tragedy. She followed in the train of the victorious army, ransacking the heaps of the slain, and with her arms covered with gore, barbarously murdering the wounded, who in vain supplicated for their lives. She lived and died in New York state.

Halleck, in allusion to the massacre of Wyoming, has the following interesting lines:

"There is a woman, widow'd, gray and old,
Who tells you where the foot of battle stept
Upon their day of massacre. She told

Its tale, and pointed to the spot, and wept,
Whereon her father and five brothers slept
Shroudless, the bright dream'd slumbers of the brave,
When all the land a funeral mourning kept.
And there, wild laurels planted on the grave
By Nature's hand, in air their pale red blossoms wave."

We find in a Connecticut paper, of 1831, an account of the recent decease of Mrs. Esther Skinner, of Torringford, in the one hundredth year of her age. Mrs. S. lost a husband, a brother, and two sons, in the war of the American revolution. She, with her family, was a resident of Wyoming, at the massacre of its inhabitants by the British, and the Indians and tories. Her two sons fell beneath the tomahawk, but the mother, almost by miracle, escaped with six of her children. Her son-in-law was the only man that escaped, out of twenty, who threw themselves into the river, and attempted to hide themselves beneath the foliage that overhung the banks. All the others were successively massacred as they hung by the branches in the river. He alone was undiscovered. The mother travelled back to Torringford, where she has led a useful life ever since—often cheerful, though the cloud of pensiveness, brought on by her sorrows, was never entirely dissipated. But one of her children survives her.

It would seem that Campbell, the poet, did not deem himself justified by the facts in the case, to picture, so severely as he did, the doings of the chieftain Brant, in the tragic massacre. In January, 1822, he addressed a letter to John Brant, Esq., of the Grand river, son of the Indian chief, wherein he makes his apologies for sundry severities upon the memory of the father; upon the ground, that he had been misinformed in following the usual printed stories of the fight; and conceding to the son, that he, the son, had convinced him of sundry misrepresentations. The truth is, that Brant, the chief, was extremely desirous of retaining the character of a humane man, and inculcated the avowal in his family, that he never did any thing savage and cruel personally; and also restrained and checked his adherents, when he could. The son declares that his father was not present at the scene of the massacre at all; but was in the rear at some distance.

When Brant was in England, after the peace of 1783, the most distinguished individuals of all parties and professions treated him with the utmost kindness and attention. In Canada the memorials of his moral character represent him as naturally ingenuous and generous; and from the premises, Campbell concludes with the assurance, that "he deems them sufficient to induce him to believe that he often strove to mitigate the cruelty of Indian warfare, and that, therefore, his opinion about him *is changed.*"

Brant was a full-blooded Mohawk, born on the Mohawk river, and educated at an Indian school in New England.

John Butler, also, often endeavoured to exculpate himself individually, from the imputation of barbarity, and it was admitted by those who knew him before the war in Sir John Johnson's neighbourhood, that he bore the character of a gentle man, and that his son, an officer under him, who was killed at the crossing of Wood creek, was far more cruel than his father.

The Delaware chief, Tedyuscung, was settled at Wyoming in 1758, at the public expense, intending thereby to place him and his people as a frontier defence. They sent on a force of fifty men, as carpenters, masons and labourers, who erected ten or twelve houses, of fourteen by twenty feet, and one for himself, of sixteen by twenty-four feet. He was an artful, wily chief, of more than common selfishness and intrigue for an Indian, and withal was intemperate and aspiring.

As early as 1742, Count Zinzendorf visited the Shawnese, then settled at Wyoming, with a missionary's wife as his interpreter. He remained among them twenty days, and while there sitting by a fire, and writing in his temporary hut, his leg was crossed by a rattlesnake, seeking to warm itself by the fire.

Wyoming, the name given by the Delaware Indians, expressed the *Large plains*, and is a corruption of the original name of Maughwau-wame. The Six Nations called it Sgahontowano, the large flats, *wano* meaning a large ground without trees. It came to be called Wauwaumia, Wiomic, and then Wyoming. The Susquehanna, on which its rests, was so called to express muddy or riley river, the word *hanna* meaning a stream of water.

The last survivor of those who were in the action of the Wyoming massacre, was Major Roswell Franklin, who after having become the *first settler* of Aurora, New York, in 1787, died there in 1843. He had fought at that battle along side of his father, and had seen his mother and sister butchered near him, and then himself and his other sister were taken off prisoners, himself, for a service of three years, and his sister for eleven years.

Pittsburg and Braddock.

In the olden time, Fort du Quesne and Fort Pitt, and the thousand tales of "Braddock's defeat," were the talk of all the land, and formed the tales of all the nurseries, scaring the hearers as oft as the tales were told.

> "The mind, impressible and soft, with ease
> Imbibes and treasures what she hears and sees—
> The tale, at first but half received,
> Till others have the fearful facts believed!"

Such facts and relations as we have occasionally gathered, and not to be found in the ordinary histories, we purpose now to give in a *desultory* manner, in the following pages:

Previous to the year 1753, the country west of the Allegheny mountains, and particularly the point which Pittsburg now occupies, was the subject of controversy between Great Britain and France.—

In the early part of that year, a party of Frenchmen from Presque Isle, now Erie, seized three English traders at Loggstown, and carried them back with them as prisoners. In the fall of that year, Robert Dinwiddie, governor of Virginia, despatched George Washington, then in the 22d year of his age, to the French commander on Le Bœuf, to demand that he should desist from further aggression. In performance of this duty, Washington arrived at "the Forks," on the 23d of November, 1753. While here he examined the site immediately at the junction of the rivers, and recommended it as a suitable position for a fort. On the next day he proceeded from this place, and called on King Shingass, near M'Kee's rocks, who accompanied him on his way to Loggstown, where they met Monakatoocha, and other Indian chiefs, and held several councils with them.

While at Loggstown, it became a question which road he should take on his way to the French commandant at Le Bœuf, and Shingass advised him not to take the road by Beaver, because it was low and swampy. Proceeding on his journey, he arrived at Le Bœuf, and learned from the French commandant that they were determined to take possession of the Forks in the spring. With this answer he left the French commandant, in company with Gist, his guide, on foot, and arrived at the Allegheny river, below the mouth of Pine creek, on the 28th of December. The next day they spent in making a raft with tomahawks, and towards evening embarked, and attempted to cross the river; but the ice driving very thick, they made very little progress, and were finally compelled to take refuge upon Herr's or Wainwright's island, where they were nearly *frozen.*

During the night it froze so hard, that *they crossed on the ice in the morning.* This circumstance affords a pretty strong inference that it must have been Wainwright's island; it lying close to the eastern shore, the narrow passage between it and the shore would be more likely to freeze in one night, than the wide space opposite Herr's island. Having crossed the river they proceeded without delay to Frazier's, at the mouth of Turtle creek. On the 31st of December, while Gist and the other men were out hunting the horses, Washington walked up to the residence of Queen Allequippa, where M'Keesport now stands. She expressed much regret that he had not called on her as he went out. He made her a present of a watch-coat, and a flask of rum, and in his journal he states that the latter present was much the most acceptable.

We here give a poetic description of first scenes at Pittsburg, viz.:

How changed the scene since here the savage trod,
  To set his otter-trap, or take wild honey,
Where now so many humble printers plod,
  And faithful CARRIERS hunt a little *money!*

How things have alter'd in this misty plain,
  Since Allequippa hunted and caught fish,
Where Mrs. Oliver and her gentle train
  Now *read* of Indians in the *Wish-ton-Wish!*

How short the time, but how the scenes have shifted,
  Since WASHINGTON explored this western wild-land,
And with his raft, and Gist, his pilot, drifted
  Upon the upper end of Wainwright's island!

'Tis seventy years ago, since that bold knight,
  With blanket, cap, and leggings, then the tippey,
Attended by his 'squire, the aforesaid wight,
  Paid his respects to good Queen Allequippa.

Her warlike majesty was quite unhappy,
  To think our courtier had not sooner come:
He soothed her feelings with a blanket capo,
  And touch'd her fancy with a flask of rum.

What changes, since from yonder point he scann'd
  The meeting streams with his unerring eye,
And, 'mid primeval woods, prophetic scann'd
  This great position and its destiny!

Since royal Shingass dwelt upon the cliff,
  Which overlooks the foot of Brunot's isle,
And angled in his little barken skiff,
  Where now for wood a steamer stops awhile.

When Shingass gave him his advice about
  The best and nearest route to Fort Venango,
And then decided for the higher route,
  Against the route by Beaver and Shenango.

But good king Shingass, it is very clear,
  Was but a royal archer after all,
And not by any means an engineer,
  And never heard or dreamt of a canal.

Monakatoocha, and the Delaware band,
  Then held their council fires of war and peace,
Where RAPP now cultivates the peaceful land,
  And sheers his sheep, and wins the golden fleece.

How changed the scene, since merry Jean Baptiste,
  Paddled his pereogue on the Belle Riviere,
And from its banks some lone Loyola priest
  Echo'd the night hymn of the voyageur!

Since Ensign Ward saw coming down yon stream,
  Where all was peace and solitude before,
A thousand paddles in the sunshine gleam,
  And countless pereogues that stretch from shore to shore.

The lily flag waved o'er the foremost boat,
  And old St. Pierre the motly host commanded·
Then here the flag of *France* was *first* afloat,
  And here the *Gallic* cannon *first* were landed.

Then here began that fatal war, which cost
  The lily banner many a bloody stain;
In which a wide empire was won and lost,
  And Wolf and Montcalm fell on Abraham's plain

Since a subaltern in old Fort Du Quesne
  Begg'd of his chief, ere yet he quit the post,
To give him but a handful of his men
  To venture out and meet the British host:

When his red allies hail'd him with a shout,
  Who led them on with Indian enterprise,
When Braddock's confidence was put to rout
  And all, but wary Washington, surprised.

But jealousy suppress'd the Frenchman's fame,
  And when his chief sent home his base report,
He cast a stigma on his rival's name,
  And got the credit to himself at court.

How changed the scene, from all that Grant did see.
  When from his bivouac on yonder height,
He waked the French with his proud reveillé,
  And challenged them to sally forth and fight.

One Highland officer that bloody day,
  Retreated up the Allegheny's side,
Wounded and faint, he miss'd his tangled way,
  And near some water laid him down and died.

'Twas in a furrow of a sandy swell
  Which overlooks that clear and pebbled wave,
Shrouded in leaves, none found him where he fell,
  And mouldering nature gave the youth a grave

Last year a plough pass'd o'er the quiet spot,
  And brought to light frail vestiges of him
Whose unknown fate perhaps is not forgot,
  And fills with horror yet a sister's dream.

His plaited button, stamp'd with proofs of rank,
  His pocket gold, which still untouch'd remains,
Do show, at least, no savage captor drank
  As gentle blood as flow'd in Scottish veins.

I think I see him from his sleep arise,
  And gaze on yonder tower with admiration!
Lo! on its battlements a banner flies,
  An unknown flag of some unheard-of nation!

Of all the features of the scene around,
  The neighbouring stream alone he recognizes;
Another such can no where else be found;
  The sun upon no river like it rises.

Does he retrace what was a blood-stain'd route;
  Through thickets of the thorny crab and sloe,
He lists again to hear the savage shout,
  Where every trace is lost of fort and foe.

But still a shorter time has pass'd away,
  Since on the Allegheny's western beach,
The lurking Shawanee in ambush lay,
  In hopes some white would cross within his reach.

Thence to the lake no white had settled yet,
  And Indian tribes still held their ancient station
When the first carrier of the old Gazette
  Took round that little humble publication.

The Muse, when she another year is older,
  May give a present picture of this place,
Which from the canvass will but rise the bolder
  That now its fading back-ground we retrace.

On the 17th of April, 1754, the French commander, Contrecœur, with three hundred and sixty canoes, one thousand men and eighteen pieces of cannon, arrived at the "Forks," where Pittsburg now stands, and compelled Ensign Ward to surrender. This invasion is very properly called, in the poetry, the *commencement of the war*, which terminated in the loss by France of all her possessions in America, east of the Mississippi.

Some incidents in relation to the subaltern who commanded the French and Indians at Braddock's defeat were derived from La Fayette, during his late visit to this country.

The account of the remains of a deceased officer which were ploughed up during the last summer, near the arsenal, are in part founded on fact. It is true that such remains were discovered, and that money and marks of military rank were found with them.

There were still some remains of the old Fort du Quesne to be found in 1834. Its site was in part occupied by a brew-house erected upwards of thirty years ago, by General O'Hara, *the first brew-house* in "the great west." The rest of the site is now filled with dwellings. It was on *the point* formed by the two rivers. Forty years ago the walls were still entire. A part of the brew-house premises fills the place which was a bastion; at a little distance from it is still there a small brick five-sided edifice, called the guard-house, erected by the British after the capture from the French. It has two ranges of loop holes through sticks of timber, let into the walls, which are a foot thick. In one of its sides, near the top, *is a relic*, a tablet of stone of two feet by fourteen inches, on which is inscribed "A. D. 1764, *Col. Boquet.*" Adjoining to this guard-house are *now* two small brick houses, which were built from the bricks taken from the walls of Fort Pitt. I saw these things in 1804. Then the area of the fort, excepting the said brew-house premises, of Shiras, was all a nearly levelled grass field, from General O'Hara's residence, where I dwelt, down to the point. In 1833, when they were excavating the ground for the foundation of the building above mentioned, which occupies the site of the bastion, they dug up several ends of the *oak* palisadoes, which were once a part of the defence on the Allegheny river side. They were of course seventy years of age or more, and yet were perfectly sound!

Braddock's battle field is seven miles from Pittsburg, on the right bank of the Monongahela. None who read of it ever think of it, as being a place near a river, or as so near to *the end* of the intended expedition!

"How cnang'd the scene, since Indian men and manners reign'd!"

The late Morgan Neville, Esq., whose acquaintance I had formed in our youth, was pleased to write some very pleasant recollections of his native place, and especially of some individuals and incidents, which it will be gratifying to preserve in these pages, to wit:

It was about the year 1796, that the Duke of Orleans, now Louis Philippe, king of France, accompanied by his two brothers, Montpensier and Beaujolais, came to the western country. On arriving in Pittsburg, then a small village, they found one or two *emigres.* who had formerly filled prominent stations under the *ancienne regime*, but who were now earning a scanty subsistence in carrying on some little business of merchandise. One of them, the Chevalier du B——c, one of the worthiest of men, and an admirable philosopher, kept a little shop, then denominated, *par excellence*, a confectionery. The articles, and the only ones, by the way, entitling the chevalier's establishment to this attractive name, were the kernels of hazelnuts, walnuts and peach stones, enclosed in an envelope of burnt maple sugar, *fabricated* by the skilful hands of the chevalier himself. Du B——c was the most popular citizen of the village; he had a monkey of admirable qualities, and his pointer (Sultan) could, like the dog in the Arabian Nights, tell counterfeit money from good; at least, the honest folks who supplied our little market with chickens and butter thought so, and that was the same thing. It was amusing to hear the master of the shop calling his two familiars to aid him in selecting the good from the bad "'leven-penny-bits." "Allons Sultan, tell dese good ladie de good money from de counterfait." Then followed the important consultation between the dog and the monkey; pug grinned and scratched his sides; Sultan smelled, and in due time scraped the money into the drawer. As there was no counterfeit "'leven-pences," Sultan seldom failed. "Madame," would my friend say, to the blowzy country lass, "Sultan is like de pope, he is infallible." Sultan and Bijou laid the foundation of this excellect man's fortune. They brought crowds of custom to the shop, and in two or three years he was enabled to convert his little business into a handsome fancy store. An attraction was then added to the establishment, that diverted a portion of the public admiration from Sultan and the monkey; this was a Dutch clock, with a goodly portion of gilding, and two or three white and red figures in front,—before striking it played a waltz. It was inestimable, this music had never before been heard in the west, and those who have been brought up amidst the everlasting grinding of our present museums, can have no conception of the excitement caused by our chevalier's clock. In those days every unique piece of furniture, or rare toy, was believed to have formed a part of the *spolia optima* of the French revolution, and most generally they were set down as the property of the queen of France. It was soon insinuated abroad, that the chevalier's clock formed one of the rare ornaments of the boudoir of the unfortunate Marie Antoinette. When he was asked how much it cost, he evaded the question with admirable casuistry. "Ah, mon ami," he would say with sincere tristesse, "the French revolution produce some terrible effect; it was great sacrifice, it is worth fifteen hundred franche guiney." That, and the dog and the monkey were worth, to the chevalier, 15,000 dollars, for he realized this sum in a few years, from a foundation of a few pounds of sugar, and a peck of hazelnuts.

Such was the Chevalier du B——c in his magazine; and he was a perfect illustration of the French character of that day; it would accommodate itself to any situation in life, it enabled the minister of marine to become, like Bedredden, a pastry cook, and young Egalité, the present king of France, a schoolmaster in Canada. But this is only one side of the picture; Du B——c, when he closed his shop, and entered into society, was the delight of his auditory. He was an accomplished scholar, possessed the most polished manners and habits of "la vieille cour." He was a younger son, or as the French people call it, he was the "cadet" of a noble family. He had travelled much, and observed profoundly. He had been to the 'Holy Land,' not exactly as a palmer, but being 'attaché a la légation Française' at Constantinople, of which his relation, Sauf Bœuf, was the head, he took the opportunity of travelling through as much of Asia as was usually examined by European travellers. Such was my early friend Du B——c, to whose instructions and fine belles-lettres acquirements, I am indebted for some of the most unalloyed enjoyments of my life, by opening to me some of the richest treasures of French literature; and such was the man whom the sons of Orleans found in a frontier American village. I do not remember the definite destination of the interesting strangers; but certain it is, that the Chevalier du B——c induced them to while away a much longer period in Pittsburg than could have been their original intention. He proposed to General N——, whose house was always the temple of hospitality, where he was in the habit of dining every Sunday, and at whose table and fireside the unfortunate *emigre* was sure to find a hearty welcome, to introduce the travellers. The general at first received the proposition with coldness. He said he had been a soldier of the revolution, the intimate of Rochambeau and La Fayette, and of course entertained a feeling of the deepest respect for the memory of the unfortunate Louis, not as a monarch; but as a most amiable and virtuous man.—He insisted that no good could spring from the infamous exciter of the jacobins, the profligate Egalité. "Mais, mon Général, (said the chevalier, with a shrug of the shoulders, and most melancholy contortion of his wrinkled features,) ils sont dans les plus grande misère, et ils ont été chassé, comme nous autres, par ces vilains sans culottes." The chevalier knew his man, and the *bon hommie* of the General prevailed. "Eh, bien! chevalier, allez, rendre nos devoirs aux voyageurs, et qu'ils dinent chez nous demain." The strangers accepted the courtesy and became intimate with and attached to the family of the kind hearted American: the charms of the conversation of the Duke of Orleans, and his various literary attainments, soon obliterated for the moment the horrible career of his father, from the minds of his hearers. If my boyish recollection is faithful, he was rather taciturn, and melancholy; he would be perfectly abstrated from conversation, sometimes for

12

half an hour, looking steadfastly at the coal fire that blazed in the grate, and when roused from his reverie, he would apologize for this breach of *bienséance*, and call one of the children who were learning French to read to him. On these occasions I have read to him many passages selected by him from Télémaque: the beautiful manner in which he read the description of Calypso's Grotto is still fresh in my memory. He seldom adverted to the scenes of the revolution, but he criticized the battles of that period, particularly that of Jemmapes, with such discrimination, as to convince the military men of Pittsburg, of whom there were several, that he was peculiarly fitted to shine in the profession of arms.

Montpensier, the second brother, has left no mark on the tablet of memory by which I can recall him; but Beaujolais, the young and interesting Beaujolais, is still before "my mind's eye." There was something romantic in his character, and Madame de Genlis' romance, the "Knights of the Swan," in which that charming writer so beautifully apostrophizes her young ward, had just prepared every youthful bosom to lean towards this accomplished boy. He was tall and graceful, and playful as a child. He was a universal favourite. He was a few years older than myself, but when together we appeared to be of the same age. A transient cloud of melancholy would occasionally pass over his fine features, in the midst of his gayest amusements; but it disappeared quickly, like the white cloud of summer. We then ascribed it to a boyish recollection of the luxuries and splendours of the Palais Royal, in which he had passed his early life, which he might be contrasting with the simple domestic scene which was passing before him. It was, however, probably in some measure imputable to the first sensation of that disease, which, in a few short years afterwards, carried him to the grave.

One little circumstance made a singular impression on me. I was standing one day with this group of Frenchmen, on the bank of the Monongahela, when a countrymen of theirs, employed in the quarter master's department, as a labourer in taking care of the flat boats, passed by. Pierre Cabot, or as he was familiarly called, French Peter, was dressed in a blanket capot, with a hood in place of a hat, in the manner of the Canadian boatmen, and in moccasons. Du B——c called after him, and introduced him to the French princes. The scene presented a subject for moralizing, even for a boy: on the banks of the Ohio, and in exile, the representative of the first family of a nation who held rank of higher importance than any other nation in Europe, took by the hand in a friendly and familiar conversation his countryman, whose lot was cast among the dregs of the people, and who would not have aspired to the honour of letting down the steps of the carriage of the man with whom he here stood on a level.

Peter was no jacobin—he had emigrated from France before the philosophic Robespierre and his colleagues had enlightened their fellow citizens, and opened their eyes to the propriety of vulgar bru tality and ferocity. Honest Cabot, therefore, felt all the love and veneration for the princes, which Frenchmen under the old regime never failed to cherish for members of the "grand monarque." I was a great favourite with old Peter.—The next time I met him, he took me in his arms, and exclaimed with tears in his eyes,—'Savez-vous, mon enfant, ce qui m'est arrivé j'ai eu l'honneur de causer avec monseigneur, en pleine rue. Ah! bon Dieu, quelle chose affreuse que la revolution.'

The brothers, on quitting Pittsburg, left a most favourable impression on the minds of the little circle in which they were received so kindly. The recollection of the amiable Beaujolais was particularly cherished; and when the news of his death in Sicily, a few years after, reached the west, the family circle of General N—— expressed the sincerest sorrow.

The Chevalier du B——c, after realizing a snug fortune by industry and economy, removed to Philadelphia, to have the opportunity of mingling more with his countrymen. On the restoration of the Bourbons, his friends induced him to return to France, to resume the former rank of his family.—But it was too late; the philosophical emigrant had lived too long in American seclusion to relish the society of Paris, or habits had changed there too much to be recognized by him. The following is a translation of a paragraph from one of his letters to his old friend, the late General N——, soon after his arrival in Paris.

"I must bear witness to the improvement and advancement of my country since the revolution; as a man, however, I cannot but mourn; the storm has not left a single shrub of my once numerous family; the guillotine has drunk the blood of all my race; and I now stand on the verge of the grave, the dust of a name whose pride it once was to trace its history through all the distinguished scenes of French history, for centuries back. With the eloquent savage, Logan, whose speech you have so often read to me, I can say, that 'not a drop of my blood runs in the veins of any living creature.' I must return to America, and breathe my last on that soil, where my most contented days were passed."

The chevalier never returned however; he lingered away his time in the different seaports of France, and he died at last in the city of Bordeaux.

We had the peculiarity and honour, in 1804, to go from Pittsburg in charge of the first sea vessel built at that place. It was then a wonder to many, that such an enterprise should be undertaken. We thought still less then of seeing a day arrive when steam vessels should navigate those waters. They did not even *then* think of running *stages* from Philadelphia, and far less of ever seeing steam cars and canals passing the mountains.

It was something *in itself*, to have made the voyage to New Orleans in such a period. It took forty-five days from the starting before reaching that city—then so different from its present character and estimation. My *MS. notitia*, while there and on the way, might make *a book* even now, if I was so minded. What I saw and observed in the descent of the river is expressed *much to my mind and feelings* in the words of another explorer, the celebrated *Audubon.* He says: "When I think of those times, and call back to my mind the grandeur and beauty of those then almost uninhabited shores; the dense and lofty forests, then unmolested by the axe of the settler; when I think of the blood spilt by many a worthy Virginian to purchase the free use of the noble rivers; when I see that no longer are to be found there any of the aborigines, and that the herds of elk, deer and buffaloes, which once pastured on those hills and valleys,—making for themselves great roads to the salt springs, have ceased to exist; now all is covered with towns, villages, and farms, where the din of hammers and machinery is constantly heard; now hundreds of steamboats glide to and fro, forcing commerce to take root and prosper in every spot; when I consider that these extraordinary changes have *all* taken place *so recently*, I pause, wonder, and can scarcely believe its reality! It *is* strange—passing strange, indeed!"

Note, *the first flat boat* that ever descended the Mississippi, went from Redstone, on the Monongahela river, in May 1782. It was owned and conducted by Jacob Yoder, of Reading, Pennsylvania, who died at his farm in Kentucky, in April, 1822, aged sixty-four years!

Pittsburg will for ever be associated with the event and circumstances of Braddock's defeat, and therefore whatever relates to him will be regarded with interest.

The Walpole Letters speak of Gen. Braddock, and say he had been governor of Gibraltar—speak of him as poor, and prodigal, and brutal, "a very Iroquois in disposition." His sister "had gamed her little fortune away at Bath, and then hung herself—after the same savage sort of temper! Braddock had had a duel with Col. Gumley, and an amour with Mrs. Upton. The ministry in England were much chagrined at Braddock's slow progress to the west, as incommoded by a needless train of artillery and road-making." So said Walpole.

In Franklin's Memoirs, there is considerable mention by him of Gen. Braddock,—of his conversation with him in Virginia, before the expedition started. He speaks of advising him as to Indian warfare, and that Braddock treated it as no obstacle; talked confidently of making of it a short work, by taking fort Du Quesne in a day; thence going quickly to Erie, and thence along the Canada line, &c. They agreed very well; and it was afterwards found by Franklin, when in London, that Braddock's letters home to the government had spoken favourably of Franklin.—[A gazette story.]

The place of conflict has since been called Braddock's field, and is situate on the north branch of the Monongahela, seven miles above Pittsburg, where the crumbling bones of men and horses long remained to mark the fatal spot.

A letter from Winchester, Va., of 3d February, 1755, (published in the New York Mercury,) says, that Sir John St. Clair and Governor Sharpe had been at Wills' creek, (*i. e.* Fort Cumberland,) where a camp was forming of one thousand men; that a train of artillery was to have arrived in Virginia from England, that transports had gone to Cork for the two regiments there, to go to America with Gen. Braddock.

February 18, Gen. Braddock and three men of war arrived at Hampton, with sixteen transports, having one thousand men. All marched off for Alexandria; but *the officers* went to Annapolis first, on the 3d April. At Alexandria, on the 13th April, Braddock and several of *the governors* met and consulted, before his going to Will's creek, then fortified as Fort Cumberland.

May 22d, 1755, Gen. Braddock and all his forces, are announced as already arrived at Wills' creek. On the 21st June, Gen. Braddock and his army were at Bear camp, near the Great meadows. [This Wills' creek runs into the Potomac, at *Cumberland*, in Maryland, at about six miles from the Pennsylvania line, and the march appears to have been very much along the line of the present "national road" to Uniontown,—near to which is Braddock's grave, and the Meadows.]

A letter from the camp at Great meadows, of July 1st, 1755, says, on the 7th ult., Sir John St. Clair marched in advance with six hundred men from Wills' creek, and two days after, the whole army followed,—*through the worst roads in the world.* Ten days after, they arrived at the Little meadows, where the whole camp was encircled by abatis, and halted three days; from thence they marched for this place. Col. Dunbar was placed in the rear with provisions and ordnance stores, and eighty wagons.

The minutes of council of the 24th of July, 1755, state that an express arrived, bringing a letter from Captain Robert Orme to Governor Morris, dated at Fort Cumberland, July 18th, 1755, from which I give these extracts, to wit: "I am so ill by the wound, that I have employed Captain Dobson to write the present letter for me. I write now, because every superior officer, whose business it was to have written concerning disaster, was either killed or wounded." [He was himself an aid-de-camp to Gen. Braddock.]

"On the 9th instant, we passed and repassed the Monongahela, by advancing first a party of three hundred men; then a second party of two hundred men; the general, with the column of artillery and the main body, passed the river *the last time* about one o'clock. As soon as the whole (twelve hundred men) had got on the fort side, (seven miles distant,) we heard a very heavy and quick fire in our front; we immediately advanced to sustain them; but the aforesaid advance of five hundred men gave way and fell back upon us, causing much confusion, and struck so great a panic among our men that no military expedient could avail to recover them. The men were so extremely deaf to *the exhortations* of the general, *and the officers*, that *they fired away, in the most irregular manner, all their ammunition, and then ran off.* [This is a different version from the common idea, for here they took their *own way* of firing, but in panic; and besides, what else could they do when they had no more ammunition left?] Leaving to the enemy the artillery, *ammunition*, provision, and baggage; nor could they be persuaded to stop until they got as far as Guest's plantation, and there, only in part; many of them proceeding as far as Col. Dunbar's party, which lay *six miles this side.* The officers were absolutely sacrificed by their unparalleled good behaviour; *advancing sometimes in bodies*, and sometimes *separately*, hoping *by such example* to engage the soldiers *to follow them*, but to no purpose. The general had five horses killed under him, and at last received a wound through his right arm into his lungs, of which he died, the 13th instant. Mr. Washington had two horses shot under him, and his clothes *shot through in several places*, behaving the whole time with the greatest courage and resolution. Gen. Braddock, having found it impracticable to advance with the whole convoy from the Little meadows, therefore, went forward with the above twelve hundred men; leaving Colonel Dunbar with the main body behind, with orders to join him *as soon as possible.* Happy it was that this disposal of them was made, else we had starved, or fallen by the enemy—as *numbers* would not have been useful." [They had along "a detachment of sailors" from the fleet! The fight "lasted three hours,"—so said many witnesses. The wagoners and pack-horse men made a quick retreat, especially from Dunbar's regiment. I saw a list of a dozen deserters from Braddock's army *before* the defeat, and the list declared, that some of them exposed his fewness of the advance number, and also his bad appointments; thereby intending to encourage the assault of the French and Indians. Their names were given.]

A letter from Col. James Burd, employed by the province to direct the opening of the military road for Braddock's army, dated 25th July, 1755, says, " We received an express from Governor Jones, from Fort Cumberland, giving us an account of Gen. Braddock's defeat and death, &c. Whereupon I went on there to confer with Col. Dunbar, and to take his orders, &c. He told me, at dinner, the facts in the case of the battle, &c., so that I might communicate them to your honour, to wit: A small body of French and Indians, say five hundred, and no more was ever on the ground, discovered on the 9th instant by the guides at a small run, called Frazier's run, seven miles this side of Fort du Quesne, being on the side of a hill on the Monongahela. Information was immediately given, when the general marched the troops and formed them. The battle began at noon day, and lasted three hours. The enemy kept behind trees and logs of wood, and cut down our troops as fast as they could advance. The soldiers then insisted much to be allowed to take to the trees, which the general denied, and stormed much, calling them cowards, and even went so far as to strike them with his own sword for attempting the trees. Our flankers, and many of our soldiers, that took to the trees, were cut off from (by) the fire of our own line, as they fired their platoons wherever they saw a smoke or fire. The *one half* of the army engaged never saw the enemy; particularly Captain Waggoner, of the Virginia forces, who marched eighty men up to take possession of a hill; on the top of the hill there lay a large tree of five feet diameter, which he intended to make a bulwark of. He marched up to the log with the loss only of three men killed, and all the time, his soldiers carried their firelocks shouldered; when they came to the log they began to fire upon the enemy; but as soon as their fire was discovered by our line, they fired from our line upon him, so that he was obliged to retreat down the hill, and brought off with him only thirty of his men out of eighty. And in this manner were our troops chiefly destroyed! The general had five horses killed under him, and was at last shot through the belly, and is buried across the road. His papers, and £75,000 in money, are all fallen into the hands of the enemy. The loss in killed and wounded is seven hundred, and about forty officers. Col. Dunbar retreated with fifteen hundred effective men. He destroyed fifty thousand pounds of powder, all his provisions, and buried his mortars and shells, &c. He had no horses with which to bring off any thing."

Another account from Winchester, Virginia, says, the Virginia officers and troops behaved like men, and died like soldiers. Out of three companies scarcely thirty men came out of the field! Captain Peyronay, and all his officers, were killed! Captain Polson was killed, and his company nearly all shared the same fate,—for *only one* escaped! Captain Stewart, and his light-horse, behaved gallantly, having twenty-five of his twenty-nine men killed!

A list of killed and wounded says, 456 killed, 421 wounded, 583 safe, total 1460 "in action *at Frazer's plantation*, the 9th July." What seems remarkable is, that all the wagoners from Lancaster and York counties returned home *but two!* Col. Dunbar got safe to Philadelphia, and encamped at Society hill, (*i. e.* Southwark,) on the 1st of September, 1755.

September 5th, 1755, it is published that the Virginia troops are to be increased to one thousand men, "under Col. Washington."

Old William Butler, of Philadelphia, whom I saw in May, 1833, in his hundred and fourth year, and who had been in the Braddock expedition, told me he was twenty-four years of age at the time he joined the Pennsylvania Greens, (faced with buff,) in Philadelphia. They were joined by the Jersey Blues, faced with red. The whole combined force was encamped in the woods then along Fifth street from Race street southward. The whole expedition of twenty-five hundred men passed through Germantown, and arrived the third day at the present Reading, where they divided and took different routes; while there at night, could see the light of the Indian fires on the mountains near them. They crossed the Schuylkill four times before getting to the mouth of the Little Schuylkill. From thence they cut their way through the "Pine swamp," so called, and made corduroy roads for the wagons; while there could hear wolves and bears; went thence to fort Augusta and Shamokin. That must have been one of the routes of that day, because C. F. Post, in his journal, says he went by that route to Fort du Quesne in 1758. They had Indian guides and followed their leadings towards Fort du Quesne.

At the time of the action, he was just off duty, near to Washington's tent. Near there, he saw Generals Braddock, Forbes and Grant talking, and Braddock *calling* out to Captain Green, to clear the bushes ahead, by opening a range with his artillery. Then Washington came out, put his two thumbs up into the arm pits of his vest, made a little circle, and came into their presence, and said, "General, be assured, if you even cut away the bushes, your enemy can make enough of them artificially to answer their purposes of shelter and concealment; it will not answer." Braddock upon hearing this, turning to his officers, said, sneeringly, "What think you of this, from a young hand—from a beardless boy!"—then but twenty-two years of age. I did not pursue this conversation any further on this point. He did not know of Braddock's having a white handkerchief tied over his hat. He was a great user of snuff, loose in a pocket! a man of middle stature and thick set.

On 23d December, 1833, I again saw William Butler, quite well still, and gleaned the following additional facts. Generals Forbes and Grant did arrive at Philadelphia, but Colonel Dunbar, a Scotchman, arrived at Baltimore. Washington had the charge of four hundred riflemen. The columns of the Pennsylvania and New Jersey lines, went in a more northern road, than the British division of regulars, after they divided at Reading. I noticed that he did not *now* seem to remember Colonel Grum, of the Virginia troops, as being colonel over Major Washington—said Washington was tall, slim and beardless—his uniform was *blue* and cocked hat. I questioned *when* they joined again. It was but two days before the battle. The lines were never in same track—were a day's march off—cut their own roads and made bridges; but chiefly went by Indian guides and Indian *tracks.* I asked him particularly *who* killed Braddock, and he answered promptly one *Fawcett*, brother of one whom Braddock had just killed in a passion; this last, who killed Braddock, was in the ranks as a non-commissioned officer; the former was a brave major or colonel, and by birth an Irishman. The soldier shot Braddock in the back, and this man, he said, he saw again in 1830, at or near Carlisle, where he was for three months, at the sickness and death of his daughter. His family confirmed this fact. His wife was by, aged eighty-three years—married sixty years. I see, too, that I have preserved a Millerstown Gazette notice in 1830, of the above meeting, and the name of Fawcett is there given also—a strong coincidence. Millerstown is near Carlisle.

The Millerstown Gazette, of 1830, speaks of the aforenamed Butler being there, and being in company with an aged soldier in their town, who had also been in Braddock's defeat, and that these two old soldiers concurred in saying that Braddock was shot by Fawcett.

A writer in the Christian Advocate—a minister, writing from the place, says "the old man died at the age of one hundred and fourteen years in 1828, who killed Braddock," and at same time, he confirms the other fact, of his brother being killed by Braddock. He lived at Laurel hill.

It is said that when the officers of Braddock's broken army got to Philadelphia, and rested there for a season, they were cruelly severe to their men, giving vent to their spleen and chagrin by beating the soldiers daily. It was a daily sight to see a dozen a day tied up and whipped; and even in the ranks the officers caned their men.

But in addition to the preceding, I may add the information I received from Billy Brown, a black man, whom I saw at Frankford, Philadelphia county, about the year 1826, in the ninety-third year of his age—possessed of an observing mind and good memory. He was present in that memorable fight as servant to Colonel Brown, of the Irish regiment, and was most of the time near the person of General Braddock. He said his character was obstinate and profane. He confirmed the idea, that he was shot by an American, because he had killed his brother. He said that none seemed to care for it: on the contrary, they thought Braddock had some sinister design, *for no balls were aimed at him!* He kept *on foot*, and had *all the time* his hat bound across the top and under his chin *with his white handkerchief*. They suspected that the white emblem was a token of his understanding with the French. He told me that Washington came up to him in the fight, and fell on his knees, to beseech him to allow him to use three hundred of his men in tree-fighting, and that the general cursed him and said, "I've a mind to run you through the body," and swearing out—"We'll sup to-day in Fort du Quesne, or else in hell!" I have full confidence in the words of Billy as far as they went, because he seemed incapable of intentional fraud, and was beside a religious man, of the Methodist profession; but above all, he had been in after life seven years a servant with General Washington, and that circumstance must have more deeply impressed the facts *as they were*, at their *first* seeing them. Braddock was shot, he said, through the shoulder into the breast, and lived some two or three days. The only words he ever uttered after his fall were: "Is it possible;"—"all is over!"

"A letter of Isaac Norris, speaker of assembly, of the date of November, 1755, to R. Charles, agent of the province in London says one of the Indian chiefs, afterwards in Philadelphia, before the governor and council, said, "We must let you know it was the pride and ignorance of that great general. He is now dead, but he was a bad man when alive. He looked on us as dogs, and would never hearken to our advice, even when we wished to tell him the danger he was in *with his soldiers.* For that reason many of our warriors left him, and would not be under his command."

In connexion with the above, I may add, that I saw the memorandum of a letter which "Major Washington" had written to the governor of Virginia, saying that the Virginians behaved bravely, but have suffered dreadfully. Many of his officers were wounded, and himself had *four bullet holes* in his clothes, and two horses shot under him! At a later period an Indian chief declared, that the Great Spirit must have reserved Washington for something important in after life, because he had aimed several shots at him without visible effect.

Braddock, after his wound, was carried forty miles and buried in the centre of the road, seven miles east of the present town of Union, and close to the northern side of the National road. The road was chosen, and the carriages and horses made to make their tracks over the grave, to prevent its discovery by the enemy. Since that day, it has never found a friend to give it a more distinguished sepulchre. The truth is, he was not sufficiently popular. He gave his chief offence to his men by not suffering them to fire as they saw opportunity, or even when aimed at, but required all firing to be done in platoons, as has been said.

The Newburyport Herald, of 1842, declares its acquaintance with Daniel Adams, an old soldier of that place, aged 82, who confirms the shooting of Braddock by his own followers. He learned the fact from Capt. Illsley of Newbury, who told him that he became acquainted with one of Braddock's soldiers soon afterwards, (under Sir William Johnston,) who was present at the circumstance. He stated that the principal officers had previously advised a retreat, which the General pertinaciously refused; that after nearly all the principal officers had been shot down, he was approached by a captain to renew the advice, whom he forthwith shot down. Upon seeing this, a lieutenant, brother of the captain, immediately shot Braddock. Several of the soldiers saw the act, but said nothing. Braddock wore a coat of mail in front, which turned balls fired in front; but he was shot in the back, and the ball was found stopped in front by the coat of mail! The editor pledged himself for the truthfulness of the man who told the facts.

Col. James Smith, of Bourbon, Kentucky, once an Indian captive, had been in his early days employed as a province man from Pennsylvania, to cut a wagon road, (in a party of three hundred men,) from Fort Loudon, to unite with Braddock's road near the Turkey foot, or three forks of Yohagana. He and his companion being alone, near Bedford, were fired at; his friend was killed, and himself taken prisoner. The Indians were from Fort du Quesne, and set out to return thither. When near it they gave the Indian shout, which was answered by the firelocks of all the Indians and

French. He had there to run the Indian gauntlet—suffered terribly thereby, and fell and fainted. When he recovered he found himself in the Fort, attended by a surgeon. They then exacted of him what they could gather of Braddock's position, force, &c. He was then befriended by an Indian who adopted him, and who soon informed Mr. Smith that they had daily knowledge of the particulars of the advance of Braddock. While at the Fort he saw the Indians and French go off to meet him—they seemed to be about four hundred men in all, as if enough to encounter the three hundred men before named. After some time, a rumor arrived to say that Braddock would be entirely cut off—that they had *surrounded* his force, and were themselves completely concealed behind trees and gullies, keeping up a constant fire; that they were falling in heaps, and if they did not *take the river* which was the only gap, and so make their escape, there would not be a man left alive at sundown! By-and-by, Indians and French were seen coming in with spoils—such as caps, canteens, bayonets, and bloody scalps; afterwards came in wagon horses, and every Indian man having his bloody scalps. Towards sundown a party came in having a dozen prisoners stripped naked; these they soon after burned to death on the river bank opposite to the fort. From the best information he could gain, there were only seven Indians and four French killed, while five hundred British lay dead on the field, besides what were killed *in the river* on their retreat. The day after the battle the artillery was brought to the fort—several of the Indians were seen moving about decked off in the dress of the British officers and men, most grotesquely proud.

A private letter to Governor Morris from Sir William Shirley, the secretary of General Braddock, conveyed by Sergeant Peters from the frontiers, before the battle, speaks of the general as "most judiciously chosen for being disqualified for his service, in almost every respect." "He may be brave and honest, but I am greatly disgusted at seeing an expedition so ill concerted originally in England, so ill appointed, and so improperly conducted since in America."

Colonel Dunbar, in a letter, says that Braddock had three horses killed under him, and was at last shot through the belly. He also said, that "by some mismanagement we had not an Indian with us, and that General Braddock could not get above eight or nine to attend him; from which circumstance he laboured under many inconveniences."

Scarooyady, an Indian chief who had been engaged to assist in the expedition, said by his interpeter, C. Weiser, to Governor Morris, that "it was the pride and ignorance of that great general that caused the defeat. He looked upon us as dogs, and would not hear any hing that was said to him by us. We often endeavoured to advise him, but he never appeared pleased with us, and *that* was the reason that many of our warriors left him, and would not be under his com mand. They were unfit to fight in the woods."

The province however, left to itself, soon showed what it could do by its own people,—as was evinced in sending out Colonel John Armstrong in 1756, with only four companies, viz.: Captains Hamilton, Mercer, Ward and Potter—these, with some frontier volunteers, made out to reach Kittaning, or Shingass town, only twenty miles above Du Quesne, (the former aim of Braddock,) and there surprised and destroyed the whole settlement, and rescued many prisoners. It was a glorious *contrast* to the other inglorious failure.

In 1758, there occurred another joyous occasion under General Forbes, the British general who made his way out to Fort Du Quesne with twelve hundred men, without mishap or molestation, for it so happened, that by the friendly treaties before made at Easton and otherwise, the Indians had become so detached from the French interest, as to leave them at the Fort to their own resources. When Forbes appeared, on the 24th of November, they *blew up* the place, and went off to their forts and settlements down the Mississippi. Under a sense of this great event, a day of public thanksgiving was appointed on the 28th of December, 1758. It was indeed a time of most hearty gratulation and cheering.

We may judge of the surprise of this unexpected good news, by the fact, that when General Forbes had advanced as far as Raystown camp, just one month preceding his triumph, he writes to the Governor as if he was then at the length of his means, and wanted, as he said, a supply of twelve hundred men to be disposed in necessary frontier garrisons—to be placed in forts, such as at Loyal Hanna, Cumberland, Raystown, Juniata, Littleton, Loudon, Frederick, Shippensburg and Carlisle—"as without these (says he) he could not secure the frontiers." But before he could be heard of again, and in the absence of all hostile Indians, behold, he gets to Pittsburg and finds the fort abandoned! Truly a lucky general, and a still more lucky province, to thus find also his calls for intermediate forts unnecessary! It was a joyful and happy result for a greatly disturbed and apprehensive people.

About the year 1770, the first settlers began to settle about Redstone Old Fort, on the Monongahela; where Capt. Michael Cressup made the *first house* of logs. The first emigration was principally from Maryland and Virginia; they supposed themselves at the time, as within the bounds of Virginia, and not of Pennsylvania, as has since been determined. In 1785, the town of *Brownsville* was laid out at this place, and great was the quantity of boats built there for the descent of the Ohio and Mississippi rivers.

Soon stores and houses began to be built, and then came the want of merchandise, all of which, including salt, was brought out on *pack horses*. These were generally led in divisions of twelve or fifteen horses, carrying about two hundred weight each, all going single file, and being managed by two men, one going before as the leader, and the other at the tail, to see after the safety of the packs, &c. These horses were all furnished with bells, which were kept from ringing during the day drive, but were set loose at night, when the horses were set free and permitted to feed and browse. The bells were intended as guides to direct to their " whereabout" in the morning. These western *carriers* were at first a great affair to their owners, as a money making concern; they starting, principally, from Hagerstown and Winchester. When *wagons* were first introduced, great was their hostility to them as an invasion of *their* rights. The first wagon load of goods which went west, went by that *southern route* (so called) that lay much along the tract of the present National road. It was the enterprise of Jacob Bowman, in the year 1789, a merchant who settled at Brownsville two years before—it was drawn by four horses, and drew about two thousand weight; the travel, going and coming, occupied about a month, and was done at an expense to the merchants of three dollars per hundred weight. Six horses since draw seven to eight thousand pounds, and go in a week, at one dollar per hundred weight.

Iron, being a matter of great importance, was first made by Isaac Meadson & Co., at Dunbar creek, fifteen miles from Brownsville.

In 1814 the *Enterprise steamer* was started, she being *the first* which descended and ascended the rivers to and from New Orleans.

In 1759, Col. Burd, with a command of two hundred men, was the first to open and cut a road from Braddock's road to the Monongahela river, where he erected a fort called Fort Burd. He passed his road along the base of Laurel hill, thence by the way of Coal run to Redstone creek, near the present Middletown.

The Indian name of Pittsburg was *Ménachkink*, a name given by them to it after it became a fort. It means with them an enclosed, confined spot of ground, such as a fort would make it.

Westward ho! Among those who have contributed their recollections of westward emigration, we may mention the facts recollected by the Hon. Judge S. Wilkeson, of Buffalo, on the Ohio. He, when young, started with his father's family from Carlisle, Pa., in the spring of 1784, to settle near the Ohio, in company with other families; and the incidents of his travel may be regarded as the picture of others, in general. His family consisted of his father, mother and three young children, with a bound boy of fourteen years of age. The road to be travelled in crossing the mountains, was scarcely practicable for wagons. Pack horses afforded almost the sole means used for transportation then, and for years after. They were provided with three horses: on one rode the mother, carrying her infant, with all the table furniture and cooking utensils; on another was packed the store of provisions, plough irons, and agricultural tools. [Even the irons for constructing mills were carried on horseback.] The third horse bore a pack saddle and two large creels, made of hickory withes in the manner of a crate, one over each side of the horse, in which were stowed the beds and bedding, and the wearing apparel. In the centre of these creels there was left a vacancy, just sufficient to admit a child in each, laced in, with their heads peeping out therefrom. Along with this company were one or more cows, which furnished them milk morning and evening. When arrived at the great mountains, the roads became extremely difficult of passage, being often along precipices, with a narrow path, where, if the horse stumbled or lost his balance, himself and burthen might be rolled down some hundreds of feet. Such paths were often crossed by many streams raised by melting snow and spring rains, and running in rapid current, in deep ravines. To these there were no bridges: great exposures and happy escapes were often occurring! When arrived, eventually, at their destination, and located in their log cabin and hastily made small clearing, they had to encounter the alarms and perils of Indian aggressions. Their men were occasionally shot, their horses stolen, and their children, if captured, were borne off and sold at Detroit, or in other cases, adopted.

Although pack horses have thus been named as the most in use, there were instances of horses and oxen being taken over these mountains drawing *wagons.* The people who went from New England in 1788, to settle at and near Muskingum, used in several cases such modes of conveyance. The "American Pioneer," an excellent work published at Cincinnati, gives several examples of such cases. Horses, four to a wagon, would progress about twenty-five miles a day; and six oxen, yoked two and two, would make a journey of twenty miles. The roads on the mountain sides were often cut into deep gullies on one side by rains, while the other was filled with blocks of sandstone. The descents were abrupt, and often not unlike the breaks in a flight of stone stairs. Some few wagons were provided with lock-chains for the wheels, but in most cases, the downward force was to be checked by heavy logs tied to the wagon, and trailing on the ground. On other occasions the road was so sideling, that it required the service of all the men, by the use of side stay ropes attached to the wagons, to keep them from turning over and falling down the mountain side. When they at last attained the Ohio, they were then to procure flat-boats in which to place their wagons and stores, and to lead their horses and oxen onward by land; going at the same time in continual watch and fear of hostile Indian surprises from the Ohio side of the river. When finally arrived, they had to depend for their safety upon log fort defences, into which they might run in cases of alarm.

In making such journeys to the west, of seven or eight weeks, they took as few articles of beds, bedding, and cooking utensils, as they could possibly do with. Their clothing and other goods were packed in wooden boxes fitted to the wagon,—the women, girls and children, would be placed inside and ride, except when they came to bad roads and mountains,—sometimes they would get scattered and create anxieties,—sometimes the horses, and sometimes the people were borne down with the current of water. None now can imagine with what dread such a long and arduous journey was then attempted from New England, and few now can have a just conception of how much they feared the ravages of wolves upon their few sheep, then held necessary for producing their clothing. The skins of the deer were often used for the wear of the men. These were arduous times for the women: they had every morning to go through wet woods and grass, sometimes a mile distant, to find their cows, by the tinkling of their bells, and to get them home for milking, for the subsistence of the family. In the mean time, the men had often to be off in considerable journeys after their straying horses, which continually showed a propensity *to leave* the wild country, and *to find their way back* from whence they came! This was a curious fact, but it was so. It might be mentioned, as a part of the scenes of western travel, that it was a common incident to meet, or to be overtaken by long strings of pack horses; those from the west bearing *peltry* and *ginseng*—the others going west, with *kegs* of spirits, *salt*, and packs of dry goods. This carrying *salt*, without which *white* people would have deemed any place uninhabitable, was an affair of great expense and concern, and which they have since *overcome* by their own inventions of *making salt*, nearer their own homes.

All these references to things past, and so fast receding from the contemplation and the view, are matters to be treasured up and *kept before the people*, for the same reasons that Virgil has inscribed the incidents in the voyage of Æneas from Troy to Italy—*they were the founders of a new state!* We must contemplate their hardihood and hardships with admiration and applause. They were a race of most daring energy of character and of fortitude—a race in every respect different from those who now occupy the same regions in opulence, ease, and splendour. Now, instead of the log house and wigwam, fine mansions exist—instead of the bark canoe, the tomahawk and scalping knife, steamboats and all the implements of comfort and convenience abound. Instead of the savage yell, the literary lecture, and the songs of Zion echo through the land. We have dwelt in a wonderful era, and have beheld amazing changes for good. Was ever people so blessed whose God is the Lord?

Frontier Towns.—Lancaster, Bethlehem, &c.

These now conspicuous and large inland towns, were long regarded in the early days of the province, as far remote in the Indian ranges and hunting grounds. The first inhabitants, who made "clearings and settlements" in those regions, were generally tolerated squatters, living rent free, for the purpose of forming a cordon, or defensive barrier, against any Indian surprise.

The earliest settlement in Lancaster, as a town, was induced by the expected advantages of the iron works near by. The first establishment of them commenced in 1726, under the enterprise of Mr. Kurtz. In 1728, the family of the Grubbs, as iron-masters, began their career; but the most extensive and successful of all was the late Robert Coleman, who amassed a great fortune thereby. Thi place was for many years pre-eminent for making and furnishing rifles for the western settlers and Indians. They also made and furnished pack-saddles for the carriers westward.

Where Lancaster now stands was once an Indian wigwam town; a hickory tree stood in its centre, not far from a spring; under this tree the councils met, and from one of these councils a deputation was once sent to confer with William Penn at Philadelphia. The Indian nation was called *Hickory*, as well as their town. When the whites began to build there, they still called it by the same name; and Gibson, at his inn, about the year 1722, had a hickory tree painted upon his sign. It was situated near where Slaymaker's hotel is now built, and the spring was in its cellar. The town, under the name of Lancaster, was not laid out until 1730; and the courts were not taken to it from Postlewaite, until the year 1734. In excavating the canal at the north side of the town, they came across the bones of the Indians massacred at the prisons, by the Paxton boys.

An Indian town once stood on a flat of land north-east of Hardwiche, the seat of William Coleman, Esq. A poplar tree was the emblem of the tribe, from whence their name was derived. Its location, and that of the town, was near the bank of the Conestoga. The Conestoga Indians were once numerous and influential. As early as 1701, we read of an embassy from Philadelphia "round about through the woods," to the "palace of the king," "where they were cordially received and well entertained at a considerable town." In the year 1721, Sir W. Keith, and his council and thirty gentlemen, went to Conestoga, to hold there a treaty with the heads of the Five Nations. An original deed from Wiggoneeheenah, of 1725, to Edmund Cartlidge, grants, "in behalf of the Delaware Indians concerned," the tract of land formerly his plantation, "lying in a turn of Conestoga creek, called Indian Point." Those Indians, under the general name of Conestogoes, continued to dwell along the Conestoga creek, until the year 1764, when fourteen of their number having been maliciously killed by the Irish settlers, the rest took shelter in Lancaster, and for their better security were placed under the bolts and bars of the prison; where, however, they were afterwards assailed and massacred—men, women and children—at midday, by an armed band of lawless ruffians, calling themselves the "Paxton boys!" The Roman Catholics, under the Jesuits, were the first who opened religious worship among the people.

In the year 1754, Lancaster had so much increased as to have then contained five hundred houses and two thousand inhabitants. A great proportion of them, then, were of German origin. The best lands of Lancaster county, and deemed, in general, the finest farms in the state, are those possessed by the German families.

Reading is of much later origin, and had, when it began, a very rapid progress—having, for instance, but one house there in 174 and in 1752 in contained one hundred and thirty dwellings! It was raised into alluring repute by the agents of the Penn-family, calling for settlers in it, as "a new town of great natural advantages of location, and destined to be a prosperous place."

The first hotel there was that of Conrad Weiser, seen in 1833, as the little white store of General Keim, on the corner of Callowhill and Penn streets, and since replaced by a great new house of fashion. It was at that place that Conrad Weiser, as Indian agent, used to deliver the Indian presents—there the war-song of the savage was sung, the war dance wound down, and the calamet of peace was smoked. The house was built earlier than the town. Lively and business like as is the present *Pottsville*, the man is now living there, in 1842, John Boyer by name, an old revolutionary soldier, now in his eighty-seventh year—born and reared at the present Schuylkill Haven, in which neighbourhood, he had often been engaged in resisting the predatory invasions of the Indians. The country around him was long a wilderness, and was often the scene of bloody massacres, much of which he had seen with his own eyes.

An old Indian war-path leading from the tribes north of the Susquehanna, crossed the mountains at Pottsville, and the few settlers who had braved all danger, and had pitched their cabins in the midst of such perils, were forced to struggle desperately at times, to save the scalps of their families from the knife. Fort Henry once stood at the head of the Swatara, at the foot of Kittatiny.

Bethlehem and Easton, formed the frontier towns on the north. The former was begun in 1743, under Count Zinzendorf, by forming there his Moravian town. As late as the year 1755, the inhabitants of the neighbouring country were driven in from their farms to the towns of Bethlehem and Easton, filled with panic and dread from marauding Indians! It was near to Lehighton, that there then stood Fort Allen, fronting on the Lehigh opposite to the mouth of Mahony creek, where the garrison was surprised and massacred by Indians. About the same time, Captain Wetherhold, who commanded a scouting party, and who used to make Allentown and Bethlehem his places of rendezvous, was surprised about six miles from the latter place, and he and his whole party were shot and scalped. On the same day a party, with one Henry Jenks, was also surprised and cut off. There was a fort there, made of logs—in command of Colonel Burd, who built his house opposite to it—the same now held by Peter Newhard, Esq., member of congress. The main street, on which it stands, now runs over the site of that fort. About the year, 1765, there used to be several skirmishes thereabout with the Indians. Mr. Newhard's father had told P. N. of these things. As late as the year 1755, the year of Braddock's defeat and alarm, there was a block-house at Harris' ferry, the present Harrisburg, and hostile Indians prowled about Shearman's valley, not far off, committing sundry depredations. Since the war of the revolution, such is the march of improvement, that Harrisburg is made the seat of government, other towns are erected in every direction, and distant places are made nigh to us in effect, by numerous turnpikes, rail-roads, and canals!

It strongly marks the rapid progress of inland improvement, to say, that several members of a family of the name of *Gilbert* are now living, who dwelt near the Lehigh, on this side of the present celebrated Mauch Chunk coal mines, who were captured in open day by a band of hostile Indians, in the year 1778, and borne off unmolested to the Niagara frontier. One of the females so captured, I have seen and conversed with only a few months before the present writing. She is a Friend, dwelling in Byberry. They then travelled through a wilderness country, unperceived by any white inhabitants, five hundred miles in twenty-six days. Now splendid stage-coaches roll over graded turnpikes, and pass through numerous prosperous towns and villages, through all the intermediate space!

A MS. journal, which I have seen, of C. F. Post, an Indian interpreter and agent, who died at Germantown, in 1785, and who made an excursion from that place, in 1758, to the Susquehanna river with sundry Indians, shows incidentally how very wild and Indian-like the intermediate country must then have been. His first stage of one day from Bethlehem was to *Hay's;* the next day to *Fort Allen*, where he met Indians from *Wyoming;* thence he went to *Fort Augusta*, on the Susquehanna, where he met sundry Indians from *Diehogo*, now called Tioga, at the head of the same river, and saw also some Indians from *Shamokin.* Coursing along the river, he came to *Wekeeponall*, and at night rested at *Queenashawakee.* The next day they crossed the river *at the Big island*, above Williamsport. In the region on the opposite side, westward, they came to several places where they saw two poles, painted red, set up as pillars, to which the Indians tied their prisoners for the night. Now how different are all those regions, brought about in a term of sixty years? Persons were lately alive in *Tulpehocken*, near Womelsdorf, who saw in that country the dreadful Indian massacre in 1755. I saw myself some that had been captured then

For further facts, see Appendix, p. 528.

INDIANS.

> "A swarthy tribe—
> Slipped from the secret hand of Providence,
> They come, we see not how, nor know we whence:
> That seem'd created on the spot—though born,
> In transatlantic climes, and thither brought,
> By paths as covert as the birth of thought!"

THERE is in the fate of these unfortunate beings much to awaken our sympathy, and much to disturb the sobriety of our judgment much in their characters to incite our involuntary admiration. What can be more melancholy than their history! By a law of their nature, they seem destined to a slow but sure extinction. Every where, at the approach of the white man, they fade away. We hear the rustling of their footsteps, like that of the withered leaves of autumn; and themselves, like "the sear and yellow leaf," are gone for ever!

Once the smoke of their wigwams, and the fires of their councils, rose in every valley, from the ocean to the Mississippi and the lakes. The shouts of victory and the war-dance rang through the mountains and the glades. The light arrows and the deadly tomahawk whistled through the forest; and the hunter's trace, and the dark encampment, startled the wild beasts in their lairs. The warriors stood forth in their glory. The young listened to songs of other days. The mothers played with their infants, and gazed on the scene with warm hopes of the future. Braver men never lived—truer men never drew the bow. They had courage and fortitude, and sagacity and perseverance, beyond most of the human race. They were inured, and capable of sustaining every peril, and surmounting every obstacle for sweet country and home. But with all this, inveterate destiny has unceasingly driven them hence!

> "Forced from the land that gave them birth,
> They dwindle from the face of earth!"

If they had the vices of savage life, they had the virtues also. They were true to their country, their friends and their homes. If they forgave not injury under misconceptions of duty, neither did they forget kindness—

> "Faithful alike to friendship or to hate."

If their vengeance was terrible, their fidelity and generosity were unconquerable also. Their love, like their hate, stopped not on this side the grave. But where are they now? Perished! consumed!

> "The glen or hill,
> Their cheerful whoop has ceased to thrill!"

The wasting pestilence has not alone done this mighty work; no, nor famine, nor war. There has been a mightier power—a moral canker which hath eaten into their vitals—a plague which the touch of the baser part of our white men has communicated—a poison which betrayed them into a lingering ruin. Already the last feeble remnants of the race are preparing for their journey beyond the Mississippi. I see them leave their long cherished homes; "few and faint, yet fearless still," they turn to take a last look of their deserted village, a last look at the graves of their fathers. They shed no tears; they utter no cries; they heave no groans. There is something in their hearts which surpasses speech; there is something in their looks, not of vengeance or submission, but of hard necessity, which stifles both—which chokes all utterance—which has no aim or method. It is courage absorbed in despair.*

If such be the traces we may draw of Indian character, being ourselves the judges, what might it not be, if told by themselves, had they but our art of letters and the aid of an eloquent press! Few or none among themselves can tell their tale of "wrong and outrage." Yet a solitary case does exist, which, while it shows their capability of mental improvement, shows also, in affecting terms, their just claims to our generosity and kindness.

The beautiful and energetic letter, of April, 1824, to the people and congress of the United States, by the Cherokee natives and representatives at Washington city, has some fine touches of refined eloquence to this effect—saying, of their communications, they have been "the lonely and unassisted efforts of the poor Indian; for we are not so fortunate as to have such help—wherefore this letter and every other letter was not only written but dictated by an Indian. The white man seldom comes forth in our defence. Our rights are in our own keeping, and the proofs of our loneliness, of our bereaved and helpless state, unknown to the eye of prejudice, having set us upon our resources, is known to those benevolent white brothers who came to our help with letters, and the lights of civilization and Christianity. Our letters (we repeat it) are our own, and if they are thought too refined for 'savages,' let the white man take it for proof, that, with proper assistance, Indians can think and write for themselves." Signed—John Ross, and three others.

The Indians were always the friends of Miquon, of Onas—of our forefathers! It was their greatest pleasure to cultivate mutual good will and kindness.—"None ever entered the cabin of Logan hungry, and he gave him no meat; or cold, or naked, and he gave him no clothes!" Grateful hearts must cherish kindly recollections of a too often injured race. We are therefore disposed, as Pennsylvanians, to treasure up some few of the facts least known of them, in the times by-gone of our annals.

We begin with their primitive character and habits as seen by

* These introductory sentiments are generally from the leading ideas of Judge Story.

William Penn, and told in his letter of August, 1683, to the Free Society of Traders.

"The natives I shall consider in their persons, language, manners, religion and government, with my sense of their original. For their persons, they are generally tall, straight, well-built, and of singular proportion; they tread strong and clever, and mostly walk with a lofty chin. Of complexion, black, but by design; as the Gypsies in England. They grease themselves with bear's fat clarified; and using no defence against sun, or weather, their skins must needs be swarthy. Their eye is little and black, not unlike a straight-looked Jew. The thick lip, and flat nose, so frequent with the East Indians and blacks, are not common to them: for I have seen as comely European-like faces among them, of both sexes, as on your side the sea; and truly an Italian complexion hath not much more of the white, and the noses of several of them have as much of the Roman.

"Their language is lofty, yet narrow; but, like the Hebrew, in signification full; like short-hand, in writing, one word serveth in the place of three, and the rest are supplied by the understanding of the hearer: imperfect in their tenses, wanting in their moods, participles, adverbs, conjunctions, interjections. I have made it my business to understand it, that I might not want an interpreter, on any occasion; and I must say, that I know not a language spoken in Europe, that hath words of more sweetness, or greatness in accent and emphasis, than theirs.

"Of their customs and manners, there is much to be said; I will begin with children; so soon as they are born, they wash them in water; and while very young, and in cold weather, they plunge them in the rivers, to harden and embolden them. The children will go very young, at nine months commonly; if boys, they go a fishing till ripe for the woods; which is about fifteen; then they hunt, and after having given some proofs of their manhood, by a good return of skins, they may marry; else it is a shame to think of a wife. The girls stay with their mothers, and help to hoe the ground, plant corn, and carry burdens; and they do well to use them to that young, which they must do when they are old; for the wives are the true servants of the husbands; otherwise the men are very affectionate to them.

"When the young women are fit for marriage, they wear something upon their heads, for an advertisement, but so as their faces are hardly to be seen, but when they please. The age they marry at if women, is about thirteen and fourteen; if men, seventeen and eighteen; they are rarely elder.

"Their houses are mats, or barks of trees, set on poles, in the fashion of an English barn; but out of the power of the winds; for they are hardly higher than a man; they lie on reeds, or grass. In travel they lodge in the woods, about a great fire, with the mantle of duffils they wear by day wrapt about them, and a few boughs stuck round them

"Their diet is maize, or Indian corn, divers ways prepared; sometimes roasted in the ashes; sometimes beaten and boiled with water; which they call *homine;* they also make cakes, not unpleasant to eat. They have likewise several sorts of beans and pease, that are good nourishment; and the woods and rivers are their larder.

"If a European comes to see them, or calls for lodging at their house or wigwam, they give him the best place and first cut. If they come to visit us, they salute us with an *Itah*; which is as much as to say, *Good be to you*, and set them down; which is mostly on the ground, close to their heels, their legs upright; it may be they speak not a word, but observe all passages. If you give them any thing to eat or drink, well; for they will not ask; and be it little or much, if it be with kindness, they are well pleased, else they go away sullen, but say nothing.

"They are great concealers of their own resentments; brought to it, I believe, by the revenge that hath been practised among them.

"But in liberality they excel; nothing is too good for their friend: give them a fine gun, coat, or other thing, it may pass twenty hands before it sticks; light of heart, strong affections, but soon spent. The most merry creatures that live, feast and dance perpetually; they never have much, nor want much: wealth circulateth like the blood; all parts partake; and though none shall want what another hath, yet exact observers of property. They care for little; because they want but little; and the reason is, a little contents them. In this they are sufficiently revenged on us: if they are ignorant of our pleasures, they are also free from our pains. We sweat and toil to live; their pleasure feeds them; I mean their hunting, fishing and fowling; and this table is spread every where. They eat twice a day, morning and evening; their seats and table are the ground.

"In sickness impatient to be cured, and for it give any thing, especially for their children, to whom they are extremely natural: they drink at those times a *Tesan*, or decoction of some roots in spring-water; and if they eat any flesh, it must be of the female of any creature. If they die, they bury them with their apparel, be they man or woman, and the nearest of kin fling in something precious with them, as a token of their love: their mourning is blacking of their faces, which they continue for a year: they are choice of the graves of their dead; for lest they should be lost by time, and fall to common use, they pick off the grass that grows upon them, and heap up the fallen earth with great care and exactness.

"These poor people are under a dark night in things relating to religion, to be sure the tradition of it; yet they believe in a God and immortality, without the help of metaphysics; for they say, "There is a Great King that made them, who dwells in a glorious co ıntry to the southward of them; and that the souls of the good shall go thither, where they shall live again."—Their worship consists of two parts, sacrifice and cantico: their sacrifice is their first fruits; the first and fattest buck they kill goeth to the fire, where he is all burnt, with a mournful ditty of him that performeth the ceremony, but with such marvellous fervency and labour of body, that he will even sweat to a foam. The other part is their cantico, performed by round dances, sometimes words, sometimes songs, then shouts, two being in the middle that begin, and by singing and drumming on a board, direct the chorus: their postures in the dance are very antic, and differing, but all keep measure. This is done with equal earnestness and labour, but great appearance of joy. In the fall, when the corn cometh in, they begin to feast one another. There have been two great festivals already, to which all come that will: I was at one myself.

"Their government is by kings, which they call *Sachama*, and those by succession, but always of the mother's side: for instance, the children of him that is now king will not succeed, but his brother by the mother, or the children of his sister, whose sons (and after them the children of her daughters) will reign; for no woman inherits: the reason they render for this way of descent is, that their issue may not be spurious.

"Every king hath his council, and that consists of all the old and wise men of his nation; which perhaps is two hundred people: nothing of moment is undertaken, be it war, peace, selling of land, or traffic, without advising with them; and which is more, with the young men too. It is admirable to consider how powerful the kings are, and yet how they move by the breath of their people. I have had occasion to be in council with them upon treaties for land, and to adjust the terms of trade. Their order is thus: the king sits in the middle of a half moon, and hath his council, the old and wise, on each hand: behind them, or at a little distance, sit the younger fry in the same figure.

"The justice they have is pecuniary: in case of any wrong or evil fact, be it murder itself, they atone by feasts, and presents of their Wampum, which is proportioned to the quality of the offence or person injured, or of the sex they are of: for in case they kill a woman, they pay double, and the reason they render is, 'that she breedeth children, which men cannot do.' It is rare that they fall out, if sober; and if drunk, they forgive it, saying, 'it was the drink, and not the man, that abused them.'

"We have agreed, that in all differences between us, six of each side shall end the matter: do not abuse them, but let them have justice, and you win them: the worst is, that they are the worse for the Christians, who have propagated their vices, and yielded them tradition for it, and not for good things.

"For their original, I am ready to believe them of the Jewish race; I mean, of the stock of the *ten tribes*, and that for the following reasons: first, they were to go to 'a land, not *planted* or *known*,' which, to be sure, Asia and Africa were, if not Europe; and He that intended that extraordinary judgment upon them, might make the passage not uneasy to them, as it is not impossible in itself, from the easternmost parts of Asia, to the westernmost of America. In the next place, I find them of like countenance, and their children of so lively resemblance, that a man would think himself in Duke's place, or Berry street, in London, when he seeth them. But this is not all: they agree in *rites;* they reckon by *moons;* they offer their *first-fruits;* they have a kind of *feast* of *tabernacles;* they are said to lay their *altar* upon *twelve stones;* their *mourning* a *year*, *customs* of *women*, with many things that do not now occur."

Gabriel Thomas, in his description of Pennsylvania, as written in 1698, says, "The natives of this country are supposed by most people, to have been of the ten scattered tribes, for they resemble the Jews in the make of their persons and tincture of their complexions. They observe new moons; offer their first-fruits to a Maneto or supposed deity, whereof they have two—one, as they fancy, above—(good) another, below—(bad.) They have a kind of feast of tabernacles, laying their altars upon twelve stones. They observe a sort of mourning twelve months; customs of women, and many other rites.* They are very charitable to one another—the lame and the blind living as well as the best. They are also very kind and obliging to the Christians. They have among them many curious physical wild herbs, roots and drugs of great virtue, which makes the Indians, in their right use, as able doctors as any in Europe."

Oldmixon says there were, in 1684, as many as ten nations of Indians in the province of Pennsylvania, comprising 6,000 in number.

William Penn held a great Indian treaty, in 1701, with forty Indian chiefs, who came from many nations to Philadelphia to settle the friendship. The same year he had also a great Indian council at Pennsbury, to take leave of him, to renew covenants, &c.

Mrs. Mary Smith's MS. account of the first settlement at Burlington, (herself an eye-witness,) thus speaks of the Indians there in 1678, saying—"The Indians, very numerous and very civil, brought them corn, venison, &c., and bargained also for their land. It was said that an old Indian king spoke prophetically before his death, and said the English should increase and the Indians should decrease!"

Jacob Taylor's Almanac of 1743 relates, that "An Indian of the province, looking at the great comet of 1680, and being asked what he thought was the meaning of that prodigious appearance, answered —'*It signifies, we Indians shall melt away, and this country be inhabited by another sort of people.*' This prediction the Indian

---

* It is scarcely possible to read these coincidences of opinion with Penn's, which precede it, without thinking of Dr. Boudinet's Star in the West, and his efforts to prove them Jewish.

INDIAN TREATY.—Page 153.

NEDOWAWAY LEAVES THE SUSQUEHANNA.—Page 181.

delivered very grave and positive to a Dutchman of good reputation near Chester, who told it to one, now living, of full veracity."

I have compiled from the work of the Swedish traveller, Professor Kalm, his notices of our Indians preceding the year 1748, to wit:

"*Of their Food and Mode of Living.*—Maize, (Indian corn,) some kinds of beans and melons, made up the sum of the Indians' gardening. Their chief support arose from hunting and fishing. Besides these, the oldest Swedes related that the Indians were accustomed to get nourishment from the following wild plants, to wit:

"Hopniss, so called by the Indians, and also by the Swedes, (the Glycine apios of Linnæus,) they found in the meadows. The roots resembled potatoes, and were eaten boiled, instead of bread.

"Katniss, so called by the Indians and Swedes, (a kind of Sagittaria sagittifolia,) was found in low wet ground, had oblong roots nearly as large as the fist; this they boiled or roasted in the ashes. Several Swedes said they liked to eat of it in their youth. The hogs liked them much, and made them very scarce. Mr. Kalm, who ate of them, thought they tasted like potatoes. When the Indians first saw turnips they called them katniss too.

"Taw-ho, so called by the Indians and Swedes, (the Arum virginicum, or Wake-robin, and poisonous,) grew in moist grounds, and swamps; they ate the root of it. The roots grew to the thickness of a man's thigh; and the hogs rooted them up and devoured them eagerly. The Indians destroyed their poisonous quality by baking them. They made a long trench in the ground, put in the roots and covered them with earth, and over them they made a great fire. They tasted somewhat like potatoes.

"Taw-kee, so called by the Indians and Swedes, (the Orontium aquaticum,) grew plentifully in moist low grounds. Of these they used the seeds, when dried. These they boiled repeatedly to soften them, and then they ate somewhat like peas. When they got butter or milk from the Swedes, they boiled them together.

"Bilberries or whortleberries (a species of Vaccinium) was a common diet among the Indians. They dried them in the sun, and kept them packed as close as currants.

"*Of their Implements for Domestic or Field Use.*—The old boilers or kettles of the Indians were either made of clay, or of different kinds of pot stone—(Lapis ollaris.) The former consisted of a dark clay, mixed with grains of white sand or quartz, and probably burnt in the fire. Many of these kettles had two holes in the upper margin; on each side one, through which they passed a stick, and held therewith the kettle over the fire. It is remarkable that none of these pots have been found glazed either inside or outside. A few of the old Swedes could remember to have seen the Indians use such pots to boil their meat in. They were made sometimes of a greenish, and sometimes of a grayish pot stone; and some were made of another species of a pyrous stone. They were very thin. Mr. Bartram, the botanist, showed him an earthen pot, which had been dug up at a place where the Indians had lived—on the outside it was much ornamented. Mr. Bartram had also several broken pieces. They were all made of mere clay, in which were mixed, according to the convenience of the makers, pounded shells of snails and muscles, or of crystals found in the mountains. It was plain they did not burn them much, because they could be cut up with a knife. Since the Europeans have come among them they disuse them, and have even lost the art of making them.—[All these remarks much accord with the speculations which I have preserved on this subject, respecting the potteries found in the *tumilii* in the western countries.]

"The hatchets of the Indians were made of stone, somewhat of the shape of a wedge. This was notched round the biggest end, and to this they affixed a split stick for a handle, bound round with a cord. These hatchets could not serve, however, to cut any thing like a tree; their means, therefore, of getting trees for canoes, &c., was to put a great fire round the roots of a big tree to burn it off, and with a swab of rags on a pole to keep the tree constantly wet above until the fire below burnt it off. When the tree was down, they laid dry branches on the trunk and set fire to it, and kept swabbing that part of the tree which they did not want to burn; thus the tree burnt a hollow in one place only; when burnt enough, they chipped or scraped it smooth inside with their hatchets, or sharp flints, or sharp shells.

"Instead of knives, they used little sharp pieces of flints or quartz, or a piece of sharpened bone.

"At the end of their arrows they fastened narrow angulated pieces of stone; these were commonly flints or quartz.—[I have such, as well as hatchets, in my possession.] Some made use of the claws of birds and beasts.

"They had stone pestles of about a foot long and five inches in thickness; in these they pounded their maize. Many had only wooden pestles. The Indians were astonished beyond measure when they saw the first wind-mills to grind grain. They were, at first, of opinion that not the wind, but spirits within them, gave them their momentum. They would come from a great distance, and set down for days near them, to wonder and admire at them.

"The old tobacco pipes were made of clay or pot stone, or serpentine stone—the tube thick and short. Some were made better, of a very fine red pot stone, and were seen chiefly with the sachems. Some of the old Dutchmen at New York preserved the tradition that the first Indians seen by the Europeans made use of copper for their tobacco pipes, got from the second river near Elizabethtown. In confirmation of this, it was observed that the people met with holes worked in the mountains, out of which some copper had been taken; and they even found some tools which the Indians probably used for the occasion. They used birds' claws instead of fishing-hooks. The Swedes saw them succeed in this way."

The Indians made their ropes, bridles, and twine for nets, out of a wild weed, growing abundantly in old corn-fields, commonly called Indian hemp—(i. e. Linum virginianum.) The Swedes used to buy fourteen yards of the rope for a loaf of bread, and deemed them more lasting in the water than that made of true hemp. Mr. Kalm himself saw Indian women rolling the filaments of this plant upon their bare thighs to make of them thread and strings, which they dyed red, yellow, black, &c.

The Indians at first were much more industrious and laborious, and before the free use of ardent spirits, attained to a great age. In early time they were every where spread about among the Swedes. They had no domestic animals among them before the arrival of the Europeans, save a species of little dogs. They readily sold their lands to the Swedes for a small price. Such tracts as would have brought £400 currency in Kalm's time, had been bought for a piece of baize or a pot of brandy!

The Indians told Mr. Kalm, as their tradition, that when they saw the first European ship on their coast, they were perfectly persuaded Maneto, or God himself, was in the ship; but when they first saw the negroes, they thought they were a true breed of devils.

The Indians whom we usually call Delawares, because first found about the regions of the Delaware river, never used that name among themselves; they called themselves *Lenni Lenape*, which means "*the original people*,"--*Lenni*, meaning *original*,—whereby they expressed they were an *unmixed* race, who had never changed their character since the creation; in effect they were primitive *sons of Adam*, and others were sons of the curse, as of Ham, or of the out-cast Ishmael, &c.

They, as well as the *Mengwe*, (called by us *Iroquois*) agreed in saying they came from westward of the Mississippi—called by them *Namæsi Sipu*, or river of fish, and that when they came over to the eastern side of that river. they there encountered and finally drove off all the former inhabitants, called the *Alligewi*—(and of course the *primitives* of all our country!) who, probably, such as survived, sought refuge in *Mexico*.

From these facts we may learn, that however unjustifiable, in a moral sense, may be the aggressions of our border men, yet on the rule of the *lex talionis* we may take refuge and say, we only drive off or dispossess *those* who were themselves *encroachers*, even as all *our* Indians, as above stated, were!

The Indians called the Quakers *Quekels*, and "the English," by inability of pronouncing it, they sounded *Yengees*—from whence probably we have now our name of Yankees. In their own language they called the English *Saggenah*.

William Fishbourne, in his MS. narrative of 1739, says the proprietor's first and principal care was to promote peace with *all*, accordingly he established a friendly correspondence, by way of treaty, with the Indians, at least twice a year. [This fact is worth remembering!] He also strictly enjoined the inhabitants and surveyors, not to settle any land to which the Indians had a claim, until he had first, at his own cost, satisfied and paid for the same; so that this discreet method engaged their friendship and love to him and his people—even while other colonies were at war and distress by the Indians.

William Penn's letter of the 25th of 5 mo., 1700, to James Logan, (in the Logan MSS.) says, that because of an injury done his leg, the Indians must go up to him at Pennsbury, along with the council, &c. Was not this assemblage for something like a treaty?

Another such assemblage of Indians met there also in 1701; for John Richardson tells us, in his journal, of his being there when many Indians and chiefs were present to revive their covenants or treaties with William Penn before his return home. There they received presents—held their cantico or worship, by singing and dancing round the fire on the ground.

In 1704, the Indians of the Five Nations (Onandago) came on to Philadelphia, to trade and make a treaty. James Logan was present.

In 1724, an Indian chief, in addressing Sir William Keith, complains that although *Onas* gave his people their lands on the Brandywine, yet the whites have stopped the river; the fish can no longer go up it; their women and children can no longer, with their bows and arrows, kill the fish in the shallow waters; it is now dark and deep; and they wish they may pull away the dams, that the water may again flow, and the fish again swim!

Mr. Carver, first settler at Byberry, became in great straits for bread stuff; they then knew of none nearer than New Castle. In that extremity they sent out their children to some neighbouring Indians, intending to leave them there, till they could have food for them at home; but the Indians took off the boys' trowsers, and tied the legs full of corn, and sent them back thus loaded—a rude but frank and generous hospitality! His great grandaughter, Mrs. S., told me of this fact as certain.

The Indians upon the Brandywine had a reserved right, (as said James Logan in his letter of 1731,) to retain themselves a mile in breadth on both sides of one of the branches of it, up to its source.

In the year 1742, (vide Peters' letter to the Penns,) there was in Philadelphia an assemblage of two hundred and twenty Indians of the Five Nations. They had come from the north-westward to get goods. While in the city, a fire of eight houses occurred, at which they gave great assistance.

In the year 1744, by reason of some strife between the frontier people and Indians of Virginia and Maryland, they aim to settle their dispute, by the mediation of the Pennsylvania governor, through a treaty, to be convened at John Harris' ferry, (now Harrisburg,) which was, however, not held there, but at Lancaster, where the affair was adjusted satisfactorily.

The last of the *Lenape*, nearest resident to Philadelphia, died in Chester county, in the person of old Indian Hannah, in 1803. She had her wigwam many years upon the Brandywine, and used to travel much about in selling her baskets, &c. On such occasions, she was often followed by her dog and her pigs—all stopping where she did. She lived to be nearly a hundred years of age—had a proud and lofty spirit to the last—hated the blacks, and scarcely brooked the lower orders of the whites; her family before her, had dwelt with other Indians in Kennet township. She often spoke emphatically of the wrongs and misfortunes of her race, upon whom her affections still dwelt. As she grew old, she quitted her solitude, and dwelt in friendly families.

A person visiting her cabin, on the farm of Humphrey Marshall, thus expressed his emotions:

> "Was this the spot where Indian Hannah's form
> Was seen to linger, weary, worn with care?
> Yes,—that rude cave was once the happy home
> Of Hannah, last of her devoted race;
> But she too, now, has sunk into the tomb,
> And briars and thistles wave above the place."

Several facts concerning the Chester county Indians, collected by my friend, Mr. J. J. Lewis, may be read on page 513 of my MS. Annals, in the Historical Society of Pennsylvania—such as their thickest settlement being about Pequa, and along the great valley In other places they usually settled in groupes of half a dozen families. The last remaining family was remembered about sixty years ago, at Kennet, consisting of Andrew, Sarah, Nanny, and Hannah, the last being the above mentioned Hannah—"last of the *Lenape!*"

As late as the year 1750, the Shawnese had their wigwam at the Beaver pond, near the present Carlisle; and as late as 1760, Doctor John, living in Carlisle, with his wife and two children, were cruelly murdered, by persons unknown. He was a chief. The governor offered £100 reward.

As it is the prejudice or misinformation of many, to regard the Indians as wholly barbaric, I herein add some elucidation of their real character as derived *now* from a living character, John Brickell, of Columbus, Ohio, who was made a prisoner in Pennsylvania when a youth, and who was given up in 1795, after Wayne's victory. He had been adopted and brought up with kindness in the family of Whingwy Pooshies, a Delaware. At his taking leave, the children all hung round him crying; and when present, before the military, his Indian father stood up and made this touching and pathetic speech, saying: "my son, there are the men of the same colour as yourself—some of them may be of your kin, or can convey you to those who are your kindred. You have lived a long time with us and I call on you to say if I have not used you as well as a father could use a son? You have hunted for me and been to me as a son. I call on you to say if you will go, or if you will still stay with me? Your choice is left to yourself." Then Brickell says, he knew its truth, and stood up some time, considerate, hardly knowing what choice to make—he thought of the children he had just left in tears—then of the Indians whom he loved—then of his own kin—and he at length answered, I will go with my kin. The Indian replied, "I must then loose you—I had leaned on you as a staff—now it is broken—and I am ruined"—he then sank back to his seat and cried, and was joined in tears, by Brickell! Such a scene was like the patriarchal relations in the Bible, and Brickell makes the remark, that many of their observances in his mind seemed to show their affinity to *the Jews.* They had their regular feasts; such as the first corn that is fit to use, was made a fruit offering, and when they started on hunting expeditions, the first game that was taken they skinned whole, observing *not to break a bone*, and leaving thereon, the head, ears and hoofs, this they cook whole and every one partakes, and *the rest they entirely burn up.* They also observe the law of clean and unclean animals. They never eat catfish, eels, or other fish *without scales*, nor beasts or birds *of prey.* They would not even eat rabbits when he had killed them. Their women, too, observed, with remarkable strictness, times of seclusion, and not returning to society, till after washing themselves and their whole apparel. In cases of deaths of husbands or wives they wore mourning apparel for an entire year. It is hardly possible to conceive that such *conformities* to Jewish rituals, among a people so long "scattered and pealed," could be the result of arbitrary choice. He shows too, that they were eminently a religious people in their own way, worshipping God, always, according to "the law of their fathers." They frequently had *family worship* in which they would sing and pray, and they had no words for profane swearing, and never used false accusation, and are always strictly chaste. Brickell remarks, that they were the best people to train up children he had ever seen; *they never whip, and scarcely ever scold, the whole family is remarkably* quiet, and much of their time they employ in instructing their youths in what they deem to be right, they say much of Maneto, much applaud before their children just actions, and greatly condemn bad examples.

That their kindness to Brickell was not an exempt case, we may know from a fact which he relates of another prisoner, one Isaac Choat. He had been but a short time a prisoner, when he was observed by his master to be sitting in a pensive mood, and being asked, what was his cause of trouble, he said, "he was thinking about his wife and children." "The Indian said, that makes me think that I should be sorry too, if carried away from my squaw and children, and I will not let you suffer, I must let you go, *but not alone* lest other Indians see you and kill you—I must go with you," and so saying, he accompained him as far as Muskingum and *set him free;* the result was, he joined his family, and was afterwards seen by Brickell.

The same Indians recaptured one *May*, a prisoner, whom they had cherished and adopted—they tied him to a tree, set a target on his breast, and shot him with many balls, and saying, "you not satisfied to live with us." This was the operation of their law, of "an eye for an eye and a tooth for a tooth." If *custom and usage* sanction the acts of others, why not justify *them also!*

Indian Visits to the City.

From a very early period it was the practice of Indian companies occasionally to visit the city—not for any public business, but merely to buy and sell, and look on. On such occasions they usually found their shelter, for the two or three weeks which they remained, about the State-house yard.* There they would make up baskets, and sell them to the visiters, from the ash strips which they brought with them. Before the revolution such visits were frequent, and after that time they much diminished, so that now they are deemed a rarity.

Such of the Indians as came to the city on public service were always provided for in the east wing of the State-house, up-stairs, and at the same time, their necessary support there was provided for by the government.

Old people have told me that the visits of Indians were so frequent as to excite but little surprise; their squaws and children generally accompanied them. On such occasions they went abroad much in the streets, and would any where stop to shoot at marks, of small coin, set on the tops of posts. They took what they could so hit with their arrows.

On the 6th of 6 mo., 1749, there was at the State-house an assemblage of two hundred and sixty Indians, of eleven different tribes, assembled there with the governor to make a treaty. The place was extremely crowded; and Canaswetigo, a chief, made a long speech. There were other Indians about the city at the same time, making together probably four to five hundred Indians at one time. The same Indians remained several days at Logan's place, in his beech woods.

As the country increased in population, they changed their public assemblages to frontier towns—such as Pittsburg and Easton for Pennsylvania, and Albany for New York, &c.

They once hung an Indian at Pegg's run, at the junction of Cable lane. The crowd, assembled there, stood on the hill. He had

---

* There was a shed constructed for them along the western wall; under it was sheltered for some time, as old Thomas Bradford has told me, old King Hendricks and a party of his warriors, just before they went to join Sir William Johnson at Lake George.

committed murder. Old Mrs. Shoemaker and John Brown told me of this fact, and said the place afterwards took the name of "Gallows-hill" for a long while. In my youthful days Callowhill street was often called "Gallows-hill street."

Indian Alarms and Massacre.

The defeat of Braddock's army in 1755, near Pittsburg, seems to have produced great excitement and much consternation among the inhabitants of Pennsylvania, even within a present day's journey from Philadelphia! £50,000 was voted by the legislature to raise additional troops. The people at and about Carlisle were in great alarm as frontier inhabitants; and Colonel Dunbar, who had the command of the retreating army, was earnestly besought to remain on the frontier, and not to come on to Philadelphia, as he soon afterwards did to seek for winter quarters. He was nick-named "Dunbar the tardy!"

To give an idea how thin the settlement of our country was at that time, it may serve to say, that such near counties as Northampton and Berks experienced the ravages of the scalping knife, by predatory parties. From Easton to fifty miles above it, the whole country was deserted, and many murders occurred. Easton town, and the Jerseys opposite, were filled with the terrified inhabitants. Some skulking Indians were seen about Nazareth and Bethlehem. The gazettes of the time have frequent extracts of letters from persons in the alarmed districts. Philadelphia itself was full of sympathetic excitement. The governor, for instance, communicates to the assembly that he has heard that as many as fifteen hundred French and Indians are actually encamped on the Susquehanna, only thirty miles above the present Harrisburg! Some were at Kittochtinny hills, eighty miles from Philadelphia. The burnings and scalpings at the Great Cove are general. At Tulpehocken the ravages were dreadful: one little girl, of six years of age, was found alive, with her scalp off! The Irish settlement at the Great Cove was entirely destroyed.

It may give some idea of the alarm which these events caused, even on the seaboard, to know, that such was the report received at Bohemia, in Cecil county, (received by an express from New Castle, and believed,) that 1500 French and Indians had reached Lancaster, and burnt it to the ground, and were proceeding onward! Three companies of infantry, and a troop of cavalry, immediately set off towards Lancaster, and actually reached the head of Elk before they heard any counter intelligence!—to wit, in November, 1755.

So sensitive as the frontier men must have felt, they became jealous, lest the Philadelphians and the assembly were too much under the pacific policy of the Friends to afford them in time the necessary defensive supplies. To move them to a livelier emotion, an expedient of gross character was adopted—it was, to send on to Philadelphia the bodies of a murdered family! These actually reached Philadelphia in the winter, like frozen venison from their mountains—were paraded through our city, and finally set down before the legislative hall—as *ecce factum!*

It seems much to diminish the idea of time to say there are now persons alive at Easton, Nazareth, &c., who once witnessed frontier ravages in their neighbourhood, or had their houses filled with refugees; and also persons, still in Philadelphia, who saw that parade of bloody massacre. Thomas Bradford, Esq., lately alive, thus wrote to me, saying: "I saw, when a boy, in the State-house yard, the corpse of a German man, his wife, and grown-up son, who were all killed and scalped by the Indians in Shearman's valley, not many miles from the present seat of government. At that time the Indians marauded all around the Blockhouse at Harris' ferry"—(now Harrisburg.)

John Churchman, the public Friend, also saw those dead bodies, and has thus spoken of them: "The Indians having burnt several houses on the frontiers, and also at Gradenhutten in Northampton county, and murdered and scalped some of the inhabitants, two or three of the dead bodies were brought to Philadelphia in a wagon, in the time of the general meeting of Friends there in December, with intent to animate the people to unite in preparations for war on the Indians. They were carried along the streets—many people following—cursing the Indians, and also the Quakers, because they would not join in war for their destruction. The sight of the dead bodies, and the outcry of the people, were very afflicting and shocking."

With the bodies came the "frontier inhabitants, and surrounding the assembly room, required immediate support."

The excitement in the assembly ran high, between those who resisted and those who advocated means for the emergency. Out-door interest too, at the same time, was great; for the citizens of Philadelphia offer, by subscription and by proclamation, 700 dollars for the heads of Shingass and Captain Jacobs, Delaware chiefs—gone over to the interests of their enemies! Among the wonders of that day for us now to contemplate, but of little notoriety then, was the presence of "Colonel Washington," on a mission from Virginia, concerning the Indians. Little did he, or any of them of that colonial day, regard him as the future president of a new and great nation!*

In the next year the scourge fell heavy upon the Indians; for Colonel Armstrong burnt their town, and destroyed their people at

---

* I heard one fact of the time, to be relied upon too:—Reese Meredith, a merchant of Philadelphia, seeing Washington at the Coffee-house, was so pleased with his personal demeanour as a genteel stranger, that he invited him home, to dine with him on fresh venison. It formed a lasting friendship, and caused afterwards, it is said, the appointment of another Meredith of the family, to be his first treasurer of the union. As this acquaintance was formed without formal introduction, it long remained a grateful recollection in Meredith's family, as a proof of his discernment. He was the father of the treasurer.

Kittaning—a great affair in that day! To commemorate it a meda[l] was struck, and swords and plate were distributed at the expense of the city to the officers, &c.

In giving the preceding notices of Indian events, made so interesting and stirring to the Philadelphians in that day, it will be appropriately followed by the history of an association formed in Philadelphia, by leading members among Friends, for the avowed purpose of preserving the former friendly relations with the Indians, without the destructive intervention of war. It had, therefore, its warm abettors and fierce opponents, as may be discerned in the following brief history of that society, to wit:

Association for preserving Peace with the Indians—Year 1756.

In the spring of the year 1755, the Indians on the frontiers of Virginia having commenced ravages on the people there, excited great alarm at Philadelphia. The pacific principles of the Friends had so long preserved the peace of Pennsylvania, that it seemed but natural that they should feel peculiar reasons on such an occasion to prevent hostilities from extending to their frontier inhabitants. They therefore united, in 1756, under the denomination of "the Friendly Association for regaining and preserving Peace with the Indians," and by their private and individual subscriptions, raised several thousand pounds to enable them to execute their friendly designs. Benevolent as their disinterested designs were, they were reproached by some; and even the government, in some instances, repelled their proffered services to preserve peace. The Edinburgh Reviewers have said, "if princes would use Friends for prime ministers, universal peace might be perpetuated," and the manner in which this association negotiated, both with the provincial rulers and the hostile Indians, seemed to verify their peculiar qualifications for such peaceful offices.

The minutes of their proceedings, containing about two quires of MS. cap paper, as preserved by Israel Pemberton, having been in my possession, I made memoranda of incidents therein, which may be consulted by the curious or the interested, in my MS. Annals in the Historical Society of Pennsylvania, pages 181 to 184.

They begin by addressing a long letter, declarative of their designs, to Governor Robert H. Morris, on the 12th of the 4th mo., 1756, and beseeching him not to declare war against the Indians until pacific overtures should be made to them, and offering to aid the same by services and money. He and his council not according with their views, they proceeded forthwith to address a long letter to the general assembly. A declaration of war was, however, made. They then address letters to bespeak friendship for their designs, and for the Indians, by directing Israel Pemberton to write letters in their behalf to Sir William Johnson, and to Governor Sir C. Hardy, at New York; copies of which are preserved—also copies of Governor

R. H. Morris' messages, conveyed by Indian agents to the Indians on the Susquehanna at Teaogon (Tioga.) With these agents the Friends made much interest; and their remark on this interference is thus recorded—" From the time of the first messengers arriving at Teaogon, the hostilities on our northern frontiers ceased, and an acceptable respite being obtained for our distressed fellow subjects, we enjoyed so much real pleasure and satisfaction in this happy event of our endeavours, as to engage us cheerfully to pursue the business we had begun, though many malicious calumnies and aspersions were cast upon us by persons from whom we had a right to expect encouragement and assistance."

They attended Indian treaties at Easton, at Lancaster, &c., and often made presents—measures which gave the Friends much ascendency over the minds of the Indians, and inclined them to peace.

The Paxton Boys, and Indian Massacre.

This was a story of deep interest and much excitement in its day —the year 1764. It long remained quite as stirring and affecting, as a tale of woe or of terror, as any of the recitals, in more modern times, of the recollections of that greater event—the war of Independence. The Indians, on whom the outrage was committed by those memorable outlaws, were friendly, unoffending, Christian Indians, dwelling about the country in Lancaster county, and the remnant of a once greater race—even in that neighbourhood where they had been so cruelly afflicted. For instance, in 1701, a letter of Isaac Norris' (preserved in the Logan MSS.) speaks thus, to wit: " I have been to Susquehanna, where I met the governor; we had a round-about journey, and well traversed the wilderness; we lived nobly at the king's *palace in Conestogoe.*" " They once had there (says J. Logan) a considerable towne"—called Indian town.

The spirit which finally eventuated in the massacre, was discerned and regretted at a much earlier period—say as early as 1729–30. Then James Logan's letter to the proprietaries (vide Logan MSS.) says, " The Indians themselves are alarmed at the swarms of strangers, (Irish,) and we are afraid of a breach with them. The Irish are very rough to them." In 1730, J. Logan complains of the Scotch-Irish in a disorderly manner possessing themselves, about that time, of the whole of Conestoga manor of 15,000 acres—saying, as their justification, (the same as they did in effect at the massacre,) that " it was against the laws of God and nature that so much land should lie idle, while so many Christians wanted it to labour on," &c. In truth, they did not go off until dispossessed by the sheriff and his posse, and their cabins burnt down to the number of thirty. They rested chiefly in Donegal, as a frontier people, at an exemption from rent, &c.

In 1764, under an alarm of intended massacre, fourteen being previously killed on Conestoga, the Indians took shelter in Lancaster, and for their better security they were placed under the bolts and bars of the prison; but at mid-day a party on horseback, from the country, rode through the streets to the prison, and there forcibly entered and killed unresisting men and women on the spot! The citizens of Lancaster were much blamed for so tamely suffering such a breach of their peace. Nothing was there done to apprehend the perpetrators. In the mean time, other Indians in amity with us, hearing of the cruelty to their brethren, sought refuge in Philadelphia, which when the Paxton boys knew, being excited to more daring and insolence by their former sufferance—like blood-hounds, stimulated to a passion for more blood by the previous taste—they forthwith resolved on marching down to Philadelphia to destroy the remainder of the afflicted race, and to take vengeance also on all their friends and abettors there. They were undoubtedly Christian professors—used Bible phrases—talked of God's commanded vengeance on the heathen, and that the saints should inherit the earth, &c. They had even writers to plead their religious cause in Philadelphia!!!

The news of their approach, which outran them, was greatly magnified; so that " every mother's son and child" was half crazed with fear, and even the men looked for a hard and obstinate struggle; for even among their own citizens there were not wanting of those who, having been incensed by the late Indian war, thought almost any thing too good for an Indian. The Paxton boys, to the amount of several hundred, armed with rifles, and clothed with hunting shirts, affecting the rudest and severest manners, came in two divisions as far as Germantown and the opposite bank of the Schuylkill, where they finally entered into affected negotiations with the citizens, headed by Benjamin Franklin, and returned home, terrifying the country as they went.

In the mean time the terrified Indians sought their refuge in Philadelphia—having with them their Moravian minister. They were at first conducted to the barracks in the Northern Liberties, by the order of the Governor. But the Highlanders there refused them shelter; and the Indians stood several hours exposed to the revilings of scoffers. This was in the cold of December. They were thence sent to Province island, afterwards by boats to League island: then they were recalled and sent to New York. In returning through Philadelphia they held their worship and took their breakfast in the Moravian church in Bread street. William Logan and Joseph Fox, the barrack master, who gave them blankets, accompanied them as far as Trenton. A company of seventy Highlanders was their guard as far as Amboy, where they were stopped by orders from General Gage; they then returned back to the Philadelphia barracks.* The alarm of the Paxton boys being near—at night too—the city is

* All these removals were measures of security, as fears were entertained from some of our own excited citizens, favourable to the Paxton boys.

voluntarily illuminated!—alarm bells ring, and citizens run for arms, and haste to the barracks! Many young Quakers joined the defenders at the barracks, where they quickly threw up intrenchments.* Dr. Franklin, and other gentlemen who went out to meet the leaders, brought them into the city, that they might point out among the Indians the alleged guilty; but they could show none. They, however, perceived that the defence was too formidable, and they affected to depart satisfied.

The Indians remained there several months, and held regular Christian worship. In time they were greatly afflicted with small-pox, and fifty-six of their number now rest among the other dead, beneath the surface of the beautiful "Washington square."

In the spring, these Indians were conducted by Moravian missionaries, via Bethlehem and Wyoming, and made their settlement on the Susquehanna, near to Wyalusing creek. There they ate wild potatoes in a time of scarcity.

The massacre of those Conestoga Indians was thus described by Susanna Wright, of Columbia, to wit: "The cruel murder of these poor Indians has affected and discomposed my mind beyond what I can express. We had known the greater part of them from children; had been always intimate with them. Three or four of the women were sensible and civilized, and the Indians' children used to play with ours and oblige them all they could. We had many endearing recollections of them, and the manner of effecting the brutal enormity so affected us, that we had to beg visiters to forbear to speak of it. But it was still the subject with every body."

No good succeeded to the actors. They were well remembered by old Mr. Wright, long a member in the assembly from Columbia. He used to tell at Charles Norris', where he stayed in session time, that he had survived nearly the whole of them, and that they generally came to untimely or suffering deaths!

Present State and Refuge of the Delaware Indians.

The Indian nation of the *Delawares*—our proper Indians—was once one of the most numerous and powerful tribes; but are now reduced to about four or five hundred souls, and scattered among other tribes. The chief place where they now hold any separate character and community is at the river Thames, in Upper Canada, about seventy miles from Detroit. There is there a placed called Moravian town—made memorable by being destroyed by our Americans in the last war, and by the death of Tecumseh, the celebrated Shawnee chief, in the battle of the "Long woods." This is at present the last and only Moravian missionary establishment among

* Among the most conspicuous of these were Edward Penington and William Logan, who were of course had under dealings by the society: but as their generous purposes were popular, their sentence was mild—only an exclusion from service in affairs of discipline.

the Indians of our country. There are there about one hundred and sixty souls under the mission of the Rev. Abram Luchenback, and his assistant, the Rev. Mr. Haman. They worship from printed books in the Delaware tongue.

The wanderings of the poor Delawares under the Moravian auspices are curious. They first collected on Mahony, a branch of the Lehigh, from whence they were driven by the French war. They then removed to near Bethlehem, where they remained till the war of the Revolution; thence they removed to Tioga; thence to Allegheny and to Beaver creek, Ohio. Both of these settlements broke up and went to Muskingum, near New Philadalphia, where, in 1821, there were but about three families remaining; these removed to the above mentioned settlement on the Thames, which was established about the year 1793.

In connexion with this renewed Moravian town, there is, higher up the Thames, a place called Bingham, occupied by Delawares; and not far from them dwell some Munsee and Chippewa Indians.

A small settlement of Delawares now reside near the mouth of Grand river, in Upper Canada, where they form a part of the Six Nations, who have a reserve of sixty miles in length on both sides of that river. Among some of these, the Methodist missionaries have wrought much civilization and moral improvement.

The Indians, formerly of Chester county, were of the Delaware or "Lenni Lenape." Of these was the tribe of the Nanticoke, which dwelt once, and lingered long along the whole region drained by the stream of the Brandywine—

> "Their home for many an age was there!"

They removed from thence in the year 1757, to the valleys of the Wyoming and Wyalusing, on the Susquehanna. At the great treaty of St. Mary's, in 1820, there were then present about twenty chiefs and warriors, of the *Nanticokes;* and among them was *one* who had withstood the storms of ninety winters, who, in most dramatic pathos, told the commissioners, that he and his people had once roamed through their own domains along their favourite Brandywine. A gentleman then present related this as fact. Ah, poor Indian! what recollections and reflections he must have had, if duly sensible of the change to him, and even to us!

> "A mighty chief, whose hundred hands
> Ranged freely o er those shaded lands;
> But now there's scarcely left a trace,
> To mind one of that friendly race!"

Tedyuscung,

A Delaware chief, a frequent visiter to Philadelphia, from 1750 to '60.—By this means, and his frequent intercourse with the whites, he had acquired a competent knowledge of our language; he was a tall, large figure of a man—always regarded himself as at home in the Norris family, where he was always welcomed; he generally had some retinue with him, and affected the character of something superior as a sovereign; he was addicted to occasional excess in drinking. On one occasion, he went with a dozen of his train to Norris' country house at Fairhill—the male part of the family being absent, the females hid themselves from terror; he, however, entered and blustered about; one of the hired girls fearing some mischief might be done to the property, for they were searching the closets for food and drink, she took up courage, and went in to restrain them; Tedyuscung affected to frighten her, saying they would kill her if she did not provide them something good; she vapoured in return—but to make the best of it, she laid them a table and refreshments, and by some finesse succeeded to hurry them off; they had much noisy mirth before going. Mr. Norris used to talk of this afterwards good-naturedly to the chief; and he used to promise no more to take possession where there were none but women to receive him.

Governor Dickinson used to relate, that he attended a treaty at Albany, where Tedyuscung was a negotiator; while there, at a time when the chief was making an ill-timed speech, being excited by a surplus of strong drink, his wife, who was present, was heard to speak in the most modest and silvery tones imaginable in the Indian tongue; the melody of her tones enchanted every ear; while she spoke, she looked steadfastly and with much humility to the ground; every body was curious to inquire of the chief what she said; he answered rudely---"Ho! she's nothing but a poor weak woman! —she has just told me it was unworthy the dignity and the reputation of a great king, like me, to show myself drunken before the council of the nation."

Isaac Still

Was a celebrated Indian of good education, a leader of the last remains of the Delawares adjacent to Philadelphia. He was a Christian man of fine morals and much good sense; and was therefore employed as agent and interpreter, in French as well as English, in many important missions to distant Indians; he was said to have travelled further over the surface of our country to the unknown wilds of the west, than any other individual, and having seen, as he said, the Rocky mountains and the white Indians; his journal of observations was deemed important, and was therefore taken down by some one for publication; but where it now is, is not known.* For a considerable time he dwelt with his family, in wigwam style, on a part of Logan's place, now called the Indian field; their only son,

* It was done while he was at Logan's place, as he said himself—and Mr. Samuel Preston has suggested (vide my MS. book,) some papers and families, where he thinks it might yet be found,—say among the papers of Logan, Dr. Barton, or H. Drinker, or E. Penington.

Joshua, in the mean time, was educated at the Germantown school house. In 1771, he moved up into Buckingham, purposing there to collect his scattered tribe, and to move them off to the Wabash, "far away," as he said, "from war and rum." This he effected in the fall of 1775, having with him about forty persons, chiefly females, as the men and the young and active (about twenty) had gone on before. Mr. Samuel Preston, who witnessed their departure, described Still as a fine looking man, wearing a hat ornamented with feathers, the women, all bareheaded, each loaded with a large pack on her back, fastened with broad straps across their foreheads, thus making their heads bear much of the burthen, they proceeded in regular form of march. Thus ended, in the year 1775, the last vestige of Lenni Lenape from the neighbourhood of Philadelphia, and from Bucks county and Jersey! Many further particulars concerning Isaac Still as an Indian, and of his services as a useful agent and ally to our cause, are told in several MS. letters from the said Samuel Preston, and may be consulted on page 556, and following, in my MS. book deposited with the Historical Society of Pennsylvania, to whom the facts therein told more appropriately belong.

Bucks county is also identified with another Indian of greatest fame, even of the renowned Tamanend, (or Tamané, as Penn spells his name,) the tutelary saint of our country! His remains repose by the side of a spring not far from Doylestown. A letter now before me from my friend E. M. says, "I have just returned from visiting the identical spot in which the celebrated Indian chief, St. Tamané, was buried. It is about four miles from this village, in a beautiful situation, at the side of an endless spring, which, after running about a furlong, empties into the Neshaminy,—the spot is worth visiting; and the reflections it awakens are worth a league's walk!" Another letter says, "I have discovered a large Indian mound, known by the name of the Giant's Grave," and at another place is an Indian burial ground, on a very high hill, not far from Doylestown."

There is some tradition existing that king Tamanend once had his cabin and residence on the meadow near the Ridge road, situated under a great elm tree on Francis' farm. The character of Tamanend is told at length in the interesting work of Heckewelder.

Miscellanea.

An original deed "from Wiggoneeheenah, in behalf of all the Delaware Indians concerned," grants unto Edmund Cartlidge a piece of ground, formerly his plantation, lying in a turn of Conestogoe creek, called Indian point [no acres or bounds mentioned,] and dated in the presence of A. Cox, witness, on the 8th of April, 1725. The Indian signature and seal are curious; the seal is of red wax impressed with a running fox, and the Indian signature, in lieu of his name, is a tolerable good drawing of a similar animal. The deed itself is among the Logan MSS. In 1722, John Cartlidge is named as killing an Indian at the same place.

In 1720, the Gazette states that a runaway man was seen last "at an Indian town, called Pehoquellamen, on Delaware river." Who can designate that place? Or who can now say where was "Upper and Lower Dinderdonk" islands, where George Fox, the Friend, was ferried across the Delaware in Indian canoes?

In 1721, Sir William Keith, the governor, his council, and thirty gentlemen, set out for Conestogoe, to there hold an Indian treaty with the heads of the Five Nations.

In the Gazettes of this period, I often observe Indians named as occasionally serving as sailors on board some of our coasting vessels. The Indians in Maine too, in fighting us, in the year 1727, coasted in an armed vessel there, and fought their cannon, &c., as well as others! At that time, too, more Indians than others were employed in all the Nantucket whalers.

In 1728, some ten or twelve Indians in Manatawna, on the Schuylkill, fell into a quarrel with the whites, and several were killed. Governor Gordon, in consequence, visits the Indians at French creek, and at "Indian town" at Conestogoe, to incite them to peace, and he proclaims, that no molestation shall be offered to any of the Indian nations then in our borders, to wit: "Delawares, Conestogoe, Ganawese, Shawenese, Mingoes." At this time, several Delawares are stated as living about Brandywine. In the same year the Indians assaulted the iron-works at Marketasoney, and were beaten off with loss.

At this time, two brothers, Welshmen, are executed at Chester for the murder of three Indians; they declared they thought all the Indians were rising on them, in the case of the above strife. They appear to have been maddened with sheer fright, and killed the first unoffending Indians they met.

About the year 1759 advertisements often appear in the Gazettes, describing children recovered from the Indians, and requesting their friends to come and take them home. Several are described as having sustained some injury; and in many cases can only tell their baptismal names, and the same of their parents!

In 1762, a number of white children, unclaimed, were given up by the Indians at Lancaster, and were bound out by order of the governor.

The Gazettes of the year 1768–9, contain such frequent and various recitals of the havoc and cruelties of the incensed Indians on the frontiers, as would, if selected, make quite a book of itself. Of the numerous calamities, Colonel Boquet, who commanded a regiment of Highlanders, and was at Fort du Quesne, (Pittsburg,) after the peace of 1763, gives a very affecting recital of the delivery up to him of all the prisoners surrendered by the Indians. Husbands went hundreds of miles in hopes of finding lost wives or children. The collection amounted to several hundred! and the sight of seeing husbands and wives rushing into each others arms, and children claimed by their parents, made the joy of all such extreme! There was also the mourning of others, who hoped to find relatives—but neither finding or hearing of them, made much lamentation. There were also Indians, who had adopted all those persons, and loved them as their children or relatives, and having then to give them up, showed great signs of distress. Some young Indians had become passionately fond of some young women, and some few women had formed attachments for them. The Indians loaded their friends at their departure with their richest gifts—thus proving they had hearts of tenderness, even to prisoners.

This same Col. Boquet when at Philadelphia, in 1756, with 500 men, threatened to billet his men on the town, with the small-pox, because he said he could not find suitable quarters.

I find among the "Proprietary Papers," so called, the speech of Lapowinso to the Proprietaries, at Pennsbury, the 9th May, 1735. Present—James Logan, Jeremiah Langhorne, Joseph Kirkbride, Thos. Freame, Wm. Piles, Joseph Kirkbride, Jr., Israel Pemberton, James Steel, Peter Lloyd, Robt. Appleton. Also, Indians, Lapowinso, Neutonies, Lesbeconk, Tiscoquam.

Lapowinso spoke and said: That as he came down the usual road to his plantation, he heard from his brethren that the proprietaries wanted to speak with him; he therefore came to shake hands with them, and was glad to see them, and presented a bundle of skins.

He desires unity and peace as usual—that he intended to come down with many of his brethren in a twelve moon's hence, to see them and to discourse further about the lands.

That a great king had a mind to have gone down with him, but was lame and could not. Next year they would come and discourse further about the bounds of the lands. That he is uneasy to be at home, to attend to a message sent him from three of the Mingo kings, who were to arrive as soon as the bark peeled, and then to go on to Philadelphia. We have a fine portrait of Lapowinso.

The proprietaries told them they were glad to see them and accepted their presents very kindly, and should always be glad to continue in peace and friendship. The skins were valued at £6 16*s.* 6*d.*

"Ask ye for hamlets' peopled bound,
With cone-roof'd cabins circled round?
For chieftains proud—for hoary sire—
Or warrior, *terrible in ire!*

Ye've seen the shadows quit the vale—
The foam upon the water fail—
The fleeting vapour leave no trace,
Such was their path, that *faded race!*"

Frontier Indians, Incidents, Hostilities, &c.

The preceding notices of the Indians are the same as were published in the first edition of the Annals, and are now intended to be much extended, for the sake of giving more enlarged views of their character and actions *in Pennsylvania;* and especially of their hostilities and ravages on the frontiers. They were once a formidable foe, and much afflicted and periled the frontier inhabitants. What we now purpose to record will, we doubt not, be new to many, although old in themselves,—

In July, 1700, there was a survey of a line from Philadelphia direct to Susquehanna, coming out nigh the mouth of Conestoga creek, a little more north, (about four miles,) near to "an old fort demolished." This was in consequence of surveyor-general Holmes' purchase of all the lands from Upland creek to Pemapecka creek, and so backward tc Susquehanna, two days' journey. The whole is said to have been bought of the Indian kings and sakamackers, for the use of William Penn—bought of Shakhoppah, Secaming, Malebore, Tangoras, Indian kings; and Maskecasho, Wawarrin, Tenoughan, Tarrecka, Nesonhaikin, Indian sakamackers. I notice that in the map of the line of survey, two Indian paths traverse it obliquely, north-west by north—the first from Philadelphia, is at Rocky run, (fifteen miles,) between the head waters of Ridley and Chester creeks, and again at thirty-eight miles, two miles beyond Doe run. These facts I found recorded in a survey book, No. 14, in the land office, and the above extracts are from the warrant of survey by Holme. Below follow other facts on the same subject, all tending to show *the treaty* by which *the lands* of Philadelphia city and county are held.

Philadelphia.

To my very loving ffriends Shakhoppah,* Secaming, Malebore, Tangoras — Indian kings; and to Maskecasho, Wawarrin, Tenoughan, Tarrecka, Nesonhaikin — Indian sakamackers, and the rest concerned:

Whereas I have purchased and bought of you, the Indian kings and sakamackers, for the use of Governor William Penn, all your land from Pemapecka creek to Upland creek, and so backward to Chesapeake bay and Susquehanna, two days' journey; that is to say, as far as a man can go in two days, as under the hands and seals of you the said kings may appear; and to the end I may have a certain knowledge of the land backward, and that I may be enabled and be provided against the time for running the said two days' journey, I do hereby appoint and authorize my loving ffriend, Benjamin Chambers, of Philadelphia, with a convenient number of men to assist him, to mark out a westerly line from Philadelphia to

* This king was one of the witnesses to Tamanend's sale, in 1683, of lands between Nesheminah and Pemapecka creeks.

Susquehanna, that so the said line may be prepared and made ready for going the said two days' journey backward hereafter, when notice is given to you the said kings, or some of you, at the time of going the said line; and I do hereby desire and require, in the name of our said Governor Penn, that none of you, the said kings, sakamackers, or any other Indians whatsoever, that have formerly been concerned in the said tracts of land, do presume to offer any interruption or hindrance in making out the said line, but rather I expect your ffurtherance and assistance, if occasion be herein; and that you will be kind and loving to my said friend, Benjamin Chambers, and his company, for which I shall, on the governor's behalf, be kind and loving to you hereafter, as occasion may require. Witness my hand and a seal, this 7th day of the 5th mo., called July, being the fourth year of the reign of our great king of England, and eighth of our proprietary, William Penn's government. THO. HOLME.

A true copy from the original, by Jacob Taylor.

With the foregoing paper is a diagram of the ground plot of the survey. It goes direct from Philadelphia city to a spot on the Susquehanna, about three miles above the mouth of the Conestoga, near to a spot marked, "fort demolished."

In the book of "Charters and Indian Deeds," (in secretary of state's office, and recorded 30 years ago,) p. 62, is given the deed of the foregoing granted lands, to wit:

We, Shakhoppah, Secane, Malebore, Tangoras, Indian sakamackers, and right owners of ye lands lying between Macopanackan, alias Upland, now called Chester river or creek, and the river or creek of Pemapecka, now called Dublin creek, beginning at a hill called Conshohockin, on the river Manaiunck, or Schoolkill, from thence extending a parallel line to the said Macopanackan, (alias Chester creek,) by a south-westernly course, and from the said Conshohockin hill to the aforesaid Pemapecka, (alias Dublin creek,) by the said parallel line north-westernly, and so up along the said Pemapecka as far as the creek extends, and so from thence north-westernly back unto the woods, to make up two full days' journey, as far as a man can go in two days from the said station of the said parallel line at Pemapecka, as also beginning at the said parallel at Macopanackan, (Chester creek,) and so from thence up the said creek as far as it extends, and from thence north-westernly back into the woods, to make up two full days' journey, as far as a man can go in two days from the said station of the said parallel line at the said Macopanackan, alias Chester creek—*For and in consideration* of 200 fathoms of wampum, 30 fathoms of duffells, 30 guns, 60 fathoms of strawd waters, 30 kettles, 30 shirts, 20 gun belts, 12 pairs shoes, 30 pairs stockings, 30 pairs scissors, 30 combs, 30 axes, 30 knives, 21 tobacco tongs, 30 bars of lead, 30 lbs. powder, 30 awls, 30 glasses, 30 tobacco boxes, 30 papers of beads, 44 lbs. red lead, 30 pairs of hawks' bells, 6 drawing knives, 6 caps, 12 hoes,—To us in hand well and truly paid by William Penn, proprietary and governor of Pennsylvania and territories—Do by these presents *grant*, *bargain*, *sell*, &c., all right, title and interest *that we or any others shall or may claim* in the same—hereby renouncing and disclaiming forever any claim or pretence to the premises, *for us, our heirs and successors, and all other Indians whatsoever*—In witness whereof we set our hands and seals, &c., this 30th day of the 5th mo., called July, and in the year 1685. (Signed)

SHAKAHAPPOH   SECANE
MALEBORE   TANGORAS.

Sealed and delivered to Thomas Holme, president of the provincial council, in the presence of us—

Great men of the Indians.	
TARECKHOUA	LASSE COCK
PENOUGHANT	MOUNS COCK
WESAKANT	SWAN SWANSON
KACOCAHAHOUS	ISM FRAMPTON
NEHALLAS	SAML. CARPENTER
TOUTAMEN	WILL ASLEY
TEPASEKENIN	ARTHUR COOK
	TRYALL HOLME.

On the 2d of 8th mo., 1685, at New Castle, a treaty is made with sundry Indians for all the lands between Quing Quingas, called Duck creek, unto Upland, called Chester creek, fronting along the Delaware river, and thence backward as far as a man can ride in two days with a horse—in consideration of, &c. [Much the same in kind, quantity and value as the above things.*] The witnesses are Peter Alricks, &c.

NOTE.—That this said Peter Alricks, "of New Castle county, gentleman," is the same to whom a grant is made by Col. Nicolls, (the conqueror of Gov. Stuyvesant, of New York,) of "surrender" of "*Matinicum island* to Peter Alricks, formerly of New Castle, with all stocks and goods thereupon." The descendants of this Alricks—say "Hermanus Alricks, of the city of Philadelphia, gentleman," and his brother Peter, both grandsons of the first Peter, "confirm," in 1734, *the signature* of their grandfather. Some of this family are now resident at Harrisburg, where two of the Alrickses are lawyers—one also a post-master in Wilmington.

We begin with several articles found recorded under their marginal dates, in the Minutes of Council, viz.

21st of 5 mo., 1685, several Indians made complaint, that the servants of Jasper Farman's plantation [probably in Bucks county] made them drunk and laid with their wives, and then quarrelled with them all. A warrant was issued for their appearance, but the

* A copy of the whole may be seen in the Germantown Telegraph of 21st March, 1838. It differed chiefly in having 100 jewsharps, 300 flints, 200 needles, 30 lbs. sugar. 5 galls. molasses, 300 pipes, and 40 tomahawks, in place of axes.

messenger returned, having lost his way in the woods! Trial was put off, and when the time arrived, the servants being present found no accusers, for all the Indians had been made drunk at home, [perhaps at the charge of the defendants themselves!]

12th of 3 mo., 1690, Lacy Cock, designing up the Schuylkill, is charged to ascertain when there, whether *the French settlers there*, (probably about French creek) have not too much ammunition, about which he is to inquire of the chief sachem of our Indians, and if so to see that the same is removed to Barnabas Willcox's store.

1706, the Minutes, say—" William Penn, when last in this country in 1700, *visited those of that place*," to wit: the chiefs of the Conestoga, Shawanese, and Ganawense Indians on Susquehanna—as also his son, after him, in order to friendship.

21st September, 1710, the queen of the Conestoga Indians, Ojuncho, and two chiefs more, and some of the *Connois* Indians, visit Philadelphia, and lay down before the council five bundles of skins and furs, making at the gift of each a speech.

The belt from the Conestoga Indians prayed, thus:—"sent from their children born and those yet in the womb, that room might be yet allowed them to sport and play, without danger of *slavery!*"

There is also messages received from several of the chiefs along the Susquehanna, about preparing for the war in Canada, *for us*, &c.

20th May, 1723, the three nations of Indians upon the Susquehanna, viz.: the Conestoga, Delawares and Shawnese, met Governor Keith at Philadelphia, to renew treaties, &c. The answer says, "by this chain, Philadelphia is joined to Conestoga and all the Indian towns upon the Susquehanna." Notices of the Indian visits to Philadelphia are very frequent.

July 4th, 1727, the Indians at Philadelphia pray that no settlements may be allowed up Susquehanna higher than Paxton, [the creek now comes out at the lower part of Harrisburg,] and that none of *the settlers thereabout* be suffered to sell or keep any rum; because, *that* being *the road* by which their people go out to war, they are apprehensive of mischief, in these parts. The same remark they also apply to the country (Allegheny) where James le Tort trades. [in 1840, a young Oneida chief, living at the old Castle New York, is named Abram le Tort.]

The answer is, that we have *not allowed* any settlements to be made above Paxton; yet the young people will spread and scatter; but to avoid collision, it is recommended that the Indians should thereafter cross *above* the mountains, [meaning above those now in sight of Harrisburg.]

May 26th, 1728, Governor Gordon, and his council, in treaty at Conestoga, met at the house of *Andrew Cornish*, about a mile from town. The chief of the Conestogoes (Mingoes) was Captain *Civility*, i. e. Taquatarensaly. They (the governor and council) refer to Penn's first treaty in *nine items*, one of which is, that "the doors of the Christian houses should be open to the Indians, and the houses of the Indians should be open to the Christians, as welcome friends on both sides," and finally this mutual amity was to exist between them for ever, or "as long as the creeks and rivers run, and while the sun, moon, and stars endure." The consideration articles given in *that* first treaty, [as I understand it] said, "we bind them with the several parcels of goods, to wit: twenty stroud match coats; twenty duffells; twenty blankets; twenty shirts; one hundred weight of powder; two hundred weight of lead; five hundred flints, and fifty knives." At the time of the meeting in 1728, the Indians upon Susquehanna are called Shawanese.

June, 1728. James Logan, in his speech in council to the Indian chiefs then present, says to King Sassoonan, king of the Delawares, that ten years before (in 1718) to quiet claims, the former treaties were confirmed with him and others by gifts, &c., and that they then signed a treaty, (then shown,) whereby they granted that all the lands between Delaware and Susquehanna were conceded from Duck creek, to the mountains on this side *Leckay*, stretching away from the forks of Delaware (below Leckay, Easton now,) to those hills on Susquehanna which lie ten miles above Paxton.*

In 1727, John Wright, an Indian trader, was killed at *Snake town*, forty miles above Conestoga, by an Indian broil, in a case of his own provocation. It is said in the proceedings, that this was the *first* accident of the kind ever heard of in the province in that settlement. It was further said, that Indian traders acted by license, well considered before the granting, and that the said John Wright's was deemed good when granted at Chester court. Wright and Burt had before been all in harmony, dancing with the Indians, and then Wright struck one of them in anger, and so lost his life by being pursued into the hen-coop.

All the foregoing are embraced in eight books of demi MS. A to M., and come down to the year 1734. I examined and extracted them pretty fully; after this the books begin and continue of large size in medium paper.

In the record of charters and treaties, I found the following concerning the two chiefs, of whom we have a present of their portraits, made in 1737, supposed by a Swede of good talent, to wit:

A treaty at Philadelphia, in 1737, made to *confirm* one before made "about three years ago at Durham," by two Delaware chiefs or sachems, to wit: Teeshakomer, *i. e.*, Tishcokenk, and Nortames, *i. e.*, Nutemus, to which were present Lappawinsse, and several other Delawares, "concerning lands more than fifty years before sold by their fathers unto William Penn;" beginning at a spruce tree by the river Delaware about Makerish Kitton, and thence west-north-west

---

* King Tamanend and Metamequan make a treaty with William Penn, on 23d 4 mo., 1683, for lands near Neshamineh creek, and thence to Pemapecka. Tamenen's mark is thus

I could find no trace of a treaty at Philadelphia, at the Treaty-tree. The Five Nations by treaty deeded the lands up Susquehanna, in 1736.

by the mountain to a corner white-oak, and thence westward to Nashamini creek, &c. The foregoing relates to Tisheohan and Lapowinsa.

I saw the original charter from the king to William Penn, it is composed of several sheets of parchment, each ornamented with wide marginal heraldic ornaments in black ink. It looks imposing and venerable.

Allentown.—This is one of the oldest settlements on the Lehigh river, and in the different wars of America, was *the scene* of *many a brave and bloody deed.* It was there that Colonel James Burd displayed such heroism in the early wars with the aborigenes. It was there that, during the revolutionary war, the bells of Christ church in Philadelphia were concealed, and it was there that John Fries, the insurgent, fomented the "Northampton insurrection," once so exciting in our annals at the time.

Indian names of places, by Heckewelder.

Schuylkill, (Ganshowéhanne,) *the noisy stream,* because of its falls and ripples.

Little Schuylkill, (Tamaquon,) the beaver stream, or place where they abounded.

Manayunk, (Meneiuńk,) *our place of drinking,* or to assemble to drink.

Makerish Kitton, applied to river Delaware, but must have been originally meant for the Trenton falls, meaning *strong, rapid,* like them.

Wissahickon, (Wisamêkhan,) catfish creek. Wisauchsican, a stream of yellowish colour.

Shakamaxon, (Schachaméksink,) place of eels.

Cohocksink, (Cuweuhackink,) *pine lands.*

Wingohocking, (Wingehácking,) fine land for planting, favourite spot.

Manatawny, (Menhattanink,) where we drank (*liquor,*) (is like Manhatten, New York!)

Tulpehoccon, (Tulpewihacki,) the land of turtles.

Wyoming, a river having large flats upon it.

Wisaukin creek, (Wisachgim,) *grapes,* the place where they grow in plenty.

Pittsburg, (Menáchkink,) a secured place, *a fort.*

Juniata, is an Iroquois word (unknown now.) The Indians said, that this river had the best hunting ground for deer, elk and beaver.

Pennsylvania, they called (Quœkelinik,) the country of Quakers!

Hoboken, (Hopoken,) a *tobacco pipe,* near New York.

Burlington, (Tschichohacki,) ancient, or oldest planted land. There they said, that they planted *their first town* on the river! It was called *Chyœs* island, (or Chygoes?) after an Indian named *Schigo* which means *widower.* The Indian tribes there, and along the river, were the *Mandas.*

Potowmak river, (Pedhámmôk,) they are coming (by water,) "sc Indians told Mr. H."

Chesapeake bay, (Tschsichwapéke,) great saltish bay.

Powhatan, the name of James river, and the chief also—the river of abundance.

Pocohantas, a run between two hills.

Rappahannok, (Lappihánne,) where water ebbs and flows.

Susquehanna, Hanna, means river, and Susque, muddy.

Temanen, probably *Temened*, (the chief?) the *affable*.

Some notable Indians, known to Heckewelder, to wit:

Nutimus, (Nútamæs,) a striker of fish with a spear, two brothers of that name, one Isaac, the other *Pontius Nutamæs*, an excellent man, was born where *Philadelphia* now stands, lived to a hundred years of age, and died at Muskingum, after thirty years' residence, in 1780. His brother Isaac, was also a chief, and a good man, and learned to work with tools, and at blacksmithing, died also near his brother in 1780.

Lawelochwelend, one who walks between two others, or the middle man. He also was born on the place now Philadelphia, he saw the first house building when about twelve or thirteen years of age; he caught fish and rabbits, and shot ducks, pheasants, &c., for the workmen—and the woman who cooked for them, and kept a little shop, gave him for them, needles, thread, scissors, knives, awl blades, &c., for his mother. In manhood he went to Ohio to dwell there, to trap beavers and otters, &c.; was made a chief there, he became afterwards a Moravian; visited Philadelphia several times and *saw its increase!*—he died at ninety years of age, about the year 1779.

Nedowaway, (Netawátees,) of the Turtle tribe, was cheated of his lands by "the Long-walk;" he was a signer to the treaty at Conestoga, in 1718—he died in 1776, at ninety years of age, in Ohio. In his possession as chief were the speeches, &c., of William Penn, and his successors. He had himself seen William Penn, and spoke of those early speeches and times with great animation to Mr. H.

Kill-buck, Jun., (Gelelémend,) as chief of the Turtle tribe, had the bag containing the wampum speeches, and written documents of William Penn, carefully preserved, till surprised near Pittsburg by bad white people, and lost the bag among them, in making his escape. He died in 1811, aged eighty years, a Christian convert.

Tedeuscung was burnt in his house on Susquehanna.

The Indian alarms and hostilities.

Secretary Peters presented in council, in Dec. 1755, a brief narrative of the incursions and ravages of the Indians in the province of

16

Pennsylvania, beginning upon the 18th of October, upon the inhabitants on Mahanatry creek, near the forks of the Susquehanna, "this being *the first inroad* ever made upon this province since its first settlement," and "thus driving in the inhabitants of all the frontier country, which extends from the rivers Potomac and Susquehanna, to the river Delaware, one hundred and fifty miles in length, and between twenty and thirty in breadth, but not fully settled, and leaving the whole entirely deserted"—"the houses and improvements reduced to ashes, and the cattle and grain carried off." All these hostile measures are imputed to the influence of the French *after* the defeat of Braddock, they gaining thereby to their interest the Delawares, Shawanese and many others formerly in our alliance, both from fear and from interest; they promising them to reinstate them in their lands, and to make the Susquehanna river the boundary of the whites, and to this end that they would build a strong fort at *Shamokin*, nigh to the confluence, or forks of the two branches of the Susquehanna.

The ravages of Indians, as told on the Minutes of Council, were as follows, to wit;

Oct. 18, 1755. A party of Indians fell upon the people on Mahanatry creek, that runs into the Susquehanna five miles below the great fork of that river, near Shamokin or Northumberland, and killed and carried off twenty-five persons, and burnt and destroyed their buildings, leaving the whole settlement deserted by the survivors.

Oct. 23d. Forty-six of the inhabitants on Susquehanna went up to Shamokin to inquire of Indians there, who they were who had so cruelly destroyed the above settlement, and on their return were fired upon by some Indians in ambush, and had four killed, four drowned, and the rest put to flight. From this cause all the settlements below, to Hunter's mill, (now McAllister's Fort Hunter,) for fifty miles along the river was deserted.

Oct. 31. An Indian trader and two other men in the Tuscarora valley, were killed by Indians, and their houses, &c. burned. The rest of the inhabitants left their plantations and fled.

Nov. 3. Two women are carried away from Conegochege by the Indians, and the same day Canalaways and Little Cove, two considerable settlements, were attacked by Indians—the houses were burned and the inhabitants put to flight.

Nov. 16. A party of Indians crossed the Susquehanna, and fell upon the county of Berks—murdered thirteen persons, burned a great number of houses, destroyed much cattle, grain and fodder, and laid waste a large extent of country.

Nov. 21. A fine settlement of Moravians, called Gnadenhutten, in Northampton county, on the West branch (Lehigh) of Delaware river, was attacked—six persons killed—their meeting-house and dwelling houses burned.

December. During all this month, the Indians were employed in burning and destroying all before them in Northampton county, even as far as within twenty miles of Easton, its chief town. It was even said that some French officers were within the same county directing the general progress of the war and the destruction.

A letter from James Hamilton, Esq., then at Easton, Dec. 25, 1755, says—"The country along the river is absolutely deserted from this place to Broadhead's, which last place was stoutly defended by his sons and others against the frequent assaults of the Indians. There are here three companies of soldiers, waiting for more arrivals, for the people here, though so injured, are very backward to engage in the service to revenge themselves; they are dispirited, and we must have men from a distance to be able to garrison these *block-houses* which we purpose to build over the hills soon.

The following notice of a reward *for scalps*, I had at first some scruples to record; but truth is truth, and on second thought I venture to give it, as it is, only adding that there were other views cherished by "the Association for preserving peace with the Indians," as organized at Philadelphia in the time of Gov. Hunter, in 1756.

At a council at Philadelphia, 6th July, 1764, present John Penn, Lieut.-Gov., Thomas Cadwalader and Richard Penn, Esqs. The council, having before agreed to give encouragement for a more successful war on the frontiers against the Indians, agreed to give a reward for scalps, &c., provided it should be approved, &c., by Sir William Johnson. His answer of 18th June, '64, is, "I cannot but approve of your design to gratify the desire of the people in your province by a bounty on scalps," &c. Whereupon the council resolved to issue a proclamation the 7th July, 1764, and to publish it in the Gazette, to wit: for every prisoner, male, delivered, 150 dollars—for every female, 138 dollars—for the scalp of every male, 134 dollars—for every female, 50 dollars, &c. &c. After this, I saw fears expressed by Conrad Weiser and others, that the reward for scalps would induce even friendly Indians to kill *white men* for their scalps. It is to be hoped that the ill-judged severity passed away without any practical operation. Gov. Hunter began it in 1756, as a proclamation, but nothing was done therefrom.]

May 5, 1758. Information is given that an Indian, William Sock, a Conestogoe, just returned from the New York country, and his comrade, a Cayuga, had for some time been tampering with the Conestogoe Indians, near Lancaster, and that they were *at the instance of those Indians* proposing to *remove* from the manor, his honour had therefore written to James Wright to inquire into the matter.

A letter was also read from Edward Shippen, Esq., of Lancaster, of 3d May, 1758, saying among other things, that "the Conestogoe Indians are going to leave their town; they say they were not kindly treated lately at Philadelphia, they being left there unnoticed, and left naked and barefooted, which was a breach of the governor's word, before given, &c.: that as they were no longer to be allowed to hunt for deer, and as they were forced to go into the wilderness to seek clothing for themselves and families, they should therefore go a little beyond Fort Augusta, and there build Indian cabins for their use, for six months or so, and then return. Mr. McKee, our friend, informs that he made it his business to inquire about these things, and that he learned from Betty Sock, the mother of William aforesaid, *that he* and some of the young men were absolutely *resolved to go and help the French.* Such being the facts, I shall use my utmost to restrain them from going, as an affair of much importance to the province."

[The foregoing statements probably explained, in part, the reason of the fears and jealousies of the Paxton men, then a part of Lancaster county, against that tribe.] Mr. Wright afterwards makes answer that the young men are going away for want of hunting grounds, and that the people here are in general greatly prejudiced against them, and so that there was some fear, even in sending old Sesane and some others, with the Cayuga, to Philadelphia, to hold a conference, which he however does, accompanied by a friend of the government. He does not palliate or excuse them, he only says he thinks they may not intend ill.

☞ I read the minute books of council down to the year 1760. The last twenty-five years, however, more superficially than the preceding ones. The last ten years were much engrossed with Indian concerns and deliberations, and with communications from Indians and Indian agents. The Indian conferences and speeches were generally of little interest; they contained no incidental history worth noticing.

We here add sundry facts gleaned from the New York Mercury, &c., from the years 1755 *to* 1763.

1755. The people settled on the west side of the Susquehanna are all alarmed and moving eastward into the settlements. The people of Juniata have all run off and left their grain to ruin—alarms also at Carlisle.

1757. We learn from Northampton county, that at Lynn township, in same county, a party of Indians assaulted Adam Clawse and his neighbours whilst cutting his corn—Martin Yager and his wife were killed and scalped; Abram Secler and a child were scalped, *but survive*; two men shot through, but still live; two children murdered; two men and two women, and a girl escaped. A party was made up and went in pursuit of them.

1757. We learn from York county, the 2d July, that a woman and three children were carried away by the Indians, and the house burnt. The farmer and his sons were abroad at work.

1757. From Carlisle, we learn, that Alexander Miller, of Antrim township, in Cumberland county, was killed in June, and two of his children carried off. His boy of fourteen years of age, shut himself in the house, and kept up such a defensive fire as to save himself by alarming his neighbours. The wife being out hid herself in the bushes—one man was killed at about six miles from Carlisle.

1757. Two men were killed in Shearman's valley—one man who was wounded made his escape into Carlisle.

1757. From Tulpehocken, July 4, one says—the Indians are murdering about six miles from my house. Last Friday three women and four children were murdered only seven miles from me. If we do not get speedy assistance all the inhabitants will move away

1757. From Heidelberg, July 9,—yesterday afternoon an assault was made upon a house in which were twenty women and children, while the men were all abroad picking cherries. They scalped one woman who still lives; another they cut terribly with a tomahawk. Three of the children they carried off prisoners.

1757. From Reading, July 12. Two Indians were seen close by the town on the 4th instant, in the evening—two were also seen before, about eight miles off. They are frequently seen in different parts of this country. We have a scheme to secure this town; and if we are not surprised *by the French*, we fear but little what the Indians can do.

1758. York county, April 5. Three Indians were seen this day near Thomas Jamieson's, at the head of Marsh creek. After the alarm was given, six men proceeded to Jamieson's house and found Robert Buck killed and scalped—all the rest of the family are missing. The same day a person going to Shippenstown, saw a number of Indians. These facts have caused much alarm.

1758. A letter from an officer at Tulpehocken, April 8th, says—We were informed last night at Shearman's valley, that a woman had been killed and scalped there—we are now setting off with soldiers in pursuit. The list of killed, with one prisoner, is as follows, to wit: At Swatara, two young men brothers; in Tulpehocken, one Levergood and wife killed; at Northkill, the wife of Nicholas Gieger and his two children, and the wife of M. Titleser—all killed and scalped. The Indians keep themselves divided in small parties through the woods.

1758. July. The Indians lately appeared near Harris' ferry, (now Harrisburg,) on the Susquehanna. One of them seized on Capt. Craig about seven miles from Harris', as he was riding along the road. The Indian cast his tomahawk and cut him in the cheek, a number of Indians at same time setting up a cry. Craig gave spurs to his horse and got off. The same day a lad, driving a plough, was shot at and one of his horses killed, the boy escaped. An Indian, at night, got his gun *through the palisade* at Mr. Harris' house, and endeavoured to fire at the people in the house, but his gun flashing in the pan, alarmed the people—on which the enemy made off.

1763. A letter from Carlisle of July, says—We have now eighty or ninety volunteers scouring the woods. The inhabitants of Shearman's valley, Tuscorara, &c., have all come over, and the people of this valley, near the mountain, are beginning to move in, so that in a few days there will be scarcely a house inhabited north of Carlisle. This letter mentions the names and places of several families attacked, and of several killed on the Juniata, and at Shearman's valley—grain destroyed—houses sometimes burnt, by small parties of Indians, only thirty or forty miles from Carlisle. The sheriff and his party overtook a party of fifteen to twenty Indians, and had a fight in Shearman's valley, and beat them off. At same time there are Indian alarms and surprises near Cumberland, in Frederick county, in Maryland. The papers contain many accounts of massacres all about the South mountain, Tuscarora mountains, &c. Retreating families pass through Fredericktown, Maryland, *daily*. The families of Fincher and of Miller, twenty-four miles from Reading, were all murdered—the Indians were pursued. At this time sermons were preached in most of the churches *in Philadelphia*, to raise funds and necessaries for the back inhabitants, and besides collections are made generally among the citizens, by going from house to house.

Indian news from Northampton county, October, 1763, says—The Indians attacked John Stinton's house, eight miles from Bethlehem, and killed some. Capt. Wetherholt from Fort Allen, (Allentown,) with his party went in pursuit. The captain and sergeant got mortally wounded.

N. Marks, of Whitehall township, and Hance Snider's families, were also assaulted—some killed and wounded. The inhabitants are all in alarm. Most of the people of Allentown, &c., have fled to Bethlehem and Nazareth, and this last is put into a state of defence. About the same time an expedition of one hundred and fifty men, under Col. Armstrong, went up the West branch of the Susquehanna to the great encampment of the Indians *at the Great island*, and they fled beyond the frontiers. The Indians appeared in Sussex county, New Jersey, on the Delaware river side, and killed several whites. On the 15th of November, the Indians killed three men, twenty-two miles from Reading, on the north side of the mountains, at the forks of the Schuylkill. They were just returning back to their plantation, which they had before deserted.

Indian ravages and incidents, near Carlisle and Harrisburg.

In the year 1807, Archibald Loudon, of Carlisle, (alive in 1835,) wrote and published a work in two volumes, 12mo., wherein he set forth his narrative of Indian wars in general, and several instances of occurrences in and near Shearman's valley, where he was born. They are curious now, as showing the rapid changes of civilization and cultivation in the same regions of country along the line of the Susquehanna, even in the short period of eighty years. When we contemplate the present state of Harrisburg and its society, we cannot but feel surprised that such a thickly populated country, so well improved, should have been so recently rescued from the terrors of predatory Indians and the horrors of the scalping knife.

James Watson and William McMullin, who lived in Cumberland county, between Conodoquinett creek and the Blue mountain, were surprised by Indians while at their barn, they endeavoured to reach their fort, where others were gathered for safety, but got wounded, overtaken and finally killed.

In the year 1756, the Indians beset the house of one Woolcomber, on Shearman's creek, at a time when all the rest of the inhabitants had gathered into the fort at George Robinson's. He being a Quaker, refused to seek refuge, saying that the Indians would be peaceable but for the Irish; while at his dinner the Indians came in, he asked them to come eat with him, but an Indian answered that they did not want food, but scalps—he then drove his tomahawk into his head. His son of fourteen years of age made off and alarmed the fort, consisting of about forty men.

July, 1756. The Indians waylaid the fort in Shearman's valley in harvest time, and when the reapers had gone out, they were about to assault it, but Robert Robinson and James Wilson, standing at the gate of the fort and firing at a mark, alarmed the Indians, so that they made off, killing a daughter of Robert Miller, the wife of James Wilson, and the widow Gibson, and taking prisoners Hugh Gibson and Betsey Henry.

Samuel Bell and James Bell, near Carlisle, in 1755–6, agreed to go to Shearman's valley to hunt deer, and were to have met together upon Croghan's gap. Before they met, however, Samuel Bell, saw three Indians in the valley, all fired at each other from their trees. He wounded one of them, and received some shot in his own clothes. The two Indians unhurt moved at same time to get him between them; in doing so, he shot one of them dead. The other Indian ran and took the dead one on his back to make escape; but he pursuing wounded the carrier, who dropped his charge and made off some distance, where he was afterwards found dead. The first wounded Indian was visited and killed. Thus one man killed three Indians within an hour. Samuel Bell was a farmer upon Stony ridge.

[The names of sundry forts were in general after the name of the owner of the farms where situate, and were stockade defences generally, for the refuge and defence of families, acting as farmers and settlers, and not for real soldiers. Hunter's fort was the same as Hunter's mill.]

In the year 1755, Peter Shaver, John Savage, and two other men, were killed at the mouth of Shaver's creek on Juniata, by Indians.

In February, 1756, Indians came to Juniata from Shamokin, to the house of Hugh Mitcheltrees, and killed his wife and a young man; they thence went and killed Edward Nicholous and his wife, and took Joseph, Thomas and Catherine Nicholous, John Wilcox, James Armstrong's wife and two children prisoners. About same time James Cotties and his boy left that party, and went to Shearman's creek, and killed William Sheridan and his family of thirteen persons!—thence they went down the creek to a family of three aged persons, and killed them. The same Cotties, in the year 1757, went to Hunter's fort, and killed a young man of the name of William Martin, whilst he was gathering chestnuts. After the war was over, the same Cotties, being at the same fort, was killed by an Indian of the name of Hambus, who reproached him for the death of young Martin.

In July, 1756, Hugh Gibson was captured from Robinson's fort in Shearman's valley—at same time killed his mother. He saw a prisoner white woman burned to death, they stripped and bound her to a stake, they applied hot irons to her, the skin sticking to them at every touch, and she screaming and crying for mercy! Several prisoners were compelled to stand as spectators.

In the year 1755, the province of Pennsylvania erected Fort Granville at Old town, situate at the junction of Kishecoquilles creek and Juniata. It was the station of a company of enlisted soldiers, when it was attacked by a body of Indians, they at same time firing it with pine knots and combustibles. The captain was killed, and his lieutenant of name of Turner surrendered; some were massacred, the others borne off, only one man escaped wounded to Carlisle. Poor Turner they burnt to death, so that he saved nothing by his too tame surrendering!

The same party next attacked Bingham's fort in Tuscarora, this they also burned, killing and capturing all that were in it. About the same time they killed Robert Cochran on his own farm, and bore off his wife and son.

The Indians, in one of their inroads into Shearman's valley, murdered a family of seven persons on the creek; thence passing over Croghan's gap they wounded a man and killed his horse. At Conodoquinett creek, in the next valley, they captured Mrs. Boyle and her two sons and a daughter.

At another time they came upon the frontiers of Lancaster county, (now that part called Dauphin county,) assaulting a family moving by wagon, killed the driver; the rest made off to a fort near by. As the men went from this fort to the next, nine miles distant, to give the alarm, they were waylaid and all killed except two, who escaped wounded.

Mrs. Boggs, of the same neighbourhood, while riding to a neighbour's house, was fired upon by the Indians, and her horse killed, she had a sucking child with her, which they killed and scalped, the mother they took away.

At Paxton, the defenceless state of the people induced four men living in one house "to erect a fort round it;" [this perhaps shows the manner of many of them named after the individual owners.] It so happened that a captain with his company had halted there to pass the night; it also chanced that the gate was left unfastened

By this means some Indians, who knew not of the accidental increase of strength, got into the enclosure and closed it, summoning at same time a surrender. The house door was opened; as they entered they were shot down, and those who fled, not being able to find the gate, were all killed!

In the spring of 1763, the Indians began to kill and scalp the frontier inhabitants, and in a short time drove them all as far as the North mountain; however, when harvest came on, some of the people of Tuscarora and Shearman's valley ventured to go back to secure their crops; but the Indians came upon them, before they had begun, and when the people, because of its being Sabbath day, were in their houses. The most of those of Tuscarora were killed. Eight persons were killed in Dodds' house, Dodds himself got off to Shearman's valley and gave the alarm. Two companies went on to bury the dead, &c., to wit: the Upper company and the Buffaloe company: as the latter were returning they were surprised by the Indians, and six of their company were killed, the remaining six persons escaped. Then the Indians went up the valley, and seeing five men approaching they concealed themselves, and killed John Logan and Charles Coil, and wounded William Hamilton, who died soon after at Carlisle.

In the second war, say on the 5th July, 1763, as told by Robert Robinson, the Indians went to Juniata in harvest time, where the people had gone back to reap their crops, while the reapers all lay upon the floor in William White's house on Sunday, the Indians crept up and shot them all, save one boy, who leaped out of the window and got off.

The same Indians, went off to Robert Campbell's, on the Tuscarora creek, surprised them in the same way, shot them on the floor where they were resting themselves. One Dodds made his escape up the chimney, and fled to Shearman's valley; thence they went to William Anderson's, and killed him; thence they went to Collins' and committed depredations, burned Graham's house, &c. They were afterwards pursued and overtaken at Nicholson's, and a battle ensued, there being twenty-five Indians, to twelve white persons; five of the latter were killed.

[In September, 1763, five persons were killed in a fight at Buffaloe creek.]

In the year 1763, a company of volunteers of one hundred men resolved to go up the Susquehanna as far as Monsey, so as by attacking them at home, they might the better drive them off from any further invasions of the settlements. They joined battle near Monsey, with two companies of Indians, supposed to be then on their way down the river for destruction—they killed their chief, called Snake, and the others dispersed.

During the Indian alarms of 1763, the congregation of Christ church and St. Peter's raised the sum of £662 for the relief of the frontier inhabitants, especially in Cumberland county. A letter at this time from their missionary, William Thomson, at Carlisle, says: "We find the number of the distressed to be seven hundred and fifty families, who have *abandoned* their plantations, many have lost their crops, and some their stock and furniture, and besides these we are informed that about two hundred women and children are coming down from Fort Pitt. The unhappy sufferers are dispersed through every part of this country, and many have passed through into York. In this town and neighbourhood, there are upwards of two hundred families, and having the affection of the small pox and flux to a great degree."

Besides the *money* sent by the vestry of the above churches, they also sent two chests of arms, half a barrel of powder, four hundred pounds of lead, two hundred swan shot, and a hundred flints; to be sold to such prudent and good people as should need them, and would use them *for their defence*. [The above facts are on the minutes of Christ church.] Contributions were made at *Philadelphia* at the same time by others.

In the year 1779, the Indians made inroads into the settlements of Northumberland county, assaulted the house of Andrew Armstrong, made him a prisoner, his wife was hid under a bed. Two families flying were attacked at Warrior's run, the men escaped, but Mrs. Durham, having her child shot in her arms, fainted and fell, and was scalped; but she revived again and got off safely. The same year, a party of Indians came into Buffaloe valley, where they fell upon two girls separated from the reapers, and secured them with one Indian, while they should try to attack the said reapers; while their Indian was lying down, one of the girls sunk a hatchet into his head, and both made off and gave the alarm.

The people of Northumberland county, to defend themselves, erected fort Freelan, also Brady's, Wallace's, and Boomes' forts. This repressed the incursions, but they killed Captain Bready while he was bringing provisions to the garrison. One of the parties of Indians went into Northumberland county, captured Peter Pence, a man and a boy. Some time after, when the Indians were asleep at night, Pence got loose, and with the aid of the boy killed two or three, and the rest, having their guns taken, fled. The white persons got to their homes.

Some of the Indian cruelties were extreme, one George Wools relates the suffering to which a young man was subjected; it was too great to be conceived of unless seen. They cut holes in his cheeks, through which they passed the cord by which he was tied to a tree, with slack enough to let him move round it. His body being naked, they seared his flesh with heated gun-barrels, and as he moved round to shun one he was met behind by another. They scalped his head and applied hot ashes and coals to his skull. Then they opened his abdomen, and taking out part of his bowels to the tree, and again compelling him to move by the touching of the hot gun-barrels, finally, as he was nearly expiring, his tormenters thrust a hot iron up to his heart, and he died!

The Indians on Susquehanna.

In the years 1744–5, the Rev. Mr. Brainard visited the Indians on the Susquehanna—he thus describes his first visit there, to wit:

In October, he started from his Indians at the Forks of Delaware, (since Easton,) accompanied by his friend the Rev. Mr. Byron, of Rockciticus; at twenty-five miles' journey they lodged at the *last house* on their road, all the rest was a "hideous and howling wilderness," nothing else but mountains, deep valleys and hideous rocks. His mare broke her legs in the rocks and had to be killed, and he went onward on foot, at night sleeping on the ground before a fire.

They arrived at Susquehanna river at a place called Opeholhauperg, consisting of twelve Indian houses—here he preached several times—had their attention, and a request to visit them again, and he returned home. [But little done.]

In September, 1745, he again left the Forks of Delaware, (Easton,) and made his journey to the Susquehanna, lodging out three nights; when he arrived at Shamokin, where were fifty houses and three hundred persons, of three tribes, speaking different languages, consisting of Delawares, Senekas and Tutelas.

Thence he travelled down the river—visited an Indian town called Juneauta, (since Juniata,) situated on an island in the Susquehanna, (Duncan's?) they were making preparations for a *sacrificial dance.* They had prepared ten fat deer for the sacrifice—they danced all night. Next day they gathered all their pow-wows, (conjurors,) to ascertain why they were so sickly of fevers and flux. [He describes the process.] Several of them understood English—they learned it in Maryland.

[The present "Clark's ferry," near Duncan's island, was called Queenashawakee by the Indians, and the Juniata, near by it, was spelled *Coniata.* This ferry was once a great fording place—a little above it, at the White rock, on the river side, John Harris had, in 1733, a house, which was complained of by the Indians. The Swedish family of Huling came originally from Marcus Hook, and settled the fine island now called Duncan's. In the year 1755, Mrs. Huling, with her two children, all on one horse, forded the river and made their escape from the Indians, down to Fort Hunter, now McAllister's place. A Mrs. Berryhill got safe to the same place, but her husband was killed and scalped. This island was the favourite home of the Indians, and there are still many Indian remains. At the angle of the canal, near the great bridge, I saw the mound covered with trees, from which were taken hundreds of cart-loads of human bones, and which were used with the intermixed earth, as filling materials for one of the shoulders or bastions of the dam

What a sacrilege! There were also among them many beads, trinkets, &c.]

August, 1746. Rode towards Paxton, (near present Harrisburg,) upon Susquehanna river; thence to Chambers', (Hunter's fort,) where he found ungodly people drinking and swearing; thence fifteen miles, to a family wholly unacquainted with God; next day travelled above all the English settlements and lodged in the woods —then he met and assembled Indians at different places—all were attentive, but few converts. September 1st, set out from Shamokin for the Great island up the North-west branch; lodged in the woods; when arrived at the Delaware town, found them drinking and drunken. Thence went eight miles to the Shawaunoes—some were attentive and some not. On the 4th September returned homewards, finding himself too feeble and unwell to remain longer. [One cannot but remark, how little all his pains and travel could effect. These journeys seemed but ill requited by the measure of success; yet his faith and zeal seem unabated.]

The Assault and Burning of Hanna's town, in 1782.

This town, now no longer such, once stood about three miles from *Greensburg*. It was distinguished in the year 1773, as the *first* county town, where justice was dispensed in legal form, *west* of the Allegheny mountains. At the time that it was made the court town of Westmoreland county, in 1773, it consisted of about thirty habitations of *log* construction. Even the court-house, and jail, and a stockade fort, were all formed of logs. Robert Hanna, Esq., was the first justice presiding in the courts, and Arthur St. Clair, Esq., first clerk and prothonotary—the same who afterwards became Gen. St. Clair. The first road opened to Fort Pitt, by Gen. Forbes and his army, passed through this town. At that place Hugh Breckenridge made his first debut as a lawyer. There were many joyous meetings at court times, when all was rustic cordiality and good cheer. Now the same grounds are annually furrowed with the plough. The summer of 1782 was a sorrowful season to the frontier inhabitants, all the country to the north-west of this town had been generally deserted from the dread of Indians, who had been killing and pursuing many of the people. On the 13th July, 1782, the memorable day for Hanna town, when sundry of the inhabitants were absent at Miller's station, two miles distant, and another part of them gone out to assist in the harvest of O'Connor's field, a mile and a half off, the alarm of approaching Indians was sounded, so that the most of the inhabitants got into the fort. The savages, provoked to find themselves discovered, sacked and burned the town—the little garrison being too weak to *assault*. They then set off to attack Miller's station—they were supposed to be about three hundred in number, assisted by some fifty or sixty *refugee* guides. There the Indians assaulted by surprise the principal house, where was a wedding party, at which were present Mrs. H. and her two pretty daughters, Mr. Brownlee, and family, &c. Some made their escape, but the *bride and groom* (think of such a state!) and several of the guests were made *prisoners*, including some of the Miller family. These were all marched off to Canada—there the beauty and the misfortunes of the Misses H. attracted attention, and a British officer loved and married the gentle Miss Marian. Brownlee, from being an active campaigner formerly against the Indians, was tomahawked on the route, while carrying his child on his shoulders—the child was killed also. A woman prisoner, who saw it, shrieking out with terror and interfering, was also killed as a warning of submission to the rest. They all remained in Canada till after the peace of 1783, and were then released—the *widow* Brownlee among the number, minus the loss of husband and child murdered! Much more in *detail* is remembered by the aged of that part of the country—one man, for instance, in running from Miller's town with his family, and carrying his little child, was so hotly pursued by the savages, that for the sake of saving his mother, he laid down his child in the field, thus saving himself and her, and strange to tell, the child, since grown up to manhood, was found afterwards safe at home asleep in bed—by what cause so restored, was never known! Is it not *now* subject of wonder, that so populous and civilized a country should, only as late as 1782, have been ravaged by predatory Indians. How easily too might some of the party have made *a book* of their sufferings and adventures in captivity, equal to that of the Gilbert family which I have herein *preserved.*

[A story of the above facts is well told in the Germantown Telegraph of 22d Nov., 1837, from an inland paper.]

Narrative of Lieut. Van Campen, showing the state of the Pennsylvania frontier, as he was engaged in it, during the Revolution.

The facts of this narrative, as he prepared it for his claim on Congress, in 1838, show that the Susquehanna was then a western frontier. It is published at large on *cover* No. 7, of Aug. 14, 1838, of Waldie's Library. It is full of legend and daring adventure in conflicts with the Indians, from the years 1777 to 1782, in the same counties now filled with a rich and civilized population.

In 1777 he was stationed three months at Big isle, under Col. Kelly. In 1778 he was sent by Col. Hunter to build a fort at Fishing creek, where they were attacked by Indians. In the same summer occurred the great massacre of Wyoming. This produced the appointment of Gen. Sullivan, with an army to push into the Indian country, in the year 1779. When near Tioga point, the Indians assembled in great force, and Van Campen, disguised as an Indian, went by night into their camp to espy out their force, &c. After this he was sent home sick with camp fever—he went to his father's farm, near the fort he had before built at Fishing creek. In March,

1780, the family was attacked by Indians, and his father and brother killed before his eyes, and himself and two relatives borne off as prisoners by ten Indians. In two or three days they rose upon these Indians when asleep, and despatched them all but one!—this was near the present Tioga. They made themselves a raft and drifted towards Wyoming. After this he was employed to keep up a constant chain of scouts around the frontier settlements, from Fishing creek to Muncey, &c.

Some Indian Facts.

At Lebanon, (one mile south of the road, westward, near to the creek Catepahilla, the former name of the settlement,) is still a stone house, altered and renewed, which was at first the *Fort house* for the neighbours, now belongs to Doctor Glovinger. There is also *in the town*, an aged woman who had been six years a captive with the Indians—taken with other children from the neighbourhood. The house had *little windows* used as loop holes for guns.

At Myerstown, six miles this side of Lebanon, is another stone house, used for a fort, and which was once bravely defended by a single woman.

At Womelsdorf, at the east end of the town, opposite to Bunker's hill, a place of fight with the Indians, is a stone house, now in part rebuilt, belonging to Mr. Schultz, and once the property of Conrad Weiser, the interpreter, (still used as a farm house,) which was the fort of the place, and maintained at one time a strong defence. An Indian burial ground is close by.

Mrs. Clemens is now alive, near Womelsdorf, who had been an Indian captive.

In the year 1736, there were a hundred Indians of the Six Nations at Stenton farm, (Logan's,) come for purposes of treaty. Stayed two days and went to the city and treated.

Conestoga Indians and Shawanese.

The Votes of the Assembly, vol. 4, p. 517—year 1755.

The committee upon the claims of the Delawares and Shawanese to lands upon *Conedoquinet*, (a creek near Carlisle,) report, that after making their best inquiries, come to the conclusion, to wit: That the Shawanese are southern Indians, who being made uneasy by their neighbours, came with about sixty families up to Conestoga, about the year 1698, by the leave of the Susquehanna Indians, who then lived there. Having afterwards consulted with William Penn, and having his permission, other Indians followed them and settled there, and also on *the upper parts of Delaware.* That as they had thus *joined* the Susquehanna Indians, who were dependent upon the Five Nations, they also became under their protection. In time, these same Shawanese were offered the lands (conditionally) upon Conedoquinet.

[NOTE.—The foregoing does not show any thing about a chief having said he had seen Penn at the treaty of the Treaty-tree, as I had published in my Tales of Olden Time, p. 208, upon the alleged extract from the above vol. 4, given by R. C.]

We shall enlarge this chapter relative to Indians, by giving a brief sketch of the narrative of the Gilbert family, captured by the Indians in the year 1780, at the place now so well known as Mauch Chunk, the present great coal district. We hope that its interest will excuse its length, *abridged* for these pages, from a still longer story. And here we must beg the reader to reflect, that this is a place but sixty miles from Philadelphia—and that secure as it then was for predatory Indians, it is now the alluring, charming and safe spot of summer travelling, and is filled with an active and prosperous population!

The captivity of Benjamin Gilbert and his family, 1780.

Benjamin Gilbert, son of Joseph Gilbert, was born at Byberry, about fifteen miles from the city of Philadelphia, in the year 1711, and received his education among the people called Quakers.

He resided at or near the place of his nativity for several years; during which time of residence he married, and after the decease of his first wife, he accomplished a second marriage with Elizabeth Peart, widow of Bryan Peart, and continued in the neighbourhood until the year 1775, when he removed with his family to a farm situate on Mahoning creek, in Penn township, Northampton county, being then the frontiers of Pennsylvania, [not far from where Fort Allen was erected.]

This family was alarmed on the 25th day of the 4th month, 1780, about sunrise, by a party of eleven Indians, whose appearance struck them with terror. To attempt to escape was death, and a portion of distress not easy to be supported, was the certain attendant on the most patient and submissive conduct. The Indians who made this incursion were of different tribes or nations, who had abandoned their country on the approach of General Sullivan's army, and fled within command of the British forts in Canada, promiscuously settling within their neighbourhood, and, according to Indian custom of carrying on war, frequently invading the frontier settlements, taking captive the weak and defenceless.

The names of these Indians, with their respective tribes, are as follow:

Rowland Monteur, 1st captain; John Monteur, second in command, who was also styled captain. These two were Mohawks, descended of a French woman.* Samuel Harris, John Huston, and

* Catherine Monteur was settled at Catherine, New York—named after her.

his son, John Huston, Jr., were Cayugas; John Fox, of the Delaware nation; the other five were Senecas.

At this place they made captives of the following persons:

Benjamin Gilbert, aged about 69 years; Elizabeth, his wife, 55; Joseph Gilbert, his son, 41; Jesse Gilbert, another son, 19; Sarah Gilbert, wife to Jesse, 19; Rebecca Gilbert, a daughter, 16; Abner Gilbert, a son, 14; Elizabeth Gilbert,* a daughter, 12; Thomas Peart, son to Benjamin Gilbert's wife, 53; Benjamin Gilbert, a son of John Gilbert, of Philadelphia, 11; Andrew Harrigar, of German descent, hired by Benjamin Gilbert, 26; Abigail Dodson, (daughter of Samuel Dodson, who lived on a farm near one mile distant from the mill,) who came that morning with grist, 14.†

They then proceeded to Benjamin Peart's dwelling, about half a mile further, and brought himself and family, viz.:—Benjamin Peart, son to Benjamin Gilbert's wife, aged 27; Elizabeth Peart, his wife, 20; and their child, about nine months old—in all fifteen persons.

The prisoners were bound with cords which the Indians brought with them, and in this melancholy condition left under a guard for the space of half an hour, during which time the rest of the captors employed themselves in plundering the house, and packing up such goods as they chose to carry off, until they had got together a sufficient loading for three horses which they took, besides compelling the distressed prisoners to carry part of their plunder. When they had finished plundering, they began their retreat, two of their number being detached to fire the buildings, which they did without any exception of those belonging to the unhappy sufferers; thereby aggravating their distresses, as they could observe the flames, and the falling in of the roofs, from an adjoining eminence called Summer hill. They cast a mournful look towards their dwellings, but were not permitted to stop until they had reached the other side of the hill, where the party sat down to make a short repast; but grief prevented the prisoners from sharing with them.

The Indians speedily put forward from this place, as they apprehended they were not so far removed from the settlements as to be secure from pursuit. Not much further was a large hill, called Mochunk,‡ which they fixed upon as a place of rendezvous: here they halted near an hour, and prepared shoes or sandals, which they call moccasons, for some of the children: considering themselves in some degree relieved from danger, their fears abated so that they could enjoy their meal at leisure, which they ate very heartily. At their removal from this hill, they told the prisoners that Col. Butler was

* Since Mrs. E. Webster, in Byberry—visited by me in 1832—a lively woman still.

† Abigail Dodson was held prisoner long—is now well settled on Susquehanna.

‡ Mochunk hill—now Mauch Chunk.

What a contrast between *things* and *places* then and now! Then so *frontier* and *wild*, now so peopled and improved!

☞ Such Indian captivity as late as 1780, at only a distance *now* of one day's ride from Philadelphia, shows the rapid settlement of Pennsylvania no great distance from them, in the woods, and that they were going to him.

The Broad mountain is said to be seven miles over in this place, and about ten miles distant from Benjamin Gilbert's settlement. Here they halted an hour, and then struck into the Neskapeck path, the unevenness and ruggedness of which rendered it extremely toilsome, and obliged them to move forward slowly. Quackac creek runs across the Neskapeck path, which leads over Pismire hill. At this last place they stopped to refresh themselves, and then pursued their march along the same path, through Moravian Pine swamp, to Mahoniah mountain, where they lodged, being the first night of their captivity.

It may furnish information to some, to mention the method the Indians generally use to secure their prisoners: They cut down a sapling as large as a man's thigh, and therein cut notches, in which they fix their legs, and over this they place a pole, crossing the pole on each side with stakes driven in the ground, and in the crotchets of the stakes they place other poles or riders, effectually confining the prisoners on their backs; besides which they put a strap round their necks, which they fasten to a tree. In this manner the night passed. Their beds were hemlock branches strewed on the ground, and blankets for a covering, which was an indulgence scarcely to have been expected from savages. It may reasonably be expected, that in this melancholy situation, sleep was a stranger to their eyelids.

Benjamin Peart having fainted in the evening, occasioned by the sufferings he endured, was threatened to be tomahawked by Rowland Monteur.

25th. Early this morning they continued their route, near the waters of Teropin ponds. The Indians thought it most eligible to separate the prisoners in companies of two by two, each company under the command of a particular Indian, spreading them to a considerable distance, in order to render a pursuit as impracticable as possible. Towards evening the parties again met and encamped; having killed a deer, they kindled a fire, each one roasting pieces of the flesh upon sharpened switches. The confinement of the captives was the same with the first night, but, as they were by this time more resigned to the event, they were not altogether deprived of sleep.

27th. After breakfast a council was held concerning the division of the prisoners, which being settled, they delivered each other those prisoners who fell within their several allotments, giving them directions to attend to the particular Indians whose property they became. In this day's journey they passed near fort Wyoming, on the eastern branch of Susquehanna, about forty miles from their late habitation.

28th. This morning the prisoners were all painted, according to the custom among the Indians, some of them with red and black, and some all red, and some with black only. Those whom they

17*

smut with black, without any other colour, are not considered of any value, and are generally by this mark devoted to death: although this cruel purpose may not be executed immediately, they are seldom preserved to reach the Indian hamlets alive. In the evening they came to Susquehanna, having had a painful and wearisome journey through a very stony and hilly path.

29th. They went in search of the horses, which had strayed from them in the night, and after some time found them. They then kept the course of the river, walking along its side with difficulty. In the afternoon they came to a place where the Indians had directed four negroes to wait their return, having left them some corn for a subsistence. These negroes had escaped from confinement, and were on their way to Niagara, when first discovered by the Indians; being challenged by them, answered, "they were for the king," upon which they immediately received them into protection.

5th mo., 1st. After crossing a considerable hill in the morning, they came to a place where two Indians lay dead. A party of Indians had taken some white people, whom they were carrying off prisoners; they rose upon the Indians in the night, killed four of them, and then effected their escape.

2d. Having some of their provisions with them, they made an early meal, and travelled the whole day. They crossed the east branch of Susquehanna towards evening, in canoes, at the place where General Sullivan's army had passed it in their expedition.

3d. They frequently killed deer, and by that means supplied the company with meat, being almost the only provision they ate, as the flour they took with them was expended.

4th. The path they travelled this morning was but little trodden which made it difficult for those who were not acquainted with the woods to keep in it. They crossed a creek, made up a large fire to warm themselves by, and then separated into two companies, the one taking the westward path, with whom were Thomas Peart, Joseph Gilbert, Benjamin Gilbert, Jr., and Jesse Gilbert's wife, Sarah; the others went more to the north, over rich level land. When evening came, inquiry was made concerning the four captives who were taken in the westward path, and they were told, that "these were killed and scalped, and you may expect the same fate to-night." *Andrew Harrigar was so terrified at the threat that he resolved upon leaving them, and as soon as it was dark, took a kettle with pretence of bringing some water, and made his escape under favour of the night. He was sought after by the Indians as soon as they observed him to be missing.

5th. In the morning the Indians returned, their search for Andrew Harrigar being happily for him unsuccessful.

6th, 7th, 8th. They continued these three days in the neighbour-

* Andrew Harrigar, after many hardships in the woods, got back " to the settlements, and gave the first information.

hood of these villages, which had been deserted upon General Sullivan's approach. Here they lived well, having, in addition to their usual bill of fare, plenty of turnips and potatoes, which had remained in the ground, unnoticed by the army. This place was the hunting ground of the Shipquagas, and whenever their industry prompted them to go out hunting, they had no difficulty to procure as many deer as they desired.

Roast and boiled meat, with vegetables, afforded them plentiful meals; they also caught a wild turkey, and some fish, called suckers. Their manner of catching fish was, to sharpen a stick, and watch along the rivers until a fish came near them, when they suddenly pierced him with the stick, and brought him out of the water.

Here were a number of colts; some of them were taken, and the prisoners ordered to manage them, which was not easily done.

9th. When they renewed their march, they placed the mother upon a horse that seemed dangerous to ride, but she was preserved from any injury. In this day's journey they came to meadow ground, where they stayed the night, the men being confined as before related, and the negroes lay near them for a guard.

11th. A long reach of savannas and low ground, rendered this day's route very fatiguing and painful, especially to the women. Elizabeth Peart's husband not being allowed to relieve her by carrying the child, her spirits and strength were so exhausted that she was ready to faint; the Indian under whose care she was, observing her distress, gave her a violent blow.

14th. The mother had suffered so much, that two of her children were obliged to lead her. Before noon they came to Canadosago, where they met with Benjamin Gilbert, Jr., and Jesse Gilbert's wife Sarah, two of the four who had been separated from them ten days past, and taken along the western path. This meeting afforded them great satisfaction; the doubt and uncertainty of their lives being spared often distressing their affectionate relations.

John Huston, Jr., the Indian under whose care Benjamin Gilbert was placed, designing to despatch him, painted him black; this exceedingly terrified the family, but no entreaties of theirs being likely to prevail, they resigned their cause to Him whose power can control all events. At their quarters in the evening two white men came to them, one of whom was a volunteer amongst the British, the other had been taken prisoner some time before. These two men brought some hominy, and sugar made from the sweet maple, the sap being boiled to a consistency, and is but a little inferior to the sugar imported from the islands. Of this provision, and a hedgehog which they found, they made a more comfortable supper than they had enjoyed for many days.

15th. In the morning, the volunteer having received information of the rough treatment the prisoners met with from the negroes, relieved them by taking the four blacks under his care. It was not without much difficulty they crossed a large creek which was in their way, being obliged to swim the horses over it. Benjamin Gilbert began to fail; the Indian, whose property he was, highly irritated at his want of strength, put a rope about his neck, leading him along with it. Fatigue at last so overcame him that he fell on the ground, when the Indian pulled the rope so hard that he almost choked him. His wife seeing this, resolutely interceded for him, although the Indians bid her go forwards, as the others had gone on before them; this she refused to comply with, unless her husband might be permitted to accompany her; they replied that they were determined to "kill the old man," having before this set him apart as a victim

16th. Necessity induced two of the Indians to set off on horseback, into the Seneca country, in search of provisions. The prisoners, in the mean time, were ordered to dig up a root, something resembling potatoes, which the Indians call whoppanies. They tarried at this place until towards the evening of the succeeding day, and made a soup of wild onions and turnip tops; this they ate without bread or salt; it could not, therefore, afford sufficient sustenance, either for young or old; their food being so very light, their strength daily wasted.

17th. They left this place, and crossed the Genesee river, (which empties its waters into lake Ontario,) on a raft of logs, bound together by hickory withes. This appeared to be a dangerous method of ferrying them over such a river, to those who had been unaccustomed to such conveyances. They fixed their station near the Genesee banks, and procured more of the wild potato roots before mentioned, for their supper.

18th. One of the Indians left the company, taking with him the finest horse they had, and in some hours after, returned with a large piece of meat, ordering the captives to boil it; this command they cheerfully performed, anxiously watching the kettle, fresh meat being a rarity which they had not eaten for a long time. The Indians, when it was sufficiently boiled, distributed to each one a piece, eating sparingly themselves. The prisoners made their repast without bread or salt, and ate with a good relish what they supposed to be fresh beef, but afterwards understood it was horse-flesh.

A shrill halloo which they heard gave the prisoners some uneasiness. One of the Indians immediately rode to examine the cause, and found it was Capt. Rowland Monteur, and his brother John's wife, with some other Indians, who were seeking them with provision. The captain and his company had brought with them cakes of hominy and Indian corn; of this they made a good meal. From him they received information respecting Joseph Gilbert and Thomas Peart, who were separated from the others on the 4th instant, that they had arrived at the Indian settlements, some time, in safety.

19th. Pounding hominy was this day's employment, the weather being warm, made it a hard task; they boiled and prepared it for supper, the Indians sitting down to eat first, and when they had concluded their meal, they wiped the spoon on the sole of their mocca sons, and then gave it to the captives. Hunger alone could prevail on any one to eat after such filth and nastiness.

21st. The report of a morning gun from Niagara, which they heard, contributed to raise their hopes, they rejoiced at being so near. An Indian was despatched on horseback, to procure provisions from the fort.

22d. As the Indians approached nearer their habitations they frequently repeated their halloos, and after some time they received an answer in the same manner, which alarmed the company much; but they soon discovered it to proceed from a party of whites and Indians, who were on some expedition, though their pretence was that they were for New York. The captain being at a distance behind, when his wife came, the company waited for him. After the customary salutations, he addressed himself to his wife, telling her that Rebecca was her daughter, and that she must not be induced, by any consideration, to part with her; whereupon she took a silver ring off her finger, and put it upon Rebecca, by which she was adopted as her daughter.

They feasted upon the provisions that were brought, for they had been for several days before pinched with hunger, what sustenance they could procure not being sufficient to support nature.

23d. The Indians proceeded on their journey, and continued whooping in the most frightful manner. Those who were behind came up, and the captain handed some rum round, giving each a dram, except the two old folks, whom they did not consider worthy of this notice. Here the captain, who had the chief direction, painted Abner, Jesse, Rebecca, and Elizabeth Gilbert, jun., and presented each with a belt of wampum, as a token of their being received *into favour*, and they took from them all their hats and bonnets, except Rebecca's.

The Indians, men, women, and children, collect together, bringing clubs and stones, in order to beat them, which they usually do with great severity, by way of revenge for their relations who have been slain; this is performed immediately upon their entering the village where the warriors reside. This treatment *cannot be avoided*, and the blows, however cruel, must be borne without complaint, and the prisoners are sorely beaten, until their enemies are wearied with the cruel sport. Their sufferings were in this case very great, they received several wounds, and two of the women, who were on horseback, *were much bruised by falling from their horses*, which were frightened by the Indians. Elizabeth, the mother, took shelter by the side of one of them, but upon his observing that she met with some favour upon his account, he sent her away; she then received several violent blows, so that she was almost disabled. The blood trickled from their heads in a stream, their hair being cropped close, and the clothes they had on, in rags, made their situation piteous. Whilst they were inflicting *this revenge* upon the captives, the king came, and put a stop to any further cruelty, by telling them "it was sufficient," which they immediately attended to.

Benjamin Gilbert, and Elizabeth his wife, Jesse Gilbert, and his wife, were ordered to Captain Rowland Monteur's house, the women belonging to it were kind to them, and gave them something to eat; Sarah Gilbert, Jesse's wife, was taken from them by three women, in order to be placed in the family she was to be adopted by.

24th. Two officers from Niagara fort, Captains Dace and Powell, came to see the prisoners, and prevent (as they were informed) any abuse that might be given them. Benjamin Gilbert informed these officers, that he was apprenhensive they were in great danger of being murdered, upon which they promised him they would send a boat the next day to bring them to Niagara.

When they left the Indian town, several issued from their huts after them, with sticks in their hands, yelling and screeching in a most dismal manner; but through the interposition of four Indian women, who had come with the captives, to prevent any further abuse they might receive, they were preserved. After reaching the fort, Captain Powel introduced them to *Colonel Guy Johnson*, and *Colonel Butler*, who asked the prisoners many questions, in the presence of the Indians. They presented the captain with a belt of wampum, which is a constant practice amongst them, when they intend a ratification of peace.

25th. Benjamin Gilbert, Elizabeth his wife, and Jesse Gilbert, were surrendered to Colonel Johnson. This deliverance, from such scenes of distress as they had become acquainted with, gave them a more free opportunity of close reflection than heretofore.

The particular attention of Colonel Johnson's housekeeper to them, from a commiseration of their distress, claims their remembrance; Benjamin, his wife, and Jesse Gilbert, were invited to her house, where she not only gave the old folks her best room, but administered to their necessities, and endeavoured to soothe their sorrows.

28th. A few days after they came to the fort, they had information that Benjamin Peart was by the river side, with the Indians; upon hearing this report, his mother went to see him, but every attempt for his release was in vain, the Indians would by no means give him up.

The British officers being acquainted that Jesse Gilbert's wife was among the Indians, with great tenderness agreed to seek her out, and after a diligent inquiry, found that she was among the Delawares; they went to them, and endeavoured to agree upon terms for her releasement; the Indians brought her to the fort the next day, but would not give her up to her relations.

29th. As the cabins of the Indians were but two miles from the fort, they went thither, and Jesse and the officers used every argument in their power to prevail upon them, representing how hard it was to part these two young people; at length they consented to bring her in next day, with their whole tribe, for a final release.

30th. They accordingly came, but started so many objections, that she was obliged to return with them.

31st. Early next morning, *Captain Robeson* generously undertook to procure her liberty, which, after much attention and solicitude, he, together with Lieutenant Hillyard, happily accomplished. They made the Indians several small presents, and gave them thirty pounds as a ransom.

When Sarah Gilbert had obtained her liberty, she altered her dress more in character for her sex, than she had been able to do whilst amongst the Indians, and went to her husband and parents at Colonel Johnson's, where she was joyfully received.

Colonel Johnson's housekeeper continued her kind attentions to them during their stay here, and procured clothing for them from the king's stores.

6th month 1st. About this time, the Senecas, among whom Elizabeth Peart was captive, brought her with them to the fort; as soon as the mother heard of it, she went to her, and had some conversation with her, but could not learn where she was to be sent to. Captain Powell interested himself in her case likewise, and offered to purchase her of them, but the Indians refused to give her up; and as the mother and daughter expected they should see each other no more, their parting was very affecting.

2d and 3d. Not many days after their arrival at Niagara, a vessel came up Lake Ontario to the fort, with orders for the prisoners to go to Montreal. In this vessel came one *Captain Brant*, an Indian chief, high in rank amongst them. Elizabeth Gilbert immediately applied herself to solicit and interest him on behalf of her children who yet remained in captivity; he readily promised her to use his endeavours to procure their liberty. A short time before they sailed for Montreal, they received accounts of Abner and Elizabeth Gilbert, the younger, but it was also understood that their possessors were not disposed to give them up.

Here they became acquainted with one *Jesse Pawling*, from Pennsylvania, who was an officer among the British, and behaved with kindness and respect to the prisoners, which induced them to request his attention also to that part of the family remaining in captivity; it appeared to them of some consequence to gain an additional friend. The colonel also gave his promise to exert himself on their behalf.

After continuing ten days at *Colonel Johnson's*, they took boat in the forenoon of the 2d, being the sixth day of the week, and crossed the river Niagara, in order to go on board the vessel (which lay in Lake Ontario) for Montreal.

[In order to condense the narrative, which contains ninety-six pages, that it may not render the perusal of it tiresome, we give the main facts, after the thirtieth page, in the follwing compendium.]

After proceeding as far as Charlton island, seeing a number of small boats, for descending the St. Lawrence, they solicited to go in one of them. They got exposed to much rain, whereby Benjamin Gilbert took sick on the passage, and for want of necessary comforts, he died of a fever, on the fourth day of their departure, and they interred him under an oak by the river side, in a coffin procured from the fort of Cœur de Lac. Finally, the widow and her two children arrived at Montreal, where they were received *by General M'Clean*, and placed in the house of Daniel M'Ulphin, for a time. Here they went severally into hired situations to procure their livelihood, and in the mean time were often favourably noticed *by the British officers*. One day, while Elizabeth Gilbert was at her ironing, she was most agreeably surprised by the unexpected entrance of her six children, just then arrived there!—to wit: Joseph Gilbert, Benjamin Peart, Elizabeth his wife, and young child, Abner and Elizabeth Gilbert. What a happy meeting after a captivity of upwards of fourteen months! These informed, that Thomas Peart, who had obtained his liberty, had voluntarily remained at Niagara, in hopes of being useful in procuring the release of the two yet detained in captivity—say Benjamin Gilbert, Jr., and Rebecca Gilbert.

We pass over considerable of incidents and facts, which attended that branch of the captives, to wit: Joseph Gilbert, Thomas Peart and two others, who were conducted by the western path, and how they finally succeeded to join the widow Gilbert, as above related. They were generally liberated through the influence and money of the British officers, and by these eventually sent to Montreal. Elizabeth Peart, the wife of Benjamin, who had the young child, being parted from her husband by those who had adoptod her, was also separated from her child by those who had chosen it. The Indians intended no cruelty by those measures, but to reinstate their family losses by their adoption. Finally, she and her child were procured, and brought again together, through the intercession and purchase of Captain Powell, at the Niagara fort. Rebecca Gilbert in her captivity was well treated, much valued, and made herself extremely useful to her Indian and legal owners, by teaching them the use of many useful branches of domestic economy.

While these events were transpiring, Benjamin Gilbert, one of the family, coming from Pennsylvania, had arrived at Castleton, near the British lines, to endeavour to procure the return of the whole family. The Society of Friends also had interested themselves in their behalf. Finally, he met them all at Montreal, after an absence of nearly three years. On the 22d of 8 mo.,1782, they all set out on their return home, and on the 28th of 9th mo. following, arrived all safely at Byberry, the place of their nativity; producing much interest and gratification to their former friends, and affording them a lively concern in the incidents of the narrative now brought to a close.

The kindness extended to this family, by the British and tory officers at Niagara, proved that humane feelings possessed their breasts, notwithstanding some of them were conspicuous in their severity against our people as warriors Colonels Butler and Brant had been conspicuous in the massacre at Wyoming, and Colonel Guy Johnson had invaded Herkemer with Indians and committed ravages there and at his former home of *Johnstown.*

The foregoing article concerning the Gilberts was sent by me to the printer at Mauch Chunk, and by him reprinted, with a promise to hunt up the old localities and families, *and to make report.*

A son of Jesse Gilbert told me that the little girl, Abigail Dodson, was detained a captive longer than the Gilberts, and is now a good liver, settled on the Susquehanna.

It would really be an interesting tour to make one's pathway along the Indian path from Mahoning to the Susquehanna, *yet left.*

One of the daughters in the foregoing narrative is now alive in Byberry, Philadelphia county, and has feelingly *confirmed* the foregoing recitals to the present writer.

What a change of country in so short a period! Now Mauch Chunk is all life and prosperity!

The Rev. Henry Smith, a Methodist minister, told in 1841, that when he was a young minister in 1793, at or near Clarksburg, on the Monongahela, the Indians assaulted the house of brother Smith, where he sometimes stopped. The preachers then wore moccasons; in their then little congregation, the two best-dressed females were clothed in short gowns and petticoats, the rest had neither short nor long gowns, and every man and woman was *barefooted!*

Indian relics, New Jersey, 1839. The skeletons of three Indians were dug out, on Benjamin Colson's farm near Rackoon creek, in Gloucester county, New Jersey, in December, 1839, by some men digging for marl. They were found two and a half feet below ground, and some of the bones still good. With them were found two pieces of gold coin of 1666, six rings, and three strings of beads.

My friend, the Rev. Doctor William Neil, (late president of Dickenson college,) a gentleman of about fifty-six years of age in 1835, when a child of two years of age, had his father and uncle killed by Indians in the same field, in day time, on a farm only nine miles from Pittsburg, on the Yougheogheney. On the same day, they also killed three sons of one Marshall, their neighbour. The Indians were a small predatory band. Such an act, *so recent* as about the year 1780, near to so settled a place as that country *is now*, must seem strange, to those who may now contemplate the great change in population and security!

In the year 1756, in the time of Gov. Morris, Benjamin Franklin was made an agent, or commissioner, for seeing to the execution of measures for the war against the Indians. At same time some regulars arrived at Philadelphia, from New York, and were ordered to be posted at Reading and Easton. Three hundred men were ordered to be posted on the west of the Susquehanna, and three forts to be built there. The governor went out to Harris' ferry, and afterwards to Carlisle, then to Easton. At same time Benjamin Frank-

18

lin goes up the Lehigh, in company with a military force, to Gnadenhutten, (Tents of Mercy,) near where he had a fort erected, called *Fort Allen*, situated opposite to the mouth of Mahoning creek. A line of communication was also opened by the same agent through the wilderness, out to the Susquehanna at Wyoming, and having a fort at mid distance, called the *Middle fort*. The old warriors of that day are forgotten, but they consisted of 550 men. When marching from Bethlehem and Nazareth, they went by the way of the gap and Uplinger's. Those named as "without the forks," were Trump's company, of 50; Aston's, 50; Wayne's, 55; Foulke's, 46; Trexler's, 48, and Wetterhold's, 44. Orndt, Craig and Martin had each a company at the Irish settlements. Secretary Peters, in his report to Lord Loudon, states, that the whole number of men raised for garrisons and patrols on the frontiers was 1400—at a cost of £70,000 currency, annually. These men were enlisted for one year, at 1*s.* 6*d.* a day. Fort Allen was surprised and taken by Indians, while part of the garrison was skating on the Lehigh. They then took and burned Gnadenhutten, and bore off prisoners, November, 1756.

There was, in the times of which we are speaking, a universal and deep excitement among the people—such as disturbed and alarmed every body. It occupied and engrossed the continued attention of the governors and legislatures in the several provinces. Governors from several of the states assembled at Philadelphia, to counsel and to concert measures with the Earl of Loudon, the commander-in-chief; and messages were continually passing to and fro, and especially to and from Sir Wm. Johnson, the chief agent for Indian affairs; Indian friends and allies were earnestly sought, and the Indian traders and interpreters were busily occupied in travelling with embassies to the frontiers, to create favourable impressions and to strengthen the frontier people. Men, women and children were every where upon the *qui vive*. They were indeed days of evil omen—every thing was sad and terrified. Long were they remembered and spoken of in later years by our forefathers. But since, their tales of woe and terror are forgotten! During all this excitement the governors and assemblies were in high disagreement about supplies, *and who should pay for them.* The Friends in the house, averse to war, would not vote for its progress; and those not in office, who ruled the meetings, believed *that they* could do better by peaceful measures. Hence the origin of "the Friendly Association for preserving peace." They exerted themselves greatly to effect their object, and contributed large sums of money. The Earl of Halifax, in England, sent out his reprimand, and censured them for interfering in Indian matters, about treaties "with sovereign princes." To this the friends made a strong case in vindication, but withdrawing, however, from any further interposition.

When the ravages of Indians were made at Tulpehocken, the panic flew to Reading, and the people there were disposed to pull down the houses of the Friends. A letter from Judge Moore, in Chester county, stated that 2000 of the inhabitants were preparing to march to Philadelphia, to compel the assembly to defensive laws. A letter from C. Weiser, then made a colonel, stated that many in Berks county were intending the same thing. Kirkbride, Hoge, Dicks and Pennock, in the assembly, resigned their seats, as Friends, at the instance of the ministry at home. It was a time of deep excitement indeed!

It will probably be interesting to many to have a right conception of the localities of *frontier forts*, *Indian towns*, and *Indian paths*, as they formerly existed in Pennsylvania, when the Indians were still among us.

A line of posts began above Easton, on the Delaware, and formed a semi-circular cordon of defence from thence across the Susquehanna at Wilkesbarre and thence by Northumberland, across the Juniata, near Huntingdon, down to Fort Littleton, near Bedford, and thence down to the Potomac.

Beginning with the semi-circle, they stood thus, viz.:

Fort Penn, on Broadhead's creek, falling into the Delaware above Easton.

Fort Augusta, at the forks of the Susquehanna, at the present Northumberland and Sunbury.

There was also another fort, once used, above it, a short distance westward of the present Wilkesbarre.

There was also a second and interior line of forts to the preceding, situate severally, to wit:

Fort Allen, on the Lehigh, opposite to Mahoning creek; next,

Fort Henry, at the head of the main Swatara creek, at the foot of the Blue mountains; next,

At Fort Halifax, on the Susquehanna, a little above Duncan's island; and Fort Hunter, a little below that island.

In returning now to the first above named exterior circle, we find next after Fort Augusta,

Fort Shirley, on Aughwick branch—a creek which empties into the Juniata, a little below Huntingdon; then comes

Fort Littleton and Fort Loudon—the former being a few miles eastward from Bedford, and the latter being a few miles south of Fort Littleton, on the Conocochegue creek, in Franklin county.

The three last named forts ranged in a north and south line, up to Fort Shirley, and from thence there went an Indian path to Fort Augusta, on the Susquehanna.

We now come to show another range of forts, going westward from Bedford, say—

Fort Ligonier; then to Hannah town, and then to Fort Pitt.

Southward from Pittsburg, on the Monongahela, at Redstone creek, stood Fort Burd, near to which there had been two Indian forts. Proceeding due north from Fort Pitt, (Pittsburg,) we find on the Allegheny, at the mouth of French creek, *Fort Venango;* and north-east from thence stood Fort Le Bœuf, at the mouth of Le Bœuf creek; and onward, a little further north, stood Fort Presque-isle, upon the margin of Lake Erie.

The Indian towns were these, viz.:

The Shawnese town, at the mouth of Fishing creek, on the north branch of the Susquehanna; next, the Wyoming town, near present Wilkesbarre; and still higher up that river, the Wyalusing town, at the mouth of the Wyalusing creek.

From these we turn to towns westward, viz.:

Bald-eagles' nest, (at the present Bellefonte,) at the entrance of Spring Creek into Bald Eagle creek, which empties into the west branch of the Susquehanna; thence westward a few miles, was Chingliomalouk, at the mouth of that creek.

Westward of the range of the Allegheny mountains, there were the following, to wit:

Shawnese cabins, a little beyond Bedford.

Conemack old town, at the head of the Kishkemanates river; on the same river, lower down, stood the town of

Blacklegs; and still further down the same, stood the

Kishkemanates town, near to its outlet into the Allegheny river.

On the Allegheny, a little below Kishkemanates river, stood

Chartiers old town; a few miles below it stood

Sewickly's town, a little above Pittsburg.

On the Allegheny, a few miles above Kishkemanates river, stood

Kittaning town, celebrated for its destruction by Col. Armstrong's expedition.

Further up the Allegheny, a few miles above Fort Venango, stood

Kushusduling and Buccaloons towns; and further up the same river, at Bigrock branch, stood Bighole town.

The Indian paths were these, viz.:

Beginning at the north boundary of the state, and with the head waters of the north branch of the Susquehanna, at a few miles westward of Wyalusing; thence southward along the range of mountains westward of Wilkesbarre, down to present Northumberland; thence to the Juniata, south-westwardly, to near the mouth of Tuscarora branch; thence up the Juniata to the present Huntingdon; thence south-westwardly, along Woodcock valley, and keeping between the mountain ranges of the Alleghenies, called "the Great Warrior's mountains," down to the south line of the state, and thence to the Potomac.

There was another Indian path, ranging parallel with the preceding, some twelve or fifteen miles more westward, beginning from the Bald Eagle and Mushanen creeks, on the west branch of Susquehanna, and proceeding southwardly along the Allegheny ranges to the present Frankstown, down to Bedford; where it was joined unto the former line of Indian paths, and guiding the traveller down to Potomac, as in the former pathway.

There was still another great Indian pathway, laying north-westward and south-eastward, beginning at Bedford, and Fort Littleton nigh by it, and going thence north-westwardly to Kittaning, on the Allegheny; and another path, still more northern in its direction, proceeded through Frankston, and from thence due north-west to Venango, still higher up the Allegheny than the former.

These several descriptions, we are aware, will be somewhat difficult of apprehension; but if those who are curious in these matters, will be at the pains to pencil-mark their maps from post to post, as herein set down and directed, they will find themselves sufficiently instructed herein.

It may serve to illustrate the character of some of our American Indians, to say, that Anthony Benezet became acquainted with a portion of them, in the back part of Pennsylvania, who, from their self-conviction of the injustice and irreligion of war, united themselves into a community, with a resolution to war no more, and asserting as their reason, "that when God made men, he did not intend they should hurt or kill one another."

Such views, entertained by them, were of course very gratifying to Anthony Benezet, and he was therefore at special pains to find out the originating cause of views so accordant with his own principles; and the facts in the case, preserved in his preface to his "Plain Path to Christian Perfection," having been kindly given to me by Mrs. Benjamin Chew, I here insert them, viz.: One of the tribe, being by a particular providence brought under difficulty and sorrow, was led, from the contemplation of the sufferings and sins around him, to think of a Creator, and to desire a knowledge of him in whom he had his being. This exercise begat in his mind a spirit of prayer. As this operation proceeded he became conscious of a good and evil principle working within him; he was at last delivered from one, and attained to the other. This man came in time to proselyte others to his own convictions, and to form his own little community averse to the principles of war. "Thus this Indian, (as says A. B.,) untaught by books and unlearned in what is called divinity, through the inshining of the light of Christ on his understanding, could explain the operation of true religion on the heart." He is supposed to have been the chief of the Delawares, named Nedowaway, who finally settled in Ohio, and who with his people united with the Moravian missionaries. See his picture in this work.

Nedowaway was an Indian chief of the Delawares, of more than common character, who had become a Christian, and died in Ohio in 1776, at ninety years of age. His name appears among the signers of the treaty at Conestoga in 1718; and in his childhood he is said to have *seen* William Penn on his second visit in 1701–2 As a trusty and discreet chief, he had been entrusted with the pre servation of all the verbal speeches, bead vouchers, and wampum, and with such writings and instruments as had come from William Penn and his early governors, &c.

He was grieved with the constant encroachments of the white men, westward, on the Indian lands; and early foreseeing that wars must ensue, and that his people must be sufferers, he resolved with his people to get far off in the west. By the advice of the Wyandot chief, he settled on the Cayahage river, where he was visited and seen by Heckewelder in 1772.

See in his picture in this work, how pensive he sits alone, and ponders in the mute eloquence of grief, upon his former well known scenes, along the mountain range traversing the Susquehanna, near Harrisburg. The picture seems to speak his inward emotions and distress at being *obliged* to leave the regions of his former *home.*

> And he felt the soul sigh, as he look'd o'er the scene,
> And remembered how once they were lords of that stream.

As a proper *conclusion* to our Indian notices, it may be well to give a little account of the present disposal of the Indian tribes, as now placed in the far west. They will make a fearful account in numerical force, if made our enemies there, and much it behoves us even now to conciliate and preserve their good will, by acts of sincere and generous friendship and support. We have selfishly placed them—many of them against their wills, where they may yet find means to consolidate and combine their strength against us! We must now look to it in time! Their localities and numbers stood thus in 1838, viz.:

The Indians now east of the Mississippi number 49,365, of which the following are under engagements to remove west of the same river, to wit:

The Winnebagoes,	4,500	Ottawas of Ohio,	100
Pottawatamies of Indiana,	2,950	Cherokees,	14,000
Chippewas, Ottawas and Pottawatamies,	1,500	Creeks,	1,000
Chickesaws,	1,000	Seminoles,	5,000
Apalachicolas,	400	Ottawas and Chippewas in Michigan,	6,500

Making in all 36,950

And those not under treaty stipulations to remove amount to 12,415, to wit:

New York Indians,	4,176	Wyandots,	575
Miamis,	1,100	Menomonies,	4,000
Ottawas and Chippewas of the lakes,			2,564

The Indians who have emigrated from the east to the west of the Mississippi (in 1838) stood thus, viz.:

Chickesaws,	549	Senecas and Shawnese,	211	Quapaws,	476
Chippewas, Ottawas and Pottawatamies,	2,191	Choctaws,	15,000	Ottawas,	374
				Pottawatamies of Indiana,	211

Creeks,	476	Seminoles,	407	Apalachico-las,	265
Cherokees,	7,911	Kickapoos,	588	Delawares,	826
Shawnese,	1,272	Peorias and Kaskas,	132	Weas,	222
Piankeshaws,	162				
Senecas,	251				

Besides the foregoing, we are to consider the force of the Indian tribes, whose former home was in the far west, which comprise an aggregate of 231,806, to wit:

Sioux,	21,600	Iowas,	1,500	Sacs of Missouri,	500
Foxes,	1,600	Osages,	5,120	Ottoes and Missourias,	1,000
Kanzas,	1,606	Omehas,	1,600	Kioways,	1,800
Pawnees,	12,500	Camanches,	19,200	Minaterees,	2,000
Mandans,	3,200	Quapaws,	450	Appaches,	20,280
Pagans,	80,000	Assinnaboins,	15,000	Gros Ventres,	16,800
Crees,	3,000	Arrepahas,	3,000	Caddoes,	2,000
Eutaws,	19,200	Crows,	7,200	Cheyennes,	3,200
Poncas,	900	Arickareas,	2,750		
Blackfeet	30,000	Sacs,	4,800		

Thus making a sum total of 332,498, as derived from official reports, made up in the year 1838. If such a mass should be set upon us as the instruments of *retributive justice*, what might not be our penalties!

THE PIRATES.

> "A bucaniering race—
> The dregs and feculence of every land."

The story of the pirates had been, in early times, one of deep interest and stirring wonder to our forefathers; so much so, that the echo of their recitals, far as we have been long since removed from their fears, have not yet ceased to vibrate upon our ears. Who among us of goodly years but has heard something of the names and piracies of Kid and Blackbeard! They have indeed much of the mist of antiquity about them; for none remember the original tales truly, and all have ceased to read, for none know where to find the book of "the History of the Pirates," as published by William Bradford, in New York, in 1724. That book I have never been able to procure, although I have some conception of it and its terrifying pictures, as once seen and read by my mother when a child. It had every character of the marvellous surely, when it contained notices of the lives of two female pirates—even of Mary Reed and Anne Bonny! Dr. Franklin tells us that he made and published a sailors' song on the capture of Blackbeard—done when he was yet a boy. Can any one bring it again to light? Many would like to see it.

Captain Kid.

Captain Kid (Robert) used to be the earliest name of terror along our coast, although I believe he never committed any excesses near our borders, or on our vessels; but partisans in his name were often named and dreaded. What countryman he was does not appear, but his residence appears to have been in New York before his piracies were known, where he had a wife and child. He most probably had been a successful privateersman, possessing then the friendship of Governor Fletcher, Mr. Nicolls, and Col. Robert Livingston; the latter of whom recommended him to the crown "as a bold and honest man to suppress the prevailing piracies in the American seas." It appears on record at New York, as early as March, 1691, that Captain Kid then reclaimed a pressed seaman; and on the 17th of August, of the same year, he is recorded as bringing in his prize and paying the king his tenth, and the governor his fifteenth, of course showing he was once every way a legalized man among them. His being called "bold," probably arose from numerous acts of successful daring, which made his name renowned while on the side of the law, and equally a subject of terror when openly acknowledged a pirate. It appears from a pamphlet of facts in the case, set forth by the friends of the Earl of Bellermont, about the year 1702, that Col. Robert Livingston and Captain Kid being both in London in 1694, the former recommended him to the crown officers, and also became his security, by whom he received command of the Adventure galley, and sailed from Plymouth in February, 1695. He came out direct to New York,* thence went to Madeira, Madagascar, and the Red sea. In the latter he began his piracies, capturing several vessels, and finally the Quedah Merchant, of 400 tons; with her he came back to the West Indies, where leaving her in charge of one Bolton, he came in a sloop† to Long Island sound, and made many deposits on shore. While in the sound he sent one Emmet to the Earl of Bellermont, then transferred from the government at New York to that at Boston, to negotiate terms of reconciliation. The Governor assured him of fair treatment, in such terms of equivocacy as ensnared him so far that he landed the first of June, 1699—was then arrested and sent home to England for trial. Finally, he was executed at Execution Dock, the 23d of March, 1701, and so gave rise to the once notable "song of Captain Kid." Col. Livingston

---

* The Modern Universal History (Edition—1763) says he left off cruising along New York and New England, because of non-success.

† The word sloop often meant a war vessel without reference to the manner of her rigging.

again attempted to befriend him after his arrest at Boston, by offering some suggestions for his relief. He was one-fifth owner of his original enterprise, in concert with some noblemen in England. The whole was an unofficial adventure of crown officers, possessing, however, the sanction, though not the commission of the king. The expedition itself being thus of an anomalous character, excited considerable political inquiry in England, and finally became, after Kid's death, the subject of parliamentary investigation. The particulars more at large have been preserved by me in my MS. book of Historical Collections, given to the Historical Society of Pennsylvania. Smith's History of New York has some few facts concerning him—see 4to. edition, p. 91. A writer at Albany, in modern times, says they had the tradition that Kid once visited Coeymans and Albany; and at a place two miles from the latter, it was said he deposited money and treasure in the earth. Two families, now of wealth and respectability, of New York, have been named to me as original settlers at Oyster Bay on Long Island, who became suddenly rich by their connexion with Kid's piracies. The story was, that they deserted from his sloop above mentioned, in the sound, after seeing the treasure deposited, and when the chief was arrested, and the expedition destroyed, they profited by the exclusive gain.

Many incidental facts of that day show that the pirates often had their friends and accomplices on shore, acting not unlike the armed vessels off our coasts in the time of the French revolution, all of whom seemed to have accurate knowledge of fit prizes to sail, or expected to arrive. The very circumstance of Kid's having a family in New York inferred his family alliances, and perhaps, if we now knew all things, we might see, even now, some of his wealthy descendants.

Tradition, about and along Long Island sound, says, that the Sachem's head, and the Thimble islands, were the rendezvous of Capt. Kid—one of these rocky islands in the sound is called "Kid's island." He deposited on Gardiner's island the same treasure which was given up to Gov. Bellermont, and of which there is a schedule in the hands of the Gardiner family at this day. It is said that a pot of $1800 was ploughed up two or three years ago in a corn field, at Martha's Vineyard, which is supposed to have been Kid's money. Kid has been sometimes called *William* Kid, and has been so named in that schedule. At Kid's island is a cave, where it is said the pirates used to hide and sleep—inside of it is cut the letters R. K., supposed to stand for Robert Kid—a hole in the rocky floor, chiselled out, is called their punch bowl for carousal. Another little island is called "Money island," and has been much dug for its treasure.

Gov. Fletcher has had the reputation of countenancing the pirates, and Nicholls, one of his council, has been handed down by tradition, as their agent.

An old account, London edition, of the Sea Rovers, from which I have seen some reprint, says of New York, about the year 1695, that "the easy access to the harbour, and the number of hiding places about its waters, together with the laxity of the newly organized government, made it *a great rendezvous for pirates*, where they might dispose of their booty and concert new schemes of depredations There they sold at small prices their rich luxuries and spoils of the *Spanish* provinces. To some at least they were welcome visiters, and for that reason, crews of these freebooters might be seen swaggering about town in open day. In time it became matter of scandal, and a public pest, and the government at home was urgently applied to [of course by the best part of the community] to suppress this evil."

It was of course a matter understood, that to make spoliations on *Spanish* provinces was so much reprisal for wrongs which Hollanders had suffered, under the cruel Duke of Alva, in their fatherland.

In 1699, Isaac Norris, Sen., writes, saying, "We have four men in prison, taken up as pirates, supposed to be Kid's men. Shelly, of New York, has brought to these parts some scores of them, and there is a sharp look out to take them. We have various reports of their riches, and money hid between this and the capes. There were landed about twenty men, as we understand, at each cape, and several are gone to York. A sloop has been seen cruising off the capes for a considerable time, but has not meddled with any vessel as yet, though she has spoken with several."

The above quoted letter, in the Logan MS. collection, goes to countenance the prevalent idea of hidden money. The time concurs with the period Captain Kid was known to have returned to the West Indies. It may have been the very sloop in which Kid himself was seeking means of conveying home his treasure, and with which he finally went into Long Island sound to endeavour to make his peace. Four of the men, landed at Lewistown, were apprehended and taken to Philadelphia; I saw the bill of their expense,* but heard no more of them, save that I saw that Colonel Quarry, at Philadelphia, was reproached by William Penn for permitting the bailing of the pirates; some were also bailed at Burlington.—Vide Penn's letter of 1701. One man of Jersey was arrested by James Logan, on his own declaration that he had so hid money on Cape May, but the case was discharged by Logan himself, as something like a hoax. William Clark, the collector of customs "down the Delaware," at Lewistown I presume, had his house robbed by pirates, as he alleged.

A letter from Jonathan Dickinson, then at Port Royal, dated the 5th of 4 mo. 1699, to his wife, then in Philadelphia, says, "Many pirates are and have been upon the coast. About two days since came news of Captain Kid's being upon our coast, being come from

* Wessell Alricks, of Newr county, (New Castle,) was paid £9, for bringing pirates in 1700, to Philadelphia, from the Whore-kills.—Logan MSS.

the East Indies with a great booty, but wants provisions. He is in a ship which he took from the natives of those parts, having thirty odd guns, with twenty-five white men and thirty negroes. There is gone hence, two days since, Ephraim Pilkerton, in a sloop well manned, to go and take him." Probably the reason of so few men on board the "Quedah" was, that Kid himself was absent in the sloop before mentioned.

An original letter, which I have seen, from John Askew in London, dated 22d of 3 mo. 1701, to Jonathan Dickinson, contains a *postscriptum* intimating the finale of this bold sea rover—saying, "Captain Kid and some other pirates are to execute to-morrow at Execution Dock, in Wapping; Kid, to be gibbetted at Tillberry Fort, Gravesend."

As a sequel to the whole, came out the ballad song of Captain Kid—a great rarity in the present day, although the pensive tones are still known to some, and have been latterly revived in much bad taste among the eccentric camp-meeting hymns—singing, "Farewell, ye blooming youth," &c. For the use of the curious, both the facts and the style of this pirate song are here preserved, from the recollections of an ancient person, to wit:

1. My name was Captain Kid,
When I sail'd, when I sail'd, } bis.
My name was Captain Kid,
And so wickedly I did,
God's laws I did forbid
When I sail'd, when I sail'd. } bis.

2. My name, &c.
I roam'd from sound to sound,
And many a ship I found,
And them I sunk or burn'd
When I sail'd, when I sail'd.

3. My name, &c.
I murder'd William Moore,
And laid him in his gore,
Not many leagues from shore,
When I sail'd, when I sail'd.

4. My name, &c.
Farewell to young and old,
All jolly seamen bold;
You're welcome to my gold,
For I must die, I must die.

5. My name, &c.
Farewell to Lunnon town,
The pretty girls all round;
No pardon can be found,
And I must die, I must die.

6. My name, &c.
Farewell, for I must die
Then to eternity,
In hideous misery,
I must lie, I must lie.

Blackbeard.

It would appear as if none of the pirates so much agitated the minds of our proper ancestors as Blackbeard—his very name raising ideas of something terrific and cruel His proper name was Teach, who acquired the *cognomen* as possessing in his person an alarming black beard, probably cherished for purposes of effect, to terrify his enemy, and as in full keeping with his black or bloody flag. His depredations in our proper seas were considerably more modern than the piracies of Kid; and after Blackbeard's career was ended in 1718, there were many, as we shall presently show, to succeed him. But we have, however, mention of a pirate, even earlier than Kid's known piracies, even as early as his privateering; for very early in the rise of our infant city, one Brown, of the assembly, a son-in-law too of the deputy governor, Colonel Markham, was refused his seat in the house on his alleged connexion with the pirates.* They doubtless found such a defenceless place a ready market to vend some of their spoil, and the naval regulations could have had little or no means to prevent clandestine commerce. The bay and river doubtless furnished them many a secure place in which they could refit or provide their necessary supplies. Perhaps as jolly sailors, full of money and revelry, they sometimes found places even of welcome, from those who might choose to connive at their real character. We find, as early as 1692, that one Babit and others stole a sloop from Philadelphia for purposes of piracy, and also committed some thefts in the river. It was, however, but a small affair, and yet, small as it was, it much excited the town.

In the year 1701, such were the apprehensions from pirates, from their depredations on the seacoast, that watches were appointed to give alarm in Sussex.

Mrs. Bulah Coates, (once Jacquet—this was the name of the Dutch governor in Delaware, in 1658,) the grandmother of Samuel Coates, Esq., late an aged citizen, told him that she had seen and sold goods to the celebrated Blackbeard, she then keeping a store in High street, No. 77, where Beninghove owned and dwelt—a little west of Second street. He bought freely and paid well. She then knew it was he, and so did some others. But they were afraid to arrest him, lest his crew, when they should hear of it, should avenge his cause by some midnight assault. He was too politic to bring his vessel or crew within immediate reach; and at the same time was careful to give no direct offence to any of the settlements where they wished to be regarded as visiters and purchasers, &c.

---

* Wilcox Phillips, who kept the inn for many years at the east end of the long stone bridge leading to the Kensington market place, (who would now be about a hundred years of age,) told an aged friend of mine that his grandfather, who lived on or about that spot, used to tell him that a pirate had actually wintered his vessel in the Cohocksinc creek, a little above that bridge.

Blackbeard was also seen at sea by the mother of the late Dr. Hugh Williamson, of New York; she was then, in her youth, coming to this country, and their vessel was captured by him. The very aged John Hutton, who died in Philadelphia in 1792, well remembered to have seen Blackbeard, at Barbadoes, after he had come in under the Act of Oblivion. This was but shortly before he made his last cruise, and was killed, in 1718. The late aged Benjamin Kite has told me, that he had seen in his youth an old black man, nearly a hundred years of age, who had been one of Blackbeard's pirates, by impressment. He lived many years with George Grey's family, the brewer in Chestnut street, near to Third street. The same Mr. Kite's grandfather told him he well knew one Crane, a Swede, at the Upper ferry, on Schuylkill, who used to go regularly in his boat to supply Blackbeard's vessel at State island. He also said it was known that that freebooter used to visit an inn in High street, near to Second street, with his sword by his side. There is a traditionary story, that Blackbeard and his crew used to visit and revel at Marcus Hook, at the house of a Swedish woman, whom he was accustomed to call Marcus, as an abbreviation of Margaret.

How long Blackbeard exercised his piracies before the years 1717 and '18, which terminated his profligate career, I am not enabled to say, but in this time the MS. papers in the Logan collection make frequent mention of him and others, as in that hateful pursuit, to wit:

In 1717, Jonathan Dickinson, at Philadelphia, writes, saying, "The pirates have not yet quitted our coast, and have taken one of our vessels at the cape, in which you happily did not ship my wine."

In August, 1718, he says, "We have been perplexed by pirates on our coast and at our capes, who plundered many of our vessels, also several from Virginia, Maryland, and New York, and some of the piratical crews are come into our province to lurk and cover themselves."

In March, 1718, he writes—"We have account from Virginia, that two small sloops fitted out there, and manned by the men-of-war's men against Captain Teach, alias Blackbeard, conquered his vessel after a bloody battle, and carried Teach's head into Virginia. We have heard too that Major Bonet and his crew, with another crew, were hanged in South Carolina; and one Taylor and his crew at Providence. But this latter wants confirmation. How these sort of men have fared in other parts we wait to hear. For these two summers they have greatly annoyed our trade. They pillaged one of my vessels, and destroyed the letters."

In another letter he writes and says, "Colonel Spotswood, governor of Virginia, formed a design with the captain of a small man-of-war to send out two of their country sloops, with about fifty men, to attack Captain Teach, alias Blackbeard, a pirate then at North Carolina, whom they took, and brought his head into Virginia, after a bloody battle, and most of them killed and wounded,"*—he also adds a sentence of peculiar character, saying, "I have to remark that papers and letters taken in Blackbeard's possession will strongly affect some persons in the government of North Carolina!"

In 1717, James Logan writes, saying, "We have been extremely pestered with pirates, who now swarm in America, and increase their numbers by almost every vessel they take—[compelling them to enter by coercion or otherwise.] If speedy care be not taken they will become formidable, being now at least fifteen hundred strong. They have very particularly talked of visiting this place; many of them being well acquainted with it, and some born in it, for they are generally all English, and therefore know our government can make no defence."

In the same year he writes to the governor of New York, saying, "We have been very much disturbed the last week [in October,] by the pirates. They have taken and plundered six or seven vessels to or from this place; some they took to their own use, and some they dismissed after plundering them. Some of our people having been several days on board of them, had much free discourse with them. They say they are about eight hundred strong at Providence, and I know not how many at Cape Fear, where they are making a settlement. Captain Jennings, they say, is their governor in chief, and heads them in their settlement. The sloop that came on our coast had about one hundred and thirty men, all stout fellows, all English, and doubly armed. They said they waited for their consort, of twenty-six guns, when they designed to visit Philadelphia! Some of our masters say they know almost every man on board—most of them having been lately in the river; their commander is Teach, who was here a mate from Jamaica about two years ago." In another letter he says, "They are now busy about us to lay in their stores of provisions for the winter."

In October, 1718, James Logan again writes to Colonel Hunter, the governor of New York, by express, saying, "We are now sending down a small vessel to seize those rogues, if not strengthened from sea. We are in manifest danger here, unless the king's ships [which seem careless of the matter] take some notice of us; they probably think a proprietary government no part of their charge.† It is possible, indeed, that the merchants of New York, some of them I mean, might not be displeased to hear we are all reduced to ashes. [Even so early it seems there were jealousies of trade!] Unless these pirates be deterred from coming up our rivers by the fear of men-of-war outside to block them in, there is nothing but what we may fear from them; for that unhappy pardon, [the same Teach before embraced,] has given them a settled correspondence every where, and

* James Logan says Governor Spotswood had before sent on to Philadelphia to get proclamations printed, offering a generous reward for pirates.

† At that time, as J. Logan writes to John Askew, in London, there was a king's ship at New York, and three or four in Virginia.

an opportunity [mark this!] of lodging their friends where they please, to come to their assistance; and no where in America, [mark this!] I believe, so much as in this town. Remember too," says he, "that one of the capes of Delaware, and half of our bay and river, are under thy government."

Such was the picture of piracy, which once distressed and alarmed our forefathers, and shows in itself much of the cause of the numerous vague tales we still occasionally hear of Blackbeard and the pirates. Here we have direct fact of his then being on the coast, well armed, with a crew of one hundred and thirty men, and waiting the arrival of another vessel, when he meditated a visit of rapine and plunder on Philadelphia itself! Think too of his crew being men generally known to captains in Philadelphia—some of them born among us,—others had been lately in the river, and the whole busily concerting schemes to lay in their winter supply of provisions; and all this through the assistance on shore of former pirates among them, who had been pardoned by the Act of Oblivion, and on the whole, produced such favour to their object, even in Philadelphia itself, surpassing any other town! Think too of the alleged force of the whole concentred outlaws—such as eight hundred in Providence, and so many at Cape Fear, in North Carolina, as to have their own governor!

As some incidental proof of "the assistance on shore" from pirates, holding their place among us under the former Act of Oblivion and Pardon, we may add, to wit: Isaac Norris, writing to his friend in October, 1718, says, "My son Harrison, moving from Maryland, had all his household goods and a value of English goods and stores, on board of G Grant's shallop, taken between Apoquiminy and New Castle, and carried off, with two valuable negro men, by eight or ten pirates in an open boat—rogues that lately came in on the king's proclamation! Grant (the owner of the shallop!) is suspected to be in the confederacy, and is in prison—having secreted goods belonging to R. Harrison, found with him, to the value of forty or fifty pounds.*

The same year, (1718,) I found that the grand jury in Philadelphia presented a case of piracy, to wit: John Williams, Joseph Cooper,† Michael Grace, William Asheton, George Gardner, Francis Royer and Henry Burton, with force of arms, viz., with swords, guns, cutlasses, &c., forcibly took the sloop Antelope of twenty-two tons, riding in the Delaware, and bore her off, &c. It was, however, marked *Ignoramus*, as not found, probably from the difficulty of procuring direct witnesses.

When we thus consider "their friends," thus "lodged among us every where," it presents additional reasons for the ideas of buried treasure of the pirates, once so very prevalent among the people, of

* This is the same family into which the Hon. Charles Thomson married; they settled at Harriton, in Merion, where C. T. lived and died.

† It may be seen in the sequel that Joe Cooper became commander of a pirate vessel, and he and his crew came to their untimely end in the bay of Honduras, in 1725.

which I have presented several facts of digging for it, under the head of Superstitions; they believing that Blackbeard and his accomplices buried money and plate in numerous obscure places near the rivers; and sometimes, if the value was great, they killed a prisoner near it, so that his ghost might keep his vigils there and terrify those who might approach. Those immediately connected with pirates might keep their own secrets, but as they might have children and connexions about, it might be expected to become the talk of their posterity in future years, that their fathers had certain concealed means of extravagant living; they may have heard them talk mysteriously among their accomplices of going to retired places for concealed things, &c. In short, if given men had participation in the piracies, it was but natural that their proper posterity should get some hints, under reserved and mysterious circumstances *of hidden treasure, if it* existed. Certainly it was once much the expectation and the talk of the times—for instance, the very old two-story house at the north-east corner of Second street and Gray's alley, (i. e. Morris' alley,) originally built for Stephen Anthony, in digging its cellar they found there a pot of money, supposed to have been buried by the pirates. This story I heard from several very aged persons. I have stated elsewhere the fact of finding another pot of money in Spruce street near Front street.

It may seem strange to us that so much aggregate depravity among English seamen could have been found, as to accumulate such numbers of pirates as alleged at Providence and Cape Fear, but they had just come out of a war in which privateering had been much fostered and depended upon by many. It presents an awful proof of the corruption of morals usually produced by the legalized robbery, called privateering, so generally conducted in an irresponsible manner. Indeed the ideas of privateersmen and pirates were so identified in the minds of people generally, that a privateer was often called the pirate.

I happen to know the fact that Blackbeard, whose family name was given as Teach, was in reality named Drummond, a native of Bristol. I have learned this fact from one of his family and name, of respectable standing, in Virginia, near Hampton. Captain Drummond was a half-crazed man, under high excitements, by his losses and imprisonment from the French. He had been a privateersman out of Liverpool, and had made several French captures, all of which he lost by their restoration at the peace. He then went again to sea and took all French vessels which he could, *as a pirate*, and eventually, being an outlaw, he captured of all kinds which he came across. His surgeon, for a part of his time, was a Doctor Cabot, who became the ancestor of a family of respectability settled in Virginia. The name of Teach, it may be observed, seems to be a feigned name, because no such name can be found in the Philadelphia or New York Directories, just as I happen to know, that the names of *Crowell*, in this country, is an *altered name*, in 1675, from Cromwell, the Protector.

When the vessel which captured Blackbeard returned to Virginia, they set up his head on a pike planted at "Blackbeard point," *then an island.* Afterwards, when his head was taken down, his skull was made into the bottom part of a very large punch bowl, called *the infant*, which was long used as a drinking vessel at the Raleigh tavern at Williamsburg. It was enlarged with silver, or silver plated; and I have seen those whose forefathers have spoken of their drinking punch from it, with a silver ladle appurtenant to that bowl.

There is at present a large marble tombstone, in a grave place half a mile out of Hampton, on the Pembroke farm of John Jones, Esq., which had been placed there by governor Nicholson in 1700, which records the death of Peter Heysham, Esq., collector of the customs, who had been killed, as a volunteer on board the king's ship, the Shoreham, in a brave encounter with a pirate on the coast; most problably, from the date, with Kidd. The action lasted seven hours, and the governor was also present. Near the same grave are three others, of like marble, with family arms, of the years 1697, 1700, and 1719. These graves had been for many years overgrown with underbrush and accumulated earth, and were lately unexpectedly brought to light, by a clearing off of the place.

In noticing the history of the pirates, there ought to be considered the cause and time of their origin, and why it appears, in the old books and accounts of them, that the Turks, Moors, and *Sallee pirates* were so often named as being dreaded on the *Atlantic*, and even in the West Indies! All these inquiries may be satisfied by noticing what has been said by Capt. Smith, in his History of Virginia, London edition, 1626.

He gives an account of the making the Moors of Barbary to become pirates. He says the long peace under King James put sea-warriors out of employ, and caused them to turn pirates—some for money, some for bravery, and some for vanity of a fearful name. They chose Barbary, because of its numerous convenient roads. Thus *Ward*, a poor English sailor, and *Danaker*, a Dutchman, first began their career there, even when the Moors scarcely knew how to sail a ship. Then followed *Easton*, who got rich—*these taught the Moors to serve them.* Then followed Jennings, Harris, Thompson and others, whose names he gives. Several were executed in time of King James, at Wapping—such as Hewes, Smith, Ellis, Collins, &c., all captains—had good ships, and well manned, but quarrelled some among themselves—finally became debauched, and so eventually the Turks and Moors took the ascendency of them, and made them serve themselves as subordinates—themselves having learned their practices, with better command of their passions and interests.

When I published the Annals, I said I could not hear of any one who then had Bradford's edition of the old pirates, in which was contained the history of Mary Read and Anne Bonney, female pirates -the former of England, the latter of Charleston, S. C., though born in Cork. I have since met with "The Pirates' Own Book," Boston edition, of 1837, which is manifestly formed from that old book, and gives the lives of those two females. From this book I find sundry additional facts concerning Capt. Robert Kidd and Blackbeard, from which I select the following additional facts, not before stated in my account of them. This is, therefore, *supplemental*—to wit:

Edward Teach (Blackbeard) was born in Bristol, England. He first was a privateersman in the West Indies, against the French. He began his piracies in a ship of 40 guns, called "Queen Anne's Revenge." Blackbeard often changed his vessels. At one time he came off Charleston, S. C., with his fellow-pirate, Richards, and one or two other vessels. There they remained some days without the bar, capturing vessels and causing much terror to the inhabitants, and stopping all trade *from* the port. While there, Teach sent in Capt. Richards, with one of his prisoners, to demand of the governor medicines, on pain of his destroying his prisoners. It was granted, and Richards and his men actually walked the town audaciously and unmolested. After this he ran ashore upon North Carolina, and made his terms of surrender to the governor. "The gold of Blackbeard (it is said) rendered him comely in the governor's eye, and through his aid he obtained a legal right to the great ship, *the Revenge*"—"the governor condemning her at Bath Town Court, as a lawful prize to the captor!" While in North Carolina, Blackbeard married a young woman of good family, the governor being present at the ceremonies! She was said to have been his fourteenth wife—twelve of whom were still living. He went off again to his piracies, and brought his captures into North Carolina, and had them again condemned—the governor and he sharing spoils! Blackbeard "passed several months in the river, giving and receiving visits from the planters," &c.—they probably not knowing his real character. In time they began to know it—and they and sundry captains of vessels made their representation to *the governor of Virginia*, as too much distrusting their own governor. The governor of Virginia hired two small vessels, and gave the command to Lieut. Maynard, who, on the 17th Nov., 1717, sailed from James river in quest, and found Blackbeard on the 21st, with but few of his men on board. A fierce fight ensued—Maynard and Blackbeard hand to hand—the latter received twenty cuts and as many shots before he fell dead. He struck off his head, and hung it on the end of his bowsprit, on his return to Virginia. They found on board the prize, letters and papers which *criminated the governor of North Carolina and his secretary.* The prisoners taken were tried and executed in Virginia, and old court records ought, even now, to show the facts. It is said of Blackbeard that he was peculiarly reckless and gay in his wickedness. For instance, he has cocked his pistols at his own banquet, and fired at one of his guests, saying, "he must now and then kill a man to make them know and fear him." He has gone into his hold with some of his men to be smoked with brimstone, "to make a hell of their own beforehand, for trial!" He had kept a kind of journal, which was found, containing remarks like these, viz.:— "Rum all out—our company somewhat sober—a d—d confusion among us—rogues are plotting—talk of separation—I must look sharp for a prize." To cherish his long black beard, he used to twist it up in portions with ribbon. In time of action he wore three braces of pistols in a sling, over his shoulders.

☞ It might be curious now to learn what family in North Carolina (like Kidd, in New York) may have had the distinguishing infamy of being descendants of the above young wife! One might ask, too, why should we not expect some one of his wives to be about the Delaware, and to have progeny?

In the year 1837, Anthony Backhouse, of Virginia, farmer, at the mouth of Tanner's creek, adjoining Pomfret, ploughed up a box of gold and silver coin, amounting to 14,000 dollars. The Norfolk Herald says, "The opinion of course has precedence, that this money was one of the *numerous* deposits made on our coast by Blackbeard."

Robert Venables, the old black man who died in 1834, aged 98, told me that he knew personally an old black man, and Carr, a drayman, in Gray's alley, both of whom had been with Blackbeard.

He had heard that Blackbeard had dealings with "Charles ——," the owner of a shallop packet to Burlington—who used, when about to start, to go around the little town, crying, "ho! Burlington, ho!" He supplied the pirate with flour, &c. Heard often of pirates' money. He knew that Murdock, Riley, Farrel and others, went to Point-no-point to dig—success not known—some said they were frightened off. Used to hear that Stephen Anthony, at corner of Gray's alley and Second street, found a pot of money in digging for his cellar. His black, Friday, first came to it in digging, and showed its outward shape. The master, to conceal and keep it, quickly sent off Friday for drink, and when he returned, the pot was gone! Such was the story. Bobert's mother, at Bridgetown, Barbadoes, knew there a Mary Read, who turned pirate.

The 11th August, 1718, Gov. Keith being present in council, (vide minutes,) presented the case of a pirate vessel arrived—being surrendered by the men. The arms and ammunition are ordered into charge—among them are "10 great guns" and "9 peteraroes," 1 doctor's chest, 1 black flag, 1 red flag, 2 ensigns, 1 jack, &c. The governor remarks, that "one Teach, a noted pirate, (Blackbeard,) had done the greatest mischief of any of the place, and was *then* said to be lurking for some time in and about *this town*;" and for that cause he had granted a warrant for his apprehension, as well as for several others hereabouts, who having received certificates of pardon upon their surrender under the royal proclamation to this and other governments, and were now said to be in active correspondence with other pirates at large, &c.

The 17th October, 1718, the governor presents a bill of £90, expenses incurred in the expedition of two sloops to the capes, in pursuit of the pirates, commanded by Captains Raymond and Naylor.

A republication of 1829, by H. Benton, of Hartford, called the "History of the Pirates," has an account of Mr. Woodes Rogers, as governor and vice-admiral of the Bahamas, going out to Nassau in July, 1718, and there granting pardon on submission of one thousand pirates on shore, they having for their Captains, Hornygold, Davis, Carter, Burgess, Current, Clark and others. To some of these the governor gave civil commissions. When the Spanish war occurred, many of them were glad again to go out *privateering*. There are not any cases of marked cruelty represented in the book. Plundering was the chief of their action, and killing, when in fight.

On the 4th July, 1726, Governor William Dummer, and his council, condemned, at Boston, Captain William Fly and three of his men, as pirates, who were hung in chains in the harbour. Captain Bellamy and seven others, about same time, get ashore at Eastham, and are captured, condemned and executed

In the proceedings of the court at Philadelphia, in June, 1697, present Governor Markham, Edward Shippen, Charles Sanders, John Farmer and Charles Sober, justices; David Lloyd, attorney general; Thomas Robinson, attorney for the Earl of Romney—the case of *James Brown*, member of assembly and son-in-law to Governor Markham, is brought up for trial; Jan Mathias, a Swede, and Peter Clawson, a Dutchman, are the witnesses against him. They give long and vague stories of their numerous voyages, all the world over, with apparent wishes to cover over any direct or voluntary piracies of their own, and neither of them present any positive culpability on Mr. Brown, who was probably favoured at last with a *nulle prosequi*, as no decision is recorded. Their story, if much condensed, would go to say, that in Africa, they were forced into Captain Avery's pirate vessel—fought a great Turk in the Red sea, took his money and let him go—did not meet with much to engage or capture, and being at length in the East Indies, in 1693–4, *James Brown*, the person indited, came on board and asked if he might be indulged in a passage home to Rhode Island, and the crew *being first consulted*, he took his passage on board; after that they fell in with no more vessels or plunder! They came across the ocean to Cat island, thence to Providence, where the witnesses and some others were discharged. Some of them went to New London and some to New York, finally to West Jersey, and then to Philadelphia, *where hearing that a man* had come to seize Avery *and all his men*, and that there was also a proclamation of pardon, they forthwith surrendered to the authorities! It came out on the whole that James Brown was also in the Red sea, and came on board from the "New Bark" from Rhode Island.

In March, 1704, Samuel Lowman, Esq., collector of the port of Lewes, (vide Minutes of Council,) claims his bill of expenses as evidence in Philadelphia, in the year 1700, against certain persons *of the port of Lewes*, who had illegally traded with Captain Kidd's ship, the Pirate, for which they were then apprehended. These pirates, about eighty in number, had before plundered Lewestown, and *threatened* to do the same at New Castle, but were hindered by the arrival of a large vessel with German passengers. The prisoners named are Robert Brandingham and William Stanton.

It would seem as if the pirates, by hook or crook, found means to escape the toils of law, so much so as to give offence to some; for I find among the *scandals* of the time, some one had set forth in a printed pamphlet, of 1703, that "these Quakers have a neat way of getting money by encouraging the pirates, when they bring in good store of gold, so that when Avery's men were here, the Quaking justices were for letting them live quietly, or else they are bailed too easily."

In the Book of Pirates, we find a few additional facts concerning Captain Robert Kidd and his compatriots. The king's commission to Kidd, while he affected to be a legal *privateersman*, incidentally named the pirates whom he was intended to capture, say Captain Thomas Too, John Ireland, Captain Thomas Wake, Captain Maze, or Mace, and other subjects, *natives or inhabitants of New York and elsewhere in America*, they being *pirates* upon the American seas, &c. [None of their histories are in the book.] Some of them were natives of New Jersey, nearest to New York. With Kidd were executed, as his accomplices, Nicholas Churchhill, James How, Gabriel Loff, Hugh Parrott, Abel Owens and Darby Mullins. It was proved that Kidd had killed his gunner, "William Moor," in a quarrel. Nicholas Churchhill and James How proved, by Colonel Bass, the governor of West Jersey, that they had surrendered to him under the amnesty, or pardon. It seems that there was a board of commissioners under the king, to grant pardons to such repenting pirates as should come in and accept. It will not fail to be observed, in the foregoing and similar cases of *names*, that none of them are of the true *Holland* race. Still it is known, that the New Yorkers, even as Dutchmen, were keen enemies of the Spaniards, who had so long devasted their fatherland. They might have been willing to wink at their aggressions on their possessions in the West Indies and South America. Even the English colonists had no aversion to their being roughly scourged, even in time of peace.

Other Pirates.

The death of Blackbeard and his immediate companions appears to have had no visible restraint on the spirit of desperate adventure in others. It doubtless broke the connexion with us on shore; but as general sea-rovers, there still continued later accounts of several, roaming and ravaging on the high seas, to wit:

In the Gazettes of 1720, there is frequent mention of our vessels encountering "pirates" in the West Indies. They are pillaged, but not murdered; nor otherwise so barbarously maltreated as now.

In 1721, it is observed that "the pirates" act generally under the colours of Spain and France. "We have advice that Captain Edwards, the famous pirate, is still in the West Indies, where they have done incredible damage," and at the same time the Gazette says, "A large sloop has been seen from hence (off Cape May) cruising on and off for ten days together, supposed to be a pirate," and three weeks later she is mentioned as running ten leagues up the bay, and thence taking out a large prize.

In 1722, mention is made of a pirate brigantine which appears off and at Long Island—commanded by one Lowe, a Bostonian. They had captured a vessel with five women in her, and sent them into port in safety in another vessel. His name often afterwards occurs as very successful; at one time he took Honduras, &c. One Evans, another pirate, is also named. While Lowe was off Long Island, several vessels were promptly fitted out against him, but none brought back any renown.

In 1723, the above "Captain Lowe, the pirate, and his consort, Harris, came near the Hook; there they got into action with his majesty's ship, the Greyhound. The two pirates bore the black flag, and were commanded by the celebrated Lowe." The Greyhound captured Harris' vessel, having thirty-seven whites and six blacks, prisoners; but Lowe's vessel escaped, having on board, it is said, £150,000 in gold and silver. The names of the prisoners are published, and all appear to be American or English. They were tried and all executed, not long after, at Long Island. What a hanging day for forty-four persons at once!

Before this action they had probably been near Amboy, &c., as it was just before announced that "two pirate vessels looked into Perth Amboy, and into New York!"

On the return of Captain Solgard to New York, of the Greyhound, he is presented the freedom of the city, in a gold snuffbox. Lowe is afterwards heard of as making prizes of twenty French vessels at Cape Breton. He is stated as peculiarly cruel, since his fight above, to Englishmen, cutting and slitting their ears and noses. There is also named one Lowder—another pirate on the banks.

In 1724, Lowe, the pirate, lately came across a Portuguese, and plundered her. His vessel is a ship of thirty guns, called the Merry Christmas; he has another ship in company as his consort. Captain Ellison, of New York, was taken in sight of Barbadoes, by Sprigg, the pirate, by whom he was well treated, though plundered some. Soon after, the Gazette announces that it is said that Sprigg, the pirate, is to come on our coast to the eastward, to careen. He is in the Old Squirrel man-of-war, which being sold for a merchantman, was taken by Lowe, and run away with by Sprigg and others of Lowe's crew. He says when he gets more men he will come and take Captain Solgard, with whom he before fought off the Hook, and who was at this time again out in the Greyhound, cruising along the coast for pirates.

The same year (1724) it is announced that they hear from Honduras by Captain Smith, that "Sprigg, the pirate," is there in the Bachelor's Delight, of twenty-four guns, in company with Skipton, in the Royal Fortune, of twenty-two guns—the same which had been commanded by Lowe, but his crew mutinying set him ashore. Skipton is a north countryman, and merciful. They promise to visit our coasts in the spring.

In 1725, it is said that Sprigg, the pirate, was put ashore by his men in the West Indies, whereby he was taken prisoner to Jamaica. From Barbadoes it is heard that Line, who was commander of his consort, was taken into Curracoa. There they were paraded to the prison, with their black silk flag! Line had lost his nose and an eye, and the wounds of his men *stank* as they walked. Line confessed he had killed thirty-seven masters of vessels!—Possibly it was boasting over-much. Skipton, the pirate, with eighty men, is stated to have been taken by his majesty's ship, the Diamond, in the bay of Honduras, together with Joseph Cooper,* another pirate vessel. When one of these vessels saw she must surrender, the captain with many of his men went into the cabin and blew themselves up.

This year of 1725 appears to have been fatal to the pirates. Their career seemed almost every where run out, and terrible and inglorious their end—"The way of the transgressor is hard!" After this the former frequent mention of pirates, in almost every weekly paper, subsides. The peaceful and honest mariners no longer fear to traverse the ocean. There were still delays of justice to some, when, as late as October, 1731, Captain Macferson and four others were tried for piracy and hanged.

THE SWEDES.

The arrival *time* of the Swedes on the Delaware has hitherto been a difficult subject to settle with certainty. I shall herein endeavour to *settle* the date at the year 1637, for the reasons which will be found below.

I had, in my former edition of Annals, set it down at the year 1631,

* Joe Cooper was before mentioned as a pirate, known and presented by the grand jury at Philadelphia, in 1718.

taking my date from Campanius. But he was not so good an authority as the Rev. Mr. Rudman's MS. account, since made public by the Rev. Mr. Clay, in his late publication, "the History of the Swedes on the Delaware." Thomas Campanius Holm, who wrote the history which he published in 1702, derived it all from his grandfather's MS. notes and papers, and may have easily mistaken 1631 for 1637; or the difference may have been a printer's error, easily made. From the same cause, Proud, who used the time 1627, may have *written* 1637, and been misprinted by ten years; just as his printer printed the 24th October instead of the 27th October, as the landing day of Penn at New Castle.

The Rev. John Campanius, who came out with Governor Printz in 1642, must have known, and have *written* the true time, if he had had occasion to have intended to mark *the time.* The history by his grandson, Thomas Campanius Holm, however, only speaks incidentally; for when speaking of the subscription and sanction of the public men to the colonization, as done in 1627, he says, "*soon after* the Swedes and Fins went to the South river"—the Delaware. At another place he says, "the Christina fort was first built *when* the Swedes arrived in 1631." From such authority, many of the subsequent writers may have been *misled.* First, Campanius Holm, may have *copied* wrongly, and from him Smith and Proud take the time of 1627; and others, like Holmes, in his American Annals,—the time *of the fort*, in 1631.

But we know from official record, still on file at New York, (quoted by Moulton) that Governor Keift remonstrated in 1638, soon after his arrival, against the building of the fort at Christina. It is dated *the 6th May*, 1638, referring no doubt to a matter *begun before* the writing of the letter; besides, as it was in old style, when the year began in March, it necessarily cast *the arrival and beginning* of the fort into the year 1637.

Acrelius, who came out as a minister to the Swedes in 1749, and published his history in 1759, assigns the time of the first settlement at the year 1638. The same period *advocated* by Moulton in his history, and also adopted by the Encyclopædia Americana. Acrelius, having published his book fifty-seven years later than Campanius, had his sufficient reasons *then*, for differing seven or eight years from Campanius, whose book he had read and considered.

It has been admitted, on all hands, that the Swedes came out here *in the reign* and under the patronage of *Queen Christina.* Thomas Campanius Holm infers, however, that it was in the time of Gustavus Adolphus, because the king's proclamation, of 1626, allowed the emigrants to depart in March and May, 1627, as he says. We know from history, that she only began to reign in 1632–3, as a minor. Of course her government could not have given sanction to any public acts assigned to 1631. She was born in 1626, and died in 1654.

The Swedish papers, *copied* from the archives at Stockholm for the

Philosophical Society at Philadelphia, as procured and sent out by our minister, Mr. Russel, have their earliest dates in the year 1640; but they *seem* to refer to an earlier date of colonization. Among them is a paper of grant of the ground, now Philadelphia, to Lieutenant Swan Schute, from Queen Christina, dated 20th August, 1653, just one year preceding her death.

Finally, we come to the notice of the *MS. accounts*, (Swedish church papers,) left by the Rev. Mr. Rudman, as lately published, *in part*, in the book of the Rev. Mr. Clay, and this authority, on many accounts, we consider as very conclusive of the year 1637–8. Mr. Rudman came out in 1697, and remained here till 1708. He purposely made inquiries, and has left us sundry results. He says, in brief, "in 1693, there had been a list taken of all the heads of families, of whom there were still alive, when taken, thirty-nine heads who had originally come from Sweden, and among them were Peter Rambo and Andrew Bonde, *who had been in the country fifty-four years;*" thus making the year of their arrival to have been in 1637–8. He says too, "upon the *authority* of old Israel Holm, and many others," that the Dutch were here *before* the Swedes, and settled on the Jersey side; and that *in the time of Queen Christina*, the Swedes came out in the ships Key, of Calmer, and the Griffin, and settled on the western side of the Delaware; there "buying their lands from the Indians, from the capes to the falls" up the Delaware. Mr. Rudman further says, that the document and the survey, by M. Kling, were both filed in the archives, and had been *seen by him* before he left Sweden in 1697.

[Thomas Budd, one of the first settlers of New Jersey, in his pamphlet, speaking of the older Indians, says "their language was, that they were injured by strong drink. It was *first* sold to us by *the Dutch;* the *next* people that came among us were *the Swedes*, and they also were blind and did not see it was hurtful to us."]

The author was the grandson of the Rev. John Campanius Holm, who went out as chaplain with Governor Printz, in the year 1642, and continued with the churches in Pennsylvania six years. The father of the author was also in the country at the same time, and from these two and sundry MSS., the author has deduced the chief part of all that he has communicated. It is not a book of so much local interest and information as we could wish; and, perhaps, the cause is in part explained, by his treating of what he never saw. Part of what he gives is derived by him from the MS. relation of Lindström, an engineer officer with the colony.

Acrelius—(the Rev. Israel,) who was in this country, a Swedish minister, from 1749 to '56, has written more interestingly, and seen correctly, concerning the earliest settlements of the Swedes. The "description" is in extracts, as follows, viz.:

The banks of the river, are inhabited by a great number of Indians of *different* nations. Their principal towns are *six.* Poatquissing, Pemickpacka, (Pennipac,) Wequiquenske, Wickquakonich, (Wiccaco) Passyunk, and Nattabakonck, (Schuylkill.) In each town there is a sachem or chief.

The Schuylkill is (we think, the same) called "Menejeck, (Manayunk,) a large creek."

Calabash is a plant growing in vines all along the river.

A monthly notice of the weather (much like the present times) is given for ten years, from 1644 to '45.

He asserts that the Swedes made the first settlement in the reign of Gustavus Adolphus, at the instance and publication of William Ussaling, a Dutchman. He *infers* that it must have been in 1627, (the time given by Proud,) because all the preparation for it was made in 1626, by the king's proclamation and grant of license to such a settlement *in that year;* the people of Sweden *were to embark* in the month of March; and those from Livonia and Finland, in May, of the year 1627. [This is the year of the birth of Queen Christina, who began, at six years of age, in 1633, to reign.]

They seemed to wonder much at our large "sea spiders," found driven ashore in our bay, by the south winds. Their description of them shows they must have been our king crabs, popularly called horse-shoe crabs.

The class of Swedish emigrants were of three kinds, to wit: the company's servants, who were employed in various capacities, and those who went there to better their fortunes; both of these were, by way of distinction, called *freemen.* The third class "consisted of vagabonds and malefactors," who were to remain *in slavery*, and to be employed in digging the earth, throwing up trenches, and erecting walls and other fortifications. With such, the freemen had no intercourse; and they (the former) had besides their particular spot for their assigned residence. Such was the earliest arrangement and purpose; but it so happened, that in the beginning of Governor Printz's administration, when a great number of those criminals were sent over from Sweden, the European inhabitants combined to refuse their admission among them; wherefore they were returned, and many of them perished on the return voyage. After this severe lesson, it was ordered, that no more criminals should be sent; wherefore, we trust that the Swedish families actually retained among us, as primitive settlers, were "all good men and true," leaving no blur upon the reputation of their descendants—several of whom may be still traced among us, as may appear by the following names, copied from a list actually taken in the year 1693, for the information of William Penn. The fact of their being in *pluralities* is, indeed, self-evident proof that none of *them* could have been *individual* criminals, to wit:

Heads of Families.	Persons.	Heads of Families.	Persons.
Peter Rambo, Senr., ...	2	Johan Rambo, ...	6
Peter Rambo, Jr., ...	6	Gunner Rambo, ...	6

Heads of Families.	Persons.
Anders Rambo,	9
Capt. Lasse Cock, (since Cox)*	11
Eric Cock,	9
Mans Cock,	8
Johan Cock,	7
Gabriel Cock,	7
Otto Earnest Cock,	5
Anders Bengtsson, (since Bankson)	9
Bengt Bengtsson	2
Anders Bonde, (since Bond)†	11
Johan Bonde,	1
Sven Bonde,	5
Johan Svensson, (since Swanson)	9
Gunner Svensson,	5
Miche Nilsson, (since Nelson)	11
Anders Nilsson,	3
Jonas Do.,	4
Brita Gostafson, (since Justice)	6
Gostaf Gostafson,	8
Hans Do.,	7
Mans Gostafson,	2
Jons Do.,	3
Nils Jonsson, (since Johnson)	6
Mans Do.,	6
Anders Do.,	4
Jon Do.,	2
Thomas Do.,	1
Hans Joransson	11
Christiern Joransson,	1
Joran Do.,	1
Staphan Do.,	5
Peter Stake,	3
Marten Martensson, Senr.,	3
Marten Do, Junr.,	10
Mats Do.,	4
Peter Soccom, (since Yocum)	9
Matts Hollsten, (since Holstein)	7
Johan Stillé,	8
Anders Wihler, (since Wheeler)	4
Eric Molica, (hence "Mulica Hill," N. J.,)	8
Jonas Kyn, (since Keen)	8
Matts Kyn,	3
Hans Kyn's widow,	5
Nils Gastenberg,	3
Eric Gastenberg,	7
Lars Johansson, (since Johnson)	6
Didrich Do.,	5
Simon Do.,	10
Peter Stillman,	4
Jonas Do.,	4
Johan Do.,	5

Heads of Families.	Persons.
Casper Fisk,	10
Peter Dahlbo, (since Dalbo)	9
Otto Do.,	7
Johan Mattson,	11
Nils Do.,	3
And. Perrson Longaker, (now Longacre)	7
Anders Frende,	4
Nils Do., widow,	7
Rainer Petersson,	2
Hans Do.,	7
Do. Do.,	5
Paul Do.,	3
Peter Do.,	3
Carl Do.,	5
Lars Do..	1
Brita Do.,	8
Anders Kindricksson,	4
Johan Do.,	5
Do. Do.,	6
David Do.,	7
Jacob Do.,	5
Lucas Stedham,	7
Lyloff Do.,	9
Adam Do.,	8
Asmund Do.,	5
Benj'n. Do.,	7
Joran Anderson,	5
Johan Do.,	9
Do. Do.,	7
Hendrich Do.,	5
Broor Seneca,	7
Anders Do.,	5
Jesper Wallraven,	7
Jonas Do.,	1
Peter Palsson,	5
Olle Paulsson, (since Poulson)	9
Bengt Do.,	5
Gostaf Do.,	6
Anders Homman, (Homans)	9
Olle Diricksson,	7
Anders Do.,	1
Johan Hoppman,	7
Frederick Do.,	7
Anders Do.,	7
Nicholas Do.,	5
Olle Pehrsson, (since Pearson)	6
Lars Do.,	1
Jacob Van der Weer, (Vandeveer now)	7
Cornelius Do.,	1
Jacob Do.,	3

* Old Moses Cox, who owned the little triangular square, at Little Dock and Spruce streets, was a lineal descendant of the Cocks—altered since to *Cox*.

† And the Rev. Mr. Clay says, they are now called *Boon*.

Heads of Families.	Persons.	Heads of Families.	Persons.
William Van der Weer, . . .	1	Lars Larsson, ...	7
Peter Mansson, ...	3	Matts Ericsson, (now Erickson)	3
Johan Do., ...	5	Eric Do., ...	1
Hendrich Tossa, ...	5	Goran Do., ...	1
Johan Do., ...	4	Eric Goranson, ...	2
Matts Do., ...	1	Matts Rapott, ...	3
Lars Do., ...	1	Nils Do., ...	3
Christian Classon, ...	7	Chierstin Stalcop, ...	3
Jacob Do., ...	6	Johan Do., ...	6
Lucas Lucasson, (since Lucas) .	1	Peter Do., ...	6
Hans Do., ...	1	Hendrich Slobey, ...	2
Peter Do., ...	1	Olle Do., ...	3
Hendrich Larsson, ...	6	Olle Resse, (Reese) . . .	3
Lars Hulling, ...	1		

There were also a few of the following surnames:—Mink, Jacob, Danielson, Schrage, Thorsson, Olsson, Talley, Iwarsson, Skrika, Grantum, Kempe, Clemson, Kuckow, Meyer, Dennis, Savoy, Fransson, Stark, Long, Knutsson, Frende, Ekhorn, Konigh, Tay, Bure, Lock, Hallton; the whole list constituting one hundred and eighty-eight families, and nine hundred and seven individuals.

I observe that the Rev. Mr. Clay's Annals of the Swedes, furnishes this same list, as being the same taken from the document *left by* the Rev. Mr. Rudman, minister from 1697 to 1708, (when he died.) The list, as so left, states one hundred and thirty-nine families, and nine hundred and thirty-nine individuals; and says, that thirty-nine of the list were *native* Swedes, of whom Peter Rambo and Andrew Bonde, had been in the country fifty-four years, (making their arrival in or near 1639.)

It may be remarked, that their names are often *compounded*, after the manner of the Welsh, by adding the word *son*. Thus Paulsson (Poulson,) is the son of Paul; Lucasson, is the son of Lucas, (Luke,) and "Goran Ericsson," is the son of Eric, and "Eric Goransson," is the son of Goran; "Svenson," is the son of Sven, i. e. Swanson, &c.

Descendants, and even acquaintances, of the foregoing names, will feel, necessarily, some interest in this exhibition of names, thus made honourable, as the proper *primores* and *magnates* of our country! They are entitled to the distinction, thus given, and let it be perpetuated. *Estu perpetua!*

The desire of the Swedish families to come out here, must have been very great, as Mr. Lindstrom observes that, when he sailed, "more than one hundred families, of good and honest men, with their wives and children, presented more than the ship could carry;" and, on another occasion, several vessels were prevented from going, by the Spaniards.

Great pains were taken, that they should be well sustained in their new home by a Gospel ministry. To this end a regular supply was sent out, and some, by the Bishop of Upsal, of "men of sound learning and approved piety."

There was a great treaty held at Printz's hall, on Tinicum island, on the 17th June, 1654, at which were present ten sachems. and a *renewal* was then made of former leagues and covenants.

We are not aware of any *place*, now known, on which any of the aforesaid Swedish families dwelt, save that of the *Stille family* in the time of its head, *Olof Stille*, which is marked in Lindstrom's map, as "*Stille's land*," in the neck. Its Indian name was *Techoherassi*, being "a place on the Schuylkill shore, and surrounded with water like an island." It was "a small plantation, built by freemen, and was much frequented by the Indians, who gave Mr. Stille the name of 'the man with the black beard,' because of his strong black beard."

The manner of living among the Swedes, as told by themselves, in a letter of the year 1693, to John Thelin, of Gottenberg, is as follows:—"We are almost all of us husbandmen, and our meat and drink is after the old Swedish custom. The country is very rich and fruitful, and we send out yearly to our neighbours on this continent, and the neighbouring islands, bread, grain, flour and oil. We have here, thank God, all kinds of venison, birds and fishes. Our wives and daughters spin wool and flax, and many of them weave. We live in great peace and friendship with the Indians; and we only wish we had good and faithful shepherds and guardians of our souls; we may add, that since we are no longer under the government of Sweden, we have been well and kindly treated by the Dutch and the English." The foregoing letter was presented to King Charles XI., who thereupon ordered three ministers to be sent with Bibles, prayer books, and catechisms. One cannot but feel curious now to know, whether any family now extant, of Swedish origin, remaining among us, has preserved any one of those royal presents. They had before lost, by death, the services of the Rev. Jacob Frabritius, a Dutchman, and had only the services of C. Springer, "a pious reader."

One of the aforesaid newly sent ministers, the Rev. Eric Biork, writes to his superiors at home, that the people received him with great joy and gratulations; but the religious services of the people were very irregular and lax, and needed reform, especially among the rising generation. He said, there were *no poor* in the country, but all provided for themselves, without any cases of want. [What can *we* say now!] The Indians he found to be great friends; more so to us than they are to the English. They call us, in their language, their "*own people.*" They are very fond of learning the catechism, which has been printed in their language, [where shall we find a copy now!] and wh.ch is to be read to their children, and taught to them by Mr. Springer. Our people live scattered among the English and Quakers; and yet our language is preserved as pure as any where in Sweden, and there being *about one thousand two hundred persons that speak it.* Many Swedes are employed in the administration of the government under Governor Markham; some are judges, captains, ensigns, constables," &c

Lewis Hennepin, quoted by Holm, states the belief, that our Indians are descended from *the Jews*, on account of *many resemblances* he finds between those natives. Hennepin, and the Rev. John Campanius, both believed that they could trace an affinity, between the Hebrew and Indian languages. The Indians then were tall, strong, nimble, and limbs well proportioned. Their faces broad—small black eyes—*flat* noses—(a mistake, surely, unless at the nostrils,) large lips—short broad teeth, and very white. Their bodies nearly naked, and of a brown or yellowish colour, anointed with bears' grease, and black paint found on the sea-shore, which enables them better to endure the heat of the sun. They make their huts of mats and of branches of trees. The mats being made of the leaves of the Indian corn matted together. They sleep on their mats and skins. They cook the most of their diet in clay kettles; and their dishes are plates of bark and cedar wood. Their drinking vessel is the shell of the calabash. Their spoons and knives were muscle shells. Their pipes were made of long reeds, and the bowl was of horn.

One might smile, to know the fact of their surprise at our *fire-flies*, "giving out light enough to show the way!" One night, they frightened all the soldiers on guard, at Fort Christina, so that they thought they "were enemies advancing with lighted matches."

One cannot but feel a melancholy pleasure, in sympathy with one of the Swedish ministers, who, in writing home of his regrets at the loss of the Swedish rule here, says, with exultation, "we have, however, retained some *lasting* memorials of our glorious *Queen*—such as the Christina church, Christina hundred, Christina creek, Christina ferry and bridge," &c. But, alas, even *these* have since been perverted to *Christiana.*

Facts and occurrences of the Swedes settled in Upland.

"The records of Upland," a folio cap book of one hundred and eighty-eight pages MS., having been lent to me by the Logan family, I have made the following extracts and *notitia* from the same, with a view to show the state and action of society, in that primitive day: say from the year 1676, when the administration of Governor Andross began on the Delaware, down to the year 1681, when it began to be the province of Pennsylvania, under William Penn. I preserve *the names* of the primitive inhabitants, as magistrates, jurors, landholders and parties in court, as they appear from time to time, for the sake of showing, *by their names*, the origin of many family names, still among us, or partially altered. The object herein is to preserve, so far as practicable now, an insight into *the ways and doings* of the little community of *primitive settlers*, who began this now affluent and prosperous country, at a period *anterior* to the arrival of Penn and his colonists. The book from which I extract will, I trust, be deposited in the Loganian library, as a venerable relic of antiquity

The book opens with a court, held "att Uppland, *in* Delaware river," by the authority of the sovereign lord, Charles II., on the 14th November, 1676.

Then follows the authority of "Edmond Andross, Esq., Seigneur of Sausmarcy, lieutenant and governor general, under his highness, James, duke of York and Albany.

Peter Cock, Peter Rambo, Israel Helm, Lace Andries, Oele Swen and Otto Ernest, [all Swedish names,] are made "justices," and are inducted under oath by the commissioners, Captain John Colier [from which we have the name, probably, of Colier's hook] and Captain Edmond Cantwell, [from which we have the name of Cantwell's bridge.]

Their power under Governor Andross reads thus, viz., "to be justices of the peace for the space of one year, and any three or more of them to be a court of judicature, and to act according to law and the trust reposed in them."

At same time Ephraim Herman is constituted "*clarke* of the court of New Castle, and also of the court att Uppland *in* the river."

Then follows, in three and a half pages, a record of *the instructions* of Governor Andross, comprised in twelve articles. Some of them to this effect, viz. The book of laws as practised in New York to be also practised *in* this river and its precincts. To have three courts—"one at New Castle—one above att Uppland, another below att the Whorekill." Each to have the power of a court of sessions, and to decide all matters under £20 without appeal. In cases above £20, and for crime extending to life and limb or banishment, to admit of appeal to the court of assizes. Cases under £5 value, may be determined by the court without a jury, unless desired by the parties, [only two or three cases of juries occur,] as also matters of equity. The court of New Castle to be held monthly—that of Uppland and Whorekill to be quarterly, "or *oftener* if occasion." All records to be kept in English. To be a high sheriff for the town of New Castle, river, and bay, and he to make under sheriffs. All rates and levies to be made by the court with the approbation of the governor, to be first obtained. It is *recommended*, that all matters under £5 be settled by arbitration, *by the consent of the parties*, and thus avoid the necessity or use of overseers and constables' courts.

The same authority orders and appoints, that in cases of *grants of land*, that *any person* desiring land shall make application to the court, which shall give order therein and certify to the governor, "for *any land* not taken upp and improved—in fitt proportions not exceeding fifty acres per head, unless upon extra occasions, where more may be allowed." Thereupon to grant a certificate of survey, which survey, when made, must be sent to New York for the governor's approbation, and to express therein the proportions of upland and meadow, so that all may have an equal chance for *proportionable shares*. Such was the original scheme of allotments of lands, which appear to have been dispensed *gratis* to all applicants intending to take up and improve the same. When William Penn arrived, he had a price per hundred acres with their quit rents, and which was of course something in the way of cost, to any then unprovided, for Swedes, or others of the former inhabitants. For the sake of a condensed view of the lands applied for at court terms, I shall hereinafter give a list, showing the times, names and qualities so granted, and their location, when expressed. The reader will soon have occasion to observe that the same names are not carefully spelled with the same letters. Names too are written familiarly, as *Lasse* for Lawrence, and *Claes* for Nicholas, &c. Surnames too, ending with sen and son, is the son of—thus Hendriksen is the son of Hendrik. The name of Cock, is since Cox, and Swen, is since Swanson. He cannot fail also to remark how generally the grounds of action are deemed good, by the verdicts going generally for the plaintiffs.

The court ordered "that Mr. William Tom, the former clarke, should deliver unto the present clarke, Ephraim Herman, the records and other public bookes and wrytings, belonging to this court." At same time the court ordered that execution should be granted against all debtors to said William Tom, for his just fees due in former actions, &c. [This Mr. Tom, gave name to Tom's river.]

Justice Israel Helm, asked recompense "for having served the river [inhabitants] often, and at sundry times, as an interpreter with the Indians for Captain Cantwell." The same was referred to the governor.

The court resolve to write a letter to the governor upon the following topics, viz.: To ask his honour to *confirm* the order about the wolves' heads. To order a means of repaying court costs and their distance of travel as justices. They state the former charge of court as it occurred at the house or place of Neeles Laerson, "for the charges of keeping a court, and for justices' diet there, 452 gilders, of which Captain Cantwell has paid 200 gilders, leaving 252 gilders still due."

The court adjourned until the second Tuesday in March next, and no soonor, *by reason* of the winter season, and so to be kept quarterly.

At a court held at Uppland *in* Delaware river, the 13th March, A. D., 1676–7. Present, Peter Cock, Peter Rambo, Israel Helm, Lacé Andries and Otto Ernest, justices. Captain Edmond Cantwell, high sheriff.

Justice Israel Helm, plaintiff—Oele Oelsen, defendant.—The defendant in an abusive and malicious manner beat and struck the justice, and with scandalous words did evil entreat him. No defendant present, the action was laid over to next term, and then if neglected to go by default.

Morten Morrenson *vs.* Mouns Staeke, for killing his ox, and for personal assault and battery. *Continued* by the court, and in mean time it is *recommended* to the parties to compose the difference themselves.

Anthony Nealson *vs.* Lace Dalboo, the plaintiff not appearing, a nonsuit ordered and costs.

The petition of Johannes de Haes, concerning his lands patented under Governor Lovelace, laying in the boght (bite or bend) between Oele Fransen and Naaman's creek, a survey is ordered.

The charge of keeping the court at Neales Laersen's house, and for the diet of the justices and commander, amount to 100 gilders, and ordered paid. Adjourned to second Tuesday in June.

Connected with the preceding court was a meeting held by the commander, Captain John Colier, upon the occasion of the news of the Sinneco [Seneca] Indians coming down to fetch the Susquehanna, that were among these river Indians. Upon the suggestion and advice of Rinowehan, the Sachomore, it was deemed best *for the quiet of the river*, that Captain Colier and Justice Helm, should go up to *Sachamexin*, where at present many Sinneco and other Indians are, and that they endeavour to persuade the whole assemblage to send severally a deputy to his honour, the governor, at New York, and that Justice Helm go with them as interpreter. The Indians continued in council four days, and incurred an expense of 250 gilders, which was paid. Thus the place of "the Treaty-tree" was then used *as a treaty place.*

At a court held the 13th June, 1677. Present six justices. Edmond Cantwell *vs.* John Ashmen, demands eight hundred pounds of tobacco, for his surveying fees for two tracts of land and their patents, &c.—so ordered.

Albert Hendricks *vs.* Andries Bertelf, demands pay for killing his boar, which had become fierce and cruel—both parties to bear equal loss.

Andries Homman *vs.* Lace Dalboo, demands redress for being beaten by Dalboo, on his own land—referred to another court term.

The high sheriff indites Richard Dúcket, the servant of Lace Cock, for his commerce with a certain mulatto woman. The fact being confessed, it was ordered he should maintain the child when he should be free.

Lace Cock *vs.* John Ashman, claims sixteen ells of serge for a black horse and a mare—confirmed and so ordered by the court.

John Stille *vs.* John Ashmen, claims a bill debt of twelve hundred and fifty pounds of tobacco of Choptank—judgement for plaintiff ordered. [This Stille is the ancestor of the present Stille family.]

Justice Israel Helm *vs.* Oele Oelsen, alias Cock, for an assault and battery, and begs as a member of the court, his respect may be maintained; after hearing witnesses of Lace Coleman and debates of both sides—fined the assaulter 210 gilders, sixty thereof for the church—the rest to the sheriff—and then to ask forgiveness of the injured party in court. The same being done, 150 gilders of the same were remitted.

The widow of Thomas Jeacock *vs.* John Ashman, claims one thousand pounds of tobacco for a horse—so ordered.

Henry Ward *vs.* Thomas Denny, claims four hundred pounds of tobacco, payable in New Castle—judgement ordered.

James Sanderlin *vs.* Oele Swensen, in an action of debt *for sixteen foxes.* The debates of both being heard; but before judgement pronounced, they had agreed mutually to compose the same, and the defendant to pay the costs.

Francis Walker *vs.* John Ashman, gone away, action by attachment on his cows and horses—judgement ordered, and Lace Cock and Mathias Holstein are ordered appraisers under oath.

Albert Hendrick, the constable, having served out his year, and asking his dismission, is succeeded by William Orian.

Jurian Hartsvelder, appeared and desired his dismission as under sheriff, he intending to live higher up the river, and his place is supplied by Michill Yzard. [This Hartsfelder is the same who came to own the chief part of the Northern Liberties, and some tracts in Germantown.]

The court was ordered to adjourn to the second Tuesday of September, and before parting, ordered a settlement of the difference about *the fly*, [a then name for marsh meadow] of the people of Carkoens-hoek, and Lacé Dalbo, by declaring that Hans Petersen and the rest of Carkoens-hoek, do mow the hay of the said fly, for the present and until the case he heard in court thereafter. Ordered that no person be admitted to plead for any other person as an attorney, without he first have his admittance of the court, or have a warrant of attorney for so doing from his client. [On a former occasion James Sanderling acted for another as his attorney, so also Edmond Cantwell.]

At a court held the 11th September, 1677. Six justices present—and Captain Cantwell high sheriff.

Claes Cram *vs.* Lace Cock, demands 20 gilders for bringing a horse, and the court ordered the pay to come from Michill Jud, the carpenter.

Morten Mortense, Jun. *vs.* Moens Staecket, declares that he chased his wife with an axe, and he, Morten Mortense, coming to her rescue, he was threatened with a gun—condemned to a fine of 50 gilders, and to be bound to good behaviour. At same time an action of slander was preferred by the father of the above plaintiff, and Moens was condemned to declare in court, "that he knew nothing but all honesty in the case."

Clerk of the court, Ephraim Herman, was ordered 200 gilders for his services for the year, to be paid out of the tax to be levied.

At a court held the 13th November, 1677. Present six justices—

John Test *vs.* Neeles Laerson, for sundry goods and merchandise to amount of 186 gilders.

William Tom *vs.* Jonas Neelson, for fees earned as clerk of this court, £6. 15*s.*, in several actions—judgement ordered.

Thomas Harwood *vs.* Hans Jurian, for balance of an account of 139 gilders—judgement ordered.

William Tom *vs.* Jan Cornelissen, for clerk fees, in the action of Peter Jegoù.

Neeles Laersen *vs.* John Test, complains that Test has been troublesome to his son about a knife, and desires to know the reason thereof; upon hearing parties, court determines no cause of action, and that the parties be reconciled, which was done in court. The plaintiff to pay clerk's and sheriff's fees.

Andries Boen *vs.* Moens Staecket, complains that, when at Badstoe, he was abused and beaten by him. The defendant desired a favourable censure of the court, as that he was in drink—fined 100 gilders.

Captain Hans Inrgrx, is ordered to warn the men belonging to his company, and with them to fit up and finish *the house of defence* at Upland, fit for the court to sit in, by the time of the next court. [This shows that the captain had citizens enrolled for general defence, and that they had a block-house which might answer for a court room. Before this they used the private house of Neeles Laerson.]

A petition signed by twenty-four individuals, of Swedish families, born in this country, ask one hundred acres each, to form a settlement just below the falls—referred to the governor.

The court take into consideration the levy or poll-tax, for defraying public expenses, and after calling over the list of tydable (tithe?) inhabitants, ordered that there be assessed and paid by each and every of them, 26 gilders. To be paid, in wheat, at 5; or if in rye and barley, at 4 gilders the scipple; or if in Indian corn, at 3 gilders; if in tobacco, at 8 stivers per pound; or if in pork, at 8; or in bacon, at 16 stivers per pound; or else in *wampum*; or skins at current prices.

The high sheriff is charged with this collection, and in case of default, to distrain the same. Then follows a list of 136 tydables, (taxables?) including their sons and servants—being the whole number then within the jurisdiction of the court in Upland. What a little community of *forefathers* then, to begin the mighty commonwealth we now possess! Notice, too, that *wampum* then was an actual money matter in traffic! The whole list consists of Swedish names, save about one dozen of more Anglified form—such as Robert Wade, Richard Noble, Henry Hastings, William Woodman, Thomas Denny, Thomas Harwood, Peter Freeman. The names are classified thus, viz.: at Taokanink, 66; at Carkoens-hoek, 24; at Upland, 17; at Marr (Marrities?) Kill, 19; and at Eastern shore, 10—total, 136.

A letter from Gov. Andross, of date 14th August, 1677, is received, read and recorded, authorizing and directing *the purchase*, of the Indians, of a small tract of land, *not yet purchased*, "*it is said*," of about two miles length along the river, between the late purchase up to the Falls—to the end that the same may be settled. He also requires that returns be made of all lands, heretofore possessed, unto the clerk of the court.

At a court held the 12th of March, 1677–8, six judges present

Luke Watson, by Edward Cantwell, his attorney *vs.* John Gray; none of the parties appearing, a nonsuit was ordered.

John Adams, in behalf of his master, Will Dervall, the attorney of John Foster, in action against John Gray, who owes 7706 pounds of tobacco to John Foster, of the island of Barbadoes, to be delivered at the Whorekill—judgement ordered against defendant.

Daniel Linsey *vs.* John Johnson—the court find both parties faulty, and order defendant to pay the debt; and as for wintering the cow and the sows, the plaintiff engaged to allow the same—each to pay half the costs.

Johannes De Haes *vs.* Wm. Orian, claims a balance for goods—claim affirmed.

Robert Hutchinson appeared, and declared that he there assigned to Israel Helm, his man-servant, William Broomfield, for the term of four years, he paying him 1200 gilders; at the same time, the said servant promised faithfully to serve his new master.

Ordered that 100 acres of land be added to the tract held for the mill at Carkoen *creeke.* [This same place is often called Carkoen *hoek*—and *hoek* means what we now call *hook*, and is often herein found connected with a creek; but it is believed properly to express *a bend*, a cove, *like a hook.*]

Anthony Nealson Long presented William Goa, a servant, whom he had bought of Moens Peterson, for three years, and asked his confirmation.

Hans Juriansen Kien, (Kean,) of Taokanink, (Tacony,) appeared and acknowledged his deed to his brother, Jonas J. Kien, (Kean,) for 200 acres, being his one-sixth portion of the original 1200 acres granted to *six* inhabitants for *the towne* of Upland, [*i. e.* Chester,] near the creek; and this lot, lying between the houses and lots of James Sanderling and Jurian Kien. Then also appeared Jonas J. Kien, and made over by deed the same tract to John Test, late of London, merchant. [This Test became the first sheriff of Philadelphia.] At same time he also conveyed to the same John Test, a certain *new block house*, near the water side of the said creek. [It is possible that *block* house may not necessarily mean a defensive place, as now, but may have been intended merely to express a house made of blocks or logs of wood.] Then also appeared John Test, and conveyed the same premises unto Marmaduke Randall, of London, merchant.

Neeles Mattson reconveys to James Sanderling, a patent for land granted by Gov. R. Nicolls, in 1668, on the north side of the Kill, next and adjoining to Israel Helm and Jorst Daniels.

On application of John Moll, president at New Castle, calling for Wm. Orian Smith, an absconded debtor, he is ordered to be apprehended and sent back.

Neeles Laerson's bill for use of his house and diet for courts is allowed at 75 gilders.

Court adjourned till second Tuesday of June, and a special meeting for a levy the 1st April.

At a court of Upland, held at the house of Justice Peter Cock, *in* the Schuylkill, the 3d April, 1678, present four justices—when they fix and determine the assessment and taxes, &c., with the sheriff, and ordered it recorded.

Adam Mott *vs.* Jan Claassen—a demand of 1300 pounds of tobacco—affirmed.

John Schackerly *vs.* Jan Claassen—a debt of f325 15—action laid over.

John Adams *vs.* Christopher Barnes—asks judgement against his plantation and crop of corn, for a debt of 1494 gilders, on mortgage—granted, and the value to be ascertained by appraisers named, and the defendant agrees in court to make delivery.

Ephraim Herman *vs.* Laurentius Carolus—demands fees as clerk of the court, 142 gilders—pay promised in October, and the plaintiff is content.

Capt. Edmund Cantwell *vs.* Neeles Laerson—for defamation, £100. Before trial, N. Laerson asked forgiveness in court, with which the captain was satisfied. At same time the court orders that N. Laerson shall repay 130 gilders, collected for head money, [poll tax,] in New Castle district, by *alleged* mistake.

Jan Cornelissen, of Amesland, complains to the court that his son Erick is bereft of his natural senses, and is turned quite mad, and he not being able to maintain him, it was ordered that three or four persons be hired to build *a little block house*, and there to confine him—expenses to be provided for in the next levy or tax.

Carell Junsen, of Marreties-hoeck, in Delaware river, (is not this the origin of Marcus-hook?) appears in court to acknowledge conveyance of land at Marrities-hoeck, adjoining to land of Jan Hendrickson, sold unto Morgan Druit, of London, mariner.

Jan Hendrickson appeared and acknowledged a deed or *transport* unto Roger Peddrik, of his land at the west side of Delaware river, as called and *known by the* name of Marreties-hoeck—the whole tract of Marreties-hoeck land being granted and confirmed by patent from Gov. Andross, on the 28th March, 1676, unto the six possessors thereof, viz.: Charles Jansen, Oele Raessen, Hans Oelsen, Oele Neelsen, Hans Hoffman, and Jan Hendricks—the whole containing 1000 acres.

Several actions are withdrawn, and mutually settled amicably.

A tax or levy of five gilders per head ordered, and to include every person upon Tinneconck island.

Adjourned to the 2d Tuesday of September.

At a court held Nov. 12, 1678, present five justices—

William Orian *vs.* John D. Haes—demands 167 gilders in account, and craves a jury; they being empanelled, brought in a verdict for 159 gilders, and the court suspends determination till next court.

Oele Dirksen *vs.* Evert Aldrets—for a debt of 71 gilders—affirmed.

Rodger Peddrick *vs.* Hans Oelsen—an action for assault and battery; striking him in the open street with an axe handle. There being no witnesses, and the defendant utterly denying the fact, the plaintiff also refusing to swear it, *the court could not come to any judgement*, but order future peace, under severe penalty.

Walter Wharton *vs.* Andries—action for 50 gilders, in wheat—judgement ordered.

James Sanderlins *vs.* John Edmunds, of Maryland—on a claim of 1200 pounds tobacco, to be delivered in Great Chaptank river; not being paid, he now moves an attachment of his great boat or shallop, now at Upland—granted, and the vendue master to make public sale, and return the same for the use of the plaintiff. She was sold to John Test for 625 gilders.

Benjamin Goodman, a servant to Oele Swenson, prays his freedom, alleging that his master says he has longer to serve. The indenture is ordered, and it being said to be lost, the court adjudges that he ought to be free.

It being taken into consideration that it was very necessary that a mill should be built in the Schuylkill, [at the present falls of Schuylkill,] "and there being no fitter place than the fall *called* Captain Hans Moens' falls"—the court decides that either the captain ought to build a mill there, (as he says he will,) or else suffer another to build there, for the common good of the parts.

And upon the request of Jan Shoetan, "the court grants him a small tract of marrish, (marsh,) lying at the aforesaid great mill fall, at the end thereof; that is to say, so much as is fit to mow four stacks of hay—and the said mill fall being *a run* that comes in the Schuylkill." [The same running from Redinger's and by Hagner's mills. The writer has in his possession the deed to Capt. Moens.]

Laurens Cock appeared and acknowledged his deed of conveyance to Elizabeth Kinsey, of 300 acres of land, lying in *Sachamexin*, "on the west side of Delaware river, *at the towne* or neighbourhood *called and known* by the name of Sachamexin—the whole dividend or quantity of land *being of late* surveyed for *the inhabitants* of Sachamexin in general, and *containing* 1800 *acres*, by which resurvey the share or interest of the said Laurens Cock, of that place, amounts to 300 acres—together with the marshes or meadows, the houses, barns, stables, stalls, fences," &c. [The above-mentioned conveyance shows the extent of the land wherein the celebrated Treaty-tree of Penn so long stood. It also seems to show a name derived from *Sacham*, i. e., a place familiar as a convening place *for Indian chiefs;* and these pages show that the *Senecas* had before assembled *there* as a preferred or chosen spot.]

The court ordered that every landholder should improve and make passable the road from neighbour to neighbour with bridges, where needful, so that neighbours on occasion may come together—those neglecting, to forfeit 25 gilders.

Peter Putco conveys by deed his land to Harman Jansen.

The limits and division between this and New Castle county are settled by this court, and John Moll, president of New Castle court, viz.: "*This county of Upland* to begin from the north side of Oele Fransen's creek, alias Steen kill, lying in the boght (bite?) above the Vedrietige-hoeck, and from the said creek over to the Single tree point, on the *east* side of this river." [Who now can mark those limits by any of the names of places set down!]

The court orders that the five gilders' tax be paid within fourteen days, as a means to pay court charges, &c.; and that each person bring the same to Tinnecong island, and pay it there to Otto Ernest Cock; and to give due notice, this shall be fixed up at *the churches* of Wicaco and Tinnecong.

Complaint being made by the *churchwardens*, that Neeles Laerson [at whose house the courts were held] had taken in some of the church glebe, *with* the lots which he had bought of *the domine*, Lasse Carolus, *here in Upland towne*—it is ordered he shall have his own due and restore the rest to the church.

James Sanderling, in behalf of the rest of the inhabitants of Upland, (Chester now,) complains that Neeles Laerson stops with his fence the old and usual way to *the fly* [to the meadow]—it is ordered that he open the way as formerly.

The court adjourns till 2d Tuesday of March.

Then follow several returns of warrants of survey put on record, as done and reported by Walter Wharton, *the surveyor*, and which are ordered to be sent to the office (of lands) in New York. [This name begins probably the family of that surname among us, and from his descendants came the old log-house, floated up the Delaware from Chester, and *planted* near the Swedes' church, and still standing in lowly style *as a relic*, little known of olden time. He died about the same time, and Richard Noble was made surveyor in his place.]

Some of the tracts may be thus noticed, to wit:

A tract of 100 acres, laid out for Michell Izard, called *Small gain*, on the north-east side of Stille's creek.

A tract of 100 acres, laid out for Anthony Nielson, alias Long, called *Long*, between Crum kill and Stille's kill.

A tract of 417 acres, laid out for James Sanderland and Laurens Cock, called Poetquessink, lying along that creek, &c.

A tract of 300 acres, laid out for Peter Rambo, Jr., a place on the north-east side of Pennapackes creek, called *Ram's dorp.*

A tract of 100 acres, laid out for Jacob Hendrickson, called Jacob's lot, on the east side of Crum's creek.

A tract of 200 acres, laid out for Henry Hastings, called Hastings' hope, above Poetquessink creek, next to land of James Sanderland.

A tract of 400 acres, laid out for John Test, called the Hopewell of Kent, on the south-west side of Upland creek, next to land of Albert Hendricks, called Lemoky.

At a court held at Upland the 12th and 13th of March, 1678–9, present four justices and the sheriff—

Wm. Orian *vs.* Johannes De Haes—complains that the account

books had been miscopied to his injury, and proves by *Doctor* Thomas Spry, who had once posted them a year before, that alterations had been made; the consequence is, that the debtors *gainsay* the accounts as they now stand—they therefore order nonsuit, on the ground that De Haes does not truly owe the sum claimed, for lack of *a due credit.*

Peter Jegou *vs.* Laurentius Carolus (the domine a minister)—demands by order of Capt. James Bollin, six scipples of wheat, which he sometimes promised and then would refuse—the court ordered payment.

Evert Aldrets *vs.* Oele Dircksen.
Wm. Clarke *vs.* Joseph Handley.
Robt. Wade *vs.* John Test.
Lasse Cock *vs.* Michell Fredericks.
} Actions withdrawn.

Johannes De Haes, by *petition*, (a common mode,) shows that he has been arrested by Wm. Orian, and forced to come three times to court—on a vexatious pretence, which has already cost him 150 gilders—the court granted his indemnification to that amount.

James Sanderling in behalf of Marmaduke Randell, by *petition*, shows that the estate of Walter Wharton, deceased, is indebted *for house rent, in Upland*, 80 gilders, which are ordered paid; also, that he owes to himself 128 gilders—which he also deemed fully proved, and ordered paid.

Edmund Draufton *vs.* Dunck Williams—on a demand of 200 gilders for teaching Dunck's children to read the Bible—employed one year, and was to have that sum by agreement, even if they learned sooner—judgement ordered.

Wm. Clarke, of Neshaminies *vs.* Jan Hendrickson—the plaintiff having entered *no declaration*; upon request of defendant, the plaintiff is nonsuited.

Pelle Dalbo *vs.* Laurentius Carolus, (the domine) for 55 gilders, for sheriff and Marshal's fees—judgement ordered.

Rodger Peddrick & Wm. Hews, joint partners with the rest of the inhabitants of Marrities-hoek, (Marcus-hook,) by their *petition*, desire that the land there, 1000 acres, be laid out and equally shared, between all the partners, by dividing equally to each the proportions of good and bad land. The court orders, that the petitioners, or those who are dissatisfied with the division, as of old hath been, may at their proper cost have the same surveyed and shared.

Moens Staeckt, by petition, complains that Andries Boen left open the fence of his land, at Calkoen's creek, to his injury—ordered that he make his fence good within four days.

Dunck Williams, by petition, prays a grant of four acres of marsh land, back of his land, at Nieshameenie's creek, in the woods above *the king's path*—granted.

John Shackerly *vs.* Jan Claasson, for a debt, 325 gilders—judgement ordered.

Peter Rambo, Senr., claims a tract of land, at Wiccaco, under a grant of this court, but which three of the Swenson's—to wit.: Oele, Swen, and Andries,—declare will invade the precincts of their patent. It is ordered that the Swenson's retain their land, and if there be any surplus, it may go to P. Rambo.

Rodger Peddrik & Hans Oelsen, appear, and *transport* (assign) their several lands, at Marrities-hoek, to Jan Hendricksen and Wm. Clayton.

Jans Justassen appeared, and *verbally* acknowledged his deed of *transport* of land to Albert Hendricks, lying between Harwicke creek and Middle creek.

In consequence of sundry persons, who were assessed 5 gilders per head, for defraying public expenses, it is ordered, that if they do not pay the same within eight days, they shall severally pay 25 gilders.

Neeles Laersen (at whose house the courts were held) was ordered to make, or leave a lane or street, from Upland creek to "*the house of defence*, or country house," (block-house,) between this and the next court day, and in default to be fined.

The court was adjourned to second Tuesday in June, and afterwards adjourned again to Sept. 6, and then again to Nov., 1679.

At a court held at Upland, 25th and 26th Nov., 1679.—Present four justices.

Peter Bacom *vs.* Capt. Xtopher Billop (Christopher B.) complains that Capt. Billop, (who voyages in a boat from St. Jonses to Burlington, 50 miles,) had taken and used his horse for four months, he claims 3 gilders per diem; also for his services six weeks, 420 gilders. The defendant not appearing, though called in three several courts, is adjudged to pay 1080 gilders. [In this and other actions James Sanderlin acts as attorney; so, also, at times, does Edmund Cantwell; but, whether they serve as attorneys in law or as *in fact*, does no appear; but it would seem as if they act as attorneys *in fact*, by reason of the *absence* of the principal.]

James Crawford, of St. George's creek, *vs.* John Test.

Michel Izard (often spelt Yzard) appeared in behalf of the plaintiff; but the plaintiff not having entered any declaration, and not appearing the next day by himself or attorney, it was, upon the request of the defendant, nonsuited.

Peter Jegou *vs.* Thomas Wright and Godfrey Hancock, in an action of trespass on the case. The plaintiff declares that, in 1668, he obtained a permit and grant of land, called *Leasy point*, lying over against Matinagcom island and Burlington, where he settled *a house of entertainment for travellers*, and there continued till 1670, when he was *plundered and utterly ruined by the Indians*, "as is well known to all the world," and having thus to seek his livelihood elsewhere. It hath since come to pass, that by the arrival of "these new-comers, called Quakers, out of England," these defendants, Thomas Wright and Godfrey Hancock, have forcibly entered upon his said lands, and there planted corn, mowed hay, cut timber for houses, &c. The defendants having declared themselves very willing to abide the verdict of the court; the court, after a full hearing and examination of the papers, do decree, that inasmuch as said Jegou had Gov. Cartret's grant, and had had possession, "*before* ever the land was sold by Sir John Berckley unto Edward Billing, and for that said Jegou had also bought the land, *and paid the Indians for the same*, he was of right entitled to the land. [This same question had before been presented before the authorities in Burlington, "who making nothing of it, the case by their consent and these defendants, was removed to this court at Upland." Thus showing how very *accommodating* and simple were then the principles of "equal justice."]

James Sanderlin *vs.* John Peers, attaches tobacco for an unsettled debt of 163 gilders.

Ephraim Herman, declares his purpose to desist (decline) his grant of land before given, so that it may lay open to others, whereupon it is requested and granted to Laers Laerson and Oele Coeckoe, (Cocke?)

John Test *vs.* Elizabeth Kinsey, demands restitution of five beavers left in her trust. [In this case John Ashton presents himself as her attorney, in her absence; but upon her coming, he desires to be dismissed and that she may manage the suit herself. He says, that she is *his mistress*—of course, making him to be her attorney or representative in fact, only.]

John Test acknowledges conveyance of his land, in Upland, to Richard Friends, of Weymouth, in England; whereupon James Sanderlin as attorney (in fact) conveys the same tract to Stephen Chambers, of the same Weymouth.

James Sanderlin and Laurens Cock convey their tract of 417, at Poetquessinck, to Walter, James and Francis Forest.

Jonas Nielson makes proof in court, that he had expended 106 gilders in the burial of Peter Veltscheerden and Christian Samuels, who were *murdered* by the Indians at Tinnagcong island, in 1672. Ordered paid.

John Test declares his conveyance of his tract at *Lamoco*, at the head of Upland creek, to Richard Boverington and John Grub, also his tract, called Hopewell of Kent, to the same persons.

It being represented to the court, by the churchwardens of Tinnacong and Wicaco churches, that the fences about the churchyards and the church buildings are much out of repair, and that some of the members are negligent to repair the same. The court orders that they be empowered to summons the members to meet and to do the said repairs, and that whosoever neglects shall forfeit 50 gilders severally, to be levied out of their goods. Court adjourned to second Tuesday of March next.

At a court held the 10th March, 1679–80.—Present six justices.

Thomas Kerby *vs.* Gilbert Wheeler, claims for work done at four gilders per diem, from October to January. The defendant says he worked not so long. The debates of both being heard, the court adjudges payment for seventy days, at 50 stivers per day.

At same time, Robert Drawton claims for sixty-three days, and the court adjudges fifty-four days at 50 stivers.

Andries Boen *vs.* Edward Williams, had contracted for thirteen hundred pounds tobacco, payable in Maryland, which the defendant shunned to deliver, and having found a horse of his now in Upland, has attached the same, and now asks a decree of the court for its sale, &c., which was ordered, and appraisers appointed to value the same.

Harmon Ennis *vs.* Andries Homman, demands the hire of a pair of oxen for one year, 45 gilders. The court adjudged 23 gilders for a shorter time.

Several actions are withdrawn, or, by the advice of the court, mutually settled.

The court declares, that whereas it incurs needful expense for diet, &c., and at same time the law allows 2*s.* 6*d.* *for every judgement* by it given, it therefore resolves, that the under sheriff shall collect the same from forty persons named, at 2*s.* 6*d.*, severally, to the amount of £5. [We thus see at what low prices they gave their services and attention.] The court adjourned to meet the second Tuesday in June next.

At a court held the 8th June, 1680.—Present four justices.

Gunla Andries, widow of Peter *vs.* Jonas Nielson, petitions to be put in possession of land, at Kingsesse—the court orders the same.

Upon the petition of Thomas Fairman, (the after owner of the Treaty-tree premises) to have a grant of 200 acres—the court orders the same where he may choose.

It being represented to the court, by the constable, that Claes Cram, lives in adultery with the wife of Bank Salung—it is ordered they shall desist, and in case of non-compliance, they shall be apprehended for the next court to act upon.

Richard Noble, the surveyor, [he became a sheriff under Penn,] made report of seven surveys of land, made by him for individuals named, that they may be sent to the *office* in New York government.

The court order, that as their former sittings at Upland creek, (Chester,) is at the lower end of the county, they will thereafter, for "the most ease of the people," meet and sit at *the towne* of Kingsesse *in* the Schuylkill.

Gunla Andries petitions, that her title to land, before disputed and now settled, may be translated from *the Dutch* and be put on the record of the court in English—granted. A part of her said land is designated by 25 "*Schrett of fence.*"

Peter Andries alleges, that the houses of Swen Gunnarson are standing upon his land. The court orders *their removal.* The witnesses are Oluff Stilla, (Stille) and Otto Ernest Cock.—Court adjourned.

At a court held at *Kingsesse*, Oct. 13, 1680.—Present five justices

Claes Cram *vs.* Hans Peters, in an action of slander, saying he was a thief, &c. Witnesses being examined, and the defendant not being able to make any proof—the court adjudge that he shall declare himself *a liar*, and the plaintiff an honest man, and pay 20 gilders.

Moens Peterson *vs.* Hans Jurian, in an action for slander. Witness proved the wrangling of the parties, and that the defendant said, You have broken my calf's leg, and Thou art a gallow's thief; other witnesses being needed the case was adjourned.

Hans Jurian *vs.* Moens Staecket, for assault and battery, done at his own door, making him bloody, and calling for a gun to shoot him. The court bind him over to keep the peace for one year, on a penalty of £40.

John Stille *vs.* Dirk Jansen, alleges, that the defendant has marked and taken his pigs, found in his cripple or swamp. The defendant allows the fact, but denies that they could have been any other than his own. The court allows a mistake, and orders a return of them with costs of suit.

Andries Inckhooren (Inkhorn) *vs.* Andries Homman, complains that the defendant pulled him by the beard and twisted his neck, and demands the reason and a reparation. A. H., being a constable, answered that he went to his house in pursuit of a whore and a rogue, and was obstructed by him, when he therefore pushed him aside. The court ordered a nonsuit.

Otto Ernest Cock (Justice) *vs.* M. P. Staecket, in an action of slander—had called him a hog-thief—the defendant says if that he did, it was in his drink, and humbly asks his pardon—and thereupon the justice said he was satisfied, and the suit was dismissed with paying costs.

Hans Moensen and Peter Jocum *vs.* Peter Rambo, Senr., complains that Rambo holds his Marsh land, and asks restitution. Witnesses declare that they knew Captain Hans Moens, to have mowed the hay on some part of that *fly*. The court orders the first patent under Governor Lovelace to possess the title, and that the defendant shall possess. [This was at Schuylkill falls, and I have the deed.]

The court appoint John Cock and Lasse Dalbo to be overseers of roads and fences, for one year. Adjourned to second Tuesday of March.

At a court at Kingsesse, March 8, 1680-1.—Present three justices.

Several tracts of land granted, and some conveyed by deed.

At a court at Kingsesse, June 14, 1681.—Present three justices.

Justice Henry Jones, and Justice George Browne, both fined £10, for non-attendance, as justices, according to law; George Brown afterwards declared he was hindered by the freshet in the creek.

Several actions mutually settled or withdrawn.

Claes Jansen brings in the ear-marks for his cattle, and desires they may be recorded—granted.

The petition of *Magister* Jacobus Fabritius, (the domine,) prays that the signers towards his maintenance shall be compelled—granted

Wm. Warner and Wm. Orian, purchasers of land of the Indians, lying in Schuylkill, (Blockley now,) being 335 gilders, pray that the other settlers there shall repay them their several proportions say eight persons, 1500 acres—granted.

An individual at the Falls, is fined £4 for selling liquor to the Indians. Adjourned to second Tuesday of September, 1681, and in mean time, the government is changed and transferred to Wm. Penn, by an order, *recorded*, from Anthony Brockholls, acting governor of New York, under date of 21 June, 1681, and commanding the peo ple to *obey* " William Markham, deputy governor," under the new government of Pennsylvania.

A list of sundry of the lands applied for and granted *gratis*, by the court of Upland, acting under the government of Sir Edmund Andross, from 1676 to 1681, to wit:

At court of 11th September, 1677.

Ephraim Herman (clerk of the court) and Pelle Rambo, 300 acres each, up the river, between Pennepekan and Poequessin creeks.

Christian Claesse, 100 acres next to Michel Shoemaker's land.

Jan Schoeven, 100 acres up the west side of the Schuylkill.

Richard Ducket, 100 acres up the east side of the Schuylkill.

John Mattson, Swen Lom, Lace Dalboo, 100 acres each, at Weissakitkonk, now Wissahiccon.

Pelle Dalboo, 200 acres, just above Tacaminik.

Jan Claasson, Paerde Cooper, 300 acres in Nishamminies creek, next to land of James Sanderling, two miles up.

Thomas Jacobse, 100 acres up Nishamminies creek, next to Claassen's.

William Jeacox, 100 acres up Nishamminies creek, next to Claassen's.

Lace Cock and James Sanderling, 100 acres each, up above Poequessink.

Captain Hans Moens, 300 acres up Pennepak creek.

Anthony Nealson and Michell Yzard, each 100 acres up above, in Cromkill.

Benjamin Goodman, 100 acres up Schuylkill, next to Richard Ducket's.

Laers Laersen and Hans Peterson, 100 acres each, up above the Mill in Amesland creek, and the place called Moherhuling.

At a court of 13th November, 1677.

Peter Rambo, 250 acres, between the land of Wicaco and land of Jurian Hartsvelder.

Lace Coleman, Pelle Laersen and Peter Erickson, 100 acres each, near the Falls of the Schuylkill.

Andries J. Inckhoeren, 200 acres in the Schuylkill, just before Beaver island.

Lace and Oele Dalbo, 200 acres in the Schuylkill, just before Beaver island.

At a court of 3d April, 1678

Thomas Nassitur, 200 acres. William Warner, 200 acres.

At a court of November 12th, 1678.

Oele Coecker, 300 acres. Henry Tedway, 300 acres.

Matthias Claassen Holstein, 100 acres. Edmund Draufton, 100 acres.

William Orian, 100 acres. Ephraim Herman, 100 acres.

Matthew Allin, 100 acres.

At a court of 12th March, 1678–9.

John Snowden, 100 acres. Hendricks Jacobs, 100 acres.

Jacobus Fabritius, 300 acres. Jurian Hartsvelder, 100 acres.

At a court of 20th March, 1679.

William Woodmancy, 100 acres. Peter Nealson, 100 acres. William Clayton, 200 acres.

At a court of 8th June, 1680.

William Clarke, 200 acres. Peter Cock, 200 acres. Thomas Fairman, 200 acres. Neeles Jonassen, 200 acres. Joseph Hardly 100 acres. Richard Tucker, 100 acres.

[The foregoing present about half of the whole list, and are here given as specimens.]

The Swedish documents sent by our minister, Mr. Russell, from Stockholm to the Philosophical Society, present two old deeds from Queen Christina, for lands at *Chester* and *Philadelphia*, of which I have a copy, to wit:

Donation to Captain John Amundson Besh, made by decree of Queen Christina, dated Stockholm, August 20th, 1653,—"that in consideration of the zeal and fidelity of the brave and courageous Captain John A. Besh, and because he has engaged to serve us with equal zeal so long as he shall live, we therefore *accord and grant* to himself, his wife, and to his heirs, and their heirs, a tract of land in New Sweden *extending to Upland Kyll*, to keep and possess the same for ever as his inviolable property." [This tract of land is said to be considered as beginning at, and appertaining to, what is now called Marcus Hook, and extended up to Chester, built upon Upland creek.]

At same time and date, a similar grant of the queen, is made to Lieutenant Swen Shute, as follows, to wit: August 20th, 1653:

For and in consideration of the good and important services rendered to us, by the brave and courageous Lieutenant Swen Shute, and because he has engaged to serve us faithfully so long as he shall live, we therefore *give and grant* to himself, his wife, and his heirs, a tract of country in New Sweden, viz.: *Mockorhultey-kyll*, as far as the river, together with the small island belonging thereto, viz.: the island of *Karinge*, and Kinsessing, comprehending also Passuming, to keep and possess the same for ever, as his inviolable property. [This tract of land is given to the person and name of him who was the proper original owner of the locality called Philadelphia, and covered the ground known by the name of Wiccaco. His name in time came to be called Swan, and afterwards Swanson, *i. e.*, son of Swan.]

The earliest dates of these Swedish papers are 1640, and seem to refer to an earlier colonization.

The early Dutch and Swedes' papers published in Hazard's Register, from the MS. in the Historical Society, are not interesting *to me* for extracts. Besides these, were several extracts from the Minutes of Council, extracted by Mr. Sargent.

I here add some facts concerning *Tinicum*, once a place of head quarters to the Swedish authorities, to wit:

Tinicum consists of big and little Tinicum islands. The larger is nine miles round, three long, and one and a half wide, and has twenty-six houses. It was on this island stood the fortress of New Gottenburg, and near it Printz's hall, (the mansion of Governor Printz,) and sundry houses and grounds of the Swedes. The house occupied by the governor is said by tradition to be the same now standing on the upland. It bears many interior marks of great antiquity, much of it was burnt by fire in 1822. The island now is worth 150 to 200 dollars an acre, and the whole island is worth $400,000, but in 1696, it was all sold for £500. It originally contained but five hundred acres, but now, by embanking and reclaiming from the water, it contains twenty-seven hundred acres, and is rendered much more healthy, and free from fevers and ague. The smaller island, "little Tinicum," fronts the other, out in the Delaware, was dry and embanked before the revolution, but in 1777 our people opened the banks to river invasion, to prevent its use by the British against Mud fort, and it still is flooded in high tides.

The following few facts concerning the Swedes, the earliest *cultivators* of our soil, may be worthy of some brief notices, to wit: Penn's letter says the Swedes and Fins came soon after the Dutch; while the latter pursued traffic the others turned to husbandry, settling chiefly about the freshes of the river Delaware. Such as Penn saw them, they were a plain, strong, and industrious people, but had made no great improvements. Their houses were full of fine children.

Numbers of Swedes lived about Kensington and on Gunner's creek, before the arrival of Penn. They had grants of land from Alexander Henoyon, the governor of New York, as early as 1664, that is the date of the deed to old Peter Cock for Shackamaxon. On that creek, three-fourths of a mile from its mouth, now so diminished, they once built large sloops, and afterwards a brig at its mouth.

The Swedes dwelt in numbers on Tinicum, calling the place New Gottenburg. At their church there, the first corpse ever buried was Catharine, daughter of Andrew Hanson, October 24, 1646.

All the Swedes, settled along the Delaware, used to go in their canoes from long distances to the church upon Tinicum island. They did the same in visiting the primitive log church at Wiccaco, almost all their conveyances were preferred by water. There was a store upon Darby to which they always went by water, even when the land route was often nearest.

The old Swedish inhabitants were said to be very successful in raising chick turkeys; as soon as hatched they plunged them into cold water, and forced them to swallow a whole pepper corn,—they then returned them to the mother, and they became as hardy as a hen's chick. When they found them drooping, their practice was tc examine the rump feathers, and such two or three as were found filled with blood were to be drawn, and the chick would revive and thrive.

Kalm, the Swedish traveller, who was here among his countrymen in 1748, has left us such notices as follows concerning them, to wit:

The ancient Swedes used the sassafras for tea, and for a dye. From the persimon tree they made beer and brandy. They called the mullein plant the Indian tobacco; they tied it round their arms and feet, as a cure when they had the ague. They made their candles generally from the bayberry bushes; the root they used to cure toothache; from the bush they also made an agreeable smelling soap. The magnolia tree they made use of for various medicinal purposes.

The houses of the first Swedish settlers were very indifferent; they consisted of but one room; the door was so low as to require you to stoop. Instead of window panes of glass they had little holes, before which a sliding board was put, or, on other occasions they had isinglass; the cracks between logs were filled with clay; the chimneys, in a corner, were generally of gray sandstone, or for want of it, sometimes of mere clay; the ovens were in the same room. They had at first separate stables for the cattle; but after the English came and set the example, they left their cattle to suffer in the open winter air. The Swedes wore vests and breeches of skins; hats were not used, but little caps with flaps before them. They made their own leather and shoes, with soles (like moccasons) of the same materials as the tops. The women, too, wore jackets and petticoats of skins; their beds, excepting the sheets, were of skins of bears, wolves, &c. Hemp they had none, but they used flax for ropes and fishing tackle. This rude state of living was, however, in the country places principally, and before the English came, who, rough as they must have also lived for a time, taught a comparative state of luxury.

The Swedes seem, however, to have retained an hereditary attachment to skin garments, for within the memory of the aged Mrs. S. she had seen old Mauntz Stille, down the Passyunk road, in his calfskin vest and jacket, and buckskin breeches.

Many Swedes settled along the western side of the Schuylkill. Matthias Holstein, a primitive settler in Upper Merion, took up one thousand acres there. Mauntz Rambo, an aged Swede, alive about sixty years ago, born near the Swedes' ford, was a celebrated hunter in his day; he killed numerous deer in the neighbourhood in his time—once he shot a panther which he found attempting to attack his dog. He remembered many Indians still among them, in his younger days.

My friend, Major M. Holstein, fond of his Swedish descent, tells me, that when he went to the Swedes' church, in Merion, as a boy, all the men and women came there on horseback, and all the women wore "safe-guard petticoats," which they took off and hung along the fence.

His grandmother, born at Molothan, four miles from Pottsgrove, remembered the Indians once about them, and that she herself, when young, had been carried some distance on a squaw's back. They then did all their travelling by canoes on the Schuylkill. When married, she and her wedding friends came down to the Swede's ford in their canoes. In the same manner they always made their visits to Philadelphia.

In 1631, the Swedes built a fort at "Fort point," the present estate of Benjamin Holmes, in Elsinborough. It was fronting upon the Delaware, and not up Salem creek. It was at this place they found the parent stock of the Elsinborough native grape. They built another at Finnsport New Jersey, opposite to Fort Delaware. They also built a fort at Elsinborough, which was afterwards destroyed by the Renappi Indians.

The Swedes settled several places on the Morris river, at Buckshutem, Dorchester and Leesburg; at the first place they had a church, but now all have disappeared, so that no Swedish names remain. Their graves, however, are still seen at Leesburg, on the brink of the river.

At Salem, one can still see remains of the earliest brick houses; they may be known, by being regularly intermixed with the glazed brick, always one-story high, with high *double* roofs. They are now generally raised into two-stories, without the glazed brick in the upper stories, and at the gable-ends may be still seen the lines which marked the former double roofs; and now the roofs have a single pitch. In the large grave ground opposite to the Friends' meeting, well filled with graves without any stones, is a very large oak tree of admirable spread and beauty in its wide branches. From being once deemed unhealthy as a residence, it has become, by the regular draining of the meadows, a healthy town, and has much of taste and beauty and neatness in the style of its houses and improvements. Philadelphians should visit it oftener, as the place where the first English emigrants began their first settlement on Delaware. It is entitled to their regard for the sake of its early associations.

THE GERMANS.

THIS hardy, frugal, and industrious portion of our population in Pennsylvania, so numerous and exclusive in places as to preserve their manners and language unaltered, are so often the subject of remark in the early MSS., which I have seen in the Logan collection, &c., as to deserve a separate notice, to wit:

When the Germans first came into the country, save those who were Friends and settled in Germantown in 1682–3, it is manifest there was a fear they would not be acceptable inhabitants, for James Logan, in 1717, remarks, "We have of late great numbers of Palatines poured in upon us, without any recommendation or notice, which gives the country some uneasiness, for foreigners do not so well among us as our own people," the English.

In 1719, Jonathan Dickinson remarks, "We are daily expecting ships from London which bring over Palatines, in number about six or seven hundred. We had a parcel who came about five years ago, who purchased land about sixty miles west of Philadelphia, and prove quiet and industrious. Some few came from Ireland lately, and more are expected thence. This is besides our common supply from Wales and England. Our friends do increase mightily, and a great people there is in this wilderness country, which is fast becoming a fruitful field."

Kalm, the Swedish traveller, here in 1748, says the Germans all preferred to settle in Pennsylvania, because they had been ill-treated by the authorities in New York, whither they first inclined to settle. Many had gone to that colony about the year 1709, [say 1711,] and made settlements on their own lands, which were invaded under various pretexts. They took great umbrage, and beat some of the persons who were disposed to dispossess them. Some of their leading men were seized by the government. The remainder in disgust left the country, and proceeded to settle in Pennsylvania. After that, even those who arrived at New York would not be persuaded to tarry, but all pushed on to Pennsylvania, where a better protection was granted to their rights and privileges. This mortified the New Yorkers, but they could not remove the first unfavourable impressions. As many as twelve thousand came to Philadelphia in 1749.

This emigration from New York to Pennsylvania is further incidentally explained by James Logan, in his MS. letters to the proprietaries. In writing to them in the year 1724, he manifests considerable disquietude at the great numbers coming among them, so numerous that he apprehends the Germans may even feel disposed to usurp the country to themselves. He speaks of the lands to the northward, (meaning Tulpehocken) as overrun by the unruly Germans,—the same who, in the year 1711, arrived at New York at the queen's expense, and were invited hither in 1722, (as a state policy,) by Sir William Keith when he was at Albany, for purposes of strengthening his political influence by favouring them.

In another letter of 1725, he calls them crowds of bold and indigent strangers from Germany, many of whom had been soldiers. All these go into the best vacant tracts, and seized upon them as places of common spoil. He says they rarely approach him on their arrival to propose to purchase; and when they are sought out and challenged for their rights of occupancy, they allege it was published in Europe that we wanted and solicited for colonists, and had a superabundance of land, and therefore they had come without the means to pay.' The Germans in after time embroiled with the Indians at Tulpehocken, threatening a serious affair.* In general, those who sat down without titles acquired enough in a few years to buy them, and so generally they were left unmolested. Logan speaks of one hundred thousand acres of land so possessed, and including the Irish squatters also.

> "Bold master-spirits, where they touch'd they gain'd
> Ascendence—where they fix'd their foot, they reign'd!"

The character of the Germans then known to him, he states, are many of them a surly people—divers of them Papists,—the men well armed, and, as a body, a warlike, morose race. In 1727, he states that six thousand Germans more are expected, and also many from Ireland; and these emigrations he hopes may be prevented in future by act of parliament, else he fears these colonies will, in time, be lost to the crown!—a future fact.

In 1729, he speaks of being glad to observe the influx of strangers, as likely to attract the interference of parliament, for truly, says he, they have danger to apprehend for a country where not even a militia exists for government support. To arrest their arrival in some degree the Assembly assessed a tax of 20 shillings a head on newly arrived servants.

In another letter he says, the numbers from Germany at this rate will soon produce a German colony here, and perhaps such a one as Britain once received from Saxony in the fifth century. He even states as among the apprehended schemes of Sir William Keith, the former governor, that he, Harland and Gould, have had sinister projects of forming an independent province in the west, to the westward of the Germans, towards the Ohio—probably west of the mountains, and to be supplied by his friends among the Palatines and Irish, among whom was his chief popularity at that time.

In later time, say about the year 1750 to '55, the Germans having become numerous, and therefore powerful as make weights in the political balance, were much noticed in the publications of the day. They were at that period of time in general very hearty co-operators

---

* It was at Tulpehocken, Conrad Weiser, a German, so often employed as Indian interpreter, was settled and died—say at present Womelsdorf, where he had his farm.

with the Friends, then in considerable rule in the assembly. A MS pamphlet before me, supposed to have been written by Samuel Wharton, in 1755, shows his ideas of the passing events, saying, that the party on the side of Friends derived much of their influence over the Germans through the aid of C. Sower, who published a German paper, in Germantown, from the time of 1739, and which, being much read by that people, influenced them to the side of the Friends, and hostile to the governor and council. Through this man, says he, they have persuaded them there was a design to enslave them; to enforce their young men [by a contemplated militia law] to become soldiers, and to load them with taxes, &c. From such causes, he adds, they came down in shoals to vote, and carry all before them. To this I may add, that I have heard from the Norris family, that their ancestors in the assembly were warmly patronized by the Germans, in union with Friends. His alarms at this German influence at the polls, and his proposed remedies for the then dreaded evils, as they show the prevalent feelings of his associates in politics, may serve to amuse the present generation. He says the bad effects of these successes of the Germans will probably be felt through many generations! Instead of a peaceable, industrious people as before, they are grown now insolent, sullen and turbulent,—in some counties threatening even the lives of all those who oppose their views, because they are taught to regard government and slavery as one and the same thing. All who are not of their party they call "governor's men," and themselves they deem strong enough to make the country their own! Indeed, they come in, in such force, say upwards of five thousand in the last year, I see not but they may soon be able to give us law and language too, or else, by joining the French, eject all the English. That this may be the case, is too much to be feared, for almost to a man they refused to bear arms in the time of the late war, and they say it is all one to them which king gets the country, as their estates will be equally secure. Indeed it is clear that the French have turned their hopes upon this great body of Germans. They hope to allure them by grants of Ohio lands. To this end they send their Jesuitical emissaries among them to persuade them over to the Popish religion.* In concert with this, the French for so many years have encroached on our province, and now are so near their scheme as to be within two days march of some of our back settlements—alluding of course to the state of the western wilds, overrun by French and Indians just before the arrival of Braddock's forces in Virginia, in 1755.

The writer imputes their wrong bias in general to their "stubborn genius and ignorance," which he proposes to soften by education—a

---

* It is true that the Jesuits at an early period founded a missionary station at Lancaster; and in 1734, Governor Gordon, from the fear of their being connected with French interests, brought the subject before the council. They also founded one at Cusshahoppen, near Summany town.

scheme still suggested as necessary to give the general mass of the inland country Germans right views of public and individual interests. To this end, he proposes that faithful Protestant ministers and schoolmasters should be supported among them—a scheme, as we shall presently see, which actually came to pass. Their children should be taught the English tongue; the government in the mean time should suspend the right of voting for members of assembly; and to incline them the sooner to become English in education and feeling, we should compel them to make all bonds and other legal writings in English; and no newspaper or almanac be circulated among them unless also accompanied by the English thereof.

Finally, the writer concludes that "without some such measure I see nothing to prevent this province from falling into the hands of the French!" The paper, at length, may be seen in my MS. Annals, in the Historical Society of Pennsylvania, pages 198 to 202. There may be consulted also, in the City Library, several pamphlets, pro and con, concerning the Germans and Quakers, printed in 1747–8—one is "Plain Truth"—"An Answer to Plain Truth"—and in 1764 appears "The Plain Dealer," and "An Answer" to it, &c.

The same writer gives a passing notice of a society in England, of noblemen and gentlemen, to raise funds for some English schools for the Germans among us; and in 1755, Benjamin Franklin published a book, entitled "A brief History of the charitable Scheme for instructing poor Germans in Pennsylvania." It is the same scheme alluded to in the Pennsylvania Gazette of 1755, saying therein, that a great society is formed in Europe for the raising of money for instructing the poor German children, and giving them ministers, &c It is patronized in Holland and England by the first nobility and gentry, and some of our first citizens are made trustees of the charity—such as Hamilton, Allen, Franklin, Peters, &c. The Rev. Mr. Schlatter is made visiting and travelling inspector and agent, and the Rev. Dr. Smith, our provost, was charged with the publication of a German newspaper. The states of Holland and West Friesland grant 2000 gilders per annum, for five years. Much is given in Amsterdam. The general assembly of Scotland gave £1200 sterling. The king of England gave £1000—the Princess of Wales £100—the proprietaries also agreed to give annually, &c. The style of the whole forcibly reminds one of the popular missionary schemes of the present day. It is all done in the name of advancing the interests of the Protestant religion—giving pious education—teaching them "to read their Bible, to sing psalms, to write and cast accounts," and also "to furnish pious instruction where they have no ministers." The whole effect of this formidable array, now that the effervescence has subsided, and the means have been fully exerted, might tempt a looker-on to suggest *cui bono!*

It appears from the Minutes of Council, of January, 1730, that the first settlers of Tulpehacka creek, were 33 families of Palatines, who came away from New York, nigh Albany, in 1713, under the allurement of Sir Wm. Keith, the governor, headed by their chief, Conrad Weiser. It appears that they did not pay the government nor the Indians for their settlement. In 1728, the Indian chief makes a claim for it of Gov. Hamilton. The names of the first families are given on page 89 of the Minutes.

The emigration of the Palatines direct to Philadelphia, by sea, are recorded as often as thirty times in one volume!

Conrad Weiser was an early and respectable interpreter, who lived once at the present Reading, and also at Tulephocken. At Womelsdorf, a town in that district, he lived and died. It is situate between Reading and Harrisburg. Himself and father were among the first settlers of Schoharie, New York; they having gone out from Germany to New York in 1712, with other emigrants, *in a long six months' passage*, under a proclamation of Queen Anne, of 1709, to take up land *free*, and no taxes. When N. Bayard, the Queen's agent, came afterwards to enrol their names, to record their metes and bounds; they became alarmed and offered resistance. Strife and apprehension ensued, so that, with some encouragement from Governor Keith, of Pennsylvania, much of the population, thirty-three families, set out for Tulpehocken, in 1713, by way of the Susquehanna river, and settled when there at Muehlback, or Millbrook. The facts are well known in the early history of Schoharie; others of the same Germans settled on the German Flats, New York.

There was, as early as 1732, to 1740, a very remarkable religious sect of Germans, formed at *Ephrata*, intended to live in a monastic life. In time it also included a separate sisterhood. They formed a considerable town, and grew in wealth by their industry and rise of value in lands. At one time they were many in number, but now have dwindled away. They were undoubtedly sincere and exemplary in their religious principles and actions. Doctor W. M. Fahnestock, of Harrisburg, who lately united himself to them, and has probably become one of their preachers, has given a long and interesting historical sketch of this people, in Hazard's Register of 1835. They were remarkable as a community in being fine Latinists—writing and speaking Latin as readily as their vernacular tongue. Men of wealth in Philadelphia, who sought good classical education for their sons, used to send them there; and I have known some educated there who used to correspond with some of the brotherhood in Latin. But above all, they were *peculiar* for their superior music and singing. It was this last attraction which first allured young Doctor Fahnestock to their meetings, and when his heart was touched, like St. Augustin's, he readily fell into sympathy with their religion—a thing in itself found needful, in some way, for all men, who come to think considerately.

Their music was so peculiar as to deserve some special mention—"not as music *for the ear*, but as music *for the soul*." One of their leaders, *Beissel*, was a first-rate musician and composer. [See p. 111 of this volume.]

These people, in general principles of religion, have come nearest to the Tunkers, and have been called Seven-day Baptists. In their early state they wore the habit of the Capuchins, or white friars—a long white gown and cowl for the men, and a cowl for the women. The men wore beards. Their inmates all assumed new names—such as Onesimus, Friedsam, &c.—after the monastic fashion in Europe. Their houses were all framed of wood, and the sides were shingled and covered. In 1740, the monks were 36 and the sisters 35 in number. The whole place is now nearly untenanted, only a few aged sisters linger about the place of their ancient recollections. Such of the society as still continue in the original principles of the first faith are settled at *Snowhill*, in Franklin county, where they have "married, and bring up families," and still *try* to execute the former *enchanting* style of singing and music.

THE IRISH.

THE Irish emigrants did not begin to come into Pennsylvania until about the year 1719. Those who did come were generally from the north of Ireland. Such as came out first generally settled at and near the disputed Maryland line. James Logan, writing of them to the proprietaries, in 1724, says they have generally taken up the southern lands, [meaning in Lancaster county, towards the Maryland line,] and as they rarely approached him to propose to purchase, he calls them bold and indigent strangers, saying, as their excuse, when challenged for titles, that we had solicited for colonists, and they had come accordingly. They were, however, understood to be a tolerated class, exempt from rents by an ordinance of 1720, in consideration of their being a frontier people, forming a kind of cordon of defence, if needful. They were soon called bad neighbours to the Indians, treating them disdainfully, and finally were the same race who committed the outrage called the Paxton massacre. These general ideas of them are found in the Logan MS. collection. Some of the data is as follows:

In 1725, James Logan states that there are as many as 100,000 acres of land possessed by persons (including Germans) who resolutely set down and improve it without any right to it, and he is much at a loss to determine how to dispossess them.

In 1729, he expresses himself glad to find the parliament is about to take measures to prevent the too free emigration to this country. In the mean time the assembly had laid a restraining tax of twenty shillings a head for every servant arriving; but even this was evaded in the case of the arrival of a ship from Dublin, with 100 papists and convicts, by landing them at Burlington. It looks, says he, as if Ireland is to send all its inhabitants hither, for last week not less than six ships arrived, and every day two or three arrive also. The common fear is, that if they thus continue to come they will make themselves proprietors of the province. It is strange, says he, that they thus crowd where they are not wanted. But few besides convicts are imported thither.* The Indians themselves are alarmed at the swarms of strangers, and we are afraid of a breach between them, for the Irish are very rough to them.

In 1730, he writes and complains of the Scotch-Irish, in an audacious and disorderly manner possessing themselves about that time of the whole of Conestogoe manor of 15,000 acres, being the best land in the country. In doing this by force, they alleged that "it was against the laws of God and nature, that so much land should be idle while so many Christians wanted it to labour on, and to raise their bread," &c. The Paxton boys were all great sticklers for religion, and for Scripture quotations against "the heathen!" They were, however, dispossessed by the sheriff and his *posse*, and their cabins, to the number of thirty, were burnt. This necessary violence was perhaps remembered with indignation; for only twenty-five years afterwards, the Paxton massacre began, by killing the Christian, unoffending Indians found in Conestogoe. Those Irish were generally settled in Donegal.

In another letter he writes, saying, I must own, from my own experience in the land office, that the settlement of five families from Ireland gives me more trouble than fifty of any other people. Before we were broken in upon, ancient Friends and first settlers lived happily, but now the case is quite altered, by strangers and debauched morals, &c. All this seems like hard measure dealt upon these specimens of "the land of generous natures," but we may be excused for letting him speak out, who was himself from the "Emerald isle," where he had of course seen a better race.

His successor, Richard Peters, as secretary to the proprietaries, falls into similar dissatisfaction with them; for in his letter to them, of 1743, he says he went to Marsh creek, in Lancaster county, to warn off and dispossess the squatters, and to measure the manor land. On that occasion, the people there, to about the number of seventy, assembled and forbade them to proceed, and on their persisting, they broke the chain and compelled them to retire. He had with him a sheriff and a magistrate. They were afterwards indicted—became subdued, and made their engagements for leases. In most cases the leases were so easy that they were enabled to buy the lands ere they expired.

* Augustus Gun, of Cork, advertised in the Philadelphia paper, that he had power from the mayor of Cork, for many years, to procure servants for America.

NEGROES AND SLAVES.

He finds his fellow guilty—of a skin
Not colour'd like his own!—For such a cause
Dooms and devotes him as his lawful prey.

In the olden time, dressy blacks and dandy *coloured* beaux and belles, as we now see them issuing from their proper churches, were quite unknown. Their aspirings and little vanities have been rapidly growing since they got those separate churches, and have received their entire exemption from slavery. Once they submitted to the appellation of servants, blacks, or negroes, but now they require to be called coloured people, and among themselves, their common call of salutation is—gentlemen and ladies. Thirty to forty years ago, they were much humbler, more esteemed in their place, and more useful to themselves and others. As a whole they show an overweening fondness for display and vainglory—fondly imitating the whites in processions and banners, and in the pomp and pageantry of Masonic and Washington societies, &c. With the kindest feelings for their race, judicious men wish them wiser conduct, and a better use of the benevolent feelings which induced their emancipation among us.

We have happily been so long relieved from the curse of slavery, that it is scarcely known to the younger part of the community how many features we once possessed of a slave-owning colony. The following facts in the case will prove new to many:

The first negro slaves ever imported into North America were brought in a Dutch ship in 1620, and sold in Virginia.

The state of slavery in Pennsylvania was always of a mild character, not only from the favourable and mild feelings of the Friends in their behalf, but from the common regard they found in families in general, where their deportment was commendable. Hector St. John, Esq., who wrote concerning the state of slavery in Pennsylvania,* as it was just before the period of the Revolution, says, "In Pennsylvania they enjoy as much liberty as their masters—are as well fed and as well clad; and in sickness are tenderly taken care of—for, living under the same roof, they are in effect a part of the family. Being the companions of their labours, and treated as such, they do not work more than ourselves, and think themselves happier than many of the lower class of whites. A far happier race among us, (he adds,) than those poor suffering slaves of the south."

The first efforts ever made in Pennsylvania towards the emancipation of the blacks proceeded from the Society of Friends in Germantown, the most of whom, at that period, were emigrants

* Vide his Farmer's Letters.

from Germany. These, in the year 1688, under the auspices of F. D. Pastorius, moved a petition or remonstrance to the yearly meeting of Friends, saying in effect, it was not Christian-like to buy and keep negroes. The meeting forbore then to give any positive judgment in the case. But inquiry was created. Cotemporary with this period, William Penn himself, whose light or reflections on the case were not equally awakened, says, in his letter of the 4th of 8 mo., 1685, to his steward, James Harrison, at Pennsbury, "It were better they were blacks, for then we might have them for life," intimating thereby, that his intended servants there were changed too often.

In 1693, the separate meeting of Friends, under George Keith, assembling at the house of Philip James, in Philadelphia, gave forth a paper declaring their sense of the duty of emancipation—"after some reasonable time of service."—Vide Gabriel Thomas.

The large original proprietors of property in Philadelphia and Pennsylvania, called "the Free Society of Traders," of 1682, although as a corporation they might be said, like others, "to be without souls," conceded an article very favourable to emancipation, saying, "If the society should receive blacks for servants, they shall make them free at fourteen years' end, upon condition that they will give unto the society's ware-house two-thirds of what they are capable of producing on such a parcel of land as shall be allotted to them by the society, with a stock of necessary tools." Then comes a proviso of rather singular character, saying, "And if they will not accept of these terms they shall be servants till they will accept of it!"

I have seen, among the earliest pamphlets extant of Philadelphia publication, one from the Friends' meeting of Philadelphia, of the 13th of 8 mo., 1693, giving "exhortation and caution to Friends concerning buying and keeping negroes." The sum of the counsel was, that none should attempt "to buy except to set free." This little address contained many of the arguments now usually set forth against slavery.

In 1696, the Yearly Meeting of Friends having concerted some measures to discourage the bringing in of more slaves, and to preserve the morals of those they had, the subject was renewed in the year 1700, on the arrival of William Penn, in consideration of his pressing upon the Philadelphia meeting his wishes concerning the same. Their sense of the subject was expressed as follows, to wit: "Our dear friend and governor, having laid before this meeting a concern that hath laid upon his mind for some time concerning the negroes and Indians, that Friends ought to be very careful in discharging a good conscience towards them in all respects, but more especially for the good of their souls; upon consideration whereof, this meeting concludes to appoint a meeting for negroes, to be kept once a month, &c."

At the same time, he introduced a bill into the assembly "for regulating negroes in their morals and marriages,"--also another "for their trials and punishments." The former was defeated by the jealousies then in the house. From the same causes an act of more security was substituted in 1705 against the negroes, entitled "An Act for the Trial and Punishment of Negroes." It inflicted lashes for petty offences, and death for crimes of magnitude. They were not allowed to carry a gun without license, or to be whipped if they did, twenty-one lashes—nor to meet above four together lest they might form cabals and riots. They were to be whipped if found abroad after nine o'clock at night without a pass, &c. At and before 1705, it had been in practice to bring Indians as slaves from the Carolinas, to the offence of the Pennsylvania Indians. This was prevented by an act.

In 1715, Mr. Isaac Norris, in one of his letters, speaks thus concerning a question in meeting respecting slaves: "Our meeting was large and comfortable, and our business would have been very well were it not for the warm pushing by some Friends, of Chester chiefly, in the business of negroes. The aim was to obtain a minute that none should buy them for the future. This was opposed as of dangerous consequence to the peace of the church, for since they could not tell how to dispose of those we have, and that many members must still possess them, and then it might fall to their lot in duty to deal with future offenders, which as it could not in itself be equitable, such must do it with an ill grace, and at best it would be a foundation for prejudice and evil speaking one of another, *so that it was got over.*" The liberating genius of Benezet has since cast better lights upon this subject, perplexed as they then deemed it.

The early efforts made to repress slavery were reiterated and numerous in our provincial assembly. As early as the year 1705, a duty was imposed on their importation; this was renewed in 1710. In 1711, they struck at the root of the evil, by forbidding their introduction in future; but the privy council in England scandalized by such liberal policy in so new and so diminutive a community, whilst their policy was to cherish slavery in so many other colonies, quashed the act in an instant. The assembly, not daunted by such a repulse, again in 1712, upon petition, "signed by many hands," aimed at the same effect, by assessing the large sum of £20 a head. This was again cancelled by the same Transatlantic policy. When the petition for the £20 duty was presented, another was offered in the name of William Southeby, praying "for the total abolition of slavery in Pennsylvania!"

Thus early were the minds of our forefathers awake to this manifest infraction of human rights, and having their consciences and feelings enlisted in the cause, though often thwarted in their purposes, they still continued to renew their efforts, so that more than one dozen of acts may be counted upon our statute books, tending directly or indirectly to repress or abolish slavery prior to our revolution. Finally, the memorable act of 1780, when we had "set up for ourselves," for ever released us from the thraldom of "sinews bought and sold!"

A letter of 4 mo., 1715, from Jonathan Dickinson, a merchant of Philadelphia, and a Friend, to his correspondent in Jamaica, says, "I must entreat you to send me no more negroes for sale, for our people don't care to buy. They are generally against any coming into the country. Few people care to buy them, except for those who live in other provinces."—Vide the Logan MSS.

Some benevolent individual, as early as the year 1722, advertised in the Mercury Gazette of Philadelphia, that "a person, lately arrived, freely offers his services to teach his poor brethren, the male negroes, to read the Holy Scriptures without any charge."

The celebrated Whitfield embraced the benevolent scheme of ameliorating the condition of the blacks he saw in our colonies. In 1739 he published his letter to the southern planters, against the practice of slavery, and in favour of the blacks; at the same time he takes up 5000 acres on the forks of Delaware, (the same sold to Count Zindendorf for Bethlehem,) in order to erect a negro school, &c. His choice of Pennsylvania for his negro colony and settlement, showed thus early his favourable opinion of the good feelings to that race in Pennsylvania.

At the same time we may perceive that, as a slave-holding colony, the odious features of slavery were necessarily to be seen among us—such as the public buying and selling,—their arrival and landing from ships, &c. I give the following facts in illustration of things as they were once among us, to wit:

Year 1736—William Allen and Joseph Turner, merchants, advertise for sale some likely negroes from Barbadoes; another about the same time advertises for sale a likely breeding negro woman and her boy of two years old.

Year 1762—Messrs. Willing and Morris advertise for sale one hundred and seventy negroes just arrived from the Gold Coast.

It was the common incident of the day to vend blacks of both sexes at public sale, at the old London Coffee-house, setting up the subject upon the head of a cask, for display to the purchasers around.

After better views and feelings had long prevailed, old recollections were strongly revived in an incident which occurred in the year 1800. The Ganges sloop of war captured two vessels engaged in slavery, and brought them into our Delaware—one had one hundred and eighteen, and the other sixteen slaves. In encamping these at the Lazaretto for the benefit of free air and health, a husband and wife, separated in the ships, never expecting to meet again, recognized each other. Their mutual recognition was passionately fond and affecting. The sudden surprise and joy was too powerful for the wife, and she became a premature mother. But, through the well directed kindness of the Abolition Society, she was restored to health and freedom.

Before the revolution it was a common incident in Philadelphia to send family servants to the jail to get their dozen lashes, for acts of insubordination. This was done at the pleasure of the master, and was usually executed on receiving a written message from the owners. An old gentleman told me of a case which he witnessed:—A master sent his servant, "Hodge's Cato," with his letter, wherein he requested to have him well whipped. The black was shrewd, suspected it conveyed some ill to him, and fell upon a device to shun it. He stretched himself on the stall at the market house near the prison, affecting to have been seized with violent cramps and pains in the bowels. When he had succeeded to excite the pity of some bystanders, he begged a black fellow near him to hurry away and deliver his letter, as it was a matter requiring haste. The appeal answered the purpose fully; for, malgre all his remonstrances, he received all the lashes bespoke for "the bearer!"

When slaves were purchased in early times with intention to be taken to other colonies, there was seen, even in Philadelphia, the odious spectacle of "the drove," tied two and two, passing through the city towards the country. Several of the aged have told me of witnessing such things even in the gentle city of Penn!

Many can still remember when the slaves were allowed the last days of the fairs for their jubilee, which they employed ("light hearted wretch!") in dancing the whole afternoon in the present Washington square, then a general burying ground—the blacks joyful above, while the sleeping dead reposed below! In that field could be seen at once more than one thousand of both sexes, divided into numerous little squads, dancing, and singing, "each in their own tongue," after the customs of their several nations in Africa.

Finally, a discerning lady, who has witnessed "the former years," and has seen the comparative happiness of the blacks—has felt, too, her strong affections and domestic relations to her family servants—thus speaks of her sense of the change produced in family comforts! "In the olden time domestic comforts were not every day interrupted by the pride and profligacy of servants. The slaves of Philadelphia were a happier class of people than the free blacks of the present day generally are, who taint the very air by their vices, and exhibit every sort of wretchedness and profligacy in their dwellings. The former felt themselves to be an integral part of the family to which they belonged. They experienced in all respects the same consideration and kindness as white servants, and they were faithful and contented." The truth is, in numerous cases where they were freed, they preferred to remain and receive their wages till their deaths.

Kalm, the Swedish traveller, speaks of the then only free negroes in Philadelphia in 1748, as having been manumitted by a Quaker master—probably referring to Ralph Sandiford, who freed all of his in the year 1733, and probably presenting to us the first instance of the kind known in our annals.

There is an ancient charity for the blacks of Philadelphia, founded as early as the year 1696, and yet, although in actual operation, is as much unknown to the mass of our citizens as if it were in Africa! It originated with the Rev. Dr. Bray, American missionary, the Bishop of London, and Mr. D'Alone, secretary to King William. Its primary object was "the conversion of adult negroes, and the education of their children" in the British plantations. Its operation with our Philadelphia blacks began about the year 1760. And in 1774, the ground rents of a large lot in our city was set apart for the payment of the expenses of two schools for blacks, one for each sex, to be educated gratuitously. "The associates" in England are per petual; and from their appointments, three of our citizens, church men, constantly serve the schools as directors and governors. Those lately in service were William Meredith, Thomas Hale, and James S. Smith, esquires. Such a charity, supported by foreigners, deserves to be better known, and especially by those blacks who may become its beneficiaries.

REDEMPTION SERVANTS.

NUMEROUS persons used to arrive every year from Germany and Ireland, who engaged themselves for a term of years to pay their passages. Some of them turned out frugal and industrious, and became in time a part of our wealthy citizens. In some few cases they appear to have been convicts from Ireland. In one case the servant was found to be a lord, and returned home to inherit his estate. The general facts are to the following effect, to wit:

In 1722, the Palatine servants were disposed of at £10 each, for five years of servitude. About this time a MS. letter of Jonathan Dickinson says, "Many who have come over under covenants for four years are now masters of great estates."

1728—An advertisement reads, "Lately imported, and to be sold cheap, a parcel of likely men and women servants." These were probably servants from Europe.

1729—In New Castle government there arrived last year, says the Gazette, forty-five hundred persons, chiefly from Ireland; and at Philadelphia, in one year, two hundred and sixty-seven English and Welsh, forty-three Scotch—all servants; also, eleven hundred and fifty-five Irish, and two hundred and forty-three Palatines, of whom none were servants.

In 1737, an article appears in the Pennsylvania Gazette to the following effect, to wit: "An errant cheat detected at Annapolis! A vessel arrived there, bringing sixty-six indentures, signed by the mayor of Dublin, and twenty-two *wigs*, of such a make as if they were intended for no other use than to set out the *convicts* when they should go ashore." Thus these convicts were attempted, under fraudulent papers and *decent wigs*, to be put off as decent servants, and especially when surmounted with wigs! Same time is advertised "for sale, a parcel of English servants from Bristol."

In 1741, public information is given to merchants and captains that Augustus Gun of Cork, bellman, has power from the mayor there, to procure servants for America for this many years past.

Such an advertisement, in a Philadelphia paper, was of course an intimation that the mayor of Cork was willing to get off sundry culprits to the colonies.

In 1750, some of our good citizens take alarm at the idea of having criminals, "unwhipped of justice," imposed upon them. They thought the offences of such, when among us, swelled our criminal list. One writes upon the subject and says, "When we see our papers filled so often with accounts of the most audacious robberies, the most cruel murders, and other villanies, perpetrated by convicts from Europe, what will become of our posterity! In what could Britain injure us more than emptying her jails on us? What must we think of those merchants, who, for the sake of a little petty gain, will be concerned in importing and disposing of these abominable cargoes." From the tenor of the preceding article it is probable they got premiums in some cases for taking off such unwelcome guests. In some cases the severity of British laws pushed off young men, of good abilities, for very small offences, who made very capable clerks, storekeepers, &c., among us. I have knowledge of two or three among us, even within my memory, who rose to riches and credit here, and have left fine families. One great man, before my time, had been sold in Maryland, as an offender in Ireland. While serving his master as a common servant, he showed much ability, unexpectedly, in managing for him an important lawsuit, for which he instantly gave him free. He then came to Philadelphia, and amassed a great fortune in landed estate, now of great value among his heirs.

When Kalm was here, in 1748, he speaks of wages of hired people as from 16 to £20 currency. A servant woman got from 8 to £10 a year, and laid up money. About the same rate of wages continued down to the period of the revolution. At such wages families were better served than now, and most of them were accustomed to remain in the same families for years.

The case of Lord Altham, who came to this country in 1728 when a lad, and served out his servitude, as James Annesley, with a farmer, on the Lancaster road, forms in itself a curious and interesting recital. The circumstance has furnished the groundwork for Roderick Random, and for the popular novel of Florence M'Cartey. The facts are as follows, to wit:

The facts concerning this singular case are taken from the evidence given on the trial, and may be depended on as authentic.

Arthur Annesley (Lord Altham) married Mary Sheffield, natural daughter of the Earl of Buckingham. By her, in the year 1715, he had a son, James, the subject of this memoir. In the next year the parents had some differences, which terminated in a separation. The father, contrary to the wish of the mother, took exclusive possession of his son James, and manifested much fondness for him, until the year 1722, when he formed some intimacy with Miss Gregory; and about the same time his wife died. Miss G. expecting now to become his wife, exerted herself greatly to alienate his affections from his son, by insinuating that he was not his proper child. She succeeded to get him placed from home, at a school in Dublin. In November, 1727, Lord Altham died; and his brother Richard, wishing to possess the estate and title, took measures to get rid of his nephew, James, by having him enticed on board an American vessel, which sailed from Dublin in April, 1728. He was landed at Philadelphia, then in his thirteenth year, sold as a redemptioner! and actually served out twelve years in rough labour, until a seeming accident, in the year 1740, brought him to such acquaintance, as led, in the next year, to his return home. The case was this: two Irishmen, John and William Broders, travelling the Lancaster road, in the year 1740, stopped at the house near the forty milestone, where James was in service with an old German. These countrymen entering into conversation, perceived they were severally from Dumaine, in the county of Wexford, and that James Annesley was the son of Arthur. The two Broders volunteered to go back to Ireland, and testify to the discovery they had made, and actually kept their word at the trial which afterwards occurred. James subsequently stated his case to Robert Ellis, Esq., of Philadelphia, who, compassionating his case, procured a passage for him to Admiral Vernon, then in the West Indies, by whom he was afterwards landed in England. But shortly after his arrival at London, James unfortunately killed a man, for which he had to stand a trial; and then Lord Altham, the unnatural uncle, exerted himself to have him convicted, but he was nevertheless acquitted as innocent. An action was brought against the uncle, and went to trial in November, 1743, and the verdict was given in favour of James, our redemptioner. The uncle appealed to the house of lords; and while the case was pending James died, leaving the uncle in quiet possession of his ill-gotten estate, showing, however, while he lived, which was not long, the spectacle of a finished villain, even in an Irish nobleman. This Annesley family, is the same by whom the celebrated *John Wesley* descended by the mother's side.

THE STAMP ACT RESISTED.

> "Society, grown weary of the load,
> Shakes her encumber'd lap—and casts them out."

THE measures of the Stamp Act in England, and the oppositions and counteractions which ensued in this country, were all so many causes combining to sever those ties of union, before existing between the parent and the offspring, and leading the latter to self-government and independence.

Many who then fell into measures of resistance had little or no conception of the termination to which it led—whilst others, as by an eye of prescience, seemed to penetrate all the hidden mysteries of the future. Such a mind as the Abbe Raynal's, before the revolution commenced, fairly wrote out our destiny, calling "the American provinces the asylum of freedom, the cradle of future nations, and the refuge of distressed Europeans!"

In November, 1765, the Stamp Act was to have taken effect at Philadelphia. John Hughes, a tradesman of Philadelphia, a friend of Dr. Franklin's, who procured him the appointment, and a member of the assembly, was made the stamp-master. He affected to decline the office, but was not deemed sincere. Wherefore, when his commission arrived (some blamed Franklin for it) all the bells were muffled, the colours hoisted half-mast, and great appearances of mobbing occurred. Hughes' house was guarded and armed by his friends, &c. In the mean time the late Thomas Bradford, from the "committee of safety," (a self-created society,) with his posse, waited on the stamp-master and compelled him to a voluntary resignation; that is, he had to say it was such.*

A newspaper of Bradford's, printed the day before the act was to take effect, was put all in mourning devices—having a death's head and × bones, for stamp a coffin, and "Liberty at an end!"

At the same time all the storekeepers in Philadelphia resolved to import no British goods, &c. William Smith opens a store for the sale of commission domestic goods, where all the patriots are invited to make purchases. The community agree to eat no lamb meat, so that the wool might be the sooner increased for home-made fabrics. Among other resolves to live in a more frugal manner suitable to the self-denying times, they determine to restrain the usual expenses of funerals, formerly conducted with a censurable "pomp of woe." In the new mode, B. Price, Esq., was buried in an oaken coffin and iron handles, and Alderman Plumstead without pall or mourning dresses.

* A long letter of his, opposing the views of his constrainers, to the commissioners of stamps in England, may be seen, with other proceedings in the case, in the Register of Pennsylvania—vol. ii. p. 244.

In the mean time, feelings of resistance were cherished by some so far as to exhibit emblems and devices diminishing the former regard to the parent country. A paper was sold about the streets called "The Folly of England and Ruin of America." In fine, the measures of resistance were so prompt, energetic and widely diffused through the colonies, that every motive of prudence urged the mother country to an equally prompt repeal. In the mean time she had granted time and occasion for organizing many civic associations, called "Sons of Liberty," &c., who thus learned, without any mishap, the hardihood and practice necessary to conduct future social and civic combinations when needful; in fact, they never fully subsided; and in the end they revived at the period of the revolution with redoubled vigour and skill.

When the news of "Stamp Act repealed" arrived in 1766, the gentlemen at the coffe-house sent a deputation to Captain Wise, by whose brig the news came, to invite him up to drink punch, and at the same time to give his whole crew presents. All was joy and hilarity. At the Coffee-house the punch was made common, and a gold laced hat was presented to the captain as a token of their gratitude. The same night every street in the city was illuminated. A large quantity of wood was given for bonfires, and many barrels of beer to the populace. Next day the governor and mayoralty gave a great feast for 300 persons, at the State-house gallery. At the same place it was unanimously resolved to dress themselves at the approaching birth-day in new suits of English manufacture, and to give their homespun and patriotic garments to the poor!

In June, 1766, being the king's birthday, and in honour of the repeal, a great number of the inhabitants of the Northern Liberties and Southwark met on the banks of the Schuylkill, then a place of arborescent shade, where 430 persons were dined in a grove. The Franklin barge, of 40 feet, and the White Oak barge, of 50 feet, both decorated with many flags, were then used with much parade. One was rowed up the Schuylkill, firing her salutes; and the other was drawn through the streets of the city, also firing her salutes *en passant*. Fireworks were exhibited at night. The whole scene was a joyous occasion, and the crowds were great. They rejoiced as well for the supposed concession as for their personal and national interests.

Dr. Franklin, who was afraid his countrymen would show too much exultation and triumph, writes in his letter of the 27th of February, 1766, to Charles Thomson, saying, "I trust the behaviour of the Americans on this occasion will be so prudent and grateful as that their friends here (in London) will have no reason to be ashamed; and that our enemies, who predict that the indulgence will only make us more insolent and ungovernable, may find themselves false prophets."

The proprietary, Penn, in his letter to Secretary Peters, says, "It was given as the softest medicine to the wound. Our friends give it as matter of great favour. Don't exult as at a great victory; but send grateful thanks, &c.—else our opposing prophets here will verify their assertion that the repeal will cause further disobedience."

Another letter of B. Franklin's to Charles Thomson, of the 11th of July, 1765, says, "I did all I could to oppose the act, but the tide was too strong. The nation was provoked by American claims of independence, and all parties joined in resolving by this act to settle the point," &c. The sequel proved how fatal was the experiment; while it helped them to feel our pulse, it also eventuated in the final dismission of the royal rulers.

The British authorities then in this country affected to neutralize the apparent exultation and triumphs at the repeal, by joining their names and persons in the displays and rejoicings. Thus the governor joined the feastings in Philadelphia; and at New York, the mansion of General Gage, in Broad street, was gorgeously illuminated with the royal arms and "Stamp Act repealed," &c.

BRITISH DUTIES AND TEA ACT RESISTED.

"Touch'd by the Midas finger of the state,
Seeks gold for ministers to sport away."

The feelings which had been excited by the Stamp Act were again much revived, in what were deemed encroachments of the British government, in their renewed attempts in 1768, to impose duties on glass, paper, &c. They wanted our money!

In September, 1768, the traders of Philadelphia, in concert with those of New York and Boston, resolved to import none of the usual goods from England, until the Act laying those duties was repealed.

In July, 1769, a load of malt arrived to Amos Strettell, whereupon all the brewers and traders held a meeting at the State-house, and there resolved unanimously that they will not purchase nor consume the same.

The papers of the year 1770, are frequent in their resolutions and appeals to the people, to adhere to the "non-importation agreement," to be persisted in until they effect a change of measures at home. The spirit is very general, and effigies are made and burnt of any dissenters of note. The spirit of liberty, under the name of "Sons of Liberty," is in full effervescence among some. Even as the opposition of the church of Rome to the reformation, then, only served to strike out new light, and to elicit more system in resistance—so in politics with us; the more we made inquiries into British misrule, the more and more we discovered the benefits of separate interests and the rights of enfranchisement.

In the year 1770, the inhabitants of New York, altered for a season, in their politics, by a most extraordinary electioneering influence, swerved from their "non-importation agreement," the only colony in the union which did it!—in consequence of which the patriots of Philadelphia meet, and resolve to make no purchases of any thing from New York—calling them at the same time, "a faction unfriendly to redress of grievances."

All the goods which came out to Philadelphia on commissions. were all rejected and had to go back, and especially those which were sent to Boston.

The desire to encourage domestic fabrics gave rise, in 1771, to the erection of a flint glass manufactory near Lancaster, by which they hoped to save £30,000 to the province. A china factory, too, was also erected on Prime street, near the present navy yard, intended to make china at a saving of £15,000.* At the same time, a piece of the finest broadcloth "ever made in America" was publicly exhibited at the Coffee-house, from the then first and only loom existing in the colonies.

In December, 1773, the tea ships, "with the detested tea," arrived in our river as far as Gloucester Point, where they were arrested from coming nearer to the city, by a committee from the general town meeting of probably eight thousand people, assembled at the State-house yard. They allowed the captain of the "Polly" to come to town, that he might see the prevalent spirit of opposition, by which he might determine whether to take the chance of remaining, or of wisely directing his voyage homeward. He chose the latter. In the mean time, the committee procured the resignations of all the consignees who had the charge to sell them.

The conclusion of the measure was, "that they had closed the important affair by a glorious exertion of virtue and spirit—by which the intended tax has been effectually broken, and the foundations of American liberty (for so they then talked) more deeply laid than ever!"

Finally, in July, 1774, the assembly of Pennsylvania, at Philadelphia, resolved, that in consequence of the long subsisting differences with Great Britain, that it is absolutely necessary to call a congress, which accordingly met at Philadelphia in September following, and held their session in the Carpenters' hall. A congress peculiarly fitted for the juncture. A body of greater men never adorned our annals—of whom Lord Chatham said to Franklin, they were "the most honourable assembly of men ever known!" Their measures, and our subsequent struggles and freedom under their guidance,

* This long row of wooden houses afterwards became famous as a sailor's brothel and riot-house on a large scale. The former frail ware proved an abortive scheme.

"*Deo juvante*," are on the imperishable pages of our history, and in the hearts and remembrance of every instructed American!

A brig called the Grayhound, commanded by Captain Allen, went for Salem New Jersey, with a load of tea, and landed it at Greenwich, the 22d November, 1774, (one year after the Boston destruction,) but young Ebenezer Elmer, (afterwards member of congress,) and others, destroyed it all by fire. Actions were afterwards brought for the recovery of its value, and failed. The whigs had half a dozen of the most eminent lawyers to favour their escape. Some were from Philadelphia.

THE GOVERNORS OF COLONIAL DAYS.

The Modern Universal History, in speaking of our colonies in the times of 1731, says, "A government in any of our colonies was scarcely looked upon in any other light than that of an hospital, where the favourites of the ministry might be till they recovered their broken fortunes; and oftentimes they served as asylums from their creditors."

Secretary Peters, in 1756, says "the governors used to get £10,000 currency a year, and the perquisites, usually, £10,000."

The following present such notices of our governors as I have occasionally met, to wit:

In 1707, I saw some reference to facts which went to show that Governor Evans, who was accused of some levities, was then reproached by his enemies with lewdness with young Susan H——. It might have been mere scandal. The Indians at Conestogoe complained of him, when there, as misbehaving himself to their women. He afterwards married John Moore's beautiful and estimable daughter, with whom he lived awhile at housekeeping at the Fairman house at the Treaty-tree. He was but twenty-one years of age, when first appointed governor. He moved back to England, where he lived a long life.

Colonel Gookin, the governor, disappointed Penn and his friends in consequence of his conduct during a considerable part of his administration. He was much under the influence of his brother-in-law, Birmingham. At one time, says the council, he removed all the justices of New Castle county for doing their duty in an action against said Birmingham—thus leaving the county without a single magistrate for six weeks! At another time, when the judges of the supreme court at New Castle would not admit a certain commission of his to be published in court, he sent for one of the judges and kicked him. In truth, his best apology seems to have been that he was certainly partially deranged. In fact, he afterwards (in 1717) made his apology to the council for several of his acts, saying his physician knew that he had a weakness in his head; wherefore J. Logan remarked to Hannah Penn, "Be pleased then to consider how fit he was for the commission he so long wore!"

1734—Nov.—The mayor exhibited an account, amounting to £9 18*s*. 6*d*., he had paid to John Newbury, for the entertainment of Colonel Montgomery, late governor of New York—ordered paid.

1736—On the death of Governor Gordon, James Logan became president of the council and ex-officio governor for the province until the arrival of Governor Thomas, in 1738. Do any know where Governor Gordon was interred?

When Sir William Keith, in 1738, published his history of the colony of Virginia, and proposed to continue the other colonies, he probably so purposed to live as an author; but as he proceeded no further, and died at London, in 1749, in poor circumstances, it is inferred he did not write our history from want of encouragement.

It may be very little known, that he, who moved with so much excitement and cabal as our governor to the year 1726, should at last fall into such neglect as to leave his widow among us unnoticed and almost forgotten! She lived and died in a small wooden house in Third street, between High street and Mulberry street—there, much pinched for subsistence, she eked out her existence with an old female; and declining all intercourse with society, or with her neighbours. The house itself was burnt in 1786.

Sir William's chief error of administration is said to have been that he early took his measures to favour the elder branch of the Penn family, (already sufficiently provided for in the Irish estate,) to the prejudice of the younger branch, who rapidly acquired riches and influence to remove and to injure him.

1746—Governor Thomas orders a day of public thanksgiving, because of the news of the pretender's defeat at the battle of Culloden. There were great rejoicings in Philadelphia—all refrained from labour and went generally to the churches. The governor himself gave a dinner to two hundred persons.

1752—Governor Hamilton celebrates the king's birth-day by giving a great entertainment at his country-seat at Bush hill, and at each loyal toast it was announced by the Association battery at Wiccacoa! In the evening there was a grand ball, surpassing all former ones in brilliancy, at the State-house, and his honour gave a supper there in the long gallery.

In 1754, Governor R. H. Morris celebrates the king's birth-day, by giving an entertainment at noon at his house in the city, and in the evening there was a great ball at the State-house, where one hundred ladies were present, and a much greater number of gentlemen. An elegant supper was given there in the long gallery.

In 1755, Governor R. H. Morris falls into perpetual strife with the assembly. Their correspondence is singular. They say "his offer was a mere idle illusion, intended first to impose on the assembly and then on the people, also to figure at home in the eyes of the ministry; and the governor is offended that we have not kept his secret." The retort reads thus: "Your very tedious message is of such an inflammatory nature, that did not the duties of my station, and justice to the people, require me to take some notice, I should deem it beneath my notice as a gentleman." Their high altercations were chiefly about the means for raising a defence against the Indians. The frontier inhabitants, thinking these controversies might impede their supplies, came to Philadelphia and surrounded the assembly room, requiring immediate support. This was all in the time of Braddock's defeat. It seems, on the whole, that the legislature acted with the sense of the people, for the members were re-elected, and Governor Morris was soon superseded by Governor Denny.

In 1756, Governor William Denny arrives, being escorted from Trenton, and when near the city, by Colonel *Benjamin Franklin's* and Colonel Jacob Duché's regiments. The mayor and corporation give him a dinner at the lodge room, in Lodge alley—cost £100 13*s.* 6*d.*; and the assembly gave him their dinner also at the State-house, at which were present the civil and military officers and clergy of the city. He took up his residence at the house called the Governor's house, in south Second street, below the present Custom-house. All this looked well, and as if something cordial might have ensued; but ere Governor Denny had fulfilled his year, he thus addresses his entertainers, saying "Though moderation is most agreeable to me, there might have been a governor who would have told you the whole tenor of your message was indecent, frivolous and evasive." The assemblies always offended by endeavoring to spare the purses of the people, and the governors always get provoked because they cannot lavish supplies to the king's service.

Governor Denny's message of September, 1757, contains these rude remarks—"If detraction and personal abuse of your governor, &c.—but I have been so accustomed to this kind of treatment, &c. I have the less reason to regret such usage, since it is obvious, from your conduct to those before me, you are not so much displeased with the person governing, as impatient of being governed at all!" The ground of offence arose from his continually asking supplies! supplies! It is really offensive to see what levies are perpetually put upon the province to help them out of squabbles generated by the courts in Europe, &c.—£50,000 for this, and £60,000 for that, and £100,000 for another. Supplies follow in such rapid succession as to have made the people feel the burthens very sensibly, and if there had not been very considerable of loyalty, it would not have been borne. In all these difficulties "Isaac Norris, speaker," gives his name to bear all the brunt of the conflict!

1759—Nov.—Governor James Hamilton arrives from abroad, and supersedes Governor Denny. He had been before governor, and was a native of Pennsylvania, and resident of Bush hill. Every body is pleased with his appointment. A dinner is given to him at the lodge. Denny's, which had lasted but three years, had had no effect but to vex the people.

In 1763, John and Richard Penn having arrived, the former, as governor, in the succeeding year gets into squabbles as usual with the assembly. The assembly among other things resolve, "That as all hope of any degree of happiness under the proprietary government is now at an end, this house will adjourn to consult their constituents, whether or not to petition his majesty to buy out the Penns' right, and take them under his immediate government!" They soon, however, got better reconciled, and Penn made a very good governor. It may be seen from a letter of Thomas Penn, of 1767, that he calls this scheme for forcing him to sell out, a measure of B. Franklin's, to which he shall not accede.

In 1768, Colonel Morris, from New York, and his lady, the Duchess of Gordon, [a very homely woman,] made a visit to Philadelphia, with several military gentlemen, and among them General Gage; they leave Philadelphia after a few days. Colonel Morris was governor of New York, and was very popular there—he soon after died, and was buried there.

In 1771, John Penn, the governor, returns to England this year, because of the death of his father, Richard. James Hamilton, as president of council, takes his place until he is succeeded by Richard Penn, who arrives in the same year. The administration of John Penn, while he stayed for eight years, was on the whole very acceptable.

In 1772, Richard Penn, the newly arrived governor, married Miss Polly Masters, of Philadelphia, and in 1773, he goes back to England, to give place to his brother, John Penn, who, after visiting England for the purpose of settling the concerns of his father, lately deceased, came again to Philadelphia in the year 1773, and again assumes the government of the province.

The aged Robert Venables, who died in 1834, aged ninety-eight years, speaking of the residences of sundry governors, told me, the first he knew was Governor Thomas, who lived where is now the Arcade, &c. Governor James Hamilton dwelt, when *first* governor, at the Slate-house on Second street; when second time governor, (after Denny,) he lived at "the Governor's house," in Second street, where is since Waln's row, below the Custom-house. There dwelt Governor Hunter Morris, and Governor Denny. Governor John Penn, he said, lived and *died* at "Stamper's row" in Pine street, between Second and Third streets. His funeral there was very great, "making quite a crowd." Said when he landed, at three o'clock on Sunday, at Chestnut street wharf, there was a great earthquake. He (Robert) was a lad at Christ church. It made much fright *there*, and he was afraid to run down the stairs from the gallery, "*they shook so!*"

The following is a List of Governors as they served in succession from the origin of the province, to wit:

1682. Oct. William Penn, proprietor, acted as governor till
1684. Aug. Thomas Lloyd, Esq., president of council till
1688. Dec. Capt. John Blackwell, deputy governor till
1690. Feb. President and council.
1693. April 26th. Benjamin Fletcher, governor.
—— June 3d. William Markham, Esq., deputy governor.
1699. Dec. 3d. William Penn acted again as governor.
1701. Nov. 1st. Andrew Hamilton, Esq., deputy governor—[a Scotsman.]
1703. Feb. President of council, Edward Shippen, till
1704. Feb. John Evans, deputy governor till
1709. Feb. Charles Gookin, deputy governor till
1717. March. Sir William Keith, Bart., deputy governor till
1726. June. Patrick Gordon, deputy governor till
1736. June. James Logan, president of council till
1738. June. George Thomas, deputy governor till
1747. June. Anthony Palmer, president of council till
1748. June. James Hamilton, deputy governor till June—[an American.]
1754. Oct. Robert Hunter Morris, deputy governor till
1756. Aug. 19th. William Denny, deputy governor till
1759. Nov. 17th. James Hamilton, till
1763. Oct. 31st. John Penn, son of Richard, till
1771. May 6th. James Hamilton, president of council till
1771. Oct. 16th. Richard Penn succeeded.
1773. Aug. John Penn—a second time governor till
1776. Sept.
1777. March. Thomas Wharton, jr., Esq., President of the Supreme Executive Council.

1778. Oct. Joseph Reed,	do.	do.
1781. Nov. William Moore,	do.	do.
1782. Nov. John Dickinson,	do.	do.
1785. Oct. Benjamin Franklin,	do.	do.
1786. Oct. Thomas Mifflin,	do.	do.

Then succeeded the New State Constitution, and the first Governor—say

1790 Oct.—was Thomas Mifflin, who served three terms of three years each, to October, 1799; after which Thomas M'Kean was governor for three successive terms of three years each.

For the sake of reference, I here add a List of Dutch and Swedish Governors, in Delaware, viz.: begun

1623. Cornelius Jacob May, }
1624. William Useling, } Dutch.
1630. Peterson de Vries, }
1631. John Printz.—Swedish.
1638. Peter Minuets, } Dutch.
1640. William Keift, }
1643 to 1653. John Printz, }
1653–4. Papegoia. } Swedish.
1654. Rintzink, }
1657. Alricks.—Dutch.
1658. John Paul Jaquet.
1659. Beekman.—Dutch.
1664. Robert Carr.—English.
1673. Anthony Colve.—Ditto.
1674. Sir Edmund Andros.—English—also governor of N. York.

OCCURRENCES OF THE WAR OF INDEPENDENCE.

"The deeds of our fathers in times that are gone;
Their virtues, their prowess, the fields they have won,
Their struggles for freedom, the toils they endured,
The rights and the blessings for us they procured."

With a view to preserve some of our local facts connected with the war of Independence, expressed in a manner more moving and stirring to our feelings than those general terms, by which our historians have generalized their facts, I had aimed to collect and preserve such *individual* and *special* incidents, as would bring back the former scenes and doings of our forefathers to our contemplation. With this purpose, I had gathered from several eye witnesses, in graphic delineations, the things they saw and did, and especially of those occurrences which transpired while Philadelphia was held under the government and conquest of General Howe and his army. I had gathered from *the reminiscences* of the aged, and the *diaries* of others of that day, several curious and unpublished facts; such as would surprise, stir, and interest the present generation.* But after

* Some of the facts were from the recollections of the late Colonel A. M'Lane, so enterprising in our "border war," along our lines,—and some from the diary of a young lady in the midst of the martial doings, &c.—all spirited and warm from the heart, with the glow of a "good whig;" some also from the diary of a widow Friend, foreboding and sad with tory sympathies and fears.

all my preparations on this matter, fully equal to fifty pages, I have found myself obliged to lay a part of it aside from the present publication. Such parts of those facts, as had been communicated to me, may be consulted on page 393 to 430, in my MS. Annals in the Historical Society of Pennsylvania.

A superficial thinker may, possibly, deem it unimportant to attempt thus to preserve some of the facts transpiring in Philadelphia, concerning the war of Independence; and especially that portion of them relative to the *entry and possession* of the city by the *British army.* Some may think the incidents so like to those of other captured cities, as to be unworthy of any special observation. But to minds of more reflection, many sufficient reasons will appear for preserving the memorial for posterity; especially in a book which is to treat of all the past events of *the city.* There are specialties of interest to be told, which no other work has or will embrace. The interest of them we conceive to be enhanced, by the hopes we all entertain, that Philadelphia will *never* again be invaded or possessed by any conquering foe. Remote as seems the extremity *from us*, the desire is more increased to conceive what were the feelings which agitated the bosoms of our kindred *in that day.* Facts, hereinafter detailed, may serve to gratify such inquirers. The general army reports, which we may have heretofore read on these subjects, have been too generalized to awaken our sympathies or feelings; but in the present exhibition, the mind will find itself brought down to *single* and *individual* contemplation, in a manner which cannot but extort its sympathetic emotions and regard. It is a duty which we owe our fathers for their rich bequests to us, that we should thus strive to appreciate their generous services, by entering into the just sense of their peril and sufferings.

I call it their generous *devotion for us*, because I think it probable that the leaders of the revolution had long cherished the idea of devoting their lives and fortunes to the *eventual independence of their sons.* The time which has elapsed, since the passions and excitements of the day drove every mind to extremities, may now be favourable to calm and dispassionate inquiry—to such as enables the honest historian to record the truth without partiality—"nothing to extenuate, nor aught set down in malice." It is not my proper business to pursue this inquiry, but traces enough may be found to invite and encourage the investigation of professed historians. It may sometimes be discovered in the answers to, and conflicts with our governors, long before the war of the revolution. It was, indeed, our policy and interest to disclaim it, and even to conceal it; and, therefore, we may not have much to expose thereon *on our records.* But in England, at the time, I suspect, governors' and agents' reports, if we knew them, would show that *they* much apprehended such a spirit and purpose in us. Several facts to that effect may be seen in the sayings and doings concerning the *Stamp Act proceedings*, as given in this book. The American Whig, begun at

New York, in March, 1768, has an article in its fifth number, imputed to William Livingston, Esq., afterwards governor of New Jersey, which shows such sentiments; it says: "The day dawns, in which the foundation of this mighty empire is to be laid by the establishment of *a regular American constitution—before seven years* roll over our heads, the first stone must be laid. As we conduct now, so will it fare with us and our children hereafter." In May, 1755, Governor Morris, of Pennsylvania, in one of his angry messages to the assembly, says, "They trifle with the king's commands and interests—thus to aggrandize themselves, and to promote their scheme of future *independency.*"

I have seen a letter from Doctor Franklin, then in London, to the venerable Charles Thomson, dated 11th July, 1765, wherein, speaking of the *Stamp Act*, he says, "None could be more concerned to oppose it than myself; but the tide was too strong. The nation was *provoked* by American *claims of independence;* and *all parties* (and we had numerous *friends* too) joined in resolving by *this act*, to settle the point," &c. And when, on the 27th September, 1766, he writes to the same, concerning the repeal, he says, "He must leave to a personal interview the causes of repeal; observing, however, that our release was chiefly imputable "to what the profane call luck, and the pious call Providence." I have, indeed, *my* conjecture, that it was the sense of these facts, among other things which I have elsewhere ascribed, that induced Charles Thomson to destroy his History of the Revolution, to the performance of which I know he was stimulated by the Hon. John Jay, "as the most competent man in the world for its proper execution."—[See his letter from Passy, of 19th July, 1783.] A paper of Charles Thomson's, which I have preserved in my collection, [see MS., book second, in Historical Society, p. 312,] shows that the proceedings of the congress of 1774, and subsequent—but *preceding* the war—purposely avoided the word *province*, and assumed the word *government*, &c. I have seen too, among the MSS. of Charles Thomson, the measures, told by me in another place, by which he and three others, of Philadelphia, overruled the people into their measures of resistance, in 1775.

Probably we felt our *maturity;* and the law of our nature prompts us, when so grown up, to cast off our leading strings, and to become parents and heads of families ourselves. It is, as Buonaparte, in his characteristic way, said to Col. Wilkes, of us: "The youth must become a man—the time must arrive when the child must cease to sleep with its mother!" I take no party side in this subject; but I have given the clue to a closer inquiry, and so I leave it.

It might, however, afford interest to some, to see at what an early time the spirit of independence in our countrymen was supposed to be operating. Although we had sufficient love and loyalty to the king and parent country, it was natural enough that we should love our own soil, and its apparent interests, still better. Some scarce works of the olden time, present some views on these topics, that may be quite new to many readers, to wit:

Evelyn, in his Memoirs, has declared the fact, that the crown, in his day, was quite jealous of its *American* possessions, as leaning too much to *independence*, even before the settlement of Pennsylvania. To this cause he imputes the establishment of those well-known state inquisitors, called the *lords of trade*, that they might take an oversight of their conduct, *in a concealed manner*, and so stand ready to report the same to the monarch—and withal be able to check in time the aspirings to independent power. *The board of trade*, says he, had their first meeting on *the 26th of May*, 1671, and were "to *advise and counsel* his majesty for the well governing of his plantations," &c. "Their first letters to the governors required them to render us an account of their present state and government; but what *we most* insisted on, (for *he* was one of the board, and is, of course, first rate authority in this case,) was to know the condition of *New England*, which appeared *to be very independent* as to their regard to Old England, or his majesty. *Rich and strong* as they now were, there were *great debates* in what style *to write to them*, and there *were fears* of their *breaking from all dependence on this nation.* His majesty, therefore, commended *this affair more expressly.* Some of our counsel were for sending them a *menacing letter*, which those who better understood the *peevish* and *touchy humour* of that colony, were *utterly against.* We therefore thought fit, *in the first place*, to acquaint ourselves as well as we could of the state of that place, by some [of the crown officers, probably,] that were newly come from thence." The same work contains other similar remarks bearing on this subject.

P. Heylin's Cosmography, London edition, 1703, contains this remark: "This plantation (New England) has ever pretended *to be more free* than any of the rest of our western plantations, and *will not be governed* by acts of parliament as the rest are, *but have set up a mint of their own*, (a two shilling piece of this coinage is now in my possession,) and trade whither they please in their own ships; and although they reverence [fear] the crown of England, and so trade not with its enemies, yet they, in the two last reigns, did *scarce acknowledge themselves subjects* till the charter was *taken* away, and a governor sent to them, on whom they wreaked their vengeance at the revolution." [This means Sir Edmund Andros, I presume.] "This, though *true of the whole*, is mostly applicable to *New Boston*, which about twenty years ago had fifty sail of stout merchant ships, and *now* (in 1692) are much more in number." "Till the reign of King James II., *they would never submit* to any governor sent from England, but live like *any free state.* But a quo warranto being sent against them in 1683, by his late majesty, they submitted to Henry Canfield, Esq., and in 1686, accepted Sir Edward Andrews [Andros] as governor." In another place, he sums us up as a people "who longed for *innovations* in *church* and *state*," and New England itself, like old Rome in the eyes of Livy: "ad quæ turba omnis ex finitimis gentibus novarum rerum cupidæ confluxit!"

Joseph Bennet, Esq., in his MS. History of New England, in possession of I. P. Norris, Esq., written about the year 1740, makes these remarks, to wit: "I remember it was talked some years ago, that the people of New England were grown so rich and powerful, that there was *danger* of *their revolting* from the crown and *setting up for themselves.*" In another place he says, "The people here affect to talk *very big sometimes*, when they think themselves *out of danger*." "It has been conjectured *by some*, that the dissenters in England had their friends in New England, with whom they hoped, in case of failing to subvert the ecclesiastical and civil government at home, they might have fulfilled their darling *schemes* of *independency* in the church, and democracy in the *state*, and *become here the founders* of some new religion as well of *a new republic*." This notion he however admits is "strongly repelled by others as malicious."

The Swedish traveller, Professor Kalm, has set down his impressions on the case, as received when at New York, 1748.—See his vol. i. p. 265. There he says: "I have been told *by Englishmen*, either born here or in Europe, that the *English colonies here*, in the space of thirty or fifty years, [the time which actually *occurred!*] would *be able* to form *a state by themselves*, entirely *independent of Old England*. But as the country which lies along the sea is unguarded, and on the land side is harassed by the French, *these are sufficient* to prevent *the breach* from the mother country. The English have, therefore, sufficient reason to consider the French in North America as the best means of keeping the colonies *in their due submission*." In another place he says: "There *is reason to believe* that the king never was in earnest to expel the French, because they being much fewer in numbers, might have been with little difficulty. The *restrictions* of the crown in its trade, &c., *was on purpose* to restrain their growth. These things [the sense of them] occasioned the colonies to grow *less tender* for their mother country; and this *coolness* is *increased* by Germans, Dutch and French, &c., settled among them."

With a design to elicit from some of our aged citizens, their recollections of incidents occurring while the British held possession of Philadelphia, from November, 1777, to May, 1778, I drew up a paper of interrogatories, not needful to be repeated here, which inquiries will account for some of the following communications taking the form of *answers*, to wit:

The Entry of the Army—as told by Captain J. C.

The grenadiers, with Lord Cornwallis at their head, led the van when they entered the city; their tranquil look and dignified appearance have left an impression on my mind, that the British grenadiers were inimitable. As I am relating the feelings and observations of a boy then only ten years old, I shall mention many things, perhaps, not worth relating; for instance, I went up to the front rank of the grenadiers when they had entered Second street, when several of them addressed me thus,—"How do you do, young one—how are you, my boy"—in a brotherly tone, that seems still to vibrate on my ear; then reached out their hands, and severally caught mine, and shook it, not with an exulting shake of conquerors, as I thought, but with a sympathizing one for the vanquished. The Hessians composed a part of the van-guard, and followed in the rear of the grenadiers—their looks to me were terrific—their brass caps—their mustaches—their countenances, by nature morose, and their music, that sounded better English than they themselves could speak—plunder—plunder—plunder—gave a desponding, heart-breaking effect, as I thought, to all; to me it was dreadful beyond expression.

Recollections of the Entry of the Army—by a Lady.

In answer to my esteemed friend Watson's queries, respecting what I can remember of the state of things, facts, and the expression of public opinion, during the memorable years of 1777 and '78, when the hostile army of Great Britain occupied Philadelphia, I will give my recollections as briefly and as simply as I can.

I can well remember the previous gloom spread over the minds of the inhabitants, from the time it was thought the enemy would advance through the Jerseys; the very darkest hour of the revolution appearing to me to be that preceding the capture of the Hessians at Trenton. The tories who favoured the government at home, (as England was then called,) became elated, and the whigs depressed. This may account for a good deal of severity that was used before the constituted authorities of that time left the city, in visiting the inhabitants, and inspecting what stores of provisions they had, taking in some instances what they deemed superfluous, especially blankets, of which our army were in great need. After the public authorities had left the city, it was a very gloomy time indeed. We knew the enemy had landed at the head of Elk, but of their procedure and movements we had but vague information; for none were left in the city in public employ, to whom expresses would be addressed. The day of the battle of Brandywine was one of deep anxiety. We heard the firing, and knew of an engagement between the armies, without expecting immediate information of the result, when towards night a horseman rode at full speed down Chestnut street, and turned round Fourth to the Indian Queen public house; many ran to hear what he had to tell, and, as I remember, his account was pretty near the truth. He told of La Fayette being wounded.

We had for a neighbour, and an intimate acquaintance, a very amiable English gentleman, (H. Gurney,) who had been in the British army, and had left the service upon marrying a rich and excellent lady of Philadelphia, some years before. He was a person so much liked and esteemed by the public, that he remained unmolested at a time when the committee of public safety sent many excellent citizens into banishment without a hearing, upon the most vague and unfounded suspicion; but contented themselves with only taking his word of honour, that he would do nothing inimical to the country, nor furnish the enemy with any information. He endeavoured to give my mother confidence that the inhabitants would not be ill-treated. He advised that we should be all well dressed, and that we should keep our houses closed. The army marched in, and took possession of the town in the morning. We were up-stairs, and saw them pass to the State-house; they looked well, clean, and well clad, and the contrast between them and our own poor barefooted and ragged troops was very great, and caused a feeling of despair—it was a solemn and impressive day—but I saw no exultation in the enemy, nor indeed in those who were reckoned favourable to their success. Early in the afternoon, Lord Cornwallis' suite arrived, and took possession of my mother's house. But my mother was appalled by the numerous train which took possession of her dwelling, and shrank from having such inmates; for a guard was mounted at the door, and the yard filled with soldiers and baggage of every description; and I well remember what we thought of the haughty looks of Lord Rawdon* and the other aid-de-camp, as they traversed the apartments. My mother desired to speak with Lord Cornwallis, and he attended her in the front parlour. She told him of her situation, and how impossible it would be for her to stay in her own house with such a numerous train as composed his lordship's establishment. He behaved with great politeness to her, said he should be sorry to give trouble, and would have other quarters looked out for him—they withdrew that very afternoon, and he was accommodated at Peter Reeve's,† in Second, near to Spruce street, and we felt very glad at the exemption—but it did not last long—for directly the quarter-masters were employed in billeting the troops, and we had to find room for two officers of artillery, and afterwards, in addition, for two gentlemen, secretaries of Lord Howe.

The officers, very generally, I believe, behaved with politeness to the inhabitants, and many of them, upon going away, expressed their satisfaction that no injury to the city was contemplated by their commander. They said, that living among the inhabitants, and speaking the same language, made them uneasy at the thought of acting as enemies.

At first, provisions were scarce and dear, and we had to live with

---

* Since the Marquis of Hastings, and who died at Malta, in 1826.

† Now David Lewis' house, 142 south Second street.

much less abundance than we had been accustomed to. Hard money was, indeed, as difficult to come at, as if it had never been taken from the mines, except with those who had things to sell for the use of the army. They had given certificates to the farmers as they came up through Chester county, of the amount of stores they had taken, and upon these being presented for payment at head-quarters, they were duly honoured. My mother received a seasonable supply in this way, from persons who were in her debt, and had been paid for what the army had taken.

Every thing considered, the citizens fared better than could have been expected, and though it was extremely disagreeable in many places, on account of the dirt, yet the city was healthy. The enemy appeared to have a great deal of shipping in the Delaware; I counted sixty vessels, that looked of large size, moored so close to each other, that it seemed as if you could not pass a hand between them, near to where the navy yard now is—and all the wharves and places seemed crowded. There was scarce any thing to sell in the shops when they came into the town, and the paper money had depreciated to nothing. I remember two pieces of silk that I saw on sale a little before their arrival, at 100 dollars per yard. Tea was fifty and sixty dollars per pound.

The day of the battle of Germantown we heard the firing all day, but knew not the result. Towards evening they brought in the wounded. The prisoners were carried to the State-house lobbies, and the street was presently filled with women taking lint and bandages, and every refreshment which they thought their suffering countrymen might want.

General Howe, during the time he stayed in Philadelphia, seized and kept for his own use Mary Pemberton's coach and horses, in which he used to ride about the town. The old officers appeared to be uneasy at his conduct, and some of them freely expressed their opinions; they said, that before his promotion to the chief command, he sought for the counsels and company of officers of experience and merit—but now, his companions were usually a set of boys—the most dissipated fellows in the army.

Lord Howe was much more sedate and dignified than his brother, really dignified, for he did not seem to affect any pomp or parade.

They were exceedingly chagrined and surprised at the capture of Burgoyne, and at first would not suffer it to be mentioned. We had received undoubted intelligence of the fact, in a letter from Charles Thomson, and upon communicating this circumstance to Henry Gurney, his interrogatories forced an acknowledgement from some of the superior officers, that it was, as he said, "alas! too true!"

One of my acquaintance, indeed an intimate one, performed the part of a "nymph of the blended rose," in the splendid festival of the Meschianza, but I saw no part of the show, not even the decorated hall where the knights and ladies supped, amidst the "grand

Salema" of their turbaned attendants; nor even the ridotto part, which was gazed at from the wharves and warehouses by all the uninvited population of the town.

The streets seemed always well-filled with both officers and soldiers, and I believe they frequently attended different places of worship, but Friends' meetings were not much to their tastes. They had their own chaplains to the different regiments, which appeared to us a mere mockery of religion. Parson Badger was chaplain to the artillery, and he was billeted at John Field's, who, with his wife, were very plain Friends, in our neighbourhood. The house was very small, and he had the front room up-stairs, and as he was a jolly, good-tempered person, he was much liked by the young fellows who used to call to see him after parades.

Even whig ladies went to the Meschianza and to balls, but I knew of very few instances of attachments formed—nor, with the exception of one instance, of any want of propriety in behaviour.

When they left the city, the officers came to take leave of their acquaintance, and express their good wishes. It seemed to us, that a considerable change had taken place in their prospects of success, between the time of their entry and departure. They often spoke freely in conversation on these subjects.

"The Honourable Cosmo Gordon" stayed all night at his quarters, and lay in bed so long the next morning, that the family thought it but kind to waken him, and tell him "his friends, the rebels," were in town. It was with great difficulty he procured a boat to put him over the Delaware. Perhaps he and his man were the last that embarked. Many soldiers hid themselves in cellars and other places, and stayed behind—(I have heard.) In two hours after we saw the last of them, our own dragoons gallopped down the street.

When our own troops took possession of the city, General Arnold, then flushed with the recent capture of Burgoyne, was appointed to the command of it, and his quarters, (as if we had been conquered from an enemy) appointed at Henry Gurney's! They were appalled at the circumstance, but thought it prudent to make no resistance, when, to their agreeable surprise, his politeness, and that of his aids, Major Franks and Captain Clarkson, made the imposition set light, and in a few days he removed to Mrs. Master's house in Market street, that had been occupied as head-quarters by General Howe, where he entered upon a style of living but ill according with republican simplicity, giving sumptuous entertainments, that involved him in expenses and debt, and most probably laid the foundation, in his necessities and poverty, of his future deception and treason to his country. He married our Philadelphia Miss Shippen.

Further Facts—by J. P. N., Esq.

I recollect seeing the division march down Second street, when Lord Cornwallis took possession of the city—the troops were gay and well clad. A number of our citizens appeared sad and serious. When I saw them, there was no huzzaing. The artillery were quartered in Chestnut, between Third and Sixth streets—the State-house yard was made use of as a Park—the 42d Highlanders occupied Chestnut below Third street—the 15th regiment were in quarters in Market street, in and about Fifth street.

When the enemy were bombarding Fort Mifflin, we could see the path of the bomb from the top of my old house. The blowing up of the Augusta was attended with a shock similar to that of an earthquake. I immediately started for Schuylkill point, where the British had a battery, and saw some firing. The officers appeared much chagrined at the events of the day. On our way down, we met several wagons with wounded soldiers—many of them in great pain—their moans and cries were very distressing. These men had been wounded before Red Bank fort.

I was present when some of the troops were going off for Germantown, the morning of the battle—they were in high spirits, and moved in a trot.

Houses entirely occupied by the soldiery were a good deal injured—their conduct, however, was quite as good as could be expected. The officers of middle age were in general polite—the younger ones were more dashing. Some of them had women with them. I recollect Colonel Birch of the horse, and Major Williams of the artillery had. They occupied houses to themselves, and were not quartered on families. All the regiments paraded morning and evening.

After the battle of Germantown, the officers who were made prisoners in that action were confined some days in the long room up-stairs in the State-house, afterwards Peale's Museum.

During the winter, prisoners and deserters were frequently brought in, and carried first to head-quarters. They were easily distinguished, as the latter always had their arms, and which they were allowed to dispose of; they were almost naked, and generally without shoes—an old dirty blanket around them, attached by a leather belt around the waist.

Deserters from head-quarters were led off to the superintendent, (Galloway,) and officers of the new corps were generally on the look out to get them to enlist.

The citizens of Philadelphia were once gratified with the full display of General Washington's whole army. It was done on the occasion of raising the spirits of the whigs, and of proportionably dispiriting the measures of the tories. As it was intended for effect, it was, of course, in its best array for our poor means, and had indeed the effect to convince the tories it was far more formidable than they expected! This martial entry passed down the long line of Front street. There, thousands of our citizens beheld numerous poor fellows, never to be seen more among the sons of men! They were on their march to meet the enemy, landed at the head of Elk

They encountered at Brandywine and at Germantown, and besides losing many lives, retained little of all those implements and equipages, which constituted their street-display in our city.

Among the things connected with the British, while they occupied Philadelphia, may be set down the following incidents:

Town's Evening Post, of 1777, says, "The British entered Philadelphia under the Earl Cornwallis—marched down Second street, and encamped to the southward of the town." The same paper says, "The fine appearance and strict discipline of the soldiers, and politeness of the officers, soon dispelled the fears of the inhabitants—kindled joy in the countenance of the well-affected." The same paper derides the attempt of the Delaware frigate and the row-galleys to annoy the city—calls it also cruel!—She got aground, and had to strike. They also deride the slight defence to resist them at Swedes' ford, where they had cast up redoubts, and allege that the affair of Germantown was ill-managed. The paper gives the copies of two letters found on board the Delaware, purporting to be written by Capt. Alexander, her commander, full *of bad spelling!* A quiz or insult?

The following advertisement, at Philadelphia, may serve to show the state of impudent profligacy of some of the British officials in our country, to wit: "Wanted to hire with two single gentlemen, *a young woman*, to act in the capacity of housekeeper, and who can occasionally put her hand *to any thing. Extravagant wages* will be given, and *no character* required. Any young woman who chooses to offer, may be further informed at the bar of the City tavern."

The Evening Post of June, '78, says, "The British army went off on Thursday morning—having before transported their stores and most of their artillery into New Jersey, where they had thrown up some works, and had some of their regiments encamped." They crossed at Gloucester point, as being so narrow. On Friday, the 19th June, General Arnold took possession of Philadelphia. It must have been foreseen by congress, because it passed a resolve on the 4th June, concerning the city in case of such an event. Yet the mass of the citizens had no such foresight.

While the British were in Philadelphia, the town boys, and boys with the British army, as drummers, &c., with a few tory boys, used to have regular battles. The town boys had their head-quarters and fortifications at the brewhouse of Morris, near the Drawbridge—a drum boy at last got killed, and a stop was put by authority.

General Knyphausen, exalted as he was in rank, used to spread his butter on his bread with his thumb! What a fancy! This was told by one of the family where he quartered. In his deportment he was gentle, and esteemed.

I add also the localities occupied by the army and officers as something unknown to the present generation, to wit:

General Howe lived in the house in High street, near Sixth street, where was afterwards the residence of President Washington. His brother, Lord Howe, resided in Chestnut street, in the house now the Farmers and Mechanics' Bank. General Knyphausen lived in the house now General Cadwallader's, in south Second street, opposite to Little Dock street. Lord Cornwallis dwelt in the house since of David Lewis, in Second above Spruce street. Colonel Abercrombie—afterwards the General, who was killed in Egypt—dwelt in the house of Whitehead, in Vine street, second door west of Cable lane. Major Andre dwelt in Dr. Franklin's mansion in a court back from High street.

Several of the British troops used to exercise in the large vacant lot appurtenant to Bingham's mansion.

The British who were wounded at the battle of Brandywine were put in Cuthbert and Hood's stores and houses in Penn street. The Americans were put into the lobbies of the State-house. The British wounded at Germantown were put into the Scotch Presbyterian church in Spruce street.

While the British remained, they held frequent plays at the old theatre, the performances by their officers. The scenes were painted by Major Andre and Captain Delancy; they had also stated balls.

They had under their control two tory presses—one the "True Royal Gazette," by James Humphreys, and the other the "Royal Pennsylvania Gazette," by James Robertson.

Sir William Howe was a fine figure, full six feet high, and well proportioned—in appearance not unlike his antagonist, General Washington. His manners were graceful and dignified, and he was much beloved by his officers, for his generosity and affability.

Sir Henry Clinton, his successor in command, was in a good degree a different man—he was short and fat, with a full face and prominent nose, in his intercourse was reserved, and not so popular as Howe.

Lord Cornwallis was short and thick-set, his hair somewhat gray, his face well formed and agreeable, his manners remarkably easy and affable—much beloved by his men.

General Knyphausen was much of the German in his appearacce, always very polite in bowing to respectable citizens in the streets, not tall, but slender and straight. His features sharp and martial, very honourable in his dealings.

Colonel Tarleton was rather below the middle size, stout, strong, heavily made, large muscular legs, and an uncommonly active person; his complexion dark, and his eye small, black and piercing.

Among their greatest feats while at Philadelphia, was that of the celebrated "Meschianza," so called. The description of which more at length is given in my MS. Annals in the Philadelphia Library, pages 300 to 305, from which I extract the present short notice, to wit:

The Meschianza at Philadelphia.

This is the appellation of the most splendid pageant ever exhibited in our country, if we except the great "Federal Procession" of all trades and professions, through the streets of Philadelphia in 1788. The Meschianza was chiefly a tilt and tournament with other entertainments, as the term implies, and was given on Monday the 18th of May, 1778, at Wharton's country-seat in Southwark, by the officers of General Sir William Howe's army, to that officer, on his quitting the command to return to England. A considerable number of our city *belles* were present; which gave considerable offence afterwards to the whigs; and did not fail to mark the fair as the "tory ladies." The ill-nature and the reproach have long since been forgotten.

The company began to assemble at three to four o'clock, at Knight's wharf,* at the water edge of Green street in the Northern Liberties, and by half past four o'clock in the afternoon the whole were embarked, in the pleasant month of May, in a "grand regatta" of three divisions. In the front of the whole were three flat boats, with a band of music in each of them, "rowed regular to harmony." As this assemblage of vessels progressed, barges rowed on the flanks, "light skimming, stretch'd their oary wings," to keep off the multitude of boats that crowded from the city as beholders; and the houses, balconies and wharves were filled with spectators all along the river side.

When arrived at the fort below the Swedes' church they formed a line through an avenue of grenadiers, and light-horse in the rear. The company were thus conducted to a square lawn of one hundred and fifty yards on each side, and which was also lined with troops. This area formed the ground for a *tilt or tournament.* On the front seat of each pavilion were placed seven of the principal young ladies of the country, dressed in Turkish habits, and wearing in their turbans the articles which they intended to bestow on their several gallant knights. Soon the trumpets at a distance announced the approach of the seven *white knights*, habited in white and red silk, and mounted on gray chargers, richly caparisoned in similar colours. These were followed by their several esquires on foot; besides these there was a herald in his robe. These all made the circuit of the square, saluting the ladies as they passed,† and then they ranged in line with their ladies; then their herald, Mr. Beaumont, after a flourish of trumpets, proclaimed their challenge, in the name of "*the knights of the blended rose*," declaring that the ladies of their order excel in wit, beauty and accomplishments, those of the

* This wharf at that time was the only wharf above Vine street, which ran out to a good depth of water. The tickets of admission (one of which I have) were elegant and curious. It had a view of the sea, military trophies, the general's crest, *Vive Vale.*

† I have in my MS. Annals an original drawing, by Major Andre, showing the style of this dress.

THE MESCHIANZA AT PHILADELPHIA.—Page 290.

whole world, and they are ready to enter the lists against any knights who will deny the same, according to the laws of ancient chivalry; at the third repetition of the challenge, a sound of trumpets announced the entrance of another herald, with four trumpeters dressed in black and orange. The two heralds held a parley, when the black herald proceeded to proclaim his *defiance* in the name of "*the knights of the burning mountain.*" Then retiring, there soon after entered "*the black knights*," with their esquires, preceded by their herald, on whose tunic was represented a mountain sending forth flames, and the motto, "I burn for ever."

These seven knights, like the former ones, rode round the lists, and made their obeisance to the ladies, and then drew up fronting the white knights, and the chief of these having thrown down his gauntlet, the chief of the black knights directed his esquire to take it up. Then the knights received their lances from their esquires, fixed their shields on their left arms, and making a general salute to each other by a movement of their lances, turned round to take their career, and encountering in full gallop, shivered their spears! In the second and third encounter they discharged their pistols. In the fourth they fought with their swords.

From the garden they ascended a flight of steps, covered with carpets, which led into a spacious hall, the panels of which were painted in imitation of Sienna marble, enclosing festoons of white marble. In this hall and the adjoining apartments, were prepared tea, lemonade, &c., to which the company seated themselves. At this time the knights came in, and on their knee received their favours from their respective ladies. From these apartments they went up to a ball-room, decorated in a light, elegant style of painting, and showing many festoons of flowers. The brilliancy of the whole was heightened by eighty-five mirrors, decked with ribands and flowers, and in the intermediate spaces were thirty-four branches. On the same floor were *four* drawing rooms, with sideboards of refreshments, decorated and lighted in the style of the ball-room. The ball was opened by the knights and their ladies; and the dances continued till ten o'clock, when the windows were thrown open, and a magnicent bouquet of rockets began the fire-works. These were planned by Captain Montresor, the chief engineer, and consisted of twenty different displays in great variety and beauty, and changing General Howe's arch into a variety of shapes and devices. At 12 o'clock, (midnight,) supper was announced, and large folding doors, before concealed, sprung open, and discovered a magnificent saloon of two hundred and ten feet by forty feet, and twenty-two feet in height, with three alcoves on each side, which served for sideboards. The sides were painted with vine leaves and festoon flowers, and fifty-six large pier-glasses, ornamented with green silk artificial flowers and ribands. There were also one hundred branches trimmed,* and

* All the mirrors and lustres, &c., were borrowed from the citizens, and were all sent home with all their ornaments attached to them as a compliment for their use.

eighteen lustres of twenty-four lights hung from the ceiling. There were three hundred wax tapers on the supper tables, four hundred and thirty covers, and twelve hundred dishes. There were twenty-four black slaves in oriental dresses, with silver collars and bracelets.

Towards the close of the banquet, the herald with his trumpeters entered and announced the king and royal family's health, with other toasts. Each toast was followed by a flourish of music. After the supper, the company returned to the ball-room, and continued to dance until four o'clock in the morning.

I omit to describe the two arches, but they were greatly embellished. They had two fronts, in the Tuscan order. The pediment of one was adorned with *naval* trophies, and the other with *military* ones.

Major Andre, who wrote a description of it, (although *his* name is concealed,) calls it "the *most splendid* entertainment ever given by an army to its general." The whole expense was borne by twenty-two field officers. The managers were Sir John Wrotlesby, Colonel O'Hara, Majors Gardiner and Montresor. This splendid pageant blazed out in *one* short night! Next day the enchantment was dissolved; and in exactly one month, all these knights and the whole army chose to make their march from the city of Philadelphia!

When I think of the few survivors of that gay scene who now exist, (of some whose sprightliness and beauty are gone!) I cannot but feel a gloom succeed the recital of the fete. I think, for instance, of one who was then "the queen of the Meschianza," since Mrs. L., now *blind*, and fast waning from the "things that be." To her I am indebted for many facts of illustration. She tells me that the unfortunate Major Andre was the charm of the company. Lieut. Andre, his esquire, was his brother, a youth of about nineteen, possessing the promise of an accomplished gentleman. Major Andre and Captain Oliver Delancey painted, themselves, the chief of the decorations. The Sienna marble, for instance, on the apparent side walls, was on *canvas*, in the style of stage scene painting. Andre also painted the scenes used at the theatre, at which the British officers performed. The proceeds were given to the widows and orphans of their soldiers. The waterfall scene, drawn by him, was still in the building when it lately burnt. She assures me that, of all that was borrowed for the entertainment, *nothing* was injured or lost. They desired to pay double if accidents occurred. The general deportment of the officers was very praiseworthy therein. There were no ladies of British officers, save Miss Auchmuty, the new bride of Captain Montresor. The American young ladies present were not numerous—not exceeding fifty. The others were married ladies. Most of our ladies had gone from the city, and what remained were of course in great demand. The American gentlemen present were *aged* non-combatants. Our young men were whigs generally, and were absent.

No offence was offered to the ladies afterwards, for their acceptance of this instance of an enemy's hospitality. When the Americans returned, they got up a great ball, to be given to the officers of the French army, and the American officers of Washington's command. When the managers came to invite their guests, it was made a question whether the "Meschianza ladies" should be invited. It was found they could not make up their company without them; they were therefore included. When they came, they looked differently habited from those who had gone to the country, "they having assumed the high head-dress, &c." of the British fashion, (vide a specimen, p. 218, of my MS. Annals, in the City Library,) and so the characters, unintentionally, were immediately perceived at a glance through the hall.—[It was in the Masonic hall in Lodge alley.] But *lots* being cast for partners, they were soon fully intermixed, and conversation ensued as if nothing of jealousy had ever existed, and all umbrage was forgotten.

The same lady was also at a splendid supper and dance given by Captain Hammond, on board the Roebuck. The ship was fully illuminated, and one hundred and seventy-two persons sat down to supper.

Miss J. C—g, who was also a knight's lady, has kindly given me her original invitation from Sir Henry Calder, (an officer of high rank,) and also an original drawing by Major Andre, (see p. 242 of my MS. Annals in the City Library,) of the dress for that fete. He sketched it to give the ladies an idea of the garb they should assume. In reality it was this:—for the Blended Rose a white silk, called a *Polonaise*, forming a flowing robe, and open in front on the waist—the pink sash six inches wide, and filled with spangles—the shoes and stockings also spangled—the head-dress *more towering* than the drawing, and filled with a profusion of pearls and jewels. The veil was spangled and edged with silver lace. She says the whole scene was like enchantment to her young mind.

The ladies of the black knights wore white sashes edged with black, and black trimmings to white silk Polonaise gowns. "The ticket" (p. 242 of my MS. Annals, in the City Library,) is surmounted with Sir William Howe's *crest*, and the shield represents the *sea*, which Sir William is about to cross—hence "*Vive Vale.*" The setting glory of the sun, and the Latin scroll, seem to indicate that although *their* luminary is thus receding from them, it shall rise again (resurgum) in another hemisphere.

Since our former publication on these subjects, we have gathered and here set down sundry other facts and incidents connected with that momentous and stirring period.

"Perseverance in struggle, and self-denial in success, should be the motto for the banners of a people that would win and wear their liberty!" Let *Americans* think of this!

The Declaration of Independence was read in the State-house yard, from a small observatory there, by Captain John Hopkins, then commander of an armed brig, a part of his father's (Ezekiel Hopkin's) squadron of three vessels. It was *formally* read on the *8th July*, at noon, "in the presence of many thousand spectators," as Town's Gazette said.

A British magazine, of 1786, says, that there was then a transfer made at the Bank of England of £471,000 to Mr. Van Otten on account of the Landgrave of Hesse, for so much due *for Hessian soldiers lost in the American war*, at £30 a head—thus making the total number lost to be 15,700 men! This was "making merchandise of the souls and bodies of men" with a witness.

We here add sundry extracts made from Town's Evening Post of 1777, &c., published in Philadelphia, which we give in consecutive dates, and which go to show the general notices of the times, and particularly the enterprises and active state of the privateers and vessels of war, to wit:

A writer who has just seen "the thousand captives of Hess," describes them as of sickly, sallow hue, with legible marks of abject slavery upon their wan countenances. Another writer says, they were distinguished for their plundering habits; that at Bordentown they were very oppressive and destructive.

The American prisoners under Lord and General Howe, and their officers, receive much severity. Captains, lieutenants, and other officers of *private* ships of war, masters, supercargoes, &c., with Indians, mulatto and negro slaves, all huddled together between decks. Their provisions are all salt, and stinted.

General Hugh Mercer, killed at Princeton, was brought to Philadelphia, and was buried with military honours, on the south side of Christ church yard; and Captain William Shippen, killed also at Princeton, was buried at St. Peter's.

Captain Nicholas Biddle, of the Randolph frigate, advertises, January 21, at Philadelphia, for "Seven deserters from on board the Randolph, lying at Fort Island." At the same time his former vessel, the brig Andrew Doria, must have been at Philadelphia, as her petty officers, seamen and landsmen, are called to their duty on board, in ten days.

The town of Providence has fitted out fifteen privateers since the war, which has brought into *that* port above seventy sail. The continental fleet under Commodore Hopkins is now there. His own ship is the Warren, of thirty-six guns.

Philadelphia, March 29th. "The Randolph frigate, Captain Biddle, having sprung a mast, is put into a 'safe port.'" [This is believed to mean Charleston;] and she had been struck with lightning. [As we have been informed.]

Boston, April 10th. The Cabot privateer was lately driven ashore at Geboge by the Milford frigate, and got off by her.

A letter from Freehold, June 24th, says, "I laid a bait last Saturday to break up the plundering *Colonel George Taylor;* it so far succeeded that I was within an ace of taking the whole; we took two men; whilst the rest were swimming towards a boat, that was coming off, we fired upon them, and killed one and wounded another.

The 4th July, being the *first* anniversary, was celebrated at Philadelphia with great display and joy. About noon all the armed ships and galleys were drawn up before the city, with their gay streamers flying. At one o'clock, all the yards being manned, they severally fired thirteen guns. An elegant dinner was given to the congress, the civil and military officers, &c. The Hessian band played some fine music, and at each toast there was a discharge of artillery. Towards evening several troops of horse, a corps of artillery, and a brigade of North Carolina forces, were drawn up in Second street, and reviewed by congress and the general officers. At night there was ringing of bells, and a grand exhibition of fireworks on the commons, and an illumination of the houses. The face of joy and gladness was universal.

At the watering place, at Staten island, there are about three hundred sail of transports!

The corps of invalids, under Colonel Nicola, is by resolve of congress, of 16th July, to be formed *at Philadelphia.*

The capture of Major General Prescott and his aid, in July, is announced to congress, by General Washington, as a fortunate event, of the particulars of which he gives in a letter from Major General Spencer, saying, "I have to congratulate your excellency and congress on the late success of Lieut. Col. Barton, who, with the number of forty, including *Captains Adams* and Phillips, and a number of brave officers, last night went on Rhode Island, and brought off General Prescott and his aid, Major Barrington." Another account calls him "*Major Adams* of the train."

Charleston, South Carolina, June. The Marquis de La Fayette, a great officer; the Baron de Kalb, major general, and several other French officers of distinction, are arrived here in a vessel belonging to the marquis, on a visit to our continent, and with an intention of entering into the American service.

For a considerable time there had been no court proceedings—every thing like regular law was suspended, until a constitution, &c., could be regularly adopted; in the mean time the chief authority seemed to vest in the executive council, and in the committee of safety.

Colonel Fanning's regiment, near King's bridge, consists of four hundred and sixty men of the British army. He was an American.

August 23d, Philadelphia. "To-morrow morning the continental army will march through this city. To proceed along Front street and up Chestnut street." They were headed by General Washington, and said to amount to ten thousand, and immediately passed over the Schuylkill. Thence to the Brandywine battle.

September 23d. It is ordered by Colonel Lewis Nicola, a Frenchman, of the invalid corps, that all vessels in the Delaware go up the

Delaware to Burlington, and down the river to Fort island; and that all smaller craft go into Timber and Ancocus creeks; all disobeying would be destroyed. This to keep them from the British.

A gentleman arrived at New York, who came from Charleston, says that the crew of the Randolph frigate, in September last, being at sea, had a mind to rise on her, and carry her to New York, a majority of her crew being British. The officers kept treble guards until they got into Charleston; and at Hobcow, on the 8th of September, she overset, and lay full of mud the 5th of October, when he left there. There was then little hope of floating her again. (See No. 423.)

No persons are to be allowed to appear abroad in the streets from 8½ o'clock to morning, without a lantern.—(A military law.)

The wood in the neck is all declared to be for the use of the king's troops, and to be reserved accordingly.—None to pass at the Jersey ferry without a pass.

Six ten-plate stoves are advertized—then a *new* thing!

Fishkill, October 23d. Last Thursday, one Taylor, a spy, was hanged at Hurley, who was detected with a letter to Burgoyne, which he had swallowed in a silver ball; but by the assistance of tartar emetic he discharged the same—a witness against himself.

Burlington, January 28th, 1778. On the 19th inst. died Francis Furgler, the hermit, in the sixty-sixth year of his age, who existed alone twenty-five years, in a thick wood four miles from Burlington, through all the inclemencies of the season without fire, in a cell made by the side of an old log, in the form of a small oven, not high or long enough to stand upright in or lie extended. It was supposed he intended this mode as a penance for some evil done in his own country. He was a German—a Catholic, and was buried in the Friends' ground at Mount Holly.—(There was a hermit close to Mount Holly—perhaps the same case.)

Congress order a monument to be erected in North Carolina to the memory of the amiable and gallant General Nash, killed in Germantown.

The tender of the Roebuck brings intelligence from the West Indies, (of course a British account,) that the Yarmouth, Captain Vincent, fell in with the rebel frigate Randolph, of thirty-six guns, and a large ship of twenty guns and three long nines, on the night of the 20th of March. These mistaking the Yarmouth for a twenty-gun ship, ran alongside and ordered her to strike; at the same time the Randolph fired a broadside into her, which wounded twelve and killed five men. The Yarmouth returned the salute with seven of her lower tier, on which the Randolph instantly blew up, and every soul perished excepting five, who were saved on a piece of the wreck, and picked up by the Yarmouth five days afterwards. They informed that the intention of this fleet was to destroy the island of Tobago.

The Adams, and Hancock, vessels of war, have been taken after leaving France. The Raleigh has made her escape from the Ariadne.

A small expedition went to Squam, where they demolished the saltworks. There were probably one hundred houses, having each six to ten coppers—one of the houses constructed by Congress at a cost of £6000—all of which they destroyed.

The Virginia frigate, in going out of the Chesapeake, in April, got aground and was captured by the Emerald, and taken to New York

An expedition, of a brig and four galleys, went up to Bordentown and captured some stores, when the people set fire to the Washington and Effingham frigates, two fine ships—two privateers, one large twenty-four-gun ship, and nine other ships, and fourteen or fifteen smaller vessels. It met with but little resistance by a hundred men. This occurred just before the British abandoned Philadelphia.

The paper of June 25th, No. 497, contains a long list of names attainted of high treason; that is to say, Tories gone off with the British.

Providence, July 4. Captain Barron, who sailed first lieutenant of the Boston frigate, we hear was lately killed in France, by means of a cannon accidentally bursting. He was an experienced and valuable officer, and his death is much lamented.

June 24th. The state ship Defence, of Connecticut, commanded by Captain Smedley, and ship Volant, Captain Oliver Daniel, sailed from Charleston.

At Philadelphia, Wednesday, the 22d of June, an elegant evening entertainment was given at the City Tavern, by the officers of the army and some of the gentlemen of the city, to the *young ladies* who had manifested their attachment to the cause of virtue and freedom by sacrificing every convenience to the love of their country.

Philadelphia, July 25th, 1778.—No. 509. The melancholy fate of the late worthy Captain Biddle, of the Randolph frigate, being as yet but little known, we give the following account of this unfortunate event, received in a letter from Charleston, dated the 29th of March last, to wit:—"Captain Clarke, of this place, yesterday received a letter from Captain Hall, of the Notre Dame, one of the fleet commanded by Captain Biddle, informing him that on the evening of the 8th of March, to the windward of Barbadoes, the fleet fell in with a large English ship of fifty or sixty-four guns: that about 8 o'clock the next morning the Randolph engaged, and handled her so roughly for twelve or fifteen minutes, that the British ship must shortly have struck, having lost her bowsprit and topmasts, and being otherwise greatly shattered, while the Randolph had suffered very little. But in this moment of glory, as the Randolph was veering to get on her quarter, she unfortunately blew up, and the whole crew perished.—One *Fanning*, of Connecticut, who arrived prize-master of a sloop taken by the Randolph, and which was converted into a tender for her, brought the letter, and confirms the account. Never was a man more sincerely esteemed or lamented than Captain Biddle."—[Simeon Fanning, above, a young midshipman then, was my uncle, and was soon after killed. His brother Joshua, was lieutenant of the Randolph, when she blew up.]

At a court-martial, Samuel Lyons, lieutenant of the Dickinson galley, Samuel Ford, lieutenant of the Effingham galley, John Wilson, lieutenant of the Ranger galley, and John Lawrence, gunner of the Dickinson galley, were convicted of deserting to the enemy, and sentenced to suffer death. The execution to be on board the galleys in the river, opposite to Market street, on Wednesday the 3d of September. The officers to be shot, and John Lawrence to be hanged.—[Only the first two suffered; the rest were reprieved.]

Young Mr. Bogert, son of Nicholas Bogert, of New York, merchant, was inhumanly killed a few days ago, by the enemy in Jersey.

The ship Governor Hancock, of Massachusetts, engaged the Levant British frigate, and the latter blew up. Captain Hardy, of the former, was killed. Seventeen of the British, only, were saved.

In October, the British, five hundred strong, went up the Little Egg Harbour river on a marauding expedition, but were repulsed by Proctor's artillery and Pulaski's legion of horse.

On the 26th of September, 1778, Captain John Barry, in the Raleigh, fought two British ships of war, off Massachusetts, and finally, to save himself from capture, succeeded to run her ashore. He fought a remarkably severe and unequal fight, taking several broadsides from a sixty-four.—(See No. 542.) The British got off the frigate. It was called a noble and daring defence of Barry's.

The Black Prince privateer returned to Boston from a cruise, having taken and manned eight prizes. The Boston, the Ranger, and another cruising vessel of the United States, sailed from Nantz the 25th of August. These and many prizes are soon expected at Boston.

Charleston, October 13th. Captain Newton, in the General Moultrie privateer, is returned from a cruise, with a prize of the Wasp brig of war.

December 2d, No. 554, contains a list of all the British vessels lost during the war.

Lord Byron having sailed with a fleet and transports from New York, said to be for the West Indies, Count d'Estaing's fleet sailed from Boston in pursuit. Dinners and parties were given to him and his officers, and parties were given on board the Languedoc to the ladies and gentlemen of Boston. Gay times, although afflicted with war and its evils.

La Fayette and other officers return to France from Boston, said, by the British, to have been recalled by their sovereign. But a letter of La Fayette's (since published) says, they returned because thev could not get commissions in our service.

Continental Money.

A gentleman has informed me, that in his youth he saw, in Philadelphia, a stuffed Paddy, wholly covered with continental money pinned on it. He also stated that a fine large lot, a little north of Lombard street, on which are since built four or five large houses (probably Barclay's row, in Front street,) was sold for £60! The money *then* had the current name of "shinplasters!"

A witty old gentleman, who kept an account of its rapid depreciation, used to say a fast trotting horse could not keep pace with it. An old merchant, who has preserved a scale of its depreciation, gave it as follows, to wit:

Value of 100 dollars in specie in continental money to wit:

Years,	1777	1778	779	1780	1781
January,	105	325	742	2934	7400
February,	107	357	868	3332	7500
March,	109	375	1000	3736	0000
April,	112	400	1104	4000	"
May,	115	400	1215	4600	"
June,	120	400	1342	6400	"
July,	125	425	1477	8900	"
August,	150	450	1630	7000	"
September,	175	475	1800	7100	"
October,	275	500	2030	7200	"
November,	300	545	2308	7300	"
December,	310	634	2593	7400	"

I give, from an original bill of my friend, Col. Allen McLane, a purchase of 1781--to wit:

Capt. A. McLane,
January 5, 1781. Bo't of W. Nicoll,

1 pair boots,	\$600
$6\frac{3}{4}$ yds. calico, at \$85 per yard,	752
6 yds. chintz, at \$150 do.	900
$4\frac{1}{2}$ yds. moreen, at \$100 do.	450 50
4 handkerchiefs, at \$100 do.	400
8 yds. quality binding, at \$4 per yard,	32
1 skein of silk,	10
If paid in specie, £18 10*s*.	\$3,144 50

Received payment in full.
for Wm. Nicolls,
Jona. Jones.

I well remember seeing the Hessian prisoners (says an elderly gentleman) which had been taken at Trenton. I stood on the porch of Pemberton's house, in Chestnut above Third street. They marched up Chestnut street past the State-house, where Congress sat. They made a long line—all fine, hearty looking men, and well clad, with large knapsacks, spatterdashes on legs, their looks were *satisfied.* On each side, in a single file, were their guards, mostly in light summer dress, and some without shoes, [in winter,] but stepping light and cheerful.

Fireworks were exhibited on the Delaware during the war, some on ship carpenters' floating stages. The greatest show remembered was that of Arnold and the Devil, carried on a wheel carriage along the streets, and burned by the latter on Market street hill.

Jacob Ritter's Facts of the Prisoners at the Walnut-street Prison.

"*The British Provost,*" so called, in Philadelphia, was the same building since called the Walnut-street Prison. It was then newly constructed and unfinished. At that place there were about nine hundred Americans held as prisoners, under the charge of the infamously cruel commissioner, Captain Cunningham, then a wicked and passionate Irishman of about sixty years of age—a florid, full-bodied man. These prisoners were those captured at the battles of Brandywine and Germantown. Numbers of them died there of *hunger and cold*, and were daily carried out and interred in the Potter's field, now the Washington square, close by. It seems strange to me that a case of such suffering to our countrymen, effected chiefly by the malignity of such a wretch as Cunningham, should not have been more spoken of by Philadelphians. We had often heard of the sufferings of prisoners at the New York provost under his control, but scarcely a Philadelphian of middle age has ever heard a word concerning our countrymen's sufferings at Philadelphia. This seems strange when compared with what I am now to relate from facts told me in May, 1833, by Mr. Jacob Ritter, aged seventy-six years, a German by descent, born near Quakertown, Bucks county, who was himself one of the inmates of that Golgotha and charnel-house in the time above mentioned—then a good man and true, and since, a public Friend.

He had been in the battle of Brandywine, and was found, while sick in a farm-house, by the Hessians, who beat and kicked him as a "*rebeller*," and bore him off to the city. At this place he and the others were *three days and nights* without any food. He saw one soldier who had eaten nothing *till his fifth day*, when he saw him get a piece of rye bread; and he actually saw him gently topple off his seat on the prison steps, dead, while he was in the act of eating!

Mr. Ritter says, he was often wantonly beaten and bruised severely by the but-end of Cunningham's whip; and at other times he was affectedly flattered and caressed, and offered many jingling guineas to join his majesty's service. He did not strike or abuse men's persons in the presence of other British officers, but on such occasions would content himself with grossly abusive language.*

On one occasion Mr. Ritter saw a poor starving Virginian, who had been several days without food, looking wistfully at some biscuits which had been sent to some newly-arrived *citizens*, prisoners, brought in on suspicion. Moved by compassion for the distress of the starving man, and almost forgetting his own similar need, he made out to slip unperceived to where they lay in a keg, and getting one, he gave it

---

* Cunningham was made a captain by General Clinton to save him from merited severity in case of his capture. He had been only a man of the ranks, and was deemed a kind of bully among the men when at New York before the war, where he got into a fight, in March, 1775, at the liberty pole—he there offending the people, they made him and his companion Hill to go down upon their knees and curse the king. They exclaimed "God bless him," and they were beaten. This rankled in his breast ever after

to the man, at same time cautioning him not to eat it all, but to break it up finely, mix it with water, and then to make it a prolonged meal by *tasting* it for a whole day. He saw this man after his release, then again a soldier, who told him he owed to his timely interference and advice the preservation of his life.

As the winter advanced, the prisoners became excessively cold. They had no extra coverings for sleeping, and the window panes being much broken, (shivered to pieces by the blowing up of the Augusta man-of-war, at Red Bank,) the *snow* and cold entered therein freely. They huddled together for warmth; but with that they also became common companions of their lice and vermin. He did not perceive any of our officers on furlough as coming among them as visiters; and he did not know of any arrangement of any of our citizens as benefactors. He had seen soup brought for them, and set down at the prison door in vessels, which, when seen by Cunningham on his visit, have been kicked over, with a curse on the rebel dogs. On such an occasion he has seen the poor, starved prisoners, when near enough to profit by it, fall upon their knees and hands, and eagerly lap up the wasted liquid! On such occasions he has looked upon the monster with painful emotions, and wondered if indeed the good God would suffer the transgressor to pass to the grave unwhipped of justice. At length his retribution day came. He was convicted of forgery in England, and came to an ignominious end.

Ritter had seen several pick and eat grass-roots, scraps of leather, chips, pieces of the rotten pump, &c., to assuage and abate their hunger. Those who had any friends in the city got to fare better, after they could contrive to let them know their wants. So he was helped by his aunt Kline, and eventually he got released, through the influence of friends pressing upon Mr. Galloway, the chief British agent, acting for the city police, &c. It was a common measure with Cunningham, when visiting them, to carry his large key, and to knock any one on the head with it who chanced to offend him. On one such occasion the struck person fell and bled, [often, perhaps, died.] Those who died, eight to twelve in twenty-four hours, were to be seen dragged by the legs along the floor to the dead carts. It was common to see several watching for the chance of rats from the rat-holes, which, when captured, were eaten, both for staying hunger, and also to make reprisals upon an enemy that often disturbed their sleep, and otherwise annoyed them.

At a subsequent conversation with Ritter, he told me, in answer to inquiries, that their supply of provisions never became regular: for instance, they never had any issue of *salt* meat. Occasionally he has seen what seemed to have been a diseased beef or cow, brought dead in a cart, and shot down on the ground in all its dung, which was eagerly cut up—by some was eaten raw, and by some was cut in strips to dry and cure, as they had no regular vessels for cooking. In his own case, after some days, he got an earthen porringer, in which he made some food by boiling, or simmering, some musty flour in water: his fire was made of old shoes and bones; (he once saw a load of chestnut come;)—he thought he never ate any thing so good as it seemed. This example was followed by others: many borrowed his porringer. In one case of their eating the rotten wood and paint from the pump, they mixed it with pump water.

Some of them let down little bags or baskets from the prison windows to the street, to get a little contribution in that way; but it was but little. They received potato skins in that way, and gladly used them. Once a small-headed man got his head out through the bars to beg; and while in the act, and unable to draw his head in again, he was seen by Cunningham, who fell to whipping him.

He never saw or knew of any of the citizens of Philadelphia ever visiting the prisoners to relieve them. Of all the Friends in the city, he never knew or heard of but one that ever came there upon benevolence to help them. He knew of no relief extended to them by the ladies or women. His old aunt was a resolute woman, who either came to assist him, or sent relief by her little son. The only act of seeming gentleness he ever witnessed from Cunningham, was upon the winning address of a starving drummer boy. He begged him to consider his case of starvation, his youth, and his inability to do the British any injury. After some inquiries by Cunningham, he said he might go if he would kneel down and kiss the prison stone steps. He did it instantly and earnestly, and claiming his reward, the persecutor let him go with a laugh. None of the American officers ever visited them. He did not know of any of the prisoners as driven to enlistment. There were times when Cunningham acted with peculiar bursts of passion, in such cases wantonly whipping, with his horsewhip, whoever came across his way. He did so particularly, when he heard of the disaster to Count Donop at Red Bank. He had his lodging rooms in the prison. His brother, a serjeant, was a moderate man.

☞ In Poulson's paper of the 25th of August, 1834, is a confirmation of the foregoing account of Jacob Ritter, told on the occasion of the death of Captain Samuel Waples, of Accomac county, Virginia, who, it states, had been taken a prisoner, as lieutenant in the ninth Virginia regiment, at the battle of Germantown, and *was confined* in the common jail of the city of Philadelphia, where he suffered many privations, being kept for *three days and nights without any kind of sustenance.*" He soon made his escape therefrom in the disguise of a Quaker, and succeeded in passing the lines, and in getting to Washington's camp at Valley Forge.

The wife of Benedict Arnold was a Philadelphian, a Peggy Shippen, and died on the 14th February, 1836, at Uxbridge, Mass., aged 83 [about the same time a sister of Major Andre, aged 81, died in England.] It seems a strange affair, that the wife of such a general should under any circumstances get back to America—to get, too, not to her own home, and with her nearest relatives, *in Pennsylvania,* but should go to Massachusetts—the same state where her first ancestor, Edward Shippen, first mayor of Philadelphia, had been publicly punished in Boston as a Quaker! Col. Burr has said that her pride and ambition perverted her husband's integrity. Their only son and daughter (he being a British subaltern) went to reside in the East Indies, many years ago. Another account, in the London Spectator, in 1838, says that two sons are then in England—say James R. and Wm. F., aged 57 and 44 -and each receive a pension of £81 a-year. *Arnold* means, in *German*, a maintainer of honour! In the Museum, at New Haven, Conn., is the identical sign, once that of General Arnold. It is thus:

B. Arnold, Druggist,
Bookseller, &c., from London.
*Sibi totique.**

He had been in London, but was born in Norwich, Conn., in January, 1740, and had been apprenticed to an apothecary in that city. He was engaged at New Haven in the trade of shipping horses and mules to the West Indies.

It might be further remarked concerning Mrs. Arnold, that she had been a Philadelphia belle, and the toast of the British officers while their army was in Philadelphia. She had been brought up in British affections—her own father, Judge Edward Shippen, was biassed on that side. Major Andre was intimate in the family, which led to a friendly correspondence between Miss Shippen and him. After General Arnold married her, he of course became acquainted with that fact, and encouraged its continuance. It was continued, until at last Arnold and Andre opened it more directly between themselves, under the names of Gustavus, for the former, and John Anderson, for the latter. The extravagances of Arnold produced the want of money; and probably the predilections of the wife for what was splendid in the British army, influenced them both to forfeit home and country for a splendid, but illusive hope!

An historical ballad of the proceedings of a town meeting at Philadelphia, May 24, 25, 1779—by Stansberry.

[Mr. Stansberry, the author of the following satire, was a young Philadelphian, of the Society of Friends. He became what was called a tory, and went off with the British. After the peace, he settled in New York, kept a china store, and became secretary of an insurance company there. He wrote other pieces of fugitive poetry. He once kept his china store in Philadelphia, opposite to Christ church, in Second street. A daughter of his married John Stille, merchant, of Philadelphia. One of his sons settled in New Jersey, and has a family there.]

* For himself, for the whole, or for all The first was his motto—for himself, indeed

CANTO FIRST.

'Twas on the twenty-fourth of May,
A pleasant, warm, sunshiny day,
Militia folks paraded,
With colours spread, and cannon too,
Such loud huzzas and martial view,
I thought the town invaded.

But when, on closer look, I spied
The speaker march with gallant stride,
I knew myself mistaken.
For *he*,* on Trenton's well-fought day,
To Burlington mistook his way,
And fairly saved his bacon.

With him, a number more appear'd,
Whose names their corp'ral never heard,—
To muster-rolls a stranger.
To save their fines, they bore a gun,
Determined, like the rest, to run
At any glimpse of danger.

The great *Mc Clenachan* bestrode
His prancing horse, and fiercely rode,
And faith, he had good reason—
For he was told, that to his sorrow,
He, with *a number more*, to-morrow
Should be confined in prison.

'Twas said, some *speculating job*
Of his had so inflamed the mob,
That they were grown unruly;—
And swearing by the "Eternal God,"
Such fellows now should feel the rod,
Resolved to "come on coolly!"†

The people's majesty of laws,
The proper, and the only cause,
Now shone in all its glory:
Morris the wise; Arnold the brave;
The *double* Mason; Wistar grave—
Confounded with the Tory.

Nor age, nor wealth, nor rank, nor birth,
Avail'd with these true sons of earth,
The offspring of the valley;
For all the lore of ages past,
What cared the statesman *with his last*,
Or hero of *the Alley?*

At close of day, no tired horse
(Covered with sweat,—with bawling hoarse,)
More gladly reached home;
Each doff'd his civic oaken crown,
First took a dram, then laid him down,
And dream'd of joys to come

CANTO SECOND.

Now Titan raised his flaming head
And drowsy sentinels to bed
Retired from irksome duty;
For they were placed, as it behooved,
To watch if tory-goods were moved,
That they might share the booty.

The most tumultuous instant seize,
With venom'd rage, on whom they please;
The People cannot err!
Can it be wrong, in Freedom's cause,
To tread down Justice, Order, Laws,
When all the mob concur?

But now, through *Mitchell's* brazen throat,
Faction, with mean, abusive note,
Proclaims *a grand town meeting*,
Where printers' devils, barbers' boys,
Apprentice lads, express their joys,
The council members greeting.

Each vagrant from the whipping-post,
Or stranger stranded on the coast,
May here reform the State:
And *Peter*, *Mich*, and Shad-row *Jack*,
And, Pompey-like *McKean*, in black,
Decide a people's fate.

The trained bands of Germantown
With clubs and bayonets came down,
And swell'd the motley train;
Resolv'd to change, like him of old,
Old rags and lampblack,‡ into gold,
Or chaos bring again.

And now the State-house yard was full,
And orators, so grave and dull,
Appear'd upon the stage:
But all was riot, noise, disgrace,

---

* General and Governor Reed—and we do not mean to endorse *the slurs*.

† The firm of Robert Morris and Blair McClenachan were reproached and threatened, and had to get into Judge Wilson's house for defence. Vide "Fort Wilson," in the Annals of Philadelphia.

‡ The materials of continental money.

And Freedom's sons, o'er all the place,
In bloody frays engage.

Sagacious *Matlack* strove in vain
To pour his sense in Dutchman's brain;
With every art to please—
Observ'd, that as the money fell,
Like Lucifer, to lowest hell,
Tho' swift,—yet by degrees,—

So should it rise, and goods should fall,
Month after month, till one and all,
Might buy as cheap as ever;—
That they lost all, who grasp'd so much,
(This, *Col. Bull** declared in Dutch,)
But fruitless each endeavour.

With solemn phiz and action slow
Arose the chairman, *Roberdeau*,†
And made the humane motion,
That Tories, with their brats and wives,
Should flee, to save their wretched lives,
From Sodom into Goshen.

He central stood, and all the ground
With people cover'd, him surround—
And so it came to pass,
That as he spoke with zeal upon it,
He turn'd his face to those in front—
To those behind, his *back*.

This gave offence—his voice was drown'd—
He should have turn'd himself all round,
Like whirligig in socket;
Or, if this did his art surpass,
At least, he should have took his *end*
And put it in his pocket.

Then *Hutchinson*, that bully calf,
(A goose has got more sense by half,)
With croaking, frog-like note,
Approved the motion, and demands
The People's sense, by show of hands,
Might save or damn the vote.

All raised the hand, with mighty burst
Of loud acclaim, (the case revers'd—
All lift their hands again,)
Blue *Bayard* grinn'd, that long-ear'd ass—
With mobs, he saw it was a farce
To reason, or explain.

But thoughtful *Rush*, and artful *Gaff*,‡
And *Bryan*, (too much vex'd to laugh,)
Were fill'd with grief and pity;
And soon dismiss'd the rabble rout—
Concluding what they met about
With choosing a Committee.

Hoping to get them more in tune
Before *the 25th of June*,
Which was the chosen day
For them to meet by sound of drum,
Unless the enemy should come,
And make them run away.

To tell their tale, with haste they speed
To their prime mover, *Joseph Reed*,
"The virtuous and sublime;"—
So virtuous, that he *cheats his friends*,
Sublimely cheats, *to gain his ends*,
And glories in the crime.

Ambition is his darling theme,
Integrity an idle dream,
That vulgar minds may draw.
At home, abroad, with friend, or wife,
In public, and in private life,
The tyrant's will is law.

Of deep resentments, wicked, bold,
The lust of blood, of power, of gold,
Possess alternate sway.
And *Johnston's bribe*§ had surely won
Rebellion's pale-faced, matchless son,
Had mammon ruled that day.

But time would fail me to rehearse,
In my poor, limping, doggrel verse,
His character divine:
Suffice it, that *in Dunlap's page*,‖
Drawn by himself, from age to age,
It shall with splendour shine.

---

* Of Chester county.

† A militia general in the war—also a board merchant.

‡ A nick-name of T. Matlack.

§ The British commissioner—who, it is said, failed to bribe Gov. Reed.

‖ Vide the letter from Cleves, on the Lower Rhine, in packet, May 25, 1779.

I have often heard it stated by persons, who went through the trials of that period, that we, their descendants, have no just conceptions of their state of suffering and deprivations. Their clothing was of the coarsest form—of home-made—made by the female's spinning done in the house; they also made all the shirting and sheeting, &c. Where so much was to be done, it was necessary that all should help; to this cause, I *know* that two lads, both afterwards commodores in the United States' navy, were both taught to be good spinners on the little wheel. Tea, coffee, chocolate, sugar, and all kinds of spices, were wholly gone in almost all country places. Sage tea and teaberry were used as substitutes. Salt was greatly needed and could not be procured. When sometimes *smuggled* into the country, it was done in women's pockets. Salt pans were settled all along the seacoast, to make salt at expensive rates. In many places where the armies passed, flour was not to be had for bread. People in Virginia and elsewhere were obliged to live on pounded corn. The mills were equally dismantled by both of the warring parties. I have known persons, in very respectable and decent families, that found very great difficulties to keep themselves even passably clothed. Women indulged in no fineries or changes then; all pretence to fashion was wholly out of the question. Wherever the armies were to pass and forage, &c., as through New Jersey, and Virginia, and the Carolinas, the farmers lost nearly all they had that was eatable or movable; their horses were pressed, and their cows and swine taken; they had no spirit to sow seed, or to till their grounds. There was no *regular* business in any thing; even apprentices were not safe, for they had to serve their turns in the several requisitions. There was, indeed, a mighty spirit of resistance raised and maintained by the *men* of that day; but the women *felt* the war extremely—and both men and women were most heartily glad, when they at last saw that their struggles were to have an end. It was an occasion of extravagant and universal joy. It could never have been borne so long as it was, but that the practice of war then gave long seasons of respite during the several *winters*, allowing time to the worn down to recruit their strength and spirits, and giving time to resort to new enterprises, and to new means of recruiting their forces, &c. Besides all this, it was almost a universal expectation, that *every next* campaign would surely *end* the *contest*. None *foresaw* or *feared* a term of *seven years!*

In our present repose and consciousness of strength and security, we can hardly conceive the state of excitement and concern daily felt in the revolutionary period. A friend of mine, who was an observant and intelligent boy, dwelling on a farm near the Yellow springs, in Chester county, has related to me some of the incidents of that time. Their ordinary religious Sabbath worship was irregular and broken up; their male neighbours, every here and there, were absent on militia service. The talk and greeting of the neigh bours, were generally about the absentees; news was very uncertain, and yet anxiously inquired after. News "by flood and field" occasionally came, which stirred and disturbed the whole community; sometimes it came saddening, of some one or other mishap befallen, to some one of their families. When the news of the landing of the British at the head of Elk, and of their advance upon the Brandywine, occurred, every family was put upon the tiptoe of expectation and alarm; besides which, new calls were made upon the people to go to head-quarters as soldiers, guides, or wagoners. In the absence of the males of the families, women and children were full of apprehension; floors were taken up, and out-houses made into concealed places for their most valuable articles of portable character. They had all undefined apprehensions of being plundered and abused. At and after the time of the battle of Brandywine, the country could be seen all in motion, in the rapid coming and going of men on horseback. In time could be seen numerous bands and parties of wearied and discomfited soldiers—none of them aiming at order, and some few of them without officers or arms. Some were going to an assigned point on the Schuylkill; but several were resolved to make their escape to their homes; many of them were beggars for some refreshments, and all was cheerfully given to them which they could spare. For many nights, the family set up all night, from wakeful apprehension. The father of the family I describe had been a Quaker, so strictly trained, that his sister, who was a preacher, would not wear her caps of any other than *brown* linen—*white* being a condemned refinement—for dress sake! Such a man, although averse to war, had by this time become so far warlike, that he had gone for the country, and was actually from home in the ranks, where he took a severe cold from sleeping on the ground, and died.

On one of the nights of apprehension, there came to the house a small company of cavalry. Their presence was disquieting any how; but when they took off their military cloaks and displayed the red coats of British officers, their dread was irrepressible. The mind said, what shall we do, and to what is this visit of the enemy to tend! They saw the dismay, and soon quieted them by saying they were American officers in disguise, out upon a tour of recognizance near to the enemy. Every now and then, after the winter campaign was deemed closed, and the British were gaily revelling in Philadelphia, the dread of British foraging parties was felt. Any thing of military aspect, and approaching them on horseback, was quickly interpreted as British assailants, and set the whole family in commotion. Sometimes they were parties of Americans, half as clamorous for needed succours, as the British themselves would probably have been. Men acting as farmers, felt as if they had no security for reaping what they might plant. The heart was heavy and reluctant at its wonted toil. Mothers, acting in the absence of their husbands, looked upon their children, and wondered if their fathers should ever return to foster and rear them. Sad forebodings were but too often true! Such facts, thus faintly expressed, have been but too true a picture all over our extended country of united colonies, wherever the approach of the hostile bands could be apprehended, or were realized. Those who lived upon the frontiers, were kept in Indian alarms; and those along the Atlantic dreaded British invasion and ravages. Their march was always a cause of desolation and anxiety, even where their discipline was intended to check any individual and family aggressions.

Among the marvels of the revolution may be mentioned the remarkable fact, that John Adams and Thomas Jefferson, *two* of the last three surviving signers of the Declaration of Independence, should both die on *the 4th of July*, 1826, at *a day* and *a period* peculiarly *set apart* as the *semi-centennial* anniversary! Jefferson was ill, and expressed a wish to live *to that* eventful day! If Mr. Carroll, the other last survivor, had also died, the epic story would have been complete.

When the mind is awakened to the consideration of singularities, it may find an increase of them: for instance, the following facts are equally peculiar respecting the *succession* of our several presidents:

John Adams died in his ninety-first year, and was eight years older than Thomas Jefferson; Thomas Jefferson was eight years older than James Madison; James Madison was eight years older than James Monroe; and James Monroe was eight years older than John Quincy Adams.

It has been *calculated*, (that Mr. Jefferson at thirty-three, and John Adams at forty, when they signed the Declaration of Independence,) the chance of their both living fifty years longer, and dying at their expiration, is only *one* in twelve hundred millions! Again, James Monroe, having strangely died on the Independence day of 4th July, 1831, makes up the *three chances* to be, by calculation, as 18,268 millions, to one mill!!

Among other peculiarities of our early presidents, it may be noticed, that the first five of them—*they being the entire number of the revolutionary men*—all ended their several terms of service in the *sixty-sixth year* of their age! and John Q. Adams himself, had he been re-elected for a second term, would have also ended in his *sixty-sixth* year! Did *he* mark *the turning point* in our national career? *Nous verrons!* The facts are these, viz.:

Washington, born February 22d, 1732—inaugurated 1789; term of service expired in the sixty-sixth year of his age.

John Adams, born October 19th, 1735—inaugurated 1797; term of service expired in the sixty-sixth year of his age.

Thomas Jefferson, born April 2d, 1743—inaugurated 1801; term of service expired in the sixty-sixth year of his age.

James Madison, born March 4th, 1751—inaugurated 1809; term of service expired in the sixty-sixth year of his age.

James Monroe, born April 2d, 1759—inaugurated 1817; term of service expired in the sixty-sixth year of his age.

John Adams was on the committee of five who were charged to draft the Declaration. He was peculiarly ardent in the cause of independence; and was considered as the *leader* therein of the New England delegates whom he held to his then desperate measures, as they were generally considered. He watched their actions, and misgivings, as a shepherd governs the wanderings of his fold! In truth, Jefferson gave the Declaration by his proper hand-writing to *the congress;* but as truly, Adams gave it *to the nation!* The place of *writing* the Declaration has been differently stated. Some have said that it was at Jefferson's chamber, in the Indian Queen inn; but Mrs. Clymer, with whom Mr. Jefferson boarded, at the south-west corner of Seventh and High streets, said it was there, and to settle that point, Dr. Mease wrote to Mr. Jefferson, and *had it confirmed* as at her house.

It may be mentioned as remarkable, the coincidence of action apparent in the conduct of those two leading and prominent states of the revolution—Virginia and Massachusetts. Both of them have supplied more public officers than any of the other states. They might justly claim parentage of the union. The great drama of the revolution *opened* in Lexington in one, and *closed* at Yorktown in the other. The first signer of the Declaration of Independence was from one; the signer of the Constitution of the United States from the other. The great leaders of the Federal and Democratic parties—Adams and Jefferson—resided in Massachusetts and Virginia, each was vice president and each was president; each a signer of the Declaration of Independence; each a negotiator of his country's treaties in Europe; and finally, both, after serving their country in their lives, were gathered to their immortality *on the same day* in which, fifty years before, they had together set their names to the freedom of their country.

I cannot but remember with what deep and stirring interest I used to sit by and hear the recitals of those who had been actors in, or observers of, the times and incidents occurring in *the revolutionary war.* It all seemed to me as a time and a drama passed by —no longer the din and the perils of war existed—all around me was peace and smiling plenty. It seemed to me like the stillness and repose after the great storm had passed by. I felt eager to look upon some of *the remains* of the desolating epoch; but little or none remained to the eye; and what I could contemplate and consider, came home to the feelings through the ear—by hearing the recitals of those who had been familiar with the incidents. What I failed thus to get at closely, concerning the war and its people concerned, I came at last, in subsequent years, to *see and feel* on other objects, seen gliding down the stream of time, like floating drift-wood, and which it has been my pleasing business, and useful occupation, to snatch from the ebbing tide, and to warehouse (or chronicle) as the relics and remains of olden time—gathering up for my own contemplation, and for the wonderment of another generation, the passing and dissolving *characteristics* of men and things of a passing and a dissolving age. "Oh, sweet is a tale of the olden time!" How grateful to the mind to have it stored with images, all its own and which others can only possess by gratefully receiving as a kindness and as a boon!

They who are now alive, and remember the termination of the *last* war—who recollect what *joy* they felt at its annunciation; and how often they felt gloomy and foreboding concerning its successful end, while in its actual progress, may have some faint conception of what the peace of 1783 was to our forefathers. Fighting with such vast odds against them as they had for seven *long* years, it then seemed as if it would never have an end! They who had screwed up their courage and their strength, again and again, for *one more*, and yet *one more still*, of exhausted efforts, looked out with perpetual *longings*—"making the soul sick with hope deferred," for some happy chance, or eventful providence, to bring their hopes and fears to *a close*. When it at last came, it came overwhelming; and was expressed, not so much in tumultuous joy, as in that comfortable sinking of the soul which one feels in fainting, after one has been struggling for life in the whelming waters, and at last reaches the shore, and then *sinks into rest*, from a sense of safety and thankfulness. Many who had *heard* of the recitals of the revolutionary war, had secretly "wished that Heaven had made them such a man," in such a time, only for the sake of seeing and feeling what our fathers did in so eventful a struggle; and when the second war came, they were not sorry to have so *lively a picture* brought home to their bosoms and interests; but when it came to questions of landings and predatory invasions, like those at Baltimore, and the threatened renewal of a landing at Elkton, and a march upon Philadelphia, it became a heart-sickening affair to many, who held up to their imaginations the successful demonstration upon Washington city, and its conflagration. Some stout hearts might sigh for the trial, in the hopes of their personal renown; but the mass, the great crowd of society, it might be seen, had sincere desires for a speedy and a lasting peace—thus proving that war is not congenial to the mass of society and business people. Some of these facts at which I have hinted should be remembered, as a sedative to any future calls of *the people* for military enterprise and glory! It *is* a bad business, for the social system, at all times!

Incidents of the Revolutionary War, as seen and noted by a widow lady of respectable character, of tory feelings and prejudices—dwelling at Burlington, New Jersey.

The following facts are taken from a MS. diary of Mrs. M. M. preserved in her family, and will comprise such *selections* as seem best calculated for the public eye.

December 6th, 1776. Being on a visit at Haddonfield, I heard from a person from Philadelphia, that the people there were in great commotion—the English fleet being approaching in the river, and the inhabitants removing into the country ; that several of good repute had been forming a design to fire the city, and being summoned before congress were strictly enjoined to abandon their purpose. My heart died within me at the news. On my journey home, I was told that the inhabitants of our little town (Burlington) were hastening away to the country, and that my nearest neighbours were already gone. I was ready to faint at the intelligence. I thought of my lonely situation, with no husband to cheer, with the voice of love, my sinking spirits—my little flock too, without a father. A flood of tears, alone, came to my relief, and I raised my heart to my God. Finally, I was favoured to reach home, and to find my family safe and well.

December 7th. A letter from my next neighbour's husband, at camp, warned her to be gone in haste—news comes from many that the British army is advancing towards us.

December 8th. Every day begins and ends with the same accounts, and we now hear that the regulars are at Trenton.

December 10th. My brother set off, but soon returned, saying he could not get away, as he heard that the Hessians were entering the town. A number of galleys have been lying before the town, for two days past.

December 11th. A party of our riflemen passed through our town going over to Bristol, saying they were forced onward before the Hessians. John Lawrence and two or three others thought best, for the safety of the town, to go out and meet them. The Hessian colonel received them civilly, and promised safety to the people. Doctor Odell made himself useful as interpreter, in talking French with the colonel. The terms were settled, that they should receive unmolested quarters and refreshments, and that none should conceal arms or ammuniton for sinister purposes. If any concealments were discovered in any of the houses, such houses should be liable to pillage. The troops remained without the town in their ranks, while the officers came into town and dined with friend Lawrence, intending to await there the determination of the commodore of the gondolas, to whom Captain Moore had been sent from the town, to confer with him for orders in our extremity. The wind being high, he could not communicate, and presently the galleys got before the town ready for firing. Then John Lawrence and William Dillwyn went down to the wharf and waved their hats, and to their astonishment, they were fired upon This result being reported to the colonel, he and his officers, and their body guard, went out to make their observations. These being occasionally seen from the gondolas, and they thinking the town was filled with Hessians, they set up a cannonade till near dark—sometimes along the main street, and sometimes across it. Several houses were struck and a little damaged, but not one living creature was injured! At night the gondolas fell down a little below the town. While these things were occurring, we, who lived upon the green bank, went with our families into the cellars.

December 12th. The men of the galleys talk of firing the town—several of them landed on our banks and told us so.

December 13th. The Hessians have been removed some miles from town, and the gondola men have been busy ashore, looking, as they say, for tories. Some of the gentlemen who entertained the foreigners were pointed out, and two were seized upon, and dragged on board their galley.

From the 13th to 16th, we had various reports of the advancing and retiring of the enemy. Some of the gondola men broke into and pillaged R. S.'s house, on the bank. About noon of the 16th, we were alarmed with the alleged advance of thousands! My incautious son, in using his spyglass, was seen from the galleys, which soon brought an armed boat on shore with a loud knocking at my house, and asking to search for the tory who had been spying at them. The captain, a smart little fellow, named Shippen, desired to be shown the spyglass; this transaction reached the town, and Colonel Cox was very angry, and ordered the men on board.

December 17th. "More news! Great news!" "The British troops at Mount Holly—guards of militia placed at London and York bridges—gondola men parading the streets, and searching for fire-arms and tories!" But a friend has made me easy, who has come from Mount Holly, who says no harm is done to any, and they only spoil the goods of some known to be in actual rebellion, *as they termed it.* The gondola men are all ordered on board, and not again to land. So far so good.

December 19th. A report prevails that General Putnam, with one thousand men, is on his march—this put all into motion at Holly. The Hessians retire to Black Horse.

December 20th. A snow storm last night has almost stopped the navigation, and has sent our guarda-costa down the river. The snow continues the next day, and much we pity the poor fellows who are out in it. Much talk now of making this *a neutral island;* but it is said that the gentlemen who visited Count de Nope, (Donop) to concert the measure, found him too much occupied to speak about it.

December 22d. It is said Putnam, with one thousand men, is at Mount Holly, and all the women are removed from the place. We hear too, that General Howe is at Trenton, and an engagement may be soon expected. A man from Mount Holly tells us, he saw there lately a great many British troops—that some of them went to the magazine there (over the Court-house) and took out one hundred canteens, and as many broken fire-arms, and piling them up in the street, ordered the men in derision to take charge of them. Several of the families which went away at the cannonading, are now returning. 'Tis said that a party of our men, two hundred strong, which marched out of Mount Holly, met a party of Hessians, and that after a fight, twenty-one of our men were killed.

December 23d. This day twelve gondolas have again visited us. The news again from Mount Holly is, that our men again met the Hessians in battle and lost ten men; and that the Hessians are in possession of the town. It is also said, that three thousand of our troops now at Bristol are to cross over to us to-night, in order to join our routed party at Mount Holly.

December 24th. The gondolas are all gone away—it is said by order of General Cadwallader, in command at Bristol. The former news about the fights is now discredited. Several of the Hessians are in the town to-day. We don't see them, because we, on the green bank, are considered *out of the town*. A pretty heavy firing is heard up the river to-day.

December 26th. A great number of flat-bottomed boats have gone up the river to-day. General Reed and Count de Nope are said to be negotiating about the *neutrality* of our place.

December 27th. A letter from General Reed to his brother informs him that Washington has had an engagement on the 25th, and taken nine hundred prisoners. It seems they were surprised while keeping their Christmas revels. How unlike Christians, in both revels and war! This evening about three thousand of the Pennsylvania militia, and other troops, landed in the Neck and marched into town, and are quartered on the people. An officer spent the evening with us, and was in high spirits. They went away the next day, when some snow again sent the gondolas down the river.

December 29. Soldiers who came last night and took up their residence in Colonel Cox's empty house, went off this morning after stopping to thank me for the food I furnished them. Soon after, another company took possession. The inhabitants are much straitened for bread and fuel.

December 30th. A number of poor, sick, and wounded soldiers are brought into town, and lodged in the court-house and private houses.

January 1st, 1777. The new-year's day has not been ushered in with the usual rejoicings. It forebodes a sorrowful year to many.

January 3d. We heard very distinctly, to-day, very heavy firing of cannon towards Trenton; and at noon upwards of one thousand men came into town in great confusion, and were quartered on the people. Several went into my next neighbour's (Colonel Cox's) house, where I went to see them, and my heart was melted to see them, lying on the floor fast asleep, although many were without blankets to cover them. I had my suspicions that they had fled the field when they should have remained, and it proved so. Among them were several innocent-looking lads, and much I sympathized with their bereaved mothers.

January 5th. I hear that Captain Shippen is killed. We hear

also that General Mercer is killed, and Mifflin is wounded; and that two thousand New-England men fell in the late engagement.

January 7th. This evening all the gondolas went from Bristol down the river.

January 8th. All the soldiers are gone from Colonel Cox's house. Only one of them came to thank me for my services to them.

January 9th. We hear to-day that our troops have driven the British to Brunswick. All the officers went out of town to-day. The weather is very cold, and the river is filled with ice. Several of the sick soldiers brought here have died.

January 11th. Weather very cold, and much I pity the poor soldiers now on their march.

January 15th. I was much affected this evening at seeing the hearse and body of General Mercer going across the river on the ice. At the same time Captain Shippen's body was also carried over—both to be buried at Philadelphia.

February 4th. To-day eight boats full of soldiers sailed up the river to join the forces. They appeared to be merry.

April 17th. A number of flat-bottomed boats went up the river and landed troops at Bristol. It is said fifteen hundred men are billeted on the inhabitants there.

May 7th. Captain Webb and his family came here, on his way to New York, he being ordered to leave the state. As he was going to bed a captain and soldiers arrived to examine his papers, and to take him to Philadelphia to the general, to answer to his being a spy. He was, however, ordered to Bethlehem.—[This is the Captain Webb who was, at that time, a Methodist minister, and was celebrated as such.] Several persons are named as suffering imprisonment as tories.

June 7th. The reports by expresses make us believe that the English army are in motion, and intending for Philadelphia.

June 13th. The soldiers at Bristol beat to march, and sail up the river.

June 14th. Before daylight the alarm guns at Princeton, Trenton, Bordentown, and Bristol were fired, and answered by those below. The gondolas, barges, and flat-bottomed boats pass up the river. We hear much firing above, and report says it is a battle. Some of the sick of the gondolas came to me for assistance, they being lodged at the governor's house (on the bank.) They had the itch fever, and I had the pleasure to see them all get well. It was grateful to observe their hearty gratitude for acts done only in duty.

Shortly afterwards there came a rough-looking man (a gondola man) to the house, and cautiously inviting me aside, he caused me at first no little alarm; but he soon said, "If I had any friends or relatives in Philadelphia, he would be glad to be the messenger, in consideration of my kindness to him when sick."—My heart was rejoiced at the opportunity, and speedily I got ready a quarter of beef, some veal, fowls, and flour, for my father and sisters there, which he called for at midnight and took into his boat. He left them at R. Hopkins', at the Point, from whence my friends sent and took them; and, two nights after, the stranger returned with a letter, a bushel of salt, a jug of molasses, a bag of rice, some tea, coffee, and sugar, with some cloth for my poor boy—all sent by kind sisters in a truly needed time. Then we remembered the poor around us, and soon the salt was distributed to the joy of many.

After this, one morning very early, we were surprised to see many hundreds of boats, filled with British soldiers, going up to Bordentown to burn all the gondolas. I felt, of course, alarmed. While looking at them, R. Sutton and his son stopped at my door, when the former said, "He was just going to join a party of soldiers going up to resist them." Poor fellow! he was killed next day. When the British returned, they fired several cannon near me at our next neighbour's house, who was a captain in the rebel army.

A rebel quarter-master who had received some kindness from us, asked me one day, if I did not wish to see my friends in the city, and said he would accompany me as far as Frankford. I readily accepted, and took along my friend A. O. We got safely to our friend Abel James' place, and next morning we had a joyful meeting with my relatives at Kensington. Our quarter-master was to call for us; but a skirmish occurring near us, he was hindered, and we had to get back by ourselves. In urging our horse over fast to make the best of it, he broke the swingle-tree in ascending the Red-lion hill, and our chair began to run back down the hill. With the help of my ribands and Nancy's garters we mended the break, and at length succeeded to get over the ferry, and finally to reach home, where we recounted our adventures to the great wonderment and grateful thanksgiving of our family friends.

☞ In conclusion, we presume it will surprise the reader, as it has ourself, to learn from the preceding how much the peaceful, quiet country town of Burlington was once stirred and excited by the haps and incidents of war. So much said of a place that has never had a mention of any thing in our revolutionary history, may serve to show how very much has been omitted by those narrators who have only aimed to speak of great and leading battles and events—and yet, herein is preserved a domestic picture of its vicissitudes and emotions, more touching and graphic than many of far more consequence. It is one thing to show the evolutions of battles, and it is another thing to show how the casualties and excitements of war affect families and individuals. Such was our war as seen and felt by a thoughtful, intelligent and peace-loving lady.

And now, by way of contrast, we shall add, from another manuscript diary, the thoughts and feelings of a young lady near Washington's camp at Whitemarsh, full of the zeal of whiggism and the admiration of the gay and chivalric spirit of martial life and array—to wit:

Incidents of the Revolutionary War, as observed and journalized by a young lady of Philadelphia, (S. W.,) residing near the American camp at Whitemarsh—to wit:

North Wales, Sept. 25, 1777. As I have no means to send letters from this our retreat to my young friend, D. N., I shall endeavour to *journalize*, for her future inspection, some of the doings, and thoughts, and observations which possess the mind of her young friend, the writer.

Yesterday, which was the 25th September, two Virginia officers called at our house, and informed us that the British army had crossed the Schuylkill. Presently another person stopped and confirmed what they had said, and besides told us, that Gen. Washington and his army were near Pottsgrove. Well, thee may be assured we were *sadly scared*. However, the road was very still until evening, when we heard a great noise at the door. All of us went out to see. It was a large number of wagons, with about 300 men of the Philadelphia militia. They begged for drink, and several pushed into the house, where some of them were saucy enough, which caused some of us women soon to make our escape in much alarm. But, after a while, perceiving that the officers were gentlemanly and the soldiers civil, we returned, and when they left we gave them our good wishes.

September 25, H. Jones came riding along, and said the British and Hessians were at Skippack road, and that we should see some of them. Our parents discredited it, but we fearful girls allowed ourselves to be much disturbed. In the evening, O. Foulke came and told us that Gen. Washington had come down as far as the Trap, and that Gen. McDougall's brigade was stationed at Montgomery. This he had from Doctor Edwards, aid to Lord Stirling.

September 26. Cousin Jesse has heard that Gen. Howe's army had moved towards Philadelphia. This excited our fears for you. After a while somebody came screaming, Sally, Sally! I ran in a moment, and behold it was the light horse come indeed! They rode up to the house, and inquired if we had horses *to sell!* The officer took two glasses of wine, and then all rode off. They belonged to Lee's troop. In the evening we heard very heavy firing, and we hear that the American army will be within five miles of us to-night. Our minds are all engrossed with these things—we think and talk of nothing else. So much for our retreating from the city to *avoid* the alarms of war!

Here passes an interval of several weeks, with nothing particular to chronicle.

October 19. Now for news and uncommon scenes! Resting in bed this morning, and ruminating, I was aroused by Liddy, and called to hear a great commotion of drums and rattling wagons. We dressed and got down stairs speedily. The news was that the British had left Philadelphia, and that our army was marching after to take possession. We went out to see the army pass. I thought it strange to feel so little fear. Soon after, several officers called to get some refreshment, but none of consequence until the afternoon, when two genteel men of the army rode up and made their salutations, and asked if they could have quarters for Gen. Smallwood. Aunt thought she could accommodate them. Then one of the officers dismounted, and wrote "Smallwood's quarters" over the door, which saved us from straggling soldiers. When left alone, we dressed for effect and adventure! Soon we had Doctor Gould, from Carolina. While he was yet present, the general arrived, with his six attendants, and having also a large guard of soldiers, with horses and baggage-wagons—quite a family! Soon there was much running up and down stairs. Presently we were introduced to Gen. Smallwood, Captain Furnival, Major Stoddard, Captain Finley, Mr. Prig, Mr. Clagen, Col. Wood and Col. Line. The two latter are Virginians, and indisposed. The general and suite are Marylanders. Some of them supped with us, the others with Jesse. What a new situation for us! I don't, however, feel afraid, although among so many officers, and the yard full of soldiers. They eat and talk like other folks, and deport themselves with elegance.

October 20. I dare say that thee is impatient to learn my sentiments of these officers—so while they are yet sleeping in their chambers, I'll draw their characteristics for thy contemplation. General Smallwood is a tall, portly, well-formed, martial man, having the deportment of a gentleman, a good understanding, and much humanity of nature. Col. Wood seems to be one of the most amiable of men—tall, genteel, a very agreeable countenance, and is a married man. Col. Line is not married, so let me be temperate in his praise. He is monstrous tall and brown, is very sensible, and agreeable in conversation. Of Capt. Furnival, I may say that he has one of the finest faces I ever saw—has a very fine person, light hair in thick profusion to help his face. But the glory of the squad is Major Stoddard, so bashful, so famous, &c. He should come before the captain, but never mind. I at first thought him cross and proud, but I was mistaken. He is but about nineteen; is nephew to the general, and acts as major of brigade. He can't be called graceful, but his mind is superior. Finley is wretchedly ugly, and went away last night. Cols. Wood and Line, and Doctor Gould, dined with us, when I dressed in my chintz, and looked smart enough.

October 26. A very rainy day, which keeps the officers in the house. In the afternoon the general and officers took tea with us. After supper I went into aunt's, and there saw the general, Col. Line and Major Stoddard. There the major got upon the notion of having me to sing—think of that! He was very facetious and clever—he has the softest voice, and never pronounces the R. [He was afterwards secretary of the navy.]

To-day arrived Col. Guest and Major Letherberry—the latter a young lawyer, who has no lack of tongue.

October 27. This evening there came a parson belonging to the army—how shall I describe him! He is near seven feet high, thin and meager—he affords no interest. Yet such as he fell in love with Liddy at sight! But he has a better rival in Col. Guest, a charming man and a brave officer.

November 1. The army has had orders to march to-day, the regulars first. The officers are all to dine with us to-day. In the evening several of them came to take of our tea.

November 2. The militia marches, and the general and his officers leave us. I feel sorry to lose their agreeable company. We saw them turn the road and go out of sight, and they have our good wishes for their safety and welfare.

December 5. Oh, Debby! I am all sensitive with fear! The English have come out to attack our army. They are on Chestnut hill, and our army three miles this side. What will become of us at only six miles distant! The battle of Germantown, and the horrors of that day, are still vivid in my imagination.

December 6. To our surprise, suddenly entered the young Major Stoddard. He could scarcely walk; poor fellow, he was sick from fatigue and cold; he looked pale and dejected; he was soon put to bed, and quickly he found rest in sleep. Next morning he rose quite renovated. He was every now and then listening for firing, and said in that case he must be off. He remained to tea, and next day he set off again to the army. He said he should always be near us in the event of an enemy's approach.

I have been reflecting how readily we can get reconciled to perils and alarms. Formerly the idea of being within ten miles of a battle ground was appalling; but now, although within six miles of two large armies, we can be easy and cheerful.

December 8. We have cause of joy—the British have returned to Philadelphia without a great fight.

December 11. I have made two new acquaintances—a Captain Lipscomb and a Mr. Tilly—the former a tall, genteel man, in delicate health, with the finest head of hair I ever saw—a light, shining auburn, negligently tied and waving down his back—"loose flowed the soft redundance of his hair." Tilly is a wild, noisy mortal, above the common size, a ruddy face, a great talker and laugher—he keeps the house in continual mirth and merriment by his oddities. Again we were surprised by the presence of Major Stoddard. While he was here we got up an admirable joke upon Tilly, by using the fine effigy of a British grenadier to be placed near his bed chamber, and to give the alarm of "the British have come!" The figure looked so real, that when Tilly saw it, he made off by a byway, and ran off a great way, to the great amusement of the family and the three or four officers present.

December 14. The officers still here, and full of their jokes on Tilly for his retreat. To-day we were visited by Captain Smallwood, a pretty little fellow, brother to the general.

December 20. General Washington's army has gone into winter quarters at Valley Forge, and we shall now have a solitude before us.

February 7, '87. We have passed several weeks without any thing of moment occurring. We had a visit from Major Jameson and Captain Howard, both of the dragoons. To-day we visited the heights of the Barren hills of Whitemarsh, and had an extensive prospect of the country, and saw there the traces of the encampment, and many ragged imitations of chimneys, and many other objects of ruin—telling the tale of what *had been.*

May 11. Paper is scarce with us, which restricts my *notitia.* I had laid aside my pen; but this evening, when seated at tea, we were aroused by the approach of light horse, and soon there followed 1600 men, under Gen. Maxwell. We thought they would pass; but soon came in the general, with Col. Brodhead, Major Ogden, and Captain Jones. The general is a Scotchman, with little to prepossess. The colonel is very martial and fierce. Ogden is genteel, with a strong nose. Captain Jones might be called a conqueror, being tall, elegant and handsome. Their brigade is to be encamped about three miles from us, where we have been out to see their encampment, and got scared by the challenge of the pickets.

June 2. Capt. A. S. Dandridge made his appearance here with his troop of horse. He is to be called the handsomest of men.

June 3. An introduction to Major Clough, Captain Swan, and Mr. Moore, all of the cavalry—they had come to dine with Dandridge. In the evening Lieut. Watts took tea with us. Saw several squads of cavalry to-day, passing off toward Skippack road. We felt at first afraid they were British. They belonged to Col. Sheldon's regiment of dragoons, and one of the captains (Stoddard) came to see us.

June 5. We have a call of a squadron of dragoons, under Major Jameson, with Captains Call and Nixon. They said they fully believed that the British were about to leave Philadelphia. After breakfast, they all set off for Valley Forge camp.

June 19. We have astonishing news, that the British have really left Philadelphia. This is delightful news! Our army is about six miles off, on their march to the Jerseys. I now think of nothing but returning back to the city, after an exile of twenty months.

Philadelphia, July, 1778. It has now pleased kind heaven to restore us back safely to our home in the city! My heart danced and my eyes sparkled with pleasure at this event. The very noise and rattle of the city was all music to my senses, so glad was I to be again *at home!*

☞ It cannot escape the observation of a considerate reader, that after all we have heard of the deprivations and sufferings of the *officers* of the revolutionary army, that we have here a fair representation of a gay and cheerful set of men, well clad and well fed, &c. We see, too, by the facts in their case, how very imposing were their easy manners and gay military array, upon the feelings and judgments of the female sex. How it affects the heart to consider withal, that the then young, gay and sportive spirits, who then so actively shone in the drama of life, are now, nearly all, no more! *Sic transit gloria mundi!*

Valley Forge Camp.—This place having been made memorable in our history by the sufferings of our army there in the winter of 1777–8, I was induced to make the place a visit fifty years after, say in July, 1828. As we approached the towering "camp hills," near the Valley Forge, what emotions pressed upon the reflecting mind! On those hills were miserably hutted the *forlorn hope* of the country in its day of gloom and peril. The name and the actions of the great father of his country, and the weight and burthen of his public cares at that place and season, pressed upon the recollection!

On these hills they constructed long rows or lines of log huts for their winter quarters, placed them on the sun side, made numerous stockades and bristling pikes for defence along the lines of trenches. To this purpose, and for their necessary fuel, they cut off an entire forest of heavy timber, which now is again covered by another growth of trees in full stature over the whole site. Poor sufferers, surrounded as they were by fuel, vain were their efforts to subdue the freezing cold of that exposed winter. Their clothes were scanty, their blankets in rags, and their feet in general without stockings, and almost shoeless! Sad are the recitals which witnesses of the neighbourhood have given of their then comfortless state as soldiers. Cases have occurred where sentinels, to keep their feet from perishing, have stood with their feet in their hats or caps.

P. S. Duponceau, Esq., who was one of the young officers of the army at Valley Forge, (aid to Steuben,) relates some facts of stirring interest. They bore, said he, their condition of *half naked* and *half famished* men, with fortitude, resignation and patience. Sometimes you might see soldiers pop their heads out of their huts, and call out in an under tone, "no bread, no soldier!" but a single word from their officer would still their complaint. He has spoken of the Washington family in such picturesque terms as makes us *see the life!* The general, partaking of the hardships of his brave men, was accustomed to sit down with his invited officers, &c., to a scanty piece of meat, with some hard bread and a few potatoes. At his house, called *Moore hall,* they drank the health and prosperity of the nation in humble toddy; and the luxurious dessert consisted of a plate of hickory nuts. There his fortitude and dignity of demeanour always gave new spirits to his officers. Even in those scenes, Mrs. Washington, as was her practice in the winter campaigns, had joined her husband; and possessing always at the head of his table her *mild,* dignified countenance. *Grave,* yet *cheerful,* her countenance and her manner reflected the feelings of the hero whose name she bore. Her presence inspired fortitude, and those who came to her with almost desponding hearts, retired full of hope and con-dence. Baron Steuben used to tell a story of his cook, who left him at that place, saying, as his justification, that where he had nothing on which to display his art, it was of no consequence *who turned the string!*—meaning the cord of the spit.

The drear of that winter was rendered the more affecting because at *that time* no nation in Europe had acknowledged our independence, wherefore all seemed to rest on the efficiency of this ill-appointed army, suffering as it was before the face of a *superior* British force: but, happily for us, then abandoned in good degree to pleasure and revelry, in luxurious quarters in Philadelphia. "Their counsels were foolishness," and the "sceptre had departed" from the sovereign who alarmed us.

A gentleman, (C. M.,) who was an officer at the camp, has told me of some of their hardships there. Fresh beef they could scarcely get; of vegetables they had none, save sometimes some potatoes. Their table was loose planks, rough, as *split* from the tree. *One* dish, of wood, or of pewter, sufficed for a mess. A horn spoon and tumbler of horn was lent round. Their knife was carried in the pocket. Much of their diet was salted herrings, in such injured state, that they would not hold together to be drawn out of the cask singly, but had to be shoveled up *en masse.* Sugar, coffee, tea, &c., were luxuries not seen. They had only continental money, and it was so depreciated it would not allure farmers to sell to them. Yet cheerless as was such a state, when they drew three months' pay, a number of subaltern officers sallied out to seek mirth and jollity, and spent a month's pay in one night of merry revelry! Sometimes, for pleasantry, you might see a squad of men and officers affecting to have received a supply of whisky—of which they were often without—and passing round the stone jug, as if filled, when lo! the eager expectant found it was only water! The fun was, that the deceived still kept the secret, in hopes to pass it to another and another unwary wight. On one occasion of alarm, the men being marched out, in several instances were so shoeless as to mark the frozen ground with blood, when General Conway, who saw it, exclaimed, "My dear fellows, *my heart* bleeds with you!"

The consequence of such hard fare was, that sickness and death prevailed greatly. Then came unavailing sighs for *home*, for all the lost comforts of domestic reliefs. The quietude of the *citizen* was sighed after. Parents, brothers, sisters, or wives and children, were remembered but to increase their regrets. The dysentery was very prevalent, and long trenches in the vale below the hill were dug and *filled* with those "whelm'd in pits, and forgotten in undistinguished mass." If such were the calamities of war, and such *the price* we pay for *self-government*, oh, how sedulously should we now preserve the *attainment!*

Revolutionary exploits of Colonel Allen McLane.—Col. Allen McLane, who died in 1829, at the age of eighty-three years, had been one of the most remarkable men, as a partisan officer, in the revolutionary war. While the British occupied Philadelphia and Germantown, he was a captain of cavalry, in the command of the scouting parties, and, as such, became known to every body as the constant hero of enterprise and daring. Having been personally acquainted with him, in his elder days, I had gathered many facts of his exploits and services, records of which may be found in pages 439 to 444 in my MS. book in the Historical Society, from which I now here make some extracts.

It was the pleasure of himself and his men to make it matter of frolic and fun to attack or alarm the enemy, wherever and as often as they could.

It was an active part of their business to intercept the market people, in the British interest, going to the city, and to turn them over to our suffering army at Valley Forge. Others he would suffer to pass, on condition of taking some supplies, and with them some messages, to brother officers, prisoners in the city. But it was their fun sometimes, when they could kill a well-fed British horse, to have their "spy butchers" carry in the choice pieces, and sell it as bullock beef for gold, which might repay, in part, the trouble and hazard of the imposition.

At one time, in the summer of 1778, going, at the break of day, into the upper end of Frankford, he was surprised by an ambuscade of British, near the Rocks. He quickly discharged his pistol at the nearest, and made good his retreat into the woods. But after gaining the open field, he discovered a troop of British horse. Finding no chance of escape, he made his advance to them as if to surrender. This put them off their guard; when he suddenly turned to the road leading to the Oxford church. Upon this, two of the troop were detached in his pursuit. When they overtook him, they took separate sides of his horse, dropping their swords in their slings, as if he was already their certain prisoner. He, no way conquered, shot his pistol into the breast of the one, and in the instant struck the other from his horse with his empty pistol. He could have brought off their horses, but that the whole troop were seen not far off, and pursued him into the swamp near Shoemaker's mill, where he eluded them. A painting of this encounter used to be exhibited at Peale's Museum.

About the same time, Captain M'Lane had an appointment to meet a citizen, disguised in woman's dress, at daybreak, at the house of one Goodman, (now Maupay's garden,) near the Rising Sun. At the moment he was on his horse, he was seen by a dozen British horsemen, who immediately urged their horses onward to his capture. M'Lane seeing his case was desperate, affected to have his men behind the house, called out to come on, and dashing up to their serjeant, fired his pistol in his face, and made his escape.

In cold weather, when riding abroad in severe nights on the lines, Captain M'Lane often used the rum in his canteen to pour into his boots, to keep his feet from freezing. Ardent spirits was very scarce and dear; and on several occasions of skirmishing, his men have been more eager to cut off the canteens of the British soldiers than to seize their persons.

When the British army entered Philadelphia, it was his business to hover close on their rear, to cut off stragglers. He thus secured several prisoners. Some of his men were disguised as British cavalry. With five of these, he entered Philadelphia in their rear, and on Second-street bridge, then over the Dock creek, he surprised and took off Captain Sandford on horseback. At the same time he was very near to seizing the British adjutant-general, with his papers, in Second near to Chestnut street. Thence he turned up Walnut street, and on the bridge over Dock creek, he surprised and took Frederick Varnum, the keeper of the jail under Galloway. As he went out Walnut street, he met old Isaac Parrish, who told him he had just seen General Howe, and several general officers, out near the Bettering-house. He pressed thither—they had gone—but he, ascending his friend Cormer's house close by, got a view of them proceeding down South street. He thought he could have seized them all, if he had had a few more minutes.

He always avoided to attack the enemy in any town, from a belief that they might be induced to fire the place. That was a reason why no attack was attempted on Philadelphia.

While the British were indulging in the festivities of the night of the Meschianza, below the city, McLane was busy with a stratagem to break them up. He had one hundred infantry, in four squads, supported by Clow's dragoons. At ten at night, they had reached the abattis in front of their redoubts, extending from the Schuylkill to the Globe mill. These divisions carried camp-kettles, filled with combustibles, with which, at the proper signal, *they fired the whole line of abattis!* The British beat the long roll, and their alarm guns were fired from river to river, and were answered from the park in Southwark. The ladies, however, were so managed by the officers as to have taken the cannonade for any thing but the fact, and therefore continued the sports of the night. But the officers in charge on the lines, understood the nature of the assailants, and gave pursuit and assault. He retired to the hills and fastnesses of the Wissahiccon. After day-light the British horse were in full force to pursue him, and finally took his picket and ensign at Barren hill. McLane was afterwards attacked, and swam his horse across the Schuylkill, when some of Morgan's riflemen appeared to his protection. He then turned upon his pursuers, driving them, in turn, into their lines near the city.

This kind of warfare, begun without necessity and without orders, from the love of enterprise and prowess, was the instinctive pleasure of such active and martial spirits to invent and accomplish. Such were the impulses which, on a former occasion, induced McLane to surprise and capture, by night, the British garrison at Paulus Hook, a circumstance already detailed in history.

McLane, at the beginning of the war, was a man of property, all of which he sold, and freely used his money to enlist and clothe a company at his own charge. His continental money went down to almost nothing in his hands; but he cared for none of these things while he could so usefully serve his country. Such a man—so dashing and valorous in his enterprise, lived to become a grave and religious character. He was the father of Secretary McLane, who was also for some time our resident minister at London.

Exploit of the Hyder Ali.—The capture of the General Monk, by the Hyder Ali privateer, on the 8th of April, 1782, by a number of volunteers, of Philadelphia, was so remarkable a case of gallantry as to deserve some special notice.

A number of gentlemen having met in the evening at Crawford and Donaldson's insurance office, in High street, and conversing together on the subject of the captures making in the bay by the General Monk, just then arrived, it was resolved to raise a loan of money by which to fit out a vessel which might succeed to capture her.

The money was obtained of the Bank of North America, upon the responsibility of sundry individuals; the Hyder Ali was purchased of John W. Stanly, and the command given to Captain Barney; a crew of volunteers, chiefly from the regular service, was engaged, and a commission of a letter-of-marque procured.

In a week, the vessel was ready, and sailed. Captain Barney disguised his vessel as a merchantman, and gave his orders, that when he should command to *board*, they should fire coolly and deliberately; and that when he should order to *fire*, then they should board. When arrived in sight, and perceiving that he could outsail the other, he hung over his drag anchors, to impede his way and to deceive the adversary. On being overhauled by the General Monk, Barney called out to prepare for boarding: the other, deceived by the call, directed his men to line the sides of his vessel to prevent them. The moment they were at their posts, Barney cried to his men to board. His men fired: the captain of the General Monk and several of his officers fell. The General Monk returned the fire, but it was too late then to retrieve; so that when Barney ordered his men to fire, they boarded without resistance. There they had a horrid sight—nearly one hundred killed and wounded lay upon the deck. The General Monk carried eighteen nine-pounders, and one hundred and fifty men: the Hyder Ali carried four nine-pounders and twelve sixes, and one hundred and twenty landsmen—four were killed and fifteen wounded.

Howe's Army.—It has probably been a surprise occurring to most *citizens*, that any country so thickly populated as ours on the seaboard, should have ever feared the force of an army small as was the British among us. Judging as peaceful citizens, estranged to the facts of war, we are apt to conceive that such a male population as Philadelphia afforded, we had only to turn out *en masse* and make a meal of the invading foe! But it is wonderful on such occasions, how *very few* of the whole can be brought out in any effect as defenders. I find I am not alone in such reflections on the case. Indeed, they are too natural not to have occurred to others. I find, therefore, that our Captain Graydon, in his memoirs, has thought of these things:—"Why so much caution (says he) against a foe in the very heart of the country? Why not rather turn out en masse, surround, and make a breakfast of Mr. Howe and his mercenaries? Could not a population of two millions of souls have furnished fighting whigs enough for the purpose! Where were the multitudes which used to appear in arms *in the commons of Philadelphia!* Where the ardent town meeting hosts! The tavern declaimers! Where the legions of New England men that hemmed in Gage at Boston! &c. Where the famed Pennsylvanian riflemen! Where the 150,000 men in arms boasted of in General Lee's letter to Burgoyne! These things promised well (on paper)—they were flattering in the extreme! Yet, on the day of trial, the fate of the country and its liberties was always committed to a handful of mercenaries—the very things which were the eternal theme of our scorn and derision. Would it have been credited, in the year 1775, (when patriotic ardour first inflamed,) that a British army of 18,000 men could have marched in perfect security from the Chesapeake to Philadelphia! That a much smaller force could have penetrated through the Jerseys! and that mere partisan bodies could have traversed the southern states in utter contempt of the *long knife* of Virginia!"—The truth is, the mass of citizens have little or no enthusiasm in such perils—they can help on the war by imposing numbers, at *resolves*, and at *the polls;* but when "sacred lives and fortunes" are needed, "*few* take the risk, and *less* the battle share!" Howe, as a martial man, knew this, and pushed his way accordingly.

Things done in Philadelphia.—It is not sufficiently known how very much our common country is indebted to *Philadelphia*, or rather to a few leading individuals therein, for those early measures which led eventually to resistance and to national independence. The acts of opposition—begun in 1774, at Boston, to the Port Bill—was altogether dependent *for its success*, as they believed, on the countenance it might receive from the *middle* colonies, of which *Pennsylvania* was deemed the chief. The spirit of Virginia was previously known to be favourable to resistance; but Pennsylvania, and especially *Philadelphia*, then the metropolis, and a great commercial city, was regarded as so far under the influence of the Quaker population and the merchants—both of whom were averse to a breach with the mother country—that little success was expected unless *Philadelphia city* could first be made hearty in the cause. The merchants had at first gone very cheerfully into *non-importation* resolutions, but when it was ascertained how very much it curtailed their business, several began to swerve. As it was thus early *ascertained* that Philadelphia was the fulcrum which turned a long lever, some leading men there, of closer observation and steadier resolution, entered into a concerted scheme to produce a great political change. These were the Hon. Chas. Thomson, John Dickinson, Esq.,* Governor J. Reed, and Gen. Thomas Mifflin.

The particulars of these facts I ascertained from the perusal of the posthumous papers of Chas. Thomson, extracts and copies of which I have given to the Historical Society of Pennsylvania.

At a general meeting, called at the Coffee-house, these gentlemen became severally speakers. Mr. Dickinson, who had the confidence of the Friends, took moderate grounds, but Mr. Thomson was so vehement and zealous for making a common cause with Boston, that he fainted and was carried out. From causes like these, they were allowed to take the rule of inofficial public measures. They soon took the expedient of calling a convention of the committees of self-created county meetings: by this they could raise a power to overawe and rule the assembly, which was in effect still too loyal for their purpose. Such "a private association, for laudable views," is spoken of in Mr. Jefferson's letter of March, 1822, to Dr. Morse, saying, "this perilous engine became *necessary* to precede the revolution." "It was a collateral power which no man should wish to see in use again"—thus showing in effect the precedent of the Paris and Jacobin clubs. That *we* did better than they, is ascribable to our better materials—men of more substantial patriotism and virtue—true sons of that "virtue" which is made significantly enough to precede in the motto-scroll of our escutcheon of *independence.*

In addition to those city measures, Chas. Thomson, and another of those speakers, made a tour through the country, under the appearance of a summer tour with their ladies, but in reality to better enlist the feelings of the back country people, and to test their disposition, in the event of a revolution.

In July, 1774, the assembly of Pennsylvania, *at Philadelphia*, resolved, "that in consequence of the *differences* which *long* have subsisted with Great Britain, and have been greatly increased by *divers* late acts, it is *absolutely necessary* to hold *a congress of deputies* from all the colonies, and that *a committee* open a *correspondence* to effect that object."

Captain Thomas Forrest.—In 1775–6, Capt. Thomas Forrest (since colonel) formed a company, which were dressed in all the style of *Indians*, with painted faces, leggings and plumes. At same time Captain Copperthwaite formed a company of young Quakers, called the "Quaker Blues." Capt. John Cadwallader (afterwards general) formed a company of "Greens," called, in allusion to the gentility of the members, "the silk stocking company." They were afterwards General Washington's guards, at New York.

Newspapers.—At the early progress of the war, much newspaper controversy appeared in the Philadelphia papers, *pro and con*, thus giving for a time the semblance of *free discussion.* "Common Sense" is controverted in several numbers, by "Cato," who in turn is answered by "the Forester" and "Cassandra."

---

* Author of the Farmer's Letters.

Arnold's Effigy.—In September, 1780, the populace of the city were drawn together in great excitement to witness the degradation and burning of Arnold, the traitor, in effigy. His figure, in regimentals, was placed on a cart and drawn through the city, to be burnt on High-street hill. He had two faces, and a mask in his left hand. Near him was the devil, in black robes, holding out to him a purse of money. Near them were some transparencies of pictures and letters describing the treachery, &c. The procession began from the rear of the present Methodist St. George's church, in Fourth street, headed by several gentlemen on horseback—by a line of continental officers—by several gentlemen in a line—and by a guard of city infantry. The accompanying music played all the way the Rogue's March!

Mrs. Darrach's Conduct.—I have very direct and certain evidence for saying that Mrs. Lydia Darrach (the wife of William Darrach, a teacher, dwelling in the house No. 177, South Second street, corner of Little Dock street,) was the cause of saving Washington's army from great disaster, while it lay at Whitemarsh in 1777. The case was this—the adjutant general of the British army occupied a chamber in that house, and came there by night to read the orders and plan of General Howe's meditated attack. She overheard them, when she was expected to have been asleep in bed, and making a pretext to go out to Frankford for flour for family use—under a pass—she met with Colonel Craig, (who afterwards shot himself,) and communicated the whole to him, who immediately rode off to General Washington, to put him on his guard. The next night, about midnight, the British army in great force marched silently out of Philadelphia. The whole affair terminated in what was called, I believe, the action of Edgehill, on the 5th December; and on the 8th following, the British got back to the city fatigued and disappointed. Lydia Darrach and her husband were Friends. She communicated all the particulars (more than here expressed) to my friend, Mrs. Hannah Haines, and others. Although she was a small and weakly woman, she walked the whole distance, going and coming, bringing with her, to save appearances, twenty-five pounds of flour, borne upon the arms, all the way from Frankford. The adjutant general afterwards came to her to inquire if it had been possible, that any of her family could have been up to listen and convey intelligence, since the result had been so mysterious to him!

Doings of Ladies.—I have heard a lady, Mrs. H———, speak in lively animation of the *feelings* of the ladies during the revolutionary war, when debarred by the patriotism of the times from the usual use of their beloved tea. Although it was proscribed from the tables of all the whigs, it was even then indulged in by some of the whig ladies. It was a practice with some, to avoid observation, by setting a *coffee-pot* upon the tea-table, even while they secretly drank their tea as from the *water-pot;* but if a stranger came in, the coffee pot was sent out (feignedly) for *more* coffee! When tea was asked for at stores, it was sold in sealed papers, under the name of cut tobacco, and similar disguises!

I have preserved an original subscription roll [vide MS. book, p. 340] of ladies who joined to contribute money to raise the bounty to the soldiery under General Washington, and to be forwarded for that purpose to his lady. This was an answer of the year 1780, to that general appeal of the general, to all the colonies, to fall upon some extra expedient to supply the army. On that occasion, the *Philadelphia ladies* set the example; and at the same time invoked all in the union to do the same. This fact gave occasion to this well expressed compliment, to wit: "We cannot appeal in vain for what is good, to that sanctuary where all that is good has its proper home---the *female* bosom!" The darkest day of our revolutionary struggle was cheered by the beams of woman's benevolence. In this city, the ladies *were distinguished* for their active benevolence; and it is a part of *our annals* of which we are most proud.

A lady of Philadelphia, writing to an officer of the British army, who had been intimate in her family before the war, thus expresses to him the patriotic feelings of her sex. The copy was found not long since in MS. among her papers. I give only a few leading extracts, to wit: "I assure you, that though we consider you as a public enemy, we regard you as a private friend, and while we detest the cause you are fighting for, we wish well to your personal interest and safety. I will tell you what I have done. My only brother I have sent to the camp with my prayers and blessings; and had I twenty sons and brothers, they should go to emulate the great examples before them. I have retrenched every superfluous expense in my table and family. Tea I have not drunk since last Christmas, nor bought a new cap or gown since your defeat at Lexington. I have the pleasure to assure you that these are the sentiments of all my sister Americans. They have sacrificed assemblies, parties, tea-drinkings and finery, to the great spirit of patriotism. If these are *our* sentiments, what must be the resolutions of our husbands *but to die or be free!* All ranks of men among us are in arms. Nothing is heard in our streets but the trumpet and drum; and the universal cry is 'Americans to arms!!'"

Philadelphia was at one time gratified with the imposing spectacle of a French army in fine style of military array, consisting of six thousand men. They came down Front street; passed up Vine street, and encamped on the commons at the Centre square. They were fine-looking soldiers, all in clean *white* uniform. They were under command of General Rochambeau, on their way to Yorktown.

When the *camp fever* was so fatal among our soldiery, they were brought into Philadelphia, and placed in any and all empty houses which could be found. In this way, eleven of them were taken to Harbeson's house in High street, near to Second street. There Mrs. Speakman, out of compassion to their sufferings, visited and refreshed them daily, and by much attention recovered the whole of them. They were young men of the Maryland line, and unbounded in their only means of recompense—"the *blessings* of those who were ready to perish." I give this instance as a specimen of a frequent incident of the time. Some striking facts of the kind, I have connected with the notices of "Carpenter's mansion."

The same lady has described to me the awful spectacles she witnessed of interring the dead soldiery from the same fever, at Pottersfield, now the Washington square. They first dug square pits for them along the western side of that square, but as they died faster, they dug a long trench on the whole length of the *southern side*—vis-à-vis Dr. Wilson's church, making two rows of *lengths*, interring double in length on top of one another, and casting the earth over them only as fast as the trench was filled up by the carts bringing the bodies from the various houses of sickness.

While Mrs. Speakman lived in High street, she saw as many as six of *our* vessels of defence float by High street in flames, set on fire by our own people to avoid the British capture. As some of their magazines blew up, it was awful—such was their "earthquake roar!" On several occasions their guns, being loaded, sent off their shot! Several balls came up High street as she looked, and then she and her family went into the cellar for greater safety. This was before the British occupied Philadelphia.

Our war, which has been called "a history of temporary devices," was replete with happy accidents, "such as the pious call providence, and the profane call luck." To instance only a few cases of "time and chance" as they occurred in the person of our financier, Robert Morris, Esq., may afford some interest.

At a time when military stores and clothing were exhausted in Washington's camp, a supply suddenly and unexpectedly arrived in a ship to Robert Morris, fully laden. These he generously gave up to the service.—At another time, when there were no cartridges but those in the men's boxes, and when, if attacked, defeat seemed inevitable, a most seasonable supply of lead arrived to Mr. Morris, in the Holkar privateer, as her ballast, all of which he promptly gave up to the army.—Finally, when the campaign of the year 1781 was concerted with De Grasse, for the investment and capture of New York, from which De Grasse so strangely and provokingly receded, against the will of Washington, on the pretext that it was dangerous for his heavy ships to act in New York bay, and that he must therefore seek his harbour in the Chesapeake, then it was that Mr. Morris gave his impulse to the army, by raising, on his own notes and credit, the means (equal to half a million of dollars) for transporting and supplying the army for its sudden remove to Yorktown, where the sequel was, the capture of the British army, and soon after the *peace!*

I met with an old manuscript letter of Robert Morris, to a friend in England, (in the hand of that gentleman,) written soon after the peace, saying, that although he suffered much loss of property by the war, that on the whole he had gone through the crisis "*about even.*" He said he had lost as many as one hundred and fifty vessels, and mostly, or all of them, without insurance, as he could not get it effected; but, as many escaped and made excellent profits, his losses were made good to him, or nearly so.

Captain Fitz—Refugee.—In the time of the revolution, there was a "British refugee" in Chester county, called "Captain Fitz," whose real name was *James Fitz Patrick.* His exploits as a robber and a depredator on the chattels and persons of the whigs, gave him great renown in his day. He kept, while he was unhung, the whole county in peril. Many parties of armed men were often in pursuit of him. He would often encounter some of them in the most daring manner. Some he would subdue, and then tie to a tree and flog them. My friend, Mr. Lewis, has written a very intereting memoir of this real *Rob Roy* of his day. It might form the basis of a romance. A more fearless spirit never lived; and he was generous and humane on several occasions. He had been an American soldier, but having received some lashes, he deserted under excited feelings of lasting hatred, which ended only with his death.

On one occasion he appeared in disguise at a public meeting, where measures were to be concerted for *his* capture! A young militia captain volunteered to take him, and vapoured much. This vexed *Fitz*, who whispered to his accomplice that he would be sure to rob him of his watch before the company should separate, and that he would do it with an iron candlestick then seen on the shelf. He took it down, and invited the militia captain aside, saying if he would come out a little from the house, he would show him how he might secure *Fitz.* There (it being night) he demanded of him his watch, and telling him he was Fitz, he *snapped* the spring of the candlestick at him, as if it was a pistol—then tied his hands behind him, and sent him back to the company.

The Doanes of Bucks county—Tories.—The Doanes of Bucks county, near Doylestown, were also the terror of their day. They were quite as famous in their section of country, and about the Philadelphia lines, as any hero of the revolution. Their father was a man of good estate, and he and his children of good reputation. When the war came on, they proposed to remain neutral; but because of their non-attendance on militia draughts, &c., and refusing to pay fines, they had their property sold occasionally, and themselves harassed. They got inflamed with their neighbours and the revolutionary rulers, and as they found themselves subjected to legal imposts and penalties, *five brothers* of them set out to live in highways and hedges, and to wage a predatory and *retaliatory* war upon their persecutors. They were men of fine figures and address—elegant horsemen—great runners, leapers, and excellent at stratagems and escapes. They were true counterparts of Captain Fitz. They delighted to injure *public* property; but did *no* injury to the weak, the poor, or the peaceful. They were in league with the British while in Philadelphia, and acted as occasional spies. They became of such importance as to have £300 a-piece offered for their heads. They went generally on horseback —sometimes separate—sometimes together with accomplices. Once with twenty-five mounted men, they *robbed* Robert Hart, the treasurer of Bucks county, of all the public treasure. Some of them were occasionally apprehended, but again broke jail. They were frequently passing between Bucks county and the British lines, and often served as guides to tory parties visiting the city. A part of them being once in a retired log-house were assailed. Two of them leaped out of the window and escaped as the assailants entered. Moses Doan, who remained, fired his pistol at Mr. Heart, which striking his pistol, glanced off into the back of Major Kennedy, of which he died. Then R. Gibson, after Doan had surrendered, shot him so that he died there in Heart's arms. Isaac Doan had his lip shot off. Abraham and Mahlon Doan, having visited West Chester, were pursued and taken by a sheriff and his posse, after having run down their horses, and stood a desperate fight on the road. These two were hung in Philadelphia. Abraham was very stout—has run away from a detachment of horse, by leaping over fences six and seven feet high. Their valour and generosity made them respected above ordinary robbers, and many temperate people in the county expressed or felt great commiseration for them.

Soldiers urging Congress.—In June, 1783, Philadelphia city was put in much excitement by four to five hundred soldiers, who came suddenly upon congress then in session, to demand their arrear of pay, &c. About three hundred of them had been in the barracks, in the Northern Liberties, and these being joined by two companies newly arrived, marched down Fourth street with martial parade, and up High street to Robert Morris's, the financiers office, at the north-east corner of Fifth and High streets. He being apprized of it, left his office in charge of his secretary, Doctor Bensell, who told me he treated their sergeants with much kindness, offering them the insight of all the books and papers, *but had no money!* They grew good-natured, and thence proceeded to Congress hall.

Colonel Garden has said, (vide his Anecdotes) that it was his misfortune to witness this outrage, and to find that too many of the men who had returned with honour from the south, forsook their officers, to join the disaffected. The leaders appeared so obstinate, that General Hamilton, who had gone into the street, endeavoured to conciliate the soldiery, returned to the hall and calmly advised them "to think of eternity, since he confidently believed that within the space of an hour not an individual of them would be left alive!" The state authorities from some cause did not think the things so desperate. They consulted the militia officers about getting out the militia to put them down, but few or none of them seemed disposed to try the measure. The governor of the state, Mr. Dickinson, seemed resolved to prefer pacific measures as equally likely to attain the end Congress, however, to show their dissent, and perhaps, some of insulted dignity, resolved on a removal to Princeton, and actually went off the same night. The *Pennsylvania Packet* of the day, in noticing the circumstance, palliates the rough measures of the men, and intimates that congress should have remained. The mutineers, however, finding themselves baffled in their hopes from congress, began to threaten to take the law in their own hands, and to satisfy their claims from the spoils of the bank. This soon aroused the general sensibility of the city, and soon force enough appeared to put them down had they made the attempt. I have heard that the sequel was, that they all returned to the barracks, and set down quietly not dreaming of harm, when they were all quietly surrounded and made prisoners, by a force under Major General Howe, who had been appointed to that measure by the congress at Princeton. This affair in the parlance of the day, assumed the imposing name of the "Expulsion of the congress from Philadelphia!"

Cornwallis Taken.—The news of "Cornwallis taken!" caused extreme joy in Philadelphia. The news came by express at midnight, and the watchmen in crying the usual hour aroused the inhabitants by adding, "*and Cornwallis taken!*" A moore cheering serenade was never heard sounding abroad in midnight air.

When "the peace" was confirmed the joy was unbounded. A great flag was hoisted on a lofty mast, on Market street hill, and the people fastened their eyes upon it by the hour, transferring to the emblem, the veneration they felt for the achievers of the peace. Great fireworks were prepared up High street, and the crowd being immense, when the arch took fire, and the rockets flew down the street among the people, a great panic ensued, and many contusions and accidents. The houses at night were illumined generally, save those of the *Friends*, which of course afforded fine sport for the rabble in breaking in the *dark panes.*

A MS. letter from Benjamin Franklin to Charles Thomson, dated Passy, May 13, 1784, once in my possession, is interesting. It gives us lasting *good advice*, &c., saying, "Yesterday evening, Mr. Hartley met Mr. Jay and myself, *when the ratifications* of the *definitive treaty were exchanged. Thus the great and hazardous enterprize* is, God be praised, *happily completed!* An event *I* hardly expected *I should live to see!* A few years of peace, well improved, will restore and increase our strength. But our future safety will depend on *our union and our virtue.* Britain will be long watching for advantage to recover what she has lost. Let us beware of being lulled into a dangerous security, and of being enervated and impoverished *by luxury*—of being weakened by internal contentions and divisions —of being shamefully extravagant in contracting private debts, while we are backward in discharging honorably those of the public—of neglect in military exercises and discipline—and in providing stores of arms and munitions of war to be ready on occasion. For all these are circumstances that give confidence to enemies and diffidence to friends; and the expenses required *to prevent a war* are much higher than those that will, if not prevented, be absolutely necessary to maintain one."

After the peace of 1783, the first American flag ever displayed in the Thames, at London, was on board the ship William Penn, (a curious coincidence of an old name, formerly connected with our *infancy* and now with the first token of *manhood!*) The widow of Captain Josiah, the commander, has told me of her being present, when she there saw the indignation of the populace at the spectacle. They saw such excitements among the people, that they so far feared a mobbing as to have had to keep up a vigilant watch, and especially at night, to guard against any violence. Mrs. J. met in company, where one of the ladies expressed her offence at seeing the flag, and her wonder at their presumption in displaying it, when she was pertinently answered, "We win gold and wear it!"

"*Yankee Doodle.*"—This tune, so celebrated as a national air of the revolution, has an origin almost unknown to the mass of the people in the present day. An aged and respectable lady, born in New England, told me she remembered it well, long before the revolution, under another name. It was then universally called "Lydia Fisher," and was a favourite New England jig. It was then the practice with it, as with Yankee Doodle now, to sing it with various impromptu verses—such as

"Lydia Locket lost her pocket,
Lydia Fisher found it;
Not a bit of money in it,
Only binding round it."

The British, preceding the war, when disposed to ridicule the simplicity of Yankee manners and hilarity, were accustomed to sing airs or songs set to words, invented for the passing occasion, having for their object to satirize and sneer at the New Englanders. This, as I believe, *they* called *Yankee Doodle*, by way of *reproach*, and as a *slur* upon their favourite "Lydia Fisher." It is remembered that the English officers among us, acting under civil and military appointments, often felt lordly over us as colonists, and by countenancing such slurs, they sometimes expressed their superciliousness. When the battles of Concord and Lexington began the war, the English, when *advancing* in *triumph*, played along the road, "God save the King," but when the Americans had made *the retreat* so disastrous to the invaders, *these* then struck up the scouted *Yankee Doodle*, as if to say, "See what we simple Jonathans *can do!*" From that time, the term of intended derision was assumed throughout all the American colonies, as the *national air* of the *sons of liberty;* even as the Methodists—once reproachfully so called—assumed it as their acceptable appellation. Even the name of "sons of liberty," which was so popular at the outset, was a name adopted from the appellation given us in Parliament, by Colonel Barré, in his speech!

Judge Martin, in his History of North Carolina, has lately given another reason for the origin of "Yankee Doodle,"* saying, it was first formed at Albany, in 1755, by a British officer, then there, indulging his pleasantry on the homely array of the motley Americans, then assembling to join the expedition of General Johnson and Governor Shirley. To ascertain the truth in the premises, both his and my accounts were published in the gazettes, to elicit, if possible, further information, and the additional facts ascertained, seem to corroborate the foregoing idea. The tune and quaint words, says a writer in the Columbian Gazette, at Washington, were known as early as the time of Cromwell, and were so applied to him then, in a song called "Nankee Doodle," as ascertained from the collection he had seen of a gentleman at Cheltenham in England, called "Musical Antiquities of England," to wit:

"Nankee Doodle came to town
Upon a little pony,
With a feather in his hat,
Upon a macaroni," &c.

The term *feather, &c.*, alluded to Cromwell's going into Oxford on a small horse, with his single plume, fastened in a sort of knot called a "macaroni." The idea that such an early origin may have existed seems strengthened by the fact communicated by an aged gentleman of Massachusetts, who well remembered that, about the time the strife was engendering at Boston, they sometimes conveyed muskets to the country concealed in their loads of manure, &c. Then came abroad verses, as if set forth from their military masters, saying,

"Yankee Doodle *came to town*
For to buy a firelock:
We will tar and *feather* him,
And so we will John Hancock."

The similarity of the first lines of the above two examples, and the term "feather," in the third line, seem to mark, in the latter, some knowledge of the former precedent. As, however, other writers have confirmed their early knowledge of "Lydia Locket," such as

"Lydia Locket lost her pocket,
In a rainy shower," &c.,

we seem led to the choice of reconciling them severally with each other. We conclude, therefore, that the cavaliers, when they originally composed "Nankee Doodle," may have set it to the *jig* tune of "Lydia Fisher," to make it the more offensive to the Puritans. Supposing it, therefore, remembered in succeeding times as a good

* Judge Martin's version of the story is only a reprint of what N. H. Carter had *before* published in his Albany Statesman. The word *Yankee*, we think, is derived from the Indian name *Yengee*, (English.)

hit on them, it was a matter of easy *revival* in New England, by royalists, against the people there, proverbially called by themselves, "Oliver Cromwell's children," in allusion both to their austere religion, and their free notions of government. In this view, it was even possible for the British officer at Albany, in 1755, as a man skilled in music, to have before heard of the old "Nankee Doodle," and to have *renewed it* on that occasion. That the air was uniformly deemed a good *retort* on British royalists, we must be confirmed in, from the fact, that it was played by us at the battle of Lexington, when repelling the foe; again, at the surrender of Burgoyne; and, finally, at Yorktown surrender, when La Fayette, who ordered the tune, meant it as a retort on an intended affront.—Vide La Vasseur's book, vol. i. p. 191.

While on this subject, it may be as well to give a passing notice of another national name just growing into common use—we mean the term "*Uncle Sam*," which first came into use in the time of the last war with England; but the cause of its origin is still unknown to millions of our people.—The name grew out of the letters E. A.—U. S., marked upon the army provisions, barrelled up at Troy, for the contractor, Elbert Anderson, and implied the initials of his name, and U. S. for the United States. It happened that these provisions were inspected there by Samuel Wilson, usually called, among his hired men, "*Uncle Sam*." One of his workmen, on being asked the meaning of the letters, E. A.—U. S., replied, archly, it meant Elbert Anderson and Uncle Sam—(Wilson.) The joke went round merrily among the men, some of whom going afterwards to the frontiers, and there partaking of the very provisions they had assisted to pack and mark, still adhered to calling it Uncle Sam; and as every thing else of the army appointments bore also the letters U. S., Uncle Sam became a ready name, first for all that appertained to the United States, and, finally, for the United States itself—a *cognomen* which is as likely to be perpetuated, as that of John Bull for old England.

Amusing Incidents.—Among the amusing and facetious incidents of the war, which sometimes cheered the heart amidst its abiding gloom, was that of the celebrated occurrence of "*the battle of the kegs*," at Philadelphia. It began at early morn, a subject of general alarm and consternation, but at last subsided, in matter of much merry-making among our American whigs, and of vexation and disappointment on the part of the British. When the alarm of explosion first occurred, the whole city was set in commotion. The housekeepers and children ran to their houses generally for shelter, and the British every where ran from their shelters to their assigned places of muster. Horns, drums and trumpets sounded every where to arms with appalling noise, and cavalry and horsemen dashed to and fro in gay confusion.

The kegs which gave this dire alarm, were constructed at Bordentown, and floated down the Delaware for, the purpose of destroying the British shipping, which all laid out in the stream, moored in a long line the whole length of the city. The kegs were charged with gunpowder, and were to be fired and exploded by a spring-lock, the moment the kegs should brush against the vessel's bottom. The kegs themselves could not be seen—being under water; but the buoys which floated them were visible. It so happened, however, that at the very time (in January 7, 1778) when the scheme was set in operation, the British fearing the making of ice, had warped in their shipping to the wharves, and so escaped much of the intended mischief. The crew of a barge attempting to take one of them up, it exploded and killed four of the hands, and wounded the rest. Soon all the wharves and shipping were lined with soldiers. Conjecture was vague, and imagination supplied many "phantoms dire." Some asserted "the kegs were filled with armed rebels—that they had seen the points of their bayonets sticking out of the bung-holes. Others that they were filled with inveterate combustibles, which would set the Delaware in flames, and consume all the shipping. Others deemed them magic machines which would mount the wharves and roll all flaming into the city! Great were the exertions of officers and men, and incessant were the firings—so that not a chip or stick escaped their vigilance! We are indebted to the facetious muse of Francis Hopkinson, Esq., for the following *jeu d'esprit* upon the occasion. I give an extract:

Those kegs, I'm told, the rebels hold,
Pack'd up like pickled herring;
And they're come down t'attack the town
In this new way of ferrying.

The soldier flew, the sailor too,
And, scared almost to death, sir,
Wore out their shoes to spread the news
And ran till out of breath, sir.

"Arise, arise!" sir Erskine cries:
"The rebels, more's the pity,
Without a boat are all afloat,
And ranged before the city."

The royal band now ready stand,
All ranged in dread array, sir,
With stomach stout, to see it out,
And make a bloody day, sir.

Such feats did they perform that day,
Against these wicked kegs, sir,
That years to come, if they get home,
They'll make their boasts and brags, sir.

[To the son of the same gentleman we have since been indebted for our two national songs, "Hail Columbia" and "Columbians all, the present hour."]

In gathering up these *scrapiana*, it occurs to the mind to think what numerous facts could yet be found among the remains of Robert Morris' office, the great financier. They have never been explored. Wherever they are, they have gone out of the hands of his family. After his embarrassments, they fell into the hands of his friend, Mr. West; but where they repose now I have not learned. That his papers should now be so hidden from the public eye, may show the strange mutability of human things. While he once filled the mouths of all men, he was a most sedulous preserver of all manner of papers passing through his hands—keeping even his own billets, &c.—saying, as his motto, to those about him, "No paper is ever to be lost in my office—they pay no taxes!"

The Gazettes.—James Humphreys, jr., of Philadelphia, being a tory, made his "Pennsylvania Ledger," with the royal arms at the head of it, into "*The True Royal Gazette.*" The whole copy is still extant in the City Library, No. 304. It is appropriately enough labelled by the binder, to wit: "Publication of the Enemy in Philadelphia." It appears to have been the individual copy preserved by Humphreys himself. It having, with the gazettes, all the extra handbills and the private marks of the numbers printed, of all such as were circulated for military or police purposes. Several of them are for the purpose of alluring our men into the British army or navy under promise of land, &c. The Gazette contains such facts, generally prejudicial to ourselves, as we wished to suppress; also statements of occurrences different from ours. They often published intercepted letters ill-spelled, &c., from small officers among us. A number of letters are given as from Washington to Lund W., and to Lady W., said to be very graphic of our poor affairs, &c. A MS. note to one of them imputes them to Mr. Randolph, then in London.

The Gazette of Hall and Sellers was *continued* by James Robertson, under the name of "the Royal Pennsylvania Gazette," at $3 *per annum.* On the 26th of May, 1778, (*his last Number*,) he says he must *suspend* its publication *for some time!* The Gazette, in his hands, frequently announced events occurring in the "rebel army," and all they state respecting the American incidents, they called *rebel* trans actions. "Rebel hills and rebel dales, by rebel bands surrounded."

ALLIANCE FRIGATE.

As Philadelphians, we are entitled to some pre-eminence for our connexion with this peculiar frigate. After the close of the war of Independence she was owned in our city, and employed as a merchant ship. When no longer seaworthy, she has been stretched upon the margin of Petty's island, to remain, for a century to come, a spectacle to many river passengers, and qualified to raise numerous associations of the past, connected with her eventful history in the revolution.

She was the only one of our first navy, of the class of frigates, which was so successful as to escape capture or destruction during the war! In the year 1781, she and the Deane frigate were the only two of our former frigates, then left to our service. She was in many engagements and always victorious—she was a fortunate ship—was a remarkably fast sailer—could always choose her combat—she could either fight or run away—beating her adversary either by fight or flight!

Twice she bore the fortunes of La Fayette across the ocean; De Noailles was also along at one time. When I presented the former with a relic of her timber, he was delighted with it for the mental associations it afforded him. Another relic, which I had given to one of our naval officers, was formed into a miniature ship, held a place at the president's palace, and now rests with General Jackson.

When coming out of the Havanna with the specie intended for founding the Bank of North America, and having for her companion the Lausanne, of twenty-eight guns, under Captain Green, they were encountered by three British frigates. Captain Barry, who commanded her, chose the smallest first, and put her to flight, he having orders to avoid an engagement for the sake of the specie. He then pursued his way. He soon left his consort far behind. He then came up with a French sixty-four, which promised him aid, when he again made back, just in time to save the Lausanne, by engaging the frigate near her, under the command of Captain Vaschan. He killed thirty-eight, and wounded fifty men, as was afterwards ascertained. The Frenchman not joining them, he then went back to her, and got a renewed promise, when they both bore down together, and all the British frigates filled their sails and fled. The Frenchman, as his excuse, said he had a million of dollars on board, and was instructed to avoid an engagement. Captain Brown, who was in the Lausanne as a lieutenant at the time, told me of these facts, and said nothing could surpass the sailing of the Alliance.

Once, when she was in the West Indies, she was pursued all day by one of the fastest seventy-fours in the British navy, and from which she effected her escape by changing her trim

THE ALLIANCE FRIGATE.—Page 338.

FITCH'S STEAMBOAT—Page 446.

She was once pursued by the Chatham ship of war, out of the mouth of the Delaware, and made her way to Rhode Island at the rate of fourteen knots an hour. In so escaping, she was intercepted by the Speedwell sloop of war, which she succeeded to run down.

When arrived off Boston, she there encountered another foe in two sloops of war, both of which Commodore Barry succeeded to capture and to get into Boston. Barry himself was wounded.

She was the favourite ship of Commodore Barry, who began his career in her by taking Colonel Laurens and suite to France; after which she made a successful cruise in the British channel, and took five or six valuable prizes.

The widow of Commodore Barry, remembering with what esteem her husband regarded this ship, had a tea-caddy made out of her wood, as a memento: and I have a picture of the ship, framed with wood from her timbers after she was laid ashore.

She was the second vessel *from Philadelphia* to Canton; the Canton, Captain Truxtun, being the first. The Alliance sailed in June, 1787, to Canton, under the command of Captain Thomas Reed, making her voyage by an unusual route, *outside* of New Holland, and discovering several new islands, returned to Philadelphia on the 17th September, 1788, when she was much visited for inspection, by many of our citizens, still alive to speak of their recollections of that fortunate vessel.

Benjamin Eyre, ship carpenter, of Kensington, purchased the Alliance in 1785, then sold her to Robert Morris; and after making her repairs, she went to Norfolk to load with tobacco for Bordeaux. She returned in the spring of 1787—sailed for Canton under Capt. Reed in June, and returned to Philadelphia in Sept., 1788. In the spring of 1789 she sailed for Cadiz with flour—returned same year —was laid up, and in the spring of 1790 was sold, *broken up, &c.*, and her remains laid upon Petty's island, after having run twelve years of service.

Such a vessel deserves some commemoration and some memorial to revive her fame. She is still a relic visibly uniting the present to the former navy, and in her single remains preserving single and alone the solitary link of union. She led those naval heroes of the infant navy, of which some remained to join their destinies with the present.

Sailors, who are fond of the marvellous, and like to be supported in their perils by the mysteries of luck and charms, should be indulged to have a relic of the fortunate Alliance chiseled into the future Philadelphia war vessels in which they may place their destinies. The magic security will be surely as good as that now attached to "Old Ironsides." Men who can "whistle for wind," love to indulge themselves in such fancies.

A more sober part of the story is, to say a few words respecting her construction, &c., which may possibly lead to useful imitation. She was 125 feet keel payable, and about 37 feet beam—making her about 900 tons. She was thought to be long, narrow, shoal, and sharp, and to be over-sparred. Her main topmast was 18 inches diameter in the cap; main yard 84 feet long, 18 inches in the slings; her topsail yard was 18 inches in the slings. As she was built up the river Merrimack, at Salisbury, Massachusetts, which had a bar at the mouth, it perhaps accounts for a part of her construction as a shoal vessel. She was first sailed in the spring of 1778, soon after her being launched, and was then commanded by a Captain Landais, a *Frenchman*, who was *preferred* to the command as a compliment to his nation, and the alliance made with us, a new people.—She was two years in building—built by John and William Hacket. Six of the persons who built her were alive at Salisbury, ten years ago, and all above seventy years of age.

All these facts may be deemed very minute; but we have our motives. Every nation forms its imaginary legends, and puts itself under the auspices of tutelary beings. We also are of an age now to construct our heroic age, and such a case as the Alliance presents a part of the material.

As Philadelphians, we are entitled to the peculiar distinction of forming the fastest sailing vessel in the world, viz.: the frigate United States, built by Col. Humphreys. With such a model we might have gone on to perfection in the art of ship construction: but our navy rulers have strangely retrograded, until we now have scarcely a good sailer to boast of. The United States frigate has outrun the fastest Baltimore clippers two miles an hour, when running nine and ten knots; but the frigate wanted ten feet more of beam to have been perfect. More beam is wanted by all our fast sailers, and they would have it, were it not to avoid the increase of tonnage duty! It is bad policy which thus induces the hazard of losing ships and lives to save a little money. Give more beam and they will not upset, and will be better sea vessels.

Our Navy.—It occurs to us to say a few words concerning the public marine of the revolution, a branch of the service which has been but little considered and known by the mass of our citizens. Like "the poor Indians," the poor sailors have had no chroniclers to preserve any adequate account of their perils, darings, and devotedness, not even among those who professedly write our naval histories. Then, those who entered the marine service took, freely, all the risks, without any provision by law for themselves, in case of being wounded, or for their families in case of their deaths. In this they wholly differed from the land service, although there were double chances against the adventurers in the sea service; for, generally, they had to make "their way in the deep," with fearful odds against them.

It is a part of our history, that it was not till fifty years after the revolution, that any provision was made by law, to reach cases of killed and wounded in the marine service of that day; and then it was only as an *incidental* measure connected with the land service, and came so late as to find few or none to benefit. Who ever heard of any *mariners*, officers or men, of the revolution, on our pension list? *It don't exist!* Of the three hundred and fifty men blown up in the Randolph frigate, only one of the families ever received any public grant!

Even those who had thus perilled their lives in a peculiarly desperate service, when they had gained prizes and brought them, in numbers, to New London and Newport, and others to the West Indies, never came to any valuable distribution. We could hear of the prize-agents getting enriched, but never the hardy combatants themselves. Such have never been told or heard of. My own father turned all of the little he got of prize-money into sets of silver spoons, still in the family. This he did, he said, to break the proverb, that prize-money *could not last.*

Before sales and settlements could be made of prize cases, the men were again off to sea, to seek more adventures. Some, more or less of them, were captured, and put to swell the masses in the prison ships of New York; and, from suffering and sickness, finally died by thousands, and were whelmed in the Wallabout. *That* was the great charnel house of our revolutionary *mariners.*

To those who would wish an insight into the perils and doings of our sea service, we commend the reading of the Memoirs of Lieut. Nathaniel Fanning, late of the United States' navy. He had been commander of several American private armed vessels in the British channel, sailing out of France. He presents a real picture of sea-peril, and cheerful enterprise and daring. Every two or three days they had a brush with something. We see, in his facts, how they had to work their way through heavy odds, always with a buoyant spirit, and always glorying in the soubriquet of "Yankee boys," and showing their "Yankee daring." He was brother to that Captain Edmund Fanning who projected our late voyages of discovery to the South pole, by Lieutenant Wilkes. Both of the brothers were residents of New York, and Connecticut-born Yankees. Colonel Fanning, their uncle, who had been secretary to Governor Tryon, was on the British side. For more concerning our navy, see App. p. 560.

THE FEDERAL PROCESSION.

"'Twere worth ten years of peaceful life—
One glance at their array."

THIS great procession took place at Philadelphia, for the purpose of celebrating the adoption of the Constitution, and it was appointed on Friday, the fourth of July, 1788, for the double purpose of commemorating the Declaration of Independence of the fourth of July, 1776. Although we have had several processions since, none have ever equalled it in the pomp and expense of the materials engaged in the pageantry. The soldiery then were not so numerous as in the late entry of La Fayette, but the citizens were more numerous, and their attire more decorative. It was computed that five thousand walked in the procession; and that as many as seven thousand were assembled on the "Union Green," where the procession ended, in front of Bush-hill.* The whole expense was borne by the voluntary contributions of the tradesmen, &c., enrolled in the display; and what was very remarkable, the whole of the pageantry was got up in four days!

The parties to the procession all met at and about the intersection of Cedar and Third streets, and began their march by nine o'clock in the morning. They went up Third street to Callowhill; up that street to Fourth street; down Fourth to High street; and thence out that street, across the commons, to the lawn before Bush-hill, where they arrived in three hours. The length of the whole line was about one mile and a half. On this lawn were constructed circular tables, leaving an area for its diameter of about five hundred feet. The tables were covered with awnings, and the centre was occupied by the "Grand Federal Edifice," drawn there by ten white horses—and by the ship Union, drawn there also by ten horses. There an oration, on the occasion, was delivered by James Wilson, Esq., to upwards of twenty thousand people: after which the whole members of the procession sat down to the tables to dinner. The supplies were abundant: no wine or ardent spirits were present; but porter, beer, and cider flowed for all who would receive them; and of these liquors, the casks lined all the inner circles of the tables. They drank ten toasts in honour of the then ten confederated states. As the cannon announced these, they were responded from the ship Rising Sun, laying in the Delaware, off High street, decorated with numerous flags.† The same ship, at night, was highly illuminated. This great company withdrew to their homes by six o'clock in the evening, all sober, but all joyful. The occasion was the strongest which could exercise the feelings of the heart in an affecting manner. It was to celebrate a nation's freedom, and a people's system of self-government—a people recently made free by their desperate efforts, the remembrance of which then powerfully possessed every mind. They then all felt the deep importance of the experiment of self-government, to which their hearts and voices were then so imposingly pledged. The scene ought not to be forgotten. We should impress the recollections of that day, and of the imposing pageantries, upon the minds of our children, and of our children's children. This has been already too much neglected; so that even now, while I endeavour to recapitulate some of the most striking incidents of the day, I find it is like

* This was then Hamilton's elegant country-seat.

† Besides this ship, ten other ships lay off the several streets, highly decorated, and each bearing a large flag with the name thereon of the State in the Union which each thus represented.

reviving the circumstances of an almost obliterated dream. I did not see the spectacle, but it was the talk of my youthful days for years after the event.

The Procession was thus, to wit:

1. Twelve axe-men in white frocks, preceded as pioneers.
2. Captain Miles' company of dragoons.
3. John Nixon, Esq., on horseback, bearing a liberty cap, and under it a flag, with the words thereon, *4th of July*, 1776.
4. A train of artillery—Claypole's corps of infantry—Bingham's dragoons.
5. Several single gentlemen, on horseback, bore silk flags, highly ornamented; one had the words "*New Era*," another, "*17th of September*, 1787,"—that being the day the Convention adopted the Constitution.
6. A car, called the Constitution, in the form of a large eagle, drawn by six white horses, in which were Judges M'Kean, Atlee, and Rush, in their robes. M'Kean bore a splendid flag.
7. Ten gentlemen, preceded by Heysham's infantry, bore each a silk flag, bearing the name of each state.
8. All the consuls of foreign states, in a car drawn by four horses, and each bearing his nation's flag.
9. A carriage bearing P. Baynton, Esq. and Colonel I. Melchor, the latter magnificently habited as an Indian sachem, and both smoking the calumet of peace.
10. The Montgomery and Bucks county troops of dragoons.
11. The "New Roof, or Grand Federal Edifice," was a most splendid spectacle. It was a dome sustained by thirteen columns; but three of these columns were purposely left unfinished. The name of each state appeared on the pedestals; a cupola rose above the dome, on which was a figure of plenty. The carriage and superstructure made thirty-six feet of height. The words, "*In union the fabric stands firm*," were very conspicuous around the pedestal of the edifice. Ten white horses drew this elegant pageant.*
12. After this edifice followed the architects and house-carpenters.
13. The Cincinnati and militia officers, followed by Rose's company of infantry.
14. The Agricultural Society, bearing a flag, followed by farmers; these had two ploughs: one, drawn by four oxen, was directed by Richard Willing, Esq. A sower followed, sowing seed.
15. The Manufacturing Society, with their spinning and carding machines, looms, jennies, &c., bearing a flag. The carriage which bore these, was thirty feet long, and was drawn by ten bay horses:

* This was afterwards placed in front of the State-house, and it is really strange that none of the numerous, elegant silken flags should have been preserved to this time. If some of them still exist, they would be very interesting in processions now. As many of them as now exist should be collected and preserved by the Penn Association, which is, in effect, our Antiquarian Society.

on this weavers were at work, and Mr. Hewson was printing muslin. The weavers marched behind this, and bore a flag of silk.

16. Robinson's company of light infantry.

17. The Marine Society, carrying a flag, trumpets, spy-glasses, &c. They preceded the *Federal Ship Union.* This elegant, small ship was a spectacle of great interest: she was perfect in every respect, and finely decorated with carvings, gildings, &c. Such a ship, completed in less than four days, was a very surprising circumstance. She was thirty-three feet in length, had been the barge of the Alliance frigate, and had been captured by Paul Jones, as the barge of the Serapis.* This ship was commanded by Captain John Green, and had a crew of twenty-five men and officers. They flung the lead, and cried the soundings, and trimmed the sails to the wind as they changed their courses. She was drawn by ten horses, and under her bottom painted canvass, representing the sea, hung over and concealed the wheels of the carriage; another vessel followed her as a pilot, and followed by all the pilots.

18. A frame drawn by four horses, eighteen feet long, contained the frame of the Union's barge, and men at work at the same. The boatbuilders followed, with a flag.

19. The sailmakers, bearing a silk flag, on which was painted the inside of a sail-loft.

20. The ship-carpenters—their silk flag representing a ship on the stocks.

To shorten this article, I briefly state, that the following professions, decorated and bearing emblematic flags, succeeded, to wit: Shipjoiners, ropemakers, merchants and traders—one carrying a ledger; cordwainers had a shop, drawn by four horses, and six men in it at work; coachpainters, cabinet and chairmakers, brickmakers, painters, draymen, clock and watchmakers, bricklayers, tailors, carvers and gilders—these had an elegant car, and men therein at work; coopers, planemakers, whip and canemakers—these had a carriage, and lads at work therein; blacksmiths had a shop, drawn by nine horses, and men therein at work, making plough-irons out of old swords; coachmakers had a shop, drawn by four horses, and men at work therein; potters—a shop and men at work; hatters, wheelwrights, had a stage and men at work; tinplate workers, glovers, tallowchandlers, victuallers with two fat oxen; printers and bookbinders had a stage, and executed printing, and cast out an ode among the people. Ten of these odes to the States, were despatched by carrier pigeons, which issued from the Mercury cap worn by the printer, habited as Mercury. Fourteen different trades then followed; then lawyers, physicians, clergy, and a troop of dragoons, concluded the whole.

I have in my possession, from the papers of the late Tench Fran-

* I had the pleasure to see this ship lying at anchor, in the Schuylkill, at Gray's ferry, where she was long preserved as an attraction to that celebrated garden and inn, and was at last sunk, in deep water, off the mouth of Mayland's creek, a little above the ferry.

cis, Esq., the bills and expenses of the procession and entertainment from which I select the following items, to wit: Federal car cost £37; triumphal car, £15; six awnings, or tents, cost £3 10*s*. to £4, severally; seven thousand feet of scantling, for frames—putting up booths, £32; Indian plate ornaments, £9; six musicians, £6 15*s*.; one hundred rockets used on board the Rising Sun, in the Delaware, £12 10*s*.; sixteen flags, £25; materials for the Federal ship, £55 7*s*.—workmanship gratis. For the good cheer of the multitude at Bush-hill, to which the procession went, there were provided—four thousand pounds of beef, at 4*d*. and 5*d*.; two thousand six hundred pounds of gammon, at 6*d*.; thirty barrels of flour, at 31*s*., and baking the same, at 7*s*. 6*d*.; five hundred pounds of cheese, at 6*d*.; 13 hogsheads of cider, at 60*s*., and one hundred barrels of strong beer, at 30*s*. No spirituous liquors were furnished, and the whole expense was defrayed by private subscription—all this to show the joy of the public at a settled constitution, produced amicably, after the toils and expenses of a long and ruinous war for liberty and self-government.

F. Hopkinson, Esq., has preserved, in his works, a minute detail of all these things, he having been much engaged in the direction of the same. Similar processions were had in New York, Boston, and other cities.

The following song has been attributed to Dr. Franklin. It is said he wrote it for the Procession of Trades in Philadelphia, at the adoption of the constitution, on which occasion a press was drawn along the streets, and copies of it distributed to the multitude.

Ye merry *Mechanics*, come join in my song,
And let the brisk chorus go bounding along;
Though some may be poor, and some rich there may be,
Yet all are contented, and happy, and free.

Ye *Tailors!* of ancient and noble renown,
Who clothe all the people in country or town,
Remember that Adam, your father and head,
The lord of the world, was a tailor by trade.

Ye *Masons!* who work in stone, mortar, and brick,
And lay the foundation deep, solid, and thick,
Though hard be your labour, yet lasting your fame;
Both Egypt and China your wonders proclaim.

Ye *Smiths!* who forge tools for all trades here below,
You have nothing to fear while you smite and you blow;
All things may you conquer, so happy your lot,
If you're careful to strike *while your iron is hot.*

Ye *Shoemakers!* noble from ages long past,
Have defended your rights with your *all* to the *last*.
And *Cobblers*, all merry, not only stop holes,
But work night and day for the good of our soles,

Ye *Cabinetmakers!* brave workers in wood,
As you work for the ladies, your work must be good
And *Joiners* and *Carpenters*, far off and near,
Stick close to your trades, and you've nothing to fear

Ye *Hatters!* who oft with hands not very fair,
Fix hats on a block for a blockhead to wear;
Though charity covers a sin now and then,
You cover the heads and the sins of all men.

Ye, *Coachmakers*, must not by tax be controll'd,
But ship off your coaches, and fetch us home gold;
The roll of your coach made Copernicus reel,
And fancy the world to turn round like a wheel.

And *Carders*, and *Spinners*, and *Weavers* attend,
And take the advice of *Poor Richard*, your friend;
Stick close to your looms, your wheels, and your card,
And you never need fear of the times being hard.

Ye *Printers!* who give us our learning and news,
And impartially print for Turks, Christians, and Jews,
Let your favourite toasts ever bound in the streets,
The freedom of speech and a volume in sheets.

Ye *Coopers!* who rattle with *drivers* and *adze*,
A lecture each day upon hoops and on heads,
The famous old ballad of *Love in a Tub*,
You may sing to the tune of your rub a dub.

Ye *Shipbuilders! Riggers!* and *Makers of sails!*
Already the new constitution prevails!
And soon you shall see o'er the proud swelling tide,
The ships of Columbia triumphantly ride.

Each *Tradesman* turn out with his tools in his hand,
To cherish the arts and keep peace through the land:
Each *'Prentice* and *Journeyman* join in my song,
And let the brisk chorus go bounding along.

SEASONS AND CLIMATE.

"I sing the varying seasons and their change."

It is intended to include in the present chapter only such notable changes of the temperature in the extremes of *heat and cold*, as was matter of surprise or remark at the time of the occurrence, and therefore most likely to arrest our attention in the present day—as a wonder of the past!

As early as the year 1683, William Penn, in his letter to Lord North, of 24th 5th month, says—"The weather often changeth without notice, and is constant almost in its inconstancy!" Thus giving us, at a very slender acquaintance, the name of a *coquettish clime!*

An old-fashioned snow storm, such as we had lately on the 20th and 21st of February, 1829, is the best thing in our country to bring to recollection olden time, when our fathers browbeat larger snow-drifts than have encumbered our fields and roads since *honesty* and *leather aprons* were in vogue! It is cheering to see the towering bank, in a sunny morning, gemmed, like the crown of a monarch, with jewels that receive their splendour from the sun's rays, and reflect them back to ornament the cold white hillock which the clouds have bestowed upon us, to awaken recollections dear, and sensations as cutting as the winter. It tells you of log fires which cheered them in the wilderness, and warmed the pottage which gave them the very hue of health. In short, as said the Literary Cadet, "a snow-storm in its severest form is a mirror, to reflect back olden time, in all its colouring, to the present!" Nor is it less grateful as a winter scene, to behold the occasional magnificent effulgence of an ice-rain, embossing in crystal glory, as if by magic hands, the whole surface of the surrounding works of nature and art.

"For every shrub and every blade of grass,
And every pointed thorn, seems wrought in glass;
In pearls and rubies rich the hawthorns show,
While through the ice the crimson berries glow.

The spreading oak, the beech and towering pine,
Glazed over, in the freezing ether shine—
The frighted birds the rattling branches shun,
That wave and glitter in the glowing sun."

It is probable that the winter of 1682, being the first which Penn saw here, must have been peculiarly mild, for he says he scarcely saw any ice at all, and in the next year, the winter of 1683, which he calls the severest before known, froze up for a few days our great river Delaware! He must certainly have been too favourably impressed by wrong information, for often the river has continued ice-bound for three months at a time. It was, however, grateful intelligence to the colonists then, and must have been a most welcome incident, ill-sheltered as they were, to have such favourable winters.

In his letter of August, 1683, to the Free Society of Traders, he thus speaks of the climate, to wit: "I have lived over the hottest and coldest seasons of the year that the oldest inhabitants remember. From the 24th of October to the beginning of December he found it like an English mild spring. From December to the beginning of March they had sharp frosts with a clear sky as in summer, and the air dry, cold and piercing. This cold is caused by the great lakes that are fed by the fountains of Canada. The air, already sweet and clear, rarely overcast, will refine as the woods are cleared off." Thus the reason of our former colder winters was then well understood. He has another shrewd remark:—"It is rare to want a north-wester; and whatever mists, fogs or vapours foul the heavens by easterly or southerly winds, in two hours time are blown away,—the one is followed by the other—a remedy that seems to have a peculiar providence in it. The winter before this (last) was mild. From March to June they enjoyed a sweet spring, with gentle showers and a fine sky. From June to August, which endeth the summer, they had extraordinary heats."

Thomas Makin's Latin description of Pennsylvania, thus describes our climate as he knew it down to the year 1729, to wit:

> "Nay, oft so quick the change,—so great its pow'r—
> As summer's heat and winter *in an hour!*"
> "*Sometimes* the ice so strong and firm, we know
> That loaded wagons on the river go!
> But yet so temp'rate are some winters here,
> That in the streams no bars of ice appear!"

Professor Kalm, the Swedish traveller, who visited us in 1748–9, has left several facts descriptive of our climate, which he derived from the aged Swedes and by his own observation, to wit:

It snowed much more formerly in winter than in the time of 1748. The weather then was more constant and uniform, and when the cold set in it continued to the end of February or till March, old style; after which it commonly began to grow warm. But in 1748, and thereabouts, it would be warm even the very next day after a severe cold—and sometimes the weather would change several times a day! Most of the old people told Mr. Kalm that spring came much later than formerly, and that it was much colder in the latter end of February and the whole month of May, than when they were young. Formerly the fields were as green and the air as warm about the end of February, as it was then in March or the beginning of April, old style. Their proverb then was "We have always grass at Easter."

The lessening of vapours by cultivation, &c., was supposed to have changed the seasons.

The winters, he understood, came sooner formerly than since. The first Mr. Norris used to say that the Delaware was usually covered with ice about the middle of November, old style, so that merchants always hurried their vessels for sea before that time. But about the year 1748 the river seldom froze over before the middle of December, old style.

An old Swede of ninety-one years of age, told him he thought he had never witnessed any winter so cold as that of the year 1697–8; at which time he had passed the Delaware at Christiana several times with his wagons loaded with hay. He did not agree to the idea of others, that the waters had generally diminished.

Isaac Norris' letter of the 8th of October, 1702, says, "We have had a snow, and now the north-west blows very hard. The cold is great, so that at the falling of the wind the river (at Philadelphia) was filled with ice." On the 10th, he adds, "there is a sign of a thaw, and he hopes vessels may yet get out."

The severity of the winter 1704–5, is thus expressed by Isaac Norris, Senr., to wit: "We have had the deepest snow this winter, that has been known by the longest English liver here. No travelling; all avenues shut; the post has not gone these six weeks; the river fast; and the people bring loads over it as they did seven years ago—[as in 1697–8 aforementioned.] Many creatures are like to perish." Kalm says, "many stags, birds, and other animals died, and that the snow was nearly a yard deep."

Early ice was thus noticed the 23d of November, 1732, saying, it has been so very cold this week past, that our river is full of driving ice, and no vessel can go up or down—a thing rarely happening so early. Many persons have violent colds.

The winter of 1740–1, a great snow. This winter was very severe during the continuance of "the great snow." It was in general more than three feet deep. The back settlers (says the Gazette) subsisted chiefly on the carcasses of the deer found dead, or lying around them. Great part of "the gangs" of horses and cows in the woods also died. Ten and twelve deer are found in the compass of a few acres, near to springs. The chief severity was in February.* Many deer came to the plantations, and fed on hay with the other creatures. Squirrels and birds were found frozen to death. By the 19th of March the river becomes quite open. Old Mrs. Shoemaker, whom I knew, told me of her recollection of that severe winter, to the above effect. Her words were, that all the tops of the fences were so covered, that sleighs and sleds passed over them in every direction. James Logan's letter, of 1748, calls it "the hard winter

* It was in February of the year 1717, that the greatest recorded "snow-storm" of Massachusetts occurred; it being from ten to twenty feet deep—compelling many to go abroad on its frozen crust from their chamber windows.

of 1741,"—as a proverbial name, saying "it was one of remarkable severity—the most rigorous that has ever been known here." Kalm says it began the 10th of December, and continued to the 13th of March, old style, and that some of the stags which came then to the barns to eat with the cattle, became domesticated thereby.

The 1st of November, 1745, is recorded by John Smith, in his journal, as the cold day—the river having frozen over at Burlington, and many boys skating on the Schuylkill.

The 17th of March, 1760, Franklin's Gazette records "the greatest fall of snow ever known in Philadelphia since the settlement!" This is certainly saying much of such a snow so late in March! [as marking the contrast the day I write this—on the 12th of March, 1829, it is mild and thundered several times!] The wind in the snow-storm was from north-east, and snow fell incessantly for eighteen hours. The minutes of Assembly show that the snow in some places gathered seven feet deep, and prevented the speaker and many members to get to town—so the house was adjourned.

The same winter another singular circumstance occurred—told to me by old Isaac Parish, to wit: The day he was married, the weather was so soft and open that the wedding guests had to walk on boards to the meeting to keep them out of the soft mire; but that night the cold became so intense that the river Delaware froze up so firmly that his friend William Cooper, married at the same time with himself, walked over to Jersey on the ice bridge on the next morning. No ice was previously in the river.

Mrs. Shoemaker, who died at the age of ninety-five, told me she had seen the deep snows of 1740 and '80; and from her recollections she said the winter of 1780 was probably as deep as that of 1740, and withal was remarkably cold, so much so as to be called the hard winter of 1780.

The winter of 1784 was also long remembered for its severity and long continuance.

The 17th April, 1797, was a severe snow-storm—when it fell two feet deep—none like it occurred again, *in April*, till the north-east snow-storm of 12th April, 1841, when it fell fifteen or sixteen inches.

Mild Winters.

The following are instances of mild winters, occurring in the years 1790, 1802, 1810, 1824, and 1828, and here severally stated in their detail for the purpose of comparison, to wit:

Extract from A. H's. Diary, for 1789 *and* 1790.

12th mo., 1789.—The weather moderate during the early part of this month. 25th, (Christmas,) a pleasant day—no ice in the Delaware. Three light snows this month. Rain from the 28th to the 31st, but the weather moderate.

1st mo. 1, 1790.—A charming day—no ice in the river and no frost in the ground.

2. This day as pleasant as yesterday—boys swam in the Delaware, and ships sail as in summer—flies common in houses.

12th. Cold—skating on the pavement this morning.

15th. Cold—snow on the ground this morning—continued snowing until 9, A. M.—wind N. E.

2d mo. 7.—Navigation stopped for the first time this winter—morning cold, with a strong wind from south.

13th. Delaware river froze very hard—weather clear and cold—wind N. W. by west.

16th. Delaware river broke up—weather foggy, very damp and warm, with a thaw—wind south-west—heavy rain at night, with thunder and lightning.

3d mo. 11.—The deepest snow on the ground we have had this winter—some ice in the Delaware.

An ancient female Friend informed me she remembered a similar moderate winter sixty years ago, in which the Delaware was not frozen; and that the ensuing summer was healthy and very plentiful, as were the years 1790, 1802 and 1810.

Extract from A. H's. Diary, for 1802.

1st mo. 12th.—Morning very cold—wind high, with flying clouds—this day the most like winter of any this season.

15th.—Remarkably pleasant, wind south south-west—no skating for the boys this winter—not one cake of ice in the Delaware, and even the ponds are not frozen hard enough to bear for two days together—prevalent winds south-west.

19th.—A very great white frost this morning.

2d mo. 5th.—And sixth of the week—by far the coldest morning this season—froze very hard last night—wind west and a very clear horizon.

6th.—Very cold—water froze in chambers first time this season—some ice about the pumps in the streets—Schuylkill froze over.

19th.—Weather moderate—a fine shad in our market this morning—this is remarkable; but what is more so, I find recorded, 1st mo. 19th, 1793, the extreme temperature of the weather exceeds all winters I have known—this day and others preceding may be compared to part of April, as one day this week a shad was caught in the Delaware.

Extract from A. H's. Diary, for January, 1810.

1st mo. 18th.—And fifth of the week—sun rose clear—a heavy white frost—wind south—soon clouded—wind south-west—some rain before noon, and some sunshine—cleared towards evening—wind shifted to north-west, with a heavy gale all night. *Jack Frost* has opened his pipes to some purpose—many people seemed to think we should have no winter, but now it appears to have begun in earnest.

The season of 1824, has been called very mild.

The year 1828. This winter of 1827–28, is remarkable for its mildness—no snow, or frost, and the plough enabled to cut the furrows! mild rains every where instead of snows. The gazettes every where teem with notices of the unusual mild weather. Even boats, in January, are descending the Susquehanna, from as far as the Bald Eagle! Even as late as the 7th of February, it is stated from the Juniata that arks were still passing down that river, and that this is the first winter ever known that the river has continued clear of ice! On the 9th of February a shad, caught near Bombay hook, was bought in the Philadelphia market for the Mansion-house hotel. This, so far, has been the rainy winter.

The mildness of the winter prevented the usual storing of ice for the fish markets, &c.—a thing unprecedented. One person laid in his ice in one day in November. On the 13th and 14th of April, 1828, came a snow storm!—much snow—not cold.

An elderly gentleman remarks on this season, that "the winter of 1827–28, is past, and such a one precisely has never occurred during sixty years of my observations. There were two events differing from any mild winters I ever remember, viz.: so much absence of the sun—but one day in December clear all day—January 20th, and 21st, clear all day—February 9th, sun rose clear and continued so all day as mild as the month of May—12th, 13th, 14th, 16th, 17th, 19th, 22d, 23d—all these days were clear, the sun shining all day—in one or two days the sun made its appearance nearly all day, and a number of days one, two or three hours--add these to the whole days and it would scarcely amount to seventeen days clear sun—this is one singular trait."

The winter of 1830–1, became just such another rainy winter—remarkable for its numerous mild rains.

The following are instances of Irregularity—to wit:

The 8th of May, 1803, was a remarkable day. It snowed so heavily as to make a wonderful breaking of the limbs of trees then in full leaf. The streets in the city were filled with broken limbs thereby—most strangely showing—"winter lingering in the lap of spring."

On the 13th and 14th of April, 1828, was a snow storm in which much snow fell, but not being cold, it soon after disappeared.

The winter of 1817 was remarkable for displaying some very vivid lightning in the month of January! No snow had fallen before this occurrence. The day preceding it fell a little, but melted the same day. At night it grew warm and rained, accompanied by vivid lightning. During the same night it blew up quite cold, and snowed about half an inch. Very cold weather immediately set in. The papers at Albany and New Hampshire spoke of vivid lightnings also on the night of the 17th of January. Good sleighing occurred at Philadelphia on the 23d of January.

On the 25th of October, 1823, was the *dark day*. There was great darkness at 9 o'clock, A. M., so as to make candlelight desirable. At Norristown they were obliged to use candles. The darkness at New York came on at about 11 o'clock, and compelled the printers to print by candlelight. It was stormy there at an earlier hour. At Philadelphia there was thunder and some rain. At Albany, at 8 A. M., same day, it snowed fast all day, forming a fall of twelve inches, but melted very fast. It thundered there at 12 and at 2 o'clock while snowing! The heavy snow broke the limbs of trees still in leaf, very much. At Newark it lightened and thundered severely, and hailed, and was very dark. On the whole, it was a widespread darkness for one and the same storm.

On the 11th of April, 1824, it thundered and lightened considerably for the first time this spring. Old people tell me they never used to see this occurrence until warm weather. But of late years it has occurred several times in the cold season, and sometimes in March. The Christmas days of 1824 and 1829 were remarkable for their coincidence of singular warmth. The thermometer in the shade at 7 o'clock, A. M., stood at 33°, and at 2 o'clock, P. M., at 63°—both days exactly alike, and on both periods having a gentle wind from the south-west.

There were in *olden time* two memorable "*hot summers*," so called, and referred to in many years afterwards—the years 1727 and 1734. I describe the latter from the gazette of the time, to wit:

July, 1734.—The weather has been so hot for a week past, as has not been known in the memory of man in this country, excepting the "hot summer" about seven years since. Many of the harvest people faint or fall into convulsions in the fields, and 'tis said in some places a multitude of birds were found dead. The names of five inhabitants dying of the heat are given. Subsequent papers confirm the extreme heat in the country, and the deaths thereby.

I ought to have mentioned too, that as early as the year 1699 Isaac Norris, Sen. [Vide Logan MSS.] speaks then of the "hottest harvest season he had ever before experienced. Several persons died in the field with the violence of the heat."

An elderly gentleman tells me that on the 1st of October, 1770, memorable as the then election day, was well remembered as a snowy day! From that time to this he has never witnessed it so early again. Since then, he thinks the earliest snows have not fallen earlier than the 1st of November. The middle of November has been regarded as an early snow. Often he has seen "green Christmas,"—that is—no snow till after Christmas, at least not such as to lay on the earth.

The night of the 11th April, 1826, was remarkably cold. It

froze so hard as to bear a wagon loaded with flour on a muddy road. Some snow on the ground at same time. On the 12th of April at sunrise the mercury stood at 24. Old people say they never saw it so cold at that season. One remembers a deeper snow on the 10th of April, about forty years ago, when he went abroad in a sled.

Comparison of time past and time present, derived from a Thermometrical Table of the years 1748 *and* '49, *compared with the years* 1823 *to* '26.

MONTHS.	YEARS. 1748.	1749.	1823.	1824.	1825.	1826.
October, ...	64°	——	58°	59¾°	64⅔°	
November, ...	54¾	——	44⅓	48½	48	
December, ...	49½	——	39½	44½	41⅓	
January, ...	——	33½°	——	41	39	40½
February, ...	——	40	——	38¾	39	
March, ...	——	50	——	44	50¼	
April, ...	——	62	——	58	58½	
May, ...	——	75	——	66	67	
June, ...	——	81	74½	74¾	78¼	
July, ...	——	87½	78½	79	83¾	
August, ...	——	85	78½	75¾	79⅔	
September, . . .	——	80½	69½	69⅓	71⅓	

I am indebted to the investigation and diligence of my friend Samuel Hazard, Esq., for sundry notices hereinafter given, respecting our winters, from 1681 to the year 1800. Besides the surprise which some of the facts will excite, they may prove useful as data for comparison with years to come. Mr. Hazard's larger collection of facts on the same subject may be found in his published book, the Register.

Winters at and near Philadelphia, from 1681 *to* 1800.

1681. December 11. The river froze over that night. The Bristol factor, Roger Drew, arrived at Chester from England, with settlers for Pennsylvania, where they lay all winter.

1704. Snow fell one yard deep.

1714. February. Flowers seen in the woods.

1720. February 23. The river is now clear of ice.

November 11. "My ink freezes, which obliges me to conclude." *Close of a merchant's letter, dated Philadelphia.*

December 20. Our river is full of ice, and the ship Prince of Orange, which is going with a flag of truce and Spanish prisoners to St. Augustine, is in great danger.

December 27. The river being now clear of ice vessels are falling down.

1721. December 19. No vessels arrived since our last, the river being full of ice.

December 26. do. do. do. locked up.

1722. January 2. River still locked up.

——— 6. Vessels get up to New Castle.

——— 9, 16, 22. River still locked up.

February 6. Vessels cleared and entered.

1723. January 1. Weather is yet very moderate, and our river open.

——— 6. Weather is yet very moderate, and river free from ice.

December. Vessels enter and clear through the month.

1724. January 18. River very free from ice.

December 15. On Thursday last a violent storm of wind and rain; tide overflowed the wharves. Two outward bound vessels returned for fear of ice, of which our river is very full.

December 22. River full of ice.

——— 29. Some driving ice, but not so as to prevent vessels going up or down.

1725. March 3. Snow fell near two feet deep last night and yesterday, which has not been known for some years.

December 21. River is very full of ice, though several vessels came up with it; no arrivals or clearances mentioned till 18th July.

1727. March 30. Weather and floods prevented the legislature from meeting at the time to which they stood adjourned.

1728. January 23. We have had very hard weather here for nearly two weeks; so that it has frozen our river up to such a degree that people go over daily, and they have set up two booths on the ice about the middle of the river.

January 30. River still fast.

February 7. Some say the ice is driving near Bombay hook. River here still fast. No clearances mentioned till March 5.

December 31. 36 vessels, besides small craft, frozen up at docks, viz.: large ships 14; snows 3; brigs 8; sloops 9; schrs. 2.

1730. January 20. We had here such a deep snow, the like not known these several years. River full of ice; no vessels can pass.

1733. January 18. Great snow at Lewes; ice driven ashore by a north-east storm.

1734. January 1. River continues open, and weather very moderate; winter hitherto as moderate as for many years past.

1736. January 6. River is fast and full of ice.

February 25. Two whales killed at Cape May.

1737. January 20. Weather very cold; persons frozen to death; a vessel below cannot come up on account of the ice.

1740. March 15. Ice broke up in the Delaware.

December 19. River unnavigable from this to 13th March.

1741. January 8. Our river has been fast some time, and we heard from Lewes that 'tis all ice towards the sea as far as the eye can reach. Tuesday and Wednesday are thought to have been the coldest days for many years.

1741. March 5. The severity of the winter complained of throughout the country. Cattle dying for want of fodder; many deer found dead in the woods, and some came tamely to the plantations and fed on hay with other creatures.

March 13. River navigable. The winter extremely long and severe.

April 19. We hear from Lancaster county, that during the great snow, which, in general, was more than three feet deep, the back inhabitants suffered much for want of bread; that many families of new settlers had little else to subsist upon but the carcasses of deer they found dead, or dying, in the swamps or runs about their houses. The Indians fear a scarcity of deer and turkeys, &c.

1742. January 22. Comet visible for some time.

February and March. Entries and clearances—no mention of ice.

December. Entries and clearances—no mention of ice.

1748. January 26. A vessel ashore on Reedy island, cut through with the ice—no entries or clearances—severe weather—a man frozen to death on a flat in Mantua creek.

1754. January 15. Our river is now, and has been for several days quite clear of ice.

1755. January 14. There is so much ice at present in the river, that our navigation is stopped.

January 21. Clearances from this date forward.

1756. January and February. Clearances through the month.

March 18. On Friday night we had a violent N. E. snowstorm, which did considerable damage to the vessels at the wharves, and probably on the coast. This is the first mention of snow. Arrivals and clearances continue through the month. There is no intimation that the navigation was interrupted this winter.

1759. January 4. Our river is so full of ice that no vessel can stir.

1760. March 20. On Sunday last, we had a violent N. E. snowstorm, when, considering the season of the year, and the time it lasted, (18 hours,) there was the greatest fall of snow that has been known, it is said, since the settlement of the province.

1761. December 24. Navigation quite stopped—measures for relief of the poor.

1764. December 31. Delaware frozen over in one night—passable next morning.

1765. February 7. On Tuesday last, an ox was roasted whole on the river Delaware, which, from the novelty of the thing drew together a great number of people.

1765. February 28. Our navigation is now quite clear, and several vessels have come up.

March 28. On Saturday night last, came on here a very severe snow-storm, which continued all night and next day, when, it is believed, the greatest quantity of snow fell that has been known (considering the advanced state of the season) for many years past, it being said to lie about 2, or 2½ feet on a level, and in some places deeper. A great number of trees are destroyed; some torn up by the roots, others broken off; and the roads so bad that there is scarcely any travelling.

1766. January 9. River quite fast since Friday last—weather very severe.

1767. January 1. Our river is so full of ice that navigation is at a stand. Thermometer, 6°; on 2d, 5°.

December 24. The cold weather of Saturday night filled the river so full of ice, that vessels could not depart; but on Tuesday there was a fine thaw accompanied with rain, and the weather is now moderate, and we hope the navigation will soon open again.

1768. February 11. Our river is now so clear of ice, that vessels get up and down.

March 24. On Saturday night last, we had a most violent snow-storm from N. E.

1769. January. Arrivals and clearances through the month.

February 23. Since our last, have had a fine thaw, warm sun, and some rain, by which our navigation is now clear.

1771. December 26. The cold has been so intense for three days past that navigation is at a stand—river full of ice.

1772. March 16. During the last week there fell large quantities of snow, in many places two feet deep—a good deal of ice in the river.

1773. January 20. River full of ice—navigation stopped.

——— 21. Thermometer in open air, on east side of the city, at 2 P. M., 8° above 0; at 4 P. M., 7°; at 6 P. M., 5°; at 10 P. M., 4°.

1779. February. Leaves of willow, blossoms of peach, and flowers of dandelion were seen.

1780. January. On Sunday morning last, at a fire at the French consul's, the weather was so severe that many of the engines were rendered useless by the intense cold. During this month, the mercury, excepting one day, never rose so high in the city as to the freezing point.

March 4. The Delaware became navigable after having been frozen nearly three months. This is denominated *the hard winter*. Ice 16 to 19 inches thick—frost penetrated the ground from four to five feet. During this winter the ears of horned cattle, and the feet of hogs, exposed to the air, were frost-bitten. Squirrels perished in their holes, and partridges were often found dead.

1781. January 27. The winter, thus far, hath been remarkably mild, so that the earth has scarcely been frozen half an inch deep, or the smallest ponds covered with ice strong enough to bear a dog.

1782. February 6. About a week since, the extremity of cold was felt here. On Tuesday afternoon the thermometer fell very low. This day the mercury was within the bulb, and in some instances it fell 4° below 0, being the greatest excess of cold experienced here for many years. It is needless to say, the Delaware, opposite the city and for several miles downward, is covered with a fixed and strong floor of ice.

1783. December 26. The navigation stopped, and in a few days the river was frozen over opposite the city, and continued so till 18th of March. 29, snow.

1784. January 13. On Tuesday and Wednesday a most remarkable thaw, attended with a warm, disagreeable, unwholesome vapour, which, in the evening, was succeeded by a sharp N. W. wind, and clear sky, so that, within a few hours, we have experienced a transition from heat to cold, of at least 53 degrees. The suddenness and severity of the frost has entirely bound up the navigation.

1785. January 3. Vessels attempt to go down, the moderate weather having so far cleared the ice; but on the evening of the 4th, the harbour was entirely frozen across.

January 20. Frozen from side to side: broke up in four or five days, and was entirely free from ice: all vessels from below came up.

1786. January 21. Our weather has been remarkably mild for the greater part of the winter, until Friday (17th) last, when it grew cold, and froze the river, in a few days, from side to side at the lower part of the city.

1789. January 3. Owing to moderate weather, the navigation is again restored, and many vessels have departed. The three lower bridges on Schuylkill were carried away by the breaking up of the ice, and one of them nearly destroyed.

1790. January 2. Such an open winter as the present has not been known in this city since it was founded—boys bathing in the river as if it were summer—wharves crowded with wood—oak 15 shillings—hickory 25 shillings.

March 10. The only considerable snow this winter—only remained on the ground three days. Yesterday morning, thermometer at 4°.

December 18. River frozen over and stands—boys skating—continued closed till 18th January

1793. January 14. Hail.

——— 18. The extreme temperateness of this season exceeds every winter remembered by the oldest inhabitants of Philadelphia, for now we have April weather.

1795. January 21. The sky has continued almost invariably without a single cloud, for a long time past. Flies were seen a few days ago. Indeed, there was an expectation with many people, that there would be no ice during the present season—about the middle of last week, however, a frost came. On Monday morning, January 19th, at 7 o'clock, the thermometer, in the open air, was so low as 12°—a great part of the river was frozen over.

1796. February 9. Navigation interrupted by driving ice for about a week past: yesterday a vessel came up. The winter to this time the most moderate I ever remember for forty-five years—very little interruption by floating ice. Schuylkill is frozen so as to bear people on it, but not very safe for many in a place.

December 6. Within ten days we have had very cold weather. The Susquehanna has closed—men and horses cross daily. It is not within man's memory to have seen the river so low of water, or to have closed so early. Snow, in Philadelphia, two inches deep.

December 24. Severe cold as remembered for forty years—snow two feet deep at the westward.

1797. January 10. River still closed—loaded wagons come over on the ice—weather as cold as remembered these fifty years.

1799. January 1. Snow—more snow in the last six or eight weeks than remembered for several winters in the same time and season, and very cold weather most of the time.

January 3. Snow. 4th, Delaware full of ice. 5th, snow. 6th, ice in the Delaware stopped, and boys skating on it—snow on the ground about three inches deep. 9th, snow.

February 9. Delaware clear of ice.

——— 25. Extremely cold. Skating on the Schuylkill, and the ice in the Delaware stopped.

March 12. Deep snow on the ground. A very long and severe winter this has been.

1800. January 1. The winter, thus far, has been remarkably open, there having been very little ice in the Delaware, and that very thin.

January 29. Last night coldest this season—the Delaware being frozen from side to side, though very little ice in it last evening.

March 8. Snow without intermission for twenty-five hours—near two feet upon a level.

December 23. The weather, except some cold nights, has been remarkably open. No ice in the Delaware—this day being remarkably warm for the season—the like not remembered since the British army were here, in 1777 and '78.

Those who are curious to examine later years, may find the record in Hazard's Register.

The Climate of Philadelphia and adjacent country

Has been much investigated by Dr. Benjamin Rush, in 1789, and revised in 1805. The facts of which may be consulted at large in Hazard's Register of Pennsylvania, vol. i, p. 151.

Among his facts are these, to wit: The climate has undergone a material change since the days of the founders—thunder and lightning are less frequent; cold of winters and heat of summers less uniform than they were forty or fifty years before. The springs are much colder, and the autumns more temperate. He thinks the mean temperature may not have changed, but that the climate is altered by heat and cold being less confined than formerly to their natural seasons. He thinks no facts warrant a belief that the winters were colder before the year 1740, than since that time. He observes, that there are seldom more than twenty or thirty days in summer or winter in which the mercury rises above 80° in the former, or falls below 30° in the latter season. The higher the mercury rises in hot days, the lower it usually falls in the night. Thus, when at 80° by day, it falls to 66° at night; or when at only 60° by day, it only falls to 56° at night. The greatest disproportion is most apparent in August. The warmest weather is generally in July; but intense warm days are often felt in May, June, August, and September. The variableness of weather in our state, he observes, lies south of 41°, and beyond that the winters are steady, and in character with the eastern and northern states. Our intense cold seldom sets in till about the 20th or 25th of December—"as the day lengthens the cold strengthens,"—so that the coldest weather is commonly in January. The greatest cold he has known at Philadelphia was 5° below zero, and the greatest heat 95°. The standard temperature of the city is 52½°. The month of June is the only month which resembles a spring month in the south countries of Europe. The autumn he deems our most agreeable season. The rains in October are the harbingers of the winter, so that, as the Indians also say, the degrees of cold in winter can be foreknown by the measure of rain preceding it in the autumn. The moisture of the air is greater now than formerly, owing probably to its now falling in rain, where it before fell in snow. Finally, he says, "We have no two successive years alike. Even the same successive seasons and months differ from each other every year. There is but one steady trait, and that is, it is uniformly variable."

Spring and Summer Occurrences,

Being such notices of facts as were deemed rare for the season at the times affixed in the following memoranda, to wit:

1736. April 22. Hailstorm near the city; hail as large as pigeons' eggs.
1750. May. This is the coldest May ever known. Several frosts, and some snow.
1772. April 2. Fell in several places six inches snow.
1783. May. A heavy hailstorm, believed the heaviest ever known here--did not extend far in width—stones fell of half an ounce—many windows were broken.
1786. May. Remarkable for the absence of the sun for two weeks, and a constantly damp or rainy weather. It continued for forty-two days, being all the time a cold north-east storm, and no sight of the sun.
1788. August 18th and 19th. There fell seven inches of rain.
1789. This spring remarkably backward—peaches failed—no cherries or strawberries—quite uncomfortable to sit without fires until June.

In July. Very hot weather—by 10 o'clock, A. M., the meats in the market putrefy, and the city mayor orders them cast into the river—merchants shut up their stores—thermometer at 96° for several days—in August fires became agreeable.

1793. April 1. Blossoms on fruit trees are universal in the city—birds appeared two weeks earlier than usual.

May 22. To the end of the month a continuance of wet and cloudy weather—wind mostly at north-east, and so cool that fire was necessary most of the time—the summer of this year was the "yellow fever" calamity.

1795. The latter end of June and beginning of July were remarkable for the continuous daily raining—perpetually interrupting the hay harvest—and then came a great flood.
1796. July 26. The most plentiful harvest remembered.
1797. April 7. The peaches and apricots in blossom.
1799. April 3. Frost last night. 11th. Some ice in the gutters. 20th. Some ice in the morning.

June 6. Black and white frost in the Neck.

1801. May 28. Hay harvest near the city.
1802. April. Several frosts this month and in May—fires agreeable.
1803. May 7. Ice—on the 8th a snow which broke down the poplars and other trees in leaf—on the 15th a fire was necessary.
1805. Summer—no rain after the middle of June, all through July—heat 90 to 96 degrees—pastures burnt up and summer vegetables failed.
1807. April 3. Snow.

June 13. Fire necessary.

August and September. The influenza prevailed.

1809. April 13. The houses covered with snow like winter.

" 26. Ice as thick as a dollar.

May 6. Ice. 13th. Grass frozen. 30th Frost—the coolest May remembered for many years.

1810. April 1. Snow on the ground. 3d. Spits of snow.
May 13. White frost for several mornings. This year was remarkable for its abundance and excellence of fruits.

1811. July 3. Warm dry weather for some time—Indian corn suffers—a finer dry hay harvest not remembered—between 3d and 9th, hot weather continued from 94 to 97°.

1812. April 13. Snow and rain.
May 4. Rain and snow. 8th. Frost. 22d. The spring very backward—fires necessary. In July the grain harvest was daily interrupted by rain, and was so long deluged that it grew and sprouted while standing.

1816. June 5. Frost. 10th. So severe as to kill beans. 11th. Severe frosts at Downingstown—destroyed whole fields of corn.

1818. July 22. Monday last rain fell four inches.

1824. July 20. Storm of rain and hail at Chester.
" 28. Unprecedented fall of rain near Philadelphia—doing much damage to bridges, &c.

1825. June 11. Severe heat at 2 o'clock—thermometer at 96° in the shade.

1827. July 20. Peaches, pears and plums in market.

1836. June. The first three weeks were cloudy and rainy every day.

1842. June. The whole month and into July—very rainy and cool.

☞ A glance at such collected instances of remarkable *irregularities* may well serve to repress the oft-repeated exclamations of those who cry, " Who ever saw the like before!" or, " An unprecedented occurrence!" &c. For, at undefined periods, the whole circle of remarkables may be found but a *repetition* of " the thing that hath been."

Indian Summer.

This was a short season of very fine mild weather, which was formerly much more manifest than of later years. It was expected to occur in the last days of November. It was a bland and genial time, in which the birds, the insects, and the plants, felt a new creation, and sported a short-lived summer, ere they shrunk finally from the rigour of the winter's blast. The sky, in the mean time, was always thinly veiled in a murky haze—intercepting the direct rays of the sun, yet passing enough of light and heat to prevent sensations of gloom or chill.

The aged have given it as their tradition, that the Indians, long aware of such an annual return of pleasant days, were accustomed to say " they always had a second summer of nine days just before the winter set in." From this cause, it was said, the white inhabitants, in early times, called it the "Indian summer." It was the favourite time, it was said, of the Indian harvest, when they looked to gather in their corn.

The known amenity of such a season was fixed upon, in olden

time, as the fittest time for the great fair at Philadelphia, which opened on the last Wednesday in November, and continued three days; thus insuring, as they conceived, as many good days before and after the term, for good travelling to and from the same. The fair in the last week of May was also chosen for its known settled weather.

Weather Prognostics.

A curious old almanac of our country, of the year 1700, gives the following rules for prognosticating the weather, to wit:

The resounding of the sea upon the shore, and the murmur of winds in the woods without apparent wind, show wind is to follow. A murmur out of caves portendeth the same.

The obscuring of the smaller stars is a sign of tempest. Also, if the stars seem to shoot, winds will come from that quarter the star came from.

The often changing of the wind showeth tempests.

If two rainbows appear, it will rain. A rainbow presently after rain, denotes fair weather.

If the sky be red in the morning, it is a sure token of winds or rain, or both, because those yapours which cause the redness will presently be resolved.

If the sun or moon look pale, then look for rain. If fair and bright, expect fair weather. If red, winds will come. If a dark cloud be at sunrising, in which the sun is soon after hidden, it will dissolve it, and rain will follow. If there appear a cloud, and after vapours are seen to ascend upon it, that portendeth rain. If the sun seem greater in the east than common, it is a sign of rain. If in the west, about sunsetting, there appear a black cloud, it will rain that night or the day following, because that cloud will want heat to disperse it.

If mists come down from the hills, or descend from the heavens and settle in the valleys, it promiseth fair hot weather. Mists in the evening show a hot day on the morrow; the like when white mists arise from the waters in the evening.

The circles that appear about the sun, if they be red and broken, it portendeth wind. If thick and dark, it shows winds, snow or rain —which are also presaged by the circles about the moon.

White and ragged clouds appearing like horses' manes and tails, foretelleth great winds—even as the sailors long have said, viz.:

Shagged clouds—like an old mare's tail,
Make lofty ships—to carry low sail.

Thunder in the morning, if it be to the south-westward, and the wind be there, denotes, many times, a tempestuous day; also, a rainbow or water gall, in the west, denotes a stormy wet day. The "sun dogs" appearing in the morning or evening, is a sign of cold, wet, windy weather—especially in winter time.

To the foregoing we might add, as a weather proverb of long standing and observation in our country, that the 17th and 18th of March have always been periods of memorable time. On the 17th, being St. Patrick's day, "he turns up the warm side of the stone"—indicating warm weather must soon follow; and on the 18th, "Shelah comes draggle-tailed," i. e. brings a wet day. In 1760, however, they concerted to bring together a most tremendous snow-storm. We add the following modern rule as a

Weather Denoter.

A wet summer is always followed by a frosty winter, but it happens occasionally that the cold extends no farther. Two remarkable instances of this occurred in 1807–8 and 1813–14. With these exceptions every frosty winter has been followed by a cold summer. The true cause of cold, or rather the direct cause, is to be found in the winter excess of west wind; every winter with excess of west wind being followed by a cold summer; and if there is no cold before, or during a first excess, then a second excess of west wind in winter occasions a still colder summer than the first. It also appears, by repeated experience, that cold does not extend to more than two years at a time. Again, if the winter excess of the east wind be great, in the first instance, the winters will be mild, and followed by mild summers; while summer excess of east wind is itself, in the first instance, always mild; but uniformly followed by cold winters and cold summers, which continue, more or less, for one or two years, according to circumstances.

Rare floods and ebbs.—In 1687, Phineas Pemberton, in his letter, speaks of the great land flood and rupture, at or near the Falls of Delaware. It occasioned much mortality afterwards.

In 1692, 27th of 2d mo., he speaks of the great flood at the Delaware Falls, which rose twelve feet above usual high water mark, owing to the sudden melting of the snow. The water reached the upper stories of some of the houses, built on low lands.

1731, February 16.—Last week we had the greatest fresh in the Delaware, ever known since the great flood at Delaware falls, thirty-nine years ago, in 1692.

In 1733, month of February, "the ice in Schuylkill broke up with a fresh, and came down in cakes of great thickness, in a terrible manner, breaking great trees where the flood came near the low land. It carried off the flats of two ferries, and the water was two and a half feet high on the ground floor of Joseph Gray's middle ferry, which is much higher than any fresh is known to have been before in that river."

1737, February 3.—Sunday night last the ice, thick and strong, broke up with the fresh occasioned by rains and melting of the snow. The water rose near six feet on the floor of Joseph Gray's house at the middle ferry, which is three feet higher than before in 1733.

March 17.—On Wednesday and Thursday last a south-east storm raised the tide higher than known for many years, which did great damage.

1738, April 6, a great storm, at east and north-east, damaged the wharves and much raised the creeks.

1754, January 22, an unusually low tide, owing to a gale from north-west.

1767, January 8.—From the great and unexpected thaw since Saturday last, the ice on Monday broke up, and at the middle ferry carried away all the boats, broke the ropes, tore the wharf, swept off some of the out-houses, &c.

1769, March 16.—Saturday last, a remarkably low tide, owing to the north-west winds. It is said to be two and a half feet lower than common low-water mark in the Delaware; and in the Schuylkill it was so low that the ferry boats could not get to the fast land on either side.

1775, September 3.—The highest tide ever known.

1784, January 13.—Great damage was done by the sudden and extraordinary rise of water occasioned by the thaw and great rain of Thursday last.

March 15.—This morning (Sunday) about two o'clock the ice in the Schuylkill gave way, but soon after it lodged, and formed a dam, which overflowed suddenly the grounds about the middle ferry, and carried off every thing but the brick house—drowning several horses and cattle, and forced the family to secure themselves in the second story till daylight, whither they were followed by a horse, that had sought refuge in the house. The waters did not subside till four o'clock on Monday afternoon* In the Pennsylvania Gazette of the 27th of March, 1784, the particulars of this event are related in the form of two chapters in Chronicles—in Scripture style.

1796, March 18.—A lower tide than recollected for many years—[say since the 26th of December, 1759, when it was lower] owing to a hard gale the night of the 16th instant, and since continued at north-west. The flood tide was two feet lower than a common ebb —the bar visible nearly across—several chimneys blown down.

1804, April 22 and 23.—A very great fresh in the Delaware and Schuylkill, attended with very high tides, occasioned by very heavy rains.

1804, March 20.—The ice gorged above the city, on coming down Schuylkill in a heavy fresh, which occasioned the water to rise to so great a height, that a man on horseback, with a common riding whip, from the Market street wharf, on this side the river, could but just reach the top of the ice piled on said wharf. The ice and

---

* There were 21 persons in the house at the time, of whom only two are now living

water found its way round the Permanent bridge on the west side, overflowing the causeway between the road and the bridge, to a depth that required boating for passengers for some hours.

1805.—This summer Schuylkill lower by three inches than had been known for seventy years—caused by the long and great drought.

1810, January 19.—Lowest tide for fourteen years.

1822, February 21.—The ice and water came over Fairmount dam to a depth of nine feet, and brought with it the Falls bridge entire, which passed over the dam without injuring it, and went between the piers of the Market-street bridge. At this fresh, the general body of water far exceeded the fresh in 1804; as the rising so much then, was owing to the ice gorging above. The fresh of 1822, from Reading down, is considered to have possessed the greatest body of water and ice ever known; at that place the river rose twelve feet high.

1824, April 7.—During the last four months twenty freshets have occurred in Schuylkill.

In 1824, the 29th of July, a very great and sudden land flood was experienced in and around Philadelphia,—the effect of a great discharge of rain, to wit:—

It commenced with light showers about nine o'clock, and from that time there were some intermissions until half after eleven, when the rain recommenced, and continued, with thunder and lightning, for the period of three hours, to pour down such powerful torrents of water, as to deluge all the low lands in the city and neighbouring districts. In these situations many cellars were filled, in some of which sugars and other perishable articles were destroyed, and other goods were damaged. The embanked meadows on the borders of the Delaware and Schuylkill were much injured, and some of the cattle were drowned. Two bridges between Holmesburg and Frankford, and the floating bridge at Gray's ferry, on Schuylkill, were carried away. The bridge at the Flat rock on Schuylkill, and Poole's bridge in Front street, were considerably damaged, and several mill-dams, and bridges across turnpike and other roads, were either carried away or considerably injured. A large quantity of lumber and drift wood was carried down the stream from the borders of the Schuylkill, and a man who was endeavouring to collect a portion of it, was unfortunately drowned yesterday morning, below Fairmount dam. The loss to the county of Philadelphia, and to individuals, must be considerable. The rain which fell, measured by the gauge, four and a quarter inches. In Germantown, it fell eleven inches.

The water rose in Cohocksink creek, four feet higher than is recollected by the oldest inhabitants in the neighbourhood. It was nine inches deep on the lower floor of a house occupied by a Mr White, and his family was apprized of the circumstance by the neighbours early in the morning, having rested in confidence of their being secured from the flood. The house is an ancient one, having been built before the war of the revolution, and during the conflict, was fired by the English; it was afterwards repaired, as many others in the vicinity of our city have been, which were burnt by order of the British.

We measured the height of the water mark left on the wall in the lower room of Messrs. Craig & Co's. cotton factory, and found it four feet above the floor. The machinery was nearly covered with it, and about forty bales of cotton goods were damaged; the dye-house belonging to the factory was inundated, and most of the dye-stuffs destroyed; much of the fencing along the creek was swept away.

At the bridge over the creek on Second street the water rose to about four feet above the crown of the arch, and from a hasty view, there appeared to be about eight or ten cart-loads of lumber across the stream at that point. It is generally believed, that the insufficiency of the tunnel of that bridge to discharge the water was the principal cause of the damage sustained: and from our own knowledge, within the last thirty-five years, the bed of the creek at Second street has been raised five or six feet, thereby lessening the tunnel nearly one-half of its capacity.

At the bridge over St. John street there were fifteen or twenty loads of lumber, casks, privies, &c., together with the plank work of the bridge, swept from its pier at Beaver street. A family residing in a small brick house near Beaver and Third streets were taken from the window of their bedchamber at about two o'clock in the morning, at which time the fresh was at its height.

When the extreme *lowest* tides have occurred in the Delaware, at the city, there have been some rocks exposed near Cooper's upper ferry, which are never seen, even in part, at other times. They were first observed bare in 1769,---then again in 1796,—and at last, again in 1810, generally on the 17th of March. These low ebbs have usually occurred in March, and have been much promoted by strong and continued north-west winds. Those rocks have been seen as much as seven or eight feet out of the water; on such occasions they have always been permanently marked with the initials and dates of visiters, &c. The rocks, in 1810, were but two feet out of the water.

1827, October.—Unusually high tides about full moon.

—— November 14.—Lowest tide recollected for many years—rocks on Jersey channel exposed to view.

1829, March 6.—The ice and fresh came over Fairmount dam five feet six inches in depth, with a very powerful flow of water, and perhaps owing to the addition of a very strong north-west wind, the awful rushing of the waters over the dam appeared, to an observer of both freshes, much more terrifically sublime than that in 1822, although at that time the depth was three feet six inches more than the recent one flowing over the dam. It is most gratifying to know that the Schuylkill navigation and canals, and the Union canal, with their locks and dams, sustained both these freshes, which have occurred since these valuable works were formed, without any injury of importance.

Storms.—1745, March 26.—Friday last a violent gust occurred, which damaged houses and cast down trees.

1747, April 30.—A violent north-east storm did much damage

1750, December 25.—A violent north-east storm last Thursday; it damaged the wharves and sunk some small craft.

1753, November 14.—A violent gale from the east overflowed the wharves, and water lodged in most of the stores.

1770 was "the great September gale," in which was a great loss of vessels all along our coast.

1786, April 1.—A north-east gale, with hail and snow, did much damage.

1788, November 10th and 11th.—A violent storm from south-east caused a heavy swell in the river; many vessels were injured.

1796, January 7.—A violent storm last night did considerable damage.

1805, December 28th and 29th.—A great storm—"a mere hurricane," by which several vessels were sunk at the wharves, and others broke loose and went to pieces.

1819, September 28.—The meadows below the city were overflowed by the great rise of the river in the late gale.

1821, September 3.—A great storm of rain and wind from the north-east destroyed many trees, blew down chimneys, and unroofed the bridge at the Upper ferry. The Schuylkill dam rose much.

The "old fashioned snow storm," (so called) of the 20th and 21st of February, 1829, the liveliest and best picture I have seen of late years of the olden-time snow scenes of my youth, came *on the 14th and 15th January*, 1831, to be far eclipsed by "the deep snow" of this last *memorable time*. It was really cheering and delightful, to rise in the snow-stillness of the *Sunday* morning of the 16th January, when,

"Earth robed in white, a *peaceful* Sabbath held—"

in a double sense,—to witness such towering pyramids and deeply piled banks of glistening snow, all resting after the subsidence of the storm, in calm repose. It cheered the men of olden days, to be thus able to show to the young of the rising generation, the unexpected, and welcome living picture of scenes oft told, but difficult to be conceived, or credited by those youngsters who had never seen them. Hardly expecting to see such another storm, in *my* future life, I determined, at the time, to preserve sundry notices of its effect, &c. throughout the country, not *now* needful to relate. It laid upon the country, and was used upon the roads till the middle of February, actually exhausting all the pleasures of sleighing by its long continuance.

There was a very remarkable storm of *rain* at Philadelphia, at midnight of the 25th of June, 1835, and continued till three o'clock in the morning. It being at time of high tide, the water sewer in Dock street filled, and the street overflowed and filled all the cellars, and even the ground floors of the houses with water. A similar heavy rain occurred on the night of the 1st July, 1842, again overflowing the sewer, and filling the cellars.

Meteors.—1737, May 7, was seen an aurora borealis.

1743, December 8, a comet visible for five or six nights.

1748, April 21, a comet visible for eight or ten nights past.

1750, February 16, a very bright aurora borealis.

1756, December 30, people much surprised with the sight of two mock suns.

1807, October 7, a comet visible.

1814, in November and December a comet is seen.

In 1749, 17th of 12mo.—There was last evening an extraordinary appearance of the aurora borealis, which moved from north-east to north-west, and back again.

In 1764, 21st of July.—There was seen at Philadelphia, at seven in the evening, a great fiery meteor, about fifty degrees above the horizon, of bigger apparent diameter than the sun, which exploded in sight of the city with a report like springing of a mine, when were seen thousands of pieces of fire to diverge.

The meteors of the 13th November, 1833, were the most remarkable ever witnessed. A beholder says, he was sitting alone in a well lighted apartment, at 4 A. M., when he suddenly saw through the window a *shower* of sparks falling past it on the outside. He supposed the house was on fire, and rushing to the door, to his extreme amazement, he found the entire atmosphere filled with *flakes* of fire, (for they fully resembled flakes of snow of a stellated or radiated form,) of a pale rose red, seemingly of an inch diameter, falling in a vertical direction, as thick as he ever saw snow! Intermingled with the smaller *stars*, were a larger kind, equal to one in a hundred of the others, of an intense sapphire blue, seemingly of three to four inches diameter. This shower continued up to broad day light. They were seen all over the United States, and have been variously described, but all agreeing that they surpassed all other known cases.

MEDICAL SUBJECTS.

To note—the thousand ills
Which flesh and blood assail.

UNDER this head it is intended to comprise such facts as have come to our knowledge respecting early diseases; to name some of the plants in use as remedies in primitive days; and to cite some facts concerning some of the earliest named physicians.

Of Febrile Diseases.

1687—Phineas Pemberton, in his MSS., states, that a great mortality occurred at the Falls of Delaware, (in 1687,) occasioned by "the great land flood and rupture."

1699—Isaac Norris, Sen., left among his papers a record, saying, "About the time of the harvest proved the hottest summer he had ever before experienced. Several persons died in the field with the violence of the heat." In the autumn of the same year, the town was visited by a very destructive fever: he says of it, "This is quite the Barbadoes distemper—[i. e., the yellow fever of modern times:] they void and vomit blood. There is not a day nor night has passed for several weeks, but we have the account of the death or sickness of some friend or neighbour. It hath been sometimes very sickly, but I never before knew it so mortal as now: nine persons lay dead in one day at the same time: very few recover. All business and trade down. The fall itself was extremely moderate and open."* Five of his own family died.

Thomas Story, a public Friend, and the recorder of the city, has also spoken of this calamity in his Journal, as being a scourge which carried off from six to eight of the inhabitants daily, and visiting the most of the families. "Great was the fear," says he, "that fell upon all flesh! I saw no lofty or airy countenances, nor heard any vain jesting; but every face gathered paleness, and many hearts were humbled."

The whole number who died was about two hundred and twenty, of whom about eighty to ninety were of the society of Friends.

1717—The summer of this year is mentioned in the letter of Jonathan Dickinson, as a time in which was "great prevalence of fever and ague in the country parts adjacent to Philadelphia."

1741—The summer of this year is called a time of great sickness in Philadelphia—Vide secretary Peters' MS. letter to the proprietary,

* In a letter of subsequent date, he says, that "three years after" the same disease became a scourge at New York, "such as they had never seen before! Some hundreds died, and many left the town for many weeks, so that the town was almost left desolate."

to wit: It was called the "Palatine distemper," because prevailing among the German emigrants, probably from their confinement on shipboard. The inhabitants were much alarmed, and fled to country towns and places; and the country people, in equal fear, avoided to visit the city. From June to October, two hundred and fifty persons died: others, of course, recovered. Noah Webster, speaking of this sickness, says, after the severe winter, the city was severely visited with "the American plague." The same disease, Doctor Bond has said, was yellow fever, supposed to have been introduced by a load of sick people from Dublin.

1743—Some of it also again prevailed in Philadelphia, says Secretary Peters, while at the same time, just such another disease visited New York, and was there considered as certainly "not imported." Joel Neaves' case, who died of it at Philadelphia, was thus described: "He had a true, genuine yellow fever, with black vomit and spots, and suppression of urine—all this from overheating himself in a very hot day, by rowing a boat. He also gave it to others about him, and they to others; yet but few of them died."

1747—Noah Webster, in his work on Pestilence, says, "This year the city was again visited by bilious plague," preceded by influenza.

February, 1748, as said by said Peters' letters, was a time of great mortality in all the provinces; it was called "the epidemic pleurisy." It thinned the country so much, that it was said that servants, to fill the places of others in town and country, were bought in great numbers, as fast as they arrived. The Indians were afraid to come to a treaty by reason of the sickness. It stopped suddenly, before the summer came.

1754—I perceive, by the gazettes, that there were many deaths by reason of the "Dutch distemper."

1755—It had often happened, that the servants coming from Germany and Holland, after being purchased, communicated a very malignant fever to whole families and neighbourhoods where they went. It was of such frequent occurrence as to be called, in the gazettes, the "Dutch distemper." This year I find it stated, that it is now settled "to be precisely the disease known as the jail fever."

Of Smallpox.

This loathsome and appalling disease was of much more peril to our forefathers than to us, in our better management now; to the poor Indians it was terrific and destructive.

The happy art of inoculation was first practised in Philadelphia, in the year 1731; and the first person of note who then devoted himself as a forlorn hope for the purpose of example, was J. Growden, Esq. The circumstance, with his character in life as a public officer in high standing, made his house a place of after notoriety, and is the same venerable and respectable-looking building (when you can see it!) now in the rear of some two or three small houses, since put up, in South Fourth street, vis-à-vis to the first alley below High street. It was then a dignified, two-story, large house, with a rural courtyard in front.

The terror of inoculation was not such in Philadelphia at any time, as seized upon our brethren of New England, and of Boston in particular, in 1721, when their doctor, Z. Boyleston, had his life menaced, his person assaulted in the streets and loaded with execrations, for having dared, with scientific hardihood, to inoculate his only son and two of his negroes.* Even sober, pious people were not wanting there, to regard it as an act of constructive murder, in case the patient died.

We, also, had our public attempts, growing out of the above facts, to forestall the public mind, and to create a religious prejudice against the attempt at inoculation. Our Weekly Mercury, of 1st January, 1722, contains the sermon of the Rev. Mr. Masley, who preached and published against the inoculation of the smallpox, which he calls "an unjustifiable art, an infliction of an evil, and a distrust of God's over-ruling care, to procure us a possible future good!"

Under such circumstances, it became a cause of some triumph in Philadelphia, to publicly announce the success of the experiment on J. Growden, Esq., made in the Gazette of March, 1731, to wit: "The practice of inoculation for the smallpox begins to grow among us. J. Growden, Esq., the first patient of note that led the way, is now upon the recovery."

1701—Is the first-mentioned occurrence of smallpox in the city of Philadelphia. In that year, one of the letters in the Logan MSS. says, "the smallpox was very mortal and general." As early as 1682, the vessel that brought out William Penn had the smallpox on board, which proved fatal to many while at sea.

1726—A ship from Bristol, England, with passengers, had many down with the smallpox; but they, with George Warner, the informant, being landed at the Swedes' church, below the town, and conducted through the woods to the "Blue-house tavern," out South street, all got well without communicating to the inhabitants of the city.

1730—Was called the "great mortality from the smallpox." That year there died of it, George Claypole and his five children. He was a lineal descendant from the Lord General Claypole, who married Cromwell's daughter. His wife Deborah lived to be upwards of ninety years of age. Vide Logan MSS.

1736–7—There are some evidences of the progress of inoculation, for the Gazettes thus state the fact, to wit: From the fall of 1736, to the spring of 1737, there have been 129 persons inoculated, viz.,

Of white men and women,	33	persons.
,, under 12 years of age,	64	,,
Of mulattoes,	4	,,
Of negroes, young and old,	28	,,

* This was the same year it was first attempted in England, after the Turkish manner, upon the daughter of the celebrated Lady Montague.

Only one child died among all the foregoing 129! The above account was framed from the then physicians of that day, to wit: Doctors Kearsley, Zachary, Hooper, Cadwallader, Shippen, Bond, and Sommers, they being the only physicians who inoculated. Doctor Græme had then no share in it, being himself confined with illness the whole time the disease was in town.

1746—Even at this late period religious scruples against the smallpox had not subsided; for I see in a MS. journal of John Smith, Esq., (son-in-law of James Logan,) that he thus intimates his disapprobation of the measure, to wit: "Two or three persons (in one month) have the smallpox, having got it at New York. Inoculation he dislikes, because it seems clear to him that we, who are only tenants, have no right to pull down the house that belongs only to the landlord who built it!"

It was probably about this period of time that Thomas Jefferson (say about 1760) came to Philadelphia, on purpose to get inoculated for the smallpox, and was placed in a cottage house, back from the city, near to the Schuylkill. It was then that Charles Thomson first became acquainted with him, and from him I derive this fact.

Samuel Preston, Esq., an aged gentleman, has given me some ideas of the fatality of the smallpox among the Indians in Bucks county. It got among the Indians settled at Ingham spring, and as they used sweating for it, it proved fatal. Several of the Indians, as they had never heard of the disease, thought it was sent by the whites for their ruin. Such as survived, abandoned the place. Tedeuscung, the Delaware chief, was among the latter.

Of Plants for Medicine.

In the olden time, the practice of medicine and the dependence of the people upon physicians in cases of ordinary sickness, were essentially different from the present. Physicians then were at greater expense for their education, with less compensation for services. Then, all accredited physicians were accustomed to go to England or Scotland to prepare themselves. The people were much accustomed to the use of plants and herbs in cases of sickness; and their chief resort to physicians was in calls of surgery, or difficult cases of childbirth. As the druggist shops have since increased in drugs and mineral preparations, the use of herbs and roots has more and more declined. We have, indeed, since then, brought the study of the names of plants into great repute, under the imposing character of botanical lectures; but the virtue and properties are too often abandoned for a mere classification of uninstructive names. In that day, every physician's house was his own drug shop, at which all his patients obtained their medicine.

I have formerly seen aged persons, not possessing more than the ordinary knowledge of plants for family medicines, who could tell me, in a walk through the woods or fields, the medicinal uses of almost every shrub or weed we passed. It was, indeed, grateful to me to perceive that nothing around us seemed made in vain!

> "Let no presuming, impious railer tax
> Creative wisdom, as if aught was form'd
> In vain, or not for admirable ends."

Thus, in the commons, the Jamestown weed was used, by smoking it in a pipe, for the asthma; the pokeberries, when ripe, and the juice dried in the sun, as a plaster of great virtue for the cancer; sour dock root made an ointment for itch and tetters; burdock leaves made drafts for the feet, to reduce and allay fevers; tea from it was made into a wholesome tonic—the roots were also used; the plant everlasting, much approved for poultices in drawing swellings to a head; of mullein was made a steam vapour to sit over, in cases of bowel diseases; motherwort was used in childbirth cases; catmint tea was used for colic; a vine which grows among field strawberries, called cinque-foil, was used as a *ptsan* for fevers; blackberry roots and berries were used for dysenteries.

In the woods they also found medicines, much of which knowledge was derived from the Indians, as G. Thomas, 1689, says, "there are also many curious and excellent herbs, roots, and drugs of great virtue, which makes the Indians, by a right application of them, as able doctors and surgeons as any in Europe." The inner bark of the oak, and of the wild cherry-tree, were their tonics. Sassafras roots and flowers were used as purifiers and thinners of the blood. People used the leaves of the beech-tree for steeping the feet in hot water. Grape-vine sap they used to make the hair grow. Of the dogwood-tree (its flowers or bark) they made a great cure for dysentery. The magnolia leaf they used as a tea to produce sweat; the berries, put into brandy, cured consumptions, and was a good bitter; the bark of it was used for dysenteries; it could cure old sores by burning the wood to charcoal, and mixing the powder of it with hogs' lard. People used the root of the bayberry-bush to cure the toothach. The cedar-tree berries were used as a tonic, to strengthen a weak spine, to destroy worms, &c. Goldenrod was deemed excellent for dysentery. Boneset, used for consumption and for agues; sweet fern for bowel complaints; pennyroyal, excellent to produce sweats for colds; dittany, for cure of a fever; alder-buds made a tea for purging the blood; elder-berries were used for purges, and the inner bark to make ointment for burns and sores. It is needless to hint at even a few of the numerous plants cultivated in gardens, and laid up in store against family illness:* many are still known. It may suffice to say, in conclusion, that they regarded the whole kingdom of vegetation as appointed for "the healing of the nations." It would be a most com-

* It was an annual concern of the ladies of the family at Norris' garden, in Philadelphia, to dry and lay up various herbs for medical purposes, to be given away to the many who called for them.

mendable adjunct of botany, if to the present exterior and superficial classification of plants, they would investigate and affix their uses and virtues.

Of Physicians.

Those who first came among us, in primitive days, were generally from Great Britain. The names and characters of those we can occasionally see in the passing events of their day, may be generally summed up in the following brief recital, to wit:

Thomas Wynn, an eminent Welsh physician, who had practised medicine several years, with high reputation, in London, and his brother, came to this country, in 1682, with the original settlers, located themselves in Philadelphia, and were the earliest physicians of the city. Dr. Griffith Owen arrived in the prime of life, and is said to have done the principal medical business in the city, where he was highly distinguished for his talents, integrity, and zeal. He died in 1717, about the age of seventy years, and left a son, who practised some time after his father's death.* Dr. Græme came from Great Britain, with the governor, Sir William Keith, in the year 1717. He was about thirty years of age when he arrived, had an excellent education and agreeable manners, and was therefore much employed as a practitioner, and greatly confided in by his fellow citizens. Dr. Loyd Zachary probably commenced the practice of medicine between 1720 and 1730, and died in the year 1756, in the meridian of life, greatly and most deservedly lamented. He was one of the founders of, and a very liberal contributor to, both the College and the Hospital. Dr. Kearsley, Senr., was for many years a very industrious practitioner both in medicine and surgery. He was not deficient in public spirit. The public are more indebted to him than to any other man for that respectable edifice, Christ church; and by his will he founded and endowed a hospital for poor widows. He educated Dr. John Redman, and Dr. John Bard, of New York. This eminent physician, Dr. John Kearsley, had been so very popular in the assembly, that on several occasions he has been borne home from the hall on the shoulders of the people; he died in 1772, at the age of eighty-eight years, having been in the city since the year 1711, happily dying just three years before he could witness the outrage offered to his respectable nephew, Dr. John Kearsley, who was obnoxious as a tory, in 1775. Dr. Cadwallader Evans was one of the first pupils of Dr. Thomas Bond, and completed his medical education in England. He was descended from a much venerated early settler, and had a great share of public spirit as well as of professional worth. In 1769, some observations appeared in the Gentlemen's

* Dr. Wynn also left a son-in-law, Dr. Jones, who enjoyed considerable repute as a physician. Doctors Wynn and Owen were of the society of Friends: the former was speaker of the assembly. To their names might have been added, Dr. John Goodson, chirurgeon, who was in the city at and before the year 1700. He was also of the society of Friends; also Dr. Hodgson.

Magazine, of London, from Dr. Kearsley, Jun., of Philadelphia, relative to *angina maligna*, which prevailed in 1746, and 1760. "It extended," says the author, "through the neighbouring provinces with mortal rage, in opposition to the united endeavours of the faculty. It swept off all before it, baffling every attempt to stop its progress, and seemed, by its dire effects, to be more like the drawn sword of vengeance to stop the growth of the colonies, than the natural progress of disease. Villages were almost depopulated, and numerous parents were left to bewail the loss of their tender offspring." An essay on the iliac passion, by Dr. Thomas Cadwallader, a respectable physician in Philadelphia, appeared in the year 1740, in which the author opposes, with considerable talent and learning, the then common mode of treating that disease. This was one of the earliest publications on a medical subject in America. Dr. Thomas Bond, about 1754, was author of some useful medical memoirs, which were published in a periodical work, in London. Phineas Bond, M. D., a younger brother of Thomas Bond, after studying medicine some time in Maryland, visited Europe, and passed a considerable time at the medical schools of Leyden, Paris, London, and Edinburgh. On his return, he settled in Philadelphia, where he enjoyed a high reputation for many years. He was one of the founders of the College, now the University of Pennsylvania. About the middle of the 18th century, Dr. Thomson published a discourse on the preparation of the body for the reception of the smallpox, and the manner of receiving the infection, as it was delivered in the public hall of the Academy, before the trustees and others, in November, 1750. This production was highly applauded both in America and Europe, as at that period the practice of inoculation was on the decline. The author states, that inoculation was so unsuccessful at Philadelphia, that many were disposed to abandon the practice; wherefore, upon the suggestion of the 1392d aphorism of Boerhaave, he was led to prepare his patients by a composition of antimony and mercury, which he had constantly employed, for twelve years, with uninterrupted success.

It was reserved for the accomplished Dr. William Shippen, and Dr. John Morgan,* to construct a permanent foundation for the medical institutions of our country. Both these gentlemen were natives

* Dr. Morgan was educated by the Rev. Mr. Finley, at his school at Nottingham, and finished his studies in the Philadelphia Academy: having studied with Dr. Redman, he went into the provincial army a short time, in the French war. In 1760 he visited Europe generally, where he mixed much with the scientific men in London, Edinburgh, Paris, and Italy. On his return home he was regarded as something extra among the people, and as having, perhaps, some of the "eccentricities of genius." The aged citizens still remember him as the first man who ventured to carry a silk umbrella—a scouted effeminacy then!—and also as an innovator in first introducing the practice of sending to the apothecary for all the medicines wanted for the sick! With Dr. Morgan was joined Dr. Chanceller, and Parson Duché, making then a rare trio, in forcing the use of sun umbrellas upon the town! Dr. Rush has said, "the historian who shall hereafter relate the progress of medical science in America, will be deficient in candour and justice if he does not connect the name of Dr. Morgan with that auspicious era in which medicine was first taught, and studied as a science, in this country."

of Philadelphia, and after receiving the usual preparatory course of instruction, repaired to Europe to complete a scientific education. Here they enjoyed ample means of qualifying themselves for the great duties of professors and teachers. Accordingly, in 1762, Dr. Shippen commenced a course of lectures on anatomy and midwifery, accompanied by dissections, to a class of ten students; and this was the first systematic course of lectures on medical subjects ever delivered in America, if we except those delivered at Newport, in 1756, by Dr. Hunter.* In 1765, Dr. Morgan returned from Europe, and was appointed professor of the institutes of medicine, and Dr. Shippen the professor of anatomy: they were the only professors of this new institution until 1768, when Dr. Kuhn was elected professor of botany. In the following year, Dr. Benjamin Rush was chosen professor of chemistry. These learned characters, assisted by the venerable Thomas Bond, as lecturer on clinical medicine zealously devoted their talents to the duties of the several departments of medical instruction. This first medical school in the American colonies, was soon after confirmed and established by the authority of the trustees of the College of Philadelphia, while Dr. Franklin officiated as their president. The Philadelphia Dispensary, for the medical relief of the poor, the first institution of its kind in the United States, was founded in 1786. The College of Physicians of Philadelphia was established in 1787, and the labours of the professors commenced under circumstances eminently auspicious to the improvement of medical science: an unfortunate competition and discord, however, between the medical college and an opposition school, for a time marred their prospects and impeded that useful progress which the friends of the institution and the public had confidently expected. But, in 1790, some important changes took place, and a harmonious union of the contending parties was effected. Dr. Rush was appointed professor of the institutes and practice of physic, and of clinical medicine. From this period the progress and improvement of the institution have been no less honourable to the venerable founders, than beneficial to the community. The commanding talents and profound erudition of Professors Rush, Wistar, Barton, Physick, Dorsey, Chapman, and others, have given the medical school of Philadelphia, a celebrity which will probably long remain unrivalled in the United States, and will enable it to vie with the most elevated seminaries of the European world. It has become the resort of students from every section of our united confederacy. Five hundred, in some seasons, have attended the various courses of lectures; and the inaugural dissertations of those who, from time to time, received its honours, have extended the fame of the school from which they have emanated. At the commencement in June, 1771, the degree of A. B. was conferred on seven, and the

* Dr. Clossey offered anatomical lectures at New York, in November, 1763; and after wards, in 1768, he, and others, proposed regular lectures at King's College, say on anato my, surgery, and physic.

degree of M. D. on four candidates. Such has been the prosperity of this medical institution, the first founded in our country, that from the most accurate calculation that can be made, up to 1830, it is computed that between seven and eight thousand young men have received in struction within its walls, since its establishment; and from this source, the remotest parts of our union have been furnished with learned physicians, who are ornaments to their profession. During the four months' attendance on the lectures, the class expends not less than 200,000 dollars in the city of Philadelphia.

As Dr. William Shippen was the first public lecturer in Philadelphia, having commenced his anatomical lectures there in the year 1762, and thus leading the van in an enterprise which has become so eminently successful to others in subsequent years, it may be curious now to learn the means by which he became qualified to be such a leader—told in all the frank simplicity and naiveté of a father (himself a physician) sending forth his son as an adventurer for knowledge abroad, and as a candidate for future usefulness and fame at home. The letters and MS. papers of the father having been under my inspection, I have gleaned as follows, to wit:

In September, 1758, Dr. William Shippen, Sen., writes to several persons in England to speak of his son William, whom he then sends to London and France to perfect him in the medical art. "My son (says he) has had his education in the best college in this part of the country, and has been studying physic with me, besides which he has had the opportunity of seeing the practice of every gentleman of note in our city. But for want of that variety of operations and those frequent dissections which are common in older countries, I must send him to Europe. His scheme is to gain all the knowledge he can in anatomy, physic, and surgery. He will stay in London for the winter, and shall attend Mr. Hunter's anatomical lectures and private dissections, injections, &c., and at the same time go through a course of midwifery with Dr. Smellie; also enter a pupil in Guy's Hospital. As soon as the season is over he may go over to France and live with Dr. Leese in Rouen, and there study physic until he can pass an examination and take a degree. Then he may return to London, revisit the hospitals, and come home." At the same time his good father does not forget "that better part," and earnestly commends his son to the spiritual guidance and oversight of his beloved friend, the Rev. George Whitfield.

Under such auspices, Dr. Wm. Shippen, Jr., was enabled to return to his country a doctor indeed, and ably qualified by his teaching to raise a school of eminent pupils in the healing art. He directed his chief attention to the department of anatomy. His first public advertisement reads thus, viz.: "Dr. Wm. Shippen's anatomical lectures will begin to-morrow evening, at his father's house in Fourth street. Tickets for the course at five pistoles each. Gentlemen who incline to see the subject prepared foi the lectures, and to learn the art of dissecting, injecting, &c., are to pay five pistoles additional."

Thus the lectures were begun in a private house in the year 1762, with only ten students. But he lived to enlarge his theatre—to address a class of two hundred and fifty persons, and to see medical lectures diffused into five branches—and Edinburgh itself rivalled here at home! He died at Germantown in 1808, and was succeeded by Dr. Wistar.

Who now knows the locality of this first lecture-room! Or does any body care to transfer their respect for the man, to the place where he began his career! It was on the premises late Yohe's hotel, in North Fourth street, a little above High street—then sufficiently out of town, with a long back yard leading to the alley opening out upon High street along the side of Warner's bookstore—by this they favoured the ingress and egress of students in the shades of night. It was at first a terrific and appalling school to the good citizens. It was expected to fill the peaceful town with disquieted ghosts—mobbing was talked of, and not a little dreaded. It was therefore pretended that they contented themselves with the few criminal subjects they could procure; which was further countenanced by a published permission to him, by authority, to take the bodies of suicides. As the dead tell no tales, the excitement of the day subsided, and the affair was dropped in general parlance—save among the boys, with whom it lingered long—

"And awful stories chain'd the wondering ear!
Or fancy led, at midnight's fearful hour,
With startling step, we saw the dreaded corse!"

The tales had not subsided when I was a boy, when, for want of facts, we surmised them. The lonely desolate house is yet standing by the stone bridge over the Cohocksink, on north Third street, which all the boys of Philadelphia deemed the receptacle of dead bodies, where their flesh was boiled, and their bones burnt down for the use of the faculty! The proofs were apparent enough:—It was always shut up—showed no out-door labourers—had a constant stream of running water to wash off remains—had "No Admittance," for ever grimly forbidding, at the door; and from the great chimney about once a fortnight issued great volumes of black smoke, filling the atmosphere all the country round with a most noisome odour—offensive and deadly as yawning graves themselves! Does nobody remember this! Have none since smiled in their manhood to find it was a place for boiling oil and making hartshorn—took thus far out of town to save the delicate sensations of the citizens, by the considerate owner, Christopher Marshall! The whole mysteries of the place, and the supposed doings of the doctors, was cause enough for ghost's complaints like these:

"The body-snatchers! they have come
And made a snatch at me;

It's very hard them kind of men
Won't let a body be!
Don't go to weep upon my grave
And think that there I be;
They haven't left an atom there
Of my anatomy!"

But more certain discoveries were afterwards made at Dr. Shippen's anatomical theatre in his yard. Time, which demolishes all things, brought at last all his buildings under the fitful change of fashion "to pull down and build greater,"—when, in digging up the yard for cellar foundations, they were surprised to find a grave-yard and its materials, not in any record of the city! A thing in itself as perplexing to the moderns who beheld the bones, as it had been before the trouble of the ancients!

In 1765, it is publicly announced that "Dr. John Morgan, professor of medicine in the College of Philadelphia, is to join Dr. William Shippen, Jr., in delivering lectures. Dr. Shippen to lecture on anatomy, and Dr. Morgan on the materia medica." Thus forming the first combination of lectures in Philadelphia, and indeed in the then colonies—a precedence to which Philadelphia still owes her renown in medical science.

In 1768, the name of Dr. Bond is also publicly announced as to lecture on clinical practice, and Dr. Kuhn on the materia medica—being so much added by the College to the two former lectures.

In 1769, Dr. Benjamin Rush is made professor of chemistry to the College, and at the same time Thomas Penn, Esq., makes a present of a complete chemical apparatus.

In looking back through the "long vista of years that have fled," the memory and the fancy can recreate the imagery of some of the men and things that were. My friend Lang Syne, whose imagination is lively, and his pen picturesque, has portrayed the remembered physicians of his youthful day, in a manner which may gratify those who are not wholly absorbed in their own contemplations, to wit:

One of the earliest, and one of the most vivid recollections in this city, by the reminiscent, is of the person of old Dr. Chovet, living, at the time, directly opposite the (now) "White Swan," in Race above Third street.* He it was, who by his genius, professional skill and perseverance, finally perfected those wonderful (at the time) anatomical preparations in wax, which, since his death, have been in possession of the Pennsylvania Hospital. These anatomical preparations, the very sight of which is calculated to fill the mind with solemn awe, while beholding not only the streets, but the lanes,

* It might justly surprise the present generation to know that, in 1778, this Dr. Chovet advertised his *anatomical lectures* to take place at his *amphitheatre* at his dwelling house in *Water* street, near the old ferry—to continue during the winter—his charge three guineas. Observe, that Water street, *then*, was the chief place of *residence* to the best families of the business class.

alleys and inner chambers of the microcosm or little world of man, was beheld by the writer only some few years since, forcing back upon the memory the once aged appearance of the doctor, contrasted with the exertions made by him, and apparent to every one who beheld him, to appear active and sprightly in business, cleaving, as it were, to his "last sand." This aged gentleman and physician was almost daily to be seen pushing his way, in spite of his feebleness, in a kind of hasty walk, or rather shuffle; his aged head, and straight white hair, bowed and hanging forward beyond the cape of his black old-fashioned coat, mounted by a small cocked hat, closely turned upon the crown upwards behind, but projectingly, and out of all proportion, cocked before and seemingly the impelling cause of his anxious forward movements; his aged lips closely compressed (sans teeth) together, were in continual motion as though he were munching somewhat all the while; his golden-headed Indian cane, not used for his support, but dangling by a knotted black silken string from his wrist; the ferrule of his cane, and the heels of his capacious shoes well lined in winter time with thick woollen cloth, might be heard jingling and scraping the pavement at every step; he seemed on the street always as one hastening as fast as his aged limbs would permit him, to some patient dangerously ill, without looking at any one passing him to the right or left;* he was always spoken of as possessing much sarcastic wit; and also, for using expletives in his common conversation, in the opinion of those who spoke on the subject, to be neither useful nor ornamental.

An anecdote, strikingly illustrative of the latter, might here be given of the doctor, and a member of the Society of Friends, who had lent him his great coat to shelter him on his way home, from the then falling rain. The coat was loaned by the Friend to the doctor, with a moral condition annexed; which, upon the return of the coat, he declared he had religiously performed—adding, in facetious vein, a supplemental remark to the Friend, descriptive of an unusual propensity he found himself to be labouring under, during the whole time he had been enveloped in a plain coat—having so said and done, they separated on the most friendly terms, with a hearty laugh on both sides.—Does none remember?

Dr. Thomas Say lived in Moravian (now Bread) street, on the west side, near Arch street. Having to pass that way frequently to school, his person became very familiar. In fair weather, he was to be seen, almost daily, standing, dressed in a light drab suit, with his arms gently folded, and leaning with one shoulder against the cheek of the door, for the support evidently of his rather tall and slender frame—now weakened by age. He was the same Dr. Thomas Say who, many years before, had been in a trance, of three days'

* In the above case of Dr. Chovet, we have a striking illustration of the changes of practice. Here was an *aged* physician doing all his visits *on foot*—but now, all think they *must* visit in their carriage.

continuance; during which time (whether in the body or out of the body, he could not tell) he beheld many wonderful matters, as is fully detailed in the "Life of Thomas Say," now extant, and written by his son Benjamin, deceased. He was of fair complexion; and his thinly spread hair, of the silvery white, slightly curled over, and behind the ears—in appearance very venerable, in his speech and manner, mild and amiable—as is well remembered concerning him, while he stood one day affectionately admonishing some boys, who had gazed perhaps too rudely at the aged man, of whom they had heard, probably, that he had seen a vision. He mildly advised them to pass on their way—pressing, at the same time, and with lasting effect, upon the mind of one of them, never to stare (said he) at strangers, and aged men.

The next aged physician of the Old School was Dr. Redman, who lived next door to Dr. Ustick's Baptist meeting-house, in Second near Arch street. The doctor had retired from practice altogether, and was known to the public eye as an antiquated looking old gentleman, usually habited in a broad-skirted dark coat, with long pocket flaps, buttoned across his under dress; wearing in strict conformity with the cut of the coat, a pair of Baron Steuben's military shaped boots, coming above the knees, for riding; his hat flapped before, and cocked up smartly behind, covering a full bottomed powdered wig—in the front of which might be seen an eagle-pointed nose, separating a pair of piercing black eyes—his lips, exhibiting (but only now and then) a quick motion, as though at the moment he was endeavouring to extract the essence of a small quid. As thus described, in habit and in person, he was to be seen almost daily, in fair weather, mounted on a short, fat, black, switch-tailed horse, and riding for his amusement and exercise, in a brisk racking canter, about the streets and suburbs of the city.

He was so well known, that in his rambles about the town, *on foot*, he would step in, without ceremony, at the first public office which presented itself to his view, and upon his seeing any vacant desk or writing table, set himself down, with a pleasant nod to some one present, and begin writing his letter or memorandum. One day, while thus occupied in his writing, he was suddenly addressed by a very forward presuming person, who wanted of him some medical advice gratis. Finding himself thus interrupted, he lifted the corner of his wig, as usual, and desired the person to repeat his question, which he did, loudly, as follows:—"Doctor! what would you advise, as the best thing, for a pain in the breast?" The wig having dropped to its proper place, the doctor, after a seemingly profound study for a moment on the subject, replied, "Oh! ay—I will tell you, my good friend—the very best thing I could advise you to do for a pain in the breast is to—consult your physician!"

These three veterans of the city, in the science and practice of medicine in the time of the colonies—like three remaining apples, separate and lonely upon the uppermost bough of a leafless tree, were finally shaken to the ground, by the unrelenting wind of death, and gathered to the "narrow house," as very readily surmised by the reader, no doubt.

My friend, Mr. P., another Philadelphian, long residing in New York, has also communicated his reminiscences of some of the Philadelphia faculty, as they stood impressed upon his boyish judgment and feelings, which I shall add, to wit:

"I wish to mention the names of a few physicians in my day. Dr. William Shippen, Sen., resided, when he left off practice, in Germantown; at the age of ninety, he would ride in and out of the city, on horseback, full gallop, without an overcoat, in the coldest weather. Dr. Thomas Bond died in 1784; *always rode* in a small phaeton; resided in Second street, near Norris' alley. Dr. Redman resided near the Baptist Meeting, in Second street; *a small black filly* had the honour to carry the doctor on his visits, and would await his return at the door of the patient; the doctor would sometimes kindly lend his creature, but she was sure to throw the rider. Dr. Chovet, a most eccentric man, full of anecdote, and noted for his propensity for what is now termed quizzing, resided in Race above Third street. The doctor was what was termed a tory; was licensed to say and do what he pleased, at which no one took umbrage. He one day entered the old Coffee-house, corner of Market and Front streets, with an open letter in his hand; it was 12 o'clock, change hour, the merchants all assembled. On seeing the doctor, they surrounded him, inquiring what news he had in that letter, which he stated he had just received by a king's ship arrived at New York. In reply to the inquiry, he said that the letter contained information of the death of an old cobbler in London, who had his stall in one of the by-streets, and asked the gentlemen what they supposed the cobbler had died worth? One said £5000, another £10,000, and another £20,000 sterling. 'No, gentlemen, no, you are all mistaken. Not one farthing, gentlemen,' running out, laughing at the joke at the expense of the collected mercantile wisdom of the city. Another time, having been sent for by the Spanish minister, Don Juan, (I forget his name,) who resided in old Mr. Chew's house, in Third, between Walnut and Spruce streets, the weather being rather unpleasant, the ambassador ordered his carriage to the door to convey the doctor home—the doctor, full of fun and joke, directed the coachman to drive by the Coffee-house, which, as he approached, was perceived by the merchants, who immediately drew up in order, hats off, to pay their respects to the Don, as minister from a friendly power. The doctor kept himself close back in the carriage until directly opposite the Coffee-house; the gentlemen all bowing and scraping, when he pops out his head—'Good morning, gentlemen, good morning; I hope you are all well; thank you, in the name of his majesty, King George,' and drove off, laughing heartily at having again joked with the Philadelphia whigs."

The few physicians mentioned in the preceding notices as having their pacing nags, or a little wheeled vehicle, are intended as rarities among the profession. It was only an indulgence awarded to the aged and infirm to submit to motive assistance. Any young man resorting to it would have endangered his reputation and practice. Dr. Rush has told his friends how often he visited Kensington on foot to serve poor sick persons, from whom he expected nothing directly, but by the fame of which, in his successful practice in their behalf, he indirectly was rewarded with his future choice of practice there.* It was not only to walk far, for smaller reward, but the time was before the fashion of umbrellas and boots, that they had to wade through unpaved lanes and alleys without defence against storms of rain, hail, or snow! As if it were inferred that men who professed to heal all maladies, should themselves be invulnerable to the assaults of disease.

In extreme olden time, occasional indulgence was enjoyed by the faculty, under an oiled linen hat cover, and a large shoulder cape of like material, called a roquelaure—it was intended as a kind of storm shed, to shield the upper works only.† Wet feet or drenched lower limbs, with the then hardy sons of Esculapius, were nothing!—or if regarded, it was only as the Indians feel for feeble children—by concluding that those who could not encounter the necessary exposures of the hunter's life, were not worth the keeping.

In tracing some of the leading features of our domestic history of medicine, there is one modern and modish change of practice which has almost subverted all former scruples of sex, and given a large accession of business to the faculty. We mean the transfer of midwifery from the hands of the grandames to professional men. This very thing shows the powerful ascendency of custom. The same ladies are still living who once, in all cases short of the extremities of death, would have resisted the approach of the man-midwife, yet came at length to submit themselves to that assistance. Its introduction as a practice (prevalent as it now is) came into use only since the year 1790. This new measure was deemed in necessary accordance with our new notions of foreign luxuries—in furniture, equipage and dress, and from the same causes, to wit: the greatly increased ability to pay for whatever was deemed modish and novel. The innovation being once adopted in high life, soon "infected downward all the graduated scale," till, finally, the whole service is engrossed by obstetric professors. Mrs. Lydia Robinson, at the age of 70 years, in 1769, had, in her services of thirty-five years, at and near New London, Connecticut, "delivered 1200 children, and never lost one." Can any skill in science surpass that!

---

* The very residence of such a man as Dr. Rush, shows by its locality how little they regarded horses or stabling then—it being a bank house on the east side of Front street, above Walnut. It was long a fashionable location for a physician or gentleman, although it had not one foot of yard.

† Old Mrs. Shoemaker, who saw them in use, said ministers also used them. It hooked round the neck and descended to the loins loose as a cloak all round.

Before this era, the crisis of all our mothers, and the hopes of all our forefathers, was committed to "female women" who, if they had not the science of their successors, had a potent and ready assistant in Dame Nature, (for reason as we will, facts are stubborn things,) and it must be conceded, that the issue, in such hands, was equally satisfactory to all concerned.

Now, the gentlemen of the profession, always men of influence and character, are known in every street and public hall; but then there was a kind of mysterious concealment of the good grandame, that made her, when rarely seen or spoken of among the younger members of the family, a being of some nondescript relation—something *sui-generis*, and as mysterious in her visits or goings abroad as her occupation itself. Some of their names and persons pass in review while we write, but we are aware that they are things not to be expatiated upon with the present generation. But as the office and the service were worthy they had their esteem in days of "Lang Syne"—even to publish elegiac praise. On the 6th of January, 1729-30, was published in the Gazette, the decease of such a useful matron, to wit: "Yesterday died Mary Broadway, aged 100 years—a noted midwife—her constitution wore well to the last, and she could read without spectacles." On this worthy woman was afterwards published an elegy, which in a short time went through tw editions. Who now can show it! Perchance from the muse of Aquilla Rose, or from the poet Keimer! With that loss we have also to deplore the extinction of the first published medical tract in our annals—an essay of the year 1740, by Dr. Thomas Cadwallader, on the iliac passion! But a more modern grandame, drawn to my hand, may close this notice, to wit: "At Second and Dock streets I would remember the house once occupied by Mrs. Lydia Darrach, a whig of the Revolution,* who assisted in increasing the census of the city more than any other lady of her profession. Finally, if they thus differed in their services afforded to our mothers, our mothers also in turn as much differed in their former mode of assisting the little strangers, by means called killing, by the moderns, maugre all which, we stouted it out and lived! "The babe then must be straitly rolled round the waist with a linen swathe and loaded with clothes until it could scarcely breathe, and when unwell or fretful was dosed with spirits and water stewed with spicery. The mother in the mean time was refreshed with rum, either buttered or made into hot tiff!"† In all this the initiated sufficiently know the marked dissimilar views and practice now!

With the increase of luxuries have come in the indolent habits of repose and table indulgences, creating a new disease quite unknown to our robust ancestors. They had never heard of the present

* Her generous whiggism may be found told under the chapter on the War of Independence.

† Memoirs Historical Society, vol. i., p. 290.

modish name of "dyspepsia." Indigestion, if it troubled them after occasional excess in banqueting, was quickly cast off by the stout efforts of Dame Nature. Men and maidens then walked much more than they rode, and pursued active employments quite as much as they read. They had not then learned to cloy themselves with the varieties of the restorateur's art:—French stimulants were unknown. Even the sedentary habits of study were then unafflicted, and the idea of a "disease of genius," now so called, had never been placed to the maladies of professional men.

The following presents a list of all the physicians and surgeons, as they existed in Philadelphia, soon after the peace of 1783, to which is affixed their residences; which are here added for the sake of showing what were then deemed their best locations for business, to wit:

James Batchelor, *Water street*, between Almond and Catharine sts.
Barnabas Binney, Arch street, between Fourth and Fifth streets.
Bond & Wilson, Second street, between Market and Arch streets.
John Baker, Dentist, Second street, between Walnut and Spruce eets.
John Carson, Third street, between Chestnut and Walnut streets.
Wm. Clarkson, *Front street*, between Union and Pine streets.
Gerrardus Clarkson, Pine street, between Front and Second streets.
Abraham Chovet, Race street, between Third and Fourth streets
William Curry, corner Second and Pine streets.
Benjamin Duffield, *Front street*, between South and Almond sts
James Dunlap, Market street, between Fifth and Sixth streets.
Nathan Dorsey, *Front street*, between Walnut and Spruce streets
Samuel Duffield, Chestnut street, between Second and Third sts
John Foulk, *Front street*, between Market and Arch streets.
George Glentworth, Arch street, between Front and Second streets.
Peter Glentworth, *Front street*, between Market and Arch streets
Joseph Goss, *Front street*, between Walnut and Spruce streets.
Saml. K. Griffith, Union street, between Second and Third streets.
James Gardette, Dentist, corner Third and Pear streets.
James Hutchinson, Second street, between Walnut and Spruce sts.
Robert Harris, Spruce street, between Second and Third streets.
John Jones, Market street, between Second and Third streets.
Michael Jennings, Moravian alley, (Bread street.)
Jackson & Smith, Second street, between Market and Chestnut sts.
John Kehlme, Race street, between Second and Third streets.
Adam Kucher, Second street, between Chestnut and Walnut sts
George Lyle, *Front street*, near Poole's bridge.
John Morgan, corner Second and Spruce streets.
John Morris, Chestnut street, between Front and Second streets.
Peter Peres, a French gentleman, north Second street, corner of Brown street, Northern Liberties.
Joseph Phiffer, a German gentleman, Second street, between Vine and Callowhill streets.

Thos. Park, Fourth street, between Chestnut and Market streets.
Benjamin Rush, Second street, between Chestnut and Walnut sts.
Fredk. Rapp, Third street, between Race and Vine streets.
John Redman, Second street, between Market and Arch streets.
Joseph Redman, Market street, between Fifth and Sixth streets.
Benj. Say, Second street, between Arch and Race streets.
Wm. Smith, Arch street, between Front and Second streets.
Saml. Shober, *Front street*, between South and Almond streets.
Thos. Shaw, corner *Front* and Callowhill streets.
Wm. Shippen, Second street, between Walnut and Spruce streets.
Benj. Vanleer, *Water street*, between Race and Vine streets.

Of the Calamities of the Profession.

A few words may be added, because exemption from error or injustice is not the lot of humanity. An annalist, without ill-nature, may tell all.

The name of Dr. E. J., chemist, has not been previously introduced to the notice of the readers as among the preceding roll, his being an exempt case, and himself *un enfant perdu.* He had the misfortune greatly to overplay his part in a case of intended merriment, which set the whole town in commotion and indignation. The circumstances are strange:—In the year 1737 an apprentice lad living with the said Dr. J. had expressed a desire to be initiated into the mysteries of masonry. The doctor and some of his friends affected to become operators, with a design to make their sport of his simplicity and credulity. He was blindfolded, and was to say certain profane words to the devil. They then administered to him a cup, which some said was in imitation of a sacrament, in which was a strong dose of physic. Being led to kiss a book to swear upon, he was made to kiss a substitute, intended to much increase the rude sport of the company. Then spirits was set on fire, having a deposit of salt, intended to cause the appearance called "snap dragon," which gives to every face near it the pale hue of death.* The lad was here uncovered so as to see them, but not being terrified, as they expected or wished, although one of the company was clothed in a cow's hide and horns, Dr. J., as if infatuated with his mischievous fancies, actually cast the pan of remaining burning spirits upon the poor lad's bosom! This fatal revel terminated in the death of the young man—for after languishing three days in delirium he died. The facts thus lengthened by the proofs in the case, have been told as they appeared in substance at the trial—for the act being a felony in its nature, caused the arrest of the doctor, and his distress in his turn. As he and his companions were withal Free Masons, it brought reproach upon the fraternity. They had therefore to repel

---

* Hanks in his late expose of masonry, says he saw this thing practised in his lodge in Virginia.

it by holding a special meeting, and publicly expressing their abhorrence of the act. On this occasion an article appeared in the Mercury of 1737–8, against Benjamin Franklin, who was privy to some of the affair, and his vindication is given in his paper, No. 479, entirely exculpating himself.

At the era of the revolution, Dr. John Kearsley, although otherwise a citizen of good character and standing, became exposed to the scoffs and insults of the people, by his ardent loyalism: being naturally impetuous in his temper, he gave much umbrage to the whigs of the day, by his rash expressions. It was intended, therefore, to sober his feelings by the argument of "tar and feathers." He was seized at midday, at his own door, in Front a little below High street, by a party of the militia, and in his attempt to resist them he received a bayonet wound in his hand. Mr. Graydon, a bystander, has told the sequel. He was forced into a cart, and, amidst a multitude of boys and idlers, paraded though the streets to the tune of the Rogue's March. The concourse brought him before the Coffee-house, where they halted; the doctor, foaming with rage and indignation, without a hat, his wig dishevelled, and himself bloody from his wounded hand, stood up in the cart and called for a bowl of punch; when so vehement was his thirst, that he swallowed it all ere he took it from his lips. "I was shocked," says Graydon, "at the spectacle, thus to see a lately respected citizen so vilified." It is grateful to add, however, that they proceeded to no further violence, thus proving that a Philadelphia mob has some sense of restraint. But although the doctor was allowed to escape the threatened tar and feathers, the actual indignity so inflamed and maddened his spirit, that his friends had to confine him for a time, as an insane. He died during the war—a resident at Carlisle. In contradistinguishing him from his once popular uncle of the same name and profession, he was usually called "tory doctor."

Of Quacks.

The forced display and quackery of medicine, as we now see it in staring capitals, saluting us with impudent front at every turn, is an affair of modern growth and patronage—all full of promise for renovating age!—

> "Roses for the cheeks,
> And lilies for the brows of faded age,
> Teeth for the toothless, ringlets for the bald!"

On topics like these, our simple forefathers were almost wholly silent. Yet we have on record some "fond dreams of hope," of good Mrs. Sibylla Masters, (wife of Thomas,) who went out to England, in 1711–12, to make her fortune abroad, by the patent and sale of her "Tuscarora rice," so called. It was her preparation from our Indian corn, made into something like our hominy, and which she then strongly recommended as a food peculiarly adapted for the relief and recovery of consumptive and sickly persons. After she had procured the patent, her husband set up a water-mill and suitable works near Philadelphia, to make it in quantities for sale. There was much lack of consumptive people in those robust days. Possibly some one may now take the hint, and revive it for the benefit of the sufferers and themselves!

About the year 1739, I saw much said in the gazettes of the newly-discovered virtues of the Seneka rattlesnake root; and while the excitement was high, Dr. John Tennant got £100 from the Virginia colony, for proving its use in curing the pleurisy.

In October, 1745, Francis Torres, a Frenchman, (probably the first, and for a long time lonely and neglected quack, in our annals) advertises the sale of the Chinese stone, with some powders, both to be applied outwardly, and to effect strange cures indeed—*all ably proved by his certificates!* The stone was a chemical preparation; when applied to the bite of a rattlesnake, or any such poison, it cured immediately. It could draw off humours, cancers, swellings, pains, rheumatisms, toothache; greatly mitigated labour pains, and pangs of the gout, &c. Might it not be a good investment to again introduce some from China? Such a stone would prove the philosopher's stone--like Midas' finger, converting what it touched to gold—the usual desideratum in those who *sell.*

Location of first Hospitals, &c.

When city physicians made their calls on foot, it is obvious that it was a convenience to have their hospital and poorhouse much nearer than they now are. The hospital, therefore, a two-story house of double front, lately standing, was the hired house of Judge Kinsey, on the south side of High street, fourth house west of Fifth street, having then much open ground and fruit trees in the rear. The poorhouse, at the same time, was near the centre of an open meadow, extending from Spruce to Pine, and from Third to Fourth streets.

In the time of the war, as has been told under its appropriate head, they made use of several empty private houses for the reception of the sick soldiery by the camp fever. The house of the present Schuylkill Bank, at the south-east corner of Sixth and High streets, then deserted by the tory owner, Lawyer Galloway, was filled with those feeble men of war. At the same time, the large building in Chestnut street (late Judge Tilghman's) was also so used.

Yellow Fever of 1793.

No history of Philadelphia would be complete, which should overlook the eventful period of 1793, when the fatal yellow fever made its ravages there. It is an event which should never be forgotten; because, whether we regard it as a natural or a spiritual scourge, (effected by the divine power,) it is a calamity which may revisit us, and which, therefore, should be duly considered, or we suffer it to lose its proper moral influence.

The medical histories and official accounts of that disastrous period are in print before the public, and, in general terms, give the statement of the rise, progress, and termination of the disease, and the lists of the weekly, monthly, and total deaths: but the ideas of the reader are too generalized to be properly affected with the measure of individual sufferings; therefore, the facts which I have preserved on that memorable occasion, are calculated to supply that defect, and to bring the whole home to people's interests and bosoms.

Let the reader think of a desolation which shut up nearly all the usual churches; their pastors generally fled, and their congregations scattered; the few that still assembled in small circles for religious exercises, not without just fears that their assembling might communicate the disease from one to the other. No light and careless hearers then appeared, and no flippant preaching to indulge itching ears: all, all was solemn and impressive. They then felt and thought they should not all meet again on a like occasion; death, judgment, and eternity then possessed the minds of all who so assembled.

Look, then, in which way you would through the streets, and you saw the exposed coffins on chair-wheels, either in quick motion, or you saw the wheels drawn before houses to receive their pestilential charge. Then family, friends, or mourners scarcely ever accompanied them; and no coffins were adorned to please the eye; but coarse, stained wood, of hasty fabric, received them all. The graves were not dug singly, but pits, which might receive many before entire filling up, were opened. In the streets you met no cheerful, heedless faces, but pensive downcast eyes and hurried steps, hastening to the necessary calls of the sick.

Then the haunts of vice were shut up; drunkenness and revelling found no companions; tavern doors grew rusty on their hinges; the lewd or merry song was hushed; lewdness perished or was banished, and men generally called upon God. Men saluted each other as if doubting to be met again, and their conversation for the moment was about their several losses and sufferings.

The facts of "moving incidents," in individual cases, prepared for the present article, have been necessarily excluded from lack of room, but may hereafter be consulted on pages 210 to 213 in my MS. Annals in the Historical Society of Pennsylvania.

THE POST.

"He comes! the herald of a noisy world;
News from all nations, lumb'ring at his back!"

THERE is nothing in which the days of "Auld Lang Syne" more differ from the present, than in the astonishing facilities now afforded for rapid conveyances from place to place, and, of course, in the quick delivery of communications by the mail. Before the year 1755, five to six weeks were consumed in writing to and receiving an answer from Boston. All the letters were conveyed on horseback, at a snail-pace gait—slow, but sure. The first stage between Boston and New York commenced on the 24th of June, 1772, to run once a fortnight, as "a useful, new, and expensive undertaking;" "to start on the 13th, and to arrive either to or from either of those places on the 25th,"—thus making thirteen days of travel!* Now, it travels the same distance in fourteen hours! The first stage between New York and Philadelphia, begun in 1756, occupied three days, and now it accomplishes it in six hours!

Nor are those former prolonged movements peculiar to us. It was even so with our British ancestors, not very long before us! We have a specimen of their sluggish doings in this matter, as late as the year 1712. "The New Castle Courant" of that year contains a stage advertisement, saying that "all who desire to pass from Edinboro' to London, or from London to Edinboro', let them repair to Mr. John Baillie's, &c., every other Saturday and Monday, at both of which places they may be received in a stage coach, which performs the whole journey in thirteen days, without stoppage, (if God permit,) having eighty able horses to perform the whole stage." Now the same distance is performed in forty-six hours! On the whole, it is manifest the whole civilized world have learned to move every where with accelerated motion! The facts, as they were in the olden time, are to the following effect, to wit:—

In July, 1683, William Penn issued an order for the establishment of a post office, and granted to Henry Waldy, of Tekonay, authority to hold one, and "to supply passengers with horses from Philadelphia to New Castle, or to the Falls." The rates of postage were, to wit:—"Letters from the Falls to Philadelphia, 3d.—to Chester, 5d.—to New Castle, 7d.—to Maryland, 9d.—and from Philadelphia to Chester, 2d.—to New Castle, 4d.—and to Maryland 6d." This post went once a week, and was to be carefully published "on the meeting-

* "Madam Knight's Journal," of the year 1704, shows that she was two weeks in riding with the postman, as her guide, from Boston to New York. In most of the towns she saw Indians. She often saw wampum passing as money among the people; but 6d. a meal, at inns, &c. Tobacco was used and sold under the name of black junk. Mrs. Shippen, soon after her marriage in 1702, came from Boston to Philadelphia on horseback, bringing a baby on her lap.

house door, and other public places." These facts I found in the MSS. of the Pemberton family. A regular act for a post-office at Philadelphia was first enacted in the year 1700.

Colonel John Hamilton, of New Jersey, and son of Governor Andrew Hamilton, first devised the post-office scheme for British America, for which he obtained a patent, and the profits accruing. Afterwards, he sold it to the crown, and a member of parliament was appointed for the whole, with a right to have his substitute reside in New York.

In December, 1717, Jonathan Dickinson writes to his correspondent, saying, "We have a settled post from Virginia and Maryland unto us, and goes through all our northern colonies, whereby advices from Boston unto Williamsburg, in Virginia, is completed in four weeks, from March to December, and in double that time in the other months of the year."

In 1722, the Gazette says,—"We have been these three days expecting the New York post, as usual, but he is not yet arrived," although three days over his time!

In 1727, the mail to Annapolis is opened this year to go once a fortnight in summer and once a month in winter, via New Castle, &c., to the Western Shore, and back to the Eastern Shore; managed by William Bradford in Philadelphia, and by William Parks in Annapolis.

In December, 1729, the Gazette announces, that "while the New York post continues his fortnight stage, we shall publish but once a week as in former times." In the summer it went once a week.

In 1738, Henry Pratt is made riding postmaster for all the stages between Philadelphia and Newport, in Virginia; to set out in the beginning of each month, and to return in twenty-four days. To him, all merchants, &c., may confide their letters and other business, he having given security to the postmaster general. In this day we can have but little conception of his lonely rides through imperfect roads; of his laying out at times all night, and giving his horse a range of rope to browse, while he should make his letter-pack his pillow, on the ground!

In 1744, it is announced in the Gazette, that the "northern post begins his fortnight stages on Tuesday next, for the winter season."

In 1745, John Dalley, surveyor, states that he has just made survey of the road from Trenton to Amboy, and had set up marks at every two miles, to guide the traveller. It was done by private subscriptions, and he proposes to do the whole road from Philadelphia to New York, in the same way, if a sum can be made up!

In 1748, when Professor Kalm arrived at Philadelphia from London, many of the inhabitants came on board his vessel for letters. Such as were not called for, were taken to the Coffee-house, where every body could make inquiry for them, thus showing that, then, the post-office did not seem to claim a right to distribute them as now.

In 1753, the delivery of letters by the penny post was first begun.

At the same time began the practice of advertising remaining letters in the office. The letters for all the neighbouring counties went to Philadelphia, and lay there till called for—thus, letters for Newtown, Bristol, Chester, New Castle, &c., are to be called for in Philadelphia.

Even at that late period, the northern mail goes and returns but once a week in summer, and once a fortnight in winter, just as it did twenty-five years before.

But in October, 1754, a new impulse is given, so as to start for New York thereafter, on Monday, Wednesday, and Friday; and in the winter once a week. This, therefore, marks the period of a new era in the mail establishment of our country. It owed this impulse, extending also to Boston, to the management of our Franklin, made postmaster general.

In 1755, the postmaster general, Benjamin Franklin, publishes, that to aid trade, &c., he gives notice, that hereafter, the winter northern mail from Philadelphia to New England, which used to set out but once a fortnight, shall start once a week all the year round,—"whereby answers may be obtained to letters between Philadelphia and Boston, in three weeks, which used to require six weeks!"

In 1758, newspapers which aforetime were carried post free per mail, will, by the reason of their great increase, be changed thereafter to the small price of 9d. a year, for fifty miles, and 1s. 6d. for one hundred miles. This was, most probably, the private emolument of the rider; the papers themselves not having been mailed at all, it is probable.

Finally, in 1774, which brings colonial things nearly to its final close, by the war of Independence, soon after, we read that "John Perkins engages to ride post to carry the mail once a week to Baltimore, and will take along or bring back led horses or any parcels."

Immediately after the second Congress met in May 1775, they appointed a committee to report a scheme of a post "for conveying letters and *intelligence* through this continent." In July following, an establishment was made under a postmaster general, to be located at Philadelphia—"he to form a line of posts from Falmouth, New England, to Savannah, in Georgia, with cross posts where needful." Such a postmaster general had $1000 per annum, and a secretary and comptroller at $340 each—*a small affair indeed then!* Benjamin Franklin was this postmaster general. In the following year, the office was conferred on Richard Bache. To carry the mails, riders were appointed for every twenty-five miles, to deliver from one to the other, and return to their starting places, they to travel day and night, and to be faithful men and true.

At the same time it was ordered that three advice boats should be established, "one to ply between North Carolina and such ports as shall be most convenient to the place where Congress shall be sitting —one other between the State of Georgia and the same port. The boats to be armed, and to be freighted by individuals for the sake of diminishing the public expense." Sometimes carrying, perchance, oysters, potatoes, apples, &c.

In November, 1776, authority was given "to employ extra post riders between the armies, from their head quarters to Philadelphia."

The pay of the postmaster general was increased to $2000, in April, 1779.

In 1779, the post was regulated "to arrive and set out *twice a week* at the place where Congress shall be sitting, "to go as far as Boston, and to Charleston, South Carolina." In consequence of this alleged *increase of business*, the postmaster general was to receive $5000 per annum, and the comptroller $4000, meaning continental money, we presume, for in September, 1780, the postmaster general actually received but $1000, and the comptroller but $500. The surveyor $533, *in specie*. Besides these two officers in the post department, there was a secretary, who acted as clerk to the postmaster general. The comptroller settled the accounts and was the bookkeeper. There were three surveyors who were *to travel* and inspect the conduct of riders, &c. There was also an inspector of dead letters, at a salary of $100 a year—now there are four clerks constantly employed at this service, inspecting upwards of a million of dead letters in a year! The post riders furnished their own horses and forage,—and when much exposed, through any country possessed by the enemy, they had an occasional military escort.

GAZETTES AND THE PRINTING PRESS.

"These mark the every-day affairs of life."

The early newspapers are by no means such miscellaneous and amusing things as our modern use of them might lead us to conceive. They are very tame, and the news, which is generally foreign, is told in very dull prose; very little like jest or mirth appears in any of them. Fruitful as Franklin was in amusing writings, it is really surprising how very devoid of *Spectator-like* articles his paper is; but very little has been furnished by his pen. He must have deemed it out of place for his paper, and therefore confined his essays to his "Poor Richard's Almanac," which was so favourably received as to call for three editions in the same year. Reflections on men and manners of that day, to which he was so very competent, would have been very interesting and judicious; but I have found nothing. Probably the "even tenor of their way," in the days of his chief residence among us, excited no cause of remarks, and that it was chiefly since the Revolution that we began to deserve remarks on the changing character of the times and the people.

But after every omission and neglect in such editors, old newspapers are still unavoidably a kind of mirror of their age, for they bring up the very age with all its bustle and every day occurrence, and mark its genius and its spirit, more than the most laboured description of the historian. Sometimes a single advertisement incidentally "prolongs the dubious tale." An old paper must make us thoughtful, for we also shall make our exit; there every name we read of in print is already cut upon tombstones. The names of doctors have followed their patients'; the merchants have gone after their perished ships, and the celebrated actor furnishes his own skull for his successor in Hamlet.

"The American Weekly Mercury" was begun by Andrew Bradford, son of William, in Philadelphia, 1719, in company with John Copson. This was the first gazette ever published in our city. It was begun the 22d of December, 1719, at 10 shillings per annum. The general object of the paper is said to be "to encourage trade." It does not seem to be the spirit of the paper to give the local news, or rather, they did not seem to deem it worthy their mention. It might have been but "a tale twice told," for which they were unwilling to pay, while they thought every man could know his domestic news without an advertiser. Foreign news and custom-house entries, inwards and outwards, including equally the ports of New York and Boston, constituted the general contents of every Mercury.

In November, 1742, the publisher, Andrew Bradford, died, and the paper was set in mourning columns, &c., for six weeks. After this it continued by the widow until 1746, when it was discontinued, probably from the cause of William Bradford, the former partner of Andrew, having soon after his death set up a new paper, called the Pennsylvania Journal.

In 1727, Benjamin Franklin projected the scheme of publishing a second, or rival paper; but his project being exposed to Keimer, he supplanted Franklin by hastily publishing his prospectus—a strange vapouring composition—and fell to getting subscribers. By this means he was enabled to start, and even to continue for nine short months, "the Pennsylvania Gazette." He had got only ninety subscribers, when Franklin and Joseph Breintnal, under the title of the "Busy Body," contributed to write him down in Bradford's Mercury. Thus won by conquest, Franklin soon managed to buy it for a trifle, as his own.

The Pennsylvania Gazette began in 1728. The braggart style of Keimer's prospectus is a little curious. His eccentric mind led him to throw it into an alphabetical order, and to embrace, in encyclopedia form, the whole circle of the arts and sciences! This arrangement was abandoned as soon as Franklin became editor. Some specimens of his braggart manner is thus displayed, to wit: "Whereas many have encouraged me to publish a paper of intelligence; and whereas the late Mercury has been so wretchedly performed as to be a scandal to the name of printing, and to be truly styled nonsense in folio, this is therefore to notify that I shall begin, in November next, a most useful paper, to be entitled the Pennsylvania Gazette or Universal Instructer." The proposer, (he says,) having dwelt at the fountain of intelligence in Europe, will be able to give a paper to please all and to offend none, at the reasonable expense of ten shillings per annum, proclamation money. So far, it possessed Dr. Johnson's character of a good advertisement: it having "that promise which is the soul of a good advertisement!"

But he transcends even the superlative degree! It will, says he, exceed all others that ever were in America, and will possess, in fine, the most complete body of history and philosophy ever yet published since the creation! Possibly he meant this extravagant praise for his intended extracts from Chambers' great Dictionary, for he adds, that a work of the self-same design has been going on in England, by no less than seven dukes, two viscounts, eighteen earls, twenty-two lords, and some hundreds of knights, esquires, &c., and withal approved and honoured by the wisest king—even the very darling of heaven—King George the First! Such advertisements could not secure patronage now, and as he eked out his great work for less than one year, it is presumed his gins did not ensnare the wary of that day. Alas! his visions of hope ended in a prison before the year had filled its term.

In October, 1729, the Gazette was assumed by B. Franklin and H. Meredith, and they promptly state in their prospectus their intention to discontinue the alphabetical extracts from Chambers' Dictionary, and from the Religious Courtship—subjects surely incompatible enough for newspaper readers. Soon after commencing, they advertise that, because of their increase of patronage, they will print twice a week,—delivering half a sheet at a time on the old subscription price of ten shillings.

The Gazette under their management gained reputation; but, until Franklin obtained the appointment of postmaster, Bradford's Mercury had the largest circulation. After this event, the Gazette had a full proportion of subscribers and advertising custom, and became profitable.

Meredith and Franklin separated in May, 1732. Franklin continued the Gazette, but published it only once a week. In 1733, he printed it on a crown half sheet quarto. Price ten shillings a year. In 1741, he enlarged the size to a demi quarto half sheet. In 1745, he reverted to foolscap folio. In 1747–8, the Gazette was published "by B. Franklin, postmaster, and D. Hall," and was enlarged to a whole sheet crown folio, and afterwards by a great increase of advertisements to a sheet, and often to a sheet and a half demi. On the 9th of May, 1754, the device of a snake, divided into eight parts, (the number of the then colonies united against the French and Indians,) was affixed, with the motto "Join or die."

In May, 1766, it was published by Hall and Sellers, who continued it until 1777 but suspended it at the visit of the British army.

Afterwards it was published once a week until the death of Sellers, in 1804. Afterwards by others.

The Pennsylvania Journal and the Weekly Advertiser.

This paper was first published on Tuesday, December 2d, 1742. It was printed on a foolscap sheet. The day of publication was changed to Wednesday. Printed by William Bradford.

About the year 1766, the imprint was changed to William and Thomas Bradford. This paper was devoted to the cause of the country, but it was suspended during the possession of the city by the British.

William Bradford died in 1791. Then the Journal was continued by his surviving partner subsequent to 1800. It was finally superseded by "the True American."

The Pennsylvania Chronicle and Universal Advertiser.—Containing the freshest advices, &c.

The Chronicle was published weekly, on Monday. The first number appeared January 6th, 1767, by William Goddard, at ten shillings per annum. This was the fourth newspaper in the English language established at Philadelphia, and the first with four columns to a page, in the colonies. The second and third years it was printed in quarto, and the fourth year again in folio. It was ably edited—having the celebrated Joseph Galloway, Esq., and Thomas Wharton, Esq., as secret partners. It gained great circulation. It became at last too tory in its bias to stand the times. It continued till February, 1773.

The Pennsylvania Packet, or the General Advertiser.

This was issued from the press, in November, 1771, by John Dunlap, once a week. In 1783, he sold out to D. C. Claypole, who printed it three times a week, for about a year, and afterwards, *daily*, making it the *first* daily paper in all the United States.

Mr. Claypole having been enriched by its publication, sold out his right to the present Zachariah Poulson, by whom it was continued in very great patronage, under the name of the "American Daily Advertiser."

Of this paper, we have a few words of special notice. It is more properly *municipal* and *domestic* than any other which we know. It seems composed to suit the family hearth and fireside comforts of good and sober citizens, never flaunting in the gaudy glare of party allurements; never stained with the ribaldry and virulence of party recrimination. It is patriarchal,—looking alike to the wants and benefits of *all* our citizens, as common children of the same city family. It is, in short, a paper like the good old times from which it has descended, and like the people of the former days, its recent most numerous readers, it carries with it something grave, discriminative, useful, and considerate. In January, 1840, it was merged into the North American.

The Pennsylvania Ledger, and Weekly Advertiser.

This Ledger was first published in January 28, 1775, by James Humphreys, Jun., at 10 shillings a year. He started to act impartially, but after the British got possession of the city, it was turned to their interest. The last number was published May 23, 1778.

The Pennsylvania Evening Post.

Was first published Jan. 24, 1775, by Benjamin Towne, in quarto, three times a week; price three shillings a quarter. This was the third evening paper in the colonies. It continued to be published till the year 1782.

Story and Humphrey's Pennsylvania Mercury, and Universal Advertiser.

The Mercury came before the public in April, 1775, and was published weekly, on Fridays, on a demi sheet, folio, with *home-made* types. It was short-lived, for the whole establishment was destroyed by fire in December, 1775.

The German Newspapers printed previously to the year 1775, *were these:—*

As early as May, 1743, a German newspaper was started in Philadelphia, by Joseph Crellius, entitled the "High Dutch Pennsylvania Journal."

By an advertisement in the Pennsylvania Gazette, of September, 1751, I find there was at that time "A Dutch and English Gazette, in both languages, adapted to those who incline to learn either.—Price five shillings per annum.

Another German paper was established about the year 1759, by Miller and Weiss, conveyancers,—the former ones being discontinued. It was printed for them about two years by Gotthan Armbruster.

Anthony Armbruster, in 1762, began a new German paper, which he published weekly for several years.

H. Miller's German newspaper was begun in 1762; and for some time there were two German and two English newspapers publishing in the city.

Der Wochentliche Philadelphische Staatsbothe.

This newspaper was first published in the German language, in 1762, by Henry Miller, weekly—afterwards twice a week, on demi size.

In 1768, the title was changed to "Pennsylvanische Staatsbothe," i. e., the Pennsylvania Post Boy. It thus continued until May, 1779, when the paper ended.

A public Journal was printed at Germantown, in the German language, as early as the summer of 1739, by Christopher Sower. Its name, Englished, read—The Pennsylvania German Recorder of Events. In 1744, it was continued by C. Sower, Jun., under the name of the Germantauner Zeitung; this continued till the year of the war of 1777.

It results from the foregoing notices of our newspapers, that sixty years ago there were only three newspapers published in the city, viz.—two in English and one in German. In contrast with the present numerous *sentinels*, watching the public weal, and their own, how diminutive the two weekly affairs of that day appear! At the present day the greatest innovation in these "folios and maps of busy life," which meet the eye, as a change for the worse, are the numerous wood-cut signs hung out from the columnar lines, like signs from their street-posts, and like them interrupting and disfiguring the whole perspective view. It is an inconsiderate as well as annoying display; for in the very nature of things it ceases to arrest attention whenever it becomes so common as to be like a wooden block set at every man's door.

The first in the colonies was the "Boston News Letter," begun in 1704; the second was also in Boston, and called the Boston Gazette, begun in 1710. The *third* was commenced in the *same year*, in Philadelphia, and called the American Weekly Mercury. New York began its first paper in 1725; Maryland in 1728; Rhode Island and South Carolina in 1732; Virginia in 1736; Connecticut and North Carolina, in 1755. At the commencement of the Revolution there were thirty-nine papers in a course of publication; and *of them* but *eight* have a present *continuance*. In 1835, there were about 1200! It may be curious to add, that these *vehicles*, now so numerous *here*, are of so modern an invention, as that the first paper in England was nearly a century after the use of printing there. "The London Gazette" began in November, 1665, as a weekly concern, and has been published on to the present day. The original *Gazette*, signifying a little treasury of news, began at Venice about 260 years ago. For the first thirty years it was only published monthly, and *in manuscript*, such was the jealousy of the government.

The Progress of the Printing Press.

Philadelphia may claim some peculiarity under this article, for Mathew Carey for many years printed his quarto edition of the Bible in standing separate types, being the first and only instance of so great a collection of standing type in the world! Christopher Sower too, at Germantown, printed in German the first quarto Bible ever attempted in the United States. Both Sower and B. Franklin were ingenious in their profession, made their own ink, and cut their own wood cuts, before either of them were attempted by others. Franklin even cast some of his own type ornaments. Jacob Bay and Justice Fox, both made type for C. Sower, in Germantown.

You may see, in my MS. Annals, in the City Library, page 282, a specimen of R. Aitkin's small Bible, of 1781, made of importance enough to require the aid of congress, and by them most formally given. It is a curiosity. There were as many as four hundred and twenty-five books and pamphlets, in original works, all printed in Philadelphia before the Revolution,—a fact in our literary annals but very little known.

I had before spoken of the press at Philadelphia being established earlier there than in Old Virginia, or in *Old* New York. I since observe a reason, of which I was not before aware. There was a fear (not felt at Philadelphia) of the too free use of it by the colonists for refractory purposes. I see that in 1683, (the time of the settlement of Philadelphia,) the governor of Virginia was instructed, *not* to allow any person *to use* a printing press upon any occasion. In 1686, Governor Randolph, of Massachusetts, forbade any one to print without *his* consent. Four years before, the general court of Massachusetts determined that there should be no press used but at Cambridge, and then only under the inspection of *two licensers:* this was "to prevent any abuse of the authorities of the country." Pennsylvania never had any such restrictions, and therefore William Bradford set up his press there as soon as the city was founded. The New York governor stopped the press in 1733, in the case of Zenger, the printer; and the governor of Virginia, when advertising a reward for pirates, had to send to Philadelphia to get the printing done, in 1718; and, on another occasion, "he thanked God that they had *no* press!"

The first successful type foundry in America was by Ronaldson, at Philadelphia; begun in 1796. He was a Scotchman by birth—acquired a fortune, and founded, near his foundry, a very tasteful public cemetery, the first of the kind among us.

Thomas Dobson gave the first impulse to book printing among us. He also came from Scotia, soon after the peace. Before his time, five or six printers used to club, to print a Testament, &c.

Robert Bell, in south Third street, in the house next north of St. Paul's church, had a bookstore and printed sundry works by *subscription*—larger works, probably, than has been supposed—for instance: I have his octavo edition of an *Appendix* to Blackstone, so printed in 1793, and he therein proposes to print his *second edition* of Blackstone's Commentaries, in four volumes, *quarto*, at three dollars per volume, and to allow gentlemen who may have his *former* edition in octavo, to return the same in part payment of the latter. At the same time, he announces that he is *then* publishing by subscription, in one volume, octavo, Furguson on Civil Society, for ten shillings.

The original printing press, used by Dr. Franklin when a journeyman in London, is preserved and owned by the Philosophical Society, in Philadelphia.

I had occasion to see and inspect the subscription list, and to note the residences of the subscribers to Goddard's newspaper, for the year 1767. It consisted of 351 individuals south of High street, 284 on the north side, and 385 in the country and neighbouring provinces—making in all 1020 persons. These facts may be deemed desirable information to modern publishers, and therefore they are here preserved.

In looking at their names, they manifestly present the elite of the city, and the men of prosperity among the tradesmen. They besides, present to our present view their "whereabouts" *then.*

I observe that High street then presented but very few names—but among them I see Charles Thomson, secretary, Dr. Benjamin Franklin, John Biddle. *Water street* is filled with the names of the gentry, such as, Reese Meredith, many of the Whartons, Sharp Delany, George Clymer, Robert Morris. *Front street*, too, was then a gentry place—having such as Nathaniel Allen, Benjamin Chew, Thomas Mifflin, James and Clement Biddle, William Peters, several Fishers and Whartons, Fishbournes, and Alexander Wilcocks. In *Second street*, Richard Penn, James and William Logan, James and John Pemberton, Thomas Bond, several of the Morris family, Benjamin Levy, Blair McClenachan. In *Chestnut street*, Benjamin and Christopher Marshall, Tench Francis, John Murgatroyd, Nathaniel Morris, Isaac Norris, John Lawrence, George Emlen, Dr. Thomas Græme, Israel Pemberton. In *Walnut street*, Joseph Galloway, Esq., Robert Harding, Priest, Joseph Beakes, Joseph Bullock. Persons "to the place native born" will readily recognize such names as among the old and respectable families of the city.

The present beautiful manner of binding books in cotton embossed cloth grew out of a case of necessity, induced by the war of 1812. The great deficiency of leather for book-binding induced those who made cheap spelling books and Testaments, and other small works, to put them up in cheap and coarse muslin. At first it was used for the backs only; finding them well received for their well-wearing, and exemption from *mould*, they began to use fine stuff and more tasteful colours, and as the favour to them increased, they went on producing better and better, until they have now become *an elegance.*

STATISTIC FACTS.

An attention to the following facts, may serve to show the progress of society, by marking its increase in population, houses, exports, &c., at successive periods, to wit:

1683.—William Penn's letter of that year, says, "I mentioned in my last account, that from my arrival, in 1682, to the date hereof, being ten months, we have got up fourscore houses at our town, and that some villages were settled about it. From that time to my coming away, which was a year within a few weeks, the town advanced to three hundred and fifty-seven houses, divers of them large, well-built, with good cellars, three stories, and some balconies." Thus settling the fact, that they built three hundred and fifty-seven houses in the first year!

1685.—Robert Turner, in his letter to William Penn, of this year, says, "The town goes on, in planting and building, to admiration, both in the front and backward; and there are about six hundred houses in three years' time."

1707.—Isaac Norris, in a letter to William Penn, says, "The province consumes, annually, of produce and merchandise of England, 14 to 15,000 pounds sterling. The direct returns were in tobacco, furs and skins; the indirect, in provisions and produce, via the West Indies, and southern colonies. In 1706, about eight hundred hogsheads of tobacco went from Philadelphia, and about twenty-five to thirty tons of skins and furs."

1720.—The taxables are stated by Proud, at 1195 persons, in city and county.

1723.—The imports from England were £15,992 sterling.

1728–9.—There were frozen up in the docks this winter, about the city, fourteen ships, three snows, eight brigantines, nine sloops, two schooners, besides shallops, &c. The whole number of churches then was but six.

1730.—The imports from England were £48,595 sterling.

1727 to '39.—From an account of the highest and lowest number of votes given at the elections, and known by the return of members of Assembly, we ascertain the votes for the county of Philadelphia to have been as follows, to wit:

Election—1727,	Highest number,	787	Lowest number,	482
1728,	do.	971	do.	487
1730,	do.	622	do.	365
1732,	do.	904	do.	559
1734,	do.	821	do	441
1735,	do.	1097	do.	517
1736,	do.	719	do.	439

Election—1737,	Highest number, 904	Lowest number, 497
1738,	do. 1306	do. 736
1739,	do. 555	do. 332

1737.—The imports from England were, this year, £58,690 sterling.—Vide Proud.

1740.—The taxables are stated by Proud, at 4850 persons, in city and county.

1741.—We are indebted to a friend for the subsequent statement of the number of taxable inhabitants of the city and county of Philadelphia for this year. They have been copied from the books of his venerable ancestor, who was assessor, &c., for several years

Statement of the number of Taxable Inhabitants of the City and County of Philadelphia, in the year 1741.

[The city was then divided into *ten* wards, and the county extended to the southern limits of Berks county, and embraced the whole of the county of Montgomery.]

Number of Taxables in the City in 1741.

1. Dock Ward,	183	*Brought over,*	880
2. Lower Delaware,	115	7. Upper Delaware,	99
3. Walnut,	98	8. High Street,	151
4. South,	105	9. Mulberry,	309
5. Middle,	236	10. North,	182
6. Chestnut,	143		
Carried over,	880	*City total,*	1621

Number of Taxable Inhabitants in the County in 1741.

[The County then contained forty-seven townships.]

Amity,	70	*Brought over,*	935
Abington,	92	Franconia,	59
Allamingle,	37	Frankford and N. Hanover,	87
Byberry,	52		
Bristol,	64	Frederick,	76
Blockley,	72	Germantown,	168
Creesham,	60	Gwynned,	93
Cheltenham,	67	Hanover, Upper,	97
Colebrook Dale,	85	Horsham,	80
Douglass,	58	Kingsess,	59
Dublin, Lower,	125	Limerick,	59
Dublin, Upper,	77	Moreland Manor,	125
Exeter,	76	Montgomery,	54
Carried over,	935	*Carried over*	1892

Brought over,	1892	*Brought over,*	2762
Maiden Creek,	75	Passyunk and Moyamensing,	78
Merion, Upper,	52	Plymouth,	46
Merion, Lower,	101	Roxborough,	38
Menatauny,	111	Sulford,	174
Northern Liberties,	151	Springfield,	29
Norrington,	25	Towamensin,	55
Oxford,	78	Whippan,	56
Ouley,	58	White Marsh,	89
Providence,	146	Worcester,	70
Perkiomen and Skipake,	73	Wayamensing,	25
Carried over,	2762	*County total,*	3422

Comparative Statement.

City Taxables, In 1741, 1,621. In 1826, 11,120. Increase, 9,499.

1742.—The imports from England this year, were £75,295 sterling.

1744.—A letter from Secretary Peters, to the proprietaries, states the population of the city, as estimated at 13,000 people, and 1500 houses. The same is confirmed in the same year, by the Minutes of the City Council.

1747.—The imports from England this year, were £82,404 sterling.

1749.—This spring the houses in the several wards were counted by the following named gentlemen, and amounted to 2076 in number, to wit:

In Mulberry Ward,	488,	by Dr. Franklin.
Dock Ward,	245,	Joseph Shippen.
Lower Delaware,	110,	William Allen.
Upper Delaware,	109,	T. Hopkinson.
South,	117,	Edward Shippen.
High Street Ward,	147,	T. Lawrence, jun.
Walnut,	104,	James Humphries.
Chestnut,	110,	J. Turner.
North,	196,	William Shippen.
Middle,	238,	William Coleman.
	1864,	
South suburbs,	150,	Edward Shippen.
North do.	62,	William Shippen.
	2076 houses.	

At the same time (1749) the places of worship were these, to wit:

1 Episcopalian,	1 Dutch Calvinist,	1 Baptist,
2 Friends,	1 Roman Catholic,	1 Dutch Lutheran,
1 Swedish,	2 Presbyterian,	1 Moravian.

The same year (1749) Proud states that twenty-five large ships arrived with Germans, bringing 600 persons each, making together 12,000 souls in one year, and that nearly as many came annually from Ireland, so as to people whole counties from those two nations.

1751.—The imports from England this year were £190,917 sterling.—Vide Proud.

1752.—Dr. Franklin stated before the House of Commons, that 10,000 hogsheads of flaxseed had been in that year exported from Philadelphia—making 70,000 bushels, and that all the flax that grew with it they manufactured into coarse linen. On George Heap's map, the exports are detailed thus, viz.: 125,960 barrels of flour, 86,500 bushels of wheat, 90,740 bushels of corn, 249 tons of bread, 3431 barrels of beef, and 4812 barrels of pork.

1753.—There were ascertained by the assessor to be 2300 houses, including the city and suburbs.

1760.—There were ascertained by the same assessor to have been in the city and suburbs 2969 houses, and 8321 taxables in the city and county. It was also officially reported that there were then 5687 taxable inhabitants in the whole county of Philadelphia, and their county tax was laid at £5653 19*s.* 6*d.* The city tax was laid at £5633 13*s.* on 2634 taxables. At the same time were reported, as within the county, the following mills, to wit:—83 gristmills, 40 sawmills, 6 papermills, 1 oilmill, 12 fullingmills, 1 horsemill, 1 windmill, and 6 forges.

1766.—Dr. Franklin, when examined this year before a committee of the House of Commons, respecting the repeal of the Stamp Act, stated the following facts, to wit:

He supposed there were in Pennsylvania about 160,000 white inhabitants, of whom one-third were Quakers, and one-third were Germans.

The taxes were then laid on all estates, real and personal—a poll tax—a tax on offices and professions, trades and businesses, according to their profit—an excise on all wine, rum, and other spirits, and £10 duty per head on all negroes imported.

The tax on all estates, real and personal, was 18*d.* in the pound, fully rated, and the tax on the profits of trades and professions, &c., made about 2*s.* 6*d.* in the pound. The poll tax on unmarried men was 15*s.* per head. All the taxes in Pennsylvania then produced about £20,000 per annum.

He said he thought our people increase faster than in England, because they marry younger and more generally, and this they did because they may easily obtain land by which to raise their families. He said the people had by general agreement disused all goods fashionable in mournings.

The imports from Great Britain he presumed to be above £500,000 per annum, and the exports to Britain he supposed did not exceed £40,000 per annum.

1767.—The exports of Philadelphia for one year were thus officially stated, to wit: 367,500 bushels of wheat, 198,516 barrels of flour, 34,736 barrels of bread, 60,206 bushels of corn, 6645 barrels of pork, 609 barrels of beef, 882 tons of bar iron, 813 tons of pig iron, 12094 hogsheads of flaxseed, 1288 barrels of beer.

1769.—In December of this year the assessor gave in the follow ing list of houses then ascertained, to wit:

In Mulberry Ward, - - -	920
Upper Delaware, - - - - -	234
North, - - - - - -	417
High street, - - - - -	166
Middle, - - - - - -	358
Chestnut, - - - - -	112
South, - - - - - -	147
Walnut, - - - - - -	105
Lower Delaware, - - -	120
Dock, - - - - - - -	739
	3318

In the Northern Liberties or northern suburbs to Second street bridge, over Stacy's run, (Cohocksinc,) 553—and in Southwark or southern suburbs to the north side of Love lane 608—making together 4474 in the city and suburbs, of dwelling-houses exclusively.

1770.—This year the number of houses was ascertained to have been—

Within the city bounds, - - -	3318
In the Northern Liberties, - -	553
In Southwark, - - - - ..	603
	4474—estimated to

contain 25 to 30,000 souls.

At the same time the number of churches was ascertained to have been 16, to wit:

3 Episcopalians,	1 Methodist,
4 Presbyterians,	2 German Lutheran,
1 Baptist,	1 German Calvinist,
1 Moravian,	1 Swedish Lutheran,
2 Papists,	

1771.—The taxable inhabitants are stated, by Proud, as being 10,455 in number for the city and county, of whom 3751 were of the city. The exports of Philadelphia, in the same year, were conveyed in 361 square-rigged vessels, and 391 sloops and schooners—making in all 46,654 tons, of which there were 252,744 barrels of flour, 259,441 bushels of corn, and 110,412 bushels of flaxseed.

1772.—The following comparative facts of several years, down to this year, have been given by R. Proud, and may serve still further to illustrate the statistics of those early days, to wit:

Of Exports.

In 1731, when wheat was at	2s. 6d.,	and flaxseed 4s. 8d.,	they amounted to	£62,584
1749, do.	5s. 3d.,	do. 10s. 8d.,	do.	148,104
1750, do.	4s.	do. 10s.	do.	155,174
1751, do.	3s. 10d.,	do. 6s. 6d.,	do.	187,457
1765, do.	5s. 3d.,	do. 9s. 3d.,	do.	422,614
1772. do.	5s. 6d.,	do. 8s.	do.	571,050

I have before noted the amounts of several annual imports from England, under their several years. The last which I stated, in the year 1751, made the amount to be £190,917 sterling; but from and after the year 1761, they sank greatly. No cause is assigned by Proud, who states the following annual amounts, to wit:

Imports of	1761,	38,099£	sterling.
"	1762,	88,228	do.
"	1763,	36,258	do.
"	1764,	25,148	do.
"	1765,	26,851	do.

As the war with France began in 1756, and ended in 1763, the trade may have been so embarrassed as to have diminished much both the ability and the safety of importation. After the peace, we know that the agitated question of "taxing America," made the people of set purpose use domestic fabrics in lieu of foreign supplies, so as by all means to diminish the trade of England with us.

1777.—In October of this year, General Howe being then in possession of Philadelphia, and many of the inhabitants gone off because of the war, or the dread of the British, an accurate census was taken by order of General Cornwallis, to wit:

Houses in the city, - - - -	3508
" in Southwark, - - -	781
" in the Northern Liberties,	1170
	5470

Five hundred and eighty-seven of the houses were found untenanted. There were 287 stores; there were also found to be 21,767 inhabitants, exclusive of the army and strangers.

Years.	City contained	N. Liberties	Southwark.	Total.
In 1790,	28,522 souls	8333	5661	42,516
1800,	41,223	16,097	9621	67,811
1810,	53,722	21,558	13,707	88,987

William Sansom, Esq., who has been for several years a minute observer of the progress of the city in its increase of buildings, has furnished the following data, to wit:

In 1802, new houses erected were		464	The detail of these houses, showing in what streets they were built, may be consulted on p. 518 of my MS. Annals, in Historical Society.
1803,	do.	385	
1804,	do.	273	
1809,	do.	205	

In the next year the total number of buildings was ascertained and found to be 20,260—say 8874 in the city, 2998 in the Northern

Liberties, and 2301 in Southwark, and their inhabitants 88,988. If we should pursue this data, it is deemed reasonable to conclude that in the last eighteen years, from 1809 to 1827, the new buildings may have averaged 600 in each year, thus producing an increase of 10,800 to be added to the former 20,260, and thus forming an aggregate of about 31,000 buildings, and a probable total of 133,000 inhabitants in 1827. I deem this estimate high enough, but the next census will check it.

In the year 1823, the churches were ascertained to be eighty in number, to wit:

13 Presbyterian,	5 Friends,
10 Episcopalian,	4 Papists,
8 Baptist,	26 of all other denominations.
14 Methodist,	(Vide Poulson's paper of 24th March.)

Philadelphia, as a great commercial city, kept a proud pre-eminence of the cities in the Union, until about the year 1820. In the year 1796, the exports of Philadelphia were above one-fourth of the whole United States, being then 17,613,866 dollars, but as quickly as the year 1820, she became as low as the seventh state in the grade of the Union! The exports of New York, in 1792, were but 2,930,370 dollars, but in 1820, they were $13,163,244! Thus, as Philadelphia has been sinking, New York has been rising, and her great canal will give her still more decided advantages, until we in turn derive our increase from our purposed inland improvements. Even the exports of Baltimore, in 1820, recent as has been her growth, were 865,825 dollars more than ours!

I since find the following facts concerning the number of burials occurring in the city about a century ago, to wit:

In 1722, the Gazette began first to record the death and burials of the month, to wit: In February, 1722, for one month, it was three of the Church of England—Quakers four, and Presbyterians, none.

In 1729 to '30, the interments in one year from December to December, were 227 in number, to wit: In Church ground 81—in Quaker 39—in Presbyterian 18—in Baptist 18—and in Strangers' ground (the present Washington Square, an adorned grave ground now for them!) 41 whites and 30 blacks. In some weeks I perceived but one and two persons a week, and in one week *none*. It is worthy of remark, that although the influence of Friends was once so ascendant as to show a majority of their population, yet it seems from the above, that the Churchmen must have been then most numerous. In the week ending the 15th of July, 1731, I noticed the burials of that week were "none!"

The tabular statement of the auditor general gives the total adjusted valuation of Pennsylvania in 1841, viz.:

The real estate in the several counties, - - -	$245,673,402
Personal property as valued, - - - - -	48,835,784
Making a grand total of - - - - -	$294,509,186

Resources of Pennsylvania—1841, the population is 1,724,033—in 1790 it was but 431,373.

We have 28,000,000 acres of land under better cultivation than any other state, and worth - - - - - - $701,000,000
300,000 houses, worth on an average, - - 300,000,000
Barns, stores, furnaces, forges, factories, mills, - - 200,000,000
1000 miles of canals, and 700 miles railroads, - 100,000,000

$1,300,000,000

The Schuylkill mines now produce 500,000 tons—the other mining districts about the same—say 1,000,000 tons a-year—nearly half of this is for exportation. Three thousand vessels a-year visit Schuylkill river to carry it away, and yet all this is in its infancy.

The Schuylkill is capable of producing four times its present quantity. The Swatara can produce as much as the Schuylkill—so can those of the Lehigh, the Shamokin and the Susquehanna.

We have, besides our anthracite, more bituminous coal (according to our state geologist) than all Europe! While Europe contains 2000 square miles, Pennsylvania has 10,000 square miles.

The western bituminous coal-field of Pennsylvania is estimated to contain *three hundred thousand millions of tons*—being ten thousand times more than *all in Great Britain!*

In one year (1838) two millions of bituminous coal was mined and *used* westward of the Allegheny mountains. Much more will be.

The quantity of iron produced in Pennsylvania is estimated at one-third of the product of the whole union. The amount of bar and pig iron produces $14,000,000.

The real estate of Pennsylvania as shown above, is one thousand three hundred millions of dollars—if taxed but three per cent. would pay off the whole state debt of thirty-five millions in *one year.*

The annual production of the state is ascertained to be one hundred and sixty millions five hundred thousand dollars—and if taxed but one per cent. would pay the interest annually of the state debt.

Who is not *proud* of such a state! She has all the resources of a great nation *within herself*—for happiness in peace, for power in war. She is capable of maintaining thirty millions of people, and feeding and clothing them herself. We produce one-sixth of all the wheat in the union. Our grain produces thirty millions of dollars a-year. Our water power is equal to the labour of four hundred millions of men! [See North American, August 12th, 1841.]

There are no people in the world who have so many advantages with so few burdens.

Colonial Statistics of New York and Philadelphia, &c., compared.—In 1769, the imports of Pennsylvania were £400,000 sterling, and of New York was but £189,000 sterling. All the New

England colonies was £561,000, and South Carolina £555,000. Virginia was the greatest of all, being then £581,000 sterling! They kept in the same relative proportion till the adoption of the Federal Constitution in 1789.

In 1791, the imports *change* thus, viz.: New York leads off at $3,222,000. Virginia is $2,486,000, and South Carolina is $1,520,000.

In 1821, the imports change thus, viz.: New York leads off at $23,000,000. Virginia is $1,000,000. South Carolina $3,000,000

In 1832, New York is $57,000,000. Virginia is $500,000. South Carolina is $1,250,000.

REMARKABLE INCIDENTS AND THINGS.

"A book wherein we read strange matters."

THE present chapter is intended to embrace a variety of miscellanea, of such peculiarity or variety in their occurrence as to afford some surprise, to wit:

Wild Pigeons.—The late aged Thomas Bradford, Esq., told me of hearing his ancestors say they once saw a flock fly over the city which obscured the sun for two or three hours, and were killed by hundreds, by people using sticks on the tops of houses. Mr. Bradford himself used to see them brought to the Philadelphia market by cart-loads. The aged T. Matlack informed me he once saw a full wagon load knocked down. A Captain Davy, who was in Philadelphia at that time, (described above,) went afterwards to Ireland, and there describing what he had seen, and giving the data for their numbers by giving breadth and time of passing, &c., some of the calculators declared they could not find numerals whereby to estimate their aggregate! They therefore declared it was a whapping lie, and ever after they gave to Captain Davy the name of Captain Pigeon.

Thomas Makin's poetic description of Pennsylvania in 1729, in Latin verse, says,

"Here, in the fall, large flocks of pigeons fly,
So numerous, that they darken all the sky."

In 1782, Hector St. John, of Carlisle, describing the country scenes he had before witnessed there, says, twice a year they ensnared numerous wild pigeons. They were so numerous in their flight as to obscure the sun. He has caught fourteen dozen at a time in nets, and has seen as many sold for a penny as a man could carry home

At every farmer's house they kept a tamed wild pigeon in a cage at the door, to be ready to be used at any time to allure the wild ones when they approached.

In 1793, just before the time of the yellow fever, like flocks flew daily over Philadelphia, and were shot from numerous high houses. The markets were crammed with them. They generally had nothing in their craws besides a single acorn. The superstitious soon found out they presaged some evil; and sure enough sickness and death came!

Fire Flies.—The first settlers and all subsequent European settlers have been much surprised with our night illuminations by our numerous phosphorescent summer flies. Makin thus spoke of them in his day—

> "Here insects are which many much admire,
> Whose plumes in summer evenings shine like fire."

Bees.—These, in the time of Kalm, who wrote of them in 1748, says they were numerous and must have been imported, because the Indians treated them as new comers, and called them, significantly, English flies. Hector St. John, at Carlisle, at and before 1782, speaks of the bees being numerous in the woods in that neighbourhood, and gives some humorous stories of their manner of finding the place of the cells, and the means of procuring the honey from hollow trees. No worms were ever known among beehives before the year 1800.

Rarities sent to Penn.—Among the presents sent to William Penn, by his request of the year 1686, were these, to wit: he saying, "Pray send us some two or three smoked haunches of venison and pork. Get us also some smoked shad and beef. The old priest at Philadelphia had rare shad. Send also some peas and beans of the country. People concerned ask much to see something of the place. Send also shrubs and sassafras," &c. In another letter he asks for tame foxes and Indian ornaments. In another he calls for furs, for coverlets and petticoats, and also some cranberries.

Flies and Martins.—I have often heard it remarked by aged people, that the flies in Philadelphia were much more numerous and troublesome in houses in their early days than since, especially in Market street. The difference now is imputed to the much greater cleanliness of our streets, and the speedier removal of offals, &c. It is said too, that the flies and flees were excessive in the summer in which the British occupied Philadelphia, caused then by the appendages of the army.

Mr. Thomas Bradford, who had been for seventy years a curious observer of the martens, has noticed their great diminution in the city, which he imputes to the decrease of flies, their proper food. In former years they came annually in vast numbers, and so clamorously as in many cases to drive out the pigeons from their proper resorts. Now he sees boxes which are never occupied. A late author in

Europe has said martens decrease there as flies and mosquitoes diminish.

Hector St. John, in 1782, speaks of his means of ridding his house of flies, in a manner sufficiently alarming to others. He brings a hornet's nest, filled with hornets, from the woods, and suspends it in lieu of an ornamental chandelier or glass globe, from the centre of his parlour ceiling! Here, being unmolested, they do no harm to any of the family, but pleased with their warm and dry abode, they catch and subsist on numerous troublesome flies. These they constantly catch on the persons, and even the faces of his children!

Locusts.—1749, June 1st—Great quantities then noticed—again in 1766, in 1783 and in 1800—in this last year they appeared first on the 25th May.

Sturgeon was remarkably abundant in the Delaware and Schuylkill rivers, and was formerly much more valued as diet among us, and especially by foreigners. The old newspapers often advertised it for sale by the city agent of one Richards, who pickled them in a rare manner at Trenton. We know from history that Sir Samuel Argal, the deputy governor of Virginia, first visited that colony in 1609, to trade and fish for sturgeon to be conveyed to Europe. Formerly there were but few families in the country but what put up one or two sturgeons every year at the shad time. In Penn's time they could be counted by dozens at a time, leaping into the air and endangering the boats!

Noxious Insects.—Several of these have appeared among us as new comers—such as destroyed perpetually the leaves of our fine elms once in the State-house yard, made their passage to this country about the year 1791, and began their wasteful career on like trees near the corner of Pine and Front streets. They were supposed to have gotten their passage in some foreign vessel making her discharge of cargo in that neighbourhood. They since destroyed like trees at Chew's place in Germantown.

"There filthily bewray and sore disgrace
The boughs on which are bred th' unseemly race."

Kalm, in 1748, speaks then of the peas being so destroyed by the bug that they then abandoned the cultivation of them, although they had before had them without such molestation in great abundance. They had to send to Albany for their annual seed, who would still use them, because the insect which also overspread New York neighbourhood, had hitherto exempted those at Albany.

It is curious, that while the worms to the peach trees, now so annoying and destructive to our trees, were formerly unknown here, they were in Kalm's time making general ravages on the peaches at Albany. Now Albany is again, I believe, in possession of good fruit. In the summer of 1750, a certain kind of worms, (so say the Gazettes) cut off almost all the leaves of the trees in Pennsylvania avoiding only the laurel bush, the leaves of which are poisonous to some animals.

Mr. Kalm made frequent mention of the excessive annoyance of the wood lice every where abounding in the woods. They were constantly brushed upon the clothes, and if you set down upon a stump or fallen tree, or upon the ground, you were speedily covered by a host of them, insinuating themselves under as well as above your clothes.

He speaks of locusts coming, as now, in every seventeen years. Caterpillars too came occasionally in such numbers as to destroy entire forests. Some such places he saw, where trees were growing up amidst the bare stalks of the old dead ones, destroyed by the worms.

Noxious weeds.—It occurs to me to mention some facts respecting some very prevalent weeds which have been introduced among us, to our prejudice, from foreign countries. The "Ranstead weed," or Anterrinum lineria, now excessively numerous in some fields around Philadelphia. It came first from Wales, being sent as a garden flower for Mr. Ranstead of Philadelphia, an upholsterer, and a Welshman.

The yellow and white daisy, or Chrisanthemum lucanthemum, also the day-wakers and night-sleepers, or star-hyacinth, botanically called Ornythegelum umbellatum. These also originally came out as garden flowers, where they multiplied, and their seed afterwards getting abroad in manure, produced a general diffusion of those pernicious plants. On one occasion, they came out in some straw packing to old Mr. Wistar, and from inoculating his farm, proceeded to others. The late introduction of the Merino wool, has brought the seed of another weed, which is multiplying rapidly among us.

Earthquakes.—In October, 1727, shocks of an earthquake were felt at night, at Philadelphia, and at New York and Boston, which set the clocks to running down, and shook off china from the shelves. The 7th December, 1737, at night, a smart shock was felt at Philadelphia, and at Conestogoe, New Castle, &c. When John Penn first arrived, on a Sunday, a strong earthquake was felt as he stepped ashore at High-street wharf. It raised some superstition, and it was, therefore, long remembered; and besides that, when he went home, a dreadful thunder-storm arose; and, finally, when he next time returned here as proprietary, a fierce hurricane came!—March 22, 1758, a smart shock was felt between 10 and 11 P. M. April 25, 1772, a slight shock felt, about 8 A. M. November 30, 1783, an earthquake felt in the city; and again, on the 1st December, a strong one was felt. January 8, 1817, the river was much agitated by the earthquake to the southward, tossing about the vessels, and raising the water one foot.

Aged Animals.—In 1823, month of June, there died on the plantation of Joseph Walmsley, of Byberry, a horse which was thirty-seven years of age. The table of "longevity of animals," states the life of a horse at twenty-five to thirty years only.

In 1824, the Pittsburg Mercury of January, declares, there is a horse then working at the brewery there, full thirty-one years of age, of full health and vigour. For the last fourteen years he has been at the brewhouse, and hauled 50,000 barrels of beer. One of thirty-one years of age is now in New York city, in a cart, and can draw 3000 lbs.—the property of John Cornish.

Two geese are now alive at Greenwich village, town of Horse-neck, eighty-five years of age each. They were hatched on the same place, and are still laying eggs.—J. Mead, owner.

John Kinsey's strange Death.—In the year 1748, died, at Philadelphia, John Kinsey, a young man, son of Judge Kinsey. His death was very singular. He was killed by his own gun, whilst resting the but of it on the bottom of a boat, in which he and his friends, on a shooting party, were crossing the Schuylkill, at Gray's ferry, on their return home. The piece, from an unknown cause, went off, and shot the load into his cheek, and thence it ascended into the brain, and he died without uttering a word. But what is peculiarly memorable is, that he had a remarkable premonition, the evening before, of his catastrophe; and he was then abroad, seeking to dissipate, by exercise and novelty of objects, the sad impressions which the occurrence had had upon his spirits.

He dreamed his cousin Pemberton had come to him, and told him to prepare to change worlds: while he talked, he thought he heard an explosion like thunder, and a flash of fire struck his cheek, [there was no thunder at the time,] and he awoke in great perturbation. The sense of the shock was deeply impressed upon his spirits. He, however, composed himself again to sleep, and was again, as he thought, (in dreaming,) visited by many spiritual beings, all of whom seemed to him to intimate his death. The influence of all these things upon his spirits was very great the next day. He communicated the facts to his family, and endeavoured to dissipate the depression of his spirits, and the constant thought of the past night, by cheerfulness. His companions were sent for to aid him in this object, and it was soon proposed to take a ramble in the woods with their guns. The mother endeavoured much to dissuade him from taking his gun; but it was overruled. They crossed the middle ferry, and in pursuing the game, he sometimes said, "I hope no accident will befall any of you, or me:" he often complained that his spirits were sad. At length, after some miles of such exercise, and when on their return, the fatal accident, above related, terminated his life! I have seen, in the possession of Mrs. D. Logan, a letter from John Ross, Esq., of the year 1748, [John Ross afterwards lived in the house next to the Farmers and Mechanics' Bank, eastward,] to his familiar friend, Dr. Cadwallader Evans, in which he details all the foregoing facts. He asserts he knows all the parties; and although greatly disinclined to superstition, he is compelled to suoscı.ıɔe to the truth of them, as indubitably true.

Varieties from the Gazettes, &c.—1726.—On the last day of De cember, Theophilus Longstreet, of Shrewsbury, of sixty years of age, met with seven swans flying over a meadow, and shot down six of them at the same shot—a shot never surpassed.

1728.—We have the following surprising, though authentic account of rum imported into Pennsylvania, during the year 1728, to wit:—224,500 gallons. In that day no other kind of spirits was used.

1735.—Some fishermen took a shark, seven feet long, above the city; the same year (March 4) great quantities of codfish were taken off the capes.

1753.—In this year the citizens of Philadelphia employed Cap-.ain Swain to go to Hudson's bay, to endeavour to find a north-west passage. He repeats his voyage the next year—both without any important result.

In 1754.—Month of June, a waterspout appeared on the Delaware, opposite to Kensington, which was carried up Cooper's creek, and supposed to break on the shore, where, it is said, considerable damage was done. A school-house was beat down, a roof blown off, and a new wherry was lifted up and broken to pieces by the fall: many trees were torn up by it.

In 1748, Christopher Lehman records, that on the 4th of May it rained brimstone! Soon as I saw this fact, I inferred it must have been the floss from the pines in Jersey; and now I lately saw a similar occurrence at Wilmington, North Carolina, from the same cause, and exciting much surprise there.

1758.—I saw a MS. letter, from Hugh Roberts to B. Franklin, then in London, which states a rare thing, saying, "Our friend, Philip Syng, has lost his excellent son John, strangely. He had been poking a stick into a kitchen sink, and holding a lighted candle in the other hand, when a vapour therefrom took fire, and so penetrated him that he lost his senses, and died in a few days.

Ruinous Speculations.—Philadelphia, in common with her sister cities, has been occasionally the victim of speculating mania. Six memorable instances have already occurred among us since the establishment of our independence. The facts concerning them severally, though too long for the present object, have been preserved in my MS. Annals, in the City Library, pages 94 to 97. Suffice it here briefly to say, speculation first began, soon after the peace, in soldiers' certificates—changing hands several times in a week, and constantly gaining!

The scrip of the Bank of the United States was a memorable event. It changed hands hourly, and went up from 25 to 140 dollars, and then fell suddenly; "It went up like a rocket, and fell like its stick!"

The great land speculation of Morris and Nicholson, in the interior lands of our state, was a most engrossing scheme of aggrandizement: very few gained any thing, and many fortunes were ruined. They themselves were desperately ruined, and for the great financier himself it provided a jail.

The public may form some idea of the extent of Morris and Nicholson's great land speculation, in the fact, that the debts unpaid by Nicholson are said to amount to twelve millions of dollars—an immense amount, certainly, for an individual in those early days!

Of the extent of those landed possessions, often bought at a few cents the acre, some conception may be formed, from the fact, that his brother Samuel reported to the government of Pennsylvania, in 1806, that the lands to which he had indisputable title, covered *one seventh* of the surface of the state! He told of one single operation of transfer of land in Georgia, for between one and two millions of acres.

Nicholson was the comptroller-general of the state of Pennsylvania, from 1782 to 1796, and in some way used the public funds to carry on his purchases. Two years after he had ceased to be comptroller, he began to show his embarrassments, and to excite a downhill preponderancy. In 1800 he died, and then the whole concern exploded. His promissory notes became virtually as nothing. Being a great debtor to the state, his lands lay under its *liens*. Many of these have since been relieved by compromise; but still, more than a million of acres remain encumbered thereby, and rendering, as a committee of the legislature declare, "titles doubtful and uncertain, retarding improvement, and keeping all concerned in endless suspense."

To remove these embarrassments, "Nicholson's Court" has been instituted, with plenary powers to relieve liens, and to adjust conflicting claims, &c. As a part of its operations, almost all the lands in Erie county is decreed to pass under its attachments; and in Beaver county, some two or three hundred tracts, exceeding 100,000 acres of the best land, and equal to one fourth of the county, are under similar process of action. Thus, at the end of forty years, does the all-grasping cupidity of one man disturb the peace and welfare of whole communities.

After the peace of 1783, deep speculation and great losses were sustained by excessive importations of British goods, beyond the means of the country to consume them, prompted by an unparalleled success in sales in a preceding year.

A deep and general speculation occurred in 1813–14. It was begun among the grocers, and, finally, influenced most other branches of business—ultimately recoiling, as it was all artificially excited, on all concerned.

In 1825, occurred deep speculations, and ruinous losses eventually, in the purchase of cotton intended for the English market. The wounds then inflicted, will long be remembered by some. It was an excited mania of gambling in the article, n[illegible] all warranted by the real want or deficiency of the article thus speculated upon.

"How oft has speculation, dreadful foe!
Swept o'er the country—laid our cities low!
The bold projector, restless of delay,
Leaves, with contempt, the old and beaten way
Of patient labour—slow and certain gain,
The fruit of care, economy, and pain:
But soon, reverses this conclusion bring,
Credit and ruin are the selfsame thing!"

Amusing Facts.—Some items partaking of singularity, and sometimes of amusement, in the contemplation, are here set down, to wit:

In 1720, Edward Horne, by advertisement, offers English saffron, "by retail, for its weight in silver!"

Same year is advertised, "best Virginia tobacco, cut and sold by James Allen, goldsmith." This union of two such dissimilar pursuits of business, strikes one as so incongruous now.

Tobacco pipes, of "long tavern size," are advertised as sold at four shillings per gross, by Richard Warder, pipe-maker, where foul pipes are burnt for eight pence per gross!

1722.—I meet with a strange expression—"*For sale by inch of candle*, on Monday next, at 4 o'clock in the afternoon, at the Coffee-house, a lot on Society hill," &c.

1723.—Josiah Quinby, of West Chester, New York, a Friend, advertises that he has discovered perpetual motion, and to be moved by the influence of the North star, &c.!! and to be combined with the influence of a well of water, over which his machinery should work!

1724.—Andrew Bradford, printer, offers a reward of £15, for apprehending John Jones, a tall, slender lad, of eighteen years of age, who stole five or six sheets of the 5 shilling and 20 shilling bills, which said Bradford was printing. He escaped after capture, from the constable, by slipping out of his coat, and leaving it in the constable's hand! He wore a light bob wig.

In 1728, some wicked fellows, in a neighbouring Presbyterian church, in lieu of another functionary, set up a large sturgeon in the pulpit, in the hot days, and the church being shut up, it was not known until it became so putrid as to compel the congregation to leave the house, and worship in a neighbouring orchard.

1729.—The Welsh having formed themselves into a fellowship appointed Dr. Wayman to preach them a sermon in their own language, and to give them a Welsh psalm on the organ—then a novelty. But their crowning rarity was, that after sermon, on the Lord's day, they went to drinking healths and firing cannon, to Davis' inn, at the Queen's Head, in Water street, each man wearing at church and in the procession leeks in his hat, &c.—"So did not St. Paul!"

1731.—A certain stone-cutter was in a fair way of dying the death of a nobleman, for being found napping with his neighbour's wife; the husband took the advantage of his being asleep, to make an attempt to cut off his head.—The wit which follows, in the reflections on the case, though showing the coarse taste of the readers then, is harmlessly left for the curious on page 118 of my MS. Annals, in the City Library.

1734.—A widow, of Philadelphia, was married in her shift, without any other apparel upon her, from a supposition prevalent then, that such a procedure would secure her husband in the law, from being sued for any debts of his predecessor. Kalm, in 1748, confirms this fact as a common occurrence, when her husband dies in debt. She thus affects to leave all to his creditors. He tells of a woman going from her former home, to the house of her intended husband, in her shift only, and he meets her by the way and clothes her, before witnesses, saying, "he has lent them."

1737.—A curious writer gives a long list of tavern expressions, used to express drunkenness among the tipplers; some are—"He has taken Hippocrates' elixir;" "he's as dizzy as a goose;" "his head is filled with bees;" "he's afflicted;" "he's made an Indian feast;" "he's sore footed;" "he clips his English;" "he sees two moons;" "has eat his opium;" "he walks by starlight;" "has sold his senses;" "has lost his rudder."

1754.—Is advertised, as just published, "The Youth's Entertaining Amusement; or a plain Guide to Psalmody: being a choice collection of tunes, sung in the English Protestant congregation in Philadelphia, with rules for learning; by W. Dawson." I give this title as a curious inadvertency, which expresses, with much simplicity of judgment, an unwary fact—that the youth, and too many of their abettors, too often resort to psalmody (which should be worship and adoration, if any thing) for mere entertainment and amusement.

1765.—There died this year, in the Northern Liberties, at the age of sixty, Margaret Gray, remarkable for having had nine husbands!

I sometimes hear anecdotes which I choose to suppress, because of their connexion with living names. I think of one which contains much piquancy and spirit, which I shall here put down as illustrating a fact which often occurred in the sudden transitions of men's conditions in the Revolution, from obscurity to elevation and renown, where accompanied with valour and ambition.—A celebrated Friend, a preacher, met an old acquaintance in the streets of Philadelphia, who had been of Friends' principles, with a sword girt on his side.—"Why, friend," said he, "what is this thou hast bedecked thyself with? not a rapier!" "Yes," was the reply; "for 'liberty or death' is now the watchword of every man who means to defend his property." "Why, indeed," rejoined the other, "thou art altered throughout; thy mind has become as fierce as thy sword: I had not expected such high feelings in thee. As to property, I thought thee had none; and as to thy liberty, I thought thee already enjoyed that by the kindness of thy creditors!"—The patriot alluded to was conspicuous in the public measures of the war; and although he never used his sword in actual combat, he directed those who did, and from that day has been a successful candidate to public offices; and finally, has raised himself a respectable name and estate.

I notice in the old MSS., that they originally called a portmanteau (as we now call it) a *portmantle*—certainly an appropriate name, as it was originally used as an intended cover for the necessary cloak or mantle, in travelling on horseback. The present word *knapsack*, I also found was originally spelled *snapsack*—an expressive name when we consider it, as it was, a sack which fastened with a snap-spring, or lock. As it was in itself a convenient pillow for the traveller when obliged to sleep abroad in the woods, it must have received the nickname of *nap* among the soldiers. The words portmantle and snapsack may be found used in Madame Knight's Journal, of 1704.—I think I have discovered the origin of the name of "Blue stockings," applied to literary ladies.* I find that, a century ago, it was a mark of lady-like distinction to wear coloured stockings, with great clocks—blue and green colours were preferred. The ladies who then formed literary clubs, being, of course, the best educated, and coming from the upper class in society, were those, chiefly, who could afford the blue stockings.—A pair of those stockings, of green silk, and broad red clocks, I have lately seen in possession of Samuel Coates, Esq. They were the wedding ones of his grandmother, in Philadelphia, and are double the weight of the present silk hose.

Sweating of Gold Coins.—The Saturday Bulletin, of the 29th of January, 1831, republishes a long article from the Lancaster Gazette, called "Reminiscences of Philadelphia:" the same is managed with considerable humour, and is intended to show, that the house of N and D., and the silversmith, Mr. D., were considerably engaged in money-making, as a *matter of commerce*, by sweating gold coin, and making it lighter thereby, for the West India trade, &c. This was during the time of the operation of Jay's treaty, which opened an extensive commerce with the British West India islands. It having been noticed that the half johannes was taken there by tale, the process of *sweating* was resorted to, by which fifteen to twenty per cent. of its value was retained. This answered sundry merchants for a time; but it becoming dangerous and disreputable as it became known, another expedient was resorted to—to make dies to construct a coin of alloyed gold. A Mr. Timothy Bingham, a die-sinker, and a Mr. Armitage, were employed in this service by sundry merchants, to whom they made their plans known. At the same time, Mr. D., the silversmith, also conceived the plan of making them, for his own market, so as to make his pieces, of six pennyweight, pass in the West Indies for eight dollars. He quit his employment as a silversmith, it is said, and moved into fashionable display, in the hopes of his splendid fortune; but a disaster at sea sunk his gold, and buried all his golden dreams at once.—[I knew the man, but I never heard of these circumstances.]

* Lady Montague's story seems too modern to account for it, and looks like a forced explanation.

This gold-sweating was done at New York, *before* the Revolution, without shame or reproach, for all gold going to the West Indies. An old gentleman told me, that he saw it often done there, when he was a lad, seventy years ago. It sweat off like water.

Potatoes.—This excellent vegetable was very slow of reception among us. It was first introduced from Ireland, in 1719, by a colony of Presbyterian Irish, settled at Londonderry, in New Hampshire. They were so slow in its use in New England, that as late as 1740, it was still a practice with masters to stipulate with some apprentices that they should not be obliged to use them! The prejudice was pretty general against them, that they would shorten men's lives, and make them unhealthy; and it was only when some people of the *better sort* chose to eat them as a palatable dish, that the mass of the people were disposed to give them countenance. At about the same time, fine salmon were so plentiful in Connecticut river, that apprentices in New England, stipulated not to eat them more than twice a week!

Big Oak Tree.—Such a tree, little noticed, is now standing on the farm of the Almshouse, near Philadelphia, probably the largest in Philadelphia county. It measures fourteen feet seven inches in circumference at the base, two feet above ground; and twelve feet eight inches at six feet from the ground. Its diameter, at one foot above the ground, is five feet four inches. The height of the tree is about fifty feet, and it has four big limbs, extending thirty-four, forty, forty-three, and forty-six feet, respectively. It appears to have increased by its annual rings, one eighth of an inch, and thus to indicate the tree to be two hundred and forty years of age. It is now, in 1837, in a state of decay, having the trunk or body of the tree hollow; but it may last as a venerable relic of days bygone, for several years to come.

Penn's Arms on Mile-stones.—There are now but few persons who are aware of these old mile-stones, made of sandstone. They stand on the Gulf road, and on another parallel road, probably the Haverford, marked 12 miles from the city—[12] in front, and on the back [ooo]. The three balls have always been called "the apple-dumplings." The stones on one of these roads were placed there by the Mutual Assurance Fire Company, as a price for their charter from the Penn family. It was a tradition of simple folk, that Penn was feasted with dumplings by King Tamany, at the Treaty-tree, and so gave rise to the balls as Penn's arms!

Ancient Coin found.—Ten pieces of silver coin, about two hundred years old, were recently ploughed up on B. C. Timmins' farm, at Chester, Burlington county, N. J. They are about the size of a dollar. No. 1, dated 1647, coined under Fred. Henry, prince of Orange: motto, "Confidens in Domino, non movetur"—(those who trust in God, shall not be moved.) No. 2, dated 1677, coined under William III., prince of Orange, with the same motto.

Milch Cows and Cowherd.—There used to be a regular gatherng of cows, by a *cowherd*, in Philadelphia, in Dock street near Second, which was continued down to the year 1795. Every morning, early, he stood at that place and blew his horn. Then all the housekeepers let out the cows in the neighbourhood—some two or three dozen, which would go directly to the point of assemblage, all standing still till the whole were gathered; then they went off with the cowherd to their field or commons for the day. In the evening he went for them and returned to the same spot; then the cowherd blew his horn, to warn the housekeepers of their return, when they opened their gates. At a signal understood, he blew his last blast, and they all dispersed to their several homes.

I know several persons, now of about sixty years of age, (in 1836,) sons of men in the best circumstances of life, who used to drive their cows out of town, daily, to pasture. [I know several of our city great ones, who would not thank me for my recollection of their names and actions.] They drove cows from as far as High street by Second and Third streets, out to the neighbourhood of Bush-hill and Girard college. I lately met one of the persons in this neighbourhood, and he inquired of me if I could recollect when *he* had charge of three such cows daily. He is now independent, and a bank director.

Tar and Feathers at Philadelphia.—In October, 1769, a man who had *informed* against some *run* wines, from an Egg Harbour shallop, was seized by some tars, and tarred and feathered from head to foot, then paraded through the street, and before every custom-house officer's door, and at the collector's. They then set him in the pillory, and afterwards ducked him in the mud of the dock, and then let him *go in peace*, to sin no more. [Similar measures were performed upon informers at New York and Boston in those days.]

A *Grave Stone* to James Porteus, dated July, 1736, now actually heads his grave in a city yard, say in Fox's lot in North Third street.

A grave-stone to M. Leader, lettered 1715, aged sixty-four years, with an hour-glass device, was dug up in 1832, in digging for a cellar, in the yard of No. 70, west side of Second street, below Chestnut street. The place was made ground, and may have been a family burial place.

Two grave-stones, of John and Rhoda Church, were dug from a cellar in Arch street, between Seventh and Eighth streets, in 1842 It had been Dr. Church's family ground.

CURIOSITIES AND DISCOVERIES.

"I say the tale, as it was said to me."

THE following facts, for want of a better designation, are arranged under the present head, although their value, as *discoveries* or *curiosities*, may have but little claim to future renown, to wit:

Kalm, the Swedish traveller, when here, in the year 1748, speaks of numerous instances of finding fragments of trees deeply embedded in the earth at Philadelphia and elsewhere. He had himself got a piece of petrified hickory, on the north-west side of the town, in the clay pits, then filled with water from a brook, where were many muscle shells—Mytili anatini. Boys gathered them and brought them to town for sale, where they were considered a dainty. Pieces of trees, roots, and leaves of oak, were often dug up from the well pits, dug in Philadelphia at the depth of eighteen feet. They also found in some places a slime like that which the sea throws on the shore. This slime was often full of trees, branches, reed, charcoal, &c. He relates similar facts from several of the Swedes at Swedesboro'—then called Rackoon, to wit: One King, a man of fifty years of age, had got a well dug on a hill near a rivulet, and at the depth of forty feet, found a quantity of shells of oysters and muscles, besides much reed and pieces of broken branches. Peter Rambo, about sixty years of age, said that in several places at Rackoon, where they had dug deep in the ground, they had found quantities of muscle shells and other marine animals. Sometimes, at twenty feet depth, they discovered logs of wood petrified, and others were charred, probably by some mineral vapour. On making a dike several years before this relation, along the creek on which the Swedish church at Rackoon stood, they found, in cutting through a bank, that it was filled with oyster shells, although it was one hundred and twenty miles from the nearest sea shore. Often in digging wells they found clams. Similar relations were confirmed by special declarations of Mauns Keen, Iven Lock, William Cobb, Aoke Helm, &c. They related that on one occasion they found, at a depth of twenty to thirty feet, a whole bundle of flax in good condition. It excited great surprise how it could get there. Mr. Kalm imagines it may have been the wild Virginia flax—Linum virginianum. Or it may have been what the Swedes themselves called Indian hemp—Apocynum cannabinum—a plant which formerly grew plentifully in old corn ground, in woods and on hills. From this, the Indians made their ropes and fishing tackle, &c. I have been thus particular in this detail, because I have myself a specimen of a "hank of hemp," as the discoverers called it, dug up from a well in the new prison, western yard, near Centre square, from the bottom of a pit or privy, at twelve feet deep.

Old Mauns Keen, a respectable Swede, told Mr. Kalm, in 1748, that on their making a first settlement at Helsinburg, on the Delaware below Salem, they found in digging to the depth of twenty feet, some wells enclosed with brick walls. The wells were at that time on the land, but in such places as are sometimes under water and sometimes dry. But since that time, the ground has been so washed away (of course old Helsinburg also!) that the wells are entirely covered by the river, and the water is seldom low enough to show the wells. As the Swedes afterwards made new wells at some distance from the former, they discovered in the ground some broken earthen vessels and some entire good bricks, and they often got them out of the ground by ploughing. These facts Mr. Kalm said, he often heard repeated by the aged Swedes. Their own belief was that the land, before their settlement there, had been possessed by some other race of Europeans, even possibly as the *Wineland* to which the old Norwegians went. The Indians, too, spoke of those wells, as being a tradition, that they had been made by another race of people some centuries before. We shall, however, see in these pages, that the Indians themselves had some rude construction of pottery, but never like the idea of real bricks. The whole suggestion and facts are curious, and may afford some speculation.

In digging a well for the house of the late David Rittenhouse, at the north-west corner of Seventh and Arch streets, they found the remains of a pine tree, at a depth of eighteen feet below ground. On the ground of Mr. Powell, within the same square, another like remains was also found; one of them was laying horizontal from the other, which seemed to be standing; they were obliged to cut off a limb to proceed with their work.

In digging a well for a pump, at Bingham's stable, back of the Mansion house, the well-digger found, at the depth of twenty-one feet, the appearance of a former surface, and several hickory nuts thereon.

In some part of Spruce street, some distance below the surface, the street commissioner, who told of it to Thomas Bradford, found there a pile of cord wood standing on its end.

The trunk of a buttonwood was found near Arch and Seventh streets, at a great depth beneath its present surface. It was embedded in black mud, and had many leaves and acorns about it.

Mr. John Moore, a brick-mason of the city, told me a fact which strongly illustrates the rapid rise of Philadelphia—to wit: that although he was but sixty years of age, he had built five hundred buildings. He gave me the following facts, viz.: About forty years ago, in digging a well thirty feet at the south-west corner of Eighth and Cherry streets for P. Waglam, they came to a pine tree, laying horizontal, which they cut through, of great dimensions. Mr. Moore has seven houses in Cherry street, on the south side, between

Eighth and Ninth streets. In digging his front well in Cherry street, at thirty feet, they came to marsh mud, and found acorns and oak leaves in abundance, and a little below them they came to fine polished coarse gravel, from the size of peas to filberts. Afterwards he dug two wells back, one hundred and forty feet southward on said ground, and at same depth came to precisely the same discoveries of acorns, leaves, and gravel. All the earth, save the first four to four and a half feet of made ground, appeared to be the natural strata of loam and sand. When he was building Mr. Girard's stores in north Water street, about thirty-five years ago, they dug out of the cellar ground, wine and beer, about one dozen bottles each, which still retained strength, supposed to have been buried there one hundred years.

Mr. Graff, the city agent for the water pipes, informed me of his having found, in digging to lay them, "near the Bank of Pennsylvania," in Second street, as I understood him, at twelve feet below the present surface, a regular pebble pavement. I should expect this to be the case in Walnut street, westward of Second street.

The late aged Timothy Matlack, Esq., told me of his having seen spatterdocks, fresh and green, dug up at eighteen feet depth, at the place called Clarke & Moore's brewhouse, on Sixth street a little below Arch street. This occurred in the year 1760, and the specimens were used by Dr. Kinnersly, in the College before his class.

At the corner of Fourth and Greenleaf alley he saw, at four feet beneath the present surface, the top of a white oak rail post, and they had to dig ten feet more for a fast foundation for a house.

Colonel James Morris, when ninety years of age, told me of his seeing turf dug up at the time of sinking the foundation of Second street bridge over Dock creek. It was a congeries of black fibrous roots. Turf also was seen in digging seventeen feet for a gravel foundation to Francis West's store in Dock street. The turf was found at twelve feet depth.

The late Jacob Shoemaker said he saw coal taken from a vein found in digging a well at a place in Turner's lane, about a quarter of a mile eastward of the Ridge road. It was, however, more probable it was such charred wood as is now found in the river bank at Bordentown.

Kensington has its foundation on quick sand, so that none of their wells will hold any depth of water.

Governor Dennie's daughter was buried in the Friend's burying ground near the corner of Third and Arch streets. What is curious is, that after she had been buried thirty years, she was dug up and found entire, but perished when exposed to the air. Her hair had grown as long as the grave-digger could extend his hands. Her broad riband was entire and was worn afterwards by the digger's daughter! Her nails were grown too. This relation is well established, and fully agrees with some other facts of the enduring quality of silk—for instance, on disinterring the leaden coffins of

Lord and Lady Bellemont at New York, in 1787, the lead was found corroded, but the silk velvet on the lid was entire. At Boston, in 1824, they disinterred a British officer; the body and clothes were perished, but the silk military sash was sound in material and colour.

Thomas Dixey, a pump-maker and well-digger, a man of seventy years of age; intelligent and respectable, a chief undertaker, in his way, for forty years in the city, having been requested to tell me all he had ever met with as curious under ground, told me, that he has often, in several places, at considerable depths, come across acorns, oyster shells, &c. He told me that in the neighbourhood of Carter's alley and Go-Forth alley he dug twenty feet, and came to oyster shells and acorns. He found a great and excellent spring at twenty-eight feet depth, at the corner of Go-Forth alley and Dock creek.

When the house, No. 72, South Fourth street, a little above Walnut street, west side, was built, they dug nine feet for their cellar, and there came to an old post and rail fence.

Mr. Dixey, in digging for a well on the north side of South street, near Third street, on the premises of Mr Reed, silk dyer, came, at the depth of twenty-five feet, across a pine limb of three inches in thickness, having its bark on it. It had petrified, and he actually ground it into a good hone, and gave it to the said Mr. Reed.

At No. 13, Dock street, the house of Thomas Shields, was found, in digging his cellar, a regular fire hearth, one a half feet below the present spring-tide mark.

Christian Witmeek, an old digger of wells in the Northern Liberties, mentioned some discoveries about Pegg's run. In Lowber's tanyard, at thirteen feet depth, cut across a small fallen tree—dug thirty-eight feet; at thirty-four feet they came to wood; full as much as twenty-four feet was of black mud. In digging a well near there for Thomas Steel, No. 81, St. John street, he came, at twenty-one feet depth, to real turf of ten feet thickness; at twenty-six feet depth they came to a crotch of a pine tree.

The clay in the vicinity of the new prison in Arch street, by Centre square, is the deepest in the city, being twenty-eight feet deep. In digging twenty-eight feet on Singer's lot near there, Mr. Groves came to gravel, and dug up a limb of an oak tree of five inches thickness, and longer than the well across which it lay. Some oak leaves, and the impressions of several were marked on the clay. Mr. Grove found an Indian tomahawk at five feet depth in M'Crea's lot, in Chestnut street, *vis-a-vis* Dorsey's Gothic mansion.

In digging a well for Thatcher, in Front near to Noble street, they came, at the depth of twenty-eight feet, to an oak log of eighteen inches thickness, quite across the pit. The whole was alluvial deposit in that neighbourhood. Turf was dug out and burnt—in digging for the drain wells of twenty-eight feet depth under the present Sansom's row, in Second street north of Pegg's run.

In Race street, between Front and Second streets, in digging the foundation of the engine house now there, they dug up an Indian grave, and found the bones.

At the corner of Eighth and Cherry streets, in digging a well, at the depth of forty feet, says Joseph Sansom, they found a fallen log

Other facts of subterrene discoveries will be found in other parts of this work, connected with certain localities spoken of severally.

In 1707–8, there was much expectation, through the suggestions of Governor Evans, of a great discovery of valuable minerals in Pennsylvania. William Penn, on hearing of it, begged an explanation, and hoped it might relieve him from his embarrassments! It proved, however, to be a deceit of one Mitchell, who had been a miner in England. He pretended he was led to the discovery by a Shawnese king. Some of the "black sand," &c., was sent to Penn to assay it.

In 1722, mine land is spoken of as having been taken up for Sir William Keith, at a place beyond Susquehanna.

In 1728, James Logan writes of there being then four furnaces in the colony in blast.

About the year 1790, John Nancarro, a Scotchman, had a furnace under ground for converting iron into steel. It stood at the north-west corner of Ninth and Walnut streets. There was also a furnace, above ground, at the north-west corner of Eighth and Walnut streets, having a large chimney, and tapering to the top. There a curious fact occurred, which, but for this record, might puzzle the *cognoscenti* and antiquaries at some future day;—such as whether the aborigines had not understood the art of fusing iron, &c. The fact was this:—The great mass of five tons of iron bars which were in the furnace, was suddenly converted into a great *rock of steel*, by reason of a fissure in the furnace which let in the air, and consumed the charcoal, whereby the whole ran into *steel*, equal to four or five tons. Some houses, of very shallow cellars, have been since erected over the place, and all are quite unconscious of the treasure which rests beneath them. It was an open lot when so used by Nancarro.

There is a curious and unaccountable vault far under ground, in the back premises of Messrs. John and C. J. Wistar,—say, No. 139 High street, north side, and between Third and Fourth streets. At fourteen feet depth is a regular arched work of stone, sixteen feet long, and without any visible outlet. In breaking into its top to know its contents, they found nothing therein, save a log lying along the whole length. They sealed it up again, and the privy wall now rests upon it. There is no conjecture formed concerning what it may have been constructed for, nor at what time it may have been made. Dr. Franklin once lived in the adjoining house, No. 141; (both houses belonged to Wistar,) whether the vault could have had any connexion with his philosophy may be a question. In rebuilding those houses five wells were found under the foundations.

In the year 1836, when digging to lay down the hydrant pipe in

High street, opposite to Decatur street, they found, under ground, *the floor* of a store or stable, out in the middle of the street; the joists were still sound and heavy. I think it must have been the remains of *the bridge* which once ought to have run across the street *at that place.*

At that run, a drunken man, who had fallen into it, was found drowned, lying on his face.

In 1738, it is announced in the Gazette, that they have the pleasure to acquaint the world, that the famous Chinese plant, *ginseng*, is now discovered in the province, near Susquehanna. It appears from the specimens sent home, that it agrees with Du Halde's account, and with Chambers' Dictionary.

Our Gems.—We are little aware of the treasure we possess among ourselves in the way of gems. The reason that they are not sought and, known is, that they cost so high to prepare them for use; so that only imported ones are now used by our jewellers. We have the chrysoprase, of a pea-green, the amethyst, the topaz, in the yellow quartz. The white or rock crystal, also the brown crystal or smoky quartz, in splendid specimens, in Lancaster county. The garnet or carbuncle, of a rich red, is found abundantly near West Chester, and some near Germantown. The calcedony, in much variety, abounds in our state and New York. Jasper is found very good at Hoboken. The beryl, splendid and perfect, is found in Chester county, exceeding eight inches in diameter. Several of the above gems are to be gathered by the handful—picking one and two here and there at a time, on the sand beach of Cape May, by the summer bathers who may pad along the strand for that purpose; they being such as are washed up in storms from the bosom of the ocean, where they may have been cast, in the whirl of waters at the first rotary impulse of the earth, when the fiat went forth—"Let the dry land appear." When we shall have lapidaries working as cheaply as in Europe, these stones may find demand—and withal, lower their market price.

The chalybeate spring, at Harrowgate, is first announced as a discovery by George Esterly, in July, 1784. After that, it became a place of public resort, as a beautiful garden, &c., and was so sustained for many years.

WHALES AND WHALERY.

"The huge potentate of the scaly train."

It will surprise a modern Philadelphian to learn how very much the public attention was once engaged in the fishery of whales along our coast, and to learn withal, that they disdained not occasionally to leave their briny deeps to explore and taste the gustful fresh waters of our Delaware—even there

"Enormous sails incumbent, an animated isle,
And in his way dashes to heaven's blue arch the foaming wave."

"The Free Society of Traders" had it as a part of their original scheme of profit, to prosecute extensively the catching of whales. To this purpose they instituted a whalery near Lewistown, and, as I am inclined to think, there was once in some way connected with the whalery a place of sale or deposit, at the junction of "Whalebone alley" and Chestnut street, on the same premises now Pritchet's. The old house which formerly stood there had a large whalèbone affixed to the wall of the house, and when lately digging through the made earth in the yard, they dug up several fragments of whales, such as tails, fins, &c. Its location there originally was by the tide-water ranging in Dock creek. Be this as it may, we are certain of the whales and whaleries, from facts like the following, to wit:

In 1683, William Penn, in writing to the above society, says, "The whalery hath a sound and fruitful bank, and the town of Lewis by it, to help your people."

In another letter of the same year he says, "Mighty whales roll upon the coast, near the mouth of the bay of the Delaware; eleven caught and worked into oil in one season. We justly hope a considerable profit by whalery, they being so numerous, and the shore so suitable."

In another letter of 1683, William Penn again says, "Whales are in great plenty for oil, and two companies of whalers, and hopes of finding plenty of good cod in the bay."

In 1688, Phineas Pemberton, of Pennsbury, records a singular visiter, saying, "a whale was seen in the Delaware as high as the falls!"

In 1696, Gov. Andrew Hamilton, of Burlington, New Jersey, authorizes George Taylor, of Cape May, to be his deputy, and to take into his possession wrecks, or drift whales, or other royal fish, that shall be driven on shore along the coast, or in the Delaware.

In 1722, deficiency of whales is intimated, saying in the Gazette, that there are but four whales killed on Long Island, and but little oil is expected from thence.

In 1730, a cow whale of fifty feet length is advertised as going ashore to the northward of Cape May, dead. The harpooners are requested to go and claim it; thus showing, I presume, that a fishery was then near there, by the same persons who may have harpooned it.

In 1733, month of April, two whales, supposed to be a cow and a calf, appeared in the river before the city. They were pursued and shot at by people in several boats, but escaped notwithstanding. What a rare spectacle it must have been to the fresh water cockneys of the city.

In 1735, month of July, some fishermen proved their better success at this time in capturing an ocean fish, such as a shark of seven feet length in a net, a little above the city. The Gazette of the day says it is but seldom a shark is found so high in fresh water. If that was strange in that day, it was still stranger in modern times, when "a voracious shark" of nine feet long and five hundred weight was caught at Windmill cove, only five miles below Philadelphia, in July, 1823. Not long after, say in January, 1824, near the same place, was taken a seal of four feet four inches long, and sixty-one pounds weight, near the Repaupa flood gates.

About the same time another was taken in the Elk river. Many years ago seals were often seen about Amboy, but to no useful purpose.

In 1736, February, "two whales are killed at Cape May, equal to forty barrels of oil, and several more are expected to be killed by the whalemen on the coast."

Finally, the last "huge potentate of the scaly train" made his visit up the Delaware about the year 1809,—then a whale of pretty large dimensions, to the great surprise of our citizens, was caught near Chester. He was deemed a rare wanderer, and as such became a subject of good speculation as an exhibition in Philadelphia and elsewhere. Thomas Pryor, who purchased it, made money by it, and in reference to his gains was called "Whale Pryor." The jaws were so distended as to receive therein an arm chair, in which visiters sat.

Two dead whales were driven on shore at Assateague beach, near Snowhill, Maryland, in December, 1833; one a hundred and seventeen feet in length, and the other eighty-seven feet in length. The cause of their death unknown. They were expected to make three hundred barrels of oil.

It is a fact but little known, that, even now, there is a family on Long beach, New Jersey, who are every winter seeking for, and sometimes capturing whales. In this business they have been engaged, the father and two sons, ever since the time of the Revolution.

In May, 1834, a young whale, of sixty feet, went into New Haven harbour—was chased, grounded, and used up.

In April, 1833, three seals were seen near Chester. One of them was caught in the shad seine, and was kept for exhibition. Some had before appeared in New York harbour near their old haunt at Robyn's reef.

GRAPES AND VINEYARDS.

NUMEROUS incidental intimations and facts evince the expectations originally entertained for making this a flourishing grape and wine country. Before Penn's arrival, the numerous grapevines, every where climbing the branches of our forest trees, gave some sanction to the idea that ours may have been the ancient *Vineland* so mysteriously spoken of by the Norwegian writers. Almost all the navigators, on their several discoveries, stated their hopes, from the abundance of grapevines, with exultation. But neglecting these we have substituted whisky!

Penn, in his letter of 1683, to the Free Society of Traders, says, "Here are grapes of divers sorts. The great red grape, now ripe, (in August,) called by ignorance the fox grape, because of the rich relish it hath with unskilful palates, is in itself an extraordinary grape, and by art, doubtless, may be cultivated to an excellent wine —if not so sweet, yet little inferior to the Frontignac, as it is not much unlike in taste, ruddiness set aside, which in such things, as well as mankind, differs the case much. There is a kind of muscadel, and a little black grape, like the cluster grape of England, not yet so ripe as the other, but they tell me, when ripe, sweeter; and that they only want skilful vignerons to make good use of them." Then he adds—"I intend to venture on it with my Frenchman this season, who shows some knowledge in these things. At the same time he questions whether it is best to fall to fining the grapes of the country, or to send for foreign stems and sets already approved. If God spare his life, he will try both means"—[a mode of practice recently obtaining favour with several experimenters.] "Finally," he says, "I would advise you to send for some thousands of plants out of France, with some able vignerons."

With such views, Penn, as we shall presently show, instituted several small experiments. He and others naturally inferred, that a country so fruitful in its spontaneous productions of grapes, must have had a peculiar adaptation for the vine. When the celebrated George Fox, the founder of Friends, was a traveller through our wooded wilderness, he expressly notices his perpetual embarrassments in riding, from the numerous entangling grapevines. The same too is expressly mentioned by Pastorius, in his traversing the original site of Philadelphia. And when Kalm was here, in 1748, he speaks of grapevines in every direction, the moment he got without the bounds of the city; and in his rides to Germantown and Chester, &c., he found them all along his way. Thus numerous and various as they once were, it may be a question, whether, in the general destruction of the vines since, we have not destroyed several of peculiar excellence, since modern accidental discoveries have brought some excellent specimens to notice,—such as the Orwigsburg and Susquehanna.

In 1685, William Penn, in speaking of his vineyard to his steward, James Harrison, writes: "Although the vineyard be as yet of no value, and I might be out of pocket, till I come, be regardful to Andrew Dore, the Frenchman. He is hot, but I think honest." This, I presume, refers to the vigneron, and to the vineyard at Springettsbury.

In another letter, he writes to "recommend Charles de la Noe, a French minister, who intends, with his two servants, to try a vineyard, and if he be well used more will follow."

In 1686, he writes to the same steward, saying, "All the vines formerly sent and in the vessel (now,) are intended for Andrew (Dore,) at the Schuylkill, for the vineyard. I could have been glad of a taste last year, as I hear he made some." Again he says, "If wine can be made by Andrew Dore, at the vineyard, it will be worth to the province thousands by the year,—there will be hundreds of vineyards, if it takes. I understand he produced ripe grapes by the 28th of 5 mo., from shoots of fifteen or sixteen months, planting. Many French are disheartened by the Carolinas, (for vines,) as not hot enough!"

About the time William Penn was thus urging the cultivation of the vine, his enlightened friend Pastorius, the German and scholar, was experimenting, as he expressly says, on his little vineyard in Germantown.

How those vineyards succeeded, or how they failed, we have no data on which to found an explanation now. We beheld, however, lately, that Mr. E. H. Bonsall was succeeding with a vineyard among us; and at Little York the success is quite encouraging.

The following description of the discovery and character of the Susquehanna grape, will probably go far to prove the superiority of some natural grapes once among us, or leave grounds to speculate on the possibility of birds conveying off some of Penn's above mentioned imported seeds! Another new and excellent grape has been discovered on the line of the new canal, beyond the Susquehanna.

About 15 years ago, there were obtained some cuttings of a grapevine which was discovered by Mr. Dininger, on an island in the Susquehanna, called Brushy island. The island upon which this vine was found is uninhabited and uncultivated, the soil alluvial, and subject to overflow. The vine runs upon a large sycamore, spreading through the top branches, to the height of forty or fifty feet from the ground, and appears to have grown with the tree, the root being from twenty to thirty feet from the tree. The wood, leaf and early shoots very much resemble what is called Miller's Burgundy, also the fruit, in colour and flavour; but in size it is much larger. It was observed, that the fruit obtained in September, 1827, was a deep brown; that of the next season, some were brown and others a deep black. The difference was accounted for by Mr. Dininger, who stated that the brown bunches were those that were shaded from the sun by the thick foliage of the tree; but those exposed to the sun were black. Some of the bunches procured that season were very fine, and set closely upon the stem—fruit the size of the Powel grape, skin thin, *no pulp*, a sweet water, seed small, flavour equal to the celebrated *Black Prince*, and not inferior to any foreign grape, for the table.

It is believed to be a truth, that no native grape was previously found, that did not possess a secondary skin, enclosing a stringy pulp, and most of them possessing a husky flavour, proving their affinity to the fox. But because this one, found on the Susquehanna, is an exception—because it possesses all the delicate sweetness, tenderness of skin, and delicious flavour of the most esteemed exotics, we are not willing to concede that it is not entitled to be classed among the native productions of our soil.

In favour of its being purely of American origin, we will state, that the island on which it was found has never been inhabited; that lying immediately below Eshleman's falls, the approach to it is difficult; and that it has rarely been visited, except by the proprietor, an aged man named Fales, lately deceased, who did not trouble himself much about grapes, native or foreign, and merely used it as a place to turn young cattle upon in the summer season. The sycamore, of which it is the parasite, appears to be about forty years old, and the vine is rooted about thirty feet from the stem of the tree, under a pile of drift wood, from which it runs along the ground, in company with three other vines of the fox or chicken variety, apparently of the same age, and, interwoven, climb the tree together. From appearances, one should judge that the tree is not older than the vine; and that the young sycamore, in its growth, carried the vine with it.

At the period in which this vine must have taken root, foreign grapes were little known in the United States, and then their cultivation was confined to the neighbourhood of the great Atlantic cities.

None of the foreign varieties we have seen correspond in appearance with this fruit; for though the wood and leaf of Miller's Burgundy are so similar as scarcely to be distinguished apart, yet the bunches and fruit of that of the Susquehanna are much larger.

Again—we have many stories related through the country, by persons worthy of credit, of the delicious grapes found upon the islands of the Susquehanna; some described as *white*, some *red*, *black*, *purple*, &c., without pulp, and all ripening in August and September. It was these reports which urged several gentlemen to the pursuit, that has been so far crowned with success, in the discovery of the kind above described. Mr. D. was one of several citizens who visited the Brushy island, in the autumn of 1827, and saw the vine, and from the observations then made, and facts that have since come to his knowledge, says, I have no doubt that there does exist in those islands a variety of grapes, equal, for the table or for wine, to any that have been imported, and that they are purely native.

Of the grape now discovered, we understand there are from two to three hundred plants, in the possession of different gentlemen in that neighbourhood, in vigorous growth, independent of those in the possession of Col. Carr and the Messrs. Landreths, of Philadelphia.

Charles Thomson used to tell, that the most luscious and excellent wild grape he ever tasted, grew in a meadow on the road to Chester. He thought the fruit so fine that he intended, at a proper season, to procure cuttings, for its cultivation; but found the stupid owner had destroyed it, because "it shaded too much of his ground!"

BEASTS OF PREY, AND GAME.

> "The squirrels, rabbits, and the timid deer,
> To beasts of prey are yet exposed here.—*Poem,* 1729.

THE following notices of the state of wild animals roaming through our woody wastes in early days, will aid the mind to perceive the state of cultivation which has since banished the most of them from our territories, to wit:

Mr. Kalm, the Swedish traveller, who was here in 1748, says that all the old Swedes related, that during their childhood, and still more in the time of the arrival of their fathers, there were excessive numbers of wolves prowling through the country, and howling and yelping every night, often destroying their domestic cattle.

In that early day, a horrible circumstance occurred for the poor Indians. They got the smallpox from the new settlers. It killed many hundreds of them. The wolves, scenting the dead bodies, devoured them all, and even attacked the poor sick Indians in their huts, so that the few who were left in health, were much busied to keep them off.

The Swedes, he said, had tamed some few wolves. Beavers they had so tamed, that they were taken to fish with, and bring the fish they caught to their keepers. They also tamed wild geese, and wild turkeys. Those wild turkeys which he saw in the woods, were generally larger than those of the domestic race.* The Indians also tamed the turkeys, and kept them near their huts. Minks were very numerous along the waters.†

* Penn speaks of turkeys weighing from forty to fifty pounds.

† Hector St. John, of Carlisle, in 1784, speaks of it as practised there, to render rattlesnakes harmless, and to keep them as matters of curiosity and amusement. If they find such a snake asleep, they put a small forked stick on their necks, by which they hold

In 1721, in September, several bears, says the Gazette, were seen yesterday, near this place, and one was killed at Germantown, and another near Darby. Last night a very large bear being spied by two amazons, as he was eating his supper of acorns up a tree, they called some inhabitants of this place (the city!) to their assistance, and he was soon fetched down and despatched by them.

As late as the years 1724 and '29, they gave a premium, by law, of 15 to 20*s.* for wolves, and 2*s.* for foxes. This was for the purpose of destroying them out of the country.

In 1729, a panther was killed at Conestogoe. It had disturbed the swine in their pen at night. The owner ran to the place with his dogs, and the beast then ascended a tree. It being very dark, the women brought fire and made a flame near it. It was shot at twice. The second fire broke both its legs, when, to their surprise, it made a desperate leap and engaged with the dogs, until a third shot in the head despatched it.

About the same time, a monstrous panther was killed at Shrews bury, by an Indian. Its legs were thicker than those of a horse, and the nails of its claws were longer than a man's finger. The Indian was creeping to take aim at a buck in view, when hearing something rustling behind him, he perceived the panther about to spring upon him. He killed him with four swan shot in the head.

In 1730, a woman in Chester county, going to mill, spied a deer, fast asleep, near the road. She hit it on the head with a stone, and killed it.

The latest notice of buffaloes, nearest to our region of country, is mentioned in 1730, when a gentleman from the Shenandoah, Va., saw there a buffalo killed, of 1400 pounds; and several others came in a drove at the same time.

1732.—At Hopewell, in New Jersey, two bucks were seen fighting near the new meeting-house, in the presence of a black doe. They fastened their horns so closely, that they could not separate, and were so taken alive! The doe also was taken. Another brace had been before caught in a similar extremity!

In 1749, the treasurers of the several counties declared their treasuries were exhausted by the premiums paid for squirrels. £8,000 was paid in one year, (says Kalm,) for gray and black squirrels, at 3*d* a head, making the enormous aggregate of 640,000! The premium was then reduced one half.

Samuel Jefferies, who died near West Chester, in 1823, at the age of eighty-seven, very well remembered a time, in his early life, when deer were plenty in his neighbourhood: and Anthony Johnson, of Germantown, tells me of often hearing from his grandfather there,

---

them firm to the ground, and in that state give them a piece of leather to bite. This they jerk back with great force, until they find their two poisonous fangs torn out. Once he saw a tamed one quite gentle. It was delighted to be stroked with a soft brush, and would turn on its back to make it more grateful. It would take to the water, and come back at a call.

of his once killing deer, beavers, and some bears and wolves in that township.

Mr. Kalm, when here in 1748, says, all then agreed that the quantities of birds for eating, was then diminished. In their forefathers' days, they said the waters were covered with all sorts of water-fowl. About sixty to seventy years before, a single person could kill eighty ducks of a morning! An old Swede, of ninety years, told Mr. Kalm he had killed twenty-three ducks at one shot! The wild turkeys and the hazel hens, (pheasants,) too, were in abundance, in flocks, in the woods. Incredible numbers of cranes visited the country every spring. They spoke also of fish being once much more abundant. At one draught they caught enough to load a horse; and *codfish*, since all gone, were numerous at the mouth of the Delaware.

In the year 1751, as I was assured by the late aged Timothy Matlack, Esq., there was killed a bear, at the square now open eastward and adjoining the late Poor-house, nine years before it was built, in 1760. He was killed by Reuben Haines, grandfather of the late gentleman of that name. He and five others had started him from near Fairmount, and chased him through the *woods* nearly five miles, when he took to a cherry tree at the square aforesaid. They had no gun, but remaining there till one was procured, he was shot down. Mr. Matlack declared this was a fact. Penn's woods, we know, were then existing thereabout.

In 1750, a woman killed a large bear at Point-no-point. She lived there with Robert Watkins, and while she was at work near the kitchen out-house, he came up to it so near, that she killed him.

These were of course deemed rare occurrences, even in that day, and have been since remembered and told from that cause.

Old Mr. Garrigues, a respectable Friend, when about eighty-six years of age, assured me that when he was a lad, and coming home one night late from Coates' woods, then in the Northern Liberties, he actually encountered a bear as he was passing over the path at Pegg's run, then a lonely place. It was moonlight, and he was sure he could not have been deceived, and he fully believed it was also a wild one. This may seem strange to our conceptions now, but as the time is seen to agree with the story preceding it, of Haines and others starting a bear at Fairmount, in 1751, there may be more reason for inferring the fact, than would otherwise be admitted. If no better reason could be found, it might in both cases be admitted to be a bear escaped from keeping. Those different parties certainly never thought of comparing their accounts, and probably never knew of each other's adventures. Their coincidence, so far as they accord, furnishes a reason which has not escaped my observation, that an annalist should not reject isolated facts, if interesting themselves, because he could not immediately discern their bearing; for other incidents may occur to give them their due interpretation at some subsequent period.

In 1816, January 1st.—A large she wolf was taken in West Nottingham, Chester county, nearly three feet high, measuring upwards of six feet in length.

1817, January 7.—A large eagle was shot fifteen miles from Philadelphia, in Moreland township, weighing eight pounds, and its wings extending seven feet. About the same time a wild cat was killed at Easton, measuring three feet.

1827, February.—A panther, measuring six feet, was killed seventeen miles from Easton.

At Bellefonte, Pennsylvania, in December, 1832, it was published that Mr. Long, of Jefferson county, Pennsylvania, called Bill Long, had killed during the hunting season, one hundred and sixty-five deer, five elks, twenty-eight bears, and thirteen wolves; one of the elks weighed seven hundred pounds. All this was done in a county within fifty miles of the great State canal, and at places but thirty miles from the great thoroughfare, the Allegheny river. So rapid is our improvement.

In October, 1834, a bear, weighing one hundred and forty pounds, was started by dogs from near the head of Joseph Lindsay's mill pond, in Chester county, and after being pursued by men and dogs, and ascending and descending several high trees, and after receiving several shots and grappling some two or three times with the dogs, was at last killed by six guns at once. Such a visiter, in so improved a county, was a strange affair, and it is supposed that it must have crossed the Delaware from the Jersey pines.

About the same time it is published, that several were seen not far from Reading, coming down from the wooded mountains, and exploring their way along the skirts of the farms.

In the same winter of 1836, a man was killed and torn to pieces by wolves, in Perry county, Liberty valley, he having first killed six of them with his knife—so it was published.

CULTURE OF SILK.

From the commencement of our annals, at different periods of time, the advantages of silk culture have been recommended or attempted.

As early as the year 1725, James Logan, in writing to the Penn family, recommends "the culture of silk in this country as extremely beneficial and promising." He says "iron-works also promise well." In the next year he speaks of silk sent to England, saying "he is glad it proves so good, and he doubts not, in time, the country may raise large quantities."

In 1734, Governor Gordon addresses the lords commissioners of trade on various objects of produce, &c., and speaks in strong terms of his expectations from the culture of silk, "as a fit return to Great Britain" for their usual importations; he says the tree is so natural to our soil, and the worm thrives so well. Some among us have shown its practicability by making some small quantities, &c.

In the year 1770, the subject was taken up in Philadelphia and adjacent country with great spirit. It was greatly promoted by the exertions of the American Philosophical Society, stimulated by the communications from Dr. Evans and Dr. Franklin in Europe. Application was made to the assembly for the establishment of a public filature at Philadelphia, for winding cocoons, and the managers to have power to grant premiums, &c., equal to about £500 per annum, for five years. The necessary incipient funds, equal to £900 were furnished by generous individuals on subscription, being generally £2 each, some £15, and Governor John Penn £20. With such means the filature was opened in June, 1770, at a house in Seventh street, between Arch and High streets, and a rate of premiums was announced.

It appears that in the year 1771, about 2300 lbs. were brought there to reel, and that of it 1754 lbs. were purchased by the managers in about two months, in July and August; nearly two-thirds of this had been raised in New Jersey. At the same time much discussion of the subject appeared in the gazettes, and many mulberry trees were planted in New Jersey and the counties around Philadelphia. The ladies in particular gave much attention to the subject, and especially after the war had begun, when the foreign fabrics of silk were cut off from their use. As early as the year 1770, Susanna Wright, of Lancaster county, at Columbia, made a piece of mantua of sixty yards length, from her own cocoons, of which I have preserved some specimens* in my MS. Annals in the City Library, page 165 and 170. She also made much sewing silk. Mrs. Hopkinson, mother of the late Francis Hopkinson, raised much cocoons. A woman in Chester county raised thirty thousand worms. To give eclat to these colonial designs, the queen gave her patronage by deigning to appear in a court dress from this American silk. The best dresses worn with us were woven in England. Grace Fisher, a minister among Friends, made considerable silk stuff; a piece of hers was presented by Governor Dickinson to the celebrated Catharine Macauley. The daughters of Reuben Haines, in Germantown, raised considerable, and his daughter Catharine, who married Richard Hartshorne, wore her wedding dress of the same material—preserved on page 230 of the MS. Annals. The late Mrs. Logan was among those who in the time of the war raised their own silk in conjunction with several other ladies, to provide for their personal or family wants.

* It received the premium of the society.

In 1772, Robert Proud, our historian, makes a MS. memorandum of his visit to James Wright's place at Columbia, where he saw one thousand five hundred worms at their labour, under the charge of "the celebrated Susanna Wright." They said they could raise a million in one season, and would have undertaken it with suitable encouragement.

About the present time, the culture of silk begins again to awaken public attention. A few families in the country are engaged in it. A Holland family, on the Frankford road, were making it their exclusive business on a large scale; and in Connecticut whole communities are pursuing it, and supplying the public with sewing silk.

SHIPS AND SHIPBUILDING.

PHILADELPHIA has long been justly renowned for her superior excellence and elegance in shipbuilding. None of the colonies equalled her; and, perhaps, no place in the world surpassed her in her skill and science in this matter. At the present day other cities of the union are approaching her excellence. When Samuel Humphreys, Sen., was visiting England, he was offered, it is said, a great sum to remain and execute models for the British navy. In early times they used to construct at Philadelphia great raft ships, of much larger dimensions than the late renowned ones from Canada, called the Columbus and Baron Renfrew, and which in the present day, have been regarded as nonpareils. A little before the war of Independence, the last raft ship was built and launched at Kensington.* Our great raft ships were generally constructed for sale and use in England, when our timber was more plentiful and cheaper. They would carry off "eight hundred logs of timber, competent to make six ships of two hundred and fifty tons each." An eye-witness, who saw one of those mammoth fabrics descend into her destined element, said she bent and twisted much in launching, but when on the water looked to the eye of the beholder much like another ship in form, &c.

Before the Revolution, a former raft ship, bearing the name of the Baron Renfrew, (probably the largest ship ever built, being upwards of five thousand tons, and double the measurement of an ordinary seventy-four) made her voyage safely into the Downs. But the pilots being unwilling to take her into the Western channel, because of her great draught of water, undertook to carry her round the

* One was launched in 1774–5, at Slater's wharf, a little south of Poole's bridge, and was navigated by Captain Newman.

Goodwin sands, where being unable to beat up against the strong north wind, got *her ashore* on the Flemish banks, near Graveslines, *where she was broken up by the heavy sea.* Nearly all her cargo *was saved.* Rafts of great size were made of her lumber, and *towed* into France, and into the river Thames. Some of them contained fifteen to twenty thousand cubic feet of timber. On the top of one of them, which was towed *to London*, was the foremast spar of this mammoth ship—being a single tree of ninety feet in length, and was there regarded with great admiration, as a noble specimen of our American white pine.

The ship-yards used to occupy the river banks, beginning about Girard's wharf, above High street, up to Vine street, and, as population increased, extended northward. As early as the days of the founder, the shipyard of William West was begun at Vine street. The activity of shipbuilding there, by which he enriched his posterity, was wonderful. He had generally more orders than he could supply, (so says his late grandson,) and mostly required for English and Irish houses abroad. William Penn's letter, of 1683, says, even then, " Some vessels have been built here and many boats."

In July, 1718, Jonathan Dickinson writes to his correspondent, saying, " Here is great employ for shipwork for England. It increases and will increase, and our expectations from the iron-works forty miles up Schuylkill are very great." The same writer calls a ship sometimes a galley, and a small vessel a hoy—of such he speaks as being used in navigating the Delaware, and going to Cape May for cedar rails, &c.

In 1721, he incidentally mentions that the sails and rigging coming to him from London for his new ship had escaped the pirates—thus showing that sails and rigging were at least preferred from abroad in that day.

In 1722, I notice as among the vessels at Philadelphia, those they call a pink, a galley, and a great fly-boat of 400 tons, all of which traverse the Atlantic ocean.

In connexion with shipbuilding, we may justly congratulate ourselves on having had the ablest ship-carver, in the late respectable and aged William Rush, that the world has ever seen. His figures on the heads of ships have excited admiration in numerous instances in foreign countries, and have been sent for from England, to adorn vessels there. We should have heard more of such facts of preference, but that the duties there were managed to cost more than the first cost of the images themselves. More concerning his talents as an artist will be found under the article " William Rush."

The frigate United States, built at Philadelphia, by Humphreys, was the fastest sailing ship ever constructed any where.

I have been often assured by competent observers, that it is a fact of which we have abundant reason to be proud, that we, as a nation, surpass all other people in the skilful construction and fast sailing of our mercantile shipping. Our constructors and captains, though self-taught, do actually cover the ocean with vessels which are nowhere equalled. In a word our *packet ships*, for superior sailing and quick despatch of voyage, do actually eclipse the world. Our sea captains, too, are the most active and vigilant of all mariners, doing double of service, in any given period of time, to any other navigators any where to be found.

PAPER MONEY.

> "Gold, imp'd by thee, can compass greatest things—
> Can purchase states, and fetch and carry kings."

In the first introduction of paper money, there was much difference of opinion concerning its eventual benefit to trade and to the community. It appears to have been first emitted under the auspices of Governor Keith, about the year 1723. Many remonstrances and counter views were urged by some.

In 1723, when Benjamin Franklin first visited us from Boston, where he had seen abundance of paper money, he noticed with surprise the free circulation of metallic money among the people. The whole of his own money then consisted of a Dutch dollar and a shilling's worth of coppers—both coins unknown among us now.

The very next year (1724) James Logan, in writing to the proprietaries, shows the quick effect of the paper emission, by saying, "No gold or silver then passes among them, because of their paper money—when they buy the former they give three shillings per £., or 15 per cent. advance in exchange for their paper."

The common fate of "paper credit" soon follows—for counterfeiters, though threatened with "death" in staring capitals, use the means which "lends corruption lighter wings to fly," by pushing their supply also into the market. Behold! they come even from Ireland!

The Gazette of 1726 announces a great quantity of counterfeit colonial bills, executed in Ireland, as arrived, and the two agents being apprehended, are soon after punished. Some of this doubtless found its use in the purchase of land for the new-comers, for the papers along to the year 1729 often make mention of its being occasionally detected in use.

About this time Governor Gordon, who succeeded Sir William Keith, emitted £45,000 on land pledged at half its value, and subject to redemption. This was increased from time to time till the whole amounted to £85,000.

In 1729, James Logan, writing to the proprietaries, thus speaks, saying, "I dare not speak one word against it. The popular phrensy will never stop till their credit will be as bad as they are in New England, where an ounce of silver is worth twenty shillings of their paper. They already talk of making more, and no man dares appear to stem the fury of the popular rage. The notion is, that while any man will borrow on good security of land, more money should be made for them, without thinking of what value it will be when made. They affirm that whilst the security is good the money cannot fall. The king's own hand should forbid this measure. Yet the last act should not be abrogated, (ill as the measure is,) because the money now out (if annulled) would occasion the utmost destruction." It may be remarked, that although the measure pleased the people, as they thought it increased riches as by magic, they knew not how, yet the crown officers were always averse to the creation of a paper medium. It may be mentioned also as a curious indication of the early times, and the actual need once felt of some kind of supply for the necessary interchanges required in the dealings among men in society—that there is now in the museum of the City Library an original petition of the people, of the year 1717, to the assembly of Pennsylvania, praying them to make *produce* a currency!

I have in my possession an original account-current of the years 1730–1, by Andrew Hamilton, Esq., one of the trustees of the General Loan office, showing the operation in those days, when no banks existed, of borrowing money upon mortgages, deeds, and other securities. It seems to show that the "credit system," even then, was required and indulged, as a useful means of improving trade and increasing property. The account begins with a detail of securities received from the previous trustees, to wit:

61	mortgages	on the £15,000 act, yet due,	£930
228	do.	on the £30,000 act,	9,438
335	do.	on the several emissions,	19,212
264	do.	on the 2d £30,000 act,	26,000

The new trustees lend out in the years 1730–1,

On 39 mortgages,	the sixth emission of 1st act,	£2,546
On 77 do.	being the first emission of the 2d remitting act of 1741,	5,481
And on a *pledge of plate*,		24

Considering the present great use of paper currency in our bank notes, and the question of their utility being sometimes agitated, it may be curious to state here the view of such money as given by the assembly as early as the year 1739, being their preamble to the act of that year, to wit: "Whereas it has been found by experience, that bills of credit, emitted upon land security, as a medium of commerce have been of great service for carrying on the trade and other improvements in this province, and money and gold being now become a commodity and generally remitted [exactly as now!] to Great Britain, in return for the manufactures of that kingdom imported hither." See Credit System, App. p. 562.

Among the emissions of later times were the bills for raising funds in 1775, for erecting "the new jail in Walnut street," and the "light house on Cape Henlopen;" both of them were decorated with pictures of the buildings, and the history of the money in both cases was, that the bills by reason of the war, &c., were never "called in," and the whole sunk in the hands of the holders!

To these succeeded the far-famed and much scouted *continental money*—an emission so immense in aggregate, so overwhelming to the payers, and so hopeless to the payees, as to make it in the end wholly non-effective to all concerned. The whole emission, as presented in a detailed official account exhibited in 1828, stated the enormous total of 241½ millions of dollars!—all issued in five years, from 1775 to 1780. We may well exclaim, "Lo, what it is that makes white rags so dear!"

In the course of the rapid depreciation which ensued, it was a common incident to hear a hundred dollars of it asked for a single yard of silk—to see children give a dollar bill for a few cakes, and finally to see 300 dollars of continental given for one dollar of silver. At one time 75 dollars of it was exchanged for one dollar of state paper. Sometimes the possession of so much nominal money, of so little worth, gave rise to many occasional freaks for its destruction—such as using it to light a pipe or a candle at a tavern; and even the soldiers sometimes, to show their recklessness of such money, or to vaunt of their abundance in it, have been known to deck off their recruiting drummers and fifers in an over-jacket formed entirely of sheets of continental money!

One of the worst uses of this money was to present it as "a legal tender," to pay with almost no value what had been before purchased for a *bona fide* valuable consideration. Many base men so acquired their property—especially when to "cheat a tory" was deemed fair prize with several. Houses still stand in Philadelphia, which, could their walls speak out, would tell of strangely inconsiderable values received for them by the sellers. The large double house, for instance, at the north-west corner of Pine and Second streets, was once purchased, it was said, with the money received for one hogshead of rum! The lot in Front, below Pine, whereon four or five large houses stood, called Barclay's row, was sold for £60 only of real value.

Many specimens of the colonial bills, now rarely seen, may be inspected in my books of MS. Annals, both in the City Library and with the Historical Society of Pennsylvania.

All of us have heard so much of "*continental money*," without having ever seen it—roughly and rudely as it was executed, and ruinous as it was to many by its rapid depreciation, (falling, in 1781, to 7000 for 100 dollars of specie, and soon after to nothing!) that it may be curious, and a novelty to many, to see a copy herein given of the impression of a seven dollar bill. Flooded as the country had been by its destructive inundations, it is matter of just surprise that so little now remains, even as a preserved curiosity. We had never seen more than the present specimen, and this we only found after

many fruitless inquiries. Such were the helps by which we carried on the war. *None of it was ever redeemed;* and those who had most of it, had the evidence in themselves how far *they* had individually contributed to its eventual success. See App. p. 551.

LOTTERIES.

> It must be told;
> These from thy lottery wheels are sold:
> Sold, and thy children dearly taxed,
> That few may win.

It must be told, that fearful as is the waste of treasure and morals by the present infatuation of many for lotteries, they were, at an early period of our city, the frequently adopted measures of "raising ways and means." It is true, they were then fairly conducted, had public benefit in design, and tickets were generally vended by disinterested citizens without reward, for the sake of advancing the public weal. It was their way, when the mass of the people was comparatively poor, and direct taxes were onerous and unpopular, to thus bring out the aid of the abler part to pay willingly for expensive public improvements, &c. The facts in the case are to the following effect, to wit:

The earliest mention of a lottery in Philadelphia occurs in 1720 when Charles Reed advertises "to sell his brick house in Third street by lottery." That house, if now known, should be the head-quarters of lotteries now, as the proper "head and front of their offending."

In 1728, the city council, averse to all private projects in lotteries, interfere and frustrate the design of Samuel Keimer, printer, and once a partner of Franklin. He had advertised his purpose to make a lottery at the approaching fair, and the council, having sent for him and heard his case, gave orders that no such lottery should be attempted, and thus the affair dropped.

In 1748 began the first occasion of a sanctioned public lottery. It was altogether patriotic. It was in time of war, when great apprehension existed that the plunder of the city might be attempted by armed vessels. Individual subscriptions and a lottery were resorted to as means for raising the "Association Battery," then constructed near the present navy yard. On this occasion, the Friends put forth their strength to discourage lotteries, and read a rule against them in their meeting. Some controversy ensued.

Christ church steeple was the next subject of public interest, awakening general regard as an intended ornament and clock-tower. A lottery for this object was first instituted in November, 1752, and the drawing finished in March, 1753, of which further particulars may be seen in the article, "Christ Church."

In the same spirit, the citizens, in March, 1753, encouraged the institution of another lottery for another steeple, viz.: "for raising £850 towards finishing a steeple to the new Presbyterian church," at the north-west corner of Third and Arch streets. The lottery was drawn in May following.

The facilities of lotteries must then have been very encouraging, as we find, about this time, that the lottery expedients are numerous. On such occasions, they invited citizens of Philadelphia and other places to contribute for quite distant places. Thus, to raise five hundred dollars to build a long wharf in Baltimore, a lottery is sold off in Philadelphia; and so to build a church in Brunswick, another is sold in Philadelphia. In Connecticut I see, in 1754, that £13,332 is raised by lottery there, to aid the building of the Princeton College, and tickets are sold in Philadelphia.

In 1754, they form a lottery of 5,000 tickets, at four dollars each, to raise a fund to complete the City Academy in Fourth street, then lately purchased of Whitfield's congregation: and in the next year a further lottery of four classes is made to raise 75,000 dollars, and net 9,375 dollars, for the general objects of the Academy, and to endow professorships, &c.

In 1760, St. Paul's church is helped to finish by a lottery. The bare walls were at first set up by subscription. First, a lottery of 5 000 tickets, at four dollars, is formed, by which to clear 3000 dollars; and the next year, another lottery, of 30,000 dollars, is formed to clear enough to buy off the ground-rent, &c

In 1761, the zeal for lotteries began to show itself as an evil. In this matter "every man did as seemed right in his own eyes." Thus, one man makes it for his store of books and jewelry, and Alexander Alexander so disposes of his forty-six acres of land on the south-west end of Petty's island, in lots, for 10,500 dollars. There are lotteries, too, announced for all the neighbouring churches: one for Bordentown, one for Lancaster, one for Middletown, one for Brunswick, one for Carlisle, Newtown, Forks of Brandywine, Oxford, and even Baltimore. Some, too, are for schools. It is even proposed to erect, by lottery, a *great bath and pleasure garden.* On this occasion, all the ministers combine to address the governor to resist it, as a place of vice.

Lotteries are also granted for raising funds to pave the streets. In 1761, 12,500 tickets, at four dollars, making 50,000 dollars, are sold for raising 7,500 dollars to that purpose.

In the same year (1761) a lottery is made to pay off a company of rangers at Tulpehauken, for services against the Indians, in 1755, on a scheme of 5,000 tickets, at two dollars each! Another lottery is made to erect the light-house at Cape Henlopen, to raise £20,000; and the house itself was begun in 1762. The bridge over the Conestogoe is erected by lottery, and also the bridge at Skippack.

As a necessary sequel to the whole, the legislature had to interfere, to prevent so many calls upon the purses of their citizens, and soon after those lotteries, an act was passed to restrain lotteries!

It would strike us as a strange location for drawing of lotteries now, to name them as in stores on the wharves: but the lottery for St. Paul's church was drawn at a store on Gardener's wharf, above Race street. And a subsequent lottery for the Presbyterian steeple, (corner of Third and Arch streets,) was drawn in April, 1761, in Masters' store, on Market-street wharf.

Lotteries having so received their *quietus*, none appear to have been suggested till the lonely case of 1768, when a lottery was granted by the legislature, in four classes, for raising the sum of £5,250 for purchasing a public landing in the Northern Liberties, and for additional paving of the streets.

The history of lotteries, since our independence and self-government, and its lately pervading evil in all our cities, is too notorious, and too generally lamented by the prudent and considerate, to need any further notice in this connexion. In the hands of the wily traffickers in these unstable wares, legal enactments have been but "ropes of sand," without power to fetter them.

STEAMBOATS.

"Against the wind, against the tide,
She breasts the wave with upright keel."

In the year 1788, the bosom of the Delaware was first ruffled by a steamboat. The projector, at that early day, was John Fitch, a watch and clock maker by profession. He first conceived the design in 1785; and being but poor in purse, and rather limited in education, a multitude of difficulties, which he did not sufficiently foresee, occurred to render abortive every effort of his most persevering mind to construct and float a steamboat, called the Perseverance.

Applying to congress for assistance, he was refused; and then, without success, offering his invention to the Spanish government for the purpose of navigating the Mississippi. He at last succeeded in forming a company, by the aid of whose funds he launched his first rude effort as a steamboat, in the year 1788. The idea of wheels had not occurred to Mr. Fitch; but paddles, working in a frame, were used in place of them. The crude ideas which he entertained, and the want of experience, subjected this unfortunate man to difficulties of the most humbling character. Regarded by many as a mere visionary, his project was discouraged by those whose want of all motive for such a course rendered their opposition more barbarous; while those whose station in life placed it in their power to assist him, looked coldly on, barely listening to his elucidations, and receiving them with an indifference that chilled him to the heart. By a perseverance as unwearied as it was unrewarded, his darling project was at length sufficiently matured, and a steamboat was seen floating at the wharves of Philadelphia, more than fifty years ago. So far, his success, amid the most mortifying discouragements, had been sufficient to prove the merit of the scheme. But a reverse awaited him, as discouraging as it was unexpected. The boat performed a trip to Burlington, a distance of twenty miles, when, as she was rounding at the wharf, her boiler burst. The next tide floated her back to the city, where, after great difficulty, a new boiler was procured. In October, 1788, she again performed her trip to Burlington. The boat not only went to Burlington, but to Trenton, returning the same day, and moving at the rate of eight miles an hour. It is true, she could hardly perform a trip without something breaking; not from any error in Fitch's designs or conceptions, but, at that time, our mechanics were very ordinary; and it was impossible to have machinery, so new and complex, made with exactness and competent skill. It was on this account that Fitch was obliged to abandon the great invention, on which the public looked coldly From these failures, and because what is now so easy then seemed to be impracticable, the boat was laid up as useless, and rotted silently and unnoticed in the docks of Kensington. Her remains rest on the south side of Cohocksink creek, imbedded in the present wharf of Taylor's board yard.

Fitch became more embarrassed by his creditors than ever; and, after producing five manuscript volumes, which he deposited in the Philadelphia Library, to be opened thirty years after his death, he died in Kentucky, in 1798. Such was the unfortunate termination of this early-conceived project of the steamboat. Fitch was, no doubt, an original inventor of the steamboat; he was certainly the first who ever applied steam to the propulsion of *vessels* in America. Though it was reserved to Fulton to advance its application to a degree of perfection which has made his name immortal, yet to the unfortunate Fitch belongs the honour of completing and navigating the first American *steamboat.*

His five manuscript volumes were opened about thirteen years ago. Although they exhibit him as an unschooled man, yet they indicate the possession of a strong mind, of much mechanical ingenuity. He describes his many difficulties and disappointments with a degree of feeling which cannot fail to win the sympathy of every reader, causing him to wonder and regret that so much time and talent should have been so unprofitably devoted. Though the project failed—and it failed only for want of funds—yet he never for a moment doubted its practicability. He tells us, that in less than a century, we shall see our western rivers swarming with steamboats; and that his darling wish is to be buried on the margin of the romantic Ohio, where the song of the boatman may sometimes penetrate into the stillness of his everlasting resting place, and the music of the steam engine echo over the sod that shelters him for ever!

In one of his journals, there is this touching and prophetic sentiment: "The day will come when some more powerful man will get fame and riches from my invention; but nobody will believe that *poor John Fitch* can do any thing worthy of attention!"

The truth is, that Fitch, like Robert Morris, lived thirty or forty years too soon: they were ahead of the condition of their country. These great projects of improvements, which we now see consummated, were beyond the means of the country to execute, and were therefore thought visionary and extravagant. Public opinion has since become better instructed, and the increase of wealth has enabled us to do what was then thought impossible.

I derive these facts from J. Fitch's MS. books in the Philadelphia Library, to wit: On the 27th of September, 1785, he gave his model and description to the Philosophical Society—which fact is also recorded on their minutes, and without proceedings or comment.—On the 1st of May, 1787, he first got his boat and works so far completed, as to make his boat perform an excursion to the satisfaction of the company then on board.– On the 12th of October, 1788, she again made an excursion with many eminent citizens on board, who much admired at their sense of its satisfactory operation.—In that winter he left the concern, and made some journeys southward. He afterwards again joined the company, and got the boat to go well, on the 12th of April, 1790. She again made a satisfactory demonstration in the summer of that year, *for her last time.* There were many intervals, in the preceding times, in which she was laid by to make repairs and alterations, and many accidents to overcome and to rectify, all tending to show the first difficulties in a new enterprise, and displaying at once his indomitable perseverance and patience.—On the 19th of March, 1791, he signs his articles in behalf of the company, with Aaron Vail, the American consul in France, the terms not expressed: but he speaks of his dissatisfaction therewith, and his fears of some intended injustice to himself.

On page 296, in my MS. Annals, in the Historical Society of Pennsylvania, is a picture of his first boat, as he invented her in the year 1786, showing the propelling paddles on the side. He afterwards quite altered its appearance, by placing the paddles behind the stern. He thus spoke of his first scheme, saying, "It is in several parts similar to the late improved engines in Europe, though there are some alterations. Our cylinder is to be horizontal, and the steam to work with equal force at each end. The mode to procure a vacuum is, I believe, entirely new, as is also the method of letting the water into it, and throwing it off against the atmosphere without any friction. The engine is placed about one third from the stern, and both the action and reaction turn the wheel the same way. The engine is a twelve inch cylinder, and will move a clear force of 11 or 12 cwt. after the frictions are deducted, and this force acts against a wheel of eighteen inches' diameter."

As remembered to the eye when a boy, when seen in motion, she was graceful, and "walked the water like a thing of life." His predilections for watchmaking machinery was very manifest; for two or three ranges of chains of the same construction as in watches, were seen along the outside of his vessel, from stem to stern, moving with burnished glare, in motion proportioned to the speed of the boat; and ornamenting the waist, not unlike the adornments about an Indian bride.

It is melancholy to contemplate his overwhelming disappointment in a case since proved so practicable, and so productive to those concerned. Some of those thousands so useless to others, had they been owned by him, so as to have enabled him to make all the experiments and improvements his inventive mind suggested, would have set his care-crazed head at rest, and in time have rewarded his exertions: but for want of the impulse which money affords, all proved ineffective. "Slow rises worth by poverty depressed!"

After Fulton and Livingston had proved the practicability of a better completion, by their boat on the North river, the waters of the Delaware were again agitated by a steam vessel, called the Phœnix. She was first started in 1809, and being since worn out, her remains, with those of Fitch's boat, repose in the mud flats of Kensington. The Phœnix, then deemed the *ne plus ultra* of the art, won the admiration of all, of her early day: but as "practice makes perfect," it was frequently discovered that better adaptations of power could be attained; and although she underwent many changes in her machinery and gear, she soon saw herself rivalled, and finally surpassed, by successive inventions; till now, the steamboats can accomplish in two hours, what sometimes took six to perform in her. For instance, the Phœnix has been known to take six hours in reaching Burlington against the wind and tide.

Such, too, was the rapid progress in steam invention, that Mr. Latrobe, who wrote a paper for the Philosophical Society to demonstrate the impossibility of a momentum such as we now witness, became himself, in two years afterwards, a proselyte to the new system, and proved his sincerity and conviction by becoming the agent for the steam companies in the west!

Most amazing invention! from a cause now so obvious and familiar! It is only by applying the principle seen in every house, which lifts the lid of the tea kettle and "boils over," that machines have been devised which can pick up a pin, or rend an oak; which combine the power of many giants with the plasticity that belongs to a lady's fair fingers; which spin cotton, and then weave it into cloth: which, by pumping sea-water and extracting its steam, send vessels across the Atlantic in fifteen days; and amidst a long list of other marvels, "engrave seals, forge anchors, and lift a ship of war, like a bauble, in the air,"—presenting, in fact, to the imagination, the practicability of labour-saving inventions in endless variety, so that, in time, man, through its aid, shall half exempt himself from "the curse!" and preachers, through steam-press printing, shall find an auxiliary effecting more than half their work!

Much of our steam invention we owe to our own citizen, Oliver Evans. He even understood the application of it to wagons—(now claimed as so exclusively British.) As early as 1787, the legislature of Maryland granted him its exclusive use for fourteen years, and in 1781, he publicly stated he could by steam drive wagons, mills, &c. Finally, he published his bet of 3000 dollars, engaging "to make a carriage to run upon a level road against the swiftest horse to be found,"—none took him up! and Latrobe, as a man of science, pronounced the idea chimerical; others said the motion would be too slow to be useful, &c. He got no patrons, and others now take his fame!—See Emporium of Arts, 1814, p. 205.

"Of each wonderful plan
E'er invented by man,
This nearest perfection approaches—
No longer gee-up and gee-ho,
But fiz—fiz!—off we go

Nine miles to the hour,
With fifty horse-power,
By day time and night time,
Arrive at the right time,
Without rumble or jumble,
Or chance of a tumble,
As in chaise, gig, or whiskey,
When horses are frisky."

A friend of mine has lately seen in Philadelphia an original letter of Mr. Fitch to Dr. Franklin, dated 12th October, 1785. It was neatly written; had some few faults in spelling, and reads in part thus:—"Steamboat navigation is, in the opinion of the subscriber, a matter of first magnitude, not only to the United States, but to every maritime power in the world, and he is full in the belief that it will answer for sea voyages, as well as for inland navigation—in *particular for packets* where there may be many passengers. She could make head off lea shore against the most violent tempests, because the machine can be made of almost omnipotent force, by the very simple and easy means of the screws or paddles, which act as oars—working on the oscillating motion of the old pumping engine, in a manner similar to that given by the human arm."

N. B. Boileau, of Montgomery county, asserts that he remembers John Fitch well as a frequent visiter at his father's house, and he *knows* that, although Fitch first used *paddles* to his boat, he also had the idea of *wheels*, for he actually showed Boileau his draught of them, and employed him as a boy to cut out of wood small water wheels as *models*, by which to construct large ones for his boat. He believes he only wanted the *money* to have had them made. He worked as a silversmith; learned to survey; went to Kentucky in 1780; left there in 1781; made a map of that country and the west, as a new land of enterprise; engraved the plate and struck off copies himself, and then sold them about the country—one of them is now with Mr. Boileau, and another is with Daniel Longstreth, at Warminster, Bucks county, Pennsylvania. For more of Fitch and steam power, see the article John Fitch, in the chapter *Persons and Characters.*

An elderly gentleman, of Philadelphia, communicates that he knew very well both John Fitch and Robert Fulton. The latter was, about the year 1770, and for several years, his schoolmate, in the town of Lancaster. His mother was a widow of limited circumstances. "I had (he said) a brother who was fond of painting. The war of the Revolution, which prevailed at that period, made it difficult to obtain materials from abroad, and the arts were at a low ebb in the country. My brother, consequently, prepared and mixed colours for himself; and these he usually displayed on muscle shells. His cast off brushes and shells fell to my lot; some of which I occasionally carried in my pocket to school. Fulton saw and craved a part. He pressed his suit with so much earnestness, that I could not refuse to divide my treasure with him; and in fact, he soon, from this beginning, so shamed my performances, by the superiority of his own, that it ended in my voluntarily surrendering to him the entire heirship to all that came into my possession. Henceforth his book was neglected, and he was often severely chastised by the schoolmaster, for his inattention and disobedience. His friends removed him to Philadelphia, where he was apprenticed to a silversmith, but his mind was not in his trade. He found his way to London, and placed himself under the patronage of his celebrated countryman, West.

"While Robert Fulton was thus engaged in London, John Fitch, a clockmaker and silversmith, was contriving schemes in Philadelphia, for the propulsion of boats by steam. He conducted his mysterious operations at a projection on the shore of the Delaware, at Kensington, which, among the wise and prudent of the neighbourhood, the scorners of magicians and their dark works, soon acquired the ominous and fearful title of *Conjurer's point.* I often witnessed the performance of his boat, 1788, '89 and '90. It was propelled by five paddles over the stern, and constantly getting out of order. I saw it when it was returning from a trip to Burlington, from whence it was said to have arrived in little more than two hours. When coming to, off Kensington, some part of the machinery broke, and I never saw it in motion afterwards. I believe it was his last effort. He had, up to that period, been patronized by a few stout-hearted individuals, who had subscribed a small capital in shares of, I think, £6, Pennsylvania currency, or 16 dollars each; but this last disaster so staggered their faith, and unstrung their nerves, that they never again had the hardihood to make other contributions. Indeed, they had already rendered themselves the subjects of ridicule and derision, for their temerity and presumption, in giving countenance, as they said, to this wild projector, and madman. The company, thereupon, gave up the ghost—the boat went to pieces—and Fitch became bankrupt and broken-hearted. Often have I seen him stalking about like a troubled spectre, with down-cast eye, and lowering countenance; his coarse soiled linen peeping through the elbows of a tattered garment. During the days of his aspiring hopes, two mechanics were of sufficient daring to work for him. Ay, and they suffered in purse for their confidence. These were Peter Brown, ship-smith, and John Wilson, boat-builder, both of Kensington. They were worthy, benevolent men, well known to the writer, and much esteemed in the city. Towards Fitch, in particular, they ever extended the kindest sympathy. While he lived, therefore, he was in the habit of calling almost daily at their workshops, to while away time; to talk over his misfortunes; and to rail at the ingratitude and cold neglect of an unfeeling, spiritless world. From Wilson I derived the following anecdote: Fitch called to see him as usual—Brown happened to be present. Fitch mounted his hobby, and became unusually eloquent in the praise of steam, and of the benefits which mankind were destined to derive from its use in propelling boats. They listened, of course, without faith, but not without interest, to this animated appeal; but it failed to rouse them to give any future support to schemes by which they had already suffered. After indulging himself for some time, in this never-failing topic of deep excitement, he concluded with these memorable words—" Well, gentlemen, although I shall not live to see the time, you will, when steamboats will be preferred to all other means of conveyance, and especially for passengers; and they will be particularly useful in the navigation of the river Mississippi." He then retired; on which Brown, turning to Wilson, exclaimed, in a tone of deep sympathy, " Poor fellow! what a pity he is crazy."

It is curious to observe, that both Fitch and Fulton should have been originally *silversmiths*. In 1785, Robert Fulton is found in the Philadelphia directory of that year set down as a miniature painter, at the corner of Second and Walnut streets—perhaps not even dreaming of steamboats, nor even making the acquaintance of the inventor, though in the same city, and *at a time* when Fitch had actually written out his views, in the above-mentioned letter to Doctor Franklin, dated 12th October, 1785.

Rumsey has been named as our earliest inventor of boat navigation by machinery; that is, so far at least as actually forming a boat with apparatus, &c., for such an operation, he probably executed one as early as 1783. A friend of mine, who saw Fitch's boat at Kensington, as early as 1786–7, saw the remains of Rumsey's boat in a rotten state in 1790, in a creek at Shepherdstown, Va., near Harper's ferry. Rumsey, it is said, went to England to procure patronage and aid, and soon after died there, poor. Some of his heirs were lately soliciting some contribution from the congress of the United States, on the grounds of Rumsey's being the first projector. Fitch, however, declared that Rumsey derived his conception from himself.

John Fitch, in his controversy with James Rumsey, respecting *priority* of claim, as set forth in his pamphlet of 1788, admits or sustains the following facts and circumstances, to wit:

That the first thought of a steamboat came to him suddenly, in April, 1785.

That in June following he went to Philadelphia, and showed his scheme to Dr. Ewing and Mr. Patterson. That in June and July he formed models, and in August laid them before congress, and in September he presented them to the Philosophical Society.

That in October he called on the ingenious William Henry, Esq., of Lancaster, to take his opinion of his draughts, who informed him that he was not *the first person* who had *thought* of applying steam to vessels, for that he himself had conversed with Andrew Ellicott, Esq., of his own views on that matter, as early as the year 1775; and that T. Paine, author of Common Sense, had *suggested* the same to him in the winter of 1778; that some time after, he (Mr. Henry) thinking more seriously of it, was of opinion that it might easily be perfected, and he accordingly had made some draughts, "*which he then showed me*," but added, that as he had neglected to bring them to public view, and as Mr. Fitch *had first published the plan to the world*, he would lay no claim to the invention. To this alleged fact A. Ellicott adds his testimony, saying that Mr. Henry did so converse with him on the subject of *steam*, and intimated his belief that it might be advantageously applied to the navigation of boats. Mr. Fitch went from Mr. Henry's, in Lancaster, to the governors of Maryland and Virginia, to see them upon the subject. He then procured laws in his behalf from the different legislatures, to wit—New Jersey, Maryland and Virginia.

He admits that he had been greatly indebted *to the assistance* of his ingenious friend and partner, Mr. Henry Voight, who had afforded him valuable hints, and had united with him in perfecting his plans; and that "to his inventive genius alone he was indebted for the improvement in their mode of *creating steam*, from a thought which struck him two years before;" for, says Mr. Fitch, *we never made a secret* of part of our works—but that a fear of departing from old established plans had made him for some time fearful of adopting it, until he (Mr. Fitch) perceived that Voight's invention of creating steam by *a condensor*, might be constructed on the *same* principles, (viz. a spiral pipe or worm,) only by *reversing* the agent—because the best means of *applying fire* to evaporate *water into steam*, must also be the best way of applying *cold water* to condense *steam*—that is, the bringing of the greatest quantity of fire into action upon the greatest surface of water, or the contrary.

Mr. Fitch asserts, and adduces his proofs, that Mr. Rumsey only began to procure *his* apparatus in the summer of 1786, and that by reason of the ice in the Potomac in the winter of that year, he could not have made any use of his steam and boat till the spring of 1787—"which was *long after* Mr. Fitch's boat was *built*, and his model of a steam-engine was *completed*." Mr. Fitch also asserts, that the certificate of Gen. Washington, of 7th September, 1784, adduced by Mr. Rumsey as his proof of an earlier period, was in relation to his earlier boat and apparatus as then shown to the general, at Bath, and which boat, as the certificate expressed it, was constructed to work against streams, by mechanism (not steam!) and manual assistance, and that she was *then* so worked in his presence.

Mr. Fitch alleges that Mr. Rumsey's application to the legislature of Pennsylvania, by his petition of 26th November, 1784, shows on its face that it was *not* a steamboat then he meditated, but "a species of boats of ten tons, to be propelled against the current of a rapid river, by the combined influence of *mechanical* powers, at the rate of twenty-five to forty miles a day."

Mr. Fitch alleges that it was an *after-thought* of Mr. Rumsey's to use and apply *steam*, and the knowledge of which he alleges he derived from himself, by seeing and hearing of his models, &c.; and that he then puts in his pretension because of the certificate of Gen.

Washington and others, to facts about his boat of 1784, as if he had been showing the same kind of boat *then*, which he could only have effected in 1787!

Mr. Fitch concludes thus triumphantly, saying, "If Mr. Rumsey claims on *his thought*, as expressed to Gen. Washington in his letter of 10th March, 1785, then he has to encounter the *prior thoughts* of Mr. Paine, Mr. Henry and Mr. Ellicott—if on former *draughts*, without exposing them to the public, he must also admit the prior draughts of Mr. Henry—but if it is to be determined by the established mode of *public declaration*, *put on record*, as was done in my case, then he must submit to *my title*, as being *prior* and indisputable."

In this publication Mr. Fitch makes the remark, that Mr. Rumsey had *insinuated* that he (Mr. Fitch) had formed his first conception of a steam vessel *indirectly* from Mr. Rumsey; because, as he hinted, Mr. Fitch got *his first thought* from a Captain Bedinger, *in Kentucky*, who went there in 1784, and who had derived his ideas, *as a secret*, from Mr. Rumsey. To this *insinuation* Mr. Fitch replies, that "he has not been in Kentucky since the year 1781."

Oliver Evans, a *blacksmith* of Philadelphia, (for steam power seems to have run most in the the heads of the *smiths*,) certainly *foresaw* the power which could be made effective from the use of steam; but when he made his assertions the public would not credit his report, and many actually believed that it was the ravings of an over-excited mind. "More than twenty years ago," says the New York Commercial Advertiser, in 1835, "we published his assertions as hereinafter written and *signed by his name*, and yet none then gave him any credence—not even the legislatures of Pennsylvania and Maryland, to which he applied for countenance and support, gave him any patronage, and he died neglected and poor! But what he then so confidently asserted is now matter of true history." I give his *published* declarations, to wit:

"The time will come, when people will travel in stages, moved by steam-engines, at fifteen to twenty miles an hour!"

"A carriage will leave Washington in the morning, breakfast at Baltimore, dine at Philadelphia, and sup at New York, *on the same day!*"

"*Railways* will be laid, of wood or iron, or on smooth paths of broken stone, or gravel, to travel as well by night as day."

"A steam-engine will drive a carriage 180 miles in twelve hours —or engines will drive boats ten or twelve miles an hour; and hundreds of boats will so run upon *the Mississippi*, and other waters, *as prophesied thirty years ago;* but the velocity of boats can never be made to equal those of carriages upon *rails*, because the resistance in water is 800 times more than that in air."

"Posterity will not be able to discover why the legislature or congress did not grant *the inventor* such protection as might have enabled

OLIVER EVANS' CAR.—Page 454.

FULTON'S STEAMBOAT.—Page 446.

him to *put in operation* these great improvements *sooner*, he having asked neither money nor monopoly of *any existing thing*."

"OLIVER EVANS."*

O. Evans was first induced to notice the powerful expansion of *vapour*, by applying his heated iron with a hammer stroke to the spittle he could cast upon his anvil; and also by heating the butend of a musket barrel in his fire, filled with confined water. He had thought of all these things in embryo as early as the period of the Revolution, and yet he and his suggestions passed for years unpatronized! Such is the too frequent fate of new and important improvements. It is in general for more fortunate men in after years to reap the harvest of such minds as Evans, Fitch and Fulton's.

In 1827 there were but two railroads, and short ones too, viz., one at Mauch Chunk and at Quincy, and *now* they are every where.

Oliver Evans not finding any one willing to promote his views for a steam-wagon, bethought himself to apply his power more profitably to mills for grinding grain, plaster of Paris, &c., and procured his patent accordingly.

In 1804, he applied his power to a machine for cleansing docks, and for that object constructed a large flat or scow, with a steam-engine; and such a one having been ordered by the board of health, he conceived that it presented him with a fine occasion for showing the public that his engine could propel both land and water carriages. He therefore set his scow, as if it were a car, upon wheels; and although it was only set upon wooden axles, and bore a weight equal to 200 barrels of flour, he actually conveyed the whole from his workshop along the streets of Philadelphia out to the Schuylkill river with great facility. Having then launched it into the river, he applied paddle-wheels in the stern, and thereby propelled it down that river *like a steamboat*, and then up the Delaware to the city, to the place of delivery.† This, it should be observed, was six years before Fulton started his first boat, the Clermont, on North river, in 1807. This was a sufficient demonstration, as he conceived, of what he had asserted, that he could make a carriage to go by steam, upon a level road, equal to the swiftest horse; and upon this confidence he offered his bet of 3000 dollars, with none to take him up! About this time he also laboured much to induce proprietors of turnpikes to introduce steam-carriages upon their roads; but none followed his counsels, although he pledged himself to construct them steam-carriages which should run *upon a railway*, or level road, at the rate of fifteen miles an hour. At the same time he published his principles of applying the same power to the propelling of boats on water and against currents.

---

* Apollos Kingsley, a young man of Hartford, Conn., about the year 1798, made and propelled through the streets of that city a steam locomotive, which he then said would in future be the means of propelling the mail stages, &c. He was not credited, died soon after, and all then went for nothing.

† See a picture of the same as it was, in this book.

Mr. Niles, of the Register, heard Mr. Evans say, many years ago, that "the child was then born who would travel from Philadelphia to Boston *in one day!*" Already they go from Boston to New York in seventeen hours, and soon they will go by the railroad to Philadelphia in six hours more, which will of course fulfil the prophecy.

Oliver Evans had at one time a great steam engine standing for six months at the corner of Ninth and High streets, where it had broken, and would *go no further!* It had been made *to go under water*, as it was said, and was to dig out river beds, and docks and shoals. It had started from his premises at Vine street, and had gone that far on the streets. To what will not steam eventually contribute!

> By the *Briarean* might thy hands supply,
> We cook, we ride, we sail, and soon shall fly!
> Mind marches;—soon the glorious day will break
>   When we may sit, our hands within our breeches;
> When steam will plough, sow, reap, grind, knead and bake,
>   And our sole task be to digest earth's riches!
> Soon iron muscle will leave nought to do,
> And slave and master both may cease from labour—
> When giant steam, with never-tiring hand
> Shall toil, the only *slave* throughout the land!

Steam power has just been doing wonders, both by land and water, for travelling facilities; but who knows how soon even these energetic auxiliaries may be superseded, and by abler and simpler inventions! Already we hear of the *electro-magnetic* combinations of Davenport and Cook, at Saratoga. This reminds us of the prophetic ken of science, as happily exhibited by Dr. Lardner: "Philosophy (said he) already directs her finger at sources of inexhaustible power in the phenomena of *electricity* and *magnetism*, and we *may expect* that the steam-engine itself may ere long dwindle into insignificance, in comparison with *the hidden powers of nature still to be revealed.* We may expect that the day will come when the steam-engine will cease to have existence, save in the page of history."—[Vide Dr. Lardner's Treatise on the Steam-engine, 1838.]

SCHUYLKILL WATERWORKS.—Page 457.

CENTRE SQUARE WATERWORKS.—Page 457.

WATERWORKS.

THE Philadelphia Waterworks were begun in the spring of 1799, by constructing a large house, for water power, near the banks of the Schuylkill, southward of High street, (of which see a picture,) and also, another edifice of marble, at the Centre square, as a receiving fountain, (of which also see a picture.) It was an ornamental structure; but with some it nevertheless bore the disparaging name of "the pepper box," in allusion to its circular form and appearance. These works had at first but little encouragement; and to induce moneyed men to adventure their capital, they were offered water free of rent for a term of years. As late as 1803, only 960 dollars was the rental of the water, although nearly 300,000 dollars had then been expended on the enterprise. At same time, one hundred and twenty-six houses were receiving the water free of cost. In 1814, there were two thousand eight hundred and fifty dwellings receiving the water, and paying a rent of 18,000 dollars. In that year, the cost of raising the water was 24,000 dollars. In 1818, the steam engine at *Fairmount* was set in operation, and raised the water at a saving of 8000 dollars, still leaving an expense of 16,000 per annum; but in 1827, such were the improvements introduced, that the expense of raising the water was but 1478 dollars, while the water rents from the city and districts had risen to 33,560 dollars, and this is still rapidly increasing. In the eventual success of these measures we owe much to the skill and perseverance of J. S. Lewis and Frederic Graff, names which will be always identified with the origin and the renown of a lasting public benefit.

Our great benefactor, Franklin, early foresaw the need of a fresh supply of water for Philadelphia, and recommended the Wissahiccon creek for that object; but that, now that the city has so much increased in population, would be drained dry in a week.

There was little or no desire expressed by the citizens of Philadelphia, for any other than their *good* pump-water, till after the yellow fever of 1793. Then, when the mind was alive to every suggested danger of ill health, the idea of pump-water being no longer good found its increasing supporters. But after river water was introduced, many were still very slow and reluctant to give up their icy-cold well water, for the tepid waters of Schuylkill. Numerous pits, however, for other purposes, in time destroyed the former pure taste of the pump-water, and led finally to their total abandonment, and the consequent increased patronage to the present necessary waterworks.

ANTHRACITE COAL.

"I sat beside the glowing grate, fresh heap'd
With Lehigh coal, and as the flame grew bright—
The many coloured flame—and play'd and leap'd,
I thought of rainbows and the northern light,
And other brilliant matters of the sort."

When the anthracite coal up the Schuylkill, at Mount Carbon, &c., was first effectively discovered—since the year 1800, it was deemed of little value, because they could devise no way to ignite it—a character which its name sufficiently denotes. About the year 1810–11, however, a practical chemist, I believe an Englishman, his name unknown to fame or me, combining science with practice, made such an analysis of the coal as convinced him there was inherent in the mass all the properties suited for combustion. He therefore erected a furnace in a small vacant house on the causeway road (Beech street) leading over to Kensington. To this he applied three strong bellows; these succeeded to give out such an immense white heat from the coal as to melt platina itself! From this experiment, at which two of my friends were present as invited witnesses, were derived such proofs as led to its future general use in our city.

It was in the year 1808, that Judge Fell, at Wyoming, made the first experiment to use that coal in a grate of his own construction; a measure in which he succeeded far beyond his expectations. Before that time they had used it only for smith-work. It was first so used in 1768–9, by Obadiah Gore, (an early settler of Wyoming,) and afterwards by all the smiths there.

The Mount Carbon coal was known to exist in the neighbourhood more than fifty years ago; and some search was made, but the coal found being so very different from any which was previously known, it was not thought to be of any value, and the search was abandoned. It is supposed to be fifty years since a blacksmith, by the name of Whetstone, found coal and used it in his smithshop. At a very early period, Judge Cooper declared his belief of the existence of coal in the district, and the Messrs. Potts explored various places along the old Sunbury road, but success did not attend their operations. A Mr. William Morris afterwards became the proprietor of most of the coal lands at the head of our canal; he found coal, and took some quantity to Philadelphia, about the year 1800; but all his efforts to bring it into use failed, and he abandoned the project, and sold his lands to their late proprietor, Mr. Potts.

It does not appear that much notice was taken of the coal from the time of Whetstone, and the search made by the Messrs. Potts, until about thirty years ago, when a person by the name of Peter

Bastrus, a blue-dyer, in building the valley forge, found coal in the tailrace. About the same time, a Mr. David Berlin, a blacksmith in this neighbourhood, permanently commenced and introduced the use of stone coal in the smith's forge, and continued to use and instruct others in its use many years afterwards. But old habits again became victorious, and appear to have held undisputed sway until about the year 1812, when Mr. George Shoemaker, a present innkeeper at Pottsville, and Nicholas Allen, discovered coal on a piece of land they had purchased, now called Centreville. Allen soon became disheartened, and gave up the concern to Shoemaker, who, receiving encouragement from some gentlemen in Philadelphia, got out a quantity of coal, and took nine wagon-loads to Philadelphia. Here again, our coal met with a host of opposition. On two wagon-loads Mr. S. got the carriage paid; the others he gave away to persons who would attempt to use them. The result was against the coal; those who tried them, pronounced them stone and not coal, good for nothing, and Shoemaker an impostor! At length, after a multitude of disappointments, and when Shoemaker was about to abandon the coal and return home, Messrs. Mellon and Bishop, of Delaware county, made an experiment with some of the coal in their rolling mill, and found them to succeed beyond expectation, and to be a highly valuable and useful fuel. The result of their experiments was published at the time in the Philadelphia papers. Some experiments with the coal were made in the works at the falls of Schuylkill, but without success. Mr. Wernwag, the manager at the Phœnix works, at French creek, also made trial of the coal, and found it eminently useful. From that time forward, the use of the coal spread rapidly, and now bids fair to become a most important and valuable branch of trade, and to produce results highly beneficial to the interests of Pennsylvania generally.

The foregoing statement may appear minute, but it is due to the individuals who laboured to force us to see the great benefit which coal is and will be to our state. We are aware that the credit of pointing out the use, and perhaps of discovering the anthracite, has been claimed by and awarded to individuals in another part of our state; but it is within the knowledge of many, that those individuals joined in pronouncing the coal good for nothing. We have abundant testimony also for the facts and dates we have given; from which it appears, that to Mr. David Berlin, George Shoemaker, and Messrs. Mellon and Bishop, we are indebted for the discovery of the use and introduction of our anthracite or stone coal.

The Lehigh Coal Company was originated in 1773, on a very small scale, and began its career by purchasing the tract of Jacob Weiss, on which is the large opening on Summit hill, nine miles up from Mauch Chunk. The difficulty and expense of transportation were however such as to dishearten the stockholders, and the property was permitted to lie idle for some years.

The *first* and *second* coal regions were then entirely unknown

Coal had only been found on the Summit hill, and at the Beaver meadows; but even there they had no conception of any continuous strata for miles. Indeed, the old coal company had offered a bonus of $200 to any one who should discover coal on their lands nearer to the Lehigh than the Summit mine, and got no claims for discovery. In the mean time, however, coal was used for the forge fires of the blacksmiths in the neighbourhood, and also in some of the bar rooms in the taverns along the roads, not distant.

The country at that time, (1800,) was extremely wild—from Stoddartsville to Lausanne—places now so familiarly known—making an intervening distance of thirty-five miles along the Lehigh, there was not one human habitation. Lands, along such a rugged and deep ravine of country, bore no selling value—for none foresaw any means to bring its timber to market. There were but thirteen houses above the Gap in the Blue mountain, including even the towns of Lausanne and Lehighton. Rafts had been sent during freshets from Lausanne downward, but none had ever come down from above that point. Since then, such has been the consumption of timber to make coal arks, as to use four hundred acres a year, and to threaten soon to exhaust the whole! From this cause, a back water navigation has been constructed along the Delaware, &c., so as to return the coal boats.

But to return to the history of the progress of coal production, viz.: In 1807, the coal company, for the purpose of bringing their coal into notice, gave a lease of twenty-one years of one of their coal veins to Rowland and Butland, *gratis*, for the manufacture of iron, from the ore and coal to be dug. *It failed of success.*

In 1813, the coal company gave a lease of ten years of their lands to Messrs. Miner, Cist and Robinson, conditioned that they should take to market annually 10,000 bushels of coal, *to their own profit.* Five arks were despatched. Three of them wrecked in the Lehigh —two reached Philadelphia, and the business was abandoned. White and Hazard gave $20 a ton for that coal for their wire manufactory, and yet it was not enough to quit costs.

That attempt, however, led to future results of permanent good: for in 1817, White and Hazard, from the need of such coal, were induced to visit the Lehigh with Mr. George Kauts, and there the three contracted with the coal company, on a lease for twenty years, on condition that they should take 40,000 tons of coal annually *for their own benefit.*

In 1818, they procured a legislative grant to improve the navigation of the Lehigh—a measure deemed almost chimerical by many. After some time they procured a stock association, and went on from year to year expending and improving—taking however but little coal to market until the year 1820—when they got to *Philadelphia* 365 tons "as the first fruits of the concern!" Little as that was, it completely stocked the market, and was sold off with difficulty! It increased each subsequent year up to 1824—making in that year a delivery of 9541 tons. In 1825, it run up to 23,393 tons, and kept along at nearly that rate until 1832, when it delivered 70,000 tons. From that time it went on regularly increasing, until now, in 1839 it has delivered 221,850 tons. And now that it has got its momen tum, who can guess where it will end!

It will be observed, that no regular sale of anthracite coal was effected in the Philadelphia market till the year 1825. It may be remarked also, that the manner of using the descending navigation by *artificial freshets* is the first on record as a permanent measure. Gen. James Clinton had, in 1779, so contrived to raise the waters of the east branch of the Susquehanna, by making a sluice dam across the outlet of Otsego lake, and so caused his division to pass onward by the raised waters.

"Dark anthracite! that reddenest on my hearth,
Thou in those inland mines didst slumber long,
But now thou art come forth to move the earth,
And put to shame the men that mean thee wrong;
Thou shalt be coals of fire to those that hate thee
And warm the shins of all that underrate thee.

Yea, they did wrong thee foully—they, who mock'd
Thy honest face and *said thou wouldst not burn,*
Of hewing thee to chimney-pieces talked,
And grew profane—and swore, in bitter scorn,
That men might to thy inner caves retire,
And there, unsinged, abide the day of fire.

Yet is thy greatness nigh. Thou too shalt be
Great in thy turn—and wide shall spread thy fame
And swiftly—farthest Maine shall hear of thee,
And cold New Brunswick gladden at thy name,
And, faintly through its sleets, the weeping isle,
That sends the Boston folks their cod, shall smile.

For thou shalt forge vast railways, and shalt heat
The hissing rivers into steam, and drive
Huge masses from thy mines, on iron feet
Walking their steady way, as if alive,
Northward, till everlasting ice besets thee,
And south, as far as the grim Spaniard lets thee.

Thou shalt make mighty engines swim the sea,
Like its own monsters—boats that for a guinea
Will take a man to Havre—and shall be
The moving soul of many a spinning jenny,
And ply thy shuttles, till a bard can wear
As good a suit of broadcloth as the May'r,

Then we will laugh at winter, when we hear
The grim old churl about our dwellings rave:
Thou from that " ruler of th' inverted year"
Shalt pluck the knotty sceptre Cowper gave,
And pull him from his sledge, and drag him in,
And melt the icicles from off his chin.

Heat will be cheap—a small consideration
  Will put one in a way to raise his punch,
Set lemon trees, and have a cane plantation—
  'Twill be a pretty saving to the *Lunch.*
Then the West India negroes may go play
The banjo, and keep endless holiday."

[See Appendix p. 517.]

WATERING PLACES.

" And when too much repose brings on the spleen,
  And the gay city's idle pleasures cloy,
Swift as my changing wish, I change the scene,
  And now the country,—now the town enjoy."

The practice of summer travelling among the gentry and their imitators, is quite a modern affair. Our forefathers, when our cities were small, and pump-water still uncontaminated, found no places more healthy than their homes; and generally they liked the country best, " when *visited* from town." From that cause there were very few country-seats in existence; and what there were, were so near as to be easily visited on foot, "not for the good and friendly too remote"—to call. Thus the Rev. Gilbert Tennant's place, Bedminister, was at the corner of Brewer's alley and Fourth street Burges' place and Mitchell's place were in Campington. Two or three were out in Spring Garden, on the northern side of Pegg's run; Hamilton's place was at Bush-hill; Penn's place was close by at Springettsbury; and lastly, Kinsey's place, were is now the Naval Asylum, and Turner's place, Wilton, was down near Girard's farm. All these were rather rarities than a common choice.

As population and wealth increased, new devices of pleasure were sought, and some *inland* watering places began to be visited, chiefly, however, at first, for the good they might be supposed to offer to the infirm. Next in order came *sea bathing*, most generally used at first by the robust,—by those who could rough it,—such as could bear to reach the sea shore in a returning " Jersey wagon," and who depended on their own supply of " small stores," sheets, and blankets, &c.—Increase of such company, in time, afforded sufficient motive to residents on the favourite beaches, to make such provision for transient visiters, as could not conveniently make their own supply. Thus, yearly, such places of resort grew from little to greater, and by degrees to luxury and refinement. It is still, however, within the memory of several of the aged, when the concomitants of sea bathing, before the Revolution, were rough as its own surges, and for that very reason, produced better evidences of positive benefits to

WATERING PLACE—SEASHORE.—Page 462.

STENTON, LOGAN'S COUNTRY SEAT.—Page 480.

visiters, in the increase of robust feelings, than they do now. But last in order, in the progress of luxury, came the last device of pleasure, in travelling excursions,—now "boxing the compass" to every point. The astonishing increased facilities of communications have diminished distances. Steamboats transfer us to far distant places, before we have fairly tried the varieties of a single day and night of their operation! Post-coaches, and fleet horses, roll us as easy as on our couches: New England and northern tours occur,—the Grand canal and Niagara are sought; westward, we have Mount Carbon, and the line of new canals; and homeward, "round about," we have the wonders of Mauch-Chunk, Carbondale, the Morris canal, Catskill mountain, and the everlasting battlements of the North river. In such excursions much is seen to gratify the eye, and much to cheer the heart.

> "The verdant meads, the yellow waving corn,
> The new-mown hay, the melody of birds,
> The pomp of groves,—the sweets of early morn."

Scenes like these, ofttimes varied, and sometimes combined with sea scenes, are ever grateful.

> "The music,
> The dash of ocean on the winding shore;"
> "How they cheer the citizen,
> And brace his languid frame!"

We proceed now to notice historically the only "*watering places*" known to our forefathers, placing them much in the order in which they occurred, to wit:

"The mineral water in the Great valley," thirty miles from Philadelphia, was first announced, as a valuable discovery, in the year 1722. In the same year, great praise is bestowed on the newly discovered mineral water at "Bristol spring."

In 1770, such was the decreased fame of the *Yellow springs*, in Chester county, that it was deplored as a public evil that it had been so deserted; although its efficacy of waters and charms of scenery and accommodation were still undiminished—at the beginning—(fifty years before.) It was stated, that from one to five hundred persons, daily, had been accustomed to be found there in the summer months.

We think "Long beach" and "Tucker's beach," in point of earliest attraction as a sea-shore resort for Philadelphians, must claim the precedence. They had their visiters and distant admirers long before Squam, or Deal or even Long Branch itself, had got their several fame. To those who chiefly desire to restore languid frames, and to find their nerves new-braced and firmer strung, nothing can equal the invigorating surf and genial air. And what can more affect the eye and touch the best affections of the heart, than there to think of *Him* who made those great waves—stalking like so many giants to the shore,—tossing their white crests high against the everlasting strand, and calling to each other, in the deep-toned moans of imprisoned spirits struggling to be free! In the beautiful language of our countrywoman, Mrs. Sigourney, we may say,—

> "Thou speak'st a God, thou solemn, holy sea!
> Alone upon thy shore, I rove and count
> The crested billows in their ceaseless play;
> And when dense darkness shrouds thy awful face,
> I listen to thy voice and bow me down,
> In all my nothingness, to *Him* whose eye
> Beholds thy congregated world of waves
> But as a noteless *dew drop*!"

"*Long Branch*," last but greatest in fame, because the fashionables, who rule all things, have made it so, is still inferior as a surf, to those above named. It was held before the Revolution by Colonel White, a British officer and an inhabitant at New York. The small house which he owned and occupied as a summer retreat, is still existing in the *clump* now much enlarged by Renshaw. In consequence of the war, the place was confiscated and fell into other hands, and finally for the public good.

That house was first used as a boarding-house by our fellow citizen, Elliston Perot, Esq., in 1788. At that time the whole premises were in charge of an old woman left there to keep them from injury. Of her Mr. Perot begged an asylum for his family, which was granted, provided he could hire his beds and bedding of others. Being pleased with the place, he repeated his visits the three succeeding years, taking with him other friends. In 1790–1, Mr. M'Night, of Monmouth, witnessing the liking shown to the place, deemed it a good speculation to buy it. He bought the whole premises, containing one hundred acres of land, for £700, and then got Mr. Perot and others to loan him 2000 dollars to improve it. He then opened it for a public watering place; and before his death it was supposed he had enriched himself, by the investment, as much as 40,000 dollars. The estate was sold out to Renshaw for about 13,000 dollars.

The table fare of those companies who first occupied the house under the old woman's grant consisted chiefly of fish, and such salted meats as the visiters could bring with them. All then was much in the rough style of bachelor's fare.

Prior to the above period, "Black point," not far off, was the place of bathing. They had no surf there, and were content to bathe in a kind of waterhouse, covered; even Bingham's great house, near there, indulged no idea of surf-bathing. The tavern entertainment at Black point was quite rude, compared with present Long Branch luxuries; cocoanut pudding, and floating-islands, &c., were delicacies, not even known in our cities!

Indeed we cannot but see, that the most of former summer excursions were but for the men. They were generally deemed too distant and rough for female participation. But later improvements in roads, and a far more easy construction of spring-carriages, have since brought out their full proportion of ladies,—gladdening the company along the route by those feminine attractions which lessen our cares and double our joys. Thus giving an air of gaiety and courtesy to all the steamboats, stage-coaches, and inns, where they enter, and thus alluring us to become the greatest travellers in our summer excursions, to be found in the world! From these causes, country-seats, which were much resorted to after the year 1793, are fast falling into disuse, and probably will not again recover their former regard. See Appendix, p. 538.

CANALS, RAILROADS, TURNPIKES.

Make freighted barks beyond the mountains stray—
New States exulting, see the flitting sails
Waft joy and plenty round the peopled vales!

In some parts of the Union a very erroneous opinion prevails, that the United States are indebted wholly to the example of New York, for the active and beneficial spirit of internal improvement, which pervades the whole confederacy of states.

The splendour of their justly acknowledged grand enterprise, appears to have eclipsed the brilliance of the numerous achievements of the other states. Hence, although *Pennsylvania* has expended several millions of dollars *more* on internal improvements, than any state in the Union, she has been but little noticed therefor.

In Pennsylvania, party spirit, as in New York, has not been brought in as an auxiliary to our public works. Hence our march, though resolute and constant, has been silent and unostentatious. If we except three of the almost uninhabitable counties in the north-western part of this state, five-sixths of every part of the commonwealth is to be intersected by *canals and railways*, leaving no *point* at a greater distance from the highways than twenty-three miles, when the works in actual progress shall have been wholly finished

We shall prove—chiefly from official documents, that from the year 1791 to July 1828, the enormous sum of $22,010,554 has been expended by the *state* and by *corporations*, on canals, rivers, turnpike-roads, railways and bridges, &c.,—and this exclusive of the sums expended by the state prior to the year 1791.

We can also show, that additional works are in actual progress, and that they will be finished at an additional expense estimated at

$12,450,000, making a grand total of $34,460,554, expended in Pennsylvania in forty years, from 1791 to 1831, (the time we pen this article,) for *internal improvements.*

From the year 1791 to 1828, 265 companies have been incorporated by the legislature for the purpose of effecting various internal improvements!

The first act passed in America for a railway for general purposes of commerce was that to Mr. Stevens and others, to make a railway from Columbia to Philadelphia—84 miles. The parties did not execute their plan, but the state has it in hands to execute it quickly. [Since finished.]

Since the year 1792, 168 companies have been incorporated to make about 3110 miles of turnpike roads—of these 102 have gone into operation and have constructed nearly 2380 miles of roads at an expense of $8,431,059.

The numerous bridges, which have been erected over almost every stream in Pennsylvania—many of them then very expensive ones, have given to us the title of "*the state of bridges.*"

Some of the county bridges have been constructed at an expense of from thirty to forty and even to sixty thousand dollars. The Schuylkill permanent bridge, was the first great structure of the kind attempted in America, executed at an expense of $300,000. The Lancaster, or upper ferry-bridge (since supplied by the wire-bridge) was composed of *one arch* of 328 feet of cord. A span exceeding any other in the world. Our wooden bridges, generally, are unrivalled in number, magnitude and scientific boldness of design.

William Penn, in his proposals for a *second* settlement in Pennsylvania, as published in 1690, alludes to the practicability of effecting "*a communication by water*," between the Susquehanna and a branch of the river Schuylkill:—A singular presentiment of a project actually commenced in one century afterwards. And at a still earlier period—say in 1613, Sir Samuel Argal wrote home to England, saying he had the hope to see a cut made between the bays of Chesapeake and Delaware. And the Modern Universal History, edition of 1763, says there is an easy communication with Maryland which comes within four miles of the Chesapeake bay—also, that a project was once set on foot for joining the river and bay by an artificial canal, (now done,) but it met with such opposition from the inhabitants of Virginia and Maryland, "that it came to nothing."

Numerous letters are now extant, which, besides their originality of views, prove beyond all doubt that the union is indebted to Pennsylvania for the *first* introduction of canals and turnpikes to the public attention. Yet this fact, susceptible as it is of every proof, is hitherto scarcely known to the mass even of our own population. Some of our citizens almost denying the existence of the works which their own means had created, and thus assisting to swell the praises of other states, to the prejudice and neglect of their own.

If Pennsylvania is to be censured, it cannot be for supineness and want of enterprise. It cannot be for sins of omission, but of commission. The fault, if any, has been that she has done what she ought to have left undone. She exercised her energies, if to blame, prematurely. She was in advance of the spirit of the age, and her example in commencing *the first canal* to connect the eastern and western waters, which, if successful then, would have stimulated other states, even then, to rivalry, proved by its failure (and all things failed under L' Enfant's engineering, although deemed a premier,) a beacon which warned them to shun her course, and withal to husband their resources, till more wealth and better qualified agents could be obtained.

Some of the correspondence above alluded to, respecting the introduction of canals, is as early as the year 1750 to '60; and although it had but little efficient power then, it nevertheless was the entering wedge which drove to important future results.

If our information be correct, we may attribute to David Rittenhouse, the astronomer, and to Doctor William Smith, provost, the credit of being the first labourers in this important measure. Afterwards Robert Morris, and still later, Robert Fulton, lent their powerful assistance.

In the year 1762, David Rittenhouse, and Doctor William Smith, we believe, at the same time, surveyed and levelled a route for a canal to connect the waters of the Susquehanna and Schuylkill rivers, by means of the Swatara and Tulpehocken creeks. The Union canal, which has since accomplished this object, passes over a portion of this route, which was surveyed *for a canal* in the time of the colonies.

The views of the projectors of this work were, if the difficulties of that period are considered, far more gigantic and surprising than have been entertained by their successors any where. They contemplated nothing less than a junction of the eastern and western waters of Lake Erie and of the Ohio, with the Delaware, on a route of five hundred and eighty-two miles. All this, too, at a period, when the country itself was comparatively a wilderness and without population—looking to the future as a means to surely realize so splendid a scheme of internal communication. Let the European journalists, who carp at our deficiencies, contemplate such facts by a new people!

In 1764, they induced the American Philosophical Society, to order a survey for a canal to connect the Chesapeake bay with the Delaware—a work now accomplished.

These laudable efforts were ably seconded by the provincial legislature, which about the same time authorized a survey on a route, extending five hundred and eighty-two miles, to Pittsburg and Erie. The result was, that the measure was strongly recommended as a feasible project, whenever the public resources should warrant the noble undertaking.

As soon after the war of Independence, as circumstances would permit, the scheme was begun. On the 29th September, 1791, a company was incorporated to effect a portion of the plan, of whom Robert Morris, David Rittenhouse, William Smith, Tench Francis and others, were named as commissioners. They were authorized to connect the Susquehanna and Schuylkill by a canal of slack water navigation. Thus *beginning* the first link in the great chain intended to connect Erie and Pittsburg and Philadelphia. The intended great union is distinctly recognized in the act as then promulgated.

Commercial embarrassments which befell some of the chief stockholders, and withal misapplied money, in a case wherein we had so little of experience, compelled a suspension of the operations. This circumstance, and the suspension some years afterwards of the Chesapeake and Delaware canal, had a most retarding effect on every other similar enterprise. Frequent attempts were made from the year 1795 to resume operations; and there cannot be a doubt, that if the state had, immediately on the first appearance of embarrassments, bestowed that liberal help—eventually proffered when too late—that these canals would have been completed.

The Union canal, intended to unite the former interests, was created by an act of the year 1811, and still preserving the ultimate purpose of extending its course to Lake Erie. Its subsequent history being an affair of much more modern time, it is not necessary to detail its progress down to its completion.

The reader who desires that information is referred to the facts as ably drawn up by George W. Smith, Esq., to whom I am indebted for much of the foregoing notices, and whose ample expose on the subject of our internal improvements, is published in the Register of Pennsylvania, vol. i. p. 405.

"The time will come, (said Fulton's letter to Governor Mifflin,) when canals shall pass through every vale—wind round every hill, and bind the whole country in one bond of social intercourse!" *And so it is even now!*

The turnpike on the Lancaster road, formed in 1792–3, was the first in the United States, and that of Germantown and Perkiomen in 1800–1, was the next in order in Pennsylvania.

It may be remarked of our citizens, that they seem more indifferent than others to that self-gratulation and public cheering which leads to great results in other communities. For instance, they go on to the accomplishment of great public works without despondency in the progress, and with little or no public display, or commemorative fetes or festivals. These remarks are elicited by contemplating the tame and unobtrusive manner in which the public officers, and public journals, announced the completion of such great works as "the Schuylkill navigation," in the year 1825, and "the Union canal," in the month of December, 1827.

No public processions or rejoicings of any kind have marked those great public events. The waters from the Susquehanna have been permitted to mingle with the Schuylkill and Delaware, without a single effort to mark the anniversary of such an auspicious event, although involving in its consequences, hopes as enlivening and cheering as " the grand canal," so called, itself.

Already has the very name of *the first boat* arriving by the Schuylkill navigation canal been lost to fame. This stint of praise and distinction is only equalled by the singularly tame and unexhilarating annunciation of the first certain completion of the Union canal. It first comes before the public eye on the 2d January, 1828, in the form of " an extract of a letter," of the 30th December, " from William Lehman to the managers," stating that " the boat Susquehanna had passed the Summit level with a load of coal from the Susquehanna, and might be expected to arrive at Philadelphia, on the 1st January." Such great news, the gazettes present without any editorial remarks, or display of their flying heralds trumpeting praise far and wide. Contented with the fact, they make no parade or flourish. Thus a great public event which in other cities gives occasion to splendid and golden books and imperial presents and letters, produces no general sensation or enthusiasm here.

We cannot but see, however, that eventually, railroads and canals are destined to become the arteries by which the life blood of our corporate body—the nation—is to be extended with equal vitality to every part. They will go on until they join us to the Rocky mountains, and thence again, beyond them, to the Pacific ocean. A universal *inland* communication is fast progressing. Never again shall we experience, in case of war with a foreign enemy, the evils before witnessed by their ascendency on the ocean, even if we should be inferior in power, in another war on that element.

Hereafter, we can transport soldiers and munitions of war, to any point of our country which may need their presence; but formerly, a foreign fleet could change its positions of annoyance at any time and place where we were least prepared, or least expected its assault.

In the war of 1812, such were the difficulties of inter-communication, that while cotton was 6 cents per pound, and sugar 3 cents per pound, in New Orleans, cotton was worth 40 cents, and sugar 30 cents, in New England. Flour, too, which could only bring $2 in the western country, was worth $15 in New England. Hereafter, such articles of home production will go from the south-west and west, to the eastern cities on the seaboard, at one to two cents a pound! What can hinder the progress and happiness of such a people as we, but our own disunion, mismanagement, or sins!

RIVER DELAWARE.

> "Not distant far the time—when, in thy solitude sublime,
> No sail was ever seen to skim thy billowy tide,
> Save light canoe, by artless savage plied."

P. HEYLIN, in his Cosmography, says the Indians called this river Arasapha, and the bay Poutaxat.

William Penn, in his letter of 1683, thus describes the fish of the Delaware, to wit: "Sturgeons play continually in our river. Alloes, as they call them, (the Jew's Alice,) and our ignorants, shades, (shad!) are excellent fish. They are so plentiful that six hundred are drawn at a draught. Fish are brought to the door, both fresh and salt. Six alloes, or rocks, for twelve pence, and salt fish at three farthings per pound. Oysters two shillings per bushel."

In the year 1733, the governor proposes to the assembly to adopt the practice of other countries, in placing buoys for the channel of the Delaware, and to appoint pilots under proper regulations. These things are said to be suggested in consequence of the difficulties of navigation, and the frequency of shipwrecks. They seem, however, to have got along awhile without them, for the buoys were not introduced into use until the year 1767.

In 1746–7, John Harding, a miller, built the wharf and made a windmill on the muddy island against the town. He, however, took a fever by working in the mud, and died. His son, who succeeded him, gave it its finish, and both expended about £600 in the works. The windmill was in operation but a few years, when it had the misfortune to have the top and sails blown off in a violent gust, and was borne in the air to Joshua Cooper's orchard on the Jersey shore! There it was seen as a play place for boys many years afterwards. This was declared by Mr. John Brown, who saw it.

At a later period a bakehouse was erected there, which, as Thomas Hood told me, did much business. They had also a frame tavern, and sold milk. In time the tavern was left untenanted, when some skating boys at night made it into a great bonfire, for the interest of the town beholders.

Captain Smith's lodgment at the north end is a modern affair, and probably better than any preceding one.

Professor Kalm, when here in 1748, said it was the remark of the old Swedes, and other oldest persons, that the rivers and brooks decreased, whilst the seashores increased. As facts, they stated, that mills which sixty years before were built on waters with a sufficiency of head, had since so little as to be kept idle but in times of rains and snows. Aoke Kalm remembered several places in the Delaware, since made islands of a mile in length, over which he used to row in a boat.

Mr. M'Clure made a scientific and minute survey of the state of our tides in the Delaware, the facts concerning which may be seen at length in my MS. Annals, page 325, in the Historical Society of Pennsylvania.

It deserves to be mentioned, as being now a remarkable characteristic of the Delaware,—the abundance of its oysters. Fifty years ago, when fewer persons were accustomed to eat oysters, and when the few that were eaten were all trundled about the streets on *wheelbarrows*, the oysters of the Delaware were scarcely thought of, or named. The good livers then only feasted on salt oysters from the seashore. As these ran out, by increased demand, those of the Delaware came into notice. Their consumption has since increased every year, and the writer, among others, began to fear they must also be exhausted; but it is not so—by a kind consideration of Providence, it seems to be their nature to increase with the disturbance and stirring of their beds; and they are also taken in deeper waters.

It has been matter of surprise to many, that our oyster beds, though so much fished, should still continue to afford a sufficient supply. Philadelphia city has increased its consumption several hundred fold, and vessels from New York are constantly supplying themselves with loads, to carry to their own nurseries. Some vessels also take them to transplant at Egg Harbour. Long Island and Egg Harbour oysters, when sold as so superior in size and flavour, are still to be regarded as natives of our own bay. Besides our own city supply from our bay, we are latterly receiving great quantities from the Chesapeake, through the Delaware canal. From the 7th October to the 16th December, 1840, there passed through that canal, for our city use, 4230 tons; and at the time of writing this fact, there is actually lying at Spruce street wharf eighteen vessels freighted with oysters;—a real fleet of luxurious diet for the city *bon-vivants!* It is said to be a fact, that much more oysters are consumed in Philadelphia than in New York, where the price, once so cheap, is now so very high.

Having been at some pains to learn something of the present and past state of our oyster beds in the bay, I have arrived at sundry conclusions, such as these:—that our fields of oysters, notwithstanding their constant delivery, are actually on the increase, and have been augmenting in extent and quantity, for the last thirty or forty years. This fact, strange to the mind of many, is said to be imputable to the great use of the dredging machines, which, by dragging over a greater surface, clears the beds of impediments, and trails the oysters *beyond* their natural position, and thus increases the boundaries of the field. These dredges are great iron rakes, attached to the vessel by iron chains, and which trail through the oyster beds, while the vessel is moving over them by the force of the wind in her sails. In this way many more oysters are dragged and loosened from the mud, than the rake will take up, and thus are left free to propagate another future supply.

It is said to be a false kindness to oysters to let them alone, as they did at New York to their famous "blue points," by a *protecting law*, which served only to have them so covered with mud, as to actually destroy them.

An old oysterman informed me, as an instance of the increase of oyster beds, that he used to visit a little one, thirty years ago, of one to two hundred feet long, and therefore very difficult to find, which now is a quarter of a mile long, and growing, known as *the new bed.* There is a field of size, also beds of size, off Benj. Davis' point, and Maurice river, N. J., and off Mahant's river, Delaware side. Since the formation of the Breakwater, lobsters and blackfish have come there in quantities. By-and-by we may expect much increase of them there! It is discovered to be a fact, in all the ponds found in the sedge marshes, lining the two shores of the Delaware, that in them are found the best oysters; and that in one of them called the "Ditch," which is an artificial canal cut into the marsh, fine oysters are always to be fished out. It has been remarked by my informant, and corroborated by others, that although oysters are found in salt water, they will not bear to be removed to water which is salter. Experiments have been made of hanging a basket of bay oysters over the vessel's side exposed to the *salter* sea water, and they have been found to die in twelve hours. Hence the necessity of planting them in waters less salt, or at least not salter than their native beds. Those caught after a copious rain are said to be much finer than those taken from the same place before the rain. The oyster is of a tenacious nature, attaching its gelatinous substance to almost all bodies with which it comes in contact—such as wood, iron, stone. When they are found attached to glass bottles, they are always found much fatter for it. The influence of mud to destroy, and of fresher water to fatten oysters, is well understood by their experience at New Haven, as told in Barber's History, page 106.

Those who make a business of transplanting, come early in the season, and carry them away in their boats to the *inland waters* about Egg Harbour, &c., from whence they are taken in the fall, *quite fat*, and carried over land to the city market, and sold as Egg Harbour oysters.

As in a good degree connected with the use and incidents of the Delaware, we here offer a graphic description of good old Burlington, intimately connected with the pleasure scenes and reminiscences of our own boyhood. Most feelingly we understand the picture as here drawn. Many must remember it.

Ah, old acquaintance! there thou art—
I hail thee with a beating heart,
I'll sing of thee, before we part,
Green bank of Burlington.

May I a passing tribute pay,
Where many a happy school-boy day,
In years for ever past away,
I play'd upon thy bank.

At early morn I thought thee fair,
At noon thou hadst the freshest air,
Thy evenings only could compare
With Eden s lovely bowers.

And most enchanting was the grace
That marked the ladies of the place,
In walk, in form, in mind, in face,
Like mother Eve of old.

Your melons were for flavour rare,
Your cream and strawberries sweetest were,
Your luscious peach, and juicy pear,
The rich and poor partook.

By pebbly shore and lofty tree,
Our good old bathing place I see,
Where school-boys all with loudest glee,
To dive, and swim, repair'd.

Lightly that batteau seems to glide,
In such a one I loved to ride,
With helm in hand, her course to guide,
While briskly blew the breeze.

'Twas sweet to leave the tiresome book,
A dozen silvery fish to hook,
Then take them home to plague the cook,
To clean and fry them all.

My tale of pleasure is begun,
We also sometimes got a gun,
Through mud and mire all day to run;
To shoot a bird or two.

Sometimes we hired a boat to speed,
On a ducking trip where wild ducks feed,
But less ducks than duckings we got indeed,
On Neshamony's marshy flats.

How spreads this river like a bay,
I've skated on it many a day,
While Bristol boys have had a fray,
And feats of skating show'd.

Keenly the crowded wharf I view,
And cannot see one face I knew,
But good Ben Shepherd's ever true,
At every varying tide.

I could have sprung from off the deck,
To give his hand a hearty shake,
For him, and for his city's sake,
My dear old Burlington.

Sadly my memory loves to trace
The kindly smile of many a face
Gather'd ere this in the resting place.
With those of ages past.

The lapse of almost forty years
Has ended all their joys and cares,
We hope they are the happy heirs
Of immortality.

No steamboat then in stately pride,
Made rapid way 'gainst wind and tide,
A shallop then its place supplied,
The goodly sloop May Flower.*

Thy sister cities have the fame,
Of battles fought, and warlike name,
Thy ancient records lay no claim
To bloody tales like these.

Thy precincts show no battle-field,
Where haughty foes were forced to yield
And many a brave one's fate was seal'd
In death upon the plain.

Ere Trenton saw the deadly fray,
Thou wast not idle in thy way;
Bold spirits suited to their day,
Withstood a tyrant's rule.

In thy Town Hall these patriots sate,
And there resolved to share the fate
Of every suffering sister state
With them to stand or fall.

I cannot see Saint Mary's fane;
It often gave me heartfelt pain
To think how oft I've heard in vain
Good Dr. Wharton preach.

Meekly as one who plainly saw
Himself condemn'd beneath the law,
He sought by love, not fear, to draw
His hearers to the Lord.

St. Mary's lifts no towering spire,
For passing travellers to admire,
Fit emblem of the Holy Sire
Who fill'd her desk so long.

* This packet belonged to Captain Myers, a well known skipper.

I hear my fellow travellers say
There is a locomotive's way,
Where school boys used to fight and play,
In Dr. Staughton's time.

And woodman's axe, with sturdy stroke
Has long since fell'd the lofty oak,
Where my poor neck I nearly broke,
To gain a squirrel's nest.

St. Mary's has a pastor new,
Young, and New Jersey's bishop too,
He needs must stand in public view,
May God save him from pride.

May he a shepherd's duty know,
To lead his flock where fountains flow,
And where perennial pastures grow,
Beneath the sacred Cross.

This steamer goes as if it flew,
The city fades before my view—
We turn, I bid a long adieu
To thee, sweet Burlington.

William Castell, in his Book of Discovery, published in 1644, says of the *Delaware river and people*, to wit: "There is another river not fully discovered, but bigger than the former, (the North river,) called the South river. It lieth west by south, towards Virginia. The entrance into it is very wide, having Cape May to the east, and Cape Henlopen to the west. The chief inhabitants lying on the east side of the river. To the east are the *Sicones* and the *Naranticones;* on the west are the *Miquans*, the *Senenquaans*, and many more."

Joshua Fisher, of Lewistown, Delaware, made the first known Bay-chart of the Delaware. The one from which all of our subsequent ones have been copied. It bears the imprint of London, 1756.

The Pea Patch *island*, now a subject of dispute, is given therein at about its present distance from New Jersey, showing no appearance of having ever been annexed to that shore. How early it may have been drawn, is not now known; but it must be inferred to have been several years earlier than 1756, because the position of Cape Henlopen is therein ascribed to the joint observation of Joshua Fisher, and *Thomas Godfrey.* The latter we know died in 1749, and had brought out his quadrant, and lent it to Mr. Fisher for trial in his surveys of the Delaware, as early as 1730.

A large chart of the Delaware bay was published in London in 1779, called Debarre's chart, from the surveys of Lieut. Knight.

It is worthy of remark, as testing the accuracy of *Godfrey*, that his position of Cape Henlopen, differs only ten miles from that now scrupulously ascertained by the United States' recent surveys. The shoals and oyster beds, as laid down in Fisher's chart, though generally in the same localities as now ascertained by the United States' survey, are very different in their lengths and breadths—and especially those nearest the main land on both sides of the bay; the present surveys, showing much more of extended shoals near the main land, than have been given in Fisher's chart In some instances, shoals then marked are now gone; and in other cases, new ones are formed.

RIVER SCHUYLKILL.

THIS name, given it by the Dutch, is said to express "Hidden river," it not being visible at its mouth as you ascend the Delaware. From the Indians it bore the name of Manajung, Manaiunk, and in Holmes' map it is called Nittabaconck. It is told as a tradition that the Indians called the river the mother, and that what is called "Maiden creek," a branch of the Schuylkill above Reading, was called Onteelaunee, meaning the little daughter of a great mother. The letter of Governor Stuyvesant, of 1644, to Colonel Nicolls, says they discovered the Varsche Rivierte—the little freshwater river, in 1628.

I have heard it conjectured that the flat ground of Pegg's marsh, and the low ground of Cohocsink swamp, are the beds of the Schuylkill, which may have passed there before Fairmount barrier gave way—one channel having come from Fairmount to Pegg's swamp, and the other from the Falls of Schuylkill by Cohocsink. The particulars of this theory may be read in my MS. Annals, p. 352, 353, in the Historical Society of Pennsylvania.

In the year 1701, William Penn writes to James Logan, saying, "Pray see the utmost of poor Marshe's project of navigating flats up Schoolkill and Susquehanna above the falls; he assuring me he could make the experiment for 40*s.* be it 50*s.* or £3. it were a mighty advantage."

In 1722, the common council this year appointed a committee to examine a route to Schuylkill through the woods, and to fix upon the site of a ferry at the end of High street, whereupon it was re solved to address the assembly for an act for the same.

The same year the corporation of Philadelphia made a causeway on both sides of the ferry, and appointed boats, &c. The ferrymen were to dwell on the western side, and to ferry persons over at one penny, horses 1*d.*, cows and oxen 1½*d.*, cart or wagon 6*d.* to 1*s.*, sheep ½*d.*, &c. The upper and lower ferries were then called Roach's and Blunston's, on private account. This one became of course "the middle ferry."

In the year 1762, we see by a minute of the council that they then leased "the middle ferry," for three years, at £200. per annum.

I am not able to say when the floating bridges were first introduced; but we know the British army made one across the Schuylkill when they held the city, which I believe they destroyed when leaving it, as it is known that Joseph Ogden built and kept a new bridge at the middle ferry, soon after they were gone.

Mr. Kalm states, that at the first building of Philadelphia, they erected sundry houses upon the Schuylkill side, which they afterwards removed to the Delaware side, on finding settlements there did not take.

The river scenery and banks of Schuylkill were once picturesque and beautiful—such as I have elsewhere described the "Baptisterion," at the end of Spruce street. Benjamin Franklin, too, said it was his custom when young to go out there with his companions, Osborne, Watson, Ralph, &c., to take a charming walk on Sundays in the woods then bordering on the river. There they used to sit down and read and converse together; now how changed the scene to a busy, bustling coal mart?

> "Receding forests yield the labourers room,
> And opening wilds with fields and garlands bloom!"

It is even now within the memory of aged men, when it was a great fishing place. Old Shrunk assured me he had caught as many as 3000 catfish of a night with a dip-net, near the Falls. Penn's letter, of 1683, speaks of Captain Smith, at Schuylkill, who drew "600 shades at a draught."

In the year 1759, there appeared in the Gazette a writer from Berks, who greatly urges the advantages to be produced by clearing and opening the river channel. Some of them were then set upon by a subscription.

The 4th of July, 1824, being Sunday, the long desired era arrived of opening the canal from Reading to Philadelphia. Many witnessed the operations near Reading with great gratification. This *is* "the consummation devoutly to be wished!"

A fact occurred in November 1832, which goes to confirm the theory before advanced, that the Schuylkill once passed from the Falls *by the way of the Cohocksink creek.* In making a coffer dam, (the first one on the eastern side,) to form the foundation of the railway-bridge at Peters' island, they came at the depth of thirty feet of excavation to *the stump* of a tree completely embedded in the soil, thus evincing that *the course* of the river has been *changed* from its original channel.—See Poulson's Gazette, of Nov. 26, 1832.

I have in my possession, a copy of a curious old deed of the 2d of May, 1681, from Peter Peterson Yocum, a Swede, to Niels Jonason, for two hundred acres of land to begin at a creek on the west side of Schuylkill above *Arromink*, called the little *Quarnes* fall, and thence, up along the river side to the *Great-hill*, being part of the original tract of 1100 acres granted by patent of Governor Lovelace at *New York* to Captain Flans Modens, i. e. Moens. [The Great hill, may be understood to be Conshohockin now—and the Quarnes, (Quarries,) the Little falls.]

The place called Swedesford, had a work of defence cast upon its margin by the Americans, in the time of the Revolution. It was the crossing place then of the army.

Near there was the Swedes' church, since rebuilt by the Episcopalians; the grave ground is well filled with Swedes, who very much

settled along the Schuylkill. The Swedes used to go to the old church in considerable numbers, in antiquated and rude style of dress. The men went on foot, or in canoes, the women on horse-back, often riding double, and always with coarse outside petticoats, which could be seen hung along the fences in dozens, while the owners were in church—their descendant daughters since scarcely know it.

COUNTRY SEATS.

It is intended herein to revive the recollection of sundry country seats nigh the city, once known to all, and now no longer arresting attention, to wit:

Bedminster was a neat country place, having a fine collection of fruit trees, at the N. E. corner of Brewer's alley and Fourth street. The same house, now an inn there, with a new gable-end, having cut off about fourteen feet once upon Fourth street. That place, when "far out of town," was the summer residence of the celebrated Gilbert Tennant. It was at another time the summer seat of the Baynton family. In the year 1755, it was advertised as "a very rural, agreeable place." Its proper front was upon the present Wood street, formerly called Brewer's alley, because of a brew-house once on that street, below Third street.

Samuel Birge had a country seat—the house still standing, with two corresponding out-houses, fronting westward, and themselves now a little west of New Fourth street, near Poplar lane. When occupied as a seat, it was surrounded with fields and woods—now it is shut in by common houses.

The Robin Hood Inn, in Poplar lane, near New Fourth street, was the summer residence of Abram Mitchell, and when occupied by a British officer in command of the British barracks, it was finely cultivated, and the woods in abundance near at hand.

Along the northern bank of Pegg's run, west of Sixth street, were several neat country houses, some of them still standing, but all their former scenery utterly obliterated by streets and houses placed near them. The present "Drover's Inn," on Sixth street, is one of them. Near the corner of Tenth and Vine streets is now the remains of what was once a distinguished seat and *farm*. The house even now, is surrounded by many old fruit and other trees—at same time—opposite to it is a long row of new and fashionable city houses—a part of Palmyra row.

Wharton Mansion, in Southwark, fronting the river, back from the present Navy-yard, was a country house of grandeur in its day. It was of large dimensions, with its lawns and trees—and, as a superior house, was chosen by the British officers of Howe's army, for the celebration of the Meschianza. Now the house and all about its grounds looks only like a deserted, decaying place.

Treveskin was the seat of Governor Gordon, down the Passyunk road, about a mile and a half below South street. It became the place of Israel Pemberton, and descended by his daughter, Mrs. Pleasants, to her family. The house is still standing.

Judge Kinsey's country seat, out South street, near to the Schuylkill, was a very superior place. The respectable looking house, surrounded by big cedars, was standing till lately, on the premises of the Naval asylum. It was, when built, the only good house between the city and Gray's ferry. It afterwards became the property of James Pemberton. On the other side of the road is now a similar country seat, built for Israel Pemberton, now the property of Mrs. Marshall, the daughter of Joseph Cruikshank, containing thirty-two acres, and used as a milk farm by Mr. Webster. Brick kilns are now all about near the place.

Wilton, the place once of Joseph Turner, down in the neck, was the *nonpareil* of its day. It was the fashionable resort for genteel strangers. Every possible attention was paid to embellishment, and the garden cultivation was superior. The grounds had ornamental clumps and ranges of trees. Many statues of fine marble [sold from a Spanish prize] were distributed through the grounds and avenues. Some of them are now on the place, mutilated and neglected, and others of them are at "Chew's house," Germantown. The mansion house and out-houses, still standing, show in some degree their former grandeur. The ceilings are high and covered with stucco work, and the halls are large. In the time of the war, when occupied by the British, it got much abused—even to chopping wood on the floors. The statues, too, made good marks for their sharpshooters, and *Pan*, now there in the cabbage garden, which long stood for the ideal presence of *Diabolus* himself, has many tokens of his fire-proof. The property, now belonging to the heirs of Henry Hill, has long been used as a rented grazing farm, and shows much of desolation and neglect, created in some degree by a long and dubious point of legal ownership.

Springettsberry, called after the name of William Penn's first wife, was once cultivated in the style of a gentleman's seat, and occupied by the Penn family. It was built, I believe, for Thomas Penn, about the year 1736 to '39, on a fine commanding situation, a little south-west of Bush-hill.

Celebrated as it was, for its display and beauty, now almost nothing remains. The Preston retreat is now on the premises, near the former house and gardens. Its former groves of tall cedars, and ranges of catalpa trees are no more. For many years the Penn family continued o have the place kept up in appearance, even after they ceased to make it a residence. James Alexander, called Penn's gardener, occupied the premises; and old Virgil Warder, and his wife, servant—blacks, lived there to old age, occupying the kitchen as their home, on an annuity (as it was said) from the Penn family—paid to them till their deaths, about the year 1782–3. For many years, the young people of the city—before the war of Independence, visited Springettsberry in May time, to gather flowers, and to talk with and see old gray-headed Virgil, who had always much to say about the Penns of former days. It was all enchanted ground to the young—

> "Where once the garden smiled,
> And still, where many a garden flower grew wild!"

In the year 1777, old Virgil had quite a harvest, derived from the blooming there—a great wonder then—of the great American aloe, which had long been nursed in the green-house. It was visited by many—and all had their gifts ready for the old black man.

The garden had evergreens, made into arbours, and nicely trimmed and clipped in formal array. There was also a seeming wilderness of shade, with gravel paths meandering through, &c. The place was in the occupancy of Robert Morris, as a country retreat, and was so used in 1784, when the mansion took fire, and was consumed.

Bush-hill, the country seat of Andrew Hamilton, Esq., near to the former place, on an elevation, commanding a fine view of the then distant city, was once kept up in fine style as a distinguished country seat—built in 1740, for Andrew Hamilton. In the rear were avenues of stately cedars—some few still remaining; and in the front was a charmingly graceful descending green lawn, gradually sloping down to Vine street. The original farm consisted of many acres, and has since descended to the family as valuable building lots. In the year 1793, the mansion-house and out-houses were used temporarily as a yellow fever hospital—and afterwards it fell into the hands of Mr. M'Cauley, and was used as his carpet manufactory.

In excavating there a new cellar for Mr. M'Cauley's use, in 1832, they came to two lines of graves parallel to each other, with about fifteen graves in each line. They were deemed to have been aboriginal. No remains were found of either bones or ornaments, but a kind of residuum of decomposed substances, which was pronounced, by geological examiners, to have been animal deposit—"it looked like gray earth in ashes." The graves were all five feet long, by two feet wide, and put at one and a half feet below the surface, and thence two and a half feet to the bottom. The rows stood north and south.

Bushhill and Springettsberry were parts of the manor of Springettsberry. James Logan early saw the prospective value of this part of the manor, so near the city, and was very unwilling to part with any portion of it, but the difficulties of the Penn family made it necessary to yield it to others. Jonathan Dickinson bought a part; and a part was given to Andrew Hamilton for needful professional services as a legal counsellor, &c., to the Penn family.

A few country seats were located along the Ridge road, having the rear of their grounds extending back to the beautiful banks of the Schuylkill. Among such were Mifflin's place, Francis' place, Peale hall, and others. Those named were all set fire to at the same time, by the British—saying, as their excuse, that they could or did serve for look-out shelters for their enemies. Two country seats on Germantown road were also burnt—say Norris' place at Fairhill, and Charles Thomson's at Sommerville.

Stenton, near Germantown, the residence of the Logan family, was originally taken up by James Logan, secretary, &c., of William Penn. The family mansion was built in 1727, in a very superior manner. At one time the fields there were cultivated in tobacco. It was used for a short time by General Howe, and at one time was preserved from intended conflagration by the British, by the adroit management of the house-keeper then there, in charge of it.

Familiar as I have been with the history and manuscript remains of the honoured proprietor, the first James Logan, I approach the secluded shades of Stenton, in which he sought retirement from the cares and concerns of public life, with such emotions as might inspire poetry, or soothe and enlarge the imagination.

In truth, I feel, with Sir Richard Steele, that on such an occasion, "I can draw a secret, unenvied pleasure from a thousand incidents overlooked by other men." A picture of the house, as now seen, is given in this work.

At the present time there are standing some three or four old brick country residences distinguished in their day. One of double front, from the road, in the lot on the northern side of the Arsenal; another stands opposite to the Arsenal, back from the road, having a circular window in the gable-end to the street, and a piazza around the whole square of the building. Another stands at the angle of the ferry-road, below the Arsenal, and shows its circular window to the road. It was built and resided in by Weiss, who inherited it from the Swedish family of Cocke. This Weiss was *the first man* to bring Lehigh coal to Philadelphia for experiment. He, bringing what he had, in his saddle-bags, and was laughed out of his hopes therein, on its being tried for ignition in his cousin Dupuy's silver-smith furnace! He died at Weissport, named Col. Jacob Weiss.

Strange to tell, a former country-seat is even *now* in the centre of Philadelphia! It is No. 2 South Thirteenth street. The same house where the five wheelbarrow men murdered a man, and were hung for it, on the Centre square.

MISCELLANEOUS FACTS.

"Made of odd ends and patches."

THE following facts have no proper connexion, and have here been brought togethei, because they had no proper affinity with any other subjects treated of severally under appropriate heads. They are shreds and patches and odd ends, here wove, into a *Mosaic* pattern—to wit:

Miscellanea.

1683, Jan. 28.—The speaker of the assembly ordered, that each member absenting himself without good cause, should pay a fine of 12*d.* sterling each time.

1685, March 16.—Nicholas Moore, (former speaker,) for contempt of the authority of the house, was expelled.

1689, March 13.—John White, a member in prison in New Castle, was ordered to be set free and to take his seat, but he was again seized by the sheriff, John Claypole, and borne off!

1695.—The Judges were allowed 10*s.* a day for their services. John Claypole alone was declared a man of ill-fame, and the governor was requested to remove him.

1701.—Juries were to be paid 8*d.* a day, and witnesses 2*s.* each. Members of assembly in after years received 4*s.* 6*d.* a day.

1702.—Solomon Cresson, going his round at night, entered a tavern to suppress a riotous assembly, and found there John Evans, Esq., the governor, who fell to beating Cresson.

1704, August 16.—The violence of the wind and rain prevented the members of assembly, out of town, from attendance. Such members usually brought their dinners with them.

——. October 15.—The assembly was required to meet on Sunday. They organized, and adjourned to Monday.

1706.—The wolves had increased so greatly near to Philadelphia, as to endanger the sheep.

1721.—Sundry persons in Philadelphia agree to receive, in payment of goods, &c., the dollars called Lion dollars at the rate of 5*s.*, the English crown at 7*s.* 6*d.*, the English shilling at 1*s.* 6*d.*, &c., proclamation money.

Four brick tenements on the west side of Front street, and with lots extending through to Second street, fronting on which are two tenements, all rent for £70. per annum, and pay £12. ground rent, bounded on the north by Clement Plumstead. who lived at the north-west corner of Union and Front streets.

1722.—The mineral water in the Great valley, 30 miles from Philadelphia, is discovered this year; and great praise is bestowed on the Bristol spring.

A public paper of the merchants at Jamaica, of July, 1722, states "that the reputation of a place, (Philadelphia,) once famed for the best flour in America, has become so corrupted, that housekeepers are scarcely persuaded to look on Pennsylvania flour." In consequence of this and other representations, an act for better inspection was passed.

The names of the grand jurors empanelled, gives one a good idea of the first inhabitants; and their original signatures to recommendations to tavern licenses, might now help many a descendant to a means of knowing the writing of their first progenitors in Philadelphia. These are still on file in the Mayor's court.

In 1722 and '23, interest was reduced in Pennsylvania from 8 to 6 per cent.

When blackbirds and crows were numerous and destructive, they gave premiums for their heads—by the act of 1704, they gave 3*d.* per dozen for blackbirds and 3*d.* for crows.

By an act of 1719, they compelled all paupers in Philadelphia to wear a letter P upon their right shoulder, to prevent them from street begging, &c.

The act for establishing a ferry to Daniel Cooper's land, was passed in 1717.

1726.—There are advertised two gray stallions suitable for a coach.

1727.—Lord De la Warr, after whom Delaware is so named, so spells his name in signing, with the other lords, the declaration of King George's death.

A lion, the king of beasts, is exhibited in Water street at 1*s.* a sight.

The king's birth-day was celebrated this year, (1727,) at the house of Wm. Chanceller, sailmaker, in whose gardens twenty-one pieces of cannon were placed and fired. Some incidental circumstances have shown that he was the friend of Sir Wm. Keith, the governor, and had from him the first grant of keeping gunpowder stored for safety.

The first loan office was opened in 1728.

1729.—J. Kempster and J. Coals were compelled to kneel at the bar of the house of assembly, and to ask pardon for offence.

1730, Nov. 5.—Monday night, one Bradley going home alone, in liquor, fell into a ditch at the upper end of Market street, where he was found dead the next morning, having been drowned in six inches of water.

It is worthy of remark, that in this early day so few co-partnerships should occur in business. In a list of 120 chief houses in trade, only two instances occur of signatures by firms.

1730.—The house of assembly ordered that a flag should be hoisted on proper days upon Society hill—such as Sundays and holidays, &c.,—and that Edward Carter be paid £10. for such hoisting, &c.

1736.—An ox is announced as to be roasted whole, for public entertainment, in the Northern Liberties—at J. Stennard's.

Mr. Derring, dancing-master, advertises for scholars. John Salomen, Latin and French teacher, advertises in Latin for pupils.

1736.—A servant man going into the river, "under Society hill," to wash, slipped beyond his depth and was drowned.

At the same place a man, attended by his wife, came to drown himself to get rid of her: but after casting himself in, at which sight she was a calm spectator, some officious persons near there rescued him, and compelled him and his wife to go home together!

1738.—Peter Poole, of Manatawna, hearing a noise in the brook near his house, supposed it was a deer in the water, and shooting at it, killed his own mother, Anna S. Poole! This family probably gave name to Poole's ship-yard and bridge.

1738.—The mayor acquainted the city council that several of the barbers of the city had applied to him to take proper measures to prevent persons exercising that trade on the first day of the week, called Sunday, and the mayor desired the opinion of the board what measures to adopt,—whereupon the board orders that they be notified to abstain from so working on that day, according to the law of the province before existing, and preventing working on that day.

1739.—One of the houses at the south-west corner of Front and Walnut streets, (held by Edward Bridges as a dry-goods store) is said to be "commonly called the Scales."

A camel is this year exhibited, the first ever shown here.

1746—"Firms" in trade now first begin to appear—say Hamilton, Wallace and Co."—"Steadman, Robertson and Co."

A storekeeper in Wilmington—say Joseph Peters—advertises his list of store goods in the Philadelphia paper. He does this often in several years, even till his death, and then his successor does the same.

In 1746, Thomas Kinnett advertises to teach the noble art of defence with the small sword, and also dancing.

In consequence of that advertisement, an article soon after appeared, signed Samuel Foulke, in which he says, "I was indeed surprised at his audacity and brazen impudence in giving those detestable vices those high encomiums. They may be proved so far from "accomplishments," that they are diabolical. This is a freedom of assault by friend Foulke, not now practised with other men's advertisements! The other does not appear to have made any defence, although so accomplished to defend himself!

1748.—The coin of the day is called pieces-of-eight—pistoles and cob-dollars.

1749.—A proclamation of Charles Willing, Esq., the mayor, commands all barbers and peruke-makers from working at their trades on the sabbath-day.

This year wood was determined, by an ordinance, that it should measure four feet in length, or be forfeited to the poor, and any person refusing to submit it to measurement, should forfeit 5*s.* per cord.

1751.—The pilot boats used to be all docked in a dock where are now Girard's stores, above High street. They were of small dimensions then. I perceive they were pinked stern, but 27 feet keel, and 11 feet beam.

1754.—By far the greatest collection of books that I have seen advertised by catalogue, even by Franklin and other printers, were published by Tench Francis, Jr., in connexion with his assortment of European and East India goods. There were then no exclusive book-stores.

William Taylor, who came from England in 1726, and settled at Darby, was the first man who ever made a pair of smith's bellows in our country.

There were great perplexities in our markets at the time of changing the computation of money from pounds, shillings, and pence, to dollars and cents, and considerable in keeping accounts, &c. It was a long time before people could get out of their old habits.

Philadelphia has long enjoyed the reputation of a peculiar cake called the *apee.* Thousands who partake of them have no conception of the origin of their name. Ann Page, lately living under another name and business, first made them, many years ago, under the common name of cakes. The aged may remember her small frame house in Second street, two doors north of Carter's alley. On her cakes she impressed the letters A. P., the letters of her name, and from this cause, ever since the initials have been disused on them, the cakes have continued to be called *apees.*

Our Philadelphia butchers are said to cut up and display their beef in a manner superior to the sister cities. At New York, they leave the lean on the chuck, which our butchers leave on the hide; and we cut the plate and the brisket more [illegible] than they do at New York or Baltimore.

In the year 1779, the Spanish ambassador, then living in Chew's large house in South Third street above the Mansion house, gave a *grand gala.* The gardens there were superbly decorated with variegated lamps, and the edifice itself was like a blaze of light.

I saw an ancient deed in the possession of Samuel Richards, which was written on very fine linen cambric, and faced on both sides with paper. It made it firm and to the eye like vellum.

The mile-stones from Philadelphia to Trenton were set up by the directors of the Company for the Insurance of houses—done in 1763, out of the funds raised by their fines. They cost £33. The particulars, as reported by the committee, may be seen at length on page 198 of my MS. Annals in the Historical Society of Pennsylvania.

I have been well assured that the stones set up along the Gulf road are marked with Penn's arms, having *three* balls. Some still remain and were seen lately. Along the Chester road, too, were once mile-stones, having some insignia of the queen's arms.

The War and Navy office of the United States, and general Post Office, when in Philadelphia, before 1800, were at the north-east corner of Fifth and Chestnut streets, and the Secretary of State's office was adjoining on Fifth street—all belonged to Simmons.

Great quantities of wood used to be brought to the city on sleds in the winter, and often sold very high; sometimes 15 to 16 dollars a cord. Since the practice of laying up wood in yards has prevailed, the winter prices are much moderated.

A city directory, and the numbering of all the houses, is a great convenience, which did not exist till about the year 1785.

A letter of James Logan, of the year 1718, states that Colonel Spotswood, the Governor of Virginia, had happily discovered passes in the Allegheny mountains, by which to conduct military enterprises, &c.

Tobacco cultivated.

In 1701, the tobacco field is spoken of, on the land of John Stacey, by the long bridge over the Cohocksinc creek.

In 1719, Jonathan Dickinson, in his letter, speaks of "several around Philadelphia who planted and raised tobacco with success."

Much of Penn's rents was paid to J. Logan in tobacco. It was cultivated at an early period on Logan's farm; also at Harriton, where Charles Thomson afterwards lived and died.

Grass and Clover cultivation.

In 1685, William Penn, in his letter to his steward, says, "Hay dust (meaning grass seed, I presume) from Long Island, such as I sowed in my court yard, is best for our fields. I will send divers seeds for gardens and fields, &c." In another letter he says, "I am glad the Indian field bore so well. Lay as much down as you can with hay dust."

Professor Kalm, who was here in 1748, says an old Swede, whose father came out with Governor Printz, said his father used to say the grass grew every where two feet high in the woods; but in Kalm's time it was much diminished. He imputes the decrease to the practice of the annual burning of the leaves.

From the letters of Jonathan Dickinson it appears he had much desire to import grass seeds; two or three times they arrived injured by the heat of the hold. In 1721, he proposes to hang it over the vessel's quarter, sewed up in tarpaulins; but before the experiment could be made, he announces himself happy to find a very simple means used by another. The seed was sealed in jars and kept air tight.

The same Jonathan Dickinson, I found in 1719, speaks of having bought up 500 pounds of red clover seed in Rhode Island, for his cultivation here—saying the white clover already tinges the roads as a natural production. Kalm afterwards, in 1748, spoke of the white clover as abundant here: and red and white as both abundant about Albany, and some about New York.

The cultivation of red clover, which proved eventually a great restorer of our impoverished lands, did not get into successful introduction and use, until it was first successfully used and publicly recommended by Mr. James Vaux, of Fatlandford, in Montgomery county, about the year 1785. John Bartram, however, the botanist, had fields of red clover in cultivation before the war of Independence.

Plaster of Paris.

When our forefathers began to work this virgin soil, they found it very productive. For the first 60 or 70 years the soil sustained itself against the exhausting manner of husbandry—producing an average of 25 to 30 or 35 bushels of wheat to the acre, as I have learned. But after the year 1750, and down to the time of the peace, frequently the former good lands could produce but an average crop of six or seven bushels to the acre. At this crisis the public became greatly indebted to the intelligence and public spiritedness of the late venerable Judge Peters. To his perseverance and recommendation we are indebted, in good measure, for the introduction and use of that incalculable renovater of our soil, the gypsum or plaster of Paris. It is now admitted that our farms now produce generally four-fold of what they used to do!

Vegetable Productions introduced.

Gardening, as an exclusive branch of business, is quite a modern concern. If any existed before the year 1793, they were without notice or emolument. But since, by introducing many new table luxuries, they have acquired reputation and profit, and this inducement has allured several to the same employment. We shall here notice a few of the more remarkable vegetables introduced among us.

As late as my mother's childhood, potatoes were then in much less esteem and use than now. The earliest potatoes, like the originals now discovered from South America, were very small, compared with the present improved stock. They were small, bright yellow ones, called kidney potatoes; and probably about seventy-five years ago, they then first introduced a larger kind, more like the present in use, which were called in New England, the Bilboa. They were, however, of slow use into families, and the story ran that they were pernicious to health; and a lover of Bilboas was said to die in five years! In Pennsylvania the same kind of potatoes were called Spanish potatoes.

In accordance with those facts, the late Colonel A. J. Morris, when in his ninetieth year, told me that the potatoes used in his early life were very inferior to the present. They were called Spanish potatoes, and were very sharp and pungent in the throat and smell. They sent occasionally a better sort from Liverpool. He said Tench Francis first imported our improved stock, which by frequent culti vation he much improved.

In 1748, Professor Kalm speaks of nightshade and privet as growing wild in our fields; of the latter several hedges were made. The squash he deemed an indigenous plant, much used by the In dians before the Europeans came. The Indians, too, had always a kind of cultivated peas. He much expressed his surprise to see our cultivated lands abounding with purslain, a vegetable which required a gardener's care in his country! He often saw, he said, asparagus growing wild in loose soils on uncultivated sandy hills. The misletoe (Viscum album) grew upon the sweet gum, the oak, and lime tree, so much so that their whole summits were quite green in winter. I believe none witness these things in our region now.

Charles Thomson, the secretary of Congress, said he well remembered the circumstance of the first introduction of broom corn into our country. Dr. B. Franklin chanced to see an imported corn whisk in the possession of a lady, and while examining it as a novelty he espied a grain of it still attached to the stalk. This he took and planted, and so we at length have got it in abundance among us.

The yellow willow among us was introduced from a similar accident, as told me by T. Matlack, Mrs. D. Logan, and Samuel Coates. All in our state came originally from some wicker-work found sprouting in a basket-state in Dock creek. It was seen by Dr. Franklin, who took it out and gave the cuttings to Charles Norris of that day, who reared them at the grounds now the site of the Bank of the United States, where they grew to great stature.

The first weeping willows were introduced into the city by Governor John Penn, for his garden, in South Third street, next adjoining to Willing's place.

The Seckel pear was cultivated first by Lawrence Seckel, and the original tree stands on the place in the Neck, once his, and afterwards Stephen Girard's, (and now the Corporation's) say five miles from Philadelphia, and about one mile above the confluence of the Delaware and Schuylkill rivers. It stands on an alluvial soil—is now half decayed—the other side sound, and bore well, in 1834. The tree had been upon the place, from the time of the father before him. For many years that the fruit had been used by the tenant, its excellence was unknown even to Lawrence Seckel himself, and at last he knew it by the chance of eating several of them at the time of their maturity. After that, he brought them to the city, and gave them out to a few of his friends. He told the father of C. J. Wistar, (my informant,) when he gave him some of the pears, that he knew not *how the tree came there*. It might be a question, whether it might not have been a Dutch or Swedish plantation of early days.

The manner of Mr. Ranstead, the upholsterer from Wales, introducing as a flower, the plant since known in abundance as the Ranstead weed, I have told elsewhere; also, in like manner, that of the day-waker, and the daisy, once deemed flowers, and now multiplied so as to be regarded as annoying weeds.

City Charter.

1684, the 26th of 5th mo., Thomas Lloyd, Thomas Holmes, and William Haignes were appointed to draw up a charter for Philadelphia to be made a borough, consisting of a mayor and six aldermen, and to call to their assistance any of the council. The charter as a city was obtained in 1691. For I find by an act of council, of 3d of 6th mo., 1691, that Humphrey Murray is recognized "as present Mayor of the city of Philadelphia." It appears, however, that in later periods the city was generally spoken of as obtaining its first charter as a city, under date of the 25th of October, 1701, that being the time of Penn's second arrival, when he granted "the charter of the city of Philadelphia."

The Northern Liberties' part was incorporated in 1803, and the Southwark district in 1794.

Several attempts, after the Revolution, were made to procure an act of incorporation for the city, before it was obtained. It was much opposed by some. Fourteen hundred citizens, in September 1789, signed and presented a memorial against it. The subject was again revived in 1786, but no act was passed until the month of March, 1789. The whole objections contained in the memorial may be read in Hazard's "Pennsylvania Register," vol. ii., p. 327. They complain that if the act contemplated should pass, they should be "subjected to an aristocratic police,"—"that the act of incorporation is in itself unnecessary,"—"that many eastern well regulated towns prosper well without incorporation,"—"on the contrary, English example affords instructive facts of the mischievous effects of incorporating."—"They object to the large powers of oyer and terminer."—"They deem the incorporation unnecessary, because the legislature, in which several gentlemen of the city are a part, will always be possessed of sufficient information respecting the provisions necessary to be made for the convenience and order of the city," &c.

Port Entries—Inward and Outward.

In the earliest newspapers, the entrance and clearance of vessels are as regularly printed for New York and Amboy, as they are at

* Since said to have been planted there by Col. Jacob Weiss, of Weissport, Pa

Philadelphia. Down to about the year 1730, they are about two or three a week inward, and two or three outward—but from and after the year 1736, they are increased to about twelve each way, in a week—being certainly a quick increase.

Funeral Pomp restrained.

In 1727, Robert Ashton, Esq., recorder and prothonotary, died, aged fifty-eight, and was buried in pomp, by torch lights at night, in Christ church ground—in the aisle of the church.

About that time, funeral cards of invitation were sent out among fashionable people, as has been lately revived. They were printed in London, having deep mourning borders, and funeral devices. Such a one is preserved in Peale's Museum, filled up in Maryland, in 1723. This ceremony was of rare occurrence.

We have some intimation of the "pomp and circumstance" of an old-fashioned funeral, in the death of *Aquila Rose*, at Philadelphia, in 1723. He was young—a printer—poet—and clerk of the assembly, and was honoured more for his merit than his wealth. His eulogium, in elegiac verse, was done by S. Keimer, "city printer," and quondam friend of Franklin—to wit:

> "His corpse attended was by Friends so soon.
> From seven at morn, till one o'clock at noon.
> By master-printers carried toward his grave,
> Our city printer such an honour gave.
> A worthy merchant did the widow lead,
> And they both mounted on a stately steed.
> Next preachers, common council, aldermen,
> A judge and sheriff graced the solemn train,
> Nor fail'd our treasurer in respect to come,
> Nor stayed the keeper of the rolls at home.
> With merchants, shopkeepers, the young and old,
> A numerous throng, not very easy told.
> And what still adds a lustre to it,
> Some rode well mounted, others walk'd a-foot.

Thus "died and was buried" in distant olden time,—

> "A lovely poet, whose sweet fragrant name,
> Will last till circling years shall cease to move."

It is not a little curious, that the original printed paper from which the above is taken is still in existence, embellished with the usual symbols of death—the head, bones, hour-glass, &c.

In 1765, it was resolved by the best families in New York, Boston, and some attempts were made at Philadelphia, to diminish the expenses of funerals—and at Philadelphia, on the occasion of the death of Alderman W. Plumstead, it is said, "he was buried at St. Peter's church, in the plainest manner according to the new mode—having no pall over his coffin, nor any of his relatives (by his request) appearing in mourning." B. Price, Esq., also, according to his will, was buried in an oak coffin, and iron handles.

The Bloody Election

Was an incident of the year 1742, and of frequent mention in the early annals as an affair of much scandal. Secretary Peters, in his letter to proprietaries, thus describes it, saying,—Young Joseph Turner gathered the sailors, to the number of forty to fifty persons, with clubs, at an open lot over against the Christ church. Thence they made an assault at the court-house, on some of the electors there. Thence went to Chestnut street, and by a back-way [for open ground seemed common then!] to the Indian King inn in High street, where, being refused any drink by Peter and Jonathan Robeson, they went back enraged to the election grounds. There they fell heavily with their clubs upon the Germans and others,—beating off the former, as many as 500. The fight became "shocking to the sight,"—"a truly mad scene and uproar,"—but the sailors were made to retreat. There was a great trial for the stairs by which the voters ascended and descended, then occupied, as formerly for several years, by Isaac Norris and his party.* The ship-carpenters clubbed together to make it their own, which they accomplished. As it produced much public feeling, it became quickly a matter of court cognizance, and even the Assembly itself, as if anticipating the courts, made it a matter of debate and business for three weeks, passing at length a bill for a riot act, &c.

Insurance.

In 1721, John Copson, the printer of the Mercury Gazette, opens "an insurance office at his office, where he will provide competent underwriters to assure any sum applied for." This was the first attempt at insurance in Philadelphia. In the former times, all insurances for sea risks, &c., were effected in London.

In 1752, was founded the Philadelphia contributionship for insuring of houses from loss by fire. It was incorporated in 1768, as a mutual assurance, and was much promoted by Dr. Franklin. In March, 1823, the capital amounted to $228,850. The number of policies out were 2273, and the sum insured, $3,620,450. What is curious respecting this ancient institution is, that they never had but one lawsuit, and that they gained! Another curious fact respecting this association is, that at an early period they insured a house which was soon after burnt, and this single loss much distressed the concerned to make it good. The annual election for directors being near at hand, at an upper room in the old court-house, no one attended but Hugh Roberts, who having waited until the

* Norris' election was always supported by the Germans.

time of choosing had nearly expired, he alone proceeded to elect twelve directors and a treasurer, all of whom he notified in due form! But for that circumstance, this institution, now so distinguished and beneficial, would have expired!

Aboriginal Trees.

For want of a better term, I have chosen so to name such primitive trees of the forest race as still remain among us, from days cotemporary with the foundation of the city. Those now standing on the northern extremity nearest the city are nigh the first gate on the Germantown turnpike,—on Wager's field or lot. There are two of them there of sweet gum, about 20 feet apart, and having a circumference of about 14 feet. Between those trees there was once deposited in the ground a quantity of stolen treasure—afterwards confessed and recovered.

On the western side of the city was a large forest elm, at the northwest corner of Race and Schuylkill Seventh streets, nearly *vis-ă-vis* to the Friends' walled-ground. An old man near there told me it looked equally as large as now, nearly fifty years ago. It was cut down in 1839.

The next nearest forest trees are three ancient gums on the north side of Vine street, fronting the Bush-hill mansion.

In the south-western section, the nearest remaining trees are a few (five) well-grown oak trees, standing in a lot at Lombard street near Schuylkill Tenth street.

At the south end, there is on Swanson street, by the water side, a great buttonwood or waterbeech, the remains of several once there, seen and noticed by Kalm, in 1748.

The above trees compose all which remain so near the city; these alone have escaped the British desolations, the axe of their owners, and time. We cannot think of them without remembering the expressive and beautiful musings of Cowper on his "Yardley Oak,"

> Survivor sole of all that once lived here!
> A shatter'd veteran,—couldst thou speak
> And tell who lived when thou wast young,
> By thee I might correct the clock of history—
> Recover facts,—mistated things set right;
> But since no spirit dwells in thee to speak,
> I will perform myself, in my own ear,
> Such matters as I may."

Other cities, as we, have their consecrated trees. On Boston common there is an elm, called the Great tree, which girths 21 2–3 feet. At Hartford they have their celebrated "Charter oak;" it girths 33 feet. At New York they venerate a group of large buttonwood trees on the ground of the Columbia College. At Providence, Rhode Island, they have their "Great Elm tree," which they publicly and solemnly consecrated "to liberty," as early as the year 1768, and at Boston, too, they had their "Liberty tree," even earlier.

Strange Transmission of Sound.

In 1707, the guns fired upon Hill's vessel, from the little fort at New Castle, were distinctly heard, by Hill's anxious wife, at Philadelphia.—Vide Proud.

On the 10th of July, 1745, "a great number of guns were heard by many people in and about town, which seemed to be at a great distance, and the next day we found by express, they were as far off as New York, at which place were great firings and rejoicings for the capture of Cape Breton!" It is probable no weight of artillery could now be heard from city to city!

Old persons have told me that before the city was paved, and when fewer carriages were employed, they found it much easier than now to hear distant sounds. Seventy-odd years ago, Cooper, on the Jersey side, had a black fellow named Mingo, who possessed a fine, clear voice, and could be distinctly heard singing in the field towards the evening—even the words of the chorus, in some cases, could be understood by those living near the water side in the city. Colonel Thomas Forrest was one who assured me of this. The aged Colonel A. J. Morris told me of his hearing Whitfield's clear voice, at Gloucester point, when he was preaching on Society hill. Captain Coates tells me that just before the revolution, when his father dwelt at the corner of Cable lane and Vine street, they could there hear the voice of his workmen at his brick-kiln, at the corner of Fourth and Green streets, cry out, "Phebe, get the dinner ready!" This may seem strange in the present thick population; but I must also add, that there are spots in Germantown, where, on occasions of overcast and calm mornings, persons can plainly hear the rattle of carts in Philadelphia, six miles off!

The guns that were fired at the battle of Brandywine were distinctly heard by persons in Philadelphia, although they were only nine and ten pounders. And the bombardment of Fort Mifflin was heard daily at Germantown. When the Augusta blew up there, Mr. Bradford told me he distinctly heard the report not far from Lancaster, and following up the line of the river, another told me they heard it near Pottsgrove. Another heard it at the forks of little Egg harbour. In Italy sound is transmitted to great distances, "because of the purity of the atmosphere."

Names of Streets changed.

In the olden time they were remarkably disposed to give popular names to streets and places, to the exclusion of their legal and recorded names. I remember very well, that when a boy, about the year 1800, we first saw index boards on the walls, to show the streets. The names of some of the streets were so new to us, that we really thought, for a long while, that they were absolutely new names. Those which have undergone changes have been as follows, to wit:

Bread street—has been called familiarly Moravian alley, because that church had its front formerly on that street.

Noble street—was called commonly Bloody lane, because a mur der had been committed there.

Garden alley—changed to Coombes' alley, because he was a tenant on the Front street corner.

Cedar street—is changed to South street, because it was the southern limit of the city. It was often called Southermost street.

Sassafras street—has been called Race street, because it was the road to the races once out there. It was also called Longhurst street, in the earliest deeds.

Mulberry street—always called Arch street, because of an arch or bridge across that street at Front street. It was also called Holmes' street, in the earliest deeds.

High street—originally called so, because of its having been the highest elevation from the river of all the other streets—changed to Market street by the popular voice, because of the markets in it.

King street—changed to Water street, because of its nearness to the river.

Branch street—changed to Sourcrout alley, and so universally once called, because the first cutter of cabbage, who made it a business to go abroad with his machine to cut for families, lived almost alone in that street.

Jones' alley—changed to Pewter-platter alley, because of such a sign (a real pewter dish of large size) once hung at the corner of Front street.

Duke street—changed to Artillery lane, because of the British cannon having been placed there.

Prime street—was called Love lane, because of a long row of lewd houses there.

Callowhill street—in 1690, was called "New street," probably because it was the first opened in the Northern Liberties.

Brewer's alley—because of Geddes' brewery there, now called Wood street.

Vine street—was at an early period called Valley street, because of its vale there between two hills, above and below it.

Chestnut street—was first called Wynn street, after Thomas Wynn.

Walnut street—was Pool street, as leading to Dock creek water.

Norris' alley—was called Hutton's lane or alley.

Gray's alley—was called Morris' alley.

Gabriel Thomas, in his account of the city as early as 1698, speaks of several other street names now not known, to wit: Shorter's alley—Yower's lane—Waller's alley—Sikes' alley—Flower's alley

—Turner's lane—all of which extended only from Front to Second street. They probably then bore the names of the chief inhabitant dwelling at or near them. The streets of larger size, he says, took the names from the abundance of such trees formerly in growth there.

William Penn, in his letter in 1683, says "the names of these streets are mostly taken from the things that spontaneously grow in the country, as Vine street, Mulberry street, &c.;" but in enumerating them, he names some not known to us, to wit: Cranberry street, Hickory street, Oak street, Beech street, Ash street, and Poplar street.

Public Spectacles.

In September, 1758, a great fire-works was exhibited at Philadelphia, on the Delaware river, in honour of the reduction of Cape Breton, by General Amherst. It represented a citadel in the centre, and on each flank a tower. On shore were other works to represent the French. Then a great exhibition of fire ensued, and the sounds of cannonade, &c. The citadel approached to storm the works on shore—they sprung a mine and surrendered. Then succeeded rejoicings by a swarm of rockets from the towers, &c. This was certainly a very grand display for so small a community, as Philadelphia then was, to effect. The truth was, the enterprise of Cape Breton was deemed an American affair of great merit—a thing in which the northern and middle colonies gave themselves great credit.

About sixty-five years ago, many hundred persons went out to the Schuylkill to see a man cross that river in a boat carried in his pocket! He went over safe, near High street. B. Chew, Esq., saw it, and told me of it, and my father saw the same at Amboy. It was made of leather—was like parchment—was about five feet long—was upheld by air-vessels, which were inflated, and seemed to occupy the usual place of gunwales. For want of a patent office, the art is probably lost. The fact gives a hint for light portable boats for arctic explorers, and suggests a means of making more buoyant vessels on canals.

The increase of public exhibitions is greater every year. We have not long since had the greatest and finest managerie of wild beasts ever before seen here, being equal to twenty animals in one collection, and containing lions, tigers, elephants, camels, &c. In 1824, we had even a mummy brought among us, from ancient Thebes, and soon after came two Roman urns, repositories for the ashes of the dead for two thousand five hundred years and more. Why do people visit such, but for their interest in relics, as a means to connect the imagination and the heart. Their heart feels the question rising like this, viz.:

> "Statue of flesh, come, prithee tell us,
> Since in the world of spirits thou hast slumber'd,
> What hast thou seen—what strange adventures number'd!"

We have also a growing practice among us, of adventurers coming from Europe—as players, singers, dancers, lecturers, and "catafeltoes wondering for their bread!"

Leathern Apron Club.

This was Franklin's club, which took the name of the Junta. In 1728, J. Logan speaks of these as being the tools of Sir William Keith's "baseness and falsehood," saying, "they are to send thee a petition, calling themselves the Leathern Apron Men, and they solicit favourable sentiments towards their master, Sir William Keith, who has raised deep contentions here"—for when he was elected into the assembly, after being no longer governor, he was escorted into town by eighty men on horseback, and guns were fired in triumph, &c. Perhaps Keith's use of the club, and Franklin's influence there, although then but young, and only a resident of the city four or five years, may present some clue to Sir William's strange seduction of Franklin to follow him in his fortunes to England, where Sir William joined "the ghosts of departed governors," as hangers on.

North-west Passage.

In 1753, the citizens of Philadelphia, especially the merchants, employed Captain Swaine, in the schooner Argo, to seek a north-west passage. At his return he got credit for his exertions, although as unsuccessful as Captain Parry's late royal enterprise.

In May, 1754, he again makes another unsuccessful voyage. The particulars of both voyages may be read on page 381 of my MS. Annals in the Historical Society of Pennsylvania, too long for insertion here; his report was, that the winter had not been so severe there for twenty-four years before. The Argo got through the ice into the mouth of Hudson strait, as far as the island Resolution, on the 26th of June; but was forced out again by ice, to sea. She cruised off with some Hudson bay ships—twenty days trying to get in again—but could not. She ran down the ice from 63° to 57°. Then went over to the Labrador coast, and discovered it plainly from 56° to 65°. Finally returned home all well, &c.

Magistrates.

Until the year 1759, it had been an occasional practice for justices of the peace to hear and decide causes at public inns; as it had a demoralizing effect in bringing so many people to drinking-places, the governor in this year publicly forbids its longer continuance. Even courts themselves, before they had a court-house, had been held there, for I see by James Logan's MS., that in the year 1702, the court at Philadelphia sat in Hall's public house.

It has been a general and frequent remark, made to me by the aged, that magistrates were, in olden time, a much more dignified and honoured class of persons than now. They were also chosen as men of the first fortune, influence, and wisdom; so that wherever they went they carried reverence, and were effectively "a terror to evil-doers." Their occasional voice, heard in the street, could instantly repress "wrong and outrage" among men, or frolic and mischief among boys. They were at the same time effective "peacemakers;" for as they never served from motives of personal gain, their fortunes being above it, they generally strove to return the parties under some mutual agreement. I can still see some of those dignitaries in my mind's eye as they remained even in my early days—a person bearing a port of authority, cocked hat, powdered hair, and a gold-headed cane, ruffles over the hand, and bowed to with reverence by all who passed them, as "His honour, the Squire."

The Dutch Riot.

About the year 1782–3, a riot was formed by numerous Dutch women, headed by Mammy Swivel, an old woman of prodigious size. It excited great interest and commotion in the northern end of the city, at the time, and led to several small law-suits. The case was this:—The square from Callowhill to Brewer's alley, and from Third to Fourth street, then lay in a field of grain, into which some hogs made their entry and depredations. The owner, for his revenge, shot three of the animals. Upon this occurrence, the German women in the neighbourhood, "called to arms." They soon gathered in strength, and fell upon the owner and beat him so severely, he had to be taken to the inn, then at the north-east corner of Brewer's alley and Fourth street, where he lay some time. In the mean time, the women, to the number of several hundreds, fell to work and tore up all his post and rail fences, making thereof a great pile, casting thereon the dead hogs, and making of the whole a grand conflagration, in the presence of great crowds of spectators—none of whom attempted to arrest their progress. It was a high exertion of female power and revenge, and long "Mammy Swivel" bore the reputation of the heroine.

Riots—There is entirely a new era in our country in this matter of riots, beginning 1834, and continuing still. It is a new spirit, waked up by the example of foreigners. They have already been so frequent, that one can scarcely preserve their remembrance. I try now to retrace them—August, 1836, to wit:

The great election riots in New York city, of 1836. Then the mob concerning the Abolitionists, and the destruction of the meeting house, &c.

The burning of the nunnery, at Charleston, near Boston.

At Philadelphia, the election of 1836, in the Northern Liberties, by an attack on the whigs—afterwards, at another election, killed one man—afterwards, burned Robb's houses, and kept the firemen off. Next a riot because of the blacks, in Moyamensing—houses and furniture destroyed.

Riot at Hamburgh, for wages along the canal, 1835.

At Natchez—the case of the man who was tried for ill-treating his wife, and *acquitted*, and thence taken from the court, tarred and whipped, and driven away.

The case of the two blacks at Alabama; condemned for killing children, to be hung, but the people took them from the court and burned them!

The case at Vicksburgh, in July, 1835, of hanging five gamblers.

The case at Livingston, in Mississippi, of self-constituted committees, hanging sundry white men and negroes, for an alleged conspiracy.

The border war of Ohio and Michigan—*people* contending *without law*, for soil!

The case of the people in Charleston, South Carolina, seizing the mail and destroying all the papers of the Abolitionists.

A mob case in Philadelphia, in July, 1835, upon the negroes, because of the assault of an insane negro, upon Mr. Stewart. Some houses pulled down.

August 8, 1835. The mob in Baltimore rise upon Glen and Johnson's houses, and kill eight persons, because of their connexion with a broken bank.

In the same month, occurred a beginning demonstration of riot at Washington city, for the purpose of putting down the abolition emissaries.

A mob at Hartford, Connecticut, pulled down the meeting house of the blacks. At New Hampshire, (Canaan,) the mob of 300 men, took off the school house of the blacks with many oxen, and placed it *out* of the town. At peaceful Burlington, New Jersey, they attacked a black man's house, and one white man got shot. At Pittsburg, the mob drove off the nunnery—at same place they tried to destroy a black barber's house. At Chestertown, Maryland, there was a gathering of the people, against the black emissaries, of several days. In Virginia, they whipped and abused an innocent man, as "an abolitionist." From the frequency of such violence, it has obtained the name of "*Lynch law!*"

Wistar Parties.

These evening parties, for which Philadelphia society is remarkable, were begun by Doctor Casper Wistar, in 1799, by his call of all the members of the Philosophical Society to his house, once a week, during the winter. They were continued to his death, in 1818, by himself alone. They were then continued by the members successively, in turn, at their several houses, ever since.

In 1835, when Job R. Tyson, Esq., became the owner and resident of Doctor Wistar's former house, at the south-west corner of Fourth and Prune streets, they were *again* begun *in that house*, and have been continued in Mr. Tyson's turn, as often as it occurs, to the present time. None but members of the Philosophical Society can be members, and they only can be such, who can come in by a unanimous vote. A limited number of guests can be invited—an indulgence more than once extended to the writer. Other societies, however, also exist, bearing the name of Wistar parties, organized by sundry social circles, in imitation of the former; and they not being enrolled philosophers, aim more to gratify the sense of good cheer and hilarity, than to discuss philosophy and intellectual abstractions. All these parties comprise only the male sex. Why don't the ladies take umbrage at the exclusion, and have their blue-stocking parties too?

Going to churches.—People of the present day, who find churches every where so near their residences, have no conception of the long walks over unpaved footways, which church-going families were accustomed to take in my early days. The writer can remember numerous families from about the Swedes' church, and far down in Southwark; and also from Kensington and the intermediate space, walking every Sabbath, in family trains of well dressed persons of both sexes, young and old—going as far as Christ church and the Presbyterian and Baptist meetings near it. Several of these were such as had their horse and vehicle, and yet they never thought of using them for such a purpose. It would have been regarded as an effeminacy or affectation.

Washington's house, in Philadelphia, having been taken down, is now built upon by three brick houses of four stories—the same now owned by Nathaniel Burt, and numbered, 192, 192½, and 194, in High street near Sixth street.

The pictures of the King and Queen of France.—In March, 1784, these large and elegantly framed *pictures* arrived at Philadelphia, in the ship Queen of France, being presents from the king. They were set up in the large committee-room of the senate, at the south-east corner of Sixth and Chestnut streets—thence went to Washington city, and were burned, I believe, by the British, under General Ross. The portrait of the king was much like Governeur Morris, who was a very fine-looking man.

"*A pond of good water*, in the driest season," is a place advertised for sale in 1784, with the land appurtenant of an entire square from Schuylkill Seventh to Eighth street, and from Walnut to Locust street. No such pond is now known.

An execution, in July, 1784, of John Martin and John Downey, occurred for a *street robbery*. What a difference from the present moderate inflictions on street depredators!

The Earl of Albion, in 1784, sends his agent to lay claim to forty leagues square of New Jersey, beginning at Cape May and extending to all of Long Island—saying, it was so patented to the Earl of

Albion, the second governor of New Jersey, *who was killed by the Indians*, and that ever since the patent had been overlooked, and therefore his agent, Mr. Varlo, now forewarns all people to avoid purchases, unless under the title of the family.

An eminent Philadelphia Quaker, who had been some time in Ireland, in June, 1784, passed through most of the streets of Londonderry habited in sackcloth, and repeatedly called on the inhabitants to repent and turn to God. He seemed a remarkably intelligent person, and declared he came from America on purpose to admonish the people of Ireland, and especially those of Londonderry.

The Philadelphiad, in September, 1784, is announced as published, " displaying some first rate modern characters of both sexes, in a friendly and satirical manner." Such a book, if now seen, might furnish something for family gossip and scandal.

Balloons.—The public Journals, about this time, are full of notices and excitement about the display of *balloons*—one of them when up took fire, and dropped its furnace, or stove, near the new play-house, in South street.

The first Directory, in 1784, gave 3570 names of housekeepers—Desilver's, in 1831, gave 26,400 names.

The Pictures for the Annals.—I have been often asked the question—how and where I became possessed of the pictures which illustrate the Annals—and it here occurs to me to answer the question, by stating the facts in the case, as being in itself something out of the usual track. One day, when riding for recreation and observation, about the hills of the Wissahiccon, I chanced to come across a Mr. W. L. Britton, carrying his port folio. In entering into conversation with him, and asking him if he was not abroad in search of the picturesque, I was indulged to see some of his sketches. He was invited to my house, and from making his call from time to time, and showing me the productions of his pencil, I was very naturally led to invite him, in time, to make sundry sketches for myself. All this was at the time without any design on my part for their publication. They were intended for my own cabinet; but as these in time multiplied, and as I eventually thought of such a work as the Annals, other pictures became necessary. In the end, he was instrumental in making the most which I needed. Thus out of a seemingly accidental acquaintance, I found a ready facility of representing pictorially such subjects as, but for his assistance, I might have never attempted. He loved the occupation as an amateur, and I needed them as a lover of the olden time, and an annalist; thus we worked into each other's hands, and the public now has the benefit. Many other equally fortuitous facilities have occurred to me, in collecting facts for this work, and would be deemed curious facts, if told.

RELICS & REMEMBRANCERS.

"These we preserve with pious care."

It may be deemed worthy of the subject, to give a special notice of those relics of the olden time, which have come to our know ledge, to wit:

Dr. Benjamin Rush had a study-chair presented to him in 1811 made out of the Treaty tree. His letter of thanks for it, as a present from Mrs. Pritchett, I have seen.

David Lewis, Esq., presented me with a piece of the mahogany beam of Columbus' house, in which he once dwelt in St. Domingo—of course of the first house constructed by a European in America. I have used parts of it in several snuff boxes of relic wood.

An elbow-chair has been made of the elm tree wood, which grew in the State-house yard. It was made in 1824, on the occasion of cutting down those once beautiful trees there, and was presented, by Adam Ramage, to the "Philadelphia Society for promoting Agriculture."

Some of the timber of the Alliance frigate has been preserved by me, as a relic of the first navy of the United States.

Some of the hair of General Washington, in my possession, is highly and justly prized.

"Yea, beg a hair of him for memory,
And dying mention it within their wills,
Bequeathing it as a rich legacy."

A writing-table of William Penn, of curious construction, of mahogany, is now in possession of J. R. Smith, Esq., of Philadelphia. Its general appearance is like a common breakfast table. By lifting up the lid, a regular writing-desk is exposed with drawers and casements, and by the use of elevators, two lids are thrown up, which furnish great convenience for placing books and papers thereon for copying from, or for writing upon. It was the gift to him from John Barron, Esq., once a venerable gentleman, who possessed large claims to lands about Philadelphia, from his progenitors.

The girder in the office of the Union canal, in Carpenter's court, is a part of the mainmast of the Constellation frigate, and has several marks of the shot it received.

I own a China plate, given to me by James C. Smith, Esq., which is the *last* of a whole set, which was the first China that ever came *direct* from China. It came by Captain Green, who sailed from New York, in 1784, and returned in May, 1785.

A piece of silver coin, marked the year 733, of the weight of ninety cents, was ploughed up by Mr. John Shallcross, at seven miles from the city, near the York road. A copy of its impression is preserved on page 64 of my MS. Annals, in the Historical Society.

The arm-chair of Dr. Benjamin Franklin is in possession of Reuben Haines, Esq., in Germantown. It is of mahogany, and the one which the doctor used as his common sitting chair.

An oaken chair of Count Zinzendorf is in possession of C. J. Wistar, Esq., in Germantown.

Autograph letters of William Penn, of the year 1677, are in possession of Henry Pemberton, of the Philadelphia bank, being a small folio book of letters from Penn to his religious friends in Holland. Among the letters is a postscript, subscribed by the initials of the celebrated George Fox. A fragment of George Fox's pen, annexed to R. Barclay's, is also with Reuben Haines, Esq.

A pewter cistern and ewer, for washing and shaving, once the property of the Penn family, is now in the possession of Thomas J. Wharton, Esq. They contain the initials of William Penn, and the family arms. It would seem as if they had been the property of Admiral Penn, from the motto being different from that of the founder—it reading "*Dum Clavium Tenens.*" This, by-the-by, is as appropriate to William Penn as the governor of a colony, as to the Admiral as the governor (or steersman) of a ship.

The tea plate of William Penn I have seen at the widow Smith's farm, near Burlington, which had descended to her husband from James Logan. The teapot was small—not to contain more than one pint—was very heavy—in fine preservation—bore the ciphers W. P.—and had a stand to set under it, in which to insert a flame heater to keep it hot or to make it boil.

Penn's book-case, formerly in possession of Nathaniel Coleman, of Burlington,—formed of English oak, veneered all over with mahogany, is now in the possession of the Philadelphia Library. Its base is formed of a chest of drawers, and a desk for writing; and above are arrangements for accounts and papers, shut in by panelled doors, having in each a looking-glass.

At that desk, I should suppose, he wrote many of those papers and publications since known to the public. It came to Coleman from the Pennsbury mansion. A sketch of it is drawn on page 105 of my MS. Annals, in the Historical Society, and the original feet of it are in my possession.

Penn's silver seal, ciphered W. P. is now in the possession of R. L. Pitman, cashier of the Northern Liberty bank,—he procured it of the above named N. Coleman, who had received it in his business as a silversmith.

Penn's clock was not long since in the hands of Martin Sommers, near Frankford, who got it from Mr. Peter Harewaggen, an aged person who lived near Pennsbury. The clock was formed of an oaken case, curiously wrought and inlaid with bone. There is another clock of Penn's, said to be such, now in the Warder family of Philadelphia.

A silver cup of Benjamin Lay, the hermit, is now in possession of Roberts Vaux, Esq.

Penn's chair, which came from Pennsbury, is now in the Pennsylvania Hospital—a present from Mrs. Crozier, through the hands of Mr. Drinker. Another similar chair is in my possession,—"a present from Deborah Logan,"—is so inscribed on its brass plate, with the addition of these appropriate words, to wit: "Fruitful of recollections—sit and muse!" Mrs. Frazier, at Chester, has the chair in which Penn sat at opening the first assembly at that place. Relics of the Treaty tree are numerous. I have myself presented several snuff-boxes formed severally of a plurality of kinds of relic wood, including the Treaty tree, Columbus' house, the Blue Anchor tavern, &c. There is, in my house, a lady's work-stand, of the Treaty tree, ornamented with the walnut tree of the Hall of Independence, and with some of the mahogany beam of Columbus' house, &c.

Joseph P. Norris, Esq., has William Penn's silver snuff-box. It is inscribed with the names of successive owners, from Governor Thomas Lloyd, downwards. He has also a watch seal of quartz crystal, set in gold, a present from an Indian king to Isaac Norris, at the treaty of 1710.

There are in my house sixteen pictures hanging up in frames of relic wood, preserved as remembrancers, to wit:

A list of my framed Relic pictures, (16 *in number*,) *July*, 1839.

1. Columbus' landing—of mahogany of his house, corners of pine, of Blue Anchor house.
2. Penn's landing at Philadelphia—of pine of Blue Anchor, with corners of Holly, at Chester landing.
3. Declaration of Independence—of pine of Table of Independence, with corners of walnut tree, once before the Hall.
4. The Hall of Independence—of pine of Table of Independence, corners of walnut tree, once before the Hall.
5. Letitia House—of oak of that house, corners of cherry tree of Pennsbury, glass of Letitia house.
6. Old Court house—of oak of its girder.
7. Treaty Tree—of elm, the ends of mulberry of Harris, at Harrisburg, corners of oak of Letitia house.
8. Washington's House—of yellow pine, of his door, and corners of mahogany of his levee door.
9. Slate Roof house—of the oak of Letitia house, the corners of cherry, from Pennsbury, glass of Letitia house.
10. The Draw-bridge and Dock creek—of pine of Blue Anchor inn, corners of oak of bridge on Chestnut street.

11 The Alliance Frigate—of oak of the Alliance, with corners of Cook's ship Endeavour, round the World.
12. The House of Sven Sener—of the buttonwood there, corners of Treaty tree.
13. The Landing of Penn at Chester—of the holly tree there, corners of cherry wood of Pennsbury, and from George Fox's oak, at Flushing.
14. The Dutch City of New York—from the pear tree of Stuyvesant, corners of Fox's oak.
15. Benezet's house and bridge—of the oak of the bridge, corners of Fox's oak, and corner pieces of Dr. Rush's cedar.
16. The Indians at Harrisburg—of the mulberry tree at John Harris', and corners of Treaty tree.

All the above are *veneers* upon frames, so as to show fronts of the relic wood named.

Besides those before mentioned as in various hands, there are attached to the pages of my MS. Annals, in the Philadelphia Library, and in the Historical Society of Pennsylvania, at the pages severally annexed, the following articles, to wit:

In my Manuscript Annals in the Philadelphia Library.

PAGE
165.—The celebrated Mary Dyer's gown specimen.
do.—Penn's bed-quilt—a fragment.
do.—Silks—made in Pennsylvania by Susan Wright and Catharine Haines.
166.—Dress silks at the Meschianza.
170.—Silk specimen of 1740, of Dr. Redman's ancestor.
do.—Red garden satin, from the Bishop of Worcester, 1720.
do.—Black silk velvet of Dr. Franklin's coat.
190.—Six gown patterns of former years, of my family.
198.—Original petition, showing all the signatures of primitive settlers of Chester, in 1704.
199.—Likeness of Penn—best done by Bevan.
206.—Likeness of James Pemberton, and costume of Friends.
215.—Paper money of 1789—of the Light house, and of the Walnut street prison, of 1775.—Specimens.
218.—Profile of a city belle of high head-dress, in 1776
do.—Specimen of a silk and silver dress of a lady.
230.—A sketch of Friends' meeting, at Centre square.
231.—Pictures of ladies' bonnets and dresses in olden time.
233 to 239, contain pictures of sundry public houses—such as Court house; London Coffee house; Jones' row; Grindstone alley; Slate house; Duche's house; S. Mickle's house; Loxley's house; Benezet's house; Governor Palmer's house; Swedes' church; Shippen's house; Washington's house; Office of secretary of foreign affairs; Friends' almshouse; Wigglesworth's house; Scene at Drawbridge, at city com-

PAGE

mons; Letitia court; Perspective at Philadelphia; Penn's treaty; the Treaty tree; a female figure drawn in colours by Major André; a pictorial invitation card of General Howe, to the Meschianza; R. Morris' great house. Generally rough sketches, made before it was determined to make accurate drawings.

240.—The first almanac of Philadelphia, (a sheet) 1687.

246.—An engraved picture of six public buildings.

247 to 252, are specimens of old colonial paper.

264.—First ground plot plans of the city, in 1793–4, by Davis.

273.—Ancient caricature and poetry, "to wash the blackamoor white." Some city gentlemen are drawn.

do.—A caricature of Friends and the Indians.

277.—Portraits of Bishop Allen and Benjamin Lay.

278.—The Association battery.

279.—Dock creek and Drawbridge scene.

280.—Pegg's run, and scenery in skating there.*

282.—Letitia house in the court.

do.—Cherry garden house.

283.—An ancient house at the north-west corner of Front and Race streets.

do.—The place called Barbadoes lot, where the Baptists and Presbyterians first held worship, corner of Chestnut and Second streets.

284.—The portrait of an oddity, known universally by the name of "M. O. Mike, H. A. Harry Hanse, Michael Weaders," and called also, "I see thee first," with some remarks on his character.

In my Manuscript Annals, in the Historical Society of Pennsylvania, are the following, to wit:

PAGE

272.—A specimen sheet of modern bank notes.

276.—Specimens of colonial and continental money.

277.—A sheet almanac of Philadelphia, 1687.

do.—Specimen of the writing of Count Zinzendorf, 1734.

278.—Slips of ancient silk dresses.

279.—An original drawing, by Kosciusko, of Miss Pollock.

296.—Picture and description of Fitch's steamboat.

296.—Gray's ferry bridge, and General Washington's passage there.

do.—Cape Henlopen Light house, and description.

342.—A slip of silk, home-made, which gained the premium in 1770, and was made into a wedding dress for Mrs. C. Roberts, in 1774.

---

* The picture, as a skating scene, is more to the ideas in my mind, than the one given in this work. There were difficulties in forming the picture of "things before," which the present artist could not overcome.

PAGE
347.—A picture of the New market, in Southwark, as drawn in 1787.
350.—A caricature print of the revolution; of "Liberty triumphant, or the downfal of oppression."
358.—Likenesses of James Pemberton and Nicholas Waln, in the costume of ancient Friends.
360.—Association battery, and windmill near.
361.—Governor Palmer's house at Treaty tree.
do.—The place of the Barbadoes lot where the Baptists and Presbyterians first worshipped.
362.—The Swedes' church.
do.—The Slate Roof house of William Penn.
363.—Shippen's great house.
364.—Alms house of Friends.
365.—Old London Coffee house.
do.—Old Court house, built in 1707.
366.—Fairmount and Schuylkill, in 1789.
do.—Bush hill, in 1788.
367.—Slate house, residence of William Penn.
368.—Davis' ground plot plan of Philadelphia, 1793–4.
370.—The same, in continuation.
371.—Holme's ground plot of Philadelphia, 1682, with explanatory remarks.
374.—A map of Pennsylvania, in 1787, curious for preserving Indian names of places, and of former frontier forts.
376.—George Heap's map of 1754, of the environs of Philadelphia, curious as showing primitive owners and localities.
378.—Old stone prison, at the corner of Third and High streets.
379.—Swedes' house of Sven Sener, and the first Swedes' church of logs, of 1669.
460.—Triumphal arches for La Fayette, and silk badge, as worn at his visit.

LIST OF UNPUBLISHED PAPERS.

These comprise such as have been purposely excluded from a publication in my printed Annals. They are, first, remarkable autographs preserved as subjects for inspection by the curious. Secondly, they are papers not expedient to be printed entire, although sufficiently useful to be preserved; and sometimes already occasionally extracted in part, under some of the divisions of the printed Annals.

In my Manuscript Annals in the Philadelphia Library, to wit:

PAGE

219.—Joseph Sansom's description of Philadelphia, in 1803, in print.

245.—A MS. petition and names, praying the king for defence, in 1743.

do.—Autograph of Count Zinzendorf, 1742.—Of his daughter Benigna, 1742.—Of Asheton, clerk of court, 1727.—Of Joseph Wilcox, Mayor, 1706.—Of James Logan, secretary, 1702.—Of William Trent, 1706.—Of William Penn.—Of Hannah Penn, 1712.—Of John Penn, in 1825.

253.—Form of a letter, by which inquiries were usually made of aged persons, having thirty-six queries.

do.—Autograph of Mary Smith—her description, in four pages of MS., of the primitive settlement of Burlington, to which she was an eye-witness.

In my Manuscript Annals in the Historical Society of Pennsylvania, to wit:

PAGE

190.—Some ancient religious scandal on Friends, by the Keithians.

252.—Autograph of Robert Fairman, of 1715, descriptive of his estate at the Treaty tree.—Singular writing.

380.—Penn's letter, of 1683, descriptive of Philadelphia then.

284.—Robert Turner's letter, of 1685, to William Penn, descriptive of Philadelphia then.

286.—Letter of P. S. Duponceau, Esq., descriptive of the office of secretary of foreign affairs.

290.—Letter of John Penn of Stoke Pogis, 1825.

294.—Autograph letter of Joseph, once King of Spain, first king ever dwelling among us.

298.—Autograph of Dr. Fothergill on Philadelphia topics.

300.— Do. of Rev. George Whitfield, 1754.

304.— Do. of Rev. John Wesley, 1772.

306.— Do. of Du Simitiere, the annalist.

310.— Do. first writ for the first assembly, 1682.

312.— Do. of the Honourable Charles Thomson, being his historical sketch of the leading incidents in the congress of 1774–5.

314.—Autograph Minute by Patrick Robinson, in a rare kind of writing, of 1693, of the proceeding of the council concerning a trespass on Schuylkill.

316.—Autograph Minute of council, of 1698, concerning duties and ports of entry.

318.—Autograph letter of William Penn, 1687, respecting his cottage in Philadelphia.

PAGE

322.—Correspondence of James Logan, proving him to have been the author of Cicero's Cato, &c., a thing imputed to Dr. Franklin.

326.—Primitive court records concerning Germantown—an extract.

328—Original account of the cost in detail of the materials and workmanship of the first court house, in 1707–8—cost £616.

332.—Autograph letter of Isaac Norris, of 1704.

334.— Do. and rare old family letter of 1693, by Samuel Flower, showing causes of emigration here to avoid woes—and signs and wonders in woful Europe.

340.—Original roll of female patriots, of 1780, of Lower Dublin, with their subscriptions and names to aid the sufferers in the war.

344.—Autograph of Dr. Franklin, in 1784, to C. T., secretary of congress, announcing the peace, and his gratification and advice on the same.

346.—Autograph of Robert Proud, our historian, concerning his birth, age, and personal history.

352.—Prosper Martin's description of his rare spring at Pegg's run, and his diagram to show the supposed former passage there of the river Schuylkill.

354.—Autograph letter of the late Joseph Sansom, Esq., of 1820, giving several facts concerning Philadelphia.

381.—A letter showing the form of inquiries addressed to the aged, by which the facts in this book were attempted to be elicited.

393 to 430.—Reminiscences and diaries of events and incidents at Philadelphia, at the time of the war of Independence, and of the acts of the British army there.

431 to 434.—Revolutionary soldiers—a tale of truth.

435 to 438.—Incidents of the war and its calamities to a family—best known to the author.

447.—Autograph signatures of the first members of "the Penn Association for commemorating the landing,"—and facts concerning the origin of that society.

461.—Autograph letter of General La Fayette of 1824, respecting his public visit to Philadelphia, addressed to Joseph Watson, Esq., city mayor.

459 to 474, contains an extended and graphic description of the public visit of La Fayette to Philadelphia, and many facts to be preserved for some future day.

486.—A printed account of Dr. Franklin's relatives at Nantucket.

490 to 496.—Printed biographical notices by Samuel Preston, Esq., of several memorable persons of Bucks county, in the olden time—such as John Watson, surveyor, Jacob Taylor, mathematician and astronomer, William Satterthwaite, poet and scholar, James Pellar, a genius, Dr. Thomas Watson, a learned and benevolent man, D. Ingham, Nathan Preston,

much concerned in Indian affairs, &c. Many local incidents are described, and the particulars of the "Indian walk" are given.

501.—A singular nomenclature of rare names of Philadelphia.

507.—The Pennsylvania Journal of 1758, containing a warning to Friends of 1758, by the Watchman, and Penn's letter of the 27th of 4th mo., 1710, admonitory.

do.—A specimen of Humphrey's *tory* Gazette in Philadelphia, 1777.

508.—Philadelphian demonstrations in 1795, for the Grand canal of New York; being a detail of the facts given by John Thompson, Esq., of his experiment and success in bringing a small schooner from Niagara to Philadelphia.

511.—A poetic description of the Delaware river and contiguous country.

516.—Reminiscences by Mrs. H.

536 to 539.—Some scrapiana of facts of our general history.

544 to 575.—Several MS. letters from Samuel Preston, Esq., generally descriptive of historical events, and persons in Bucks county,—say of Thomas Jenks, Thomas Penn, and Lady Jenks, of the Indian walk—of E. Marshall, and his discovery of silver—of Richard Smith, botanist, and traveller among the Indians,—of the noted Indian, Isaac Still, and his tribe in Bucks county, and of Frederick Post, the interpreter.

576 to 580.—A detail of facts concerning Godfrey's invention of the quadrant,—in print.

Here I would mention, as a closing and general remark, that several communications made to me by aged persons, of *all* they knew or remembered, have been used by me under various *distributions*, but *the whole together* of what they said, which may hereafter interest their immediate friends, may be found in my MS. Annals in the Philadelphia Library—such are those from J. P. Norris, T. Matlack, John Brown, Sarah Shoemaker, Davenport Merrot, Owen Jones, Isaac Parrish, William West, Samuel Richards, Samuel Coates, Thomas Bradford, A. J. Morris. Those by Lang Syne, pages 520 to 530, and by Samuel Preston, are to be found in my MS. Annals in the Historical Society,—also there, Penn's letters to James Harrison, his agent from 1681 to '87, page 164 to 171; the Loganian MSS. at Stenton, pages 222 to 260; Secretary R. Peters' letters to Penns, page 266 to 269; extracts of the minutes of the Association of 1756 for preserving peace with the Indians, pages 180 to 183.

CONCLUSION.

We come now to our conclusion; not that we have fully said all which could have been written from what we possessed, but that we have given so much as we considered of sufficient importance to interest the mass of readers.

What Philadelphia and Pennsylvania may hereafter become, we shall leave to other chroniclers to notice. Some two or three ages hence, when all of *us* shall have passed away, and when "new men and manners reign," they may have an equal opportunity to display their own times in contrast with the present. To such a work, they will receive readier helps than we possessed. They will find abundance of public journals, but too scandalously minute, wherein daily incidents of every kind are amply disclosed;—some to our credit, and some sufficiently repulsive to our moral sense. They will have, too, abundance of pictorial representations of dress, fashions, equipages, houses, edifices, public works, public men, and picturesque views of scenes and places,—such as never existed to aid us, in our researches into the past.

We advertise the reader, that this work having been written out and *concluded in July*, 1842, as signified at the preface, it is to be considered that all references to any given past time, as "so many years ago," are all to be regarded as referring backward from *the year* 1842, and *not* from the date of the imprint, on the present or future title pages.

APPENDIX.

Having on hand sundry facts further illustrative of our early history, and sundry articles of places, in which we, of Philadelphia and Pennsylvania, are sufficiently interested as occasional visiters, or lookers on, tending to describe things as they were, and from which they are now yearly changing, we herein connect them as an appendix to this work, viz.:

Landing day of William Penn, at New Castle.

On the 27th day of October, 1682, arrived before ye towne of New Castle, in Delawar, from England, Wm. Penn, Esq., proprietary of Pennsylvania, who produced twoo certain deeds of feofment from ye illustrious James, Duke of Yorke and Albany, etc.: for this towne of New Castle, and twelve myles about itt, and also for ye two lower counties, ye Whorekills and St. Jones'; wch sd deed bore date 24 August, 1682, and pursuant to the true intent, purpose and meaning of his Royll highnesse in ye same deed, hee, ye sd William Penn, received possession of ye towne of New Castle, ye 28th of October, 1682.

The testimony of Richard Townsend—a public Friend—delivered about the year 1727.

In the year 1682, several ships being provided for Pennsylvania, I found a concern on my mind to embark with them, with my wife and child. I went aboard the Welcome, in company with my worthy friend, William Penn, whose good conversation was very advantageous to all the company. His singular care was manifested in contributing to the necessities of *many who were sick on board, of small pox*, of whom as many as *thirty died*. [What a loss!] After a prosperous passage of two months, having had in that time *many good meetings on board*, we arrived there.

At our arrival, we found it a wilderness; the chief inhabitants were *Indians*, and some *Swedes*, who received us in a friendly manner, and though there was a great number of us, the good hand of Providence was seen in a particular manner; in that provisions were found for us by the Swedes and Indians, at very reasonable rates, as well as brought from divers other parts, that were inhabited before.

Our first concern was to keep up and maintain our religious worship, and in order thereunto, we had several meetings in the houses of the inhabitants; and one boarded meeting-house was set up, [the place of the bank meeting,] where the city was to be, near Delaware, and where we had very comfortable meetings; and after our meetings were over, we assisted each other in building little houses for our shelter—[meaning such as the caves and cabins.]

After some time, I set up a mill on *Chester creek*, which I *brought ready framed*, from London, which served for grinding corn, and sawing of boards; and was of great use to us. Besides, I, with John Tittery, made *a net*, and caught great quantities of fish, which supplied ourselves and many others; so that although three thousand persons came in the first year, we had no lack. We could buy a deer for two shillings, and a large turkey for one shilling, and Indian corn for 2*s*. 6*d*. per bushel. The Indians were to us very civil and loving.

As soon as Germantown was laid out, I settled my tract of land, which was about a mile from thence, where I set up a barn and a corn mill, which was very useful to the country round. But there being few houses, people generally brought their corn upon their backs, many miles. I remember, one man had a bull so gentle, that he used to bring the corn on his back.

In this location, separated from any provision market, we found flesh meat very scarce, and on one occasion we were supplied by a very particular providence, to wit: As I was in my meadow, mowing grass, a young deer came and looked on me while I continued mowing. Finding him to continue looking on, I laid down my scythe and went towards him, when he went off a little way—I returned again to the mowing, and the deer again to its observation. So that I *several times* left my work to go towards him, and he as often gently retreated. At last when going towards him, and he not regarding his steps, whilst keeping his eye on me, he struck forcibly against the trunk of a tree, and stunned himself so much as to fall, when I sprang upon him and fettered his legs. From thence I carried him home to my house, a quarter of a mile, where he was killed, to the great benefit of my family. I could relate several other acts of providence, of this kind.

Being now in the eighty-fourth year of my age, and the forty-sixth of my residence in this country, I can do no less than return praises to the Almighty for the great increase and abundance which I have witnessed. My spirit is engaged to supplicate the continuance thereof; and as the parents have been blessed, may the same mercies continue on their offspring, to the end of time.

RICHARD TOWNSEND.

The Declaration of the German Friends of Germantown, against Slavery, in 1688.

While the Annals are in the progress of publication, there has been found, for the first time, among the papers of the Philadelphia yearly meeting, of 1688, *the original MS. declaration;* being the same addressed to the monthly meeting of Friends, then held at the house of Richard Worrell, in Dublin township. It is in itself *a curiosity*, and as such is here published. So intelligible a paper, written by Germans, then only four or five years in our country, is something remarkable in itself, viz.:

This is to the monthly meeting held at Richard Worrell's:

These are the reasons why we are against the traffic of men's body, as followeth: Is there any that would be done or handled at this manner? viz.: to be sold or made a slave for all the time of his life? How fearful and faint-hearted are many at sea, when they see a strange vessel, being afraid it should be a Turk, and they should be taken, and sold for slaves in Turkey.* Now what is *this* better done, than Turks do? Yea, rather it is worse for them, which say they are Christians; for we hear that the most part of such negers are brought hither against their will and consent, and that many of them are stolen. Now though they are black,† we cannot conceive there is more liberty to have them slaves, as [than] it is to have other white ones. There is a saying, that we shall do to all men like as we will be done [to] ourselves; making no difference of what generation, descent, or colour they are. And those who steal or rob men, and those who purchase them, are they not all alike? Here is liberty of conscience, which is right and reasonable; here ought to be likewise liberty of the body, except of evil-doers, which is another case. But to bring men hither, or to rob, [steal] and sell them against their will, *we stand against*. In Europe, there are many oppressed for conscience sake; and here there are those oppressed which are of a black colour. And we who know that men must not commit adultery—some do commit adultery *in* others, separating wives from their husbands, and giving them to others: and some sell the children of these poor creatures to other men. Ah! do consider well this thing, you who do it, if you would be done in this manner—and if it is done according to Christianity! You surpass Holland and Germany in this thing. This makes an ill report in all those countries of Europe, where they hear of [it,] that *the Quakers* do here handel men as they handel there the cattle. And for that reason some have no mind or inclination to come hither. And who shall maintain this your cause, or plead for it? Truly, we cannot do so, except you shall inform us better hereof, viz.: that Christians have liberty to practise these things. Pray, what thing in the world can be done worse towards us, than if men should rob or steal us away, and sell us for slaves to strange countries; separating husbands from their wives and children. Being now this is not done in the manner we would be done at, [by]; therefore, we con-

---

* The very apprehension before expressed by F. D. Pastorius, of himself, while at sea, in his communication to Governor Lloyd's daughters.—Vide the article *Pastorius*, in vol. i. page 518 of this work.

† A colour not familiar to them, at home, as Germans.

tradict [oppose], and are against this traffic of men's body. And we who profess that it is not lawful to steal, must, likewise, avoid to purchase such things as are stolen, but rather help to stop this robbing and stealing, if possible. And such men ought to be delivered out of the hands of the robbers, and set free as in Europe. Then is Pennsylvania to have a good report, instead it hath now a bad one, for this sake, in other countries. Especially whereas the Europeans are desirous to know in what manner *the Quakers* do rule in *their* province; and most of them do look upon us with an envious eye But if this is done well, what shall we say is done evil?

If once these slaves (which they say are so wicked and stubborn men,) should join themselves--fight for their freedom, and handel their masters and mistresses, as they did handel them before; will these masters and mistresses take the sword at hand and war against these poor slaves, like, as we are able to believe, some will not refuse to do? Or, have these poor negers not as much right to fight for their freedom, as you have to keep them slaves?

Now consider well this thing, if it is good or bad. And in case you find it to be good to handel these blacks in that manner, we desire and require you hereby lovingly, that you may inform us herein, which at this time never was done, viz., that Christians have such a liberty to do so. To this end we shall be satisfied on this point, and satisfy likewise our good friends and acquaintances in our native country, to whom it is a terror, or fearful thing, that men should be handelled so in Pennsylvania.

This is from our meeting at Germantown, held ye 18th of the 2d month, 1688, to be delivered to the monthly meeting at Richard Worrell's.

GARRET HENDERICH,
DERICK OP DE GRAEFF,
FRANCIS DANIEL PASTORIUS,
ABRAM OP DE GRAEFF.

At our monthly meeting, at Dublin, ye 30th 2d mo., 1688, we having inspected ye matter, above mentioned, and considered of it, we find it so weighty that we think it not expedient for us to meddle with it *here*, but do rather commit it to ye consideration of ye quarterly meeting; ye tenor of it being related to ye truth.

On behalf of ye monthly meeting,

JO. HART.

This, above mentioned, was read in our quarterly meeting, at Philadelphia, the 4th of ye 4th mo., '88, and was from thence recommended to the yearly meeting, and the above said Derick, and the other two mentioned therein, to present the same to ye above said meeting, it being a thing of too great a weight for this meeting to determine.

Signed by order of ye meeting.

ANTHONY MORRIS.

Mason and Dixon's Line.

This is a locality, marking a boundary line between Pennsylvania, Maryland and Virginia, much referred to in modern times, by political disputants, and but little understood by the mass of the people.

It refers to a line of division between those states, run and settled as such, by Mason and Dixon, two English surveyors who run and determined it in the year 1761. Previous to that time, it was a subject of frequent controversy, and hard feelings for many years, between William Penn and Lord Baltimore and their several successors, from the time of the grant of Pennsylvania to William Penn, in 1680.

The king of England made his grant of Pennsylvania to William Penn in 1680, beginning at the 40th degree of north latitude up to the 42d degree—bounded by the Delaware on the east, and to extend westward *five degrees of longitude.* On the south a previous grant had been made to Lord Baltimore, in 1632, including *all* of the 40th degree, as far west as the meridian of the "first fountain" of the River Potomac, which made the five degrees of west longitude to extend beyond the meridian of the Potomac. William Penn conceded the width of a degree to Lord Baltimore, as the older grantee, but claimed that portion west of his meridian, down to the completion of the 39th degree of latitude, five degrees long, and from thence in a line parallel with the River Delaware, in all its meanders, to the 42d parallel of latitude.

Virginia, meanwhile, claimed, that the western boundary of Pennsylvania should be a *parallel of five degrees* west of the River Delaware, *where the 42d parallel cut that stream.* This involved, as the great subject of controversy, *the right to Fort Pitt,* which had been garrisoned by Virginia, as its own domain, in 1752. Their ensign and his command of forty men were there captured by the French, and then they in turn were made prisoners by General Forbes, acting for the British government, in 1758. It was afterwards evacuated and stood defenceless, until the year 1773; when John Conally, acting under Lord Dunmore, as the governor of Virginia, took possession. Conally was arrested as a trespasser, by Arthur St. Clair, (afterwards a general,) then a justice of the peace for Westmoreland county. Lord Dunmore, the governor, then contended that Pittsburg was fifty miles *within* the colony of Virginia, to which the Ohio country was supposed to belong. On the other hand, the governor of Pennsylvania proved, by surveys, that it was *six miles* within the five degrees of longitude from the River Delaware, due east from the fort. Conally, who had given his bond to the court, being released on bail, returned to the court at its sitting, on 5th April, 1774; but, to their surprise, brought with him 150 armed men, and actually broke up the court! Troops were thereupon raised, and mutual arrests, and releases by force, ensued for a time. But after much mutual recrimination, a line was agreed upon *by commissioners*, fixing it as it now stands.

The Maryland line was produced to five degrees of longitude, measured upon that parallel, being 39° 43′ 42″ north, and for the west line of Pennsylvania a meridian of longitude was drawn to Lake Erie. If William Penn's construction of the grant to him had been adopted, the state of Ohio would have approached *within six miles of Pittsburg*.

To those who are minutely curious on the subject, there is a lengthened *memoir* by James Dunlop, Esq., published in the papers of the Historical Society of Pennsylvania, which they may consult with profit. See, also, the case as stated by W. Murray, of 1737, reprinted in Hazard's Register, vol. ii., page 200, in 4 pages royal 8vo.

Lord Baltimore alleged that the 40th degree of north latitude had been ascertained, and part of the line run, in 1681, in pursuance of a letter of the king; but Penn denied that any such line had been ascertained. The claims of Maryland were asserted with continued acrimony, violence and occasional bloodshed, until they were finally abandoned in 1760, by the mutual agreement of the parties.

The original parties had two personal interviews in America, but with no satisfaction to either of them. At length, in 1685, one important step was taken by a decision of King James' council, which ordered "that for avoiding further differences, the land lying between the bay of Delaware, and the eastern sea on the other side, and the Chesapeake bay on the other, *be divided* into equal parts, by a line from Cape Henlopen to the 40th degree of north latitude."

Mutual agreements were made between the successors or heirs of the parties, on the 10th May, 1732. By this *celebrated agreement* it was determined, that a semicircle should be drawn at twelve miles around New Castle;—that an east and west line should be drawn beginning at Cape Henlopen, (Cape Cornelius,) and to run westward to the exact middle of the peninsula; and thence northward, so as to form a tangent with the periphery of the semicircle at New Castle, drawn with the radius of twelve English miles; and that from such semicircle, it should be run further northward, until it reached the same latitude as fifteen English miles due south of the city of Philadelphia;—and from the northern point of such line, a due west line should be run across the Susquehanna river, and twenty-five miles beyond it, and to the western limits of Pennsylvania, when occasion, and the improvements of the country, *should require it*. This agreement, however, became the subject of much after litigation and cavil, as may be frequently noticed on the records of the Minutes of Council, if consulted.

The Penns were evidently gainers by the agreement, inasmuch as they made no concession of territory; and but for it the Maryland claim would have reached so far as to cover several parts of the present counties of Philadelphia, Chester, Lancaster, York, Adams,

Franklin, Bedford, Somerset, Fayette and Greene. Finally, the matter in dispute, went into Chancery, and was not decided until 1750, when the lord chancellor decreed a performance of the articles of agreement, as being their best guide and foundation, as a measure *before fixed by themselves.* Some subsequent cavil however ensued,—when finally, Frederick, Lord Baltimore, tired of the litigation, entered into articles of agreement with Thomas and Richard Penn, in 1760, which at length effectually *closed all further altercation and dispute.*

In consequence of such agreement, Jeremiah Dixon and Charles Mason were appointed to run the unfinished line, in 1761; and they extended the western line between the two provinces 230 miles, marking 130 miles of the same by stone pillars. It was called in subsequent history "Mason and Dixon's line," to distinguish it from the "Temporary line," so called,—run in 1739.

In the controversy, it is seen, that William Penn and his successors manifested the most tact and patience—by which they eventually made the best of the bargain. Some of the *original* papers in these matters are not now to be found, but the facts in the case are admitted in our courts, as evidence without *proof.*

To our forefathers, the controversy, while it lasted, was as stirring and exciting, as a state of actual war, on a small scale.

Doctor Thomas C. James' account of the discovery and use of Anthracite Coal.

It was some time in the autumn of 1804, that the writer and a friend started on an excursion to visit some small tracts of land that were joint property on the river Lehigh, in Northampton county. We went by the way of Allentown, and, after having crossed the Blue mountain, found ourselves in the evening unexpectedly bewildered in a secluded part of the Mahoning valley, at a distance, as we feared, from any habitation; as the road became more narrow, and showed fewer marks of having been used, winding among scrubby timber and underwood. Being pretty well convinced that we had missed our way, and, as is usual with those who are wrong, unwilling to retrace our steps, we nevertheless checked our horses about sunsetting, to consider what might be the most eligible course. At this precise period, we happily saw emerging from the wood, no airy sprite, but, what was much more to our purpose, a good substantial German-looking woman, leading a cow, laden with a bag of meal, by a rope halter. Considering this as a probable indication of our being in the neighbourhood of a mill, we ventured to address our inquiries to the dame, who, in a language curiously compounded of what might be called High and Low Dutch, with a spice of English, made us ultimately comprehend that we were not much above a mile distant from Philip Ginter's mill, and as there was but one road before us, we could not readily miss our way. We accordingly proceeded, and soon reached the desired spot, where we met with a hospitable reception, but received the uncomfortable intelligence that we were considerably out of our intended course, and should be obliged to traverse a mountainous district, seldom trodden by the traveller's foot, to reach our destined port on the Lehigh, then known by the name of the *Landing*, but since dignified with the more *classical* appellation of Lausanne. We were kindly furnished by our host with lodgings in the mill, which was kept going all night; and as the structure was not of the most firm and compact character, we might almost literally be said to have been rocked to sleep. However, after having been refreshed with a night's rest, such as it was, and taking breakfast with our hospitable landlord, we started on the journey of the day, preceded by *Philip*, with his axe on his shoulder, an implement necessary to remove the obstructing saplings that might impede the passage of our horses, if not of ourselves; and these we were under the necessity of dismounting and leading through the bushes and briers of the grown-up pathway, if pathway had ever really existed.

In the course of our pilgrimage we reached the summit of the Mauch Chunk mountain, the present site of the mine or rather quarry of anthracite coal; at that time there were only to be seen three or four small pits, which had much the appearance of the commencement of rude wells, into one of which our guide descended with great ease, and threw up some pieces of coal for our examination; after which, whilst we lingered on the spot, contemplating the wildness of the scene, honest Philip amused us with the following narrative of the original discovery of this most valuable of minerals, now promising, from its general diffusion, so much of wealth and comfort to a great portion of Pennsylvania.

He said, when he first took up his residence in that district of country, he built for himself a rough cabin in the forest, and supported his family by the proceeds of his rifle, being literally a hunter of the back-woods. The game he shot, including bear and deer, he carried to the nearest store, and exchanged for the other necessaries of life. But, at the particular time to which he then alluded, he was without a supply of food for his family, and after being out all day with his gun, in quest of it, he was returning towards evening over the *Mauch Chunk* mountain, entirely unsuccessful and dispirited, having shot nothing; a drizzling rain beginning to fall, and the dusky night approaching, he bent his course homeward, considering himself as one of the most *forsaken* of human beings. As he trod slowly over the ground, his foot stumbled against something which, by the stroke, was driven before him; observing it to be *black*, to distinguish which there was just light enough remaining, he took it up, and as he had often listened to the traditions of the country of the existence of coal in the vicinity, it occurred to him that this, perhaps, might be a portion of that "*stone coal*" of which he had heard. He accordingly carefully took it with him to his cabin, and the next day carried it to Colonel Jacob Weiss, residing at what was then known by the name of Fort Allen. The colonel, who was alive to the subject, brought the specimen immediately with him to Philadelphia, and submitted it to the inspection of John Nicholson and Michael Hillegas, Esqs., and Charles Cist, an intelligent printer, who ascertained its nature and qualities, and authorized the colonel to satisfy Ginter for his discovery, upon his pointing out the precise spot where he found the coal. This was done by acceding to Ginter's proposal of getting through the forms of the patent office the title for a small tract of land which he supposed had never been taken up, comprising a mill-seat, on which he afterwards built the mill which afforded us the lodging of the preceding night, and which he afterwards was unhappily deprived of by the claim of a prior survey.

Hillegas, Cist, Weiss, and some others, immediately after, (about the beginning of the year 1792,) formed themselves into what was called the "Lehigh Coal Mine Company," but without a charter of incorporation, and took up about 8 or 10,000 acres of, till then, unlocated land, including the Mauch Chunk mountain, but probably never worked the mine.

It remained in this neglected state, being only used by the blacksmiths and people in the immediate vicinity, until somewhere about the year 1806, when William Turnbull, Esq., had an ark constructed at Lausanne, which brought down two or three hundred bushels. This was sold to the manager of the waterworks for the use of the Centre Square steam engine. It was there tried as an experiment, but ultimately rejected as unmanageable, and its character for the time being *blasted*, the further attempts at introducing it to public notice, in this way, seemed suspended.

During the last war, J. Cist, (the son of the printer,) Charles Miner, and J. A. Chapman, tempted by the high price of bituminous coal, made an attempt to work the mine, and probably would have succeeded, had not the peace reduced the price of the article too low for competition.

The operations and success of the present Lehigh Coal and Navigation Company must be well known to the country; the writer will therefore close this communication by stating, that he commenced burning the anthracite coal in the winter of 1804, and has continued its use ever since, believing, from his own experience of its utility, that it would ultimately become the general fuel of this, as well as other cities.

Doctor John Watson's account of the First Settlers of Bucks county.

This account having been written as a contribution to the Historical Society, and having sundry notices of the state and progress of society, in Bucks county, from its earliest settlement, may present a picture of the past, which may prove interesting to many, viz.:

The township of Buckingham, situated near the centre of the county of Bucks, is the largest township in the county, containing 18,488 acres.

Solebury lies between Buckingham and the river Delaware, and contains 14,073 acres.

The whole of the two townships in early time was called Buckingham, being a favourite name with our first worthy proprietor, *William Penn.* The name was first given to the township and borough now called Bristol, but transferred here perhaps about the year ——, before Cutler's resurvey; by which it appears, that the two townships were divided by a north-west line from the lower corner of Thomas and John Bye's tract, extending to the upper corner of Randal Blackshire's tract.

It appears, by an enumeration of the inhabitants taken in 1787, that Buckingham contained 173 dwelling houses, 188 out-houses, 1173 white inhabitants, and 13 blacks. Solebury, 166 dwelling houses, 150 out-houses, 928 white inhabitants and no blacks.

The first settlers generally came from England, and were of the middle rank, and chiefly Friends: many of them had first settled at the Falls, but soon after removed back, as it was then called, into the woods. As they came away in the reigns of Charles, James, William and Anne, they brought with them not only the industry, frugality, and strict domestic discipline of their education, but also a portion of those high-toned political impressions that then prevailed in England.

Friends had suffered much under the Stuarts; and though promised much by the Oliverians and a republican equality, they experienced but little relief from either. They therefore equally disliked the Presbyterians and the Pretender; and were loyally attached to the protestant succession in the house of Hanover.

Many of the early settlers of Buckingham and Solebury had been educated in what may, with some propriety, be termed good style; and though not great scholars, yet were great men. The exercise of their personal and mental abilities was excited into a high flow of energy, by the bold enterprise of settling a new country, under so many novel circumstances, of much importance to themselves and their posterity. The women were generally good housekeepers; or, at least, their industry and frugality made proper amends for whatever might be deficient, in respect to such improvements and refinements as were not so well suited to their circumstances of mediocrity and equality.

At that early period, when our forefathers were building log-houses, barns, and sheds for stables, and clearing new land, and fencing it chiefly with poles or brush, it has been said that a *hearty, sincere good will* for each other generally prevailed among them. They all stood occasionally in need of the help of their neighbours, who were often situated at some distance through the woods.

Chronic ailments were not so frequent as at present; which was, perhaps, in part owing to the wholesome diet, brisk exercise, lively manners, and cheerful and unrefined state of the mind. But acute disorders, such as fevers, in various degrees—those called "long fevers, dumb agues, fever-and-agues," sore throats, and pleurisies, were then much more common than now. The natural small-pox was peculiarly distressing—was mostly severe, and often mortal—and nothing strange that it should be so. The nature of the disorder being but little known, it was very improperly treated by the nurses, to whose care the management was chiefly committed. A hot room—plenty of bed-clothes—hot teas—and milk punch, or hot tiff, were pronounced most proper to bring the eruption out, and to make it fill well: and the chief danger was apprehended from the patient taking cold by fresh air or cold drink.

As money was scarce, and labourers few, and business often to be done that required many hands, friends and neighbours were commonly invited to raisings of houses and barns, grubbing, chopping, and rolling logs, that required to be done in haste to get in the crop in season. Rum and a dinner or supper were provided on those occasions; and much competition excited in the exercise of bodily strength and dexterity, both at work and athletic diversions.

Reciprocal assistance, being much wanted, was freely afforded and gratefully received—and notwithstanding the rude and unpolished state of mind and manners that may be expected to have prevailed in the first settlers in a wilderness country, and in a much more marked degree in those who succeeded after them, yet from their mutual wants and dependencies, the social and active vivacity of simple nature, and perhaps more than all these, from their hearty and honest zeal in a religious bias of the mind, a kind and unaffected friendship formed a principal feature of their general character. Their equality of circumstances, similarity of views and pursuits, and union in religious and civil principles, and the acquisition of new acquaintances far from their former connexions, all tended to unite them in habits of sociability, and to form impressions of sincere regard.

When false impressions, (or indeed ignorance,) have once so far gained ground as to influence general habits and customs on an erroneous principle, it requires much labour, and a long time to wear them out. This appears evident in the use that is made of spiritous liquors and tobacco. It is probable the first settlers used these articles to ward off infection; and spirits principally to prevent the bad effects of drinking water to which they had not been accustomed in Europe. They imagined the air and water of this hot climate to be unwholesome. The immediate bad effect of cold water, when heated with exercise in summer, and the fevers and agues which seized many in the autumn, confirmed them in this opinion; and not having conveniences to make beer that would keep in hot weather, they at once adopted the practice of the labouring people in the West Indies, and drank rum. This being countenanced by general opinion, and brought into general practice as far as their limited ability would admit, bottles of rum were handed about at vendues, and mixed and stewed spirits were repeatedly given to those who attended funerals—

"So fast the growth of what is surely wrong."

A concern arose among Friends on the subject, and a stop was put to this evil practice in a short time. I call it evil, because it produced effects that were hurtful in a high degree to individuals, and also to society in general.

An act of assembly was passed, prohibiting the giving of spirits at vendues; and though the law was not much regarded for many years, and the practice continued, yet this mischievous and dishonest practice is almost wholly disused.

In early times, weddings were held as festivals; probably in imitation of such a practice in England.

Relations, friends and neighbours were generally invited, sometimes to the amount of one or two hundred; a good dinner was provided, and a lively spirit of plain friendship, but rather rude manners, prevailed in the company.

They frequently met again the next day, and being mostly young people, and from under restraint, practised social plays and sports, in which they often went to an extreme folly; but in those times such opportunities of promoting social acquaintance might be in some degree proper, though otherwise wrong.

At births, many good women were collected; wine, or cordial waters, were esteemed suitable to the occasion for the guests; but besides these, rum, either buttered or made into hot tiff, was believed to be essentially necessary for the lying-in woman. The tender infant must be straitly rolled round the waist with a linen swathe, and loaded with clothes until he could scarcely breathe; and, when unwell or fretful, was dosed with spirit and water stewed with spicery.

When wheat and rye grew thick and tall on new land, and all was to be cut with sickles, many men and some women became dexterous in the use of them, and victory was contended for in many a violent trial; sometimes by two or three only, and sometimes by the whole company for forty or fifty perches. About the year 1741, twenty acres of wheat were cut and shocked in half a day in Solebury. Rum was drunk in proportion to the hurry of business, and long intervals of rest employed in merry and sometimes angry conversation.

The imposing authority of necessity, obliged the first settlers and their successors to wear a strong and coarse kind of dress: enduring buckskin was used for breeches and sometimes for jackets; oznabrigs, made of hemp tow, 1*s.* 6*d.* per yard, was much used for boy's shirts; sometimes flax, and flax and tow were used for that purpose;

and coarse tow for trowsers; a wool hat, strong shoes, and brass buckles, two linsey jackets, and a leathern apron, made out the winter apparel. This kind of dress continued to be common for the labouring people until 1750.

Yet a few, even in early times, somewhat to imitate the trim of their ancestors, laid out as much to buy one suit of fine clothes, as would have purchased two hundred acres of pretty good land. The cut of a fine coat, (now antiquated,) may be worthy of description. Three or four large plaits in the skirts—wadding almost like a coverlet to keep them smooth—cuffs vastly large up to the elbows, open below, and of a round form. The hat of a beau was a good broad-brimmed beaver, with double loops, drawn nearly close behind, and half raised on each side. The women, in full mode, wore stiff whalebone stays, worth eight or ten dollars. The silk gown much plaited in the back; the sleeves nearly twice as large as the arm, and reaching rather more than half way from the shoulder to the elbow—the interval covered with a fine Holland sleeve, nicely plaited, locket buttons, and long-armed gloves. Invention had then reached no further than a bath bonnet with a cape.

Something like this was the fashion of gay people; of whom there were a few, though not many, in early times, in Buckingham and Solebury. But the whole, or something like it, was often put on for wedding suits, with the addition of the bride being dressed in a long black hood without a bonnet. There was one of these solemn symbols of matrimony made of near two yards of rich black Paduasoy, that was lent to be worn on those occasions, and continued sometimes in use, down to my remembrance. Several of these odd fashions were retained, because *old*, and gradually gave way to those that were new. The straw plait, called the bee-hive bonnet, and the blue or green apron, were long worn by old women.

The careful housewifery, and strict domestic discipline of many honourable mothers, has had an influential effect down to the present time; so that whatever there may have been, or that now remains as valuable traits of character in the inhabitants of these parts of the country, is chiefly owing to the virtues of the first settlers; especially in those families, (which are many,) who remain to the present time.

The first adventurers were chiefly members of the Falls meeting; and are said to have frequently attended it, and often on foot. In the year 1700, leave was granted by the quarterly meeting to hold a meeting for worship at Buckingham; which was first at the house of William Cooper, (now John Gillingham's.) They soon after removed to the house of James Steiper, (now Benjamin Williams',) and in that time, and for some time after, some of those who died in the new settlement were buried on his land, I believe near the line in the old orchard: others were taken to the Falls, or Middletown. In a short time they removed again, and held a meeting at Nathaniel Bye's, where his grandson, Thomas Bye, now lives.

In the space of time from the first improvement until 1730, perhaps a period of more than forty years, many circumstances and occurrences may be worthy of remark, and especially the difficulty of beginning in the woods. Building a house or cabin, and clearing or fencing a field to raise some grain, were the first concerns; procuring fodder for their small stocks was next to be attended to: for this purpose they cut grass in plains or swamps, often at several miles from home, stacked it upon the spot, and hauled it home in the winter.

One of the first dwelling houses yet remains in Abraham Paxson's yard, on the tract called William Croasdale's, now Henry Paxson's. It is made of stone, and is dug into the earth where there is a moderate descent, about twenty feet by ten or twelve. At the end fronting the south-east was a door leading into the dwelling-room for the whole family, where there was a sort of chimney; and a door at the other end, also level with the ground, led into the loft which must have been the lodging room.

Until a sufficient quantity of grain was raised for themselves and the new-comers, all further supply had to be brought from the Falls or Middletown; and until 1707, all the grain had to be taken there, or to Morris Gwin's, on Pennepac below the Billet, to be ground. In that year Robert Heath built a grist-mill on the great spring stream in Solebury. This must have been a great hardship—to go so far to mill for more than seventeen years, and chiefly on horseback. It was some time that they had to go the same distance with their plough-irons and other smithwork. Horses were seldom shod; and blocks to pound hominy were a useful invention borrowed from the natives. After all their care and industry to provide for the winter, they must have struggled with many difficulties, and suffered much hardship in passing over that tedious and rigorous season, when the snow was generally deep, and the winds piercing cold.

In 1690 there were many settlements of Indians in these townships—one on the lowlands near the river, on George Pownall's tract, which remained for some time after he settled there—one on James Streiper's tract, near Conkey hole—one on land since Samuel Harold's—one on Joseph Fell's tract—and one at the Great spring, &c.

Tradition reports that they were kind neighbours, supplying the white people with meat, and sometimes with beans and other vegetables; which they did in perfect charity, bringing presents to their houses, and refusing pay. Their children were sociable and fond of play. A harmony arose out of their mutual intercourse and dependence. Native simplicity reigned in its greatest extent. The difference between the families of the white man and the Indian, in many respects, was not great—when to live was the utmost hope, and to enjoy a bare sufficiency the greatest luxury.

About 1704, several new settlers arrived; among whom was my great-grandfather, Thomas Watson. His certificate is from Pardsey

Cragg, in Cumberland, G. B., dated 23d, 7th mo., 1701. His wife was Eleanor Pearson, of Probank in Yorkshire, and their two sons, Thomas and John. He first settled at a place then called Moncy hill, near Bristol; and settled finally, about 1703 or 1704, on Rosill's four hundred acres in Buckingham.

John Watson became the deputy surveyor in this county; and by the force of a suitable docility of mind and quickness of perception, rather than from constant application, he acquired among learned men the character of a great scholar. At the time of his decease, which was in 1761, he was employed, in company with Purdie and Dixon in running the line between Pennsylvania and Maryland. Being seized with the influenza, and having taken cold while in a fever, in extremely hot weather, he rode upwards of sixty miles in a day to William Blackfan's, where he died.

It appears in an old account book of my grandfather, Richard Mitchel, who had a grist-mill and store in Wright's town, 1724 to 1735, that his charges are as follows:—wheat from 3*s.* to 4*s.*; rye one shilling less; Indian corn and buckwheat, 2*s.*; middling, fine, 7*s.* and 8*s.*; coarse, 4*s.* 6*d.*; bran, 1*s.*; salt, 4*s.*; beef, 2*d.*; bacon, 4*d.*; pork was about 2*d.*

Improved land was sold generally by the acre, at the price of 20 bushels of wheat. Thus, wheat 2*s.* 6*d.*, land £2 10*s.*; wheat 3*s.*, land £3; wheat 3*s.* 6*d.*, land £3 10*s.*; wheat 5*s.*, land £5; wheat 7*s.* 6*d.*, land £7 10*s.*; wheat 10*s.*, land £10. When provender could be procured to keep stock through the winter, milk, butter, and cheese became plenty for domestic use. Swine were easily raised and fattened. Deer, turkeys, and other small game made a plentiful supply of excellent provision in their season. Roast venison and stew-pies were luxurious dishes, which the hunter and his family enjoyed in their log cabins with a high degree of pleasure.

Having generally passed over the era of necessity that attended the first settlement, about 1730, and for some time before, they mostly enjoyed a pretty good living, were well fed, clothed, and lodged; and though all was in the coarse way, yet their fare was wholesome and nourishing, their clothes fine enough for labouring people, and no doubt they slept as sound on chaff beds on the floor in the loft, as they could have done with all the finery that the inventions of later days have introduced. The domestic management that fell to the share of the women was generally well ordered. As soon as wool and flax were raised, they manufactured good linen of different kinds and degrees of fineness, drugget, linsey, worsted, &c., sufficient to clothe themselves and families; were very industrious and frugal, contented to live on what their present means afforded, and were generally well qualified to make the most proper use of what they had.

Notwithstanding the engagements at home, and the difficulty of travelling in those early times, yet visits of friendship were frequent, not only to relations, but others. On these occasions, cider, metheglin, or small beer, toast of light biscuit made of fine wheat flour, and milk, butter, cheese, custards, pies, made an afternoon's repast. Chocolate was sometimes used; and in lack of other materials, the toast was sometimes made with rum and water. For common living, milk and bread, and pie, made the breakfast; the milk being boiled, and sometimes thickened in winter; good pork or bacon, with plenty of sauce, a wheat flour pudding, or dumplings, with butter and molasses for dinner; and mush or hominy with milk and butter and honey, for supper. Pies of green or dried apples were the universal standard of good eating, especially with children. When milk was scarce, small-beer thickened with wheat flour and an egg, or cider in that way, made an agreeable breakfast.

Wheat was the principal article for making money. Butter, cheese, poultry, and such articles were taken to market on horseback. There were but few stores in the neighbourhood, and those kept but few articles.

Most of the original tracts were settled and improved before 1720, and in 1730 the lands up the Neshamony and in Plumstead were settled; and in New Britain by Welsh generally. Large fields were cleared and pretty well fenced; low and swampy land was cleared out for meadow; and but little seed of any kind of foreign grass was sown, as the plough was seldom used to prepare for meadow; and red and white clover were only propagated by manure, after they were first somehow scattered about on the new settlement.

From 1730 to 1750, as the people were industrious, the land fresh and fertile, and seasons favourable, their labours were blessed with a plentiful increase; so that many plain dwelling houses and good barns were built, convenient articles of househould furniture were added by degrees, and by the means of productive labour, moderate riches increased insensibly. The winter of 1740–41 was very severe. The snow was deep, and lay from the latter end of December to the fourth of March; and in the period above mentioned, there was generally more snow, and that lay longer on the ground through the winters, than of latter years. Easterly storms of pretty heavy rain, lasting mostly two or three days, were also much more frequent.

Northern lights, I believe, are not so common of late years as formerly; but of this I am not certain.

Indian corn, not being an article of trade, was not attempted to be raised in large quantities before 1750, nor until some years after. It was dressed by ploughing and harrowing between the rows, the hills all moulded nicely with the hoe when the corn was small, and, after ploughing, hilled up again with the hoe. For wheat, open fallows were preferred, which were generally ploughed three times during the summer; but in this way, unless corn and buckwheat had preceded, the blue grass, not being killed, became injurious to the crop. Hence, what was called double cropping became common; which is sowing oats on the corn-stalk and buckwheat ground, and then sowing wheat in the fall. This practice effectually killed the grass, and impoverished the land; large fields being sown, and but small portions manured. Liming answered a good purpose, which kept the soil in better heart; but, on the whole, wheat crops were on the decline, growing poorly in the fall, being eaten by lice or small flies; and, in wet land, being frozen out by the winter Mildew and rust sometimes destroyed it near harvest. On all these accounts, spring grain was more cultivated; and, as horses, cattle, and pork bore a better price, served in part to make up the deficiency. But the land generally suffered by a bad method of farming.

Before this time, no cross occurrence happened materially to disturb the general tranquillity; every thing, both public and private, went on in an even and regular routine; moderate wishes were fully supplied; necessaries and conveniences were gradually increased; but luxuries of any kind, except spiritous liquors, were rarely thought of, or introduced; either of apparel, household furniture, or living. Farm carts were had by the best farmers. Thomas Canby, Richard Norton, Joseph Large, Thomas Gilbert, and perhaps a few more, had wagons before 1745; and a few two-horse wagons from then to 1750 were introduced; some who went to market had light tongue-carts for the purpose. These were a poor make-shift, easily overset, the wild team sometimes ran away, and the gears often broke. John Wells, Esq., was the only person who ever had a riding chair. He and Matthew Hughes were the only justices of the peace, except Thomas Canby, who held a commission for a short time; and there were no taverns in the two townships, except on the Delaware, at Howell's and Coryell's ferries, (which was owing probably to the disposition and manners of the inhabitants,) and but one distillery a short time.

The preceding account will apply with general propriety to the state of things until 1754, when a war began between England and France concerning lands on the west and north-west of Pennsylvania. Col. Washington was defeated and taken prisoner on Wills' creek; and, in the ensuing summer General Braddock was defeated and killed in that country. When the Indians attacked the frontiers of this province, four or five hundred thousand pounds were granted in a few years for the king's use; money was also sent in from England to purchase provisions, and in general the war introduced a more plentiful supply of cash. Trade and improvements were proportionably advanced; the price of all kinds of produce was increased, wheat was from six shillings to a dollar a bushel, and a land tax was raised to sink the debt; yet the burden was not sensibly felt, as there was such an increasing ability to bear it.

As the quantity of cash increased during the war, so also there was a much larger importation of foreign goods. Bohea tea and coffee became more used, which were not often to be found in any farmer's house before 1750. Tea, in particular, spread and prevailed almost universally. Half silks and calico were common for women's wearing; various modes of silk bonnets, silk and fine linen neck-handkerchiefs; in short, almost every article of women's clothing was of foreign manufacture. The men wore jackets and breeches of Bengal, nankin, fustian, black everlasting, cotton velvet, as the fashion of the season determined the point, which changed almost every year. Household furniture was added to, both in quantity and kind; and hence began the marked distinction between rich nd poor, or rather between new-fashioned and old-fashioned, which has continued increasing ever since. The first beginning was by imperceptible degrees; I believe tea and calico were the chief initiating articles. Tea was a convenient treat on an afternoon's visit, easily gotten ready at any time; and calico a light agreeable dress that would bear washing. On the whole, present calculation decided against homespun of almost every kind, and in favour of foreign manufactures, which were to be had in the city, or in country stores, so cheap, and often on credit.

The subject of old and new fashion bore a considerable dispute, at least, how far the new should be introduced. Some showed by their practice that they were for going as far as they could; some stopped half way; and a few, trying to hold out as long as they could, were not to be won upon by any means more likely to prevail than by the women, who had a strong aversion to appearing singular; so that at the present time, and for these twenty years past, there are but few men, and fewer women, left as perfect patterns of the genuine old-fashioned sort of people.

State of the Country at Swatara, Pottsville and Mauch Chunk in 1829, *as seen, and journalized by an observer.*

The MS. from which this is taken, being a picture of things as they were, and from which they are continually changing by population and improvement, may serve to preserve some tokens of their former wilderness state, to wit:

On Monday, 3d August, 1829, I started in the mail stage, at three o'clock A. M., for Reading. Found a full company of agreeable travellers—went twenty-six miles to Troy's, to breakfast. Giving time for a devouring appetite.

We approached Reading by 11 o'clock. High hills and mountains seem to encircle it. We look down upon it as in a vale below us. It covers a wide extent of ground, and presents a mixture of log houses and finely built three story brick buildings. The place has an air of business.

The first hotel there was the house of Conrad Weisser, seen in 1829, as the little white store of General Keim, on the corner of Callowhill and Penn streets, and since replaced by a great new house of fashion. It was at that place that C. Weisser, as Indian agent, used to deliver the Indian presents—here the war song of the savage was sung, the war dance wound down, and the calumet of peace was smoked. The house was built earlier than the town

Here I took my seat for *Lebanon*—to go along the line of the Union canal through the Tulpehocken country. The Tulpehocken country ranging along the line of *the creek*, to Lebanon, is a rich valley country, with high mountains in the distant view. The cultivation and scenery always fine. This was the favourite *home* of the Indians, and of their supplanters, the *Germans*. To this land went Conrad Weisser, the Indian interpreter,* he settled *his farm* at the present Womelsdorf, where we arrived at half-past two o'clock—a town chiefly of log houses, on a rising ground. There I inquired for Weisser—he has been buried there many years—his grandson is still there—Old Willick Seltzer, now alive there, remembers to have seen and talked with Conrad. He was a good man, the favourite of the Indians, who invited him to go and settle at their home. C. Weisser, as magistrate, married the *first* German minister there. The present aged Reverend William Hendel is said to have many facts of the primitive settlers. The whole face of the country looks *German*—all speak that language, and but very few can speak English. Almost all their houses are of squared logs neatly framed—of two stories high. They look to the eye like "Wilmington stripes," for the taste is to white-wash the smooth mortar between the logs, but not the logs themselves, thus making the house in stripes of alternate white, and dusky wood colour. Much I wanted to make every house entirely white, with the white-wash of their abounding lime. The barns were large and well filled, generally constructed of squared logs or stone, but all the roofs were of *thatched straw*—a novelty to my eye—said to last fifteen years. Their houses were shingled with lapped shingles. Saw *no* stately or proud mansions, but all looked like able owners. This character of houses and barns, I found the same throughout my whole range of tour.

As I rode through the Tulpahocken, much I thought of the former Indian owners—

> "Whose hundred bands
> Ranged freely o'er those shaded lands,
> Where now there's scarcely left a trace,
> To mind one of that tawny race."

Some few of them still clung about their former home till the period of the Revolution, and then suddenly withdrew. How it surprises the mind to consider the present rich harvest fields, decked all over with houses—canals and turnpikes running through former wilds. This in a place which in 1755, after Braddock's defeat, was so *new*, so *frontier*, so possessed by the Indians, that the massacres and ravages there were dreadful—one little girl was found alive, of six years of age, who had been scalped. The city gazettes of the day teemed with accounts of Indian devastations, at Tulpahocken—

---

* See Proud's History. Post and Tedyuscunk, and Indians stopped there, in 1758—next at Fort Hunter, on the Susquehanna.

in Berks—in Northampton—scaring the inhabitants into such towns as Lancaster, Easton, &c. The story ran that 1500 French and Indians were encamped on the Susquehanna, only thirty miles above the present Harrisburg!

I found all the aged with whom I talked, in my travels, had Indian stories to relate when questioned. Near Pine grove is an aged woman now, who was nine years a prisoner with the Indians from that neighbourhood.

All the population we see are Germans of coarse manners and education. Uninformed as they are, they are powerful enough in the interior to sway the election, and to give us *German rulers.* This seems strange to contemplate, as we were originally *English* colonists.

We arrived at Lebanon at half-past four o'clock, P. M., a large-looking modern town—having a large court-house, prison, and three churches with steeples—the whole of a city aspect. Even here the talk of the street was still German, and occasional English.

This place is famous now as the *Summit* level of the Union canal. I found the whole region a very *level* plain. Six miles of the canal here was cut through hard limestone rock, found a little below the surface; it leaked greatly—they resorted to clay and puddling; finally planked the whole six miles as tight as a tub! A very expensive concern!

All along my rides, I noticed every where fields strewed with flax laid to dry—for every where German women still use the spinning wheel! Cheapness of manufactured goods will not allure *them* from their olden habits of making home-made stuffs.

I start along the Union canal, *on foot*—go by the celebrated *tunnel* cut out of solid rock, through a hill. There I bathe in the canal; finally see sixteen descending locks in seven miles—reach Mrs. Jeffries' good brick house, called "Mount Union hotel," near the romantic banks of the Swatara. There see a long and deep reservoir, used as a "*feeder*," by water works there, which by steam power pump up and *send back* the water before used at the Summit level. It is sent back by a framed trough six miles long! A good supper and bed here were charged only *2s. 6d.!* From the mount near here, I looked northward over a very richly cultivated plain, formed along the stream of the Swatara. It had mountains near it. It lay in squares of various coloured fields, like the sections of a chequer board. From the canal here issued forth a beautiful cataract of forty feet, tumbling into the Swatara, nearly drained out below.

Having heard much of the *great feeder*, formed in the gaps of the Blue mountains, a few miles off, I started before sunrise to go along the line of the canal leading to it, by Jones' town, four miles off. This I also undertook *on foot.* It gave me much better chances of observation and the means of keeping close to the canal. It led through a romantic looking country, of alternate woods and farms, along the margin of the Swatara. I every where found more *cultivation* than I had expected. At length I was much charmed, when I expected no such art of man, to see at a distance, gleaming through the trees, a kind of magnificent bridge across the Swatara, which on nearer approach proved to be a fine *aqueduct* to the canal, over which I went to the opposite side. Afterwards I passed a well finished bridge, at Jones' town; I saw at a distance the place where the dam of the feeder was forming between the base of the two mountains—closing in the Swatara fifty feet deep, three-fourths of a mile wide, and seven miles long! A big affair indeed! An expense hereafter to be avoided, by inclined planes, as at Morris canal.

About forty houses in Jones' town, and a steepled church, on a level ground. Some locust trees before old houses.

Here I sought a horse and dearborne to convey me to the Blue mountain pass. Went through Stump town, a small log house town—rich and cultivated, in the county of Lebanon. All Germans, none along the road could answer me in English. They are a heavy, toilsome race—saw women at thrashing—heard no where the songs of the nursery—no mothers joyful with their children, all was dull and money-making.

I went across the Blue mountain on foot—I was desirous to *feel*, as well as see its slow ascent and descent. It took about four to five miles to get across it, although itself at the lowest point leading to "Pine grove." The whole of it was covered with broken fragments of big stones and forest trees growing between—seemed a good den for rattlesnakes, but I saw none, nor any kind of trace of wild animals! At meridian I reached the summit of the road, and sat me down on a stone in the shade, and there wrote this page of my book *on the Blue mountains!*

The tops of hills below me, covered with woods, look like a level vale covered with green velvet, and fields between of various cultivated hues. I hear distant dogs bark, cows low, and sheep bleat, and tinkle. See readily at forty miles' distance, where all the horizon seems bordered and shut in by green mountains towering as my own, and through these are occasional 'passes,' where I see still further, twenty miles or more, to other mountains, *blue* with distance. From this resting stone, where I sit, once looked out the Indian wanderer, looking abroad as from the home of his Great Spirit. From hence they saw their smoking wigwams—knew their corn fields, and felt the love of *their homes.* In such still regions as this, they sought the bear and deer. All this walk over the mountain was through constant shade of lofty trees. The country towards Pine grove, after my descent, was in good tillage.

As I cross another branch of the Swatara, observed another instance of the usual bungling signs of the country, all done by country artists "unknown to fame." Here I read on a finger post, "PEINT GRoF," which, being interpreted, stood for *Pine grove!* I before observed a sign lettered thus, to wit: "Sheuin work & al wagons"—which stood for all kinds of wagon work and horse shoeing! All the usual signs of inns, with heads of generals, or horses, bulls, or bears, were clumsy daubs, often marking the genius of the host himself.

Wednesday, 5th August,—began this day before sunrise, by walking four miles to Schuylkill Haven, all along a good road and among farms—feel rejoiced to see myself so near to the head of the Schuylkill navigation. Here thought of Penn, when he first rejoiced to see the Schuylkill, near to Philadelphia—looked forward to its future usefulness in uniting our commerce to the Susquehanna. Yet little he or they then knew of the region where I now stand and ponder. How often, and how many Indians, but half a century ago, were familiar with this water as their favourite haunt—near here I see the canal, a work every where reducing savage wildness to level or modelled paths, &c. Along this I make my walk, all is still in early morn, the songsters of the grove are vocal, the sun just begins to gild the scene, and to give brilliance to the dew drops—canal boats are moving to and fro, the rush and fall of waters are heard in the locks, the boatmen's horns resound—half-tunes are blown abroad, and all the scene opens on the senses, from my former silent walk, like the spells of enchantment. As I proceed along a well-beaten canal path, passing lock after lock, and boats after boats—I see much romantic beauty and scenery, down the acclivity beneath my walks, in the closely adjacent and continuous Schuylkill, which here for a long distance adheres closely to the canal. As I approached to Mount Carbon, the high hills came in view—in time they surrounded me; and when I reached the proper *landing place*, or the head of the navigation, I see myself in a busy town, at the water side, and at the narrow base of mountains of 1000 feet in height, covered all over with woods. Wagons appear all along the road, drawing coal to the landing—there are great wharves for its deposit, and boats about them to convey it to Philadelphia. Several warehouses, numerous boats building on the stocks—all noise, bustle and enterprise. Onward half a mile in ascending line, come to the general town called *Pottsville*, named after the original proprietor, whose blazing furnace still is there for melting ore and casting iron.

Took my breakfast at eight o'clock, at Troutman's hotel, where I found my valise of clothes, before sent on from Reading.

Pottsville is another Rochester in rapidity of rise; seems to be now a town of 100 houses, and constantly adding, buildings are every where going up. It is a high ground, but in front and rear close shut up with coal mountains of 1000 feet high. The Sharp mountain and its range is ever in the eye—much city people here, all the storekeepers are from cities; no German characters here, save among the wagoners of the coal, and the country visiters. The Schuylkill is in sight, then hides itself between the mountains. Then I visited several coal mines; the North American was worked into 1700 feet, others usually 600 or 700 feet. I saw the process of the railway cars. The houses are generally plastered in imitation of stone, or white, and several are of brick; lots and houses bring great prices--much speculation abroad in lots and in coal acres. Only *one* old *log* house in the place, some are of white frame. Saw two rattlesnakes which had been killed in the neighbourhood. The hotels here are large. The coal wagons are constantly going along the street, making it *black* thereby. A rail road is forming along the river, on the other side, which will take off this annoyance. All the conversation here at present is about coal—one Gothic church, Presbyterian, and one Roman chapel.

Lively and business like as is the present *Pottsville*, the man is now living here, John Boyer by name, an old revolutionary soldier, now in his eightieth year, born and reared at the present Schuylkill Haven, in which neighbourhood, he had often been engaged in resisting the predatory invasions of the Indians. The country around him was long a wilderness, and was often the scene of bloody massacre, much of which he had seen with his own eyes.

An old Indian war-path, leading from the tribes north of the Susquehanna, crossed the mountain at Pottsville, and the few settlers who had braved all danger, and had pitched their cabins in the midst of such perils, were forced to struggle desperately at times, to save the scalps of their families from the knife. Fort Henry once stood at the head of the Swatara, at the foot of Kittaning.

On Thursday, 6th August, early in the morning, I started from Pottsville in a dearborne, having Mr. L. as a companion, to go across to the "Mung Chung" coal mine, said to be twenty miles off by the shortest route, over an *unfrequented* road, much in primitive wildness. We have no guide, but are told to go *between* the Sharp and Broad mountain range, till we reach our end. We pass Port Carbon, Middle Port, and Upper Port, on Schuylkill; towns now *on paper*, but intended to rival Pottsville, by their coal regions; they have only a house here and there. I am told Maiden creek was "Ontalaunee." This ride was through wild regions, over hills and down into ravines, and here and there a farm, or saw-mill. The last third of our route was rougher and ruder, much woods—cypress swamps, high hills, Tuscarora mountains, Wild-cat mountains, Panther creek—wild names! The road almost obliterated with bushes—had often to get out and walk beside our dearborne. We breakfasted at Middle Port, a half-way house. Along here is forming a rail road, down to Pottsville. The Schuylkill here is dammed across for Casner's saw-mill, a good head—Schuylkill has two heads, being *springs*, each eight miles off. We again passed another branch of the Schuylkill, near another Casner's saw-mill, and there we undressed and bathed in the stream; after this our progress was very wild. Broad mountains and Sharp mountains 1000 feet high, on either side, and our way along a wilderness suited for deer, and "leather stocking" hunters. It was all a place to interest the feelings of any unaccustomed eye; yet, in this lonely region, we once in a while broke upon some German cottage. In one of these we made a dinner of bread and milk, and fed our horse. We did not hurry, we rather walked our way; early in the afternoon we reached the Mung Chung coal mountain. It was on the summit of a flat mountain, 1000 feet high, and nine miles from the village of Mung Chung. Here the mine was all quarried *open*, forming a great open area of five acres, quite different from those at Pottsville, which go *into* the side of the mountain, working the way by a subterraneous path, &c. Here the region is denuded of trees. Houses for the miners make a small town. After seeing all the strange operations, and much ingenuity in machinery, &c., we join the cars to make our descent on the rail. We began our descending career in several divisions, fourteen cars to each coal division; I chose my lot with the mule division—twelve of these were in cars, three mules abreast, munching their hay, while we went off ten miles an hour, and sometimes, for change sake, at twenty miles—could go at sixty miles, and more. This is a very grateful ride, so rapid, feel so much air, and yet see trees so still—go along the side of a declining mountain, and see *down* amidst trees far below us; or over to other high mountains beyond us. As we proceeded we saw gathering vapour rolling along the ridge of mountains, and curling and circling to the vale below; then a general mist succeeded, and quickly rain in pelting patter came over us, wetting us beyond our wishes. On the whole we got on well enough, and descending by the hill from the stopping place, we came to Kimball's capacious and elegant hotel in time to sit down to a welcome supper, with a company of about thirty ladies and gentlemen. The house is three stories—has two ranges of galleries. It is set into the base of an impending mountain 900 feet above it.

On the opposite side of the Lehigh is a mount, 900 feet in height, and the canal along its base; near the bridge is a dam across the river. Looking up or down the river is very picturesque; all the scenery is very romantic. A grist-mill of great power is in the town, and two or three saw-mills. The boat-building is a curiosity, Here four men make a coal ark for twenty-five tons of coal, in thirty minutes! They plane the joints of the pine boards, with a plane of nine *irons*, turned, to give it *power*, by a crank; twenty spikes of six inches length are driven home at a stroke, one at a time; every thing in this region shows *invention*, so much so, that it looks like enchantment, and Josiah White himself is the great wizard! At his house, on the side of the hill, he has a deer park. The rush and roar of the water here are sensible *to the ear* day and night. The river goes up seventeen miles higher to Pine swamps, whence they send down rafts, on which ladies and gentlemen make pleasant parties. Every thing here delights *ladies*, there is so much *adventure*—looking hazardous, but without harm; for *them* to descend on cars—or on rafts over rapids, is very exciting. While I write now under a forest shade, at my hotel, I see up the river, ladies rowed about in a small boat, shouting with joy as they go. We have trout at table caught up the river.

Friday, 7th August, I prepare at midday to make a start for Easton, at the mouth of the Lehigh, and to ride in the stage along the romantic banks of the river, in sight of the excellent canal. There we see many miles, as we ride amidst towering trees, running up the rocky mountains high above our road. Often we see the Lehigh dammed across, and the schutes, as they were formerly made by the inventive Josiah White, for the deepening and use of the river. Came to Lehighton, where we took a dinner-snack—a small place—saw there the place of *Fort Allen*, now having only *its well* remaining there. At that fort, in 1758, C. F. Port, the interpreter, records his stopping with his Indians. It seems not long ago, and yet now all has been civilized and settled. At Lehighton we went over a bridge, close by the former fort, to the northern side of the river. There we ride close alongside of the canal. These canals so closely adhering to the sites of the streams which they rob of water and bear off their fame, strikes me as something *parasitical.*

We finally leave the canal as we come through the lofty *water gaps.* There is there a great reservoir of water retained by a dam. We now proceed through the country farms leading towards Easton; the country looks but tame, hills diminish, finally we reach Easton by moonlight. This day we have a passenger who carried with us a rattle snake in a box, with a glass plate; it took the jolts and company very quietly, but rarely shaking his rattles, or seeming to care for us!

Former state of Beasts of Prey, Deer, &c.

Our inland country was originally well stocked with bear, wolves, deer and turkeys. The flesh of the two last was not only a luxury, but a necessary article of food. Deer skin breeches, and deer skin facings to woollen pantaloons, (after one season's service,) were the height of country fashion. The wolf made great havoc with the few sheep introduced; committing depredations at the same time upon the wild deer. He has been known to attack cows. The bear confined himself to hogs; and many instances are given of his boldness in capturing and carrying away provisions of this kind. He springs suddenly upon his victim, grasps him in his arms or fore legs with a force which is irresistible, erects himself upon his hind legs like a man, and makes off in an instant with his load. The piercing squeal of the hog is the first warning of his presence, to the owner. A large bear, which meets with no obstruction, will make his way through a thick wood in this manner, with a hog of good size, faster than a man on foot can follow. The groans and struggles of the animal in his embrace become weaker and weaker, and soon cease entirely. One of these creatures took a shoat from a drove belonging to J. H. in his presence. He followed him closely, but the bear evidently gained in the race till he came to a brush fence, and not being able to climb it with sufficient expedition, dropped the dying pig in order to secure himself. Mr. E. S. was chopping on his land, when one of his hogs was taken near by. After a severe contest with clubs, Mr. S. recovered the body of his hog, and, using it as a bait, afterwards caught the offender in a trap. Another seized a full grown hog belonging to A. W near by, and notwithstanding men were near and made close pursuit, he carried it off without difficulty.

When Mr. E. C. lived in his log house, his hogs were fed across the road at a trough in the field. One morning, as he returned from feeding them, a large bear fell upon the hogs before he had reached the house. By the time he had seized his rifle and recrossed the road, the bear had secured one, and as he rose, preparatory to a retreat, received a bullet in the chest. He then let the hog fall and made fiercely at Mr. C.; but, in making an effort to scale the bars, fell backward and died.

Mr. J. C. and his dogs fell in with one of a moderate size, while traversing the woods in search of horses. An engagement followed in which the bear had apparently the advantage. To an early settler, the loss of a dog, his companion and faithful sentinel, was a misfortune that affected, not only his interest, but the best feelings of his heart. Mr. C. had nothing in hand but a bridle, and could therefore bring no weapons to the assistance of his friends but such dry clubs as lay about him. The animal paid very little attention to these, but at length finding a young sapling, he broke it into a good stick, and managed to give several hard knocks repeatedly on the same spot, just behind the ear. By this means he was killed, and the dog released.

By the assistance of a large and valuable wolf dog, Mr. D. P. and Mr. D. F. killed one with clubs and stones.

If the body of a hog was recovered partly eaten, the same bear could generally be taken in a trap within the next twenty-four hours. He invariably returned for the remainder, and showed little or no sagacity in avoiding his fate. For this purpose a heavy steel trap was used, with smooth jaws, and a long drag chain, with iron claws at the extremity. It was not fastened to the spot, because the great strength of the animal would enable him to free himself, but as he ran, after being snared, the claws would catch upon the brush, retarding his flight, and leaving a distinct trail. He was generally overtaken within two miles, exhausted of strength. Here the dogs were first allowed an opportunity to exhibit their courage and natural animosity, before the rifle put an end to his degradation and sufferings. In these conflicts, if the shackles were upon his hind legs, leaving the fore paws free, there were but few dogs desirous of a close combat the second time.

In the winter, the inhabitants of this and the adjoining townships determined to make an effort to clear the country of the bear and of the wolf at the same time. There were four *drives*, or large hunts, organized during the winter. They were frequently got up in the new country by those who were not professed hunters, for the purpose of taking a few deer and turkeys, then so common. A large tract of wild land, the half or fourth of a township, was surrounded by lines of men, with such intervals that each person could see or hear those next him, right and left. The whole acted under the command of a captain, and at least four subordinates, who were generally mounted. At a signal of tin horns, or trumpets, every man advanced in line towards the centre, preserving an equal distance from those on either hand, and making as much noise as practicable. From the middle of each side of the exterior line, a blazed line of trees was previously marked to the centre as a guide, and one of the subofficers proceeded along each as the march progressed. About a half or three-fourths of a mile from the central point, a ring of blazed trees was made, and a similar one at the ground of meeting, with a diameter at least equal to the greatest rifle range. On arriving at the first ring, the advancing lines halted till the commandant made a circuit and saw the men equally distributed and all the gaps closed. By this time a herd of deer might be occasionally seen driving in affright from one line to another. At the signal, the ranks move forward to the second ring, which is drawn around the foot of an eminence, or the margin of an open swamp or lake. Here, if the drive has been a successful one, great numbers of turkeys may be seen flying among the trees away from the spot. Deer, in flocks, sweeping around the ring, under an incessant fire, panting and exhausted. When thus pressed, it is difficult to detain them long within the ring. They become desperate, and make for the line at full speed. If the men are too numerous and resolute to give way, they leap over their heads, and all the sticks, pitchforks and guns raised to oppose them. By a concert of the regular hunters, gaps are sometimes made to allow them to escape. The wolf is now seen skulking through the bushes, hoping to escape observation by concealment. If bears are driven in, they dash through the brush in a rage from one part of the field to another, regardless of the shower of bullets playing upon them. After the game appears to be mostly killed, a few good marksmen and dogs scour the ground within the circle to stir up what may be concealed or wounded. This over, they advance again to the centre with a shout, dragging along the carcasses which have fallen, for the purpose of making a count. [The foregoing facts were communicated by a friend.]

Wolves were taken with difficulty in steel traps, but more readily in log pens, prepared like the roof of a house, shelving inwards on all sides, and containing the half devoured carcass of a sheep, upon which they had made a previous meal. The wolf easily clambered up the exterior side of the cabin, and entered at the top, which was left open; but once fairly within it, he could neither escape or throw it down.

Turkeys were taken in square pens, made of lighter timber, and covered at the top. They entered at an open door in the inside, which was suspended by a string that led to a catch within. This string and catch were covered with chaff, which induced them to enter, and while engaged in scratching about the chaff to get at the grain mingled with it, some unlucky companion would strike the catch and let the door down behind them all.

Sea-shore watering places—Cape May—Long Beach, &c., 1822–3.

We are enabled by access to some MS. journals, to portray in some degree, a former state of the sea-shore watering places, which may serve to mark things as they were, to those who shall come after us, and may behold things in another aspect of improvement and luxury, to wit:

These pages shall be appropriated to catch some of the fleeting images and things, which may flit across the mind or press upon the sight, in an intended excursion to the sea-shore, at Cape Island.

Behold us safely pushed off from the wharf, and going at a rate of ten miles an hour! What variety of images crowd upon the mind! We turn to friends at home, and instinctively sigh farewell—we think how far we shall be off at the close of the day, and the new society we must encounter. We look among the numerous passengers, (forty of different sexes,) and feel that we form opinions of our companions from our transient glances at their exterior. Some we recognize as plain sober persons; others, as young and sprightly dashers—all anticipating the fulfilment of their several hopes. Here and there a pale languid frame indicates its forlorn hope from a sea bath—doing what they can to arrest the tide of their ebbing life; others, all nerve and sinew, seem going to make life more sportful. What sights of ships, boats, and busy life upon the waters! How independent *we feel* whilst thus conscious that the mighty frame of such a ponderous vessel is set in motion, with all the men thereunto connected, to minister to *our* pleasures and to *our* comforts. What elegance in such a vessel of accommodation and comforts! How rapidly the passed objects fade from the view—and with what interest we look ahead to discern the new things breaking upon our vision! With what remarkable ease and quiet, the captain gives and executes his orders and purposes. A *ship* of equal magnitude could only be urged on with a load of curses. No swearing in this vessel! There is something *sublime* in contemplating this *wonder* of the genius of *Fitch* and *Fulton*, making such a mighty fabric fly like a dart through the pressing waves. Man "shall have dominion" over all the things which God has made. How destructive an element is fire, and yet to what purposes of *steam*, of health, warmth and comfort, does it not minister!

As we pass in rapid succession the fleeting objects, I remember my impressions, respecting *the same things*, when a lad; I perceive that all the places on the Delaware then appeared of more importance than they do now—and even greater—hills looked bigger then.

We come off the *high lands of Christiana*, seen at a long distance—its extreme verdure and proper mixture of woods and fields is very beautiful to the eye. Its gradual elevation from the river presents a very interesting scene, and makes us surprised that in such beautiful scenery, there should be no appearance of elegance, as of country seats, in the mansions, &c.

Come to at New Castle—a number of sea vessels at anchor here. The spire to one of the churches, although plain, is very conspicuous at a great distance on the water. Went ashore, into the main front street, to see the house built in 1687, after the manner of the houses in Holland, of brick said to have been then imported from thence. The bricks are very small, yellowish, and now rough-cast with plaster. It presents its gable-end to the front street—the roof is remarkably steep, making two stories in itself. The *end* walls are higher than the roof, and have regular steps on their upper surface above the roof. The year, 1687, is in iron letters, as clamps, on the front wall. One feels a sentiment of veneration at seeing such a vestige of antiquity. The generation to which it belonged, and those who successively inhabited it, have all gone to join "the nations beyond the flood."

After this place, till we reach the cape at six o'clock, the same evening, the river or bay becomes wider and wider, till it at length forms "*the bay*," and sometimes leaves us out of sight of land on one side or other, alternately. We pass many ships and brigs to and fro. Some after long voyages, earnestly anticipating the pleasures of an arrival to greet long absent friends; and others bound abroad to distant climes, filled with hopes and fears for their eventual success therein.

As we near the beach, we see many carriages in waiting to bear us to the boarding houses, three miles off, on the opposite sea beach. Before sundown, we arrive at our boarding house, (Aaron Bennett's,) at Cape Island. We take the house nearest to the surf, because we wish, while we stay, to be salted and pickled with sea air. We find the three houses very full of guests, containing together perhaps near two hundred persons. ☞ The time will come when, from the natural advantages of this place, there will be much more resort here, and much improvement in the accommodations and entertainments.

Our first night we were crowded, so that I had to take up my rest on a pallet of wood; an old settee and a pillow, made me to rest myself in very sound sleep through the night. The last comers had to accept the roughest fare. I have a heart for these things; and when the mind is in favour of conforming ourselves to our condition, we readily make rough things smooth. *I intend to be pleased with all I cannot mend;* and I have no doubt I shall *much increase my comforts thereby.*

The sea here often encroaches on the houses—several acres of the lawn in front of the house (Bennett's) have been gradually, or by storms, washed off into the sea. The distance now from the house is one hundred and sixty-five feet. In 1804, as then measured by Captain Decatur, it was three hundred and thirty-four feet off. It was formerly three hundred feet still further off—say sixty or seventy years ago—[so old men, present, told me.]

The ladies, at appointed hours in the forenoon and afternoon, go into the surf, at which time gentlemen do not walk on the banks. The ladies wear flannel and other woollen dresses—none go out above half their depth.

The sea *diet* is not so good as we expected—the variety of fish is not great nor frequent. We ask often for crabs—and the oysters are small.

It is sometimes curious to observe the variety of men and manners, and the very different interest we feel in faces and persons. Some possess that frank and open unreserve that seems to invite and ensure sociability; whilst others seem to forbid such freedom of approach—therefore, with some we seem at home and free; whilst others we seem to be likely to know no better after seeing them here, than if we had never broken bread in their society.

Some parties have been made up to go off Indian river, fifty miles off, to fish. Sometimes they catch several hundred fish—at other times ladies and all go to the shore and see the fishing with a seine.

Cape Island is a village of about twenty houses, and the streets are very clean and grassy; but our walks are generally up and down the beach. I generally walk a mile at a time, and several times in a day.

What a sublime and awful contemplation is the great deep! How wonderful the power of *Him* who made it such. What vast and unexplored treasures lie concealed beneath its ample bosom! How it teems with animal life—and withal how useful to man! To see the constant succession of outward and inward bound vessels, is very interesting. What various thoughts and enterprises must engage the numerous breasts, which compose the inmates of those floating habitations! Some feel buoyant with the hopes of seeing wives, sisters, husbands, or brothers, they may never see. Some are emigrants, forsaking all their former connexions, coming to new lands to seek happiness and wealth, and perchance to die. Some, having amassed fortunes abroad, are returning to spend the fruits of their foreign enterprise *otium cum dignitate* among their friends—and perchance some of ruined reputation and-ill gained riches are coming to seek a quiet and a refuge denied to them where known. How easy to extend the thoughts of all those who are thus busily thinking for themselves! How astonished and confounded we should all gaze upon one another, if all our thoughts were *necessarily* as open and unconcealed as our visages; or our hearts were as exposed to each other as before God.

Thursday, the 8th August.—Have now been here since Monday night—it really seems long, although there is no disrelish to any thing here; but time seems long when one is broken off from their usual habits. Last night one of the gentlemen played dancing tunes on his flute, and several made themselves merry with dancing in the dining hall. They were so well pleased, that to-night a more regular ball is to be given, and the ladies and gentlemen from the other boarding houses (McKinsey's and Hughes',) are invited. Several riding parties go off to day along the beach and other places. I can perceive that even pleasure sates: for several that have now stayed out their time, express much desire to see the steamboat again to take them home. The arrival of new company, and the departure of some of the old, twice a week, produces a wonderful bustle for the first night, while both parties remain in the house, and leave several of the gentlemen to take their rest on tables, chairs and settees.

Several of us have a desire to engage a pilot boat to take us on to Tuckerton beach—we expect in such a trip of sixty miles a more direct experience of the sea and the tossing waves. Several may get sick, and if the wind is fair, we shall be transported to an entire new company in six or seven hours.

Among our few amusements—we swing—gather curious shells and pebbles upon the strand—walk the piazza, and converse. A curious and laughable exercise is to try to walk blindfolded to any given object in a direct line. It is impossible to conceive how very much we are prone to deviate to the right or left. Some would almost describe a semicircle, whilst they thought they were walking straight to the mark. Ladies and gentlemen exercise at this. Some pitch quoits—some play *domino.*

Among the subjects of novelty and interest got up here, we were indebted to the enterprise of a Mr. Woolston, from near Wilmington, for a draw of a seine for catching sharks and porpoises. This cost *us* by subscription thirty dollars—say twenty dollars for twenty men, &c. The seine used is of great weight and strength, and made of best *rope.* The original materials cost $1500; and the whole belongs to a company, who, in the proper season, make it a business here to catch schools of porpoises, and render their livers and fat for lamp-oil, at one dollar per gallon. Early in the morning, the seine was drawn off about one-sixth of a mile from shore; and a boat at each end was anchored there to wait till porpoises should attempt to pass between them and the shore. Several schools came near; but none went inside. They remained off all day. In drawing it to land in the evening, it brought ashore six sharks and two large fishes of the skate kind, very like *bats* in their form and appearance. One or two of the sharks were eight feet long. They had great muscular vigour after their heads were off; and their heads for several hours after they were off—if stood up upon their base, and a stick thrust into their throat, would snap violently, and with much strength, their teeth into the wood. It is strange that these sharks occupy *the same waters* in which we bathe, and yet never molest us. Even when some go out swimming and floating beyond their depth.

Last night the gentlemen at Hughes' gave a ball in return for the one at our house the night before. (Ours cost the contributors $1 62½ for each gentleman.) We were all indiscriminately invited —but few, however, went. The ladies made up a great many ornamental decorations with green branches and flowers from the gardens. Some were wild, and some were sunflowers. The chandelier was made of oak hoops from casks, and covered with evergreens plucked from some neighbouring bushes.

It is worthy of remark how very much of the timbers and wrecks of vessels we see employed in all the fences and sheds in the village. They may be known by their marks of *rust* from spikes, &c., in the wood. When one considers the heartaches and terrors of those who must have been their companions (if they lived) who came floating with them on the tempest surges, we must feel a measure of gloom and sympathy to look upon them, and to think that this or that *plank* was a poor sufferer's last refuge.

I have been much interested in hearing the relation of the incidents of the late war at this place. The British, by commanding the ocean, were frequently off these capes. The main fleet would lay off Cape Henlopen; but their tenders, launches and smaller vessels, made such frequent threats of landing, and ravaging the country for supplies of cattle, &c , as to make a connected guard along the whole coast necessary. They would frequently capture small vessels, and immediately set them on fire. They sometimes landed with flags of truce to exchange or land prisoners. Once they attacked a large American privateer, and the fight was very interesting on both sides, and close to the shore. She got on the breakers and went to pieces. I felt, whilst I heard these recitals, as if I should have been much interested to have been present.

Whilst at church, I saw a gentleman with a shark-cane. It was formed from the spine bones of the shark. I observed, that persons took out all the spines of those we lately took. The cane had a *steel* elastic wire run through its whole length—was varnished and had a neat silver head. Its general appearance was that of the Indian reed-cane.

Monday night brought us the arrival of the steamboat with new company, and much bustle. We had just sat down to supper when we received ten new guests, chiefly Quaker ladies. To these were soon added a company of fifteen men and five women, from Cape Henlopen, to sup and spend the night. They had a fiddle, and some an excess of drink. After supper, they set to dancing, and to rude mirth, and kept it up till midnight. I went to bed, and slept through the midst of their shuffling and boozy mirth.

The entire exemption which one feels at a watering place, from all the usual family concerns of housekeeping or business, is a state which a care-crazed man of business should *feel* to arrive at any just conception of it. It would make us bad and useless members of the community to live thus freed (*constantly*) from the concerns and obligations of life; but a man, who labours ordinarily much for himself and others, should occasionally step into such a new state of existence. The *transition* is so extreme, that it is capable of producing mental and bodily emotions, calculated to loose him from many morbid and nervous afflictions of body. Let the closely confined city drudge, by all means, visit such a *sans souci* establishment, and abandon his mind and body to absolute freedom of both. It will make him a more ethereal being.

The season of bathing at Cape May begins about the 8th of July, and continues to the last week in August.

Cape May must, at some future day, be the great resort of the southern gentry. All those who live in Maryland and Virginia, nearest to the city of Baltimore, will ride there, quit their carriages, or send them home, and take the steamboat to Frenchtown and New Castle where they can, the *same day*, join the steamboat from Philadelphia. In this way Marylanders and Virginians will get to Cape May *on the same day from Baltimore*. All the gentry of Delaware and Philadelphia will find it to their advantage to go to Cape May of course. The beach is so decidedly preferable to Long branch that it must be preferred, whenever the boarding houses at Cape May shall have made enough to enable them to make such improvements as are needful there.

I predict, too, that the time will ere long come, when pilot boats will be engaged for 15 to $20 to take parties of fifteen to twenty people as often as once a week to the houses of entertainment at Tucker's and Manahawkin beach, sixty miles. All those who want to *see* and *feel* the exercise of a sea voyage and sea-sickness, and to get out of sight of land, will become parties to such excursions. I was the first who proposed this; and if a pilot boat had come to land while I talked of it, I had a dozen persons ready to embark, and to come home to Philadelphia by the Tuckerton stage.

A Trip to Long beach Seashore, 1823.

The country from Evesham down to Tuckerton has all the appearance of its original wildness—few houses or settlements appear. Pine and oak woods on both sides of the road perpetually; and for at least 30 miles of the road, the bushes on either side fill up the whole road, which is scarcely the single path which *one* wagon fills. We met nothing almost on the road to turn us out. I could thus have a very good conception of how the country looked in the hands of the aborigines, some few of whom still linger about.

Was much interested to see the formidable ruins of Atsion iron works, (27½ miles). They looked as picturesque as the ruins of abbeys, &c., in pictures. There were dams, forges, furnaces, storehouses, a dozen houses and lots for the men, and the whole comprising a town; a place once overwhelming the ear with the din of unceasing ponderous hammers, or alarming the sight with fire and smoke, and smutty and sweating Vulcans. Now, all is hushed; no wheels turn, no fires blaze, the houses are unroofed, and the frames &c., have fallen down, and not a foot of the busy workmen is seen.

Little Egg harbour, (now a poor country and population,) was once a place (in my grandfather's time, when he went there to trade &c.) of great commerce and prosperity. The little river there used to be filled with masted vessels. It was a place rich in money. As farming was little attended to, taverns and boarding houses were filled with comers and goers. Hundreds of men were engaged in the swamps cutting cedar, and saw-mills were numerous and always in business, cutting cedar and pine boards. The Forks of Egg harbour was the place of chief prosperity; many shipyards were there; vessels were built and loaded out to the West Indies; New York and Philadelphia, and the southern and eastern cities, received their chief supplies of shingles, boards, and iron, from this place. The trade too, in iron-castings, while the fuel there was abundant, was very great. The numerous workmen, all without dependence on cultivation of the soil, required constant supplies of beef, pork, flour, groceries, &c. from abroad. Even the women wore more of imported apparel than in any other country places. Merchants from New York and Philadelphia went there occasionally in such numbers that the inns and boarding houses could not contain them, and they had to be distributed among private houses. On such occasions they would club and have a general dance, and other like entertainments.

Sometimes rich cargoes came ashore on the beach, and were brought up the river for public sale, and brought there many traders to buy.

The vessels from New York and New England on trading voyages were numerous before the Revolution. The inlet was formerly the best on the coast; and many vessels destined for Philadelphia in the winter, because of the ice in the Delaware, made into Egg harbour river, and there sold out their cargoes to traders from New York and Philadelphia.

In these times Great Egg harbour had little or no distinction. Its inlet and advantages were not good. It since enjoys more than Little Egg harbour. Now both those places do their chief business in taking cord wood, especially pine, to the cities; but formerly they did none of that, when fuel was cheaper and easier procured.

In the time of the revolutionary war, Little Egg harbour river was a good refuge for our privateers, or their prizes. Many sales were made there of prize goods. The British, aware of it, endeavoured to avenge themselves. They entered it in light vessels and destroyed Chestnut neck, a town of about 20 houses, which have not been since rebuilt.

Count Pulaski, with his legion was down there, and had an action with the British in the Revolution.

There used to be a considerable exportation of *sassafras* from Egg harbour. Some vessels went direct to Holland with it "north about," to avoid, I believe, some British orders of trade therein. The Dutch made it into a beverage which they sold under the name of *sloop*. This commerce existed before the war of the Revolution.

When I ride over these lands and see so much soil whitened and glistened in the sun, especially in the woods where vegetation cannot conceal, I am forcibly persuaded that all these Jersey lands were once traversed by the finny monsters of the great Atlantic deep; and where the formal pine trees tower, there the billows rolled!

We arrived safely at Tuckerton at 7 o'clock in the evening. It proved to be a much neater and more civilized place than I expected. Several houses were painted, and were of boards, save Tucker's store, which was of brick. I should suppose it contains fifty buildings; twenty houses are on the main street. It has a Methodists' and Friends' meeting house; a mill dam and grist and saw-mill, and near it a wind-mill to make *salt*. This last arricle is made with much success and profit. The work cost $4,000. The people here have several fields planted with the castor-oil plant, and have two or three mills to grind it. They find it very profitable. Their chief export has been pine wood.

Friday morning, at 7 o'clock, I left Tuckerton with Capt. Horner, to go to Horner's house on the Long beach. Had head wind, and arrived at about 10 o'clock: fare 25 cents! The price of going in this vessel to sea or elsewhere is 25 cents, when company is made. As I came out of the creek my eyes were arrested with a considerable mound, on which three or four large cedars were growing. It was a hill of oyster and clam shells, left there by the aboriginal Indians long since. They dried their clams. What numbers they must have consumed to have made such a hill!

Horner's house, at which I have sat down for the present, is a new house, built and set up by a company of gentlemen in Philadelphia for the purpose of sea-bathing. It is all made for good cheer and free and easy comforts, without any attempt at elegance. None of the floors are planed, and the side walls are rough boards, and the ceilings are white-washed. Its appointment of liquors and table is very good. It is set down on an extremely desolate beach, full of broken and small sand-hills, without a solitary tree. Its very desolation increased my sense of comforts! I the more enjoyed the solid diet of the table; its zest was heightened by contrast! Its desolation too, was so isolated as to cut me off from all the *world*, and seemed to make me begin there an entire new existence! Thus *I* found charms where others might have been disgusted. But it is a manifest disadvantage that the bathers have to walk half a mile to the shore across the sand, and the ladies to ride in a cart. This company intend to increase its benefits and comforts. As it has fine shooting and fishing, and a grand surf, it will always best suit gentlemen who love rough and vigorous fare. The beach is twenty miles long, and to the northward has several houses, and so much of cedar wood as to shelter red foxes. The tables are a cover which is set on trussels and moved out of the room. The room is about twenty-six by fifteen feet. The proprietors intend to build a large house next summer. [This is since done, and every thing is in more refinement.] This establishment is quite new. They have dug and found a fine well of fresh water at ten feet depth near the house. It had never entered the mind of former people that good water could be found. In great sea storms, the sea has covered this whole beach, and the water came quite up to the ground floor of the house. The inlets and the beach have much altered in fifty years. It was once covered with cedar trees. Now all are gone. The inlets in the war of the Revolution admitted two frigates to come in, and now there is only water for small vessels.

This is a great place for the killing of ducks and geese in the winter. They have nothing else to do, and use decoys and ambush, and very often lay out to shoot as the flocks fly over them. The house at Tucker's beach is a cluster of three houses built at different times. The original house of the celebrated Mother Tucker is a one-story house, with a hipped roof, and front piazza. When you enter this piazza you are struck with the display of *names* cut in the boards of the house by the summer visiters; and probably one hundred clams are nailed up, of large size, having names inscribed on them. The house stands about the length of five hundred feet from the seashore. The salt meadow comes close up to the house, and the house is elevated on a heap of sand and shells. The room in which I lay on my cot and write this is open directly to the ocean. I see the vessels buffeting the waves, and the roar of the bellowing surf seems to lie just below me.

These beaches are much more dreary in the aspect than Cape May. Nothing seems to grow upon them but wild and scattered tufts of grass. But one feels comfort in the increase of appetite, and the consciousness of high cheer and good provisions.

How often have the landmarks of this shore been sought out by the approaching mariners of distant voyages, seeking, with anxious and distrustful eye, the first glimpse of the doubtful coast. Many this day, in the distant verge of the sinking horizon, would give great gifts to be once more on *terra firma.* Women passengers, sick of their confinements, listen with eager attention to the conjectures about land, which by their *soundings* is known to be near at hand; and the terrors of possible stranding and shipwreck are pictured to their labouring imaginations. It might do one good to see such objects land, and to regale them with the delicacies of the season, untasted by them for months.

Sundry of us made a sailboat excursion up the sound to the other boarding house on the same beach, twelve miles off, to the large house, called *the Mansion of Health*, (of which see a picture.) We found it well kept and supported by a goodly number of inmates.

The house, a hundred and twenty feet long, stands about one tenth of a mile from the surf. The original house once there was at one half the distance, and had numerous cedar and oak trees nigh it. The great "September gale," of 1821, swept over the whole island at this place, and tore up or blew over those trees, so that none now remain nigh, although the stumps of many are still seen. The whole island is twenty miles long, being from Tucker's to Barnegat inlets. At its northern end are still many trees and high hills, wherein foxes burrow.

As a riding vehicle to the surf and along the beach the ladies use an ox-wagon, wherein they amuse themselves greatly in a rustic novel way.

I was surprised to learn here from old Stephen Inman, one of the twelve family residents of the place, that he and his family have never ceased to be whale catchers along this coast. They devote themselves to it in February and March. They generally catch two or three of a season, so as to average forty to fifty barrels of oil apiece. I saw their look-out mast, their chaldron and furnace for rendering the oil, their whale-boats, &c. He has taken some whales of ninety barrels of oil. The whale bones of large size lay about bleaching in the sun. About his place are many oak and holly trees. Gunners go there much, in the season, for wild geese and ducks. Inman has killed twenty-four geese in a day. Sheep, mules, and horses are pastured and browsed on the northern end of the island, by himself and others. His house having formerly been the winter quarters of the gunners, is fully cut with the names of his visiters, made on the outside boards, under the piazza.

The coasting trade along these shores must be great. Sometimes we could count twenty sail, all going onward, eastward and southward. Their white sails looked like villas set along a highway.

Sometimes I think and wonder at what *could* have been all the features of this place before civilization and European eyes scanned it. I peopled it in imagination with Indians, seeking here and finding a summer home for their unrestrained supply of fish, shell-fish, birds' eggs, &c. In these sounds they had often "*wigwassed*" for sheep heads, of whom we learnt the art of *bobbing*, as even now practised successfully, with flaming torch at night.

The beach at this place is certainly *the best* along our coast, and to be so shut up on an island, makes every thing of sea character still more like sea-shore. The very desolation of the sands around us makes the table refreshments still more estimable by a feeling sense of contrast.

As we sail back to our boarding house, we notice many fish in the waters we traverse, such as we might have speared, if we had been so disposed, and had had the needful instruments.

Monday, August 17.—This begins a new epoch. Awake at five

o'clock, and found the wind fair at S. W. I determine therefore to try for Long branch by sea. I am taken off in the bay to Capt. Rogers' sloop Jane, loaded for New York, and near to the New Inlet We arrived at New York the next day with a delightful sail

"*Reminiscences of Philadelphia.*"

We here give an article from the pen of "Lang Syne," (often quoted in this work,) as a specimen of his manner and tact in giving subjects of by-gone days. It may serve to show to others, what they may imitate in the way of tales of olden time, from the use of the materials, so abundantly preserved in the foregoing pages. For the character of the writer, Mr. M'Koy, (now no more,) see page 182 of vol. i. of these Annals. On the present subject he says, to wit:

The contemplation, occasionally, by your reminiscent, of the astonishing increase in population, wealth and splendour, now exhibiting every where throughout our beloved city; its lengthened pavements and splendid buildings, very frequently cause a reversion of the mind, back upon the period when, on Monday mornings in particular, he crept lazily to school, stopping here and gazing there, upon the "moving panorama" around him. The images of characters then existing in the city, and the situation of things, are as palpable as was the "air drawn dagger" of Macbeth, but without the horror. They float upon the memory rather as "Thistle down moving," or the motes (sometimes mingled and convolved) discernible only in the sunbeam. Ere they vanish for ever, as the curling mist, or the flitting ghost at cock-crow, it is intended in this communication to collect a variety of them hastily together, in one groupe, so that those who have a relish for the modern antique, in by-gone days, may see them

"Come like shadows, so depart."

An elderly domestic in the Pancoast family, who always named himself Me Mo Michael Hans Muckle Weder, although moving in an humble sphere, his person and character were familiar to every inhabitant. When sent on an errand he could scarcely proceed a square in an hour, being continually surrounded by all sorts of people, some viewing him, and listening to him, and some asking him over again, the same question which had been asked a thousand times. Whether the question (repeated) came from the child or the man, he was sure to answer them, every one, with an unbroken smile, extending from cheek to cheek, (sans teeth,) with unwearied patience, idiotic simplicity, and an affectionate tone of voice. To astonish them, he sometimes changed his usual amiable appearance and expression of countenance, to a hideous frown and an awful squint; his two eyes gazing at each other, and his long tongue hissing like the serpent from between his boneless gums, causing the juvenile spectator to shrink away from the horrid sight, which was but for a moment—then resuming his usual benevolent smiling look, he would say, "that's the way to frighten the Indians, so it is." He claimed as sweethearts, all the fashionable unmarried young belles in the city. He had "fifty hundred, twenty hundred and sixteen" of them; and when any one of them married, he was sure to go the next day after the wedding, to claim his forfeit, always cheerfully given to him, which was a half crown, and a glass of punch from the lady's own hand, which, said he, was all the same, as though I married her myself.

A partially deranged, elderly, spectre-looking maiden lady, tall and thin, of the Friends' persuasion, named Leah, was somewhat remarkable from the circumstance, that she used sometimes to pass the night, wrapped in a blanket, between the graves of the Potter's field, (now Washington square,) for the benevolent purpose of frightening away "the doctors."

Collector Sharp Delany, in the front part of his family residence, transacted the whole custom house business of the port of Philadelphia, at the south-east corner of Walnut and Second streets, at present occupied by the Delaware Insurance Company.

George Baynton, a native of the city, was, without controversy, acknowledged to be the most admirable among the fashionable young gentlemen of his day—being of proper age and height, and of most astonishing beauty. "The beautiful Fatima," as described by Lady Wortley Montague, in her letters from Adrianople, and George Baynton, should have been brother and sister. Boys and men would turn and gaze after his splendid personal appearance—"many a bright eye fell beneath his glance," and followed his receding footseps with admiration. Fame had assigned to him all the bounties of nature, beyond the reach of art,—and every youthful manly grace, accompanied by the fascination of the serpent, towards the devoted fluttering bird. He deceased in the fever of 1793.

The uptown and the downtown boys, at this time, used to have, according to the streets, their regular night-battles, with sticks and stones, making the panes of glass to jingle on the pavement occasionally—but the appearance of Old Carlisle and the famous West, the constable, would scatter them into all the hiding places, peeping out from hole and corner, when the coast was clear.

The sign of the Three Jolly Irishmen, a tavern kept at the north-east corner of Race and Water streets, and whose locality ('twas said) was familiar in places across the ocean, used to be notorious throughout the city, as a primary resort of the "new comers," and at times, one continued scene and sound of daily riot, and night brawl, making it dangerous to meddle with them, even by course of law. A little old German watchman, who stood in his box hard by, his shoulders bending under the pressure of years, and his chin and nose almost in contact—on being foolishly applied to one night, and questioned why he did not go and quell the riot there, answered as follows—"Bless my soul, gentlemen—bless my soul, wass can I do wid dem."

White sand for floors, being at the time an important article of consumption, the old sand man, for the northern part of the city, was looked for the same as the milkman. For the amusement of his customers, on being requested so to do, he would send his horse onward, the length of the square, then call after him by his name, causing the horse, with the load of white sand, to turn about and come to him—he trolling the song of "White sand, ho!—a shilling a bush, *soft 'oder'* hard money."

Turkey carpets were spoken of, and only to be seen upon the floors of the first families for wealth. Parlour floors of very respectable people in business used to be "swept and garnished" every morning with sand sifted through a "sand sieve," and sometimes smoothed with a hair broom, into quaint circles and fancy wreaths, agreeably to the "genius for drawing" possessed by the chambermaid.

The Old Loganian Library, a one story brick building, shaped gable-end fashion in the front, stood solitary and alone, within a post and rail fence on the west side of Sixth street, midway between Chestnut and Walnut streets. Behind the house, and on the grass, the scholars belonging to the Quaker Academy, in Fourth street, used to have the regular "set to." Sometimes in the grapple, after being "brought to the scratch," the following exclamation might frequently be heard by one of the combatants—"Don't tear my shirt—tear my skin—but don't tear my shirt."

The Northern Liberties, about Camptown and Pegg's run, used to be in agitation almost every Saturday night, by the regular, irregular, tavern, rough-and-tumble, smash fighting, between the ship-carpenters, from Kensington, and the butchers from Spring Garden; the public authority not even attempting to hinder them.

A bank note at this time, signed by Thomas Willing, president, and countersigned by a long row of hieroglyphic, perpendicular hair-strokes, only discoverable by the close inspection of microscopic power, to be the name of Tench Francis, the cashier, was a kind of "caviar to the multitude," and not to be seen, as now-a-days, in the hands of every one. It used to be viewed as a thing totally different from the continental paper money—as something unfathomable and puzzling to the brains of people, in its very nature—it being considered as so much cash in gold and silver, to be had in a moment. The strength of the paper caused a *bet* to be made, that in its *material* it consisted of either silk or Russia sheeting; and that three of the notes twisted together would lift a fifty-six pound weight from the ground. On trial, the notes broke by the weight; a convulsive laughter ensued among the crowd. A consternation seized the owner of the notes, whether or not by having torn them, he would be able to recover their amount from the primitive national bank. There were three banks in the thirteen United States, at the time, and the banking system was spoken of as a great mystery, known only to the "great financier," Robert Morris, and the precious few. The number of banks at present distributed throughout the now twenty-four United States, being three hundred and sixty-five, the great mystery has been proportionably unraveled.

Persons living towards the Delaware, and speaking of the house, No. 322 Market street, (then standing by itself, above Ninth street,) by way of designating the distance, would say "away out at Marcoe's."

Story books for children consisted in Goody Two Shoes, Giles Gingerbread, Tom Thumb, Peter Pippin, and Robinson Crusoe abridged, all printed and published originally in St. Paul's Church Yard, London, by Carrington Bowles, and resold here at sixpence.

The people being numbered about this time, the population of the city, in round numbers, was said to be above 50,000; which act of numbering was supposed by many pious persons—speaking on the subject, after it had happened—to be the procuring cause of the judgment of *the fever*, with which the city was afterwards afflicted. Even, they said, as was the judgment of pestilence upon the Israelites, for numbering the people in David's time.

Continental Money.

It may interest many to see a brief notice of the history and progress of our continental money,—because so few of the present generation, have ever been rightly informed respecting its operations and details. It is in itself something, properly appertaining to an illustration of our chapter of "the War of Independence," and as such we here give it, to wit:

In June, 1775, was made the first emission of 2,000,000 of dollars. Before the close of that year, 3,000,000 more were issued. In May, 1776, 5,000,000 more were issued, in the autumn of that year 5,000,000 more, and in December, 5,000,000 more. Such frequent and large emissions began to reduce their value in the confidence of the people. In the mean time, the power of taxing was virtually denied to the Confederation. They could only *recommend* the measure to the states.

The whole amount issued during the war was 400,000,000 dollars! but the collections made by the continental government in various ways, cancelled from time to time about one half of it, so that the maximum of valuation at no time exceeded $200,000,000; nor did it reach that sum, until its depreciation had compelled congress to take it in, and pay it out at 40 dollars for one of specie.

It kept nearly at par for the first year; as it was then but about equal to the amount of specie held in all the colonies. But the quick succession of increase tended to depreciate it, till it reached

500 for 1, and finally 1000 for 1,—when it ceased to circulate for any value at all.

Congress, after a time, exchanged forty for one, by giving the holders loan office certificates *at par*, and had offered to redeem the whole in the same way at 1000 for 1 when it was down at that price! but as those loan office certificates had themselves gone down to 2*s*. 6*d*. on the pound, or eight dollars for one, very few were found to avail themselves of the offer. That was their misfortune, to have been so distrustful, or so needy!

Public securities of similar character, bearing various names, such as loan office certificates, depreciation certificates, final settlements &c., were also given to the public creditors, for services, supplies, &c., and thus constituted *the public debt* at the end of the war. All these were worth but eight for one, until the adoption of the present constitution in 1789, when they were funded and rose to par, and *thus made fortunes for many!*

The whole revolutionary debt, as estimated on the journal of Congress, the 29th April, 1783, *not including* the paper money, stood thus, viz.:

Foreign debt to France and Holland, at 4 per cent.,	$7,885,085
Domestic debt, in various certificates, as above,	34,115,290
At four and six per cent. interest,	$42,000,375

Making an interest of $2,415,958 per annum,

To the foregoing the Secretary of the Treasury afterwards added, for claims held by several of the States $21,500,000 and then *funded* the whole, putting a part on interest at six per cent., postponing another part without interest for ten years, and the remainder bearing an immediate interest at three per cent.

The foregoing, with arrears of six years of interest being added, and with some other unsettled claims, made the whole debt amount to ninety four millions, which soon went up to par!

The statesmen of the Revolution were well disposed to pay their paper obligations, and alleged, that they also had the ability to do so: but against these, stood the inability of the people to pursue the profitable employments of peaceable times, and therefore their inability to pay taxes, even if the Congress had had the power to impose them. They could only *recommend* the measure to the States. They had all agreed at one time to exact an impost of 5 per cent., on all imported goods, but Rhode Island resisted the measure to the last, and without *unanimity* it could not be adopted!

The campaign of 1778 and '79, with an army of thirty to forty thousand men, was sustained by emissions of paper money to the amount of 135,000,000, of dollars. Thus "making it by wagon loads!" In the same time, the amount of specie received into the public Treasury was but 151,666 dollars, a weight but about a ton of coal if all put into a cart for its carriage!

It has been said that so great a sinking of paper money, was not so injuriously felt among the people as might be imagined;—and it has been reasoned thus, viz.: The largest sum by which they could have been affected, might be estimated at 300,000,000 at 20 for one, which is only half of the rate fixed by Congress. This would give 15,000,000 of sound money; and this, having been a currency for six years, gives an annual average of 2,500,000; which, to a population of 3,000,000, would make, in point of fact, a poll tax of but about one dollar to each; or if they be estimated by families of six persons each, would be an annual loss, to such severally, of but five dollars each! So easy it is by figures to diminish losses, which *we* of the present generation have never felt! Yet it was a painful and onerous loss to our forefathers, now all gone beyond its influence!

Those who are minutely curious on this matter may consult, with profit, a late paper in the proceedings of the Philosophical Society of Philadelphia, by Samuel Breck, Esq.

Fort Allen.

It was near to Lehighton that the fort once stood, fronting on the Lehigh, opposite to the mouth of Mahony creek. There the garrison (while some of them were out skating) was surprised and massacred by Indians. Nothing now remains of it but its deep well. About the same time, Captain Wetherhold, who commanded a scouting party, and who used to make Allentown and Bethlehem his place of rendezvous, was surprised, about six miles from the latter place, and himself and whole party shot and scalped. On the same day, a party, with one Henry Jenks, was also surprised and cut off.

Indian Settlement—Inland.

The Indian hunter here his shelter found;
Here cut his bow and shaped his arrows true,
Here built his wigwam, and his bark canoe,
Speared the quick salmon leaping up the fall,
And slew the deer without the rifle ball.

Here his young squaw her cradling tree would choose,
Singing her chant, to hush her swart pappoose;
Here stain her quills, and string her trinkets rude,
And weave her warrior's wampum in the wood.

No more shall they thy welcome waters bless,
No more their forms thy moonlit banks shall press;
No more be heard, from mountain or from grove,
His whoops of slaughter, or her song of love.

Spinning Wheels and Looms.

These wheels are now so out of fashion and use, as hardly to be known by their names, among the modern city belles, as former articles of household thrift. They must, therefore, be told, that the first is the name of an old fashioned piano with one string and one melody—the other was a big house-organ with but few stops. They sometimes joined their melodies and sung, most cheerily, airs of olden time, like these, viz.: "The diligent hand maketh rich." "She provideth both wool and flax." "She stayeth at home," &c.

Battle of Germantown—Incidents.

Lieutenant Whitman, of Reading, was left on the field, supposed to be killed, or mortally wounded. After a while, he made out to crawl on hands and knees, to the second house, on south side, in Washington lane. There he was sheltered by the resident, and was visited by Doctor Witt, who soon pronounced his case incurable; but at the earnest begging of the lieutenant, he continued to try to save his life. He recovered surprisingly for a time, when a British officer coming to hear of him, he made him and his host both prisoners. While so held, Lieutenant Whitman found a chance to get to speak with Major Andre, who procured him a release. He then went to live with Mr. Hergesheimer, where he was nursed and fed, till the time of the retreat or withdrawal of the British from Germantown. While he was there hiding himself, for fear of a second capture, the American horse appeared, when he claimed their help and protection. Just then, they captured a country *Friend* coming in to sell butter to the British; and as his punishment, they made him take up Lieutenant Whitman, in his chair, to Reading. He lived many years afterwards.

Battle of Germantown, as stated by General Wilkinson.

General Wayne, who was in the battle and led the first onset along the main street, writes afterwards from White Marsh, on 21st November, 1777, to General Gates, (vide Wilkinson's Memoirs,) and says, "At Germantown, fortune smiled on our arms for *full three hours;* the enemy were broken, dispersed, and flying in all quarters; we were in possession of their whole encampment, together with their artillery park, &c. A wind-mill attack was made on a house into which six light companies had thrown themselves *to avoid our bayonets;* this gave the enemy time to rally; our troops were deceived by the attack, taking it for something formidable, they *fell back* to assist in what they deemed a serious affair; the enemy finding themselves no further pursued, and believing it to be a *retreat*, followed; confusion ensued, and we *ranaway* from the arms of victory *really open* to receive us. We shall be therefore obliged to leave Mr. Howe to his occupancy of easy winter quarters, whilst we shall be reduced to the hard necessity of making a winter campaign *in the open field* with naked troops. But I do not despair; if our worthy general will but follow his own good judgment, without listening too much *to some counsel.*"

General Wilkinson, in his Memoirs, gives his facts concerning the disposition of the troops, vol. 1, page 351. He says:—"When he visited the camp at Whitemarsh, the battle of Germantown was then the prevailing topic and conversation; and there were *many versions* and *opinions* of the same, and much too many censures by subalterns, who could not know the facts which governed the conduct of their superiors and themselves. Some charging it to the tardy movements of the left; others to defective vigour on the right; but those who had been most warmly engaged, ascribed it to the halt at Chew's house, which was imputed to the counsellors of the commander-in-chief, among whom I perceived, that General Greene was the most prominent object of jealousy, and yet a gentleman well able to advise and most efficient to act, and positively the first captain of his day, a most worthy pupil of Washington too."

He gives General Armstrong's letter to General Gates, from the Trapp, of 9th October, 1777, saying:—"The British were encamped chiefly at Germantown, and the foreigners principally betwixt the Falls of Schuylkill and John Van Deering's mill. We *could not* take off, (as was designed,) but beat the enemy's pickets, so that *the surprise* was not total, but *partial.* We attacked at the head of Germantown with vigour, and *drove* the British, who frequently *rallied*, and were *drove again and again*, about the space of *two miles*, when some *unhappy spirit of infatuation* seized our troops almost universally, whereby they began to retreat and fled *in wild disorder*, without orders from the general, and beyond *his power to prevent.* [Note.—Colonel Forrest told me, it was caused by our drummers striking a beat for *a parley* at Chew's house, which was understood by the men to mean a *retreat*, and that nothing could correct it.] So that a glorious victory already *eight tenths won*, was *shamefully* and *mysteriously* lost; for none *now can* give any *good reason* for the flight! The *conjectures* are these—the morning was foggy, and so far, unfavourable. It is said our men took the manœuvres of part of our people for large reinforcements of the enemy, and thereby took fright at themselves or at one another! Some unhappy officer is said to have called out *we are surrounded!* The enemy, in their flight, a part of them, took into a church, and a large body into Mr. Chew's house, where we made an ill-judged delay. There was a flag sent in and insulted, and the bearer (Lieutenant Smith) was wounded. My destiny was against the foreigners, rather to divert them with the militia, than to fight their superior body, which we did, until the general, seeing his men retreat, *sent for me*, with the division. I followed a slow cannonade several miles, but found him not—then fell in the rear of the enemy, still supposing them a vanquished party, and *that we had victory.* We gave them a brush; but their artillery, well directed, soon obliged us to file off, near *two hours* after our troops had left the field. I lost but *three* and nine were wounded."

General A. St. Clair, writes from Whitemarsh, November 21, 1777, to General Gates, saying:—"The battle happened in his absence. There was *strange* mismanagement, and it *has produced infinite court martials*, and made us dread the *superiority* of the British *discipline*, which gives me much concern. It is melancholy *that Congress*, so lately so august, so truly venerable, should in so short time be so visibly altered. Certainly we much need *reform in these matters!*"

General Wilkinson gives us sundry facts of the arrangement of the battle, and disposition of the troops, most of which he learned from Colonel Forrest, who confirmed several facts, and with whom he travelled over the localities and made his observations and reflections, at the time he was in Germantown, in 1815–16, writing and publishing his Memoirs. They are to this effect, to wit:

The main body of the British occupied ground nearly at right angles with the main street. The *front* line on the school-house lane to the west, and the church lane (its opposite) to the east. The park was in the area, south of the market-house, and fronting the house of David Deshler, [now S. B. Morris',] in which General Howe had his quarters. The *second* line formed a parallel, at about one-fourth of a mile in the rear, and flanking the road near the old six-mile stone, before the door of H. Conyngham, Esq. The *advanced* body, consisting of the second battalion of British light infantry, with a field train, occupied the height in front of Beggarstown, [Bonsall's place,] on the left of the road, and at two miles advance from the main body, with an out-lying picket at Mount Airy. The 40th regiment, commanded by Colonel Musgrave, was in a field, eastward of Chew's house.

The Americans marched all night, in a dark atmosphere, having as an advanced patrole, the horse of Captain Allen M'Lane, who attempted to surprise their picket, but fell in with double centries, whom he killed, with the loss of one man, and soon after routed the guard.

The surprise was complete, and *Wayne's* brigade *commenced the action* with the British light infantry, who resisted manfully, but were forced to retire, leaving their artillery on the ground; but preserving some order in their retreat, and making a scattering fire as they fell back. Colonel Musgrave's regiment, being soon after attacked, retired into Chew's house. In the mean time, General Wayne pressed the retreating light infantry, and *continued* to overthrow every thing in his way. Our men, as is common with raw troops, expended their ammunition lavishly, soon run short, and sent to the rear for a supply. General Washington, with General Sullivan, and the troops who followed Wayne, having reached Chew's house, from which Musgrave was delivering a random fire, from the upper windows, at the corps passing on the road, who might be heard, *but not seen*, because of the distance of the house and the density of the fog, called a consultation, (as he understood,) when it was determined to attack the house, a measure which caused a halt of the centre column; but having no effect on those approaching on the right and left. It was reported that Colonel Laurens, an aid of General Washington's, attempted with a party to force the main door, through which the party within shot out many bullets. About same time, Major White, aid to Sullivan, got mortally wounded by a shot from the cellar window, in his attempt to fire a window shutter. These attacks being withdrawn, because of the severity of the resistance, a parley was ordered to be beaten, when Captain Smith, of the Virginia line, got shot as he was advancing with a flag to demand a surrender.

General Wayne, in the mean time, continued to pursue the retreating enemy. General Armstrong was engaged with the Hessians near the Schuylkill, and a part of General Green's column had reached the church lane, and met the right wing of the enemy's front line. At this time Colonel Stewart, with his regiment, and Colonel Matthews, with the 9th Virginia regiment, got warmly engaged, though not in concert, and were soon overpowered. Stewart made good his retreat, and Colonel Matthews, with his corps, were made prisoners.

During these operations, Lord Cornwallis was advancing rapidly from the city with the grenadiers, and the left wing of the British front line had got in motion, under Generals Gray and Agnew.

At this time, the front of the American troops had nearly reached the market-house, [midway of the town,] when hearing *the parley* in the rear, and mistaking it for *the retreat*, some one cried out, "they beat the retreat,"—when the exclamation spread like wild fire—a sudden panic ensued, and troops which had met with *no check*, fled in wild disorder, in spite of the exertions of their officers to rally them!* The fog still continued heavy, and the left column had become entangled, and was falling back, and the right had made no impression. Captain Forrest, then of the artillery, was, before the time of beating the parley, setting off from General Knox to the front, to say the ammunition wagons were at hand, and had nearly got up with the front, when the beat was made, and the consequences followed under his own immediate observation.

General Agnew was not killed in the general action, but had come with his brigade from the left wing to give *his support*, when our troops gave way, and while advancing at the head of his column, he was shot down by one of some lurking party.

Finally, had Washington pressed forward with the centre, fatigued, and exhausted of ammunition, he would have come into contact with the *main body* of the enemy, fresh for action—against a force of 10,000; and it cannot but be feared, that he must have met with a still greater disaster. On the whole, it must be regarded, evil as it seemed to have been, another manifestation of the Divine Providence in behalf of these states.

---

* He notices such panics, as occurrences, happening to the best troops, such as those in the battle of Friedlingen under Villars, &c.

Adventures of a "Collector," and Reminiscences of the Year 1800

Young persons engaged in commercial trade, have little or no conception of the changes which have been effected in their pursuits, since the short period of forty years. To illustrate something of what we mean, we propose to give some facts of the incidents which usually befel, at the time mentioned, those young clerks and apprentices in the dry-goods trade,—y'clept "collectors."—To give the picture of one such, we shall draw from our recollections of one who was our cotemporary.

At the beginning of this century (the year 1800) this friend of ours was still "a 'prentice hand" with one of the six or eight *only* great notables in the city of Philadelphia, in the dry-goods importing way. They consisted of Fries, Chancellor, Wistar, and Ashton, in High street; and of Field, Thompson, Hartshorne, and Large, in Front street. All beside these were comprised in the little world of small dealers below them. At that time, all their remittances from the West, came in, in "hard dollars," and were generally carried, after their arrival, to banks for deposit, like the iron money of Lycurgus, in wheel-barrows! These large dealers had their regular seasons of country collection, in mid-winter and in mid-summer. 'Twas in the former season that my friend once started from Philadelphia, to go to Harrisburg and Carlisle to the westward, and round about to Virginia and home, as collector of one of the houses before named. He was mounted on horseback, wrapped up in a great Fearnought over-coat, his legs and feet muffled up in woollen "leggins and over-shoes." It was a mild time for the season, and so mild that the frost was out of the ground, and the roads were bad beyond the conception of the present race of travellers. For instance, we have known it to be a fact, that four hours have been consumed in going by the road from Philadelphia to Germantown, the saddle or team-horse sinking to the knees and deeper in many places, before the turnpike was made. At the hill at Germantown, it was much steeper than now, and so narrow as to admit of but one carriage at a time. It was even the practice of the stage to cause its passengers to get out and walk up the hill; and all wagoners used to stop and unite their teams to draw up loaded wagons, both there, and also at the hill at Norris' place nearer the city.

Our collector had been carefully forewarned to keep a good lookout for *the ripples* at "the fording places;" for then, be it remarked, we had few or none of our present good bridges. When he got near to Harrisburg, having forded the Swatara, by the course of its *ripple*, he met with an old customer in the form of an elderly widow, who had just got a young husband, in the person of a German musician. The lady was extremely afraid of fording, and as our young traveller had now acquired some skill therein, he offered to lead the way, if they would follow in their old fashioned chair. The offer was accepted, and they went on very well until about the middle of the stream, when lo! the horse which had been but imperfectly tied at the collar, actually walked out of his gears, drawing out the wedded groom by the reins into the water, and letting down the shafts! thus leaving the lonely lady screaming with fright, with her feet under the water in her chair! In the mean time the big trunk of merchandise, which had been set up in the forepart of the chair, was floating down the ebbing stream. Time and money were lost to procure assistance to regain the trunk, and to draw out the lady and the chair!

Harrisburg, at which he next arrived, was a rough and rude affair. compared with its present improvement and enlargement. The crossing of the Susquehanna, at the then "Harris' ford and ferry," was *occasionally* a terrible affair. He had actually to remain there *nine days* to get even a chance to pass over amidst the driving ice. When he did start, the boat, which had twenty inches of ice frozen to its bottom, became an unmanageable clump among the floating masses, and drove down the stream some miles, before they could effect their landing. Now, the same river is traversed by a grand bridge in two divisions, making an entire mile in length! It ought to be remembered, that at this time there were no bridges in all the route to the West!

Carlisle was then chiefly remarkable for its rigid religious feelings, and especially in its deep silence in the streets and at the inns on the Sabbath. The Scotch Presbyterians then had all the sway to themselves.

On one occasion of travelling beyond Carlisle, the passage of the Yellowbreeches' creek was so swollen as to stop the passengers for a couple of days. He at length procured a man, who, for the consideration of four dollars, contrived to set him over at a place above the ford. He used a canoe to which he tied and swam the horse; he then took off the wheels and the body of the sulkey, and ferried them over separately.

Sometimes these tours extended to the "far West," and at other times through the western parts of Virginia and North Carolina. As there were then no stages and no banks inland, there were of course no means of remittances, and, therefore, *the collectors* were expected to call generally upon their customers. When they had succeeded to gather their silver in quantities, they bought pack-horses to serve as their carriers; each horse taking bags containing two thousand dollars, placed upon little wooden-formed saddles, much in the shape of a sawyer's wood-horse and set upon the horses' backs. These horses when they arrived at Philadelphia were sold. It was in this way of horse-back travelling, you could sometimes see officers of the Western army "coming into the settlements," as they called it, even on to Philadelphia. In this way of travelling, we can well remember, when, about the same time, the present *Philip, king of France*, rode out High street, with his young brothers, as explorers and visiters of the Western regions.

We might justly be surprised, *now*, to contemplate a young man, quite alone, with his half a dozen horses laden with silver, travelling the lonely wilds of our woods and the rugged heights of our Alleghanies, unmolested by robbers, and almost without fear! No accidents then occurred, for surely men were less enured to crime. The pack-horses used to be severally unladen at nights, and the silver carried into the traveller's bed-room, in the low log-house inn. The collector had indeed his pistols; but what were they to the power of the landlord and his friends, if they had been evil disposed! The money was, however, a serious charge, and we could, if we had room, give some amusing anecdotes of false alarms.

Such facts, so recent in our history, should not be forgotten by those who now enjoy such remarkable improvements in our transportation conveyances, by steamers, railroads, and comfortable coaches drawn upon turnpikes.

The Revolutionary Navy.

The Revolution was begun without a single armed vessel. In 1775, Rhode Island *began* by fitting out two small schooners to defend the coasting trade, and Connecticut had *also* two small vessels for the same object. Rhode Island was the first to recommend *to congress* the formation of a naval force; and in December, 1775, congress commissioned several vessels—say thirteen in number, and thus *commenced* our gallant little navy. In the spring of 1776, Massachusetts fitted out several armed vessels, the white flag of which bore a figure of a pine, or liberty tree, with the motto, "We appeal to Heaven." The first naval battle took place about three weeks after the battle of Lexington; and a Captain *Wheaton* was the first to cause *the striking* of the British flag on the ocean. At the time of this early career on the sea, General Washington undertook to get up and send to sea an expedition of six vessels, and was obliged in his instructions to address them *as a part of the army*. This because no congressional laws then existed for the creation of the navy.

At this early period of our naval enterprise, the middle and more southern states seem to have started with the device of the rattlesnake, on their flag. The earliest vessels seen of the Virginia outfit, at Norfolk and Hampton roads, contained thirteen stripes, and a rattlesnake in its coil with head and tail erect, and thirteen rattles—with the motto, "Don't tread on me." *

The earliest frigate, from Philadelphia, the Alfred, Captain Hopkins, of which Paul Jones, was lieutenant, showed a flag of thirteen stripes of red and blue, with a rattlesnake, in a running attitude, with mouth open and sting projected, under it the motto—"Don't tread on me." That same flag, says Sherburne, in his Life of Jones, was borne by the Alliance frigate, under Paul Jones, when she dashed through a British fleet of twenty-one sail of war-vessels in the North sea, receiving their fire and making her escape.

* It is commended by the London Morning Chronicle, of 25 July, 1776.

Memoranda from Lewis Evans' Journey in 1743, *going from Philadelphia by the Schuylkill and Susquehanna, to Lake Ontario, to wit.*

About 24 miles west of the wagon ford, is the passage through the first ridge of the Kittocktinny Mountains, (since Blue Mountains.) From the top of this pass we have a view of the vale ten miles across, varied here and there with swelling hills, looking at a distance like cleared land, but are covered with dwarf oaks, about shoulder high, and bearing acorns, or the best gall-nuts of any we have. Count Zinzendorf gave to this vale the name of St. Anthony's Wilderness, and designs, as Mr. Conrad Weiser tells me, to bring over some Germans to settle it. The soil is but poor and ordinary, except on the Swatara, and there is at present *no practicable* road over the mountain by which the vale may communicate with the settled part of the province. [The foregoing description must apply to Schuylkill county generally.] He speaks of a settlement of Indians, five families of Delawares, at the confluence of the two branches of the Swatara;—marking the place since Jones Town, on the main road to Harrisburg. [How things are since altered.—The Wilderness of St. Anthony is no more such, but is now "a beautiful and variegated valley above the Kittatinny Mountain," which mountain stretches from the junction of the Susquehanna and Juniata rivers, over Dauphin, Schuylkill, and Northampton counties.]

Shamokin (now Sunbury) is called *an Indian town* of Delawares, who have their groups of wigwams pretty near together, and many more scattered here and there over a very fruitful spot of ground of about 800 acres.

Early travelling in Pennsylvania, inland, 1762.

Heckewelder tells us of his travel from Litiz (Lancaster) with C. F. Post and others, to the Indians at Muskingum. They started on horseback, singing a hymn. Their going so far was deemed perilous. Put up first night at Middletown; next day crossed the Susquehanna at Harris's ferry; the river was risen fearfully by the melting of much snow, the ferrymen feared to cross; at length they got over, but were carried down the stream two miles by the rapid current. Stopped at Carlisle to meet and talk with Indians; in two days reached Shippensburg, where they saw the *last* of the white settlements. Then came the howling wilderness, and every where they saw the blackened ruins of former houses and barns, and remains of chimnies, the sad memorials of French and Indian devastations in the war of 1756, and after, of which they heard many horrid recitals from eye-witnesses. Eleven miles beyond Shippensburg, Post struck into a mountain path, as a much shorter route than by the wagon road. The path was hardly discernible, and the ascent steep and rocky. After a travel of several days, they arrived at the Juniata crossings, incurring much danger over the rapid stream. Soon after they passed "Bloody Run," where a body of soldiers conveying provisions to Fort Pitt, had been surprised and killed. Seven miles further, they came to Fort Bedford, where was a strong garrison. On the 30th March they began to cross the Alleghany mountains; then the ground was covered with snow 3½ feet deep. Saw there many carcases of horses scattered along the mountain path, more snow was falling, and they feared to be covered with it; after a painful ride, they gained the summit of the mountain. At last, after a hard day's journey, they came to the cabin of a hunter (Jack Miller) in Edmond's swamp. As soon as nightfall the wolves came round and began their dismal howl, *the night music* of the place, all the year round. Miller (called "Fancy Jack") had no stable, and to guard the horses from the wolves, ward and watch was kept up all the night by the hunter and his sons. In the morning they started and soon reached Stony Creek, where the small steam was too swollen to be crossed. The small garrison, and the few settlers were on the other side. In time a *Sugar trough* was brought from the woods, and they ferried over, but their horses narrowly escaped destruction. Afterwards they crossed Laurel Hill and Chestnut Ridge, and reached Bushy Run on the 1st April, from whence they pushed on diligently to go 25 miles to Fort Pitt, before night. When within seven or eight miles of that Fort, they found themselves on Braddock's field, known as the place of action on the 9th July, 1755, by the dreadful sight of so many scattered skulls and bones of the slain, which lay so thickly around, as to be continually stricken by the hoofs of their horses and awaking dismal recollections of the slain. At length they reached the Fort, and were once more among their fellow men. The then only private dwelling was at the point, owned by two traders, Davenport and McKinney, who received them into their house with the most friendly hospitality. In the command of the Fort, was Colonel Bouquet, who, with his officers, treated them with much civility.

[Such as the preceding, was the nature, toil, and exposure of an inland travel, in 1762, and for several years afterwards. It is something now, to be thus informed by actual travellers, what was once the rough and wilderness state of a country, since so settled, productive and flourishing!]

Western Pioneers, as recollected by Rev. Mr. Doddridge.

The first settlements along the Monongahela, commenced by his father, with others, was in 1772. In 1773, they extended even to the Ohio. First settlers came mostly from Maryland and Virginia; they generally went by the route of Braddock's TRAIL,

Some which went from Pennsylvania, went by the military road, *via* Bedford and Ligonier. Their removals were generally on horses with pack-saddles. Settlement entitled men to land, 400 acres free. They called the same "Tomahawk's rights," because with it they barked and deadened the trees around their bounds of location. They usually chose grounds having a hollow for the house and barn, and the hills near, making them as settled in a basin, intending thereby that "whatever comes to the house, comes down hill."

Usually, settlers came in the Spring, the male part only, and after clearing and planting corn, &c., went back for their families, and brought them out in the Fall. Small families came out at once in the Spring. They depended much on lean venizon and wild turkeys, and often the flesh of the bear. Anxiously they looked out for the first growth of the potatoes, pumpkins, squashes, &c. When the young corn came it was a perfect jubilee to use them for roasting ears, and afterwards when hardened by age, to grate them on a tin grater for "Johnny Cakes." (Journey cakes.)

At this time, the settlers lived in peace with the Indians, but in the year of 1774, all was brought into confusion and peril by the war of Lord Dunmore, all brought on by the atrocious murder of the peaceable, inoffensive Indians at Captina, and Yellow Creek. They had, in consequence to move the women and children into Fort, wherein they had small hovels; the men, in the mean time, had to risk the knife and tomahawk, in occasional attention to their fields, to guard their families from eventual starvation.

These original settlers had to be their own mechanics, for all which they needed. The hommony block and hand-mills were found in most of their houses. The block was hollowed out at top by burning, and the play of the pestle ground the corn. Sometimes they used the sweep of 16 feet to lessen the toil, in pounding corn into meal for cakes and mush. At some places where they had saltpetre caves, they made their own gunpowder by means of those sweeps and mortars. In making meal, they also used a domestic contrivance called a grater; it was a plate of roughly perforated tin, on which they grated their grain. The hand mill was another and a better contrivance, made with two circular stones, the under one being the bed stone, and the upper one the runner. These were placed to run in a wide hoop or band, with a spout for discharging the meal; the runner was moved by a staff passed through an upright affixed in the runner. Such mills are still used in the Holy Land, as alluded to by our Saviour, when he said "two women shall be grinding at a mill." &c.

Their water-mills were tub-mills, made readily with little expense, consisting of an upright shaft, at the lower end of which a wheel of 4 or 5 feet was attached, the upper end passed through the bed stone and carried the runner in the manner of a trundle-head. Sifters were used in lieu of bolting cloths, and were made of deerskins as a parchment, stretched over a hoop and pierced with holes made with hot wire.

As to their clothing, it was spun by women in every house; almost every woman could weave their linsey-woolsey and make the clothes.

Every family tanned their own leather; their tan vat was a large trough sunk in the ground; bark was shaved and pounded, ashes were used in place of lime, for taking off the hair. Bear's and hog's lard and tallow, answered in place of fish oil. The currying was done with a drawing-knife; the blacking was made of soot and hog's lard.

Most families had their own tailors and shoemakers; those who could not make shoes could make shoe packs, made like moccasons, of single pieces of leather, save the tongue-piece, on the top of the foot, all was fitted by gathering stitches. They made ploughs of wood, harrows with wooden teeth, they also made their own cooper ware of staves. Some who could not do some of these things for themselves, gave their labor to those who could, and so all were profited and mutually accommodated. Rough times indeed!

For a long time after the first settlement of the country the inhabitants married young. There was no distinction of rank, and very little of fortune; on these accounts the first loves resulted in marriage; and a family establishment cost but a little labor, nothing else. Marriages were celebrated at the house of the bride, and the incidents were usually these, viz.: It created a general sensation, it was looked to by all, old and young, as occasion for frolic and fun, and being almost the only means of producing a gathering, except where labor was required, such as reaping, log-rolling, house building, or campaigning; they went to it with double zest. The groom party started from the house of the father early, so as to reach the house of the bride by noon, the intended time of marriage,—for it was always to precede the dinner. The company there assembled being frontier people, without a store, tailor, or mantuamaker within a hundred miles, came dressed accordingly. The gentlemen were dressed in shoe-packs, moccasons, leather breeches, leggins, linsey hunting shirts, and all home-made. The ladies dressed in linsey petticoats, and linsey or linen bedgowns, coarse shoes, stockings, handkerchiefs, and buckskin gloves, if any. The horses were caparisoned with old saddles, old bridles or halters, and pack-saddles, with a bag or blankets thrown over them; a rope or string was the usual girth. The procession march on such an occasion was intended to be in double file, where the horse paths, for they had no roads, would permit. Such paths were occasionally interrupted by fallen trees.

and sometimes so done from mischief, and by interlocking grape vines and sapplings to frustrate the company. Sometimes a posse of neighbors would be resting in ambush to fire a *feu de joie*, so as to cover the party with smoke, and to create surprise and shrieks among the riding ladies, and the chivalrous bustle of their partners. If some got a sprain, they bound it up with their handkerchief, and cared little more about it; they had no doctors to help them, nor to help consume their gains. As the procession neared the house of the bride, it would sometimes occur that two young men would start on horseback, full tilt, to win the bottle of whiskey, which, it was previously understood, would be hung out for the gain of the first arrival. The start was announced, by an Indian yell; the more the route was encumbered by logs, brush, muddy hollows, &c., the better for the rival parties to show their horsemanship. The bottle gained, the winner returns to the party, and first hands it to the groom, and thence it goes on from one to another, giving each their draught of a dram, the ladies included.

For the repast of such a party, the table, made of a large slab of timber hewn out with a broad-axe, and set on four sticks, was spread with beef, pork, fowls, and sometimes deer and bear meat. There might be some old pewter dishes and plates, but the rest were wooden bowls and trenchers. A few pewter spoons were to be seen, but the most of them were made ot horns. If knives were scarce, the deficiency was made up by using their scalping knives, taken from the belts of their hunting shirts.

After dinner dancing commenced, and usually lasted till the next morning. The figures were reels, or square sets, and jigs. The commencement was always a square four, which was followed by what was called jigging it off; none were allowed to steal away to get sleep, and if girls got tired, they were expected, for want of chairs, to sit upon the knees of the gentlemen.

At 9 or 10 o'clock at night, some of the young ladies would steal off the bride. That was sometimes to a loft, above the dancers, going there by a ladder; and such a bride's chamber, was floored with clap boards, lying loose and without nails. Some young men, in mean time, stole off the groom to his bride. At a later period, they sent them up refreshments, of which *black Betty*, so called, was an essential part, as she stood, in their parlance, for a bottle of whiskey.

Such entertainments sometimes lasted for several days, none giving over till fully fagged down. If any neighbors felt themselves slighted, by not being invited, it would sometimes occur, that such would show their presence by cutting off the manes, foretops, and even tails of the horses belonging to the wedding party, everything being rude, like the regions which surrounded them! All those scenes and all those kinds of people have passed away.

First Western Settlements.

Wm. Darby, speaking of his early recollections of Pittsburg, and the adjacent country, (beginning 25 years after Braddock's defeat,) after speaking of his wonderment at the changes effected in 55 years of absence, says, that the Indians were before his time, most clustered about that vicinity. That it was there that Shingas, King of the Delawares, occupied the spot chosen by Washington as the agent, for the site of a post for the Ohio Company. The other part of the proximate country was inhabited by the Mingoes and Shawanoes. When the French were obliged to abandon their position at the forks of the Ohio, the greater part of the Indians moved further west; so that when settlements first began to be made there by the Whites from Virginia and Pennsylvania, the whole country was an unsettled wilderness. It was between the years 1735, and '50, that the Whites passed and seated themselves "few and far between," beyond the Blue Ridge. The oldest town in the Great Valley, is Winchester, Va., which had probably been an Indian village before. It was a trading station as early as 1730; Hagerstown was also another out-trading post. Salt at that time was worth $5 per bushel to frontier people, and the difficulty of getting it continued for 30 years afterwards. The great era of Western settlement began in 1752, under the auspices of Gov. Dinwiddie; it was he that gave the impulse and encouragement westward, extending from Wyoming in Pennsylvania, to Holstein river in Virginia. In Virginia, the Alleghany was not passed by the settlers until 1749, when some isolated habitations were formed in the Green Brier county. In 1750, Christopher Gist was sent out by the Ohio Company, with instructions to examine the country, and to report the practicability of settlements along the Ohio river, and thence down to the Falls of Ohio. He made his journey up the Potomac, thence up the valley to where Fort Cumberland was afterwards made; thence to the Franktown on a branch of the Juniata, thence to Loyalhannon, and thence out to the Ohio, at the Forks. When he got to Muskingum, he saw the King's colours there hoisted, and George Croghan (Indian trader) at the head of the few Whites found there, and holding a council with the Indians. It was from Winchester, Va., that Thos. Merlin and John Salling undertook a journey of discovery up the Great Valley. They went as far as the head of the Roanoke, where Salling was captured by the Cherokees, and carried to the present Tennessee; from thence he escaped in a hunting excursion in Kentucky. At his return home, *via* New Orleans to Williamsburg, he gave such fascinating accounts of the fine lands seen that he inspired John Lewis and John Mackay to accompany him westward. Lewis made his settlement near the present

Taunton, and gave his name to Lewis creek, a branch of James river; and Mackay fixed himself (where his dèscendants now reside,) in the Forks of the Shenandoah. At that time their hunters could find buffaloes to kill, now no longer seen.

First Settlers of New Jersey.

Of the first settlement of Newton township, old *Thos. Sharp*, a friend, has left a quaint account, to wit: Let it be remembered, that it having wrought upon ye minds of some friends that *dwelt in Ireland*, but such as came thither (there?) *from England*, and a pressure being laid upon them for some years, from which they could not remove until *they gave up* to leave their friends and relatives there, with their comfortable subsistence, to transport themselves and families into this wilderness. In order thereto, they sent *from Dublin* in Ireland, to one Thomas Lurtin, a friend in London, commander of a pink, who came and made his agreement to transport them into *New Jersey*, viz: Mark Newby, Thomas Thackara, William Bate, George Goldsmith, and Thomas Sharp, (the writer) then a young man and single. But while the ship lay at Dublin, Thomas Lurtin getting sick, remained behind, and put the command under his mate, John Daggar, who set sail the 19th 9th mo., 1681, and arrived at *Elsinburg* in Salem Co., upon the 19th 11th mo., (two months) following, where they were well entertained at the houses of the *Thompsons*, who had before gone from Ireland in 1677. [The time of the first Thomas Watson.] These had attained to very good living by their industry. From there, we went to Salem, where were several houses that were *vacant* of persons who had left the town to settle in the country. In these we resided for the winter, which proved to be moderate. At Wickacoa (Philadelphia) we purchased a boat of the Swansons [sons of Sven the Swede] and so went to Burlington to the Commissioners, of whom we obtained a warrant of survey, from the then Surveyor General, Daniel Leeds. Then, after some considerable search to and fro in what was then called *the third* of *Irish* tenth, we at last pitched upon the place then called Newton, [up Newton creek, and now gone,] which was *before* the settlement of Philadelphia. In the Spring of 1682 we all removed from Salem, together with Robert Zane, who had before come with the Thompsons, and was also *expecting* us. So we began then our settlement; and although we were at times pretty hard bestead, having all our provisions as far as Salem, *to fetch by water*, yet through mercy of God, we were preserved in health, and from any extreme difficulty. A meeting was immediately set up at the house of Mark Newby,*

* This Newby brought out many half-pence of 1680, which were called *Patrick* money, and some of them are now preserved by Joseph O. Cooper in Newton.

and in a short time it grew and increased—unto which Wm. Cooper and family that lived at the Poynte, resorted; and sometimes the meeting was kept at his house, where he had been settled some time before. We had then zeal and fervency of spirit, although we had some dread of the Indians as a salvage people, nevertheless, ye Lord turned them to be serviceable to us, and *to be very loving* and kinde. Let then the rising generation consider that the settlement of this country was directed *upon an impulse*, by the spirit of God's people; not so much for their ease and tranquillity, *as for their posterity*, and that the wilderness being planted with *a good seed*, might grow and increase. But should not these purposes of the good husbandman come to pass, then they themselves shall suffer loss. These facts I have thought good thus *to leave behind*, as one having had knowledge of these things *from the beginning*.*

[The aforesaid Thomas Sharp was a surveyor and clerk of court, the same who laid out and surveyed the old "Town of Gloucester," and so called at the time, (1689,) and the place previously Hermaomissing and Arwames by the Indians, and Nassau by the Dutch and Swedes. There was once there a chalybeate spring, much visited by Philadelphians, where they also regaled on strawberries.]

"At yon salubrious fount to sip,
Immured in darksome shade,
Around whose sides magnolias bloom,
Whose silver blossoms deck the gloom,
And scent the spicy glade."

[Vide Rev. Nathaniel Evans' poems.

Thomas Sharp's name is often seen in Isaac Mickle's Reminiscences of Old Gloucester, (an interesting little work.) It was from this family of Sharps, that we have derived the Elsinborough grape, near Salem.

Becket's notices of Lewis Town and the adjacent country of Delaware as done from 1727 *to* 1743.

Having been favored in the year 1838 to peruse a MS. book of 190 pages, as written by the Rev. Wm. Becket, church missionary at Lewis Town, from 1727 to 1743, being his notices of sundries, his letters, his poetical compositions, &c., I take therefrom the following items.] He went from London to Lewis Town in 1721, was born in Cheshire.]

He proposes that the Society for Foreign Missions in London, should apply to the crown to procure the grant of the lands in the three lower counties, comprising 200,000 acres, inasmuch,

* Thomas Sharp's letter above, is preserved as a just counter-part to the letter of Richard Townsend, a public friend, who wrote and described incidents at Philadelphia, in the early settlement. Let them live side by side *for posterity*.

as they were *not* included in the grants to Pennsylvania or Maryland, although the two proprietors were then contending for it in London. "Sundry persons who have present titles from one or the other, are uneasy, and would willingly have the Church for their landlord, as a majority of the people are of the Church of England. With such means of money at command, support might be raised for a suffragan, much wanted here."

He demurs to marriage licenses being equally in the hands of the Presbyterians as well as in the Church—saying it was an *innovation* first introduced by Gov. Sir George Wm. Keith, to improve his desperate fortune.

His parish comprised the whole county of Sussex—having four churches, and having service every Sabbath alternately, The first was built in 1707 at Cedar Creek. St. Peter's at Lewis Town was erected in 1722,* chiefly by gifts made in *Philadelphia.* The first settlers were generally churchmen from England—some few were Dutch. "Since then, the Scotch Irish came into Sussex, have two meeting-houses, and are very *bigotted.*"

The proportion of inhabitants in Sussex in 1728, were 1,075 of church people, 600 of Presbyterians, and 75 of Quakers; making together 1,750 *souls*, the whole estimated population. In Lewis there were 58 families. The negroes in Sussex were 241. School-houses were usually built of logs, done in *one day* by all the neighbourhood, by the side of a wood.

Mr. Becket wrote poetry very readily, and left several examples. It was his practice to ride on horseback fifty miles a week, to visit the churches and people.

The early prevalence of Church of England doctrine in Sussex, —not much altered till the time of Whitefield, tended much to preserve there "the love of Church and State" among a majority of the people, even down to the time of the Revolutionary war. That event produced many *Tories*, so-called, who were nevertheless very well meaning and respectable people. They aimed to live neutral, but being sometimes persecuted, they would sometimes leave their homes, and take refuge in the Black Swamp, and had considerable sufferings there.

Earliest Iron Trade and Furnaces, Pennsylvania.

These were begun as early as 1715. Exportations were made in 1717. Some jealousy was thereby excited in the mother country, so that in 1719 a bill was introduced into Parliament to prevent the erection of rolling and slitting mills,—but was then rejected. In 1750, however, such an act was passed; but allow-

* There was a still earlier congregation at Lewis Town,—one which appears of record as early as 1707.

ing the exportation of pig metal to England, free of duties. Pig metal exported in 1750, was 3,425 tons, and 390 tons of bar iron. The cheapness of wood and labour here, gave great advantage to the American furnaces,—which they thus enjoyed from 1750 to the period of the Revolution.

The first built furnace of Pennsylvania, was that of Colebrooke Dale, (Berks Co.,) built in 1720, by Jas. Lewis and Anthony Morris, of Philadelphia. The Reading furnace was built in 1730, and the Warwick in 1736. The Cornwall furnace in Lebanon county, was built in 1741-2, by Peter Grubb, and greatly enriched all the owners. In 1798 it became the property of Robt. Coleman, who also acquired a great estate thereby. The price of pig iron at this place in 1780, was £300 Continental money, and in 1785 was £6 10 shillings, Pennsylvania currency or $17¼. The Mount Vernon furnace erected in 1800, by Henry B. Grubb, produced 50 tons a week. The Mount Hope furnace, built by Peter Grubb in 1786, yielded about 900 tons of pig metal per annum.

Red Bank, and the War of the Revolution.

Job Whitall, who lived at Red Bank, in a large brick house fronting the river, (next below the redoubt where Count Donop fell,) kept a MS. Diary, from the year 1775 to 95, wherein he noted daily events, relating to himself. From that book I have made sundry extracts, hereinafter given, which may serve to show some of the incidents of the war at and near his place in 1777-8. A large cannon ball went through his house, while his wife was spinning. She then took the wheel and herself into the cellar.

1777. 10th Month, 22d. This day pleasant and fair—he and his father hung the gate—then finished the stacks. Then got up horses and wagon, and loaded their goods, to move them, —because the English troops (in the river) were coming nearer. Himself, wife and children, after eating dinner, went off to uncle David Cooper's [near Woodbury.] Cooper sent his wagon to aid in moving the goods. They drove away 21 head of cattle. The *people in the Fort* drove away from father and I, 47 sheep, into the Fort.

10th Month, 23d. The Americans filled the house at his father's, so that we were forced to move out, and we took loads of goods to John Murdocks, in Woodbury, [three miles off.]

25th. The soldiers pressed his mare, by order of Col. Greene.

26th. We haul away the wheat and grain,—then fill four rooms with goods, locked up.

27th. These rooms the soldiers broke open, and took away some potatoes.

11th Month, 1st. The soldiers took his mare and four loads

of rye—he gets off some of his horses. His neighbours assist to carry some of his produce, hay, &c.

4th. The soldiers press his oxen, as they were in the act of hauling away. The soldiers went to his uncle David Cooper's and there pressed J. Whitall's sorrel.

7th. He and family went to Woodbury meeting (of Friends,) found it was in use as an hospital for sick soldiers; but Friends held a solid, satisfactory meeting out of doors. The militia soldiers were quartered at Gibbs' house, and filled it. Paid for beef then at one shilling and sixpence per pound.

9th. The soldiers at Woodbury steal some of Whitall's pigs—in meeting time, while the family is at meeting.

10th. He goes to "the Bank," (his homestead,) and gets a load out of his cellar. Now he moves again, (from Murdock's, in Woodbury,) to Gibbs' for safety.

15th. He went over to his house at Red Bank, to bring away a load, but *there* was so much firing there, that nothing was done by him. To-day he killed his fat cow, and in the night the soldiers came and pillaged a part of it.

16th. We held our meeting at Mark Miller's house.

21st. He staid at home to-day, because of the English soldiers, *then* arrived there. They took his two mares both with foal, and while the army was passing by, they came and took their bread, pies, milk, cheese, dishes, cups, spoons,—also their shirts, sheets, blankets, &c., then drove out the cattle from the brick shed, all of which, however, came back again, save one ox.

22d. The soldiers took one of his pigs, and cut and hacked others. A great number of soldiers went by to-day, partly peaceable, they only took some gears and some potatoes.

23d. The soldiers took some of his hay, slung on their horses, and also took ten sheep.

24th. A warm pleasant day. The English soldiers all moved off in the morning from Woodbury. He walked to the camp ground—found there his big kettle, and the hide of his brown ox. He then walked to Woodbury, and found that they had opened his smoke-house, and taken five flitches. They also had used of his boards a thousand feet, and burned two or three thousand of his staves.

27th. Observes a northern light and records its appearance.

30th. Goes to Friends meeting, then held *again*, for the first time, in the meeting house.

12th Month, 15th. He goes over to Red Bank to spread and gather flax, being a residue left by the soldiers, who had before used some of it for tents.

1778. 2d Month, 10th. Went to "youths' meeting" at Woodbury—a great gathering, and many public Friends, and a very grateful time there to many.

4th Month, 20th. He moves back to Red Bank, and drives

back his cattle, after an absence, and precarious living, for upwards of six months.

☞ The place of Job Whitall, now held by his grandson Louis Whitall, is an old family homestead of ninety acres held upwards of a century. It was first settled there by Henry Treadwell, in 1683; after sixteen years, was bought by the ancestor James Whitall, and there used as his farm. The brick house was built there in 1748. Col. Franklin Davenport, of Woodbury, said that all of Col. Greene's command were black men. The present owner, Louis Whitall, has the scull of Count Donop; he took me to his grave—sunken, and marked with a coarse stone, inscribed with his name, when killed, &c.; he also led me over the remains of the old redoubt. It was, at the time, in an apple orchard; which was cut down to make room. There are remains of two breastworks—the first one was on too large a scale to man it, and they therefore made a smaller one within the other, *on one side of it.* The outer fosse is still a deep ditch, and all the premises are now all overgrown with tall and thick set pines, and some other trees. The monument is placed some distance northward from the redoubt, on the line of the next land owner, as the Whitalls did not wish it on their ground, because of predatory companies visiting the ground, and using their melons and fruits, &c.

[I visited the place and took the above notes and memoranda, the 26th and 27th of June, 1847.]

Whitall's house was used as an hospital after the battle, to amputate the wounded. Mrs. Whitall, was a character, and being present when they complained of heavy foot-falls on the floor, said they must not complain, who had brought it on themselves! She was, however, kind-hearted and useful to them. One night, while seated at sewing or knitting, she saw the lower limbs of a thief, going up stairs, she followed up immediately—found him under the bed, ordered him out, led him by the collar down stairs, and slapped his face and bid him begone.

Our Advancement and Prosperity.

Being remarks induced by the perusal of Macaulay's England, Vol. 1, Chap. 3d.

However we, of this age, may smile at the rustic simplicity of the past—so often set forth in the present work, we are only to read such a book as Macaulay's England, at the time that Pennsylvania began to be settled, to perceive how like the early settlers here, was the condition of the home country which they had left. Macaulay's extended 3d chapter, is replete with notices of all such leading *changes* of men and things *there*, as these Annals of our country have aimed to note and observe *here*. He remarks very justly that "we must never forget that the country *then*, was a very different country from that in which we *now* live."

We here give a summary of facts, for example, to wit. "The Army and Navy, then, were small neglected concerns. The sheep, oxen, and horses, were diminutive. They had no race horses, as now. Their manufactories were few. Agriculture was ill understood, and little practised:—they had few gardens and flowers. Coal and salt mines were not worked. The roads were bad. Stages were few; going only two or three times a week to principal towns. The chief land carriage was with pack horses. Their country gentlemen and gentry made few or no visits to London. London itself, was coarse and grotesque in its buildings of wood and plaster. They had only small gazettes of weekly publication; and the mass of the people had no reading but in the form of ballads. There were no political readers—no free discussion; and very few who were able to read and write. Few books were printed and read. The people were coarse and cruel in their sports. The country clergy were ill paid, and little regarded. Few humane and charitable institutions existed. The poor were ill paid,—but four to seven shillings per week, and their comforts generally neglected. They had no hospitals for their sickness. The Post-office was but little used, and merchants lived in confined closes, &c. They were without libraries. Philosophy, medicine, chemistry, mechanics, were studied by very few. The elegant places now about London, were then rude uncultivated commons, having in many locations, heaths, fens, and morasses. Highwaymen then beset most of the roads; and travellers went mostly on horseback.

From the premises, we of this country, cannot but perceive, that *our* progress in improvement, preceding the period of our Revolutionary war, much surpassed the time of the two Charles' and Cromwell's governments. A result which we should be inclined to impute to our self-movements, and self-inspired impulses, impelling to all that was useful and ameliorating. As Americans, let us consider!

Old Congress and First Prayer.

John Adams has given in a letter of Sept., 1774, at Phila., his graphic description of the cause and manner of the first prayer in the then First Congress. Writing to a friend, he says "When the Congress met, Mr. Cushing motioned that it should be opened with prayer. It was opposed by Mr. Jay and Mr Rutledge, because we were so divided in religious sentiment—Some Episcopalians, some Quakers, some Anna-Baptists, some Presbyterians, and some Congregationalists, that we could *not join* in the same worship. Mr. Samuel Adams rose and said that "he was no bigot, and could hear prayer from any gentleman of piety and virtue, who was at the same time a friend to his country—that he was a stranger in Philadelphia, but had heard that Parson Duché deserved that character, and therefore he moved that he, an Episcopalian clergyman, might be desired to read prayers before the Congress to-morrow morning." The motion was affirmed. Mr. Randolph, our President, waited on him—he appeared with his clerk, and in pontificals, read several prayers, and then read the order of Psalms for the 7th September a part of which was the 35th psalm. You must remember, this was the next morning, after we had heard the rumours of the horrible cannonade of Boston. It *seemed* as if Heaven had ordained *that* psalm to be read on *that* morning! After this, Mr. Duché, unexpectedly to every body, struck out in extemporary prayer, which filled the bosom of every man present. I must confess, I never heard a better prayer, or one so well pronounced—done with such fervour—such ardour—such correctness and pathos, and in language so elegant and sublime, for Congress, for the Province of Massachusetts Bay, especially the town of Boston. It had an excellent effect upon every body here. I must beg you to read that psalm, to wit: "Plead my cause, O Lord, with them that strive against me—stand up for my help—say unto my soul, I am thy salvation. Let them be turned back and brought to confusion that devise my hurt—and my tongue shall speak of thy praise evermore." If there is any faith in the *sortes Biblicæ*, it would be thought providential. The whole scene and crisis—was enough to melt a heart of stone. I saw the tears gush into the eyes of the old, grave, pacific Quakers.

Congress, and Seat of Government at Princeton, July, 1783.

The Rev. Ashbel Green, in writing to his father—says: "We have the gentlemen of the Congress for fellow-students, they, however, exercising by themselves in the library. We are made now alive and bustling; the quiet of the village is broken up—carriages and wagons and chairs, now rattle every where; oranges, pine-apples, and lemons, and other luxuries, are all the cry now. They have had a great public dinner, at 6 o'clock, having present sundry foreign ministers. In the evening, sky-rockets and fireworks. The papers, brought by the Congress, filled six wagons."

My Annals—a picture of Colonial Times.

I have sometimes said, and still oftener thought, that my Annals should afford interest abroad—even in Europe, itself, as showing the early domestic and homebred history of *our Anglo-Saxon race*, destined perchance, with Britons at home, to *anglify*, under Providence, the other nations of the globe! I see some of my thoughts, lately, well expressed in the London Christian Examiner—to wit: "Trace the principles and institutions of the Pilgrims in their development, operation and results. Not only 'the little one has become a thousand, and the small one a great one,' but those institutions, civil and sacred, have found throughout a congenial soil. In *these* stand *the glory of America;* under any other dynasty that country could never have risen. On her present position we must look with intense interest. Her whole history is interwoven with the fate of Europe—America holds no common place. Her conduct and influence in morals and religion, is in unison and co-operation with that of Britain, and is destined to change the whole aspect of society every where. The superstitions and errors of ages are melting away. In her future progress she is destined, in common with Britain, to carry along with her the destiny of the species. The world is not only to receive a new language, a new philosophy, a new religion; but to take its entire type and impression from these two nations. In moral power and resources, America not ony rivals, but far exceeds the European States, England alone excepted. No force can crush the *sympathy* that already exists and is continually augmenting, between Europe and the New World. We are deeply interested *in the progress* of her power and greatness; for she is *descended* from ancestors who, like the Father of the faithful, for the sake of truth, went to a land which they knew not; and like the children of Abraham, have truth in their keeping—in common with us; and are destined to carry it by their commerce and British principles of civilization, to the end of the earth." [Are not Britons, then, peculiarly interested in examining those traces of our domestic history, those pictures of our rise, progress, and advancement to present greatness, which have been pictorially drawn from facts, such as I have traced and recorded? Let Britons examine and consider! Americans too, of whatever State, and however distant from Philadelphia, or New York, have a direct interest in such recitals as I have aimed to preserve, as being a picture of those *Colonial days*, when we as Colonists were all of homogenous character, and in each and every Colony, presented an honest, frugal, contented, and homebred race.]

Memoranda of Historical Works concerning our olden time.

The most ancient is that of *John de Laet*, of Antwerp; a resident of Leyden—himself a scholar—he wrote very accurately from what he heard. He knew personally, Capt. De Vries, and had seen the MS. journals of Hendrick Hudson, Adrian Block, Capt. May, and probably other voyagers to the New Nederlands. He had much enthusiasm for the interests of our New World—he formed, probably, the earliest chart of the Delaware. He describes the tribes of Indians, from the Capes to the Falls at Trenton. He published in 1625, and died in 1649.

☞ A translation of the part relating to the New Netherlands has been published in the first volume of the New York series of the New York Historical Collections--he published in black letter, in Dutch and Latin. Which last was, of course, for the *savans* of Europe.

The next in order comes the *Royal* Beauchamp *Plantagenet*, who published in 1648, his "description of *New Albion*, made up from his two pamphlets, of 1637 and '42. Though carelessly written, it seems to be the result of an actual residence, by certain English settlers, (among whom was Master Evelyn,) under the grant to Sir Edmond Ployden, his friend.* He had marked out the country for several *nobles* of his family, and he and his compatriots, for a while held a settlement on the Jersey side of Delaware, somewhere below Red Bank, supposed at Billingsport. But one copy of this most remarkable work is believed to exist, and that is in the Philadelphia Library, [and which is intended to be copied, *as a curiosity*.]

The "description of New Sweden," by Campanius, may be regarded as the third book in point of order of our antiquities. For although not printed at the time it depicts—yet it contains facts about locations along the Delaware, collected by Thomas Campanius, and Peter Lindstrom, the Engineer, contemporary with Gov. Printz, in 1642 and subsequent. This Campanius was the Swedish clergyman who lived in New Sweden six years. He was born in Stockholm, 1601, from which cause he has been called Thomas Campanius *Holm*. He made a catechism into the Indian Language, printed in 1696, he died in 1683. The notes which he wrote at Tinicum, were edited by his grandson, also named Thomas Campanius Holm, and published at Stockholm in 1702. It has lately been done into English by Mr. P. S. Duponceau, at the instance of the Historical Society of Pennsylvania, and a small copy of Lindstrom's map of the Delaware, accompanies the work, a large chart of 27 inches is also preserved in the Philosophical Society.

The next of the historians and geographers is *Adrian Van der Donck*, who bore the honours of Doctor of civil and common law, from the University of Leyden. He enjoys the distinction of being the first lawyer in the New Netherlands, and the first sheriff of Rensselaerwyck. He came out in 1642, and afterwards printed at the Hague in 1653, his "Description of the New Netherlands." From the second edition of 1656, Mr. Johnson of Brook

* Ployden calls himself *Earl Albion*, as having land enough here to give him an Earldom! It all went down as to claim and title; but in 1788, we saw in the public papers, a claim to New Jersey and Long Island, as belonging to the Earl of Albion's family—it died away unnoticed.

lyn, has made *his translation.* Although in himself a scholar, he preferred to write in his vernacular tongue, the Dutch. His map of 1656, so far as the Delaware is concerned, seems very correct.

In 1655, was published, in Dutch, a work by *David Pieterzen de Vries*, master of artillery, his "Brief historical and journalized notes of several voyages to the four quarters of the globe." This De Vries is the same person who appeared in command at Fort Nassau, N. J. He was concerned with his friends De Laet and Van Rensselaer in planting colonies in New Netherlands.

☞ A portion of his work has been translated *into English* for the New York Historical Society, by Mr. Troost, and also some fragments of it have been preserved by Du Simetiere.

In 1698, Gabriel Thomas, published in London "an historical and geographical account of the Province of *Pennsylvania* and of West New Jersey." The part relative to Pennsylvania, I have given in my Annals. The New Jersey part, I have not seen—the book is now very scarce, and hard to be obtained—the Jersey part has been reprinted here lately.

Peter Kalm, was a professor of Botany, born in 1715 in Sweden, who visited our Swedish settlers in 1748, and remained among us three years; he published his travels among us, in an English translation in 1770,—died in 1779, much distinguished as a Botanist.

In 1796, the Rev. George Acrelius published at Stockholm, "A description of the present and former state at the Swedish congregations in New Sweden," which was translated by Nicholas Collin, D. D., of Swedes' Church, Philadelphia. Acrelius had been a minister at the Christiana Church in Delaware, for several years. He returned to Sweden in 1756, and lived at Fallinsboro in Sweden, when his book was published.

The Wissahiccon.

This romantic Creek and scenery, now so much visited and familiar to many, was not long since an extremely wild unvisited place—to illustrate which, I give these facts, to wit: Enoch and Jacob Rittenhouse, residents there, told me in 1845, that when they were boys the place had many pheasants, that they snared a hundred of them in a season—they also got many partridges. The creek had many excellent fish—such as large sunfish and perch. The summer wild ducks came there regularly, and were shot often—also, some winter ducks. They then had no visitors from the city, and only occasionally from Germantown. There they lived quietly and retired—now all is public and bustling—all is changed.

John S. Hutton, of Philadelphia, aged 109 years.

Longevity, and List of Names and Ages.

The frosts of ninety years have passed
  Upon this aged head—
It seems a fine old relic cast
  From days that long have fled.

Mrs. Betsey Frantham, died at Maury county, North Carolina, on the 10th January, 1834, aged 154 years! She was a native of Germany, and arrived at North Carolina in 1710. At the age of 120 her eyesight became almost extinct; but during the last twenty years of her life, she could see as well as when 20 years of age! She had come out in 1710 among a number of German emigrants, to whom Gov. Lynte was directed to give 100 acres of land severally, as motives to settlement. She was for several years unable to walk, and it was their practice for several years to keep her lying between two feather beds, to keep up the essential temperature to the preservation of her life. She had lost the sense of taste and hearing, for some time before her death.

Died at New Brunswick, N. J., (Aug. 1834,) Hugh Henderson, aged 104 years; a native of the Highlands of Scotland. He could take long walks, and enjoyed his health and spirits till February last, when he broke his leg by a fall on the ice. His bones were set and reunited firmly.

Died in Chester county, 1831, Nathaniel Mercer, of that county, aged 101 years.

Died at New York, September, 1834, of Cholera, a poor coloured woman, aged 109 years. She lived and died in Orange street. There is now living in Washington street a coloured man who is aged 104 years.

Joice Heth, a negro slave, is exhibited alive at Pittsburgh, aged 161 years! She retains a vivid recollection of the scenes of her youth, and is to be brought on to Philadelphia, New York, &c. It is said that she once belonged to General Washington's father, and had been the nurse of the General. A post mortem examination in 1835–6, seems to prove her to be *not more* than 90 years old.

Col. W. Drake, died at New Haven, on the 11 Sept. 1796, in the 100th year of his age, and having his faculties sound to the last.

Wm. Butler died at Philadelphia in May, 1838, aged 108, "the oldest inhabitant of Philadelphia."

Died at Fairfield, S. C., 3 Jan., 1835, Jennings Allen, aged 117 years, had served with Braddock, and also in the Revolution.

General Washington, his providential preservation.

Sundry circumstances in the early life of Washington, while a *Colonel* in the western *wilderness*, have not been sufficiently noticed, as marking him even from the beginning, as "*the man of destiny*," as one *providentially preserved* for the subsequent salvation of his country. For instance, in the case of his exposure of person in the battle of Braddock's defeat. His letter to his mother of 18 July, 1755—says, "The Virginian troops"—to which he belonged—"showed a great deal of bravery, and were nearly all killed. I luckily escaped without a wound, though I had four bullets through my coat, and had two horses shot under me. The general's two aids being early wounded, I was the *only person* then left to distribute the general's orders. At the same time he requests to inform his brother John, that he has not been *killed*, as had been before reported in a circumstantial account. He added, "By the all powerful dispensations of Providence, I have been *protected* beyond all human probability or expectation, while death was levelling my companions on every side." Such remarkable perils, and such acknowledgments of a divine protection therein, are things which should be impressively considered.

Besides the foregoing, it came to pass afterwards, when Washington was out in Ohio in 1770, to explore some wild lands near the Kenawha river, he there met an aged Indian chief who told him, that during the battle in Braddock's field, he had singled him out at several times to bring him down with his rifle, and ordered his young warriors to do the same; but none of the balls took effect! He was then convinced that the young hero was under some special guardianship of the Great Spirit, and he had therefore desisted from firing. He had now come a long way to pay his homage to so peculiar a man—as *one saved by Heaven!* Surely, if the poor Indian, could thus discern the protection from above, much more readily should we, who profess to understand a God "who rules in the affairs of men."

In the year 1753, Major Washington, returning from his visit to Fort Le Bœuf, roughing it all the way like a perfect woodsman, urging his lonely way through the depths of the forests, in the depth of the winter, fell into a fearful dilemma, which ordinarily would have cost the life of any other individual. He had left his horse and heavy baggage, and for the sake of greater dispatch, had undertaken *to foot* his way, with his friend Mr. Gist, for his companion. Being tied up in his watch coat, with his better clothes off, and his papers and provisions tied in a pack slung to his back, (think of that, for the great General Washington, afterwards President of the United States;) they urged their lonely way through the woods, each with gun in hand and momentarily exposed to Indian surprise. That surprise came from a party of French Indians laying in wait—one of them fired upon them not fifteen steps off but missed, and then they seized him, (mark it, that they were too humane to kill an enemy in possession!) and at night let him go; they in mean while *walking* all night, as their best security for getting beyond the reach of the party on the morrow. They then continued walking all next day—when they reached the river two miles above Shannopins—which they had hoped to have found *frozen*, from the keenness of the cold which they had braved. The ice there, however, was drifting in vast quantities, and they had no way to pass it but *on a raft*, which they themselves were obliged to construct, with only one poor hatchet. In such a necessary and hurried work, they were diligently employed all day—exposed to cold in their persons; and with continued apprehensions from the pursuing Indians, probably near them! On such an occasion did Washington, probably, remember the prayers which he may have been taught by a mother's care in his youth. Can we suppose that he did not ejaculate something from the heart, for Divine support and protection! He was protected. For soon after they had embarked on their frail log structure, "they got jammed up in the ice, and *momentarily expected* their raft to sink, and themselves to perish!" Just at their extremity, when Washington was setting his pole to save his position, he was jerked out into 10 feet water! They had then no alternative, but to make their way to an island, leaving their raft to its fate. There they had to pass the whole night in mid-winter!—their clothes soaked with iced water and stifly frozen;—so frozen, that his companion, Mr. Gist, had all of his fingers and some of his toes frozen! Mark the providence! Washington though equally, or more exposed, was not frozen; and the very severity of the freezing made them a formidable bridge of ice, by which they safely passed over to the main land on the next morning, and soon after reached the wigwam of Queen Allaquippa, where they were refreshed! Surely as many of us as may regard Washington as bestowed upon us, as a nation's deliverer, must herein see and confess the hand divine, which led his footsteps in his youth, and guided him in future years, through a long, perilous and eminent life. We know of nothing in the whole career of Washington, which has been to us such moving cause of emotion, as the contemplation of these earliest scenes of Washington. Scenes, however, which have been least noticed by others. We can't think of his rugged and severe backwood struggles—his exertions for life and honour, without thinking how little he then could have dreamed of his country's Independence, and himself the appointed Leader! We row *backward* when we go ahead! So dark and mysterious are the counsels which sometimes lead and rule in the affairs of men!

It may be imputed to the good tact and good sense of Gov. Dinwiddie who came out to Virginia in 1752, to have first brought out the proper estimation of the talents of young Washington; and still more are we indebted to the discernment of the Rev. Samuel Davis, (afterwards President of Princeton College,) who at his sermon preached the 17 Aug., 1755, before the Hanover volunteers of Capt. Overton's command, to excite them to the war, just after the defeat of Braddock—He says, "shall these savages go on unchecked, and must our unhappy brethern on our frontiers go unassisted and unpitied? No! No! Thank God, he has been pleased to diffuse some sparks of the martial fire through our country—in you it begins to kindle, and may I not produce you, my brethern, who are engaged in this *volunteer* expedition as instances of it?" He then gives as an episode or note, saying, "I may point out to the public, that heroic youth, Col. Washington, whom I cannot but hope Providence has hitherto preserved in so signal a manner for some important service to his country." Doct. Davis' text, in the foregoing sermon, was from 2d Saml. x. 12. "Be of good courage, and let us play the men for our people, and for the cities of our God: and the Lord do that which seemeth him good."—*See Davis' Sermoms, vol.* 5. *Edn.* 1818.

Passing Changes of Men and Manners.

We have been sometimes urged to bring out another volume, wherein we should so dispose of facts of *changes* passed and passing upon society, as should by emphasis of remark, arouse the indolent or inconsiderate reader to a due sense of the real importance of the changes produced. We feel that we have *done enough;* and the reader, therefore, by his own reflections and notices, must supply needful amplifications.

We, however, think of sundry prevalent and modish actions of society, such as did not, and could not, formerly, find toleration. They are just so special and striking as to form a proper and closing chapter to these Annals. Not for the sake of censorship, or objection, but as marking an era, in "the progress of enlightened civilization," to be remembered.

The generation of elderly ladies have not yet passed away, who made a part of that society which could not behold such things as opera-dances and waltzes with complacency. They felt, as females, an instinctive, inherent modesty, precluding them from such publicity. The encroachments upon female modesty have been progressive, and may continue.

The first most effective inroad upon the instinctive modesty of the sex—as is still remembered by them, was the modish introduction of *man*-midwifery. Against its practice we urge no complaint: nevertheless, it is remembered as of record, that Mrs. Lydia Robinson of New London, Conn., who died in 1769 at the age of 70 years, had been for 35 years a successful female midwife for 1,200 children, and *never lost one.* After the change of such practice, to male hands, women felt a hardihood, which prepared them to permit other influences upon female character.

Such came latterly, in the form of opera dancing, waltzing, and circus riding, wherein performers in the display of limbs and individual symmetry, had the countenance of society; and yet we have among us still, many who can well remember their first emotions of confusion and blushes, at first seeing some of these spectacles. In time, they also fell in with the fashion of the times, and subdued their scruples.

To what they did eventually submit, and bring themselves to witness, we may portray form such exhibitions as Perrot, and the figurante Taglioni, could display. If it were not so graceful it would be indecent; but they understood the philosophy of their art, it was to throw around sensuality such a colouring of refinement as might divest it of its grossness. Look! there she comes from the back of the stage, turning round and round with the speed of a teetotum, in indescribable and fascinating grace—she pirouettes—she springs and vaults, her scanty drapery flying upwards, discloses to her enraptured admirers, among the young men, the beauty of her limbs. See! she now rests before the foot-lights, on the very point of her toe, the other limb highly elevated, depressing and elevating her body with infinite grace and ease, and smiling and looking modest as an angel—meanwhile, affording to enraptured male beholders, the opportunity of scrutinizing the grace and proportions of her figure. Next, see the impersonation of Perrot, he comes and leaps about as if his feet were made of India rubber, and spins around upon the point of his toe like a top. He joins the figurante, and they twirl away and glide along, holding eloquent discourse with their pliant limbs, after the manner of waltzing. He, wonderful for grace and beauty of person, is as much the idol of the ladies, as is the other the goddess of the gentlemen. The applause on all sides is deafening, save from some few youthful innocent girls who have never beheld the like before. Look at some of them who have come with their friends to see something new—undefined, vague, glimmering and wonderful—

> ———"Oh! the joy
> Of young ideas painted on the mind
> Of objects not yet known, when all is new!"

It is a "Ballet"—a thing which rank and fashion has countenanced and sustained. Their conductors and companions are persons of unblemished reputation and virtue, and therefore cannot be wrong. Look at any one of these novices—the face betrays that she has seen enough to crimson the visage and neck with the blush of shame—she instinctively hides her head from a sight which has shocked her former sense of decency. There is no affectation here. It is nature out, and comes without bidding. While thus confused she hears the enraptured plaudits of all around her, and begins almost to feel ashamed that she has felt confused. She almost fears that her emotions might be imputed to awkwardness—to prudery—to anything else than the truth, she therefore labours to arrive at such mastery over self as the manners of society impose.

The exhibition of figure, grace, &c., having thus found public favour, came in time to give idea to the exhibition of living models, as statuary subjects for artists, amatuers, &c. To show forth from life, selected individuals of both sexes, as models of perfection in bodily configuration,—veiled only, with invisible or flesh colour tissue. They found for a while some spectators of both sexes, others thought it too gross, and the curtain was dropt. Whether posterity will raise it again, they shall see. The time was, when, even real statuary—dead cold marble, with its vacant eye, could not be exposed where females were to be met or seen; and the same influence is measurably so still. But while circus riders, of both sexes, can be tolerated to appear in seeming nakedness of limb and bodily form, the nudities of images, as in Italy and France, may come to be a future common exhibition.

With the operas have come in, a new style of singing, such as our forefathers knew not. It does not profess to be natural but highly artificial, measuring its excellence by its difficulty of execution. Its prevalence, so far, has changed all manner of singing now heard in social intercourse, it aims at anything but sweet melody, and seems like an affectation of something else. But all are not thus disposed, for those who judge of music and its charms, from natural instinct, adhere earnestly to nature's dictates, and therefore give all favour to coloured ministrels, who profess to follow nature's mode. They teach harmony to natural ears and tastes, and successfully burlesque the operas, with all their exalted screams, trills and intonations. That some opera singers should get into choirs of some churches is another innovation of the age; and with it comes the other innovation, with some, of *singing*, what should be *praying* responses, ' meekly kneeling on the knees." This we are bound to say, was not always so.

One most obvious and most embarrassing change, which has "come over the face of our affairs,," is the increased and increasing difficulty of providing acceptable employment for growing-up sons—of such as aim at what they deem genteel occupation. They find the Bar and medical profession, already surcharged; and if they aim at wholesale stores and business houses, they find them scarce, and few and far between. The result is, that young men are not, and cannot be, prepared for early marriage, and settlement, or else they seek to find fortunes where they should not. Too many are therefore driven to live upon contingencies and chance, and are liable to be seduced into criminal stratagems, at a rate of number never before so witnessed. A time must therefore come, when men of sense will educate and train their surplus sons to husbandry, and others to mechanic arts requiring skill and education. Architecture, for instance, in houses and ship construction, can open many avenues for further employment, and the elaboration of metals can be carried out into many channels of elevated and enlightened mechanicism. Gentlemen, by *combination*, could so determine to place their sons, and thus elevate the standard of character, just as readily as the same class, could determine recently, to make what was free schools for poor children, *common schools* to themselves and all other tax prayers. Make it the fashion that young men should be so disposed of, and the object is attained. Men, who by elevation lead society, may in this matter set the example of so disposing of their sons, and not forcibly constrain them into positions where society draws another way, and affects to exclude them. It is not the labour, but the exclusion, which operates on their minds. Our forefathers, when society, was more equalized, experienced no such difficulties in the acceptable disposal of their sons. They found readily places for all positions where their education and training inclined them.

It is thus, by comparing the present and the past, we arrive at some apprehension of what our forefathers did in former times, and at some appreciation of the changes which may be induced in the future. We are thus pleased and satisfied in proportion to the images which can be created for our contemplation—while facts can be educed for consideration, the imagination and the heart must be affected. What the world will come to hereafter, we may all know, as being within the compass of all past history Society moves in a circle of changes. If we are in pride, pride will bring arrogance and war—War will produce poverty—Poverty humiliation and Peace—Humiliation will induce Repentance and Reform—Reform, economy and wealth, as at the beginning, &c.

The Revolutionary Navy.

Where so much has been done for the glory of our country, in the times which tried men's souls—it is desirable to say a few words—to wit.

We have many reasons for believing that the officers of our first, or revolutionary navy, were in many respects different from the present—different, we should say, in dress, manners, and mind. Their habits were simpler—their manners plain, and their intercourse frank and familiar. In their dress, there was little aim at show and grandeur. They wore small cocked hats without lace—hair powdered and cued—coats with ample skirts, and foul-anchor buttons—small clothes—hose and shoes. Their dignity and sternness, when they aimed at any, was not before their countrymen, but before the enemy. In that relation, they showed themselves men of great tact, and of most indomitable spirit and courage. They had all been practical seamen, in the merchants' service and thus came out in their new relation, for the occasion. Indeed our earliest officers for our subsequent navy, which produced officers such as we have seen to earn a fame for themselves and their country by their gallantry, in actions since the revolution, had also been drawn from the mercantile marine.—Such were Bainbridge, Porter, Chauncey, Hull, Perry, Preble, &c. They had not been originally bred for drawing-rooms and courtly display; but they had no deficiency in polished circles, when called to the exercise of their rules and usages.

Army Officers.

The speaking of navy officers above, stimulates me to say a few words of army officers, such as they were down to the year 1800, while the seat of government was at Philadelphia. They were frequently seen abroad in the streets, and always in their uniform. It was less expensive and splendid than now, and thus made an easier affair of daily wear. They arrived, generally from the west, on horseback, with a servant, and their baggage under a bear skin, on another horse. It was gratifying then to the citizens, to see military men thus willing to show their colours—and it gives a hint to similar professional men to do the same now.

American Scenery.

Willis has well told wherein our American scenery differs from European; and since the scenery has been depicted by Bartlett, and put upon steel plates, we cannot but perceive how *equally* grand and imposing are many of *our* river and lake scenes, compared with the best of the European—"having no parallel in Europe or on earth."

"It strikes the European traveller (says Willis) at the first burst of the scenery of America on his eye, that the new world of

Columbus is also a new world from the hand of the Creator—the vegetation is so wondrously lavish, and the outlines and minor features are struck out with so bold a freshness. The Minerva-like birth of the republic—its sudden rise to independence, wealth and power, and its continued and marvellous increase in population and prosperity, strike him with the same surprise, and leave the same impression of a new scale of existence, and a fresher and faster law of growth and accomplishment." Travellers, who have exhausted the *unchanging* countries of Europe, now turn their steps to the novel scenery and *evershifting* aspects of this. It is *in river scenery*, however, that America *exceeds all other lands;* and "here (says Bartlett) the artist's labour is not *as in Europe*, to embellish and idealize the reality; he finds it difficult *to come up to it.*" Let this concession be considered and remembered by Americans!

The Credit System.

It has been said that "to the system of *bills of credit*, Pennsylvania owed more of her provincial prosperity than to any other cause—it gave her a facility in effecting *exchanges* not otherwise attainable." The mother country opposed this system, and when the colonial assembly had passed acts for such emissions, they were negatived by the crown as soon as the acts permitted—say in two years. To meet this obstacle the assemblies restricted their acts to two years at a time, and thus managed to make the emissions *continual.* Since then we have often effected great and lasting good by the credit system—accomplishing numerous great enterprises. All this while it was held under wholesome restrictions and restraints. We have also greatly abused it when used as a means of excessive stock-jobbing, and extravagant speculations. Like fire and water, which are so useful and necessary in their legitimate use, they can be *mismanaged* to a tremendous amount of evil. Benjamin Franklin, in his early days, was the first person in Philadelphia who wrote and published *in favour* of creating paper money; and he says, that he was strenuously opposed by all the monied men; but they continued to discuss it in the *junta*, and it carried with the people—and after the first trial in was sc liked, as to make calls for more.

FINAL APPENDIX OF THE YEAR 1856.

NOTES AND REFLECTIONS ON SOCIAL CHANGES AND PROGRESS IN GENERAL.

"Now othor men and other manners reign."

Since the publication of the preceding pages, fourteen years ago, (in 1842,) showing the State of Society in Olden time,—and considering *now*, the wonderful *changes* continually passing upon men, and things in the course of "Progress," it seems to become a needful comment on the past, to bring up to the notice of the present *entering* generation, some of the leading changeful features of the present day,—i e "the Progress of Social life"—as said Daniel Webster, —"a history of our Firesides and the changes—from age to age of our homes."

We shall therefore aim to present to our readers—by way of *contrast*, such *comparisons* of the present and the past, as shall best exhibit the *points*, in which the measures of *change* and *progress*, have been most conspicuously manifested;—and which are indeed, so strikingly wonderful, when told, as should,—if duly considered,—make us a wonder unto ourselves.

Without such an Expose, we cannot but believe, that, the mass of the people,—so familiar and cognisant in every-day things now,—could not realise the position from which they have been taken. They are but too prone to think, that the life that *now is*, is the life that has always *been*. In these matters, we might say with Sidney Smith, on a like occasion,—"It is some importance at what period a man is born. A young man alive at this period, hardly knows to what changes, and improvements of human life he has been introduced;"—And with Macauley's recent history say, "We are to consider that the history of such a given past epoch, is no longer the history of the country, *as we now see it.*"

Let us therefore to facts: Such as will be shown under the following heads to wit:

General remarks on our changes.

It is pleasing to see,—amidst such passing events, that there is a growing interest in *preserving* the Annals and Reminiscences of the past. The great changes of the present, *compared* with the past, adds to their picturesqueness; and from this cause it is, that those who discard the use of all past modes and forms,—and who habitually supercede them by new things,—are nevertheless gratified in reading the record of their preservation *in books*. We have received many written notices of these facts from various correspondents,—and as a proof in point, we here extract from one such letter, received from the author of the History of Norwich, Connecticut; —saying, "A new and fascinating department of literature is growing up amongst us, having for its basis, not merely bare facts and dates of our domestic history, genealogy and biography, but also, *all* that is instructive, beautiful and shadowy of the past;—for 'posterity (as said John Q. Adams) delights *in details*;'—such as your Annals have so vividly displayed—Truly, I sympathise with you, and every one, who like you, is engaged in reviving and keeping fresh the deeds and memorials of our forefathers."

What wonderful things do we now behold, "not before dreamt of in our philosophy!" Rail Roads and Cars—annihilating space —Telegraphic wires, conversing at unlimited distances—Steamers traversing every Sea—Steam-Engines and power adapted to all kinds of manufactures—Inventions of machinery (in the Patent office) to supercede almost every kind of former labor—Stereotyping everything on paper—Daguerreotypes cheapening the likenesses of every body. Chemical developments, for the supply of every thing required in the arts, and opening the arcana of nature to the use of all—ascertaining the elements of combinations in nature— and so seperating the parts, as to show new sources of power and profit—*forecasting* the fact, that in time, *Water* may be used as a *Fire*! In the mean time, the ingenuity and devices of Crime, becoming more and more apparent—and compeling new efforts of counteraction from all those who regard the progress of Religion and Virtue, in the world.. We see too, the great exaltation of the Anglo Saxon race, as a species destined to carry out civilization and christianity, to all the dark corners of the globe—The conquest of Mexico, by us—the opening trade of California and Oregon—the discovery of gold and quick Silver—the Commerce of the Pacific and the access there to China—the opening of a Rail Road across the Isthmus, and a great Rail Road across our Continent, all tend to open some grand developments of Providence, in the coming half Century—they who shall succeed us, shall behold still greater wonders!

The parade and success of Foreign Artistes, become more and more astounding—So much of our money contributed to their reward! All kinds of new devices for making money—It is new to make public readings of Shakespeare, as introduced by Mrs. Fanny Kemble —*Operas* are now fostered—supplanting *natural* music—Immodest exposure of female limbs in dancing Polkas, and the like—our mothers and grand mothers, were too modest to behold such things— Circuses, Menageries, and human Models (libidinous) find favour— Riders and Beasts, multiply in all our cities &c.,

Our People are fast changing.

From being once a domestic, quiet people, content to rest in their fireside comforts, and indoor society,—they are being all drawn abroad to seek for spectacles and public wonders! Now there are puffing advertisements to draw them abroad every night and day in the week—and this is not all—the whole must be indulged at so much expense;—One sees that it is working a serious evil;—but who knows *how* to stay it! It is changing and corrupting society here, and is alluring from abroad all manner of foreign artistes—to batten on, and impose themselves upon our credulity, prodigality and habits of display. The temptations to employ means for such occasions, is what must demoralize the mass. The aged among us, perceive and deplore these things,—but the young, who never saw our former golden age of moderation and virtue, feel that we are in their way—as a grave incumbrance, and earnestly wish us off the Stage! Posterity shall see and consider!

To all this add, the *rivalship* of grandeur in houses—expensive furniture—immense and luxurious hotels—elegance and costs of Passenger vessels—and Passenger Cars—costly carriages—costly dresses for ladies and jewelry.—Pride and not comfort give favour to immense hotels, as some think.

I should also say as evidences of our fast changing character—That the whole aspect of society as I now see it, is different from what I saw it everywhere in my earlier life. All is now self-exalted and going upon stilts. It all comes from *foreign* influence—our addictedness to *imitate* what is foreign and modish. The big *Cities* on the Sea board, set the pattern and example—and the inland Towns follow. No wonder we are thus enslaved to foreign views, when we consider, the propensity of our big Cities to arrogate to themselves, the right to dictate and controul,—Take for instance the practice of New York, as " The Empire City and State"—and consider *now* the appalling fact that the late *City* census there, gives nearly *the half* of the whole City population, as foreigners!—How can such a state of Society claim to be an *American* City!—Say 237,000 foreigners—against 278,000 Americans!—

There is another remark on this subject—Every one as old as myself, sees and notices, the general clatter from crowds of people and confusion now along the streets—no room now to turn or look about—once it was peaceful—pleasant and safe to walk the streets,—now tall houses, are crowded with numerous working tenants—formerly, they were in smaller houses and in bye places.—'Tis terrible now to sicken and die at crowded streets, where the rattle of omnibuses is unceasing.

We have become an excitable people.

One cannot but notice the great change in this matter, that has come over us as a people—we are wholly different now, from what we were half a century ago. The noticed changes have been growing upon us ever since the introduction by the Press of " every day's report of wrongs and outrage"—The readers of the daily Press, usually look first to Police reports, at home and abroad, for something strange, revolting or wonderful--Even quite aged persons, so seek for something *new*, or exciting--and if nothing, or nearly so, is presented in that department, they regard the papers as "dull or uninteresting." It is not a healthy condition of the mind, we are sure:—And much it needs some remedy.—At present it manifestly "grows on what it feeds—"It is a failing which is perpetually stimulated, by individuals, and by cliques, and parties, for selfish aims and purposes—Advertisers, and sundry Monopolists, work the machinery with striking effect. Americans are being "*puffed*" out of their common sense. One feels vexed and jaded to see how the people are *managed* and jilted out of their money, "at auction prices," for Jenny Lind, and her vocal wonders! To sell choice seats, (if such there are,) at auction, might pass, but to sell "Promenade tickets," where all must *stand*, and all on *common* ground, has no reason for an *advanced price;* and especially to sell *all* such tickets, to one or two *Speculators*, who may again raise them at their pleasure, on the people! If the people would only *combine*, by Town meeting, and buy no such tickets, it would be but a just rebuke. But where is the *Press*, that would allow such a suggestion to appear in their columns, while the *advertisers* pay so well for "*puffs*" of a counter character—and having at one concert, "seventy free seats, for the gentlemen of the Press." The Press is, indeed, a mighty engine for Weal or Woe!

Our anti-social character.

We can perceive that we are fast growing into this characteristic. —There is scarcely any thing now, as it once was—It is mainly produced by the vanity of doing all things upon a great and grand scale. If it is by travelling vehicles, the people must go by hundreds where they can only stare at, and scan each other without speaking —When located at places, it must be in big Hotels and Palaces,— where all must keep aloof, and look askance at each other. Look at houses like Astor's Girard's, Tremont's—They only serve til. they can be *surpassed* by others, still greater. Think of the Cape May Mansion house, the Mount Vernon—There people were expected to give up all things like home and quiet, and to congregate into masses of three thousand at a house—wheu! People going under pretence of seeking health and the free breath of Heaven and its glorious sea air, to breathe in the surroundings of perpetual cookings —and the discharged atmosphere of three thousand lungs, in little bed-chambers.

One house presents at Table, one Salmon from Boston, at a cost of 41 dollars and puts it in the paper! My countrymen pay for all this unblessed extravagance. Are we not scandalized by all such apings of Royal magnificence, and prodigality, as avowed equalizers—of Republicanism? Would the vain of expensive renown, instead of congregating in Palace Hotels, think of the numerous boarding houses, of many suffering widows,as in former times, how different would be their reward?

Changes of houses.

At this time, I am called to the consideration of the fact, that Philadelphia, (like New York,) is *now* taking quite a *changed* aspect in its buildings.—The former good houses, are so fast, *passing away*, along the several principal streets, and are so numerously supplied by new, and *taller* structures, of another style; as to very visibly efface the appearance of what before was.—To my eye, the whole aspect is changing.—It is indeed, already, another City—*A city building on the top of the former!* All the houses now, above *three* stories—present *an elevation* so manifest, as to *displease the eye*;—and particularly, where several, *go up* so exalted, as to break the former *line* of equality, and beauty.—Even such edifices, lately constructed, as the Banks of North America, Philadelphia and Western Bank, are struck down by the still later, *towering* business houses and hotels, &c., near them.—The next generation, will see nothing of Philadelphia as I saw it, generally, in the year 1800, and subsequently. Another remark, belonging to this subject is,—that young married people, and without family, must have their houses as large, or even larger, than their parents had, when full of children! *All go now on stilts*!

Nothing so much attracts the notice of Europeans, visiting our country, as the general newness and freshness of the architecture of all our cities, and towns.—All seem to them new in aspect, and bright and gleaming. Indeed our own passion for change—"to pull down and build greater"—seems likely to preserve nothing which now might be called, old and venerable;—The rust of antiquity, so much embodied in foreign literature, is not a thing that *is*, with us. We must add years to our progress, before we begin to environ our localities with poetry and tale. *Improvement is our motto now!*

Our great cities.

Our great cities, are fast realising the characteristics of "great deserts." This fact is imposed upon our notice continually,—Formerly, the greatest houses among us, intimated families of superior grade; and all who dwelt in such, were deemed as exempt from the care and bustling strife of business.—They were, essentially *genteel*, by education, affluence, and long-standing family consideration;—Now we see far more expensive and showy edifices, the result of fortunate persuits—The inmates aim at more show and grandeur. One sees readily, how they aim to surpass and eclipse each other.—In the meantime, store-keepers are everywhere, buying up and driving out the long planted respectable residences—leaving no place for retired, quiet grandeur;—but turning the whole city into a great city mart of trade,—bustle, display and rivalship.—They seem to push out and exclude from *cities*, any really dignified residences, for really dignified aristocracy—These in time, will have to contrive country homes, of centralized localities, where trade and its sequences may not annoy them, or invade their own desired exclusiveness,—Who shall see this?

Change of market supplies &c.,

Philadelphia—once so famous for its abundance. cheapness and excellence of marketing, is wonderfully changed,—Formerly, every one going to market, could have his choice of all manner of poultry—country meats and butter &c., not so now—The hucksters now, go far into the country and buy up all manner of supplies. Country men are agreed to this trafic—at less prices, because of the increased difficulty of getting their wagons and horses, in proper places for safety, and care in the city. The success of great hotels and eating houses now ingross the first and best supplies in market—and speculators go there and buy largely for New York markets, to send on by railroads &c.,—Formerly, none but real country farmers sold their productions in our markets,—now the stalls are very much held by hucksters. Many now go into the country, and buy up the whole productions of farms—others buy up by contract, all their butter, milk, potatoes—poultry, calves, &c.,—House-keepers feel perniciously this great change for worse!

Extravagance of living and prices.

There is much to interest the philosophic mind—fond of unriddling the characteristics of our nature,—in looking into the actions of men—To consider the why and wherefore, of so many becoming the willing victims of imposition, practised upon vanity. See how readily, men go to highest charges—for table-diet—for board—for carriages—display for clothing—for show and display in everything.
See at watering places, how readily they submit to be spunged in everything—how reckless they affect to be to cost.—Think how readily *they* submit to exalted prices for alleged Champaigne, made of Cider of Wines adorned with blue strings, and gilded labels,—and sold at four prices as forty years old—So too of Brandies, made of our whiskey, and marked Bordeaux Vintage of 1830—And finally of Alleghany whiskey, selling by wholesale, at thirty-five to forty cents—marked very old and very good, at two to three dollars a gallon—How those who profit by the imposition, must laugh in their sleeve, to see the success of their craft upon the credulity and vanity, of those who live for show. Some lookers on, see and know these things. While such submissives to practised frauds, spoil and enhance the price of everything "to everybody!" As some confirm-

ation to the preceding, we here annex an article from the "Pennsylvania Inquirer," of the thirtieth of June, 1855.

"There is another form of extravagance to which public attention ought to be directed, for which the ladies are not so much responsible. It is seen in the present style of our public steamboats and hotels. It is neither necessary nor expedient for any of the substantial purposes of the travelling community, that our steamboats should be floating palaces, and that every person who dines at a hotel, should be made to pay for a sumptuous feast, involving all attainable luxuries, whether he wishes them or not. It would be of great public advantage, if our hotels should adopt the European plan of furnishing only what should be specially ordered. There is a manifest absurdity, as all will grant, in making every person who dines at a public table pay for wine which he does not use; but no greater than in making every guest pay the cost of a sumptuous meal, while he partakes only of the plainest dishes, and desires no other.

"Another evil of this system is, that at these public tables, the example of luxury and extravagance, is set which promotes the same in private life. This is one of the many forms in which habits of luxury are gaining upon our people, and from which we must be reformed, or be ruined. The innocent in such a case suffer with the guilty. If the extravagant only beggared themselves, the evil were less to be deplored. But their habits are the source of those great commercial disasters which press most heavily upon the poor, who are thus thrown out of employment, and cut off from the means of earning their bread. Such extravagance is one of the forms of public wrong, of injury to the Commonwealth, of violence to the general humanity; and every sentiment and precept of Christianity is against it."

Travelling now-a-day.

The mass of the travelling public now, have no conception of the things they have lost, by the modern means of going by *Railways*. They go too rapidly for country observation, and pass too, through *low* grounds, and avoid going through towns, &c.,—whereas, formerly going by Stage they saw all of the best Villages, Inns &c.,—The passengers too, not exceeding a dozen at a time, became sociable in the route—were feasted and lodged at Inns, by the way—There was then much to interest, by sight-seeing; but now, they go to Boston, or to Niagara &c., and find all between places an entire blank.

Changes on Ocean voyages—now present a new era.

Now we build vessels of 3,000 tons, (and even of 5,000!) to traverse between our coasts and Europe—as Packets &c.,—In 1818, Jeremiah Thompson of New York, built Packets of 300 tons—and in 1821 he added one of 500 tons, which was disused, as too large for the then trade! In former years, when the influence of the Gulph Stream, as a *warmer* of the atmosphere was less known and understood, vessels leaving England were used to go South to the coast of Africa, to take trade winds and make across to Charleston, South Carolina—making it a necessary intermediate place—Vessels too, arriving off the coast of New York in winter, if the ice and frost were severe, used to put back to Charleston or the West Indies, there *to thaw*, and to stand out *till Spring*.—But *now* Vessels only put off to the Gulph Stream and there loosen their icy fetters, and return back to New York &c.,—Log books of 100 years ago, show that the average rate of sailing, (so says Lieut: Maury.) between New York and the West Indies, *did not exceed one mile per hour*,—because the action of the Stream Currents, were so powerful and little known—Doctor Franklin, is said to have first suggested the idea of avoiding the action of that stream *against* vessels—in 1748, when Kalm, the Sweedish naturalist, visited our country, he came from Gravesend, August 15, and arrived in 41 days, and called that, "the shortest passage ever known!"

Steamers now, are in full operation every where! What changes in thirty years of time!—Even *I* have seen *two ages*, with more of strange passes, than has been before witnessed!

Wonderful is the progress of Steam Vessels—only take a few facts of the past, to compare with things *now* and progressing!—

Previous to the year 1800, some eight or ten keel boats, of 20 to 25 tons, performed the carrying trade between Cincinnati and Pittsburg.—In 1802 the first government vessel appeared on Lake Erie,—In 1811 the first Steam boat, (the Orleans) was launched at Pittsburg—Previous to 1817, about twenty barges of about 100 tons, constituted the force of transport—from Orleans, along the River up to Louisville and Cincinnati—They made but one trip a year—From the Falls (Louisville,) up to Pittsburg, about 150 keel boats of about thirty tons, did the carriage of freight &c., about 1815-17.—They used six or seven weeks in making the passage to and fro. In 1818 the first Steam boat ("Walk in the water,") was built on Lake Erie—In 1826, the water of Michigan was first ploughed by a Steam boat visit.—Now what are Steam vessels doing?

A wonderful change is latterly effected of having ships as Packets and Steamers, to sail *certainly* on a given day—Such accuracy was never before aimed at, or expected—Another great change is, that ships come and go from wharves, without noise, oaths and curses—Formerly, Captains had to be full of passion, and bustle—And very often when they came up to the wharf, there was to be *a crush*, of something—to be afterwards repaired.

Lately too, it is found out, that Seamen can sail without grog and drunkeness—and that it is not indispensable to their usefulness and service, that they should be ignominiously *flogged*! Too long they have been treated as dogs—henceforth as men!

Change of Postal concerns.

This is a great affair for all the people;—Mails passing with such celerity and at *so little of charge.* This is something that everybody feels, and rejoices in. A letter, big enough for two of former letters, (half an oz.) going all the way to California and Oregon, for only ten cents! No one now-a-days, has occasion to encumber a private conveyance anywhere.—To contrast these easy means of intercourse, with what the men of the Revolutionary period experianced, is indeed a wonderful change. Then the conveyances by mail, was hazardous—infrequent and expensive. Families then, seperated by the War, and living in the country, reserved themselves, almost exclusively to private chances—and scarcely aimed to exchange letters, but about once in a year—Nothing was more common, than for men in the public service to write some two or three times, before even one would be received. Not long since, when postage was twenty-five cents, per letter to towns in the West, or to New Orleans—the last occupying a month in transit, the tax of postage was a heavy item,—when all outside of one sheet, was taxed double —Now *double* letters can pass as single, to those who will write without *useless* Envelopes. Formerly it was deemed of real importance, in case of needed proof of identity, to secure to each letter, the Post mark of date and place.* A time may be expected to occur when the absence of such Post marks, may be found of much moment in some court trial. I have never yet used an Envelope.—News Papers, now so universally scattered every where, and so grateful in remote places, was in the past times, almost wholly unknown—They went out to Publishers, for their use, in republications of Local Journals. There are no people on the earth, who have such chances of general knowledge—To this we may add, that the editorials and communications are generally of superior composition and style. A man who reads much, is necessarily inducted into an improved style of writing, by what he reads.

The Progress of the Daily Press.

In April 1775, there were thirty-seven news-papers in the colonies. Of this number, only eight of them were devoted to the home government.—Of those which did not take sides, five of them went over to the Tory party during the war. The five States of Maryland, Virginia, North and South Carolina and Georgia, taken together, had but one more news-paper than Pennsylvania, and only three more than Massachusetts.

In the year 1798, there were two hundred news-papers in all the United States—Of these 178 or 180 supported the Washington and Adams' administrations—The twenty others, were mostly under the controul or influence of aliens, and *opposed* to the leading measures

* Mrs. Barker, of Philadelphia saved 80.000 Dollars in Court, by such mark!

of the Executive—chiefly by French merchants—strongly biased to French interests abroad.

The Daily Penny Press—Nothing is like this rapid improvement in offering cheap information to the People—It was deemed a perilous adventure, when the Ledger first began its career, fourteen years ago—Then all the daily papers of Philadelphia printed but 7000 copies to subscribers—now the Ledger alone prints off 40,000 impressions—Other cities now have well-supported penny papers—To this, add the fact, that all our youth are to be educated at the public expense, and surely we shall become the greatest readers in the world!

Our once Wooden Country.

Not long since, our woods were so abundant, as to be deemed an incumbrance—It sold in the cities at low rates for fuel—And Mulbery and Maple for use for furniture, was scarcely looked at or regarded —Now pine for combustion, and white pine for all kinds of construction, are rising in prices and alarmingly becoming scarcer and scarcer—Iron is beginning to supply the place of many things formerly used in white pine—Coal is supplying the place of fire wood, a happy discovery in a needed time—Rags and paper having become scarce, we have now discovered fibrous plants and wood as a capital substitute. Truly, the human mind, enlightened, is competent to provide for all its actual wants · Our heaviest inconvenience, is provision for our luxuries—These give us constant annoyances—in inflated expenditures—adverse "balances of trade" &c., The world is made up of wrong doers.—And *the proud*, as well as *the poor*, are always with us.

Politics.

Politics as a profession and employment, steadily advances—It is seized as the road to advancement. It is looked to, by active men, as a means of living and support. They aim to *divide* us as a people, and to keep us in opposition, that they may severally divide the spoils. There needs some great, national, cheap paper, sustained by disinterested, able and patriotic men, to show us *truth*, and to show the sinister designs of all selfish politicians—Such a measure, can only be effected by a combination of able, disinterested men,—Men free from the tramels of party, and nobly aiming at the good of the whole. Shall we not yet see this? The press as it now operates, will not publish anything against those who are liberal contributors for advertisements, &c., They are not willing to disoblige *such*.

Elections,—These are now made affairs of display and excitement, wholly different from the quiet of former times.—They had no music, placards or banners, as now; and no such thing as omnibuses to pick up voters—No taverns for assembling in wards--and no stump orators, travellling round districts to win proselytes and partizans.—We are *worked upon* by every contrivance—which selfishness, if not patriotism, can devise!

Luxury and Wealth.

Are daily presenting new forms of display—in furniture, dress, equipages and table indulgence. All old forms are passing away. —Nothing of the revered past, is allowed to remain. Think of ladies dresses now costing 1200, to 1500, dollars! and the wives of *Commoners,* having jewelry to the amount of 15,000 to 2),000 dollars, and more.--Evening parties, too, among such, to be boastfully paraded at an expense of 1,000 dollars for a night! We are certainly a fast changing people. Whether for weal or woe, posterity shall judge.

It is often observed, that the *young,* in fashionable life, are far more arrogant and assuming in companies of display and exhibition, than they used to be.--They are far less reverent to the aged than in former times,—pushing them aside, from counsel or controul. Former shame-facedness of youth, is regarded as awkard *mauvaise honte* and not to be tolerated in "good society," so called. Europeans even now, among us, wonder at the unrestrained freedom of talk and action, of our young females.—They now have their social Soirees to themselves,—all young together.

The *increase of Wealth,* produces an abundant overshare of Professional men—in Law, Physic, and Army and Navy. It is greatly needed to exalt the character of Tradesmen (so called) so as to lead many of good means to enter therein—especially to elevate the class of architects—of carpenters and shipwrights—manufacturers of metals—of machinery &c.—great room now exists for educated Farmers.—The Clergy serve *by call.*

Extravagance in Dress.

At this time a fashionable dry goods store advertises, a lace scarf for 1500 dollars! Another, has a bridal dress for 1,200 dollars—Bonnets at 200 dollars are also sold. Cashmeres, from 300 dollars and upwards, are seen by dozens along Broadway. And 100 dollars is quite a common price for a silk gown.—Think of such a scale of prices for "un-ideaed" American women! Can the pampering of such vanities, elevate the character of our women? Alas! the women who live for such displays—who give their whole attention to diamonds and dress, are fast becoming unfitted for wives or mothers —and are operating the ruin of husbands and parents.—Do we not greatly need voluntary sumptuary laws and restraints! History records, that when the Roman matrons fell into similar extravagances the Empire itself, felt the deterioration, and fast fell into its decline

Will any consider! One serious consideration is, that prudent thoughtful men, cannot engage in matrimonial alliances—In this, the ladies themselves will become sufferers:—And men themselves, driven from hopeful marriages, will be induced (several of them,) to resort to concubinage. What a fearful extremity for the future! Let the really elite of "upper tendom," reform this thing. as a *patrictic* measure, and all the lower world will follow—Who will consider?

At Christmas, in New York, an Opal breast pin, set in a circle of diamonds, was bought for a lady for 4,500 dollars! A leader, in the Pennsylvania Inquirer and the Public Ledger of the eighth of November, 1856 are strongly confirmatory of all these remarks.

The Pennsylvania Inquirer, of the thirtieth of June, 1855, thus notices "Popular Extravagance:"—

"Our Christianity and our love of Country should put us upon fitting remedies for some of the alarming habits of extravagance which prevails among us. One of the sources of this manifold evil has been fairly put in the following remarks of a wholesale merchant and importer, as given in the Annual report, of 'The American Woman's Education Society:'"

"You have got hold of a great matter, sir, I hope you will succeed. The women are wrong, sir. They are not educated rightly. They are going to bankrupt the country unless there is a change.—More is thought of show than substance. We pay scores of millions annually for ladies ornaments, which are of no use. We cannot afford it. It is worse than sinking the gold in the sea! We are paying more duties on artificial flowers than on railroad iron! God help you to elevate the position and the aim of woman."

"The fact that a store in this city, employed in the sale of laces and other superfluities in that line, pays a rent of ten thousand dollars a year, is a significant comment upon this speech. There is no cure for such an evil, though it threatens ruin to the country, and greater ruin to Christian character, but in something that shall divert the ambition of the female mind to something better worthy of rational and immortal beings, than this rivalry in expensive dress and outward show."

Hoops Again!

We had hoped that our ladies would never again be brought to use such ill-looking, useless and deforming appendages to their dresses —They are, as seen along our streets, a Misdemeanor. They are so suggestive of immodest thoughts, both while worn and also when seen dangling from stores along the streets, just like so many parsachutes. One feels as if they must be scanning them, to conjecture how and where the limbs therein could be found! They are too, so annoying and engrossing of place and room in omnibuses—Rail Cars, and in church pews and aisles—and *why* all this; but as spell bound *subserviants* to some *foreign* spell—one feels scandalized for "the Land of the Free!" Nor is this all—Ladies who profess to be christians and communicants too, *pledged* "to renounce the vain pomp and vanities of the world, and *not to be led thereby*," go up to the sacramental altar, showing before the eyes of all beholders—an unseemly vanity!

When we think of "the human form divine," as fashioned in the purpose of the Creator;—when he gave us also, our abiding appreciation and sense of the beautiful, so fully expressed in the *Grecian* models, so universally adopted by all subsequent Sculptors and Artists: And think also of that same human form as prevalent in the year 1800 and afterwards, and as then universally approved by the whole Beau Monde. What must be the feelings of the former beaux and other beholders now, at this modern expose of a "monstrous novelty and strange disguise!" Women then, presented as *they ever should*, specific notices of individual figure—such as Heaven made and designed them; and the present artificial rotundity and expansiveness, were just the kind of personages, who then carried themselves at a discount—Don't many remember!

Presents at Weddings.

This has lately come up, as a fashionable extravagance, to the amount of many thousands of dollars—The practice with the haut ton now is, for the Bride to have them set off for display in a guest room, where the articles are paraded for exhibition, with appended notices from the Donors—Both the bride and the Donors, obtain their shares of renown and report, on such occasions.—All of the invited, very naturally become contributors, and some feel the tax thus imposed, somewhat unwelcome—on some ultra occasions, 15,000 to 20,000 dollars are said to have been contributed—But after that, comes the reaction;—for those thus cheered by benefactors, must come in *their turns* to disburse all their gains in equally ambitious gifts to after marriages in their circles. (Some of these are shrewdly suspected of being loaned from jewellers at high fees!)

Wearing of Beards.

Looking at numbers of men who now wear beards, and seeing, of course, their countenance with many, one cannot but look back upon a time in our youth, when not worn by any citizens; one cannot but remember a time, when the Tunkards and Menonists of inland Pennsylvania used to come to the city, wearing their beards—They were then a repulsive spectacle to boys and ladies, universally—and it required no little resolution in the wearers to bear them as they then did, for Christian profession sake—Now others do the same thing cordially for fashion's sake! "Les fous font les modes."

Opera Music.

Such as men once used with human voice, is greatly altered—natural voices and tones, such as nature impressed, are passing away, for unnatural efforts, making strange display—such as proceeds from *Opera singing*—by strained efforts—All of our singers, in social circles, now show much of affectation.—That it is not according to man's nature and bias, is abundantly proved by the plaudits every where bestowed upon Public Singers, who burlesque the others, and sing with good voices, *natural* airs—Such as the Virginia and Orleans Minstrels—the Hutchinson family &c., Some itching ears, have even introduced affected singing into churches! So did not Luther, who was himself a good musician—he adapted all his tunes to their subjects—Solemn, grave, severe, or gay.

Tho' musical I am—I never could
Fall into raptures o'er Italian singing;
Songs without words I never understood,
Tho'soft and sweet as " harp of houris stringing—"
Nor would I ask a lady for a song
Unless the poetry has beauty in it.

Our artificial Music, considered—We having before stated how much we spoil our music by artificial refinement, we have set down a confirmation, given by another hand—to wit: " All music that paints nothing is only noise! and were it not for fashion, which *unnatures* every thing, it would excite no more pleasure than a sequel of harmonious and finely sounding *words without any order or connection*—" " Those airs which paint images—and called speaking airs, will always surpass the most labored refinement of art—such as ' Roys wife,' 'John Anderson &c.,'—fascinate the soul, because they are *melodies* of *nature*." Mr. Barnum has created a new era in public excitability—He uses the press with such dexterity to *puff* himself and his exhibitions, as to make himself the focus of all that is popular. —all to make his own fortune!—None but himself could have ventured on such a great amount of money to Jenny Lind for her visit—Think of so much being awarded for *singing*! Is it possible that it is, indeed, so super-human and exalted as to be really worth the contribution—or is it excited phrenzy! The very splendor of her reception at New York is to forestall public opinion, and to come eventually out of the peoples' pockets! See her at Irving house having there for herself, a parlor, drawing-room, dining room, and two bed-rooms—all newly fitted up in a most gorgeous style, at a cost of 7,000 dollars! One really sighs at such extravagance in republicans—225 dollars is bid for an admission ticket! and at Boston, the first ticket bid off at 625 dollars, and her suite of rooms cost for decorations, 13,000 dollars!"

Our Manufactures—of all kinds.

Our improvements and inventions, in all things needful for our use and, comfort, is boundless—Formerly we depended for *every thing* upon importation. Now we fabricate every thing needed for clothing, in cotton and wool,—and all kinds of metallic implements and iron-mongery. In chemical, and articles of materia medica, the quantity home made, is wonderful—our productions in glass, iron and metallic substances are very great and very perfect.

The *changes* already effected, would fill a volume in enumeration. Now we make Wall papers, carpets, paints—(See a book now publishing by Freedly, on this subject.)

The Chemical productions—as now got up by our manufacturers, would if told in extension, make a curious and interesting work—They have so cheapened the prices of drugs, and paints and colours, before imported, and had so many obstacles to surmount, to gain favour and beat down prejudice, that their history in popular style, would be quite entertaining.—Almost everything in this department was formerly imported. I have myself endeavored to procure facts. but those concerned, make money too fast to spare time for detail, for *my* use and notice!

The Casting of Iron, is undergoing vast improvements—from once being extremely rough and unsightly, we now see *beauty* of castings in all forms.—Our Pine woods are used far beyond reproduction—other woods must hereafter supply—The Pines of North Carolina &c., are now using for camphine fluids for lamps &c, The formation of gas—for lighting streets and houses, is a modern affair:—and it is supposed that *water* will some day be found to supply its place! The introduciion of the use of India rubber and Caoutouche, for all manner of things—as for clothing &c., is wholly a new affair of wonder.

Necromancy and Magnetism, &c.

Necromancy, Fortunc-telling &c., by *advertising* men, professing to be philosophers, and proceeding by Nativities &c., is a new affair and seems to find employers.—Slight of hand, by Blitz,—the man of Ava, &c., are new and very successful enterprises—"wondering for their bread!" They are really wonderful in concealment and deception; but by their honest confessions of illusion, serve to do away former conceptions of Demoniacizm.

Witchcraft is gone—exploded, and the nearest approach and illustration of former deceptions, seem now developed in Animal magnetism; and the powers possessed, by manipulation and passes, to influence the actions of others, compelling them to sit, stand, walk and do, according to the will of the operator. Operators, too, working from powers in nature, and used by honest men, on other men, sincere and true as themselves.

Increase of Wrong and Outrage.

Really my country, is so much increased in crime of all kinds and characters, as makes me feel heart-sick to think of its progress—and the state of society to which I am to leave my heirs.—It really makes life of far less value to live it—and almost makes one sigh for a change into another and better world.

Combinations of Wicked Boys—These combinations of lawless lads in the cities of Philadelphia and New York, under indicative names—signifying outlawry and mischief,—is wholly a new manifestation of progress:—Such as have made "houses of Refuge" indispensable for the security of Society against their crimes and encroachments. The good people of the Olden time, had no such disturbers of their peace—All boys worked at something *useful* in their times. Cheap Theatres and Comic allurements, are now their visited night schools.

> "Because inquity shall abound.
> The love of many shall wax cold."

The year 1852 has been a season of most appalling crime—so many gross murders—rapes—cruelties, See the book, *Hot Corn* of New York. Excessive destruction of life, by "Accidents," &c.,—One who fears God, may well fear his judgment,—unless we repent and turn.—There has been a morbid sensibility for criminals—a desire to screen them from the merited gallows—This encourages wickedness—Religion itself, seems not to have the same hold and influence, on the mass—Men grow up by example to forget God.

Objections to Capital punishment, is a new thought, gaining ground fast.—It is made an affair of religious obligation—It may be expected to prevail for awhile—but probably not permanantly—Because its tendancy will be to encourage crime. God, who is *unchanging,* once declared that—"thine eye shall not spare or pity, the murderer," and the new Testament, said, "the *sword* of justice, was not used in vain," and St. Paul, said, "he was willing *to die*, if he committed things *worthy* of death," meaning thereby, that some offences were so regarded by him. Legislators exempt *from death,* (by executions) even while they fine our sons, for not serving in military duty *to kill* our enemies—So inconsistent are we! A better rule is,—"Society shall *shake* its encumbered lap, grown weary of the load!" It is a weary load to find imprisoned homes for lawless criminals. Will not another age restore Capital punishment?

What became of John Fitch.

The above is the heading of an article and letter in the Journal of the Franklin Institute, of March, 1853; as given in the following words—which go to *confirm*, what *I* had *before* published—to wit: Letter from Alexander M. Mc Dowell—

Demopolis, Alabama, July 6, 1852.

" As it is to this day an unsettled point, of what city of the East had the glory of being the birth place of Homer, so it has been equally undetermined as to the place in the great West, where the mortal remains of one greater than Homer, have their resting-place; I mean the great embodied *genius of Steam* ;—the indigent, friendless machinist *John Fitch*—the co-worker and adviser of Rumsay and Fulton. &c., &c., &c., The writer of this having occasion some twenty-five years ago to bury a little nephew at *Bardstown*, Nelson County, Kentucky—and having discovered in the crowded little protestant graveyard, near the County jail, an open space of twenty or thirty feet square, not occupied by graves, commenced digging the nephew's grave there; when he was stopped by the aged sexton Mr. Alexander Mc Keown, who said that spot ' contained the bones of John Fitch, the great Steam man'—and that the space was left thus large to build a monument to his memory by the State of Kentucky. The Hon. Ben: Hardin and Doctor Burr Harrison, of whom inquiry was made, corroborated the statement of Mr. Mc Keown, and states that a resolution to erect a monument over Fitch had passed the Legislature of Kentucky, of which they had been members, but that no appropriation had ever been made to carry the resolution into effect. The aged Sexton must long since have passed from earth, and it is probable there are now few, even in Bardstown, who could point out the grave of John Fitch.

Signed, Alexander M. Mc Dowell.

Such are the facts as given by Mc Dowell, and it frets me while I write, to think how little the public will give heed to what we have severally written to bring the remains to storied, monumental fame—President making, and Foreign Artistes, are more engrossing!—McDowell, would doubtless like to know what I have done in *the same* object. I wrote to him per mail and heard nothing—

Romanist Religion among Us.

The Romanists are, at the present, establishing themselves throughout our whole land, and we mean to state *the fact* as it is without reproach.—This is done by erecting churches, schools, and nuneries, (by aid of Foreign funds,) in all places. Many are disturbed by their presence. But the press will be too free and expansive to allow them to take undue ascendency and domination, and will urge their conductors also to divest themselves of many of their assumptions and pageantries, as fostered and indulged in foreign countries. Romanist people here, cannot be governed with absoluteness, as abroad. The result may be, that Romanism, will be improved, and true Religion, among themselves, will be better diffused.--It may come to take the type of *Puseyizm*(a new thing)and both together may catch the affections of those who desire pomp and circumstance in splendid Religion and love the imagination to be exercised in "decent ceremonials," dramatic displays, Opera singing and music, &c.,

The Treaty Elm.

There was taken as a scion from the treaty tree, by S. Coates, a young tree, which sprung up from the roots of the fallen tree, which he planted in the grass lot, Westward of the Hospital Wall on Ninth street. It there grew to be a large tree (high as the three storied house)—but when they opened Clinton street, it left that tree standing out in the street, two feet beyond the curb—At my request of the lot owners it stood there awhile after the pebble pavement was made—but now I see they have cut it down as *an incumbrance*, alas! how little many care for *our antiquities*! It is vain to argue with money interests—It stood about the sixth house, North side, from Ninth St. —I have just learned from Mr. S. D. Bowers, that there is now alive a large Elm tree, upwards of sixty years of age, standing on the street, at the place long known as the dwelling house and ship yard of his father, taken by his father, Samuel, when a young man, sixty-five years ago, as a shoot, from the celebrated Treaty tree.—There he nursed and cherished it, during all his life-time, and at this time, it is now in full vigour. Long may it survive, as a grateful *historical* remembrance! It is indeed strange, to be so little generally known. It stands a little South of where the British had their River battery, in the Revolutionary War, and on the river street, "Penn" as then there. (Samuel Bower died in 1834, at seventy-five years of age.) The tree stands on the West side, fronting Rowland & Co—Iron works,—and is midway between Maiden on the North, and March or Poplar on the South. Before the death of Samuel Bower--a limb of fifty feet across the street, got broken by a storm--It was strengthened and stood a few years, when another storm broke it off—The tree now spreads sixty feet.

Consolidation of Philadelphia.

This is indeed, a wonderful event--effected by mutual concessions of various included towns and districts—It will be a very benificial improvement. By working as a *Unit* hereafter, it will *unite* many former seperate interests. The full history of the *means* used by which the measure has been effected, would make *a book* of itself.—Even political parties, laid aside, for the occasion all of their local interests; and patriotism and disinterestedness was allowed for the special occasion, to *govern* for the good of the whole! The men of my youth, never looked forward to such a growth of their city—It is a wonder!

Germantown Changes and Improvements.

When I had succeeded to influence many to plaster the fronts of their houses—I next came to stimulate lot owners to *pave* their foot ways.

I began this article to say, that we are indebted to Robert H. Thomas, for the impulse, *first* given by *him*, to increase the houses and population of the place. He proved by his own success, in laying out new streets, and selling lots and building cottage houses, that he had a power to attract business men, and men of money, to seek a residence for Country air, &c., He began his first operations some twelve years ago along Centre street; next he bought, and laid out the lots on Kelly's farm—His example set the two Prices—Eli and Philip—to buy the grounds of Wunder, and to lay out Price street, —where I live.—Germantown now, is no longer, Germantown as it was! It now goes on in building fancy cottages for city business men, &c.,

Germantown once the seat of Government of the United States!

In the year 1789, a *Resolution* passed the House of Representatives then in session in New York, that the permanent seat of government, ought to be on the banks of the Susquehanna, in *Pennsylvania*; but it was amended in the Senate by fixing upon Germantown, *as its site.* Upon being returned to the House, the amendment was approved and sent back again to the Senate, for a slight amendment, providing that Pennsylvania laws, should continue in force, in such Federal district, *until* Congress should legislate otherwise—Thereupon, the subject was postponed, until the next Session;—and thus, our old Germantown, after being thus fixed upon by both houses, was wholly laid aside!—The influence of Robert Morris, the Financier, was said to have led to its being fixed in Philadelphia City,—where it settled *at the S. E. corner of Sixth and Chestnut streets.* The same now occupied as Court Rooms.

We well remember to have seen in our boyhood, *a caricature* published by the New Yorkers, who were averse to its removal from that city,—wherein Robert Morris was shown in the foreground, drawing with a rope the Congress to Philadelphia!—To our young mind, it was *a queer* picture! What a picture might not a fruitful imagination, *now construct*, of possibilities now, if such a location had been so settled. Things would have been so very different now both in Washington city.—The city of distances; and the present *granite heights* of cottage-embellished Germantown!—Washington itself, at some future day, may be removed, more to *the centre* of population—and St. Louis itself, become the seat of the American Empire! We are all in a state of Progress!

Germantown and its old grave stone.—In May 1856, there was found. four feet below the surface, at the rear of Charles Waiss' Coal yard, a marble flat laid stone, indicating the place of burial of Godfried Lehman, and beneath it his bones —The stone inscribed him, as dying in his sixty-eighth year, in the year 1756, (one hundred years ago,) as born in Germany—and as being buried in his own garden. He was thehead of the present Lehman family in Germantown—and Benjamin Lehman, conveyed the remains and marble stone, to the Tunker's grave ground—It arrested considerable attention—

Log Prison and ancient group of houses in Germantown.—The picture, which we have given of *the last* of the oldest houses still remaining in Germantown,—now belonging to the family of John Green, present a very picturesque groupe,—and stand in interesting *contrast* with many modern houses, built there. They would seem to have been built at several intervening periods—The front house on the right of the picture, now faced with white mortar is the original Log house—It was brought and placed there, as the dwelling house of John Adams Hogermoed, who had before passed a night in it—for some occasion of intemperance, while it occupied the Market square as the Prison. When it was afterwards sold, the same Hogermoed became the owner. One of the higher houses in the rear, it may be seen, is diagonally boarded.—The whole groupe seems to be formed of *four* different constructions—a part is of stone, All such *remains* of the primitive times, are fast fading from the things that be!

Germantown Railroad.—This, now popular Road, was originated about the year 1830, by Jesse Torrey, then a temporary resident of the place—It was sustained at the time, by sundry Essays in Mr. Freas' paper—An act was soon after procured, for its Charter, and met with a ready subscription, especially from sundry City Brokers—with whom the Scrip found a ready advance of price--Some time after the whole concern met with a severe depression, by the defalcation of its President—It lingered on a great while, while shares sold often as low as one dollar—An Act was procured in February 1847, for the relief of its creditors, whereby, stock owners and creditors, agreed to consolidate their claims at from thirty-five to eighty per cent reduction, according to their class—After which, the Road, including to Noristown, went on progressively rising, till it has risen above par, and has given twelve per cent of Dividend.

Brother Jonathan.

This name as a personation and name of our countrymen of New England—and sometimes—abroad, for all Americans, is a designation said to have been first used by General Washington, as the appellation he gave to his friend Jonathan Trumbull, the Governor of Connecticut—in the period of the Revolution. When upon an occasion of importance, Washington said—" We must consult brother

Jonathan, first"—Officers present, came to use it as a bye word—and as the phrase circulated more and more,—it came eventually to be the pass word of the people, generally.—

Great Fire.

On the ninth of July, 1850 at four P. M. occured the *greatest* fire ever witnessed in Philadelphia, commencing near Vine St. on Water St. and burning up to the East side of Second, and from New St. to Callowhill—no house escaping. Among the houses, were some of the most respectable residences of the olden time—say Friends meeting House in New St. (Keys Alley)—Wests' House, N. W. corner of Vine and Front Sts. several from thence along the North side of Vine to New Market St.—and at that N. W. corner, the *Two* respectable houses of the Messers Whitehead, John and James, brothers—The corner house was once the residence of our Governor Mifflin, and in the War of the Revolution it was the residence of Col. Abercrombie of the British Army—afterwards General Abercrombie who was killed in Egypt.—Up Front St.—West side, was the residence of Col. Coperthwaite and other respectable men of the Revolution.

Old Furniture.

A modern freak of fashion—began at Boston and brought here, has been the revival of old furniture, found in garrets and lofts:—by the art of *varnishing*, they have been brought out with display—the gathering of such, came in time, to such a demand, as to call for new-making much of chairs &c., in imitation—It is queer that those who thus profess to venerate such old family articles, are the same class who before scouted them from sight—Even now, the class, are not those who read " Annals of Olden Time"—They go for them, because the fashion is so! very well.

Walnut Wood, as used for Cabinet furniture, has now become a *fashion*—just because it is getting scarce and dearer, and withall looks so like Rose wood—But in former days Walnut was the *common* furniture wood—as being second to Mahogany—As men got more wealthy it was discarded—it became cheaper and cheaper, and was sold as common fuel in my time—But now, it is again a wood of luxury—as is also curled Maple and Birch. This improvement comes from the use of Varnish, which helps the display of the grain.—

General Education.

General Education for all the people is a new affair—taxing all the people therefor. Before this time it was held ungenteel to accept of free education—But when men of large estate saw how heavily they were taxed to pay for the children of others, and for schools of such elevation and excellence as the High Schools, sundry of the upper class *combined* in a resolution to send their children to the same schools; then everybody aimed to include their children—The result is, that Americans, are coming to be the most generally instructed people in the world. This advantage, with cheap news papers and cheap printing and book-making, seem destined to so free our minds, as to enable us forever hereafter, to surmount all assumptions of future power to debase, and enthral the human mind, whether in church or state.

Education now, is the same up-hill work it ever was, with very little reform—save the non use of the strap and lash—but some day they will *reverse* the order of acquiring *languages,* and will learn words —words, *first,* and *afterwards* Grammar.—Nature says so.—They will also say *it is enough,* for common schools, to teach only, reading writing, arithmetic and grammar

Pins, what becomes of them?

Considering the millions made every day—the people wonder what becomes of them! This subject brings to mind their state in a former age—When they were all imported and cost more than now. It was a consideration to save them all, by picking them up when seen—This was a peculiar operation of the boys—Two special reasons concurred with them—They were their capital, for the play of the game of *push pin,* and for their surplus they could get pennies, at home—It was a common sight to see boys with a line of pins stuck in their sleeve cuffs.—Men too, always had a place for some, stuck in a line, at the head of the lappels of their coats.—It showed how far we were once a frugal, conservative people.—It was of the same characteristic, as that of wearing Cloths, *over again* by turning garments.

Family Stockings and Shirts.

Now stockings are made too cheaply to permit of knitting them; but in former times, mothers and daughters were always busy at their knitting, while sitting in attention to calls from visitors—They not only, were proud to knit their own wear well, but they also, made coarser ones for the boys and servants—made of thread and woollen yarn—and if in large families they *could not* do all, they hired women helps, to do them—Young ladies, then, truly, could not get time for Pianos, Opera, Theatre and spectacles.

Stores for sale of shirts and drawers—is a modern affair.—Such a thing would not have succeeded when females, universally, in families worked out such articles—Now females—very genteel, have not the time!

Land of the Swen Family.

"A grant was issued on the third of May, 1671, by Francis Lovelace, Esq,. Governor General, under the Duke of York, *confirming* to the family (as granted by the *Dutch* governor,) the former grant from Queen Christina, bearing *before* then, the names of Swen Gunderson, Swen Swanson, Ole Swanson and Andries Swanson the Wiccocoe Tract, containing eight hundred acres, at a quit rent of eight bushels of Winter wheat to his Majesty—Its boundary is as follows, to wit:—Beginning on the Delaware, a short distance North of Shippen St.;—thence Westward, verging towards Cedar street, striking it between eighth and ninth streets; thence along the South side of Cedar street to a point about six perches East of Shippen *Lane*; thence Southward, *parrellel* with Shippen Lane, to a corner a short distance South of Federal, and West of twelfth street,—probably the N. W. corner of the parade-ground lot; thence along the *said Creek* to the Delaware; and thence to the place of beginning"—The Eastern portion of the tract, bounded by the Passyunk was erected into the district of Southwark, March 26, 1762." —Think of such a tract of eight hundred acres—to one family once, —and *now* no exalted heirs!

Schoolkill River.

The origin of this name has never been satisfactorily explained—It has been referred to *Dutch*, as expressive of hidden river—;—But I have an original idea, that it was from the beginning of *English* form and origin—It was a combined word—having *kill*—for creek or river; because it was a common *English* manner once, to call all the small waters, *kill*, from the early Dutch settlers—*School* was added, to express the peculiar place where *schools* of emigrating fish, resorted up its waters to spawn their young.—Thither went every summer the shad and herrings to its source—and in *that* river, was always the greatest fisheries known in our waters—far surpassing the Delaware itself. Its waters were colder than the Delaware, and therefore it allured thereto the finest, earliest and largest fish.

Original Shore of the Delaware.

At present, there is no longer, any evidence or view of the original shore—and wharves being everywhere extended out into the river—the passage to Smith's Island &c., is now much abridged.—But *I* have seen the original shore at several places, down to the year 1800 —It came up to the *east* side of Water street, so I saw it, at Pooles Bridge—at Taylor's dock, below Callowhill St.—at the North side of Dock St. creek—and at the end of the street North of Swedes church.—

Britsh Defences of Philadelphia.

British Defences at Philadelphia in the Life of General John Lamb pp. one hundred and ninety-one, are described—to wit:

Because of the increase of Washington's army at White Marsh, in November '77—they began to fear some attack from him; Richard Platts letter to General Lamb, says: "They have thrown up very strong lines across—from River to river, besides these, ten or twelve very strong redoubts, ditched, friezed, picketed and abbatised; every one of which cross fire and flank their lines." "Judge then, if any attacks will be made by our army this winter"—[I suppose, these were made *so strong after* the Battle of Germantown, fourth of October '77. A picture of the same is here given.]

Conventions and Congresses.

It is a fact but very little considered, that the idea of these, came not up at first, as an invention of the Revolutionary War—It is was only the *renewal* of similar gatherings on other previous colonial associations—So many colonies—speaking the same language, and subject to the same *Parent* authority, naturally felt sympathies and mutual interests, though of different constitutions; and when occurrences from the French and Indians, produced mutual dangers, they instinctively called Conventions to consider their proper and harmonious action, even for the benefit of the Crown—While these meetings were congenial to its interests, the officers of the crown, both in America and England, looked on complacently—There were several of such calls of the Colonies, *before* the Revolution.

Sleds, Sleighs and Skates.

These are now quite altered affairs—Sleds were once made of boards and low, but now they are all set on runners like little sleighs.——Their skates now have iron foot rests (formerly of wood) and all with turn up, high fronts—not very safe in case of breaking through ice—formerly, the skates were called Dumps—having the irons no longer than the foot.—With this notice, we might notice, the numerous little wheel carriages made by Bushnel—So that all little folks have now something ornamental.—The Boys formerly, had far rougher things.—

Sleighs.—are far more showy, than in days of olden time—The small affairs called *jumpers*—such for two persons, with their *curved* upward fronts, present appearances of cost, far beyond the general former straightly boarded sides, and *triangular* fronts, for the stand, of the *upright* driver, of the times now by gone—Then they were made for whole families, with woolen, gay coverlids for the backs—Now they pass well for *courting* vehicles, and *tete-a-tetes.*

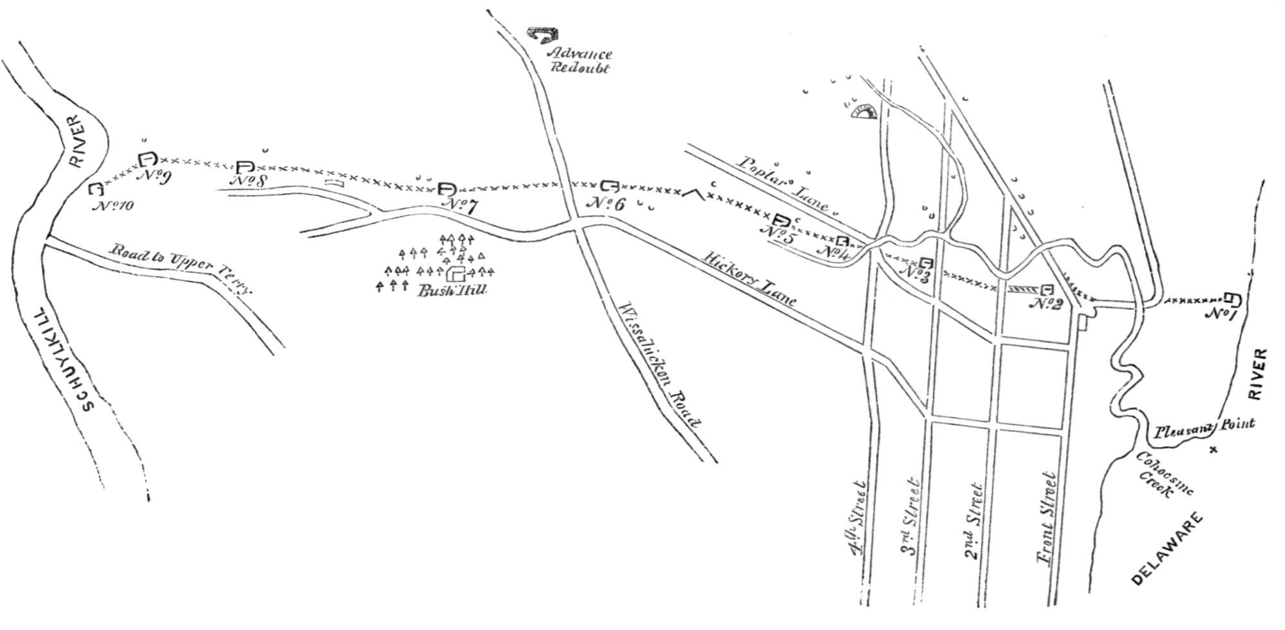

BRITISH DEFENCES OF PHILADELPHIA.—Page 610.

Name of Egg Harbour.

I think, I ascertained at Absecum beach, called Atlantic City now, from "the oldest inhabitants," why we have had the name of Egg-Harbour, for the long sea coast of Jersey—It meant, the Egg-*shelter*—a place of pre-eminent security for Birds, and their eggs—Many kinds of large birds, as seen there, only thirty years ago, built their nests in the tops of the numerous trees, once growing along the front beaches of the whole New Jersey Coast,—so that an individual standing on the top of the front line of sand mounts, (cast up by the winds) could look into the nests and see many large eggs, good for eating—These, and the grape vines, hanging to every tree, made the region of Sea coast—both the *place of Eggs*,—and also, as the *Northmen*, called it, the *vinland.* The former big birds and their eggs, are now greatly gone—The Mud hens, were once very numerous throughout the whole area of marsh grass in the Sound, being seven miles over in width—There the hens—raised piles of Mud—two feet high—in the tops of which they laid their eggs—But now the hens and nests, are rarely found. What a time, must once have been, for the "poor Indian," to have been gatherers of such cheap and ready food! and how ready there, for their use, oysters, clams, crabs, fish—Alas, poor Indian now westward driven! Such their destiny—such our inheritance now! One cannot reflect upon the *vast changes* affecting, without emotions of wonder! What cannot *enlightened* man effect! By and bye, we shall see Railroads traversing our continent from the Atlantic to the Pacific—How much wiser to preserve *Peace relations*—for benefitting mankind, than to *exhaust* all of *our* means in senseless Wars! An hundred millions wasted in War, would build Railroads across our Continent! Let us sedulously cultivate and preserve peace. Such was my spontaneous reflections while standing on the Sand hills of great Egg Harbour.

Cold and Snow of January, 1856.

This month it is alleged, in the Inquirer, has been the *coldest* for thirty-four years preceeding, say January 1821—then ten degrees below zero, by the records of the Thermometers—The mean temperature of January, as kept by J. Mc Allister has been twenty-eight degrees—and is far ahead of its predecessors—The snow, too, which began about the fourth and fifth has continued for sleighing, all through the month and into February.

The thermometer was down to ten degrees below zero—some two or three times at night. The ice, and skating and sliding on the Delaware was continued also—Doctor Rush had published that in his life he had not seen more than four degrees—below zero—I have not seen any degrees of cold set down to the memorable hard winters of 1740 and '80: but we saw then more mention of injuries by cold to cattle, swine, squirrels. Birds, Deer &c., The ice in the western waters and down the whole length of the Mississippi, go beyond all former years. The deep snow of the fourteenth and fifteenth of January 1831—caused good sleighing till the middle of February—The present sleighing lasted till the end of February also—and began the fourth and fifth of January—of course the *longest snow.*

The Year 1856—*Annus Mirabilis.*—This year has been wonderful —as stated in the "Evening Bulletin"—The last Winter so co d; this summer so hot and dry.—So many terrible calamities—of Ocean —Flood and Land :—Such accidents of Steamers and Railroads—A year of the terrible and effective.

"*Who Reads an American Book?*"

This sneer uttered in England a few years ago, is now well answered in the annexed article—as stated in 1856—at Crystal Palace, New York.

"Book publishing in this Country.—The Secretary of the Book Publishers' Association, in his valuable address at the Crystal Palace, said: 'Let it be remembered that the aggregate number of the *new* books first manufactured in a single year is not less than two millions four hundred thousand. Putting aside school books, Bibles. and society publications, the number of volumes printed and reprinted. will reach eight millions! The school-books alone will swell the number twelve millions more. The number of volumes issued yearly from the gigantic establishment of the Messrs. Harper alone, has been estimated at more than a million of volumes; and the Philadelphia house of Lippincott, sends forth books at an average of fifty cases per day, the year round. And consider, besides, the enormous bulk of reading matter issued by our 200 periodicals, and 2,000 newspapers! Think of the 18,000 double or 36,000 single reams of paper required yearly for a single magazine, which courses over the country, unprecedented in cheapness and attraction, at the rate of 150,000 per month. The wildest imagining at home or abroad, twenty years ago, would not have stretched so far as this. Why sir, the sheets from our book-presses alone, in a single year would reach nearly twice round the globe, and if we add the periodicals and newspapers, the issue of our presses in about eighteen months, would make a belt, two feet wide, printed on both sides, which would stretch from New York to the moon!'"

VARIETY OF PASSING BRIEF FACTS. VIZ:

News Papers at one cent a piece, were a wonder for cheapness, when first out.

It is new to use professional singers in churches—

It is still newer to sing responses while *kneeling*, as in the ten commandments.

The use of Cloroform in painful surgical operations, is new and assisting wonderfully.

Dentists are arriving at great improvements in "saving and preserving teeth.

Private penny posts, for delivery of letters in the city,—and express carriages for carrying heavy parcels about the cities,—and omnibuses for carrying people at small charges, are all new enterprises and succeed. The vending of clothing for gentlemen, *ready made*, is a new enterprise.—

Dispepsia and Spinal Diseases.—Dispepsia in men, and spinal diseases in women, are new forms of diseases, coming in, as a consequence of luxurious and indulgent living.

Boquets, (flowers) at Parties—is new—so also Boquets, on the Centre tables,—The tables themselves, are also new—Suppers to such parties. is also new.

Slate roofs, is now a beginning affair—because Cedar shingles come so high now.

—*Cedar Posts*, too, are becoming so high as to induce the use of Iron posts.

Building brick houses, in the City, in *Winter*—is a new enterprise, to save time.

Envelopes for Letters.—It is new to put letters under an envelope —It is a useless adjunct and will destroy the *evidence* of Post marks to letters.—The courts will some day complain of this.

We are invaded with new rules and new forms by Fashion's invisible Agent.—Who knows who first imposes the cuts of our dresses!

Use of Granite and Iron posterns.—The use of Granite and Iron posterns and pedestals to house fronts, is new.

The cutting of our garments, as now, is an entirely new device, and capital, too.

The planeing, jointing and grooving of boards, by Steam power, is wholly new.

Great signs to houses and some elevated upon roofs for display— and signs to read perpendicularly—and the formation of new forms of Sign letters—is all a new contrivance. So also, is various imitations of grained wood—such as oak, maple, mahogany &c.,—they were all began first in New York and then followed here.—

It is new to cover houses with plaster, in imitation of marble—brown stone and yellow &c.,

It is new to cover roofs of houses with zinc, tin, and slate.

The numerous wholesale Silk stores, exclusively of silk and ribbons from France, is new. So too, the importations from France of cloths and cassimers, is new—also French boots.—

Eating houses and Refectories is new among us,—especially oyster houses.

Paving foot ways, with flag stones—is a new affair—adopted from New York, when they had not good bricks.—The paving the streets with blocks of wood and blocks of stone—for carriage ways is new.—

Ship Launching Now.—They have now changed the way of launching ships—They now slide them off without the use of a girdle of *wedges*—by heavy hammers—That was a means far more interesting to hearers and spectators, than now.

The Pegging of Shoes and Boots, is a modern affair—so also of *turning* lasts—The wood pegging was the invention of Joseph Walker, *now alive,* at Hopkinton Massachusetts. He lives to see the trade of that State in shoes and boots, equal to eighteen millions of dollars!

Steeples—wherever built, were universally *white,* so as best to be seen furthest—and among trees.—Lately has come up a new conceit, of having them *brown* and chocolate—Aheu!

Carriers.—It is a modern thing to send home parcels from the stores, for purchasers,—and equally new for Butchers to send home meats purchased.—Men and women took home their own marketing; and many boys of good families, went with wheel-barrows, and stopt near the markets till filled—One remembers well, many young ladies of good families, who used to do all the marketing—Stores did not formerly have porters to cary parcels, and make fires, and sweep, &c.,—That was always done by the apprentice merchant. Boys are far prouder now, than they used to be, and more dressed in business.

The only known Gibbet Left.—The only known *gibbet* now in the United States—of the olden time remains, is now kept as a relic at the Moyamensing Prison.

Samuel Breck's Letter.—He describes our poverty, and our depression of spirit, at the conclusion of the War of the Revolution—and shows how wonderfully, all things revived and flourished, by the adoption of the Federal Constitution.—A charter which some proud and angry men are now disposed to annul and destroy! Read it—Read it! in the "North American," of the eleventh of February, 1851.

Mild Winter of 1850-51.—*The Past Winter*—of 1850-51, is one to be remembered for its mildness—The mean temperature of February—has been (though usually one degree the coldest in winter) 41¼ degrees, which is eleven degrees above the common mean average—very litlle of snow and very littie of frost has been seen—At this time, (March 1,) vegetation is one month ahead of ordinary seasons.

Flags of the Revolution. There are now at Alexandria, Virginia —The Hessian Flag, captured at Trenton —dated 1775, of embroidered silk—Also the Flag of the seventh Regiment, surrendered at York Town—Also the Flag of Washington's Body guard—is of silk and has the motto "Conquer or die."

"*Macpherson's Blues.*"—This corps of infantry originated in 1794, at this time I am furnished with a copy of the Roll of names, being four hundred and twenty-nine in all.—I joined the same corps, a minor, in 1798-9—and now I see that all are gone, to be no more, except seventeen persons, now "oldest inhabitants."

Henry Gideon, the last of Washington's Life Guard.—He died at New York, on the fifteenth of March, aged one hundred and one years—he was laid out in state, at the City Hall.—He is the same person, whom I formerly knew in Arch street, Philadelphia—above fifth street—He was called, as I remember, Washington's trumpeter —He had a fine-looking daughter.

Segars.—Men of the present age, seeing the immense use of segars, might think they were always so used; but not so—They began with the fever of 1793—and were first used, along the streets, to keep off the yellow fever.

Improvement of Street Paving.—In August, 1852—I wrote a letter to the City Commissioners—offering for the public good, my suggestion for an easy means of making the pebble pavements, more enduring—It was simply to *underlay* with cheap, *rough*, flat stone—With such underneath, the pebbles could not sink as now, and form wheel routs,—For a beginning trial, let them only underlay the usual wheel routs, and prove them—afterwards underlay the whole crown —leaving the side alone, as least used.—

General Thomas Harrison, the Regicide—I saw lately his portrait, in possession of Doctor Charles Willing of Philadelphia—It is a fine *cavalier* face and dress—with pointed beard and moustache—a face of about forty years—His three sons, Samuel, Benjamin and Joseph, came to this country at the earliest settlement—*Samuel* settled at Gloucester—New Jersey—and has left descendants there, known to me—Joseph was killed by a horse, at Crosswicks, New Jersey.—They have also an old Pear tree on the farm—brought out at first coming, and still alive and bearing fruit. *Benjamin* settled in Virginia—and was the progneitor of General Harrison, President of the United States.—

Swedes on the Isle of Kent.—I came to the knowledge of the fact that there were Swedes settled on this Island as early as 1653.—Among them was Swan Swanson, Andrew Hanson and Valerious Leo, who appear named there in 1655—Swanson had his grant from Queen Christina, for Wiccoca at Philadelphia, 1653.—

The Year 1854, "*A Year of Terror.*"—In this year it has been estimated as losses, to wit: Property destroyed by fires, twenty-five millions of dollars—with one hundred and seventy-one lives lost thereby—one hundred and ninety-eight Rail-road accidents, caused the death of 186 persons, and wounded five hundred and eighty-nine; forty-eight steam boats sunk or burned, killing five hundred and eighty-five and wounding two hundred and twenty-five. There were eighty-two murders and eighty-four executions—Add to all this loss of life and property by ship wrecks,—by burning of Ocean steamers, pestilence in many places, would constitute a vast amount of the horrible, for this eventful year.

Undertakers for Funerals.—This is wholly a modern affair—It was formerly the case, that long trains of Friends—male and female, walked in procession—It seemed more solemn than now—and when the coffin was accompanied by pall and pall-bearers for respectable funerals, it was more dignified and imposing—It was a kind of willing homage of friends,—who thereby signified a willing respect and regard to the deceased.

"*God Willing.*"—This was once of universal declaration, in announcing forth-coming sermons to be preached at given places—Now it is almost as universally discontinued and ministers come, and go, without any such rest on contingencies—No cause has been published for the change, from Nisi Dominus frustra.

Shipments of Specie, abroad.—The Jeremiads, so repeatedly given in our public journals—of the amount of the last shipments of Specie abroad, is a very *queer* affair.—as being, as alleged, a matter to concern me and every man—Why should *I or they* lament over this, if it was not *our money!*—How would we individually suffer by it—Or even the nation itself—if it was not our own?

Recent Discoveries.—In 1807, the first *effective* Steam boat was by Fulton—now there are more than four hundred in our rivers and lakes. In 1825 the first rail-road was put in acceptable operation—Now there are over twenty thousand miles of them in the United States, at an outlay for building of three hundred millions of dollars. In 1845, the Electric Telegraph was started successfully. In 1839, Daguerre, showed his invention of printing from sunbeams—Since then we have Gun cotton and chloroform working their wonders. Look, too, at Hoe's admirable printing press productions, turning off twenty thousand copies in an hour.—Gas, which was only made known in 1809, is now lighting up our streets and halls, every where—How all these things, manifest the operations of our truly fast and progressive age—Who can sufficiently appreciate the coming future?

City Police.—What a change is there wrought also, in having now eight hundred policemen to hang and lounge about the great Town, to be ready to suppress outbreaks, and to preserve the peace of the city!—What a change, since a few constables, could answer equally well. The fire men too, of the present day, so much more numerous, and so much given themselves, to outbreaks and violence—So different in men and morals, from the grave, substantial householders, of the earlier Fire companies—"What a falling off was there!"

ANTHONY'S HOUSE.—Page 618.

Artificial Ice.—A machine has been completed at Cleveland, Ohio, capable of producing a ton of solid ice in twenty-four hours and to sell ice at five dollars a ton—It was done in an apartment where the mercury stood at eighty degrees—We, ourself, had conceived the idea of making Ice in winter, at any given places, by ejecting spray from hydrants and fountains so as to freeze readily as it rested in their wettings on a prepared floor.

Last Log House.—The last original Log House, is out Spruce St. South side, near Willow St. and near to Schuylkill River—It is a two storied, white plastered house, on its Spruce street front. Such a house was originally built, from using the forest trees, once near by.

"*Social and Fireside History.*"—Daniel Webster, in one of his speeches,—said, as if to commend our kind of notices—"There is still *wanting* a history which shall trace the Progress of social life—We still need to learn how our Ancestors in their houses, were fed, lodged and clothed, and what were their employments—We wish to see and know more of the *changes*, which took place from age to age in the homes of first settlers &c.,—*We want a History of Firesides!*"

N. W. corner of Ninth and Green streets.—This place where is now a Tavern and Freight Depot of the Railroad Co.—was in former time a brickkiln pond—fifteen or sixteen feet lower than the general surface now. And at the next square above—from Tenth to Eleventh Sts. and from Spring-Garden Sts. up to Wallace St. was a very fine apple orchard—as still remembered by the Ancients.—

Log Prison and Ancient Group of Houses in Germantown.

The picture which we here give of *the last* of the oldest houses, still remaining in Germantown,—now belonging to the family of John Green, present a very picturesque groupe,—and stand in interesting *contrast*, with many modern houses, built there. They would seem to have been built at several intervening periods—The front house on the right of the picture, now faced with white mortar is the original Log house—It was brought and placed there, as the dwelling house of John Adams Hogermoed, who had before passed a night in it—for some occasion of intemperance, while it occupied the Market square as the prison.—When it was afterwards sold, the same Hogermoed, became the owner. One of the higher houses in the rear, it may be seen—is diagonally boarded—The whole groupe seems to be formed of *four* different constructions—a part is of stone.—All such *remains* of the primitive times, are fast fading from the things that be!

The Aged Mrs. Maddox.

Having before noticed several of the remarkably aged of our country, we feel here inclined to notice, one, who besides her advanced age, had also, characteristics of mind and person, which made her a peculiarity in her day—"the observed of all observers."—We allude to *Mrs. Mary Maddox,* who died at the age of one hundred and two years, on the fifth of August, 1783, at the country seat of John Wallace Esq., in Somerset County, N. J. She was the daughter of John Rudderow of New Jersey; and had lived in Philadelphia, from her early life, till the period of the Revolutionary War, when she moved to the banks of the Raritan. During her long life, she enjoyed uninterrupted good health; and preserved to the last, a freshness and clearness of complexion, with scarce a wrinkle on her visage, which made her the wonder of the sitters at Christ Church, where she was a long approved communicant—never missing an attendance in thirty consecutive years. Her mind, memory and enlightened conversation, were strong and vigorous, even to the verge of her last illness and death. She was the wife of the Hon. Joshua Maddox Esq., one of the Provincial Judges of Pennsylvania.—Both of these persons, now lie buried in Christ Church ground, at the S. E. corner of Fifth and Arch Sts.—very near to the grave of Franklin.

Anthony's House,

In the fast changing construction of houses in Philadelphia, as residences of the respectable inhabitants, it is a satisfaction to give the present picture of a house, once respectable for its size and indwellers therein—It stands at the N. E. corner of Gray's Alley. and Second St.—below Chestnut St. It bore for many years the name of " Stephen Anthony's house,"—who died in 1763. In truth, it may have been originally built by him, for on page 223 of this Volume, it may be seen, that it was built so near the time of Blackbeard's career, who was killed in 1717, that when Stephen Anthony was having the cellar dug for it, about the year 1729, his black man Friday, then working there, came to a pot of money, which might have been hidden there by Pirates. The name of the Alley, was perhaps received from Gray, who had a large brewery on the North side of Chestnut St. between Third and Bank Alley.—In contemplating the House, we must mark its superiority in its early day, because it is ornamented with drops under its eaves—and its superior form of dormer windows—As a dwelling house, it shows the marks of where once ranged an entire extension all round it, of pent house we must remove present store windows, and set before the house its former street porch--The bricks too, now all *painted* red, were originally regularly intermixed with the blue glazed bricks,—a token, only belonging to the grades of best houses. All the three first houses in the Alley, were also marked with the drops under the eves, and were also built with the alternate intermixture of blue glazed bricks—Probably, one of them, built for, and dwelt in, by Gray the brewer; and so early too, as to have given the name to the Alley.—Such Alleys as that, and Carter's opposite, and Norris' near there, were at first chosen and dwelt in, in preference to wide main streets; because free from general travel, and therefore not liable

THE WILLING HOUSE.—Page 619

to be cut up, by wheels; and they were easier swept clean, at a period, before the existence of paved streets. Norris' Alley, was always remarkable, for its very notable cleanliness. Another thing to be contemplated in the picture is, that the frame house adjoining on the left side was once the residence and home of the subsequently renowned personage, Robert Fulton—when an apprentice to Duffel a Silversmith. There he probably lived as unconscious of "the divinity that stirred within him," as it rested before his time in another City visitor, who came in time to be equally famed, in Benjamin Franklin. The whole group, and their spontaneous associations, furnish much of ready consideration to the thinking and excursive mind. Such a house as Anthony's, and the Lætitia house of William Penn, in Lætitia Court, present the best, *last remains,* of what was the original feature of Philadelphia.—Now, successful traders, far surpass them all, and live in costly luxury. *Tempora mutantur!*

The Willing House.

We give a picture of this once respectable family residence of the Willing family, at the S. W. corner of Third street and Willing's Alley, taken down "to build greater," for the Reading Railroad Co. in 1856. It was originally built in 1745 for Charles Willing, after the pattern of the former homestead in Bristol, England. It was afterwards occupied as the family residence of his son, Thomas Willing, a member of the Congress of 1776—and afterwards the President of the first Bank of the United States. When first erected it was on "the hill," so called, "beyond Dock Creek:" and was then deemed a Rural home "outside of the Town,"—having connected with it, on its southern aspect, a large enclosure of Oak trees, of forest remains, with ample space of grass ground, extending from Third to Fourth streets. While in its prime, it was a fine specimen of rural elegance and family affluence;—A pleasant retreat from the throng and bustle of the early City avocations. Now, its location, has come to be a thronged place, of many genteel residences.—Near by it, southward, was the large enclosed grounds, and elegant mansion of William Bingham, Esq., who was a senator of the United States, while it held its session in Philadelphia, in 1800. That house, of two elevated stories of brick, of double front—most elegantly adorned, with door and window embellishments, was in its day, the wonder of the mass of passing travellers;—and Mr. Bingham, having married the elegant daughter of Mr. Willing, made the whole area along Third St.—to Spruce St, a kind of family distinction of both families for many years—Now all the same grounds, are fully filled with blocks of many dwelling houses.

The Early Emigrants to Pennsylvania.

These have been recently noticed, and *all named* in a book published by J. D. Rupp, at Harrisburg—Such a book, should be peculiarly interesting to those whose forefathers are therein shown, when they arrived and where they settled &c.,—Giving therein as many as thirty thousand named persons.—From that book, I select the following facts, viz:

From 1682 to 1776, Pennsylvania was the *central point* of emigration from Germany, France and Switzerland.—From 1682 to 1702, comparatively few Germans arrived—not above two hundred families, and they mostly located at Germantown—But the period from 1702 to 1727 marks an era in the early German emigration.—Between forty and fifty thousand left their native homes in exchange for homes here. Because of the relentless persecution and oppression in Switzerland, a large body of defenceless Mennonites fled from the Cantons of Zurick of Bern, and Schaffhausen in 1672,—and took up their abode in Alsace on the Rhine, where they remained till they emigrated to London and thence to Pennsylvania—about the year 1709. —They lived sometime at Germantown.—In 1712, they purchased of Penn's agents in *Pequœ*—Lancaster Co.,—There this swiss settlement formed the nucleus and centre of a growing population of Swiss, French and Germans.—All there, contributed to make it the Eden spot of Pennsylvania—From such a head-land, they sent out M. Kendig as their Agent to Germany and Switzerland, to invite others to follow them:—Wherefore in 1711 and 1717, and a few years later, so many more came over, as even to alarm the officials here. lest the Country might become a German population, rather than an English one. From such a course of action, it was made the law of Pennsylvania, that no emigrants should be allowed to settle, unless they previously took, severally, an Oath of Allegiance —Their compliance, became therefore a matter of record, and from this fund of names and arrivals, the compiler, Mr. Rupp, has formed his book of Emigrants.

From and after the year 1716, the Germans, some French, and a few Dutch, began to penetrate the forests more inland,—Large German settlements were commenced at different points within the present limits of Montgomery and Berks Counties. At Goshenhoppen, there was a German Reformed Church organized in 1717. Some Low-Dutch Mennonites settled along the Skippack some few years later.—Some German and French, located themselves on the fertile lands of Wahlink,—where an opening was made for others of the persecuted Huguenots.—Of these, the most prominent families in order, were the De Turcs, Bartolets, Delaplaines, Levans &c., Some of these became Pietists.—Among the early settlers of Alsace, now *Elsace* township in Berks County were many French reformed or Huguenots; also Swedes, who were Lutherans—About the year 1728-9, the Germans crossed the Susquehanna, and located within the present limits of York and Adams Counties.—Besides these,—they passed into Maryland, and settled in Washington and Frederick and at Hagerstown &c.,—In 1738, some Moravian Germans arrived and settled at Bethlehem Pennsylvania.—Before them. there had arrived a number of Schwenekfelders, who settled in Bucks and Montgomery Counties, and in Berks and Lehigh.—

Thus from the year 1735, the settlements in Pennsylvania increased rapidly—extending over much Country West of the great Susquehanna,—whither the Scotch Irish had before led the way.—Many had gone into Cumberland Valley. Prior to 1770, German settlers had gone out beyond the Alleghany Mountains—some in present Westmoreland, and some on the Monongahela in Fayette County.

It is impossible to contemplate these primitive explorers and pioneers seeking a resting place from the sufferings and perplexities of ‘woeful Europe," without a sense of thankfulness, that such men, "of like passions with ourselves," should have eventually established such comfortable, even affluent homes, for their posterity. Let any one now visit their land, and see how prosperity and happiness abounds—We see indeed, "the Wilderness to blossom as the Rose." *Laus Deus!*

Rowdy Assassinations.

The frequency of these deathly assaults on fellow citizens, without compunction, by those who have gone into the use of Colt's pistols, and the Bowey knife,—are wholly affairs of modern times—The fatal instruments, and their terrible effects, are of latter day origin. We once used to contemplate assassinations as almost wholly confined to Spaniards:—And we had undefined dreads of Spanish ports in Cuba and South America. Every American visiting such Ports, held himself, very cautious in his walks about their towns and suburbs—Now they have become familiar, to our ears, as of frequent occurrence among ourselves, in almost all parts of our extended Country. While so many are essaying to put down public executions for deadly crimes, few or none came forth in strength to abate the number of impulsive assassinations. The oldest inhabitants, still alive, may well remember the execution at Philadelphia of "young Reed," about the year 1791-2 for the murder of a man on High St. wharf, by stabbing him fatally, in his passion, with his pocket knife—The whole city was moved thereat. Every body thought it terrible—All thought that passion could not justify the fatal result; and although he had strong and respectable family friends, no possible move of the public, offered any hope that he could be rescued from the ignominious Gallows! "Life for life," was the rule then.

The Environs of Philadelphia.

It having been lately my fancy, to travel about the surroundings of the City, it may be curious, to others, of Younger years, to have the knowledge of some of the *changes* wrought out in the life of an "oldest inhabitant," like myself. All the Streets and houses, over in Kensington, from the Stone bridge over the Cohocsink, out to the New York Rail-road Depot,—now all covered with compact houses, was in my early days, all fields, open grass lots, and rural vegetable garden enclosures.—At the same time. all the area, from Franklin Square—Northward and Westward, was in like manner, open grass grounds—called Commons—All out from the head of Fourth St.—at Craig's Mill, Northward and Westward, were in Commons and in Sundry Rope walks—with here and there, a small cottage, with kitchen gardens—The West side of Philadelphia from Ninth and Tenth Sts. to Schuylkill were in commons and brick kilns.—On the South, beginning at South St. from Fourth St. Southwestward you entered into the proper Country dotted with a few Rope walks, and having many little places—here and there, engaged in Cultivating Vegetables for the City market. At that time, it was deemed to be a great way, to go as far out as the Schuylkill River,—or as far as Bush hill, *North*-westward;—or as far out *South*-westward, as the present Naval Asylum,—In all the preceding routs, every body went by cross-cuts to nearest points—seeing few or none of present streets as their landmarks.—It was all a different world, from any thing and every thing, of present observation,—The brick ponds, everywhere scattered about, were the skating places of all the boys —Now the former boys are *non est*; and the present boys and girls, can see almost nothing of what we once saw.

Then think, of the abounding flocks of Sheep—the wandering, grazing Milch kine,—the straggling worn out horses, the many flocks of killdeers and plovers, seen on the wing or on the grass, and the sharp shooters sometimes in their pursuit.—The many boys and girls, seen gathering unlimited quantities of mushrooms;—Parties of men and boys at their pastime sports,—such as shinny, Bat-ball, Prison-baist, foot racing &c., Oh! it was a joy to see their excited fun and glee. The whole area was then their *Gymnasium*, without expense and withont paid "Instructors."

Waste lands—laying in Commons, were not then subjects of speculation, and Sale, at exalted prices—as now, by *the foot*. Their owners then, were unknown to the mass,—The same areas are now all supplanted by piles of profitable brick and mortar.

In those days too, an out town drive, was of ready attainment—no going over the long streets of cobble stones—always uneasy and noisy—Then the Country air was easily and quickly found. On such *changes*, the pen of "*Sam Slick*," could find themes to fill a book. Do none remember!

Marriage Obstructed.

The increase of luxurious living, is operating powerfully against early marriages, as mothers and daughters may readily notice—The *Home Journal*, speaking of this subject, instances, the ascertained fact, that although the year 1856 has been a privileged Leap year, there was, at Boston 20 per cent less of marriages there, than the year preceeding. The *cause* is indeed to be found in the fact, that the shrine to love and marriage is crushingly draped with silks at from 3,00 to 15,00 dollars a yard—It is festooned with laces at prices to cause terror to hear it—expensive jewelry flashes through the meshes, everywhere.—Silver plate, paved thick upon leases of "genteel residences," support the altar;—and Milliners' and other bills, litter the base of it.—Great sighs heaved from the bottom of prudent but hopeless hearts, are all that is given to Hymen. Marriage is becoming a luxury to men—And those, whose means are limited, are as much prohibited from its adoption as by a police regulation:—Do we not really need, a "Retrenchment Society," which shall make economy fashionable?—O, for a restoration of ginghams and prints! Is there no deliverance from the silken web of evil, which French looms are weaving for us?

In addition to the above, We here add, from the North American of third of January 1857,—to wit: "Sundry Religious and Secular papers have begun a regular foray upon the extravagances of female dress. They say justly, it interposes a powerful obstacle with young men to marriage and tends to increase vice. The fault lies in Parental indulgence—and the remedy must be administered from the same quarter."—It might have added that the evil is effected by a class who never earn any part of such expenses! See also, Harper's Weekly of the same date—We are glad thus to see our *former* suggestions: so likely to be sustained—The Ladies "Dear Women," must look to these things, even for their own, eventual interests!

The first Effective Locomotive.

The first in our country—(like the first Steamboat) was that called "Old Ironsides," built in 1832-3, the first artistic construction of M. W. Baldwin—When she began her first operations along North Ninth St.—for the Philadelphia Germantown and Norristown Railroad Co.,—she ran a mile in a minute, and was the wonder of assembled hundreds of people, gathered at and near the Depot. That same Engine is still in operation in Vermont. She ought to be preserved as a relic.

Ladies and their affairs in Olden time.

The memoirs of Mrs. Joseph Reed (the wife of the Governor and General) tells us of sundry things as she found them in Philadelphia in in and about the year 1770.—She had been Miss De Bert of London —and found things different then from her former home—said the houses were low—and found but one street of business like home where she liked then to go, for the sake of her recollections of Thames Street, London—She visits Boston, and goes all the way on horse back, think of *that*, ye moderns! She liked Old England least, for its luxuries and conveniences;—but resolves to keep, her preferences to herself. In time her feelings came over to the American and whig cause. She then expects generally, to, order her fineries from London,—and orders from her family there,—to have a fine damask Cloth for 21 shillings—a neat fan of leather mount for 25 shillings —Also, needles No. 5 to 10.—She sends for four pair of black Calma shoes—eight dozen of eight bowed Cap wires—asks for a handsome Spring silk; and proposes to send a gown to be dyed over, of any colour which it will best take. Says Miss Pearson makes money by visiting London once a year, for its fashions. She praises our climate, and finds the people very Civil—and much accustomed like country people, to acquaint themselves with the affairs of their neighbours. Says Burlington, has the reputation of a very sleepy place—dull and quiet. She says, Men in trade, are in their habits, cheerful and gay,—especially at their tables,—being also acute men of business, in their Counting houses and stores. In her letters home, she shows much of such feelings of sacrifice, for a time, as we may now witness, from our own ladies, who leave gay homes, to become wives in California, or in the far West.

Through in Nineteen hours.

This is the promise of the advertisement of the new route from Philadelphia to Pittsburg, and I believe it is fulfilled every day. What that journey *has* been, I have some opportunity of knowing from a manuscript journal kept by Matthew Clarkson, Esq., in the year 1766. Mr. Clarkson was a merchant of Philadelphia—for several years Mayor of the city—and appears to have gone westward on behalf of some company with which he was connected, whose object was to carry on trade between Philadelphia and the Mississippi. He set out on horseback, with a servant, August 6, 1766. On the first day he met wagons loaded with skins coming from the west and overtook others "loaded with pork going for the king's use to Fort Pitt"—the name of the settlement which the English gave it in the place Du Quesne, and which was afterwards changed to Pittsburg. He lodged at "The Ship." 35 miles from Philadelphia.

The next day (Aug. 7,) he dined at "The Duke of Cumberland," and reached Lancaster in the evening. On the 8th crossed the Susquehanna at Wright's ferry, and reached York. On the 9th crossed Conewaga creek, and arrived at Carlisle, where he rested till the 12th, when he resumed his journey with a stronger horse, dined at Shippensburg, and lodged seven miles further on. On the 13th at the "Burnt Cabins," he overtook thirty-two horse loads of flour on the way to Fort Pitt, and mentions cattle going in the same direction, and "skins," coming eastward. "This day's journey [thirty-four miles] has been extremely tedious and fatiguing; the road, except the first ten miles, was nothing but hills, mountains, and stones, until you pass the Burnt Cabins, when it is tolerable, but hilly."

Aug. 14th.—From Littleton to breakfast at the foot of Sideling hill; dined at the crossings of the Juniata; lodged at Bedford. Here he stopped for a day, and purchased an interest in five tracts of land in Cumberland valley, Danning's creek, and Woodcock valley, mostly in the vicinity of Bedford, containing in all eighteen hundred acres, for one-half of which he paid £90, ($240.)

Aug. 16th.—At the foot of the Alleganies he found an encampment of Indians, under the command of Capt. Green, who were engaged in gathering and drying whortleberries. Lodged at Stony creek. Next day, dined at Ligonier, and lodged at the Twelve-mile run. 18th.—To Brushy run, Turtle creek, and reached Fort Pitt just after dark.

Thus he got "through in ten days," without counting stoppages, happily without being tantalized, as he jogged along under the hot sun, with the fore-knowledge that his grand-children would make the same journey "through in nineteen hours." His journal mentions indeed a "conductor of the trail," but it was of Conestoga wagons, not of cars and crates.

When he reached the embryo city of smoke, he found no sumptuous hotels inviting him to repose. Upon his arrival, he says: "I was stored away in a small crib, on blankets, in company with fleas and bugs." He took a walk to "the ship-yard; found four boats finished and in the water, and three more on the stocks; business going on briskly." Palmy days, those, in Pittsburg; said boats being probably batteaux, not much greater than such as are now slung at the stern of the steam-monsters that lie or ply by hundreds on her waters.

The fort was under the command of Major Murray, who gave Mr. Clarkson his lodging in the barracks; but, on account of the miserable accommodations for boarding, he usually made his meals on bread and milk "at the store." The other officers of the garrison were Captain Belneavis, Lieutenants McCoy, McIntosh, C. and G. Grant, and Hall. Doctor Murdock and Reverend Mr. McCleggan, chaplains, who preached alternately in Erse [Scotch] and English."

In an afternoon's ride from Fort Pitt he found an Indian settlement of the Mingoes. He mentions the arrival of a Seneca chief, who had been to the Illinois, and brought from that barbarous region, over his own post track, a packet of letters to the civilized east, from the commander at Fort Chartres, near the present St. Louis. The latest date was June 21st. The news of the day was that provision was scarce and dear: Indian flour being at 5 shillings per hundred; ordinary buffalo meat at 3 shillings per pound. "The French on the opposite side of the river in plenty." The mail from Fort Pitt was sent monthly by soldiers, to Shippensburg which was the nearest post office. Mr. Clarkson mentions the breaking of his thermometer as an irreparable loss. In these days it would probably be accounted too small an article for the great blasts of the glass furnaces to condescend to make. "No ropes for painters here, and no prospect of being able to supply this defect."

Mr. Clarkson was engaged in loading boats at Fort Pitt to transport merchandise down the Ohio to Fort Chartres, on the Mississippi. He engaged a Seneca chief to accompany him; probably, as a guide, interpreter and protector through the tribes along the river, some of whom were not in a friendly state. Before consenting to go, Kayashuta "said he must first see his family at the White Mingo town, and warm the hearts of his nation, and know how things stood with them. For this purpose he wanted a couple of bottles of rum." This article was not so easily obtained in Pittsburg as it is now. "Sixteen kegs of spirits arrived on pack-horses." On the 3d of September the wagons arrived from the east with the merchandise for the loading of the boats. The Indian and a companion were to have "forty bucks," for their services, besides an interpreter at 12 dollars a month. At this point the cooper's shop was burnt, and the traders had "no other way of procuring casks to pack the flour in." About this time the Reverend Messrs. Duffield and Beatty arrived "on a message among the Indians to preach the gospel." On the 16th September the boat left Fort Pitt, and on the 11th of December arrived at Fort Chartres. The trade of the boats seems to have been chiefly with the Indians for peltry. They bought beaver, minx, otter, bear, deer, muskrat, wolf, panther, martin, raccoon, fox, wild cat.

A memoranda made at Fort Chartres says, "the boats from New Orleans of the largest size carry about eighty hogsheads of claret; twenty-two to twenty-four men, who have about 400 livres each. Three months are accounted a good passage. A hogshead of claret on freight pays 300 livers." This mention of claret is explained by remembering that the Mississippi was at that date a French river, as to its settlement.

The Pioneers of Seventy Years ago.

"*Monument to a Pioneer.*—The citizens of Harrisburg, Pennsylvania, are taking measures for erecting a monument over the grave of John Harris, the first settler on the banks of the Susquehanna river, and after whom has been christened that town." This causes this letter from William Darby Esq.,

Sir:—The preceding epigraph I cut from your paper of the 9th instant. I hope you will do me the favor to reinsert it in the *Republic*, with some remarks, which will explain why I give you the trouble. One is personal to myself. I was born in that part of old Lancaster county, Pennsylvania, now Dauphin; and in the autumn of 1781, with my parents, crossed the Susquehanna a

Harris' Ferry. Though only between the ages of six and seven, I remember distinctly coming to and crossing the river. There was then Harris' Ferry-house on the east bank, and Kelso's Ferry-house on the west. When either Dauphin or Lebanon counties, then included in Lancaster, were made separate counties, I have no date. The village of Lebanon, then of some extent, preceded Harrisburg. The notice of an intention to erect a monument to the founder of Harrisburg excited in my mind many recollections which I cannot embody in words. One was that Mr. Harris very narrowly escaped being murdered by savages on the very spot where Harrisburg stands. No one having a heart will ascribe it to vanity when I state that I was born, 1775, twelve miles from Harrisburg, then really frontier. The notice enclosed is, however, in one part an error! There were white settlers no doubt at both Sunbury and Wilkesbarre, and also other places on east Susquehanna, many years before at Harrisburg. My own personal knowledge of the place and its leading names go back beyond the foundation of Harrisburg as a town. There are some descendants of that family on the Susquehanna. I am inclined to think.

There was, during more than a century previous to the treaty of Grenville, on the frontier settlemeuts of that part of the United States, a most admirable body of men, whose names have already in great part been sunk to oblivion. These men, under the title of Spies or Rangers, were the terror of the savages. With all the wily watchfulness of the Indian, the spy had the resources of civilzation.—Such men were John Harris, and, within my own remembrance and personal acquaintance, Lewis Wetzel, Martin Wetzel, Henry Jolly, and I might name more, who were the true and brave champions of the early progress of an immense region on which I have trod when in great part a wilderness; and what is its aspect now? A region of imperial extent, glowing with life. Could any or all of the men I have named, rise from the grave and hover over the scenes of their invaluable services, how ecstatic would be their feelings.

Henry Jolly was a man of education and extensive reading; in manners dignified, and in the discharge of his duty as a "*Spy*," a true model of cool and collected self-command.

He was one, and a most efficient one, of a body of men whose names and even existence as a corps, are now lost in great part, to human memory, and the extent and value of whose services could not, were they even known, be estimated. I cannot, ought not, to omit one curious trait observed in the manners of the frontier spy—taciturnity. This fact was in my hearing noticed and accounted for by Henry Jolly in words to the following import:—"***Habitual watchfulness, when on their duty, in the then interminable forests.***"

Peace and honor to their manes!

Wm. Darby

Camden New Jersey.

This place now a city, and covering so much of ground in its Squares, was, in my boyhood, a Country place of open Commons, and fenced fields, and was only known as a place of *three ferries*—of upper, middle, and lower—having in connection with them, severally, Taverns, and Stores, for the use of the market people resorting there—And all, long held by the three Coopers—Joseph, Daniel, and Joshua. The open grass commons, back from the River side, were generally in the state of their former Corn hillocks—left so, uncultivated for years, after their being so made fenceless, by the British in the War. Back, from the upper ferry about half a mile, was a raised Redoubt, made there by the same Military.—The common woods—began at about ½ of a mile from the River, and extended without houses, far back into the Country.—Back from the ferries were long rows of large trees of black cherries, and here and there, were Persimmon trees:—all for the use of the Philadelphia boys—From the lower ferry (Joshua's) down to Gloucester point lay *impassable*, swampy meadows,—with here and there, invasions of River water.—Like wet grounds, lay between the middle and upper ferries—All much decked with gay and towering wild-rose bushes, and Alders,—Now the whole of the former aspects are changed—The lands are made dry, and many buildings occupying the same—

The passages from Philadelphia to Camden, at that period, were wholly by Wherries and horse-boats—using Oars and sails. And, in the winter, when the ice was fixed or driving, the wherries were often seen on the ice, drawn along by the oarsmen and passengers. With their sharp bows, they often broke the ice through the floating cakes by lifting and sinking them, for that purpose—or if strong enough, raising them on to the floats, and sledding over them, into the next water.

This mention of ferries, reminds one of the equally unimproved position of Brooklyn, New York, which at the time referred to above, had but *one* Ferry house, and no appearance of a Town there;—and having an abrupt bluff covered with original forest trees, and Shrubs,—the whole—wholly rural. Jersey City, was a Ferry house, surrounded with wet marsh.

Our Boys are habitual Destructionists.

The proof of this, is every where manifest, in their habit of effacing every thing ornamental and beautiful, which they can reach, to mar and destroy. They show it even in their primary schools, in chipping and destroying desks, benches, balustrades &c.,—They love to disfigure newly painted Walls,—and fences along the streets, and in public walks. We are sorry to say, that such boys are peculiarly belonging to the Saxon race; for it is to be observed, that French, Spanish, and Italian boys, have no such propensities: on the contrary, they very early manifest an ambition to appear everywhere as little men, (" petit maitres.") They affect to dress and act as men—They are therefore to be seen very early at Balls, &c.,—among grown up persons; and always to avoid street gatherings and rough outdoor plays &c., While, we talk of learning them gymnastics &c.,—should not Parents and Teachers, rather aim to learn them *Conservative* affections! Let them know themselves better, and learn to forebear. Will parents consider?

The State of our maiden ladies.

The Newburyport Herald, in moralizing upon their state and prospects thus states their position in " the land of steady habits:" And we may add, such are the strictures of many Editors, in many other Cities. May not wary Citizens, proceed to organise associations, which may assume the responsibility of forming Sumptuary laws, which might embrace themselves and families as persons boldly " renouncing," the extremes of the day; and cordially *refusing* to be ruled " or led thereby?" If men, were to go into the same scale of expenditure for personal display, should we not soon find ourselves undone! Will not Parents and others consider?

The Herald, thus deplores our position, to wit:

Our fathers used to tell of the profligacy of Paris; their children tell of the mysteries of New York, a city not far behind any in Europe. And making proper allowance for size, how far is New York ahead of our other cities and towns? Once was a time when a wife was " help meet." We boast of our system of education; we have female high schools, female colleges, female medical schools. Our girls are refined, learned, wise; they can sing, dance, play pianos, paint, talk French and Italian, and all the soft languages, write poetry, and love like Venuses. They are ready to be courted at ten years, and can be taken from school and married at fifteen, and divorced at twenty. They make splendid shows on bridal tours, can coquette and flirt at the watering places, and shine like angels, at winter parties. But heaven be kind to the good man who marries in the fashionable circles. What are they at making bread and boiling beef? Why, how thoughtless we are—to be sure they will board, or have servants. What are they at mending old clothes? But there we are again; the fashions change so often, that no body has old clothes but the rag men and the paper makers now! What are they at washing babies faces, and pinning up their trowsers? And here is our intolerable stupidity once more; having children is left to the Irish! What lady thinks of having nasty children about her now?—or if she is unfortunate, don't she put them to wet nurses to begin with, and boarding schools afterwards?

We repeat—we have come to a point, where young men hesitate and grow old before they can decide whether they *can* marry, and afterwards keep clear of bankruptcy and crime. What is the consequence? There are more persons living a single life—are there more leading a virtuous life? It is time for mothers to know that the extravagance they encourage is destructive of the virtue of their children; that all the foolish expenditures making to rush their daughters to matrimony, are, instead of answering that end tending to destroy the institution of marriage altogether. We find now, that in the town of Hancock, with more than eight hundred inhabitants, no marriage is recorded for the year 1855; and in Cheshire, Middleton, Munroe, Montgomery, Roxborough, Halifax and Rutland, with populations varying from two hundred and seventeen to fifteen hundred, but one marriage is reported in each. But moralizing apart.

During the year the youngest male who was married was a youth of sixteen to a bride of seventeen. Seven grooms of the age of seventeen years were united to brides severally, one of fourteen, sixteen, seventeen, and nineteen each, and three of twenty-one. The youngest female was a girl, of thirteen years to a man of twenty-one. One male of sixteen years of age, seven of seventeen, fifty-three of eighteen, one hundred and forty-seven of nineteen, and ninety of twenty, were married for the first time; and ten females, of fourteen, forty-three of fifteen, and seventy-three of sixteen, were married also for the first time.

More than four sevenths of the marriages are among the *foreign* born; and this, because, it is argued, the foreign born *can afford* to get married, and the native born can not: and this must be so long as our extravagant modes of life continue.

It is quite a modern affair to advertise—as now Sometimes occurs, for Wives and husbands—A queer affair in itself, and a hopeless refuge too.

A Lady's Traveling Wardrobe.—A few months since a lady from a neighboring city passed through Baltimore en route to Washington, expecting to be absent from her home for two days. In the rush of travel about that time, two trunks, containing her wardrobe, were missed; and as she held the checks of one of our railroads for them, the company of course were liable for the contents. She was requested to give, as far as she could remember, a list of the articles and their value; when the following list was forwarded, and is now among the archives of the office:

One diamond bracelet and pin, 459 dollars, one hair bracelet, 60 dollars, one ditto, 20 dollars, one heavy gold bracelet, 110 dollars, two heavy gold rings, 20 dollars, one coral bracelet and pin, 35 dollars, one pearl fan, 15 dollars, one gold chain, 20 dollars, one brilliant pin, 10 dollars, two small coral bracelets, 7 dollars, two pearl card cases 15 dollars. Artificial flowers, 30 dollars. One set honiton laces, 20 dollars, one set valenciennes laces, 20 dollars, one set applique laces, 20 dollars; other collars and sleeves, 40 dollars; one handkerchief, 12 dollars, one ditto, 5 dollars, one ditto, 8 dollars, one ditto, 7 dollars, one ditto, 5 dollars, one ditto, 3 dollars; others amount to 30 dollars. Bouquet holder, 10 dollars; Opera cloak, 30 dollars; Ermine furs, 30 dollars. One velvet mantilla, 30 dollars. one parasol, 5 dollars; two embroidered skirts, 40 dollars; one black flounced dress, 45 dollars, one pink flounced dress, 55 dollars, one buff flounced dress, 45 dollars, one buff plain silk, 10 dollars, one blue brocade, 25 dollars, one ditto, 20 dollars, one white muslin flounced, 35 dollars, one ditto 30 dollars, one brown merino, 30 dollars. One black silk basque, 18 dollars, one black satin basque, 12 dollars, one plain ashes of rose basque, 12 dollars. Two lace skirts, 25 dollars. One morning dress, raw silk, 25 dollars. One drab woolen skirt, 8 dollars, one white embroidered skirt, 10 dollars. Two long night-dresses, 10 dollars; one pair drawers, 2 dollars; two chemises, 5 dollars; one pair corsets, 3 dollars; two pair white silk hose, 6 dollars, one pair black silk hose, 3 dollars, three pair lisle thread hose, 3 dollars, five pair cotton hose, 6 dollars. One pair white kid gaiters, 4 dollars, one pair brown and bronze gaiters, 6 dollars, one pair walking boots, 7 dollars, one pair red kid slippers, 2 dollars, one pair bronze kid slippers 2 dollars, one pair black prunell slippers, 2 dollars. Two ivory stick fans, 7 dollars, one white paper fan, 1 dollar; one shell comb, 4 dollars, one dressing comb, 4 dollars; one brush, 3 dollars; one braid hair, 4 dollars; one set curls, 7 dollars;. one head dress, 10 dollars, two ditto, 10 dollars; three night caps, 2 dollars; one book, 1 dollar; one opera-glass, 18 dollars; two hand mirrors, 2 dollars; one glove box, 3 dollars; seven pair of gloves, 7 dollars; two pair mitts, 6 dollars, one ditto, 5 dollars; five plain skirts, 10 dollars, two flannel skirts, 4 dollars; one black silk basque, 12 dollars; one all wool delaine dress, 7 dollars, one brown poplein dress, 7 dollars, one night dress, 2 dollars. Plain skirts, 1 dollar. Trunk, 30 dollars, ditto, 15 dollars. Portfolio, 4 dollars. Flounced skirts, 5 dollars. Letter paper, pens, water-colors, drawings, letters, bills, &c., Total, 1,765 dollars.

The forgoing catalogue was given as all that could be remembered at the time, but the next day another list was received, enumerating articles to the value of 300 dollars, making the grand total of the value of a young lady's wardrobe over 2000 dollars independent of the dresses, jewelry, &c., which she was wearing at the time the trunks were lost Fortunately, however, for the company, the missing trunks were found, having been miscarried, and their contents all safe.—*Baltimore American—May* 1857.

The reader should observe, how little there is, of real necessary clothing—Say, only one pair drawers, and two Chemisettes.

Our Shad Fisheries.

It is interesting to consider the present *exclusive* prices of Shad in our markets, and their *common* former prices. About the period of the Revolutionary War, they could be commonly bought at the wharves, in Shad time, at 3 to 4 pence a piece; and 12 shillings and 6 pence per hundred. Colonel Anthony I. Morris, told me, that he had seen shad sell, in several successive years—Say about ninety years ago, at ten shillings the hundred. At the beginning, when William Penn was present, he wrote of their great abundance; and said that "six Alloes or Rock, could be bought for one shilling." With their small Seines then, it was common to take five hundred, at a haul.

Contemplating such former facts, it may be interesting to a present reader, to learn our present position, from facts now published in our Public Ledger, to wit:

At each of all the large fisheries on the Delaware, there are employed from fifty to sixty men. The Season of fishing is from the first of April to tenth of June. They make five hauls in twenty-four hours; and the hauls, occupy from two and a half to three hours. The large size Seines are five hundred fathoms long,—admitting a Sweep of nearly half a mile,—It is drawn to the shore by a windlass on the shore, in an operation of an hour and a half. Their largest hauls number from eight hundred to nine hundred shad. Rock, perch and catfish, are often found in the hauls, in large numbers. There are about two dozen of such Fisheries—one of the best of them at Fancy Hill brings a rental of 1200 dollars—The whole of the Fisheries, employ about one thousand men; and they obtain about twenty thousand of fish, in each twenty-four hours.

The Herrings are taken in the low-water hauls—and produce from two thousand to four thousand severally.

In the present "Progressive times," we have to give for two to three shad, *one dollar!*—a price which tends to exclude them from the tables of Common life. We feel sorry for ***any exclusion***, from so great a good!

We overtax our energies.

To buttress this opinion, we here give—the words of the ***Philadelphia Ledger*** to wit:

"If we go on with the life we have lived for the last generation, we shall exhaust ourselves, prematurely.—Why are we, as a race, so nervous? Is it not because our mode of life exhausts our vital energies prematurely.—We work too hard, we think too hard, seek pleasure too hard—We are moderate, in short, in nothing, [our very overgrowth of spirit and energy, makes us so readily take to fillibustering and its perils.] Now, though this superabundant energy enables us to excel other nations, in whatever we undertake, it also wears us out more rapidly. At forty, our men are as old as Englishmen or Frenchmen at fifty-five; and our women at thirty, are as faded as European ones, at forty. A month of sober methodical life in a quiet Country place, is worth a whole season of dancing, banqueting &c., at the Watering places. The rush for excitement is sapping their lives; and must entail weak Constitutions on the rising generation."

The Evening, Bulletin, says,—"to our *Extravagance* we owe all our embarrasments. Our importations of the French and other European markets—(especially since the reduction of the Tariff,) have been the cause of our past troubles; and the predictions of trouble to come, are all based upon a continuance and an increase of these importations—We have a host of Speculators at work, and pushing for Western lands, with no proportionate settlers and cultivators of the Soil—The result is, that the fruitful West, has not, in many places, a sufficiency of Edible productions to supply their own wants."

We can thus perceive, how very much we are our own tormentors! We *must* Supply the *remedy*, or work our own griefs.

Conclusion.

The reader, who may have gone through the reading of the foregoing pages, may have noticed, that we have been chiefly busy with *Facts*;—And sometimes, with Facts which may not have been wholly grateful to our self-love and self-respect. Among the many things highly creditable to ourselves as a Community, have been, occasionally interspersed, Facts, which should be corrected and reformed. As a truthful recorder, We have been governed by the rule of "nothing extenuate, nor aught set down in malice." Let the good be cherished and diffused; and let the bad be corrected and reformed.—

With this *last* address to his Countrymen, the Author takes his final respectful leave. He feels that his aim has been, to "do the State some service,"—by the preservation of these fleeting and perishing Memorials of the past; snatched, like drift wood, from the stream of the ever ebbing tide of time.

He wrote not for fame or recompense, but *Con amore*;—because he found it grateful to his heart, to thus notice and record the doings and the characteristics of a notable race of forefathers. Olim meminisse juvabit!

THE AUTHOR.

PARTICULAR INDEX OF VOL. II.

Particular Index.

Particular Index.

INDEX OF APPENDIXES.

Index of Appendixes